LEGACIES

Using Children's Literature
in the Classroom

LEGACIES

Using Children's Literature in the Classroom

LIZ ROTHLEIN

University of Miami

ANITA MEYER MEINBACH

Dade County Public Schools

 HarperCollins*CollegePublishers*

Executive Editor: Christopher Jennison
Cover Illustration: Christine Orlando
Electronic Production Manager: Angel Gonzalez Jr.
Manufacturing Manager: Willie Lane
Project Coordination and Text Design: Ruttle, Shaw & Wetherill, Inc.
Electronic Page Makeup: Ruttle, Shaw & Wetherill, Inc.
Printer and Binder: RR Donnelley & Sons Company
Cover Printer: The Lehigh Press, Inc.

For permission to use copyrighted material, grateful acknowledgment is made to the copyright holders on pages 531–532, which are hereby made part of this copyright page.

HarperCollins® and ® are registered trademarks of HarperCollins Publishers, Inc.

Legacies: Using Children's Literature in the Classroom
Copyright © 1996 by HarperCollins College Publishers

Library of Congress Cataloging-in-Publication Data

Rothlein, Liz.
    Legacies: using children's literature in the classroom/Liz
Rothlein, Anita Meyer Meinbach.
        p.   cm.
    Includes bibliographical references and index.
    ISBN 0-673-46985-9
    1. Children's literature—Study and teaching (Elementary)—United
States. 2. Children—Books and reading. I. Meinbach, Anita Meyer.
II. Title.
LB1575.5.U5R67   1996
372.64´044—dc20   94-34987
                                                          CIP

97 98   9 8 7 6 5 4 3

can be used to teach children to read, and that literature has an important place in the curriculum.

At last, the tremendous value of literature is being recognized; many districts and states have made literature use a top priority in revitalizing reading and language arts programs. Literature, however, goes far beyond reading and language arts, cutting across all content areas and life experiences. Literature should be intrinsic to the study of any topic, adding dimensions to students' understanding.

The primary goal of *Legacies* is to serve as a guide for elementary teachers, parents, and librarians who wish to bring quality literature to children and instill in them a lifelong love of reading and an appreciation for the thoughts and

---

Reflections of . . .
Zena Sutherland

As is true of the literature of older countries, the books that come out of our own culture reflect its experiences and its beliefs. In books for children there are also echoes of what society thinks children should know and not know, and of how these precepts should be taught.

The United States is a young country; it is a vast land, and its white settlers, huddled on the east coast, were imbued with Puritan morality and with the idea that they were entitled to occupy a wilderness that they persisted in viewing as "uninhabited." The theological dominance of early, gloomy books for the young was weakened by new perceptions of what children enjoyed reading (even by the idea that enjoyment was appropriate) and by the resultant spate of adventure stories that incorporated the qualities demanded by frontier life: courage, initiative, and industry.

In the years after the Civil War, precepts of Victorian morality abounded, especially in books for girls. Louisa May Alcott's *Little Women* (the first family story to become an American classic) preserved such moral concepts without the maudlin sentimentality of books like the Elsie Dinsmore series. Increasingly, there were reflections, in the body of published literature, of the diversity of its readers—many of them from emigrant families—and of the fact that free public education was creating more readers.

In no other country has there been such a mutually effective relationship between the publishing world and the librarians who were emerging from a growing number of library schools. At first most of them (whether school or public librarians) were women, and they were pioneers in the critical reviewing of children's books. Many became editors in the burgeoning new children's departments of publishing houses. The production of children's books has become very big business; until the last decades of the twentieth century most of its sales were institutional, but the increase in sales to the public is evident both in the proliferation of children's bookstores and in the expanded size of the children's book sections of many general bookstores.

Preface

The world of books is truly a gift, a legacy to our children. Books become their friends, their mentors. Books are the wings on which their imaginations soar. Books dare them to dream, nourish their curiosity, and challenge their ideas. Through the pages of books, children travel the far corners of the world, explore space and the depths of the oceans. Through books children travel in and out of time, reaching back to the very beginnings and to the farthest edges of tomorrow. Books give children insight into human nature and motivation. They discover that others have often experienced joys, sorrows, and fears similar to their own, and they gain new perspectives. Books are an adventure, and those who work with children have the privilege and responsibility of guiding them on an unforgettable journey that will last forever.

Legacies: Using Children's Literature in the Classroom is intended for all adults who are interested in bringing children and literature together. It is specifically designed for preservice and inservice teachers, kindergarten through grade eight. *Legacies* was developed as a text for college-level children's literature, reading, and language arts classes and as a practical source book for teachers. It is also valuable for parents and librarians who wish to expose children to good literature.

For too long, quality works of literature generally have been read only outside the classroom. They have been read after the "real work" was completed. Despite advances in education, teachers have not been successful in bringing children and books together. Between 1958 and 1980, 95–99 percent of American teachers used basal readers to teach reading (Koeller, 1981), and while children developed reading skills, they did not develop positive habits and attitudes toward reading. Research on illiteracy has given added impetus for changes in education. One of the changes that has gained popularity is the use of quality literature in the classroom.

Numerous studies have compared literature-based reading programs with basal reading programs. Eldredge and Butterfield (1986) studied 1149 students, comparing a basal approach with five experimental methods, including two literature-based programs. They found that "the use of children's literature to teach children to read had a positive effect upon students' achievement and attitudes toward reading—much greater than the traditional methods used."

Similar results have been obtained in studies focusing on students at risk of failure (Larrick, 1987), students in economically depressed rural communities (White, Vaughan, and Rorie, 1986), and remedial readers (Chomsky, 1978). There is no doubt that literature-based reading programs work, that literature

Primary Level (Science)   432
Intermediate Level (Geography)   439
Intermediate Level (Social Studies)   451
Related Literature   458

CHAPTER 14: **Assessment and the Literature-Based Curriculum   463**

Principles of Whole Language
    Evaluation   464
Forms of Authentic Assessment   465
Professional Resources   473

CHAPTER 15: **Reaching Beyond the Classroom   475**

Libraries   476
Parent Involvement   480
Professional Resources   495

Appendixes:

A. CHILDREN'S BOOK AWARDS   497

B. RESOURCES FOR TEACHING
LITERATURE   513

C. PUBLISHERS AND ADDRESSES   516

D. CHILDREN'S PERIODICALS   520

E. TEACHER PERIODICALS   524

F. BINDING BOOKS   525

G. RESOURCES FOR PARENT LEND-
ING LIBRARY   530

CREDITS   531

INDEX   533

CHAPTER 6: **Independent Reading   203**

The Importance of Independent Reading   204
Selecting Independent Reading Materials   205
Establishing an Independent Reading Period   208
Paired Reading   210
Professional Resources   213

CHAPTER 7: **Storytelling   215**

The Importance of Storytelling   216
Selecting the Story   217
Preparing the Story   219
Guidelines for Good Storytelling   221
Choosing Appropriate Props or Media   223
Organizing a Storytelling Festival at School   224
Children's Literature   227
Professional Resources   228

CHAPTER 8: **Diversity and Children's Books: Finding the Right Book   231**

Students with Special Learning Needs   232
English as a Second Language Students   239
Cultural Diversity in a Literature-Based Classroom   246
Children's Literature   253
Professional Resources   262

PART III
Words and Worlds of Wonder: Interacting with Literature   271

CHAPTER 9: **Responding to Literature Through the Language Arts   275**

Speaking and Listening   276
Readers as Writers   291

The Writing Process   294
The Language Experience Approach   313
Children's Literature   314
Professional Resources   315

CHAPTER 10: **Responding to Literature Through the Arts   317**

Dramatic Responses   318
Visual Arts   326
Children's Literature   334
Professional Resources   337

CHAPTER 11: **Celebrating Literature: Alternatives   339**

Multimedia Alternatives   340
Children's Literature   350
Professional Resources   350

PART IV
Windows to the World: The Literature-Based Curriculum   353

CHAPTER 12: **A Literature-Based Reading Program   359**

Components of a Literature-Based Reading Program   361
Creating Literature-Based Lessons and Units   383
Literature and the Basal Reading Program   389
Organizing the Literature-Based Classroom and Materials   393
The Classroom Library   400
Children's Literature   403
Professional Resources   404

CHAPTER 13: **Literature and the Curriculum: A Thematic Approach   405**

Toward a Thematic Approach   407
Thematic Units   422
Primary Level (Social Studies)   424

Contents

PREFACE   XI

ACKOWLEDGMENTS   XVI

PART I
The World of Books: Discovering Good Literature   1

CHAPTER 1: **Exploring Genres   7**

Picture Books   8
Realistic Fiction   25
Historical Fiction   38
Fantasy/Science Fiction   45
Traditional Literature   50
Poetry   60
Informational Books   68
Biographies   74
Children's Literature   80
Professional Resources   106

CHAPTER 2: **Selecting a Variety of Genres   109**

Interest Inventories   110
Monthly Topics   111
Current Events   111
Author, Author   111
Calendar of Genres   113
Genre Units   113
Children's Literature   125
Professional Resources   125

CHAPTER 3: **Exploring Literary Elements   127**

Characterization   128
Plot   135

Setting   140
Theme   143
Point of View   146
Style and Tone   149
Evaluating Genres and Their Elements:
   A Synthesis   151
Censorship and Children's Literature   152
Children's Literature   157

PART II
The World Through Books: Bringing Together Children and Books   159

CHAPTER 4: **The Read-Aloud Program   163**

The Importance of Reading Aloud   164
Preparing a Read-Aloud Program   169
Guidelines for Reading Aloud   170
Assessing the Read-Aloud-Program   174
Suggested Read-Aloud Books   174
Children's Literature   174
Professional Resources   183

CHAPTER 5: **The Shared Reading Experience   185**

The Importance of the Shared Reading
   Experience   186
Approaches to Shared Reading   187
The Shared Book Experience   187
Shared Poetry Reading   195
Creating Big Books   195
Commercial Big Books   196
Suggested Big Books   196
Professional Resources   201

Books are the legacies that a great genius leaves to mankind, which are delivered down from generation to generation, as presents to the posterity of those who are yet unborn.

Joseph Addison
The Spectator, No. 166, September 10, 1711

ideas presented in literature. We hope that reading this literature will enable children to break beyond everyday boundaries, to wonder, imagine, and explore life's endless possibilities.

In keeping with this goal, *Legacies* presents approaches and strategies for using children's literature as the basis for the reading program and as a framework throughout the curriculum. The text is divided into four parts, which work together to enrich children's lives through reading and responding to quality literature.

Part I: The World of Books: Discovering Good Literature

Children must be introduced to quality literature and need to be guided in selecting the best literature has to offer. Chapter 1 describes each of the genres and suggests activities for using each genre in the classroom and activities to help teachers become familiar with a variety of literature in each genre.

Chapter 2 describes ways to encourage children to read books that represent different genres. Three genre units illustrate ways to introduce and highlight specific genres.

Chapter 3 describes the elements of literature—characterization, plot, setting, theme, point of view, style, and tone—and offers a selection of activities that will involve students in exploring these elements.

Part II: The World Through Books: Bringing Together Children and Books

Chapters 4–7 describe the approaches that have been most effective in literature-based programs to stimulate children's interest and involvement in reading: the read-aloud program, shared reading, independent reading, and storytelling. Benefits of each approach are described, guidelines are offered to help implement the approach, and activities are suggested to use the approach most effectively.

Chapter 8 is designed to help teachers use literature with various special populations, including students with special learning needs and English as a second language students. The chapter introduces the unlimited literary works that focus on various cultures and offers suggestions for creating a multicultural classroom.

Part III: Words and Worlds of Wonder: Interacting with Literature

Literature affects each child differently, and the approaches and activities detailed in Part III encourage children to interact with literature and respond in a multitude of ways. Chapter 9 emphasizes those responses that foster and develop speaking and listening skills. Specific questioning approaches, from those that encourage a more aesthetic or personal response to literature to those that develop skills in critical thinking and problem solving, are described. Additional approaches, such as book talks and literature circles, are detailed and suggestions for their use in the classroom are offered. The second part of Chapter 9 focuses on readers as writers. Approaches such as the writing process and language experience are described and ideas for connecting reading with writing are explained. Various strategies for encouraging students' written responses to literature are included.

Chapter 10 is dedicated to dramatic and artistic responses to literature. Activities and approaches such as creative drama, story theater, readers theater, choral reading, music, and puppetry that involve students in dramatic interpretations are described, as are methods for encouraging students to learn more about artists and experiment with a variety of artistic media.

Chapter 11 offers multimedia alternatives to the traditional book report. Activities are outlined that challenge students to extend their understanding of selected literature and encourage them to share literary works they've read with others.

Part IV: Windows to the World: The Literature-Based Curriculum

Part IV details the planning and implementation of a literature-based reading program along with ways that literature provides a framework for the total curriculum. Chapter 12 describes the whole language philosophy—its elements, organization, and implications for learning. Components of a literature-based reading program are outlined, as are ways to weave together various approaches and elements to provide a literature-rich program that promotes all aspects of the language arts within a meaningful context. Sample lessons and schedules are provided to illustrate how to develop a two-hour reading/language arts program to enhance the benefits of literature and provide skill development as student needs dictate.

Literature is the perfect vehicle for encouraging children to face issues and problems on an individual basis and from a more global perspective. Thematic units are the perfect vehicle for connecting literature and the curriculum. Chapter 13 outlines how to develop thematic units and offers a comprehensive list of sources for locating appropriate literary works. Comprehensive interdisciplinary units written for primary and intermediate levels combine theory and practice, as children read for real purposes and make connections between what they are reading and what they are studying. It is hoped that the understandings they gain will stay with them long after the last page is read.

One of the most overwhelming concerns of educators is how to evaluate student growth in literature-based programs. Traditional methods of testing do not adequately assess student development, nor can they analyze the processes students use to read, write, and perform other tasks. Chapter 14 describes methods that can be easily adapted to any classroom setting to assess student growth, processes, skill development, and attitudes toward learning.

Informal and formal forms of authentic assessment and the creation of student portfolios are discussed.

The tremendous importance of parent involvement in children's education has long been recognized. Chapter 15 includes many suggestions for involving parents and family members in their child's learning. Activities from reading aloud with their children to using the library are described to encourage parents to take an active role in bringing literature into the home.

Appendixes

The appendixes provide a wealth of information, including a listing of children's book awards; resources for teaching literature; a list of publishers and their addresses; periodicals for children and teachers; resources for parents; and step-by-step procedures for binding various types of books.

References

Chomsky, Carol. "When You Still Can't Read in Third Grade: After Decoding, What?" in S. Jay Samuels, ed. *What Research Has to Say about Reading Instruction.* International Reading Association, 1978.

Eldredge, J. Lloyd, and Dennie Butterfield. "Alternatives to Traditional Reading Instruction." *The Reading Teacher* 40: 32–37, 1986.

Koeller, Shirley. "25 Years Advocating Children's Literature in the Reading Program." *The Reading Teacher,* 34: 552–556, 1981.

Larrick, Nancy. "Illiteracy Starts Too Soon." *Phi Delta Kappan,* 69: 184–189, 1987.

White, Jane H., Joseph L. Vaughan, and I. Laverne Rorie. "Picture of a Classroom Where Reading Is for Real." *The Reading Teacher,* 40: 84–86, 1986.

Acknowledgments

Legacies: Using Children's Literature in the Classroom was truly a collaborative effort. In writing it, we stood on the shoulders of those who tirelessly worked to spread the message of the importance of children's literature. We stood on the shoulders of those teachers who brought literature into the classroom and whose ideas and initiatives made learning a joy. We stood on the shoulders of all those authors and illustrators whose words and art have stimulated our imaginations and nourished our souls, whose work has caused us to laugh, cry, and wonder and filled us with awe.

Our appreciation to Natalie Babbitt, Russell Freedman, Jean Craighead George, Lee Bennett Hopkins, Myra Cohn Livingston, Rebecca Lukens, Milton Meltzer, Walter Dean Myers, Sam Sebesta, Maurice Sendak, and Zena Sutherland, those authors and illustrators whose essays appear throughout the pages of *Legacies*. Their words, always thought-provoking and inspiring, leave us asking for more. We thank them for sharing a bit of themselves.

Our thanks to Tony Fredericks, our colleague and friend, for the imaginative ideas and support he lent to this work.

Our thanks to our editor, Christopher Jennison, for his steadfast belief in this project and all the wisdom he shared. Our thanks, too, to Shadla Grooms, editorial assistant, for her dedication and efforts on behalf of this book.

We are most appreciative to the following reviewers of the text. Your suggestions have truly made a difference.

Sara Ann Beach, University of Oklahoma
Kathryn Castle, Oklahoma State University
Victoria Chou, University of Illinois at Chicago
Darwin Henderson, Purdue University
Carol A. Hodges, Buffalo State College
Joan Nist, Auburn University
Annetta Probst, University of Victoria
Sam Sebesta, University of Washington
Sylvia M. Vardell, University of Texas at Arlington
Jerry Watson, University of Iowa
Derek Whordley, Duquesne University
Bonnie Campbell Hill, Seattle Pacific University

Finally, our appreciation to all teachers using *Legacies*. It is our hope that you will join with us, standing on the same shoulders as we have, to bring the world of literature to students—a legacy of riches and magic, of hope and love.

PART I

The World of Books: Discovering Good Literature

CHAPTER 1 • **Exploring Genres**

CHAPTER 2 • **Selecting a Variety of Genres**

CHAPTER 3 • **Exploring Literary Elements**

There is no frigate like a book
To take us lands away.
Nor any coursers like a page
Of prancing poetry.
This traverse may the poorest take
Without oppress of toll;
How frugal is the chariot
That bears a human soul!

Emily Dickinson

Walking into a library we are struck by the rows and rows of titles. Which to select for our students should not be left to chance. There is a debate raging today as to what children should be reading. Do we encourage children to read anything they wish, in the belief that eventually they will become more discriminating in their selections? Or do we take the position of Myra Cohn Livingston (1988, p. 21), who wrote, "If we as librarians, teachers, parents, and children's literature advocates are content to let children read anything in the belief that reading per se is good, we lay ourselves wide open for generations with feeble vision and crippled imaginations."

We believe those who work with children and books are in a position to affect children's reading habits and feelings about reading for a lifetime. We are reminded of a fifth-grade student, typical of many. He could read well, but rarely did so. That is, until the end of fifth grade, when his teacher assigned him *Island of the Blue Dolphins* (O'Dell, 1960). The child was touched by the story in a way no book had ever touched him. He cried with Karana and shared with her the triumph of survival. He sought other books by O'Dell and books with a similar theme, such as *Julie of the Wolves* (George, 1972). And he began to read! His experiences mirrored Livingston's belief that "Literature, the best of the best, must certainly touch a wellspring within reader or listener. . . ." (1988, p. 21).

It is vital that teachers, parents, and librarians understand not only children, but also the criteria to apply when selecting and evaluating literature. As they are exposed to quality literature, children will begin to have a feel for what is "the best of the best" as they make their own reading selections and find the book or poem that is just right for them. The right book could be that one special story that opens the door to the world of literature for a reluctant reader, stimulates a child's curiosity, or helps a child who is going through a troubled time to not feel so alone. Between the covers of books, children can visit the past, explore the wonders of the universe, feel pride in who they are, and meet special friends. Books invite children to become one with the characters and vicariously experience their joys, sorrows, hopes, and fears. The "right book" will stay with them, exciting their imaginations and challenging them to search for another book that is "just right."

Part I of *Legacies* is designed to help teachers familiarize students with the tremendous variety of literature available and help students develop the skills and understanding necessary to select the best literature has to offer. Chapter 1 describes the various genres of books. Children's literature is commonly divided into picture books, realistic fiction, historical fiction, fantasy/science fiction, traditional literature, poetry, informational books, and biographies. A book's genre is often easily established, but some fit the criteria of more than one genre. Although these classifications are often subject to debate, they do introduce the scope of books available and emphasize the importance of exposing children to the wealth of literature that exists. From poetry to picture books, from fantasy to biography, each is valuable and each holds unlimited possibilities.

Chapter 2 offers a wide spectrum of activities for using literature in the classroom and for extending the teacher's knowledge of the quality literature available in each genre.

Each genre contains elements of literature—characterization, plot, setting,

---

Reflections of . . .

Russell Freedman

When I begin a new book, I often think of a story my father liked to tell about himself.

Dad was a small child when his family moved from New York City to a rockbound farm near Windsor, Connecticut. One afternoon, as my father would tell it, he ran across a field to meet *his* father, who soon would be coming down the road with his horse and wagon. As my father waited and dawdled, he noticed a big stone on the other side of the field. He ran over and picked up that stone, which was almost too big for him to hold. Then he started carrying it back toward the road, stopping here and there to put the stone down and catch his breath, then picking it up again and carrying it a bit farther. When he reached the side of the road, he carefully put the stone down for good.

When his father—my grandfather—came rolling down that dirt road and climbed out of his wagon, my father said: "Do you see that big stone? I picked it up and carried it all the way across the field!"

"Why did you do that?" his father asked.

And my father replied: "God put the stone down over there, and *I* moved it over here!"

My father loved to tell that story because it signified to him that he had the power to effect change—and that everyone big or small has that power. Today, when I begin a book, I'm hoping to move a stone or two myself. I'm hoping to change the landscape of the reader's mind, if just a little—to leave the reader with a thought, a perception, an insight, perhaps, that he or she did not have before.

That's especially important if you are writing history or biography for an audience of impressionable young readers. Your book may be the first they've ever read on that particular subject. They will come to it with great expectations, eager to be surprised, to be enlightened, to be changed. If you do a good job as author, your book may still be alive in their memories 50 years from now. I try never to forget that.

theme, and point of view—but these elements are developed differently depending on the nature of the genre. Chapter 3 describes literary elements to help develop in children an awareness of the way they interact to weave the magic that is good literature. An understanding of the elements of literature helps children establish a schema for the structure of each genre and encourages critical thinking skills as they compare the elements of various literary works. Children who are exposed to various literary forms are better able to use these different forms in their own writing (Eckhoff, 1983). Chapter 3 also describes motivating activities to further children's understanding of genres and their elements. Activities give students an opportunity to apply their knowledge of literary elements, especially in their own writing, and to evaluate specific works of literature based on appropriate criteria.

References

George, Jean Craighead. *Julie of the Wolves.* Harper & Row, 1972.

Eckhoff, B. "How Reading Affects Children's Writing." *Language Arts,* 60: 607, 1983.

Livingston, Myra Cohn. "Children's Literature Today: Perils and Prospects." *The New Advocate,* 1: 18–28, 1988.

O'Dell, Scott. *Island of the Blue Dolphins.* Houghton Mifflin, 1960.

JOYFUL NOISE

Poems for Two Voices

PAUL FLEISCHMAN

illustrated by Eric Beddows

CHAPTER 1

Exploring Genres

Picture Books

Long before they can decode the written word, young children are fascinated by picture books. A good picture book is a source of delight and enrichment. The pictures leap off the pages, weave magic tales, and spark the imagination.

Reflections of . . .
Maurice Sendak

I was the youngest of three children growing up in Brooklyn, and when I got a book from my sister, about the last thing I did was read it. A book, for me, was for sniffing, poking, chewing, licking. The first real book I ever had was Mark Twain's *The Prince and the Pauper*, illustrated by Robert Lawson, whose work I still admire. I treasure that book, although I don't know if I ever actually read it.

Children have a sensuous approach to books. I remember one letter I received from a little boy who loved *Where the Wild Things Are*. Actually, I think the letter was written by the boy's mother, and he sent me a picture he had drawn. So I wrote him back and sent him a picture. Eventually, I received another letter, this time from his mother: "Jimmy liked your postcard so much he ate it." That letter confirmed everything I'd ever suspected.

I seem to have been blessed, or cursed, with a vivid memory of childhood. This is not supposed to happen. According to Freud, there's a valve that shuts off the horrors of childhood to make room for the horrors of adolescence. I must have a leaky valve, because I have these torrential memories. From a career standpoint, I guess that's been a good thing. Socially, it's been nothing short of disaster.

I profited as a child from the dynamics of my family. My brother was a writer, and I was allowed to illustrate his stories. With alarming regularity, our home would be invaded by these galumphing people called relatives. My brother would be called upon to read his latest opus, and I would hold up illustrations that I had done on shirt cardboard.

I remember one story called "They Were Inseparable." It was about a brother and a sister who loved each other so much that they planned to get married. You see, Freud never came to Brooklyn. At any rate, I could understand my brother's feelings. Our sister was very beautiful, in a Delores del Rio way. But he must have had a hint that this would never work, because his story ended with a terrible accident in which the brother was permanently damaged. I did very well at illustrating the blood and bandages, but not nearly so well at creating the kissing scenes.

I was a sickly child and spent a lot of time looking out the window. There was a little girl across the street named Rosie, and I must have 40 sketch pads filled with Rosie pictures and Rosie stories. She was incredible. She had to fight the other kids for attention, and she had to be inventive. I remember one time when she came up with an explosive line: "Did you hear who died?" Rosie started telling the kids that she had heard a noise upstairs—a noise like someone falling, furniture breaking, and gasping, choking sounds. She went to investigate, and her grandmother was on the floor. Rosie had to give her the kiss of life—twice. Her grandmother managed to whisper "Addio Rosie" before dying. While Rosie was talking, her grandmother came up the street, carrying groceries from the market. The kids waited until she had gone into the house before turning to Rosie with the request: "Tell us how your grandma died again."

Rosie's stories became the basis of *Really Rosie*, an animated film, for which Carole King set my words to music. Then Arthur Yorinks and I formed The Night Kitchen, a children's theater company, and we cast *Really Rosie* for the stage. Then we planned to collaborate on a production of *Peter Pan*.

J. M. Barrie left the copyright of the play with a children's hospital in London, so I visited the hospital to ask for permission to produce the work. While I was there, I visited some of the children. You might be surprised to learn that most of the children who are terminally ill know that they are. I was asked to go see a little girl who was dying. She had heard I was in the hospital, and since her favorite book was *Where the Wild Things Are* she had asked to see me.

I sat down by her bed and started drawing. Before long, she was sitting so close to me that her face was practically on my elbow. She was saying, "Put the horns on; put the teeth in" and ordering me about. She was wonderful and funny, and I drew very slowly to give her as much pleasure as possible. But after a while I became aware of something. I saw a look on her mother's face. The girl was engrossed in the drawing, and the mother was watching her child with a look that said, "How can she be so cheerful and lively when we all know . . ." It was a puzzled, confused, lonely look. Suddenly, without glancing up, the girl reached out until her hand touched her mother's. Without looking, she took her mother's hand and squeezed it. Children know everything.

The Night Kitchen theater and my books are written for and dedicated to children like Rosie and this little girl. Children who are never satisfied with condescending material. Children who understand real emotion and real feeling. Children who are not afraid of knowing emotional truth.

Generally, books for young children are referred to as picture books. Illustrations play an integral part in these books. Instead of simply being an extension of the text, illustrations are necessary for understanding the book's content. The elements of a picture book are heightened by the way the illustrations create mood, depict characters, and develop action. Almost every artistic medium and technique has been successfully used in picture books, from watercolors to collage and pen-and-ink sketches, photographs, and linoleum prints.

Usually children's first books, picture books, encourage an appreciation and love for reading as they allow children to participate in the literate community. As children listen to picture books being read, or as they "read" them aloud, they are developing their reading readiness skills and language development. Since so much of their speech and vocabulary has been developed by the time they are 6 years old, it is vital that young children be provided with literature to stimulate and nurture language development.

Picture books are an excellent vehicle through which children learn about the world of books. They illustrate writing styles and techniques and expose children to a variety of literary genres. As they listen to, read, and compare the literature in picture books, even young children begin to recognize literary elements, such as plot, character, setting, and theme. Picture books provide emergent readers the schema for literature, a way to understand its organization and elements. Finally, picture books provide children with picture clues that aid them in obtaining meaning from the written text.

Teachers need to build a classroom library filled with picture books. While they were originally designed for younger children, picture books should be shared with children of all ages and can be used to expand concepts in different curricular areas. The many informational picture books available today can be used to supplement text or trade books. Older children can also appreciate picture books from an aesthetic point of view. For example, Graeme Base's alphabet book, *Animalia,* with its elaborate illustrations, fascinates all children. Older students are captivated by the imaginative pictures and format and often use it as a model for their own alphabet books.

The classification of picture books is a subject of debate. Is it a genre of its own, or is it subsumed within other genres? A case can be made for either point of view: picture books have certain qualities in common, yet, because of their subject matter, they cross into other genres. For example, *Where the Wild Things Are,* by Maurice Sendak, is a picture book, but the text would be classified as fantasy, while *The Snowy Day,* by Ezra Jack Keats, is a picture book that could also be classified as realistic fiction. *The Magic School Bus at the Waterworks*, by Joanna Cole, and others in the Magic School Bus series are excellent examples of informational picture books, while Robert Frost's "Stopping by Woods on a Snowy Evening" illustrated by Susan Jeffers, becomes a picture book.

To focus on the qualities, benefits, and appeal of this special group of books, we treat picture books as a distinct literary genre. There are a variety of types of picture books: alphabet books, counting books, books of Mother Goose rhymes,

toy books, concept books, wordless picture books, predictable books, easy-to-read books, and picture storybooks.

Alphabet Books

In an alphabet book, each letter of the alphabet is matched with an illustration of an object that begins with that letter. The illustrations must clearly match the key letters and the objects pictured must be easily identifiable.

One of the primary benefits of alphabet books is that they help children identify letters and corresponding sounds. Children may also recognize the printed words that accompany the objects pictured. Alphabet books help develop visual literacy, stimulate object definition, and enhance vocabulary development.

There are several types of alphabet books. The most common have a word-picture format in which each letter of the alphabet corresponds to words and pictures beginning with that letter. Alphabet books of this type range from the simple to the complex. In *Eating the Alphabet,* Lois Ehlert presents fruits and vegetables beginning with different letters. In *Anno's Alphabet,* by Mitsumasa Anno, each letter is painted as if it were made of wood and is matched with an imaginative, clever picture. Woven into the borders are additional pictures of objects beginning with that letter. For example, the kangaroo is surrounded by kings and keys, knives and knots.

Another type of alphabet book includes simple narratives. Anita and Arnold Lobel's Caldecott Honor book, *On Market Street,* inspired by seventeenth-century trade engravings, is the story of a young boy's journey along Market Street. On his trip, he meets merchants created by the items that they sell. Readers delight in the incredible new people they discover—the woman made of clocks, the man made of fresh vegetables, and the ice cream man with banana split feet.

Some alphabet books are organized around a specific theme, such as animals, modes of transportation, or flowers. *Anamalia,* by Graeme Base, presents a fantastic animal world from A to Z. With each letter of the alphabet, children meet exotic and familiar creatures set in unusual landscapes. Children are fascinated by "an armored armadillo avoiding an angry alligator" and laugh at "zany zebras zigzagging in zinc zeppelins." In *Ashanti to Zulu,* Margaret Musgrove introduces diverse African cultures and traditions, with explanations of 26 customs from 26 different African tribes.

This alphabet book explains that Ally Alligator, his family, and six of his best friends went to the fair. From: Christianna Rose Cannon, *The Ally Alligator Alphabet Book,* Bright Elementary, Dade County Schools, Miami, Florida

Eric said he'd rather eat.

Frank freaked out.

Ike inhaled deeply

Alphabet books can help young children with reading and writing, while older children can explore them as a literary form. And, no matter what their age, children love to create their own alphabet books.

Activities to Use with Alphabet Books

1. Have students create a personal alphabet book, using each letter to describe something about their personality or likes and dislikes.
2. Have students select a favorite alphabet book and use the same style and format to create a new book. For example, students can visit different shopkeepers in *On Market Street*.
3. Have students create an alphabet book based on a topic being studied. They can create tongue twisters for each letter or write corresponding words or phrases.
4. Have younger students use materials such as velvet, corduroy, satin, or leather, to create letters for their own alphabet book. They can then draw or cut out pictures to place on the appropriate pages.
5. Create the ultimate alphabet book with as many words and objects as the students can find for each letter.
6. Encourage students to create an alphabet book with words from another language(s), as in Muriel Feelings's *Jambo Means Hello*.

Counting Books

Counting books present numbers and number concepts in a variety of ways. Often, numbers are matched with illustrations of familiar objects, with the number of objects depending on the number or concept being stressed. It is important that both numbers and objects are clear and easily identifiable. Extraneous details in the illustrations should be avoided so children readily understand what is being counted and can focus on the objects and number concepts.

Counting books such as Tana Hoban's *1, 2, 3* develop the concept of one-to-one correspondence and aid in the development of sequential counting, usually one through ten. More complex is *Anno's Counting Book* which helps build number concepts and higher levels of thinking, and also includes the concepts of time, seasons, and sets. Counting books become increasingly more complex as children become involved in addition, subtraction, and other numerical operations. For example, *The Doorbell Rang*, by Pat Hutchins, involves two children, a plateful of cookies, and more and more guests among whom to divide the cookies. As each guest arrives, the children have to refigure how many cookies each guest receives.

Many counting books incorporate the concepts of size and shape. Language development is enhanced when rhyming is used to convey the message. For example, *Can You Imagine,* by Beau Gardner, includes rhyming patterns as well as number concepts. *Over in the Meadow,* Ezra Keats' version of the classic Appalachian counting rhyme, introduces children to the numbers one through ten as they meet animals and their young "over in the meadow." The verses lend themselves to song as well and children can dramatize the actions of the animals as they dig, dive, and buzz.

Activities to Use with Counting Books

1. Create a counting book on the topic of nature. Assign each pair of students a number from 1 to 15. Take the students to a park and allow them to plan a page for the counting book, using elements of nature, based on the number each pair was assigned (one leaf, two blades of grass, three pebbles, etc.). As each page is completed, take a picture of it. When the pictures are developed, affix them to paper labeled with the corresponding number and bind the pages together.
2. Have children use objects such as blocks, cubes, and crayons to imitate the number concepts in the counting book being read.
3. Have children create a multicultural counting book using pictures and drawings of objects related to various cultures. Have them look at several other counting books to help determine the organization of the new one.
4. Have children select their favorite counting book, read the book with a partner, and then, using the same style, add several pages to the book.

Mother Goose Rhymes

Mother Goose rhymes are usually a child's first introduction to the literary world. Their appeal lies in their fast-paced action, rhyme, rhythm, mood, and nonsensical verse. Mother Goose rhymes contain a variety of characters and subject matter and they create various moods. Humor and musical qualities are important aspects. These rhymes are magical. Children react spontaneously to the verse by laughing, clapping, or singing along.

The varied language patterns allow children to experiment with sounds and uses of words as they develop their own language skills. In addition, these well-loved nursery rhymes instill a love of poetry, prepare young readers for more sophisticated forms of poetry, and acquaint them with poetic devices such as alliteration, repetition of initial sounds, as in "Baa baa, black sheep" or "Wee Willie Winkie," and onomatopoeia (imitation of natural sounds in word formation), as in "Pat-a-cake, pat-a-cake." It is wonderful to watch young children at play, unconsciously singing their favorite Mother Goose rhyme. The verses become a common bond among children. No matter what their background, culture, or heritage, all children can share in the magic of Mother Goose.

Many editions and versions of Mother Goose rhymes have been published. Tomie de Paola's *Hey Diddle Diddle* contains more than 200 rhymes accompanied by his incomparable illustrations. Other favorite Mother Goose editions include *The Oxford Nursery Rhyme Book*, compiled by Iona and Peter Opie, containing more than 800 verses and pictures from old chapbooks and toy books, and *The Orchard Book of Nursery Rhymes*, compiled by Zena Sutherland. Selected rhymes are the subject of individual books, such as Peter Spier's *London Bridge Is Falling Down*.

Activities to Use with Mother Goose Rhymes

1. Read students a large selection of Mother Goose rhymes. Ask each student to select and illustrate a favorite rhyme and compile a class book entitled *Rhymes from Mother Goose.*
2. Have students make up new Mother Goose rhymes by replacing characters and actions. For example, "Hickory, dickory, dock" could become "Hickory, dickory, dawn, the cow ate up the lawn."
3. Have students present short plays of various Mother Goose rhymes, using puppets, flannel board cutouts, and other materials.
4. Enlarge and laminate the pictures from a Mother Goose story. Have groups of students put the pictures in sequence without talking. (This can also be done with words on sentence strips.) Have the group perform the rhyme for the rest of the class as they show the pictures (or sentence strips).
5. Encourage students to tap out the rhythm of favorite rhymes using student-made musical instruments.
6. Introduce older students to poetic devices such as alliteration, rhyme, and onomatopoeia. Have them create an "encyclopedia" of poetic devices with examples from Mother Goose.

Toy Books

Toy books employ an unusual way of presenting content. They include pop-up books, cardboard books, cloth books, finger puppet books, and flap books. Toy books are becoming increasingly popular. They entice children to become involved with the text as they explore letters, numbers, concepts, rhyming words, and plots. Their unique format encourages involvement with the book: children open doors, look under flaps, and unfold pages to discover hidden secrets. In Eric Carle's *The Very Hungry Caterpillar*, for example, children put their finger through the holes and count. In Carle's *The Very Busy Spider*, children can actually feel the spider's web and trace its growth. Dorothy Kunhardt's *Pat the Bunny*, first published in 1940 and still a favorite, encourages children to use all their senses. *Goodnight Moon,* a classic children's story, has been adapted into a pop-up book, *The Goodnight Moon Room.* As they turn the pages, children pull, lift, and rock the "quiet old lady who is whispering 'Hush.'"

Activities to Use with Toy Books

1. Demonstrate to students how to make a pop-up book (see Appendix) and have them create a book based on a favorite Mother Goose rhyme.
2. Hold a toy book fair to which students bring all types of toy books to share with their classmates.
3. As a class, select a favorite picture book with limited text. After examining several toy books, assign each pair of students a different page from the picture book to redo in their favorite style, such as pull-tab, fold-out, or pop-up.

Concept Books

Concept books make concrete and abstract ideas more easily understandable by representing them with pictures. A good concept book presents objects clearly and includes examples to foster understanding of the concept. The concepts being emphasized may be taught through the story line or explained through repetition of examples and ideas or comparisons. Concepts such as color, shape, and size lend themselves to demonstration, whereas concepts such as position and emotion are more difficult to explain.

Concept books foster cognitive development. Children seek to identify relationships as they become aware of the differences and similarities among objects and transfer these newly integrated concepts into other areas. The books stimulate vocabulary and language skills as children match words with pictures of objects. Children may become active participants as they underline, point, or verbally respond to various items in response to a teacher's or parent's directions. Affective development is also enhanced through the use of books based on children's values, feelings, and everyday events in their lives.

Many well-known writers and illustrators of children's books have created concept books. Tana Hoban, for example, has a long list of concept books to her credit, including *Of Colors and Things, Shapes and Things, Is It Larger? Is It Smaller?*, and *Exactly the Opposite.* These books emphasize and reinforce a specific concept through stimulating photographs. Peter Spier's *Fast–Slow High–Low: A Book of Opposites,* Aliki's *My Hands* and *My Feet,* and Shirley Hughes's *All Shapes and Sizes* teach children about themselves and their surroundings.

Concept books are actually children's first informational books. They expand children's understanding, helping them see relationships between and among people, places, and things. Through concept books children gain insight into the concrete world and the abstract as they add to an ever-expanding awareness of their world.

Activities to Use with Concept Books

1. Select several concept books on a similar concept, such as *Look Around! A Book About Shapes,* by Leonard Everett Fisher, *Shapes,* by John Reiss, Tana Hoban's *Circles, Triangles and Squares,* and Bill Gillham and Susan Hulme's *Let's Look for Shapes.* Assign different groups of students different shapes and have them create their own page for a concept book on shapes. (The same strategy can be adapted to concepts such as color and size and abstract concepts such as happiness and love.)
2. Take pictures of children performing activities such as walking through a door, sitting on a chair, and lying under a table and create a book that teaches the concept of spatial relationships.
3. Read several concept books on the same subject and have students demonstrate their understanding of the concept. For example, the concept of opposites can be expanded as students find objects that are big/small, tall/short, sharp/dull, and so on. The concept of color can be demonstrated as students find red, blue, green, and yellow items in everyday things around them.

Wordless Picture Books

These books tell a story through illustrations alone. Wordless picture books have become increasingly popular, appealing to a society of youngsters who delight in television, comic books, and other visual forms of communication. If a story line is intended, the pictures must be properly sequenced and the action clearly drawn. Wordless picture books take many forms; they can be humorous or serious, informational or fictitious.

These books offer many benefits. They are instrumental in developing left-to-right progression, the concepts of top and bottom, the turning of pages, and an appreciation of and respect for books. Wordless picture books foster oral and written language development as children use details and make their own interpretation to produce text to accompany the pictures. Teachers may record the generated text and use it in language experience lessons or children may produce their own text. As children create their own versions of the story, wordless picture books provide a catalyst for creative thought processes.

Comprehension skills are also developed as children "read" the story. Children analyze the author's intent, identify main ideas, and recognize details as the story unfolds.

Wordless picture books also familiarize children with the elements of a story, using illustrations to provide information and enable children to make predictions. While reading *Tuesday*, by David Wiesner, the 1992 Caldecott Award winner, children can respond to the following: What is the story about? What do you think will happen next? Identify the main events of *Tuesday*. What do you think some of the characters are thinking?

As children discuss the story, they become authors, weaving a tale that combines the elements of plot, characterization, setting, and so on with the mood, story line, and characters established by Wiesner's humorous and inventive illustrations. No two narratives will be the same as children use their own creativity to interpret the events of Tuesday evening and Tuesday night as a group of frogs soar silently above the city and in and out of homes.

Activities to Use with Wordless Picture Books

1. Share *Tuesday* with students. Have them create a similar wordless book called "Next Tuesday, 7:58 p.m.," beginning where Wiesner left off, when pigs fly!
2. Have students share a favorite wordless picture book with a buddy.
3. Have students create a wordless picture book that tells about an important event in their lives. Encourage them to bring in photographs to help tell the story.
4. Create a "listening station" and have students tape their narration of a favorite wordless picture book. Encourage several versions to accompany the same book. Allow students to compare their interpretations.
5. As a class, develop a text for a wordless picture book and create a puppet show to retell the story.

Predictable Books

Predictable books include repetitive language patterns, phrases, or questions, refrains, strong rhythm and rhyme, sequences of numbers or days of the week, and so on to help the emergent reader gain meaning from the text. Predictable books allow children to participate actively by joining in on a repetitive change or chorus. From an early age, children become part of the story as they repeat such memorable phrases as "Not I," from *The Little Red Hen*, by Paul Galdone, or "Goodnight moon, Goodnight moon, goodnight cow jumping over the moon," from Margaret Wise Brown's *Goodnight Moon*. In Wanda Gag's classic, *Millions of Cats*, children become more and more excited (and louder and louder) as they chant the repeated phrase, "Cats here, cats there, cats and kittens everywhere, hundreds of cats, thousands of cats, millions and billions and trillions of cats." This repetition is important, because words need to be repeated many times before they become part of a child's reading vocabulary.

Through repetition, children quickly learn language patterns. Repetitive story patterns help children predict the action in the plot. In *The Very Busy Spider*, by Eric Carle, the spider constantly turns down invitations to join the other animals who invite her to "chase a cat" or "catch a pesky fly." After each invitation, as the text explains, "The spider didn't answer, She was very busy spinning her web." Children begin to recognize the response and chant along. In predictable books, the outcome can be imagined very easily. After reading a few pages, children can tell what they think will happen next or predict how the story will end. It's not surprising that at the end of *The Very Busy Spider*, "the spider caught the fly in her web . . . just like that!"

Predictable books also provide great models for writing. After reading *Brown Bear, Brown Bear, What Do You See?* or *Polar Bear, Polar Bear, What Do You Hear?* children can follow the same rhythm, pattern, and style as the author, Bill Martin, Jr., substituting their own content to write their own version.

Another type of predictable book is the cumulative tale. These stories have repeated phrases that become longer with each new character or event. Most of us can remember cumulative rhymes from childhood, such as "Old MacDonald Had a Farm" and "I Know an Old Lady Who Swallowed a Fly," and we remember the overconfident Gingerbread Boy as he escaped an ever-increasing assortment of characters. *Drummer Hoff*, adapted by Barbara Emberly, begins with the simple phrase, "Drummer Hoff fired." With each page another character and an action is added, until, in the last page, "General Border gave the order, Major Scott brought the shot, Captain Bammer brought the rammer, Sergeant Chowder brought the powder, Corporal Farrell brought the barrel, Private Parriage brought the carriage, but Drummer Hoff fired it off."

Activities to Use with Predictable Books

1. Read a predictable picture book aloud. Once students are familiar with the repeated phrase(s), have groups create their own mimes to accompany the phrase(s).
2. Once students are familiar with a predictable story, create sentence strips with the repeated phrase(s). Have assigned students hold up the phrase at the appropriate time.
3. Have students write "Good Morning Sun," modeled after *Goodnight Moon*, by Margaret Wise Brown.
4. Seat students in a circle and have them create a cumulative tale as they go around the circle. You may wish to write the tale on chart paper as students dictate it.

Easy-to-Read Books

Easy-to-read books are designed to allow children with beginning reading skills to read independently. Similar to picture books, easy-to-read books contain a large number of illustrations that are suggestive of the text. Unlike other picture books, which are written at various reading levels and designed for adults to read to children, easy-to-read books are often written with a con-

trolled vocabulary, easily understandable words, and limited sentence and text length. Generally, they are a bridge between the basal reader and the trade book.

Easy-to-read books can be fact or fiction. They can be humorous, even non-sensical, like many of the Dr. Seuss stories, or quite serious, dealing with child-hood issues. Many are written as a complete story, while others, such *Frog and Toad Are Friends*, by Arnold Lobel, provide separate stories in one book. While some easy-to-read books are written with a controlled vocabulary, others, such as the Frog and Toad series are not. However, easy-to-read books demonstrate that quality can be achieved even with limited or controlled vocabulary.

Whether mystery or sports, fact or fantasy, easy-to-read books give chil-dren an opportunity to make their own selections based on their own needs and interests. Using these books, children practice and reinforce their reading skills. They feel a sense of accomplishment and independence as they actually read a book. Easy-to-read books provide the vehicle for such independence.

Activities to Use with Easy-to-Read Books

1. Place students in pairs and allow them to select an easy-to-read book to read to one another.
2. Read chapters from an easy-to-read book and have students come up with titles for each chapter.

3. With the students' participation, make a list of class favorite easy-to-read books. Duplicate the list for parents and encourage them to check these books out of the public library.
4. Assign groups of students an appropriate easy-to-read book (a book with a strong plot and little dialogue). Have them prepare a story theater.

Picture Storybooks

A picture storybook conveys its message through illustrations and text, both of which are equally important to the story. A well-written and well-illustrated storybook gives children a sense of what constitutes good literature. Good picture storybooks contain elements intrinsic to other literary forms: well-structured plot; well-defined characters that, whether human or animal, display human qualities to which children can relate; style that has movement; authentic, accurate settings; and interesting themes. In addition, these books are original and imaginative and provide stimulus for creative thought. Since most picture storybooks are read to children, the language is authentic. As with other good literature, picture storybooks foster an appreciation of language, encourage oral communication, expand cognitive thought processes, foster the expression of feelings, and increase sensitivity to the arts.

Picture storybooks cover a wide range of topics and themes, often based on everyday experiences with which children can readily identify. Many picture storybooks reflect a child's reality, such as the wish for the security of home, as in *Where the Wild Things Are,* by Maurice Sendak, in which Max wishes "to be where someone loved him best of all," or the need to succeed, as in Robert Kraus's *Leo the Late Bloomer. Alexander and the Terrible, Horrible, No Good, Very Bad Day,* by Judith Viorst, reminds children that everyone experiences disappointments, "Even in Australia."

Picture storybooks are also written to deal with difficult subjects. *The Fall of Freddie the Leaf,* by Leo Buscaglia, and *I'll See You in My Dreams,* by Mavis Jukes, deal with the subject of death in a sensitive manner and at a level to which children can relate. Books such as *Rose Blanche,* by Roberto Innocenti, and *The Wall,* by Eve Bunting, recall the untold sadness of war. The former, set in Germany during World War II, is about a young girl who makes secret journeys to a concentration camp to give children whatever food she can find. The latter describes a young boy's visit to the Vietnam Memorial in Washington, D.C.

Picture storybooks such as Chris Van Allsburg's *Just a Dream* are written to sensitize children to nature and the responsibility each of us has to protect our environment. In *Owl Moon,* Jane Yolen reminds us of the beauty and quiet of nature and the need to respect our environment. *Fireflies!,* by Julie Brinckloe, tells us that sometimes we have to set something free in order to keep it: "I held the jar, dark and empty in my hands. The moonlight and the fireflies swam in my tears, but I could feel myself smiling."

Picture storybooks often are children's first introduction to different ethnic and racial groups and to relations between generations. From an early age, it is important that children learn to recognize, understand, and appreciate the differences and sameness among all people. In *Abuela,* by Arthur Dorros, Rosalba and her grandmother take an extraordinary trip. Both English and Spanish phrases narrate the journey. Faith Ringgold, in *Tar Beach,* awakens our childhood fantasy of breaking free of all boundaries. In this magical story, the stars lift Cassie Lightfoot from the rooftop of her Harlem apartment building and carry her over the city.

Picture storybooks cover every genre—traditional literature, fantasy, poetry, realistic fiction, and historical fiction. There is a recent trend toward picture storybooks dealing with biography and informational subjects. Whereas biographies in the past were written about superheroes—those men and women who appeared to be almost perfect—today's authors introduce children to more complex heroes, recognizing that even heroes embrace positive and negative qualities, such as Columbus as projected in Jane Yolen's *Encounter.* Informational books also are written on all subjects, from Joanna Cole's Magic School Bus series, which takes the reader on incredible journeys through the solar system, the human body, and the waterworks, to Peter Golenbock's *Teammates,* the story of Jackie Robinson, the first African American man to play on a major league baseball team, and the Brooklyn Dodgers.

No matter what the need, the topic, or the theme, there is a picture storybook available on the subject. Picture storybooks, though originally conceived for younger children, are being read by older students as well. The magic of a good storybook knows no boundaries.

Activities to Use with Picture Storybooks

1. Invite parents, grandparents, and friends to a "picture-perfect picnic." Together with their child, have them select a favorite picture storybook and read it to one another during a picnic lunch at school. (Invite community guests to pair with children whose family or friends can't come.)
2. Organize a "favorite character parade," in which children dress up as their favorite storybook character. After the parade, have a "meet the character party," in which each character tells a little about himself or herself and his or her adventures.
3. Select a favorite picture storybook author of the month and decorate your classroom door with book jackets, illustrations, and so on that reflect the author and his or her work.
4. Have students re-create a favorite scene from a Caldecott Award–winning picture storybook. Mount pictures on construction paper or cardboard and label it with the author, title, illustrator, and year it won the Caldecott Medal.
5. Invite local artists and illustrators to share their expertise in a specific technique. Share books with students in which illustrations are created with this technique.

6. Gather picture storybooks that reflect different cultures, such as *Why Mosquitoes Buzz in People's Ears,* by Verna Aardema, *Arrow to the Sun,* by Gerald McDermott, or *Tar Beach,* by Faith Ringgold. Assign each group of students books relating to a specific culture. As they read the books and study the illustrations, have them list ideas and perceptions about the culture.

7. Give groups of students different picture storybooks. Ask the students to cover the text and, looking only at the illustrations, write a brief summary of the plot, setting, characters, and mood. Have them read the story and compare their summary with the text. Discuss what they discover about the illustrations in a picture storybook.

Selecting and Evaluating Picture Books

Certain criteria must be considered when selecting and evaluating picture books. The following checklist may be helpful. (Not all 10 criteria apply to all types of picture books.)

❑   1. Do the pictures extend the text, rather than conflict with it?
❑   2. Are the pictures clear and easily distinguishable? Are extraneous details avoided?
❑   3. Do the illustrations enhance the setting, plot, mood, and characterizations?
❑   4. Will children be able to identify with the characters and the action?
❑   5. Are the style and language appropriate for young children?
❑   6. Do the illustrations avoid stereotypes?
❑   7. Is the theme significant?
❑   8. Is the concept or theme appropriate for young children?
❑   9. Have a variety of books been chosen to reflect multicultural awareness?
❑ 10. Have books been chosen that reflect a variety of genres?

Extending Your Knowledge of Picture Books

1. Keep a file divided by type of picture book (alphabet, counting, Mother Goose rhymes, toy, concept, wordless, predictable, easy-to-read, and picture storybook). Locate 10 books that fit into each category and create an index card for each, listing bibliographic information, a brief summary, and an evaluation based on the criteria for selecting picture books.

2. Select several topics that would be of interest to your students. Create a card file of picture storybooks relating to each of these topics. *The Bookfinder,* by Sharon Spredemann Dreyer, is an excellent resource that indexes, and reviews children's books on more than 450 topics. Other valuable resources are listed in Professional Resources at the end of the chapter.

3. Create a mini-unit based on a favorite picture storybook. An excellent framework for creating this unit is provided in Chapter 12.

4. Read aloud to students several picture books and ask them to tell you why they did or didn't like it. Keep a record of these evaluations, along with bibliographic information, for future reference.
5. Compare and evaluate several versions of Mother Goose collections.
6. Prepare a survey that asks elementary-school teachers to list their favorite picture books and to make suggestions for using them in the classroom.
7. Create your own list of Caldecott Award winners or honor books, organized by artistic medium used. Add to each category five titles that did not win the award but which you believe are deserving.
8. Select five authors and/or illustrators of children's picture books and create an annotated list of books written and/or illustrated by each.
9. Many have criticized Mother Goose as being sexist. Survey Mother Goose rhymes for this and other stereotypes. Consider ways to use these rhymes to make children aware of stereotypes and to alleviate them.

Realistic Fiction

Childhood is a special time of wonder, joy, and growth. Yet growing up is an often difficult and sometimes painful process. Children face many of the same hopes, fears, and doubts as adults and they need reassurance and help in dealing with their feelings. Through books of realistic fiction, children can identify with certain characters and situations and thereby gain understanding and insight into their own lives.

Also referred to as contemporary or modern realistic fiction, this genre includes books that are imaginatively and realistically written and that deal with all aspects of life. Books of realistic fiction have certain qualities in common. While they are fictitious, they are set in a plausible place and time, and they contain believable characters involved in situations that could conceivably happen. Many stories of realistic fiction focus on problems, issues, and feelings encountered in daily living, such as family relationships, security, the need to belong, survival, interpersonal skills, growing up, and sexuality. There is a recent trend to include stories in which the protagonists are members of minority groups (see Chap. 8), reflecting the multicultural world in which we live and giving readers an opportunity to see the world through the eyes of those from different backgrounds. It is hoped that this will result in a generation of individuals who are more open and appreciative of others, more empathic, and more caring.

Realistic fiction offers children an opportunity to understand themselves better. Through the experiences of characters in books, children realize they are not alone and that there are others who have felt as they feel, dreamed the same dreams, and faced similar problems. They gain perspective on their own reality and their own roles in society. For example, many children have had to move, whether to another end of town, another state, or another country. They can identify with Leigh Botts, the main character in *Dear Mr. Henshaw*, by Beverly

Reflections of . . .

Walter Dean Myers

College was supposed to provide my son with an education and give him a decent start on the rest of his life. As it turns out, the only thing he has accomplished so far is the ability to argue with his beloved father (me) and to question the very work that provides the money (a lot) for that education.

What he questions is my claim of writing realistic fiction. According to him, my life isn't even realistic, so what do I have to base my stories on? My life? Not realistic? Hey, I was raised in the streets of Harlem and attended the school of hard knocks!

"But inside your head you're always playing sports, or involved with some fantasy," he said, smugly. "I can tell by the way your hand goes up every now and then with an imaginary jump shot, or the way your eyes kind of glaze over and you miss half of our conversations at times."

"There was a big game on last night," I countered. "Naturally I was thinking about it."

"And sometimes when I walk into a room I see you having imaginary conversations with people only you can hear!"

"Maybe it's old age," I mumbled.

"Granddaddy said you used to do the same thing when you were 9."

"Imagination is good for you once in a while," I said, looking for an escape valve.

"But if you're always leading an imaginary life," Mr. Know-It-All said, "On what are you basing your so-called realistic fiction?"

"You have a limited understanding of realism," I said. "You seem to think it only means something physical. What you think is real, too! I think, therefore I am!"

"Granted, but if you spend most of your life reading what someone else has imagined," he said, parking his size fifteens on the couch, "and another part of it in your own little imaginary world, then your reality is mostly not the kind of reality they mean when they speak of realistic fiction. Admit it!"

"Wrong! Wrong! Wrong!!!" I said, snatching the remote control from his hand. "I have to imagine the world around me in order to recreate it in my books. So I turn the real world into an imaginary world so that it becomes real to my reader. In turn, my reader has to be able to imagine the world I'm creating in order to understand what I'm saying. Do you get it?"

"So you're going to write about that imaginary jump shot you're always making?" he asked, a crooked smile on his face. "The one that always wins the Big Game?"

"Well . . . no, I guess not."

"Aha! Then I'm right!" he bellowed, an evil glint in his eye.

"No!" I bellowed back, triumphantly. "Not only are you wrong, but you're also imaginary!"

And with that I stopped thinking about him and he was gone.

Cleary, a child who misses his old home, old friends, and old life and who must come to terms with his parents' divorce. In *In the Year of the Boar and Jackie Robinson*, by Bette Bao Lord, the reader is introduced to a character who must make a new life for herself in a new land where customs and lifestyles are strange and the people unfamiliar. In Laurence Yep's *Child of the Owl*, a Chinese American child discovers her roots when she goes to live with her grandmother in San Francisco's Chinatown. And in Jerry Spinelli's *Maniac Magee*, the title character roams from place to place searching for the one place where he can belong, the one place he can call home.

Realistic fiction can also help children discover and experience the unfamiliar to help prepare them for the inevitablities of life, such as aging and death. In Tomie de Paola's *Now One Foot, Now the Other*, children experience first sadness and then triumph as a young boy's love and patience bring his grandfather back from the devastating effects of a stroke. Children mourn with the characters who must face the death of someone they love in Tomie de Paola's *Nana Upstairs, Nana Downstairs* or Judith Viorst's *The Tenth Good Thing About Barney*. Through the experiences of Jess in Katherine Paterson's *Bridge to Terabithia*, children learn about the courage they need to face death and life. They share Jess's grief as he comes to grips with the death of his best friend, and as Jess draws strength from her legacy of friendship and love they begin to understand that even in death a person lives on in our hearts. *I'll See You in My Dreams*, by Mavis Jukes, is a picture book about having to say goodbye.

Realistic fiction can also help children better understand their environment and the role they have in preserving it. Books such as *Hatchet*, by Gary Paulsen, and *Water Sky*, *Julie of the Wolves*, and *The Talking Earth*, by Jean Craighead George, deal with survival based on the ability to interact with the environment and encourage a respect for the delicate balance of nature. These books also allow children to discover the capability each has to sustain life and take control of their destiny.

Mysteries, sports stories, animal stories, and humorous stories are all examples of realistic fiction. These forms lead to a better understanding of the human condition and are favorites of children of all ages who vicariously share in the adventure. For example, humorous stories, such as those by Peggy Parish about Amelia Bedelia, the maid who takes everything literally, often cause the reader to laugh out loud. In *Play Ball, Amelia Bedelia,* Amelia looks for a clothing tag when she's told to "tag Jack."

In realistic fiction, children not only see themselves in various situations and characters, but they also discover ways to deal with their own problems as they make choices and become aware of the consequences of these actions. Children learn about themselves and others and find meaning in their lives as they explore the world in which they live and establish their own place in it.

The tremendous scope of realistic fiction makes it possible to find something for everyone. The table on page 28–30 lists just a sampling of the diverse themes developed in realistic fiction books. Because most deal with more than one issue, it is often difficult to place them in just one category. For example, the themes developed in *Dear Mr. Henshaw* include divorce, moving and starting over, and growing up. Therefore, several books are listed more than once.

REALISTIC FICTION

LOOKING DIFFERENT	Author	Grade Levels
Blubber	Judy Blume	4–6
Freckle Juice	Judy Blume	3–6
Nothing's Fair in the Fifth Grade	Barthe DeClements	3–6
Look Who's Beautiful!	Julie First	4–6
Get On Out of Here, Philip Hall	Bette Greene	4–6
The Runt of Rodgers School	Harold Verne Keith	4–7
Anastasia Has the Answers	Lois Lowry	4–6
Crow Boy	Taro Yashima	1–3

GROWING UP		
Are You There, God? It's Me, Margaret	Judy Blume	4–6
The Secret Garden	Frances Hodgson Burnett	5–9
Dear Mr. Henshaw	Beverly Cleary	3–6
Staying Nine	Pam Conrad	2–5
Desdemona—Twelve Going on Desperate	Beverly Keller	4–7
Anastasia Krupnik	Lois Lowry	3–6
Arthur, for the Very First Time	Patricia MacLachlan	3–6
Be a Perfect Person in Just Three Days	Stephen Manes	3–6

ACCEPTANCE AND BELONGING		
The Hundred Dresses	Eleanor Estes	2–5
Harriet the Spy	Louise Fitzhugh	4–6
The Outsiders	S. E. Hinton	6+
Scorpions	Walter Dean Myers	5+
Call It Courage	Armstrong Sperry	4–7
Maniac Magee	Jerry Spinelli	3–6
Shadow of a Bull	Maia Wojciechowska	4–7

FAMILY RELATIONSHIPS		
The Pinballs	Betsy Byars	4–7
The Not-Just-Anybody Family	Betsy Byars	4–6
Where the Lilies Bloom	Vera and Bill Cleaver	6+
Peter's Chair	Ezra Jack Keats	K–3
Anastasia on Her Own	Lois Lowry	4–6
Baby	Patricia MacLachlan	2–6
Jacob Have I Loved	Katherine Paterson	6+

FAMILY RELATIONSHIPS	Author	Grade Levels
Stevie	John Steptoe	K–3
Dicey's Song	Cynthia Voigt	6+
A Chair for My Mother	Vera B. Williams	K–3
FRIENDSHIP		
The Cybil War	Betsy Byars	2–5
May I Bring a Friend	Beatrice Schenk de Regniers	K–3
Aldo Applesauce	Johanna Hurwitz	4–6
Onion John	Joseph Krumgold	4–7
Bridge to Terabithia	Katherine Paterson	4–7
Rosie and Michael	Judith Viorst	K–3
DEATH AND DYING		
Nana Upstairs, Nana Downstairs	Tomie de Paola	K–3
Now One Foot, Now the Other	Tomie de Paola	K–3
You Shouldn't Have to Say Goodby	Patricia Hermes	K–6
I'll See You in My Dreams	Mavis Jukes	1–4
Mama's Going to Buy You a Mockingbird	Jean Little	3–6
A Summer to Die	Lois Lowry	4+
Bridge to Terabithia	Katherine Paterson	4–6
Parks Quest	Katherine Paterson	5+
Missing May	Cynthia Rylant	4–6
The Tenth Good Thing About Barney	Judith Viorst	1–4
SURVIVAL		
Monkey Island	Paula Fox	4–7
Julie of the Wolves	Jean George	4+
The Talking Earth	Jean George	5+
From the Mixed-Up Files of Mrs. Basil E. Frankweiler	E. L. Konigsburg	4+
Hatchet	Gary Paulsen	5+
The Sign of the Beaver	Elizabeth George Speare	4+
Call It Courage	Armstrong Sperry	5+
GENERATIONS		
How Does It Feel to Be Old?	Norma Farber	K–3
The Hundred Penny Box	Sharon Bell Mathis	2–6
Through Grandpa's Eyes	Patricia MacLachlan	K–3
Annie and the Old One	Miska Miles	K–4
The War with Grandpa	Robert Kimmel Smith	4+
MULTICULTURAL		
M.C. Higgins, the Great	Virginia Hamilton	5+
Zeely	Virginia Hamilton	3–6
. . . And Now Miguel	Joseph Krumgold	6+
In the Year of the Boar and Jackie Robinson	Bette Bao Lord	3–5

MULTICULTURAL	Author	Grade Levels
ustin and the Best Biscuits in the World	Mildred Pitts Walter	3–7
Child of the Owl	Laurence Yep	5+
PREJUDICE AND DISCRIMINATION		
Sounder	William Armstrong	5+
About the B'nai Bagels	E. L. Konigsburg	4–6
Felita	Nicolasa Mohr	3–6
Journey to Jo'berg	Beverly Naidoo	3–6
With My Face to the Rising Sun	Robert Martin Screen	4+
Sea Glass	Laurence Yep	4+
DISABILITIES		
The Summer of the Swans	Betsy Byars	4–7
Golden Daffodils	Marilyn Gould	4–6
Mine for Keeps	Jean Little	4–7
Welcome Home, Jellybean	Marlene Shyer	4–6
The Alfred Summer	Jan Slepian	4–6

Selecting and Evaluating Realistic Fiction

When selecting and evaluating realistic fiction books, all the standards of good literature must be met. In addition, the following criteria should be considered.

- ☐ 1. Can the child identify and relate to the characters or situation as portrayed in the text and illustrations?
- ☐ 2. Is the content presented honestly and realistically?
- ☐ 3. Does the child have an opportunity to gain insights and understanding into problems and situations?
- ☐ 4. Are a variety of cultures and lifestyles represented?
- ☐ 5. Are the characters and actions plausible?
- ☐ 6. Is there a hopeful, positive, and mature approach to dealing with a problem or situation?
- ☐ 7. Is there enough information to allow the child to draw his or her own conclusions?

Activities to Use with Realistic Fiction

The activities outlined below illustrate ways students can be encouraged to build personal frameworks as a result of their own responses to the literature and their own experiences. Similar activities can be developed for any work of realistic fiction. Many of the activities and discussion forums described in Part III can easily be adapted to encourage and enhance responses to books of realistic fiction.

Looking Different

1. In a world in which people are judged first by their physical appearance, many children feel inferior if they aren't as thin, as tall, or as perfect as currently popular models and actors. Read aloud the following books by Judy Blume:

   Freckle Juice—the story of a boy who wants to look like his peers so badly that he eventually paints freckles on his face so he can look like his friend

   Blubber—the story of the cruelty of children toward each other

   After reading one or both of these books, respond to the following questions: What problems did the main character have? How did the main character deal with the problem? In what other ways might this character have dealt with the problem? What advice would you give him or her?

   Have students collect pictures of people with different physical attributes—those who are tall, short, thin, and heavy; people who wear glasses, who have freckles, large and small noses; people who have blond hair, black hair, and no hair. Have them make a collage of these pictures and then write a poem or short story that reflects their feelings about differences in appearance. For example:

   People

   Tall people, short people,
      Thin people, fat;
      Lady so dainty
      Wearing a hat.
   Straight people, dumpy people,
      Man dressed in brown,
      Baby in buggy,
      These make a town.

   Author unknown

2. Read *The Hundred Dresses,* by Eleanor Estes, the story of Wanda, a young girl who is constantly ridiculed by the other kids. Although Wanda always wears the same old clothing, she tells them about the hundred beautiful dresses hanging in her closet. It isn't until she moves away that the other children discover that Wanda is a talented artist and designer and the hundred dresses are a hundred drawings that Wanda has created. Ask students to write letters to Wanda, as if they were in her class, to explain why they acted toward her as they did and how they felt after they received her father's letter.

Growing Up

1. Read *Desdemona—Twelve Going on Desperate,* by Beverly Keller, in which Desdemona faces a series of disasters as she grows up and faces life's challenges. Ask students to list the various "catastrophes" Desdemona had to face. What do they consider the highlight of her life? The lowest point? What event do they think was a turning point in her life? Ask them to imagine a book was being written about them and to create a title using the title of this book as a model: _____ (student's name) _____ (student's age) Going on _____ (adjective). Have them write a beginning for the book, telling about a significant high point, low point, or turning point in their life.

2. Read *Be a Perfect Person in Just Three Days,* by Stephen Manes. Have students discuss the reasons being perfect is like "sipping weak tea."

Acceptance and Belonging

1. Read *Maniac Magee,* by Jerry Spinelli, the story of a 12-year-old orphan whose amazing feats have earned him the nickname Maniac. Of all the amazing things he can do, most amazing is the way he brought two parts of a racially divided town together in acceptance and friendship. Have students imagine they are one of the characters in the book and are establishing a special award to be given to Maniac, the "Maniac Award." Let each student deliver a speech to the class to explain why Maniac has been chosen as recipient of the award.

   Establish a "Maniac Award" for your school to be given annually to the person who has done the most to further harmony and acceptance in the school. Have students design a medal to present to the winner.

2. In *Call it Courage,* by Armstrong Sperry, Mafatu has a terrible fear of the sea and, as a result of his cowardice, feels as if he were an outcast in his tribe. After reading the book, read the letter on page 33 to the class and ask them to write a response. Have students share their letters with their classmates and discuss the advice given.

3. Ask students to think of a time they felt as if they weren't accepted by others. Have them role-play the situation with other students. Discuss what happened.

4. Peer pressure is a very real and often a very deadly phenomenon. Read *The Scorpions,* by Walter Dean Myers. Have students research the lure of gang membership to discover why people their age join groups and what they believe to be the pros and cons of gang membership. Based on the insights gained from *The Scorpions* and from the research, have students hold a "talk show" in which students pretend to be gang members and de-

July 22, 1989

Dear Advice Columnist,

I am nine years old and I don't know what to do or who to go to for help. I feel like such

a failure because I can't live up to the expectations of being an island chief's son. I am

supposed to be brave, but I am not! I am afraid of the sea because it killed my mother

when I was a baby, and yet I live on this seafaring island where the people worship

courage. People call me a coward. I even heard my best friend, Kana, call me a coward,

and now I feel as if I have no friends. Please tell me what I can do.

Signed,

The Coward

scribe their experiences. Invite school counselors and psychologists to be part of the panel.

Family Relationships

1. Read *Where the Lilies Bloom,* by Vera and Bill Cleaver, or *Dicey's Song*, by Cynthia Voigt. Have students discuss the importance of family in these stories and the commitment that held them together. Have students create a family tree using a variety of materials. If possible, have them obtain pictures to put on the tree as well as a phrase that captures the essence of each member of their family. The family tree should go back as far as possible and should include the student and his or her siblings.
2. Read *The Pinballs*, by Betsy Byars, or *The Great Gilly Hopkins*, by Katherine Paterson, which deals with children who are in foster care yet yearn for a permanent family and home. Form discussion groups in which the following issues are highlighted:
   a. The positive and negative feelings associated with foster care

b. The qualities that allowed each character to survive new situations

c. The characteristics of the character the students admire most

d. Insights gained about life and family relationships

Friendship

1. Have students read one of the books about friendship and explain why they would or would not like the main character in the book for a friend.

2. Have students read one of the books about friendship and create a recipe, based on what they learned in the book, for making and/or keeping good friends.

3. Ask students to think about the books they read that dealt with friendship and make a list of events from the books that exemplified true friendship. Have students as a class create a mural that illustrates what friendship means to them.

Death and Dying

1. Read *Nana Upstairs, Nana Downstairs,* by Tomie de Paola. Tommy's mother tried to help him understand Nana's death by telling him his grandmother would live on in his memory. Have students develop a questionnaire to discover how people have dealt with the death of someone close and, from the information gathered, create a book to help others deal with death.

2. Read *The Tenth Good Thing About Barney,* by Judith Viorst, in which a family holds a funeral for Barney, their dog. At the funeral, a eulogy was delivered. Have students create a eulogy for a pet they have loved.

3. Read *Bridge to Terabithia,* by Katherine Paterson. In dealing with death most people go through certain stages, as Jess did. Have students create a story-map or timeline to show the stages Jess went through. Have them research the stages of dealing with death by talking to doctors, nurses, or those who have had to deal with death.

Survival

1. Read *Water Sky,* by Jean George. Have students write a newspaper article that explains the importance of the whales to the Eskimo people or an editorial that addresses the issues of protecting whales from extinction.

2. Read *Call It Courage,* by Armstrong Sperry. Have students discuss the ways Mafatu used his skills and resourcefulness to survive against nature and the elements. Have them select and research a natural phenomenon (hurricane, tornado, flood, earthquake, lightning storm, volcanic eruption, etc.) and create a brochure to give people the information needed to sur-

vive (ways to stay safe, where to find shelter, how to protect their homes, food supplies, etc.).

3. Read *The Talking Earth*, by Jean Craighead George. Have students discuss the meaning of "the balance of nature" and what Billie witnessed in the Everglades that illustrates the way humans are upsetting this balance. Have them discuss problems related to the environment that Earth faces today. Ask them to select one and write a plan to help eliminate this danger. Have them send letters outlining their ideas to congressional leaders, the local newspaper, or environmental agencies.

Generations

1. Read *The Hundred Penny Box*, by Sharon Mathis, which tells the story of Michael's great-great aunt Dew who was 100 years old and kept an old box filled with pennies, one for each year of her life. Have students make their own Hundred Penny Box, putting in one penny minted in each year of their life. Have them create a log that tells the most significant events of each year, both global and personal.

2. Read *The War with Grandpa*, by Robert Kimmel Smith. Have students write a journal entry that tells about a special time or event involving their grandparents or other older members of their family.

3. After reading a book dealing with generations, have students make a list of interview questions to ask grandparents and other members of their family that will tell future generations what their lives were like. The questions should elicit responses about their childhood, traditions and celebrations they remember, anecdotes, problems faced, work and work conditions, and so on. Encourage students to capture the interview on videotape or cassette.

Multicultural Understanding

Books dealing with various cultures should be a part of each topic issue studied. In addition, you can create a special unit on various cultures by dividing students into groups and allowing each to select a different culture, for example: African American, Hispanic, Native American, or Asian American. Have each student in the group select a different book related to the culture. Plan a week of activities for each of the cultures studied in which students:

1. Read special portions of the books aloud.
2. Deliver character monologues or skits to promote understanding of the customs, values, or significant issues/problems of the culture.
3. Share special foods of the culture.
4. Invite guest speakers.
5. Role-play some of the situations described in the books.

Prejudice and Discrimination

After reading one of the books on the subject of prejudice/discrimination, ask students to think about how the character(s) were treated. For example, in *Sounder,* by William Armstrong, the father was discriminated against because he was a sharecropper. Have students think of how other people who suffer from prejudice have been treated.

1. Have students write a poem that answers one or both of these questions: What is prejudice? What is acceptance? (See below, page 37, and page 39.) Their poems should include information gained through the book they read. For example, the poems below were written after students read Jane Yolen's *The Devil's Arithmetic,* a work of historical fiction which describes the life of a girl who travels back in time to experience the holocaust.
2. Ask students to think of prejudice in another way and *become prejudice.* Have them describe what they look like, how they influence people, what their life is like, and how they are responsible for certain things that have occurred. Have them write the story of their life, including reasons for their long survival and explaining how they can be eliminated (see page 38).

Disabilities

1. Read *The Summer of the Swans,* by Betsy Byars, in which Sara's brother is mute. Have students discuss the problems people such as Charlie face each day. Have them select one type of disability and learn more about it by spending time with a person who has this disability. Ask them to make a list of changes that need to be made in their school/classroom to make life easier for people with this type of disability. Have them discuss their

What is Prejudice?

Written by: **Jillian Robinson, Age 11**

North Dade Center for Modern Languages
Dade County Schools, Miami, Florida

Prejudice is a swan, unearthly but ignorant.
a strong disliked scent,
winter, cruel and harsh,
frustration and stress,
unfair, cold, and agony.
prejudice is a Devil's Arithmetic,
unpredictable and hipocrisy,
It could be anywhere and everywhere.

That is Prejudice.

Acceptance

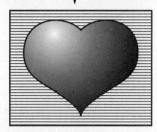

Beyond the horizon of hatred
Behind the door of racism
In between love and hate
Inside the hearts of stone
After the storm of prejudice has passed
After the wounds of hate are mended
There lies a small golden box filled with love,
forgiveness and acceptance

By: Laurean Robinson, Age 11

North Dade School for Modern Languages
Dade County Schools, Miami, Florida

list with experts in the field and send a copy of their suggestions to the local school board urging these improvements be implemented.

2. Read *The Trumpet of the Swan,* by E. B. White, in which Louis the Swan, born without a voice, uses other abilities to do great things. Have students discuss what Louis has in common with people such as Helen Keller, Louis Braille, Beethoven, Stevie Wonder, and Marlee Matlin. What qualities do they all seem to possess? What message does *The Trumpet of the Swan* give regarding disabilities? Have students create a poster that reflects this understanding.

Extending Your Knowledge of Realistic Fiction

1. Create an "interest inventory" to help you identify books of realistic fiction that will appeal to a selected group of students. Questions in the inventory might focus on students' family, siblings, interests, favorite sports, pets, travel, heroes, other favorite books, favorite television shows, goals, and so on.

2. Create a filing system for realistic fiction by dividing books according to theme or topic. Complete a file card for several books that fit these

I AM PREJUDICE

By Jennifer Herrera, Age 11

North Dade School for Modern Languages
Dade County Schools, Miami, Florida

I am prejudice and proud of it. I am the reason why many riots start. The definition of me is hate.

I come from all different countries. I come in different shapes, sizes, and genders.

I hate Whites, Hispanics, Jews, Blacks, and anyone else who differs with me. I've caused the death of six million innocent Jews. I am the reason that different races still fight against one another. I am also the reason women are still fighting for equality.

When I see two different races in conflict it gives me a sense of satisfaction. If I am able to continue on my path, I will destroy families, friends, and societies as we know it.

The three words that cause a chill to run down my spine are friendship, forgiveness, and peace. The three words that give me power are bigotry, sorrow, and pain. The reason why the word love doesn't cause a chill to run down my spine is because I love hate. I also love war. You can't kill me by calling me names or throwing punches. That's what makes me so powerful.

I haunt the air. I am your worst nightmare. I am any pain that comes upon you. The only way the world can get rid of me is if there was peace everywhere.

I AM PREJUDICE

themes/topics, listing theme/topic; bibliograpic information; a summary; something special about the book; appropriate age levels; and to whom the book would probably appeal (see page 40).

3. Select a popular author of children's realistic fiction and create a file of interesting information about the author and summaries of his or her books. Resources such as *Something About the Author* and *Yesterday's Authors of Books for Children* can provide valuable information. Create 5–10 activities you could use in a classroom if you were planning a special tribute to this author.

4. Create a story unit based on a specific book of realistic fiction. This unit should contain a story summary; a brief introduction to the author; a prereading activity to set the stage and motivate reading; questions to involve students in a discussion of the story and foster higher-level thinking; activities that relate to the book and its theme (for small groups, individuals, and the entire class), activities that foster development of skills in all areas of the curriculum; and a bulletin board idea that gives students an opportunity to display their work related to the book.

WHAT IS

PREJUDICE ?

Prejudice is . . .

exploding bombs

the devil's arithmetic

death, slow and agonizing

a barred door between races

a war declared on the universe

the destroyer of love, the producer of hate

a slimy water moccasin spitting venom into your unguarded mind

THAT'S PREJUDICE

by: Bronwyn Steinberg, Age 11

North Dade Center for Modern Languages
Dade County Schools, Miami, Florida

5. Compare several examples of classic fiction with books of modern realistic fiction. What are the similarities and differences?
6. Create a list of relevant, meaningful activities that will involve students in sharing a favorite book of realistic fiction. Include activities that involve such areas as drama, art, music, writing, and speaking. Encourage the use of videotapes, audio cassettes, computers, slides, photography, and so on.
7. Select a favorite book of realistic fiction. Locate literature in other genres that deal with a similar subject.
8. Select a specific minority group. Locate at least five books written before 1960 and five books written between 1960 and today that include characters representative of the minority groups. Compare the ways the minority group is portrayed.

Historical Fiction

Time travel is possible. Children can be transported through the centuries to another age. They can become part of the past, taking part in long-ago events and meeting people who, though different in many ways, are fundamentally the same as their contemporaries. Children don't need a time capsule or magic carpet for this adventure. They simply need books that are rich in history and vivid

Literary File Card: Realistic Fiction

Theme/Topic:

Title:

Author: Publication date/publisher:

Summary:

Something special about book:

Appropriate age levels:

This book would probably appeal to students who:

in detail, that artfully combine fact and fiction—books that are classified as historical fiction.

Historical fiction is a realistic story set in the past. By reconstructing life in another time, these stories allow the reader vicariously to experience past events. The author of historical fiction researches the setting of the story, both place and time, using a variety of sources, from newspapers to diaries and interviews to books. The details of life, such as food, clothing, and transportation, must be portrayed naturally to bring the past to life in a realistic, believable manner. The elements of time and setting are important influences on the central plot and characters. In addition, the author must establish a tone that holds the reader's attention. Elizabeth George Speare, one of the most respected authors of historical fiction (*The Witch of Blackbird Pond, Calico Captive, The Sign of the Beaver*) relates that her research for a book can take a year or more.

There are different types of historical fiction stories. One type uses fictional characters and does not refer to known people or recorded historical events. For example, in *Caddie Woodlawn*, Carol Ryrie Brink, through Caddie, a 12-year-old fictional character, takes the reader back to the Wisconsin frontier in 1864. No real people or actual historical events are identified in this story, yet the reader gets a feeling for life on a farm in the 1800s. Similarly, through the characters and setting in *Sarah, Plain and Tall,* by Patricia MacLachlan and *Prairie Songs,* by Pam Conrad, the reader gains a sense of the beauty and vastness of the prairie.

Another type of historical fiction involves actual people and recorded events. Esther Forbes's *Johnny Tremain* is an example. Johnny, Paul Revere's apprentice, lives during the prerevolutionary days and early wartime in Boston. Both a real person (Paul Revere) and a recorded event (the Revolutionary War) are vividly and accurately portrayed. In *Shh! We're Writing the Constitution,* Jean Fritz introduces the reader to the men charged with the awesome responsibility of shaping a form of government that would guide the new nation.

Perhaps the greatest value of historical fiction is that it allows the reader to experience the past. Books of historical fiction have captured the spirit of past times and allow us to relive the victories of the human spirit as well as the defeats caused by human weaknesses and prejudice. Books of historical fiction allow us to journey across America in the wagon trains that carried pioneers who ventured west and introduce us to the colorful and rich heritage of the immigrants who sought a new life in a new land. Children become settlers as they share in the adventures of Constance in Patricia Clapp's *Constance: A Story of Early Plymouth.* They will be able to imagine what it was like to stand on the deck of the Mayflower and view America, their new home. Children learn about George Washington and his times through Phoebe's experience in Judith Berry Griffin's *Phoebe and the General.* In the many books that comprise the Little House series by Laura Ingalls Wilder, the reader becomes part of the Ingalls family and travels with Ma, Pa, Mary, and Laura from the little log cabin on the edge of the Big Woods of Wisconsin, across the country by covered wagon through Kansas, Minnesota, and the Dakota Territory. The stories vividly recollect the days of the pioneer and the challenges that waited at every turn. Through reading *Dragonwings,* by Laurence Yep, inspired by the account of a Chinese immigrant who made flying machines, children experience a more recent past, a time when thousands of people came to the United States in search of a better life. Readers will empathize with Moon Shadow, who initially faces persecution and prejudice as he tries to hold on to his heritage, yet make his way in a land of strangers.

Through books of historical fiction, children learn about the events that changed the course of history. For example, *Sarah Bishop,* by Scott O'Dell, recounts the story of a family torn apart because of the Revolutionary War. Sarah's father is a Tory and her brother is a Patriot, and Sarah finds herself alone and pursued by the British. The Civil War and the flight from slavery are recounted in such books as Virginia Hamilton's *The House of Dies Drear* and Faith Ringgold's highly acclaimed picture book, *Aunt Harriet's Underground Railroad in the Sky.*

Through historical fiction, children's sense of decency and fair play is heightened as they empathize with characters who have been persecuted. From books such as *Number the Stars,* by Lois Lowry, which deals with the bravery of the Danish people determined to protect their Jewish citizens during World War II, and Roberto Innocenti's picture book *Rose Blanche,* readers learn about the devastating effects of prejudice and apathy. Mildred Taylor's *Roll of Thunder, Hear My Cry* introduces children to the courage and nobility of an African American family surrounded by prejudice in a small Mississippi town during the 1930s. Elizabeth George Speare's *The Witch of Blackbird Pond*, set in New England in the 1600s, deals with religious intolerance and the witch hunts of earlier centuries. Books such as these often give children a deeper understanding of human nature.

Finally, books of historical fiction allow us to look at the past with the advantage of historical perspective. For example, most books that tell the story of Christopher Columbus and his journey to the New World view his contributions through rose-colored glasses. They perpetuate the glory of the discovery and hail the perils that were overcome. Yet in *Encounter*, by Jane Yolen, the contributions of Columbus are seen through the eyes of a young Taino boy who witnessed the destruction of his tribe at the hands of the Europeans. Native Americans have historically been characterized as vicious and uncivilized, but more recent books give insight into the plight of the Native Americans who were exploited in the name of progress. For example, King David, the main character in *Save Queen of Sheba*, by Louise Moeri, realizes what it means to the Sioux Indians to have white settlers on their land. Most books that deal with the Revolutionary War portray the colonists who revolted as "knights in shining armor" and the British as evil. However, *Sarah Bishop*, by Scott O'Dell, allows the reader to observe the shades of gray. Through most accounts of history we see the bombing of Japan as the solution to ending World War II. However, in *Sadako and the Thousand Paper Cranes*, by Eleanor Coerr, we become involved in the life of Sadako, a Japanese girl who contracts leukemia as a result of the radiation from the atomic bombs. We are inspired by her courage and we see the dark side of nuclear power.

More books of historical fiction are being published than ever before, a trend caused in part by the recent trend to use literature to teach and enhance curriculum topics and concepts. Books of historical fiction can be found to extend any social studies lesson, in such diverse areas as discovery and exploration, war, becoming a nation, pioneer days and the westward movement, colonial times, immigration, and survival.

Many resources are available to help locate and use that special book that will bring history to life. A few of these resources are listed below. Numerous books develop specific works of children's literature to teach specific social studies content and themes as well as content throughout the curriculum. Through historical fiction, children can experience the past first-hand. They read about events and the way they have shaped our world and can compare them with the present. They read about people who have learned to overcome problems, work out differences, accept challenges, and learn alternative ways of handling situations. Historical fiction provides the vehicle through which children can learn from the past to improve tomorrow. And through their vicarious journey, children may be better equipped to cope with the everyday realities of life today.

Sources for Locating Children's Literature in Social Studies

Gillespie and Gillespie. *Best Books for Children: Preschool through the Middle Grades.*

Huck, Hepler, and Hickman. *Children's Literature in the Elementary School.*

National Council for the Social Studies. *Notable Children's Trade Books in the Field of Social Studies.*

Norton, Donna E. *Through the Eyes of a Child: An Introduction to Children's Literature. A Reference Guide to Historical Fiction for Children and Young Adults.*

Sutherland and Arbuthnot. *Children and Books.*

VanMeter. *American History for Children and Young Adults: An Annotated Bibliographic Index.*

Selecting and Evaluating Historical Fiction

As with any other literature, when selecting and evaluating historical fiction, the standards of good literature must be met. In addition, the following special criteria are important.

❑ 1. Are past events depicted accurately and authentically?
❑ 2. Are the details of the times portrayed accurately and authentically?
❑ 3. Do the characters reflect the values of the times?
❑ 4. Is the plot consistent with the times?
❑ 5. Is the language appropriate to the times, yet interesting to present-day readers?
❑ 6. Does the theme provide insight into and understanding of past events?
❑ 7. Does the story provide a perspective of the way the past affects the present and the future?
❑ 8. Are fact and fiction blended in an interesting manner?
❑ 9. Is the past brought to life?

Activities to Use with Historical Fiction

1. Ask students to select a book of historical fiction and list five facts they discovered about the time and place in which the book is set. Involve them in research using informational books to ascertain the accuracy of the facts presented in their books.
2. After they have read books of historical fiction that describe a significant event in history, have students dramatize a scene from one of the books or prepare a monologue in which the main character describes his or her impression of the historical event. For example, a student can be Thomas Jefferson or Patrick Henry describing his experiences as the Constitution is planned, based on *Shh! We're Writing the Constitution,* by Jean Fritz.

3. Have students select a favorite period from the past. Based on information they discover in books of historical fiction, have them create a newspaper that might have been written during that time period. It should include sections such as world news, local news, weather, advertisements, editorials, an advice column, and household hints.

4. After they have read books set in a particular time period, have students create "time period graffiti," in which they draw pictures and write phrases and words that reflect the events and sentiments of the people of the time covered.

5. Have each student keep a simulated journal, written as if he or she were a character from one of the books of historical fiction. In their journals, have them react to the different situations described in the book.

6. Have students write a story set in today's world that will be the historical fiction of tomorrow. Encourage them to incorporate information found in newspapers, magazines, letters, television programs, surveys, and so forth, to help their stories accurately reflect life as it is today.

7. After they've read a book of historical fiction, have students create a humorous skit or a more serious documentary to describe the life or time period presented in the book.

8. Read to elementary students a book of historical fiction that relates to something they have been studying. Ask them to respond to one of the following, in oral, written, dramatic, or artistic form:

   a. What if you were president of the United States when the story took place? What one law would you have tried to pass? How would it have changed life at the time?
   b. What if you could change the outcome of one event described in the book? What would you choose, and how would the event turn out?
   c. What if you were a character in the book who suddenly traveled through time to today's world? What advice would you give other children?

Extending Your Knowledge of Historical Fiction

1. Make a list of different periods in U.S. history. Create a card file of books of historical fiction that reflect each of these. Each card should include bibliographic information, time period, and a brief summary of the story.

2. Read the books you located on one of the different time periods (see 1, above). Which book gives the most insight into the period? How was this accomplished?

3. Discuss the message of the quote by George Santayana: "Those who cannot remember the past are condemned to repeat it." Select several books of historical fiction and relate their theme to the present to discover what lessons we have or have not learned from the past.

4. Create a unit on an individual war or war in general. Read books of historical fiction that deal with the war(s), such as *Early Thunder*, by Jean Fritz (Revolutionary War), or *Cyrus Holt and the Civil War*, by Anna Gertrude Hall, or *Number the Stars*, by Lois Lowry (World War II). Create activities that will encourage students to analyze the events leading up to the war(s), the reasons for war, the issues involved, the aftermath, and so on.

5. Select a topic and locate several books of historical fiction and several informational books that deal with the same topic. What are the similarities and differences in the treatment of the subject?

6. Select a well-known author of historical fiction, such as Clyde Robert Bulla (*A Lion to Guard Us*), Alice Dalgliesh (*The Courage of Sarah Noble*), Jean Fritz (*Early Thunder*), Laura Ingalls Wilder (the Little House books), Patricia Clapp (*I'm Deborah Sampson*), Elizabeth George Speare (*The Bronze Bow*). Read several books by this author and research the author to learn how he or she prepares to write a book of historical fiction. What makes their work such outstanding examples of historical fiction?

7. In preparation for a unit on a specific event or time in history, create an "artifact box." Artifacts can include objects, news articles, photographs, and so on that relate to this subject as well as a collection of books of historical fiction.

8. Select a chapter in an elementary social studies textbook. Locate several books of historical fiction that deal with the same topic. Discuss how the trade books bring the topic to life and the impact of these books on children's understanding and motivation for learning.

Fantasy/Science Fiction

In the world of literary fantasy, anything can happen and the impossible becomes believable. In a world of talking beasts and underground kingdoms, of secret immortality and mysterious wizards, children learn to make sense of their own lives. One definition of *fantasy* is "the willing suspension of disbelief." Lloyd Alexander, one of the most popular writers of fantasy, wrote, "Fantasy and realism aren't polar opposites, but simply two modes of expressing the same thing. Both draw from the same source, the world we live in . . ." (1988, p. 75). Fantasy allows the reader to explore the past, the future, and the worlds that coexist in the present. It combines the elements of the impossible and the possible to make the incredible appear credible.

Fantasy books take on many forms—stories of enchantment, humorous tales, stories in which animals and toys are personified, tales of science fiction, and so on. Fantasy includes stories of extraordinary worlds and imaginary kingdoms, the supernatural and magical happenings, stories that reshape the present and give us a glimpse of the future. The common thread that distinguishes fantasy from realistic fiction is the blending of the fantastic with realistic detail. Good fantasy weaves at least one element of the impossible into a framework of reality, while realistic fiction may include a situation that only seems improbable.

The elements of literature—setting, characterization, and theme—are important in creating fantasy. Fantasy may be set in the distant past, the future, or the present. *Knights of the Kitchen Table,* by Jon Scieszka, for example, takes place in ancient times; three boys magically become knights battling giants and dragons. *The Giver,* by Lois Lowry, tells of a futuristic society that protects its citizens from pain, from war, and ultimately from the ability to make their own choices. The story may take place in strange new worlds that make the strange seem familiar, as in Eleanor Cameron's *The Wonderful Flight to the Mushroom Planet,* or in realistic surroundings that make the familiar seem strange, as in Mary Norton's *The Borrowers.* Fantasy carries the reader to a setting that is beyond real-life constraints. The characters—whether animate or inanimate, human or animal—possess qualities and experience situations with which children can identify. For example, the animals in *Charlotte's Web,* by E. B. White, and the toys in *The Velveteen Rabbit,* by Margery Williams, feel and express love, hate, joy, and sadness with the same intensity as human characters. Fantasy depends on the ability to honestly convey emotion and portray the human condition, leading the reader to new insights and understanding. The themes of fantasy are universal and often quite serious, involving social and political issues and human values, emotions, and motivation. The battles between good and evil and greed and unselfishness, exemplified in Laurence Yep's Dragon series and C. S. Lewis's Chronicles of Narnia series, are common themes in fantasy. The meaning of life and death is frequently explored, as in *Tuck Everlasting,* the haunting tale of immortality by Natalie Babbitt. As the story of the Tuck family unfolds, the reader sees death as a natural part of life and explores the moral and social implications of a world in which people are immortal. As do many books of fantasy, *Tuck Everlasting* encourages the reader to face life's challenges. After discussing the book, one fifth grader remarked, "I know I can't live forever, but I'm going to do something special with my life so that I can be immortal."

Modern fantasy has its roots in traditional literature such as myths, legends, and folk tales. For example, Hans Christian Andersen, one of the earliest modern writers of fantasy, borrowed from the old fairy tales to create such fantasy classics as *The Ugly Duckling* and *The Emperor's New Clothes.* Many contemporary authors have also borrowed from traditional literature. Jane Yolen used many elements of the folk tale genre to create such tales as *The Girl Who Loved the Wind,* and Holly Hunter based *The Mermaid Summer* on legends of the past.

Within the story, regardless of the setting, characters, plot, or theme, well-written fantasy must be consistent. The images, language, experiences, and details must combine to make the plot, characters, and setting logical and believable. After reading fantasy, children often feel as if they have been to wherever the book is set; the settings and the characters become real to them. In fact, they often wish that what they have just read were real.

Fantasy helps children deal with their lives and gives them new ways to look at old problems. As fantasy stretches their imaginations; children become more creative in their ideas and problem-solving techniques; a vital part of the divergent thinking process. For example in Lois Lowrys Newberry award–winning book, *The Giver*, the reader explores the issues of governmental control, censorship, and the importance of memory as they witness the metamorphisis of a future society. They learn to be more accepting and open-minded as they analyze different viewpoints, and more spontaneous. Finally, as fantasy makes the impossible seem possible, they dare to dream.

Science fiction is an important subgenre of fantasy; because of its importance and value to the world of literature, it deserves special attention and analysis. The main factor that determines whether a piece of literature is science fiction or pure fantasy is whether scientific laws or principles are stressed. In science fiction, the scientific world, with its technological advances and possibilities, is of paramount importance. Good science fiction contains the same elements that are intrinsic to good fantasy. It must center around well-defined characters involved in human conflicts or problems. The setting, though often another place and time, must seem possible within a framework of realistic detail. The details contain many scientific truths and possibilities, while the conflict and solution rely on scientific content.

Science fiction looks at life and explores possibilities and human ability to solve problems. As technology advances by leaps and bounds, what was science fiction years ago is today's reality. Jules Verne, for example, wrote of atomic submarines and rockets that journeyed into space. He wasn't writing realistic fiction: his books were considered science fiction when they were written more than 100 years ago! Science fiction writers work within the context of scientific laws but allow their imaginations to challenge reality. For example, André Norton and Dorothy Madlee's *Stat Ka'at* allows children to imagine the rescue of all the earth's cats, as a superior breed of cat sweeps down on earth, before the world destroys itself.

Science fiction allows children to hypothesize about the future by imagining that certain events, conditions, or findings exist. In Jill Paton Walsh's *The Green Book*, for example, a family and others escape earth on a spaceship before "the disaster" occurs.

Science fiction paves the way for "a brave new world" by pointing out how the past and present affect the future and by helping explain often-incomprehensible technological advances. A good example is H. M. Hoover's *This Time of Darkness*, in which pollution and the uncertain quality of the outside atmosphere force people to live in underground domed cities for protection.

Science fiction explores moral questions as well as social issues. Human relationships, conflict, and solutions to problems and fears can also be explored through science fiction. In *The Fallen Spaceman*, by Lee Harding, children are vividly drawn into the friendship of Tyro, from outer space, and Eric, an earthling. Though Eric is initially frightened by the creature from outer space, he overcomes his fear. In *The Martian Chronicle,* by Ray Bradbury, the reader is forced to explore social problems such as aging and atomic warfare.

Science fiction challenges children to believe and confirm that they can achieve almost anything their minds can conceive. It enables them to evaluate how they might live their lives and what types of changes would have to be made and helps them come to terms with moral and ethical issues. For example, based on science fiction dealing with the colonization of outer space, students may discuss: How would they colonize other planets? Who would rule? How would they determine who is to live there? How could they prevent today's problems from occurring in the new world? What would the quality of life be? How would they deal with other civilizations? Science fiction stimulates the imagination, asking children to think creatively, to open themselves to all possibilities.

Selecting and Evaluating Fantasy/Science Fiction

Good works of fantasy, as with other genres, must meet the standards of good literature. In addition, the following criteria should be considered.

- ❒ 1. Is the setting authentic and integral to the story?
- ❒ 2. Is the language appropriate and consistent? Does it add credibility to the fantasy?
- ❒ 3. Is the plot creative, believable, and ingenious?
- ❒ 4. Does the story blend fantasy with reality, making the impossible seem possible?
- ❒ 5. Are the details consistent with the plot, setting, characters, and viewpoint?
- ❒ 6. Is the element of time authentically represented?
- ❒ 7. Are the details so vivid that the reader becomes one with the story?
- ❒ 8. Are emotions conveyed honestly? Is the human condition portrayed honestly?
- ❒ 9. Is the reader led to new insights and understandings?
- ❒ 10. Does the story contain worthwhile themes?
- ❒ 11. In works of science fiction, does the story contain scientific laws, principles, and technology that give plausibility to the situations and solutions?

Activities to Use with Fantasy/Science Fiction

1. After reading several stories of fantasy based on fairy tales, discuss the elements of these stories. What do they seem to have in common? Using tales such as those by Hans Christian Andersen, have students create their own modern fantasy tales.

2. After reading a book of fantasy/science fiction, have students create several "What ifs" based on the story. For example, based on *Tuck Everlasting*, by Natalie Babbitt, students might respond to the questions "What if you had the opportunity to become immortal?" or "What if no one ever died?"

3. Have students compare several books of fantasy/science fiction that include similar elements, for example two books that personify animals, such as *Winnie the Pooh*, by A. A. Milne, and *Charlotte's Web*, by E. B. White.

4. Writers of fantasy manipulate the element of time, allowing characters to explore times in the past, present, or future. For example, Hannah, in Jane Yolen's *The Devil's Arithmetic*, suddenly finds herself transported in time to the Poland of World War II. Have students list times, such as the year 2010, the 1960s, or the 1700s; settings, such as the Old West, imperial Rome, or the South at the beginning of the Civil Rights movement; and characters, such as a rocket scientist, an aging circus clown, or a teenager who wants to be a famous artist. From these lists, have students select a time, a setting, and a character and then briefly outline a story involving that time, place, and character. They may work individually or in groups.

5. Children who read *Where the Wild Things Are*, by Maurice Sendak, are captivated by the characters. Encourage the class to create a flip book to develop new and unusual "wild things." This activity can be done using any memorable, unique characters from books of fantasy.

6. Many tales of fantasy take place in strange new worlds. One such world, Narnia, is introduced in *The Lion, the Witch, and the Wardrobe*, the first book in C. S. Lewis's Chronicles of Narnia series. After reading such a fantasy book, have students create a new world of their own. Have them consider what it looks like, how you get there, and who lives there. Once the students have planned this new world, have them re-create it using any artistic medium. They might then introduce their new world to others in a short story.

7. Many tales of fantasy involve talking beasts and objects that think and feel as humans do. Develop a lesson on personification and have students select animals or objects as a basis for poems that use the technique of personification.

8. Have a brainstorming session about the problems of the future as predicted in books of science fiction that students have read. Have them select one of these problems as the basis for a problem-solving activity (see Chapter 9) in which they determine the best way to prevent these problems from occurring.

9. Science fiction is considered a vehicle for helping us prepare for the future. After reading several books of science fiction, have students create a future newspaper that reflects the scientific advancements, technology, problems affecting Earth, and other issues described in the books they have read.

10. Create a classroom "fantasy festival." Turn the room into a strange new world. Decorate with mobiles representing different books of fantasy the students have read. Have students create their own book jackets for stories of fantasy they've written. As part of the festival, have students use readers theater, story theater, or other creative dramatics to retell a favorite fantasy tale.

Extending Your Knowledge of Fantasy/Science Fiction

1. Read several examples of books of fantasy that contain eccentric characters, extraordinary worlds, suspense and the supernatural, time shifts, folk tale elements, personification of inanimate objects, imaginary kingdoms, and struggles between good and evil. For each book, create a journal entry that includes bibliographic information, a brief summary, and a brief reaction to the events, characters, setting, and so on.
2. Read several books of science fiction that explore other worlds, visitors from other worlds, or the future. Compare the way the books deal with the subject.
3. After reading several books of fantasy, complete the phrase, "Fantasy is _____."
4. After reading several books of science fiction, consider whether today's science fiction can become tomorrow's reality. Discuss your ideas.
5. Perform a survey to determine the favorite books of fantasy/science fiction of girls and boys at different grade levels. What generalizations can you make based on their responses?

Traditional Literature

They are the tales of our youth: the tales of wicked witches, beautiful princesses, and fearless heroes. They capture the magic of childhood, the belief that anything is possible. They have sheltered our dreams and provided cherished moments of enchantment, wonder, and hope. They are the works of literature rooted in humanity: folk tales, fables, myths, and legends.

Traditional literature has formed the foundation for modern literature. Its origins can be traced to the origins of humanity itself. Stories were passed orally from generation to generation, each culture making the stories their own. Timeless and universal themes dealt with peoples' needs to understand themselves, the world around them, and their place in the world. Many tales were written in response to the times and mirrored peoples' feelings regarding social castes and the struggles of the poor. Kindness, patience, and hard work were seen as qualities that would, in time, be rewarded; good would eventually triumph over evil and the power of love would prevail. Traditional literature reflects society, providing insight into the human condition and representing the good, bad, strengths, and flaws in all of us.

Folk Tales

Folk tales include epics, ballads, folk songs, and legends. They relate the plausible and implausible adventures of humans and animals. Often, the situations and characters are based on historical people and places and draw from a people's religious beliefs, customs, and values. Folk tales are classified into various subtypes—cumulative tales, *pourquoi,* or why tales, humorous tales, beast tales, magic and wonder tales, and realistic tales. Most popular, especially with children, is the fairy tale, a folk tale for the child in all of us.

All folk tales share certain characteristics. They are usually written in a simple, direct manner. The characters, plot, and setting are established in just a few lines, as in this introduction to the Grimm Brothers' *The Twelve Dancing Princesses:*

> Once upon a time there was a king who had twelve daughters, each more beautiful than the other. They slept together in a hall where their beds stood close to one another. At night when they had gone to bed, the king locked the door and bolted it. But when he unlocked it in the morning, he noticed that their shoes had been danced to pieces, and nobody could explain how it happened.

The plot is often simple, filled with fast-paced action, and includes repetition. Humor, rhyme, and repetition can be enjoyed in such tales as Paul Galdone's *Henny Penny* or *The Pancake* as children join in during the refrains or practice repeating alliterative words and phrases. Situations and other elements are also repeated, usually in threes; often there are three children, three wishes, three chances, and so on. The conclusion usually immediately follows the story's climax. For example, as Sleeping Beauty is kissed by the prince, the kingdom awakens, all is restored as it once was, and they live happily ever after.

The settings are vague—"Once upon a time in a faraway land . . ."—allowing the reader to imagine that the action could happen any place and at any time. The characters are often stereotypes—the good and beautiful princess, the cruel and powerful stepmother, the poor, hard-working, virtuous hero. Often the characters possess special qualities that lead to the denouement.

Folk tales appeal to children's sense of justice. In *The Old Traveler,* kindness is rewarded while greed is not. In the end, good triumphs over evil. Folk tales also help resolve moral issues. In *Jack and the Beanstalk* greed is depicted as an undesirable quality; in Charles Perrault's *Cinderella* unselfishness is rewarded while selfishness brings unhappiness.

Many of life's lessons are learned through folk tales. In *Budulinek,* for example, a small boy learns to obey his granny and never open the door to strangers. In *The Husband Who Was to Mind the House,* the husband learns that his wife's job is not nearly as easy as he thought. From *The Fisherman and his Wife,* we learn to appreciate what we have. *Zlatch and the Goat and Other Stories* is a collection of folk tales by Isaac Bashevis Singer. The tales are timeless and filled with wisdom for all ages.

Since many folk tales have their origins in other cultures, children can learn a great deal about specific cultures and their people—what they value, their goals, and their dreams. Verna Aardema's *Why Mosquitoes Buzz in People's Ears*, an African folk tale, relates the problems that occur because of the tall tales Mosquito tells the animals of the jungle. As a result, Mosquito learns her lesson and gives up telling the tales, "To this day she goes about whining in people's ears: 'Zee! Is everyone still angry at me?'" Comparing folk tales is an excellent strategy to allow children to discover the sameness as well as the differences among people. For example, hundreds of versions exist of the tale of Cinderella, including Ai-Ling Louie's *Yeh-Shen* (China), John Steptoe's *Mufaro's Beautiful Daughters* (Africa), and Lynette Dyer Vuong's *The Brocaded Slipper* (Vietnam). While depicting the universal value of good over evil, each story varies in significant ways, such as the type of punishment delegated to the stepsisters. Resources to locate variations of the same basic tale include Margaret Read McDonald's *The Storyteller's Sourcebook*. The Table on page 53 lists just a sample of the different versions of a number of favorite folk tales.

The folk tales of different cultures, woven together with the experiences of people who have immigrated to America, have recently been published. They are folk tales that offer hope and express the sorrow, loneliness, and fear of a people. In *The People Could Fly*, Virginia Hamilton has collected the tales that "represent the main body of black folk tales . . ." (p. xi)—stories that tell of a rich heritage and of the strength and perseverance of a people. In *The Rainbow People*, Lawrence Yep has collected the tales of Chinese Americans: "Although all but one of the tales is set in China, each seemed like a lens that helped focus on some facet of Chinese life in America" (p. xi).

In the United States, tales have evolved that tell of the exploits of the lumberjacks, railroad workers, and sailors who helped to make the country strong. Tales of these heroes match the vastness of the country, and their accomplishments are told in hyperbole. Calamity Jane, Annie Oakley, Paul Bunyan, Captain Stormalong, Mike Fink, Daniel Boone, Davy Crockett, Johnny Appleseed, Windwagon Smith, John Henry, and Pecos Bill extolled the American virtues of courage, fortitude, and ingenuity. Some of these heroes were real people; others, embodying a cornucopia of qualities, became real through the yarns spun about them. These uniquely American tales are often called tall tales, and many children's books, such as Aliki's *The Story of Johnny Appleseed*, Steven Kellogg's *Paul Bunyan, Pecos Bill*, and *Johnny Appleseed*, and Ariane Dewey's *The Narrow Escapes of Davy Crockett* retell the stories of these well-loved heroes.

Many unusual variations of folk tales have also been written, each transforming one of more elements of the original. In John Scieszka's *The True Story of the Three Little Pigs*, the tale is told from a different character's point of view: the wolf explains how he was only trying to borrow a cup of sugar to bake a cake for his poor, dear granny. As he explains, he was framed and the victim of

A COMPARISON OF FOLKTALES

FOLK TALE	COUNTRY OF ORIGIN
Rumplestiltskin	Germany
Tom Tit Tot	England
Duffy and the Devil	England
Sleeping Beauty in the Wood	France
Briar Rose	Germany
The Queen of Tubber Tintye	Ireland
Henny Penny	England
The Hare that Ran Away	India
Johnny Cake	England
The Wee Bannock	Scotland
The Pancake	Norway
Tom Thumb: His Life and Death	England
Little Tom Thumb	Russia
Le Petit Poucet	France
Little One Inch	Japan
Cinderella and the Glass Slipper	France
Little Burnt Face	Milmac Indians
Kari Woodengown	Norway
Yeh-Shen	China
The Brocaded Slipper	Vietnam
Cinderella, or the Little Glass Slipper	England
Mufaro's Beautiful Daughters	Africa
The Egyptian Cinderella	Egypt
The Maid of the Glass Mountain	Norway
Red Riding Hood	Germany
Lon Po Po	China

journalistic hyperbole. *Ugh,* by Arthur Yorkins, sets the story of Cinderella during caveman times. Children love to compare these versions with the originals and in doing so gain additional insights. These stories motivate students to create their own versions of folk tales, manipulating characters, setting, plot, point of view, and style. Sipe (1993) presents an excellent annotated bibliography of transformations of traditional stories and suggests ways students can create their own transformations.

As with other forms of traditional literature, folk tales stimulate artistic expression. Children are often motivated to illustrate, dramatize, or write a creative piece based on the plot, setting, or characters. As they become involved in these activities, they can better relate to the characters and gain an understanding of languages, dialects, and customs.

Selecting and Evaluating Folk Tales

The following criteria should be used in selecting and evaluating folk tales.

- ❏ 1. Is the plot suspenseful and fast-moving?
- ❏ 2. Is the setting timeless, one that can occur anywhere or any time?
- ❏ 3. Is the sequence of events easy to follow?
- ❏ 4. Is a problem described in a simple and direct fashion?
- ❏ 5. Can a child identify with the characters?
- ❏ 6. Does the conclusion immediately follow the climax and reflect a logical outcome?
- ❏ 7. Is there repetition, either of responses or of situations?
- ❏ 8. Is it entertaining?
- ❏ 9. Does the story provide an outlet for the expression of feelings?
- ❏ 10. Does the story express universal values?

Activities to Use with Folktales

(See pages 113–115 for a folk tale unit that involves students in reading and writing folk tales.)

1. Involve students in reading several versions of the same folk tale to compare the stories and illustrations. For example, students can consider whether the illustrations are authentic to the culture and whether they add to the story. Have them select their favorite version and prepare a book review to encourage others to read the tale.
2. Have students select a favorite folk tale and write a story of their own based on a specific event. For example, they can write their own version of *Cinderella*, "When the Clock Struck 12:00."
3. Folk tales often reflect a culture's traditions, customs, and values. Read aloud folk tales from various cultures and have students help fill in the chart on page 55 after each tale is read. Have students compare this information with their own family's values, customs, and so on. What similarities and what differences can be discerned?
4. Create a class-illustrated anthology of favorite folk tales. The book can be divided into cumulative tales, talking beast tales, humorous tales, realistic tales, tales of romance, tales of magic, and tales in which characters are transformed.
5. Have students create a class newspaper by developing articles and accompanying art for sections such as world news, the editorial page, advertisements, comics, and an advice column. The newspaper can focus on a specific folk tale or folk tales of a specific culture or can include articles based

Title of folktale				
Country of origin				
Values reflected				
Qualities respected				
Customs				
Other				

on any number of tales. For example, the news story "Amazing Beanstalk Stretches to the Sky" could include a "factual" account of Jack's adventures with the giant. An editorial could focus on opinions as to whether or not Goldilocks was actually trespassing. Advertisements can be written for a magic wand that turns pumpkins into coaches, and letters to "Dear Abby" can ask for advice about what to do after you've eaten an old woman's cottage.

6. Many folk tales lend themselves to being acted out in a mock trial, such as the case of Momma and Poppa Bear versus Goldilocks, or the mosquito in Verna Aardema's *Why Mosquitoes Buzz in People's Ears* could be charged with annoying the iguana. Select a folk tale in which the character's motives and final actions can be questioned. Select students for the roles of judge, defendant, plaintiff, attorney for the defense, attorney for the prosecution, witness for the defense, witness for the prosecution, and jury members.

7. Have students select a favorite folk tale and transform it into a rap song. You may first wish to have students listen to versions of rap. Scholastic publishes a Rap Tales series that includes books and cassettes of well-known tales put to a rap beat. Students will love these new versions. As a variation, students may write ballads based on America's tall-tale heroes.

8. Have students dramatize a favorite folk tale or involve them in a story theater to retell the tale. Have them create musical accompaniment that reflects the origin of the story.

Fables

According to legend, Aesop was a slave who lived in sixth-century Greece. Although little is known of Aesop, the tales long synonymous with his name have entertained us for centuries and have given us reason to pause and ponder. Fables are brief tales that, in the end, startle us with truth that is so simple yet often difficult to ascertain in everyday life. Other sources of fables include *Jatakas*, animal stories of a man living briefly as an animal, the *Panchatantra*, the oldest known collection of Indian fables, and *The Fables of LaFontaine.*

Fables are based on human nature, and although their characters are often animals, the animals personify humankind. The characters are usually one-dimensional: the fox is always clever, the mouse always small and rather weak. Unlike fairy tales, in which the poor, unsung hero wins the hand of the beautiful maiden, characters in fables basically remain the same. However, as the fable unfolds, each character learns, as does the reader, a valuable lesson in life. Everything revolves around the moral, which is the rationale for the fable's existence.

A knowledge of fables should be a prerequisite for cultural literacy, since their influence is so pervasive. How often have we caught ourselves repeating a lesson from a fable as encouragement to ourselves or others, such as "necessity is the mother of invention" (*The Crow and the Pitcher*) or "slowly but surely" (*The Tortoise and the Hare*)? How often have we strived to keep our priorities firmly established by reminding ourselves that "precious things are for those who prize them" (*The Cock and the Jewel*) or "do not pretend to be something you are not" (*The Ass in the Lion's Skin*)?

Fables encourage children to reflect on the strengths and weaknesses all humans possess, and they clarify their understanding of human motivation and human nature. From *The Fox and the Grapes*, for example, children can better understand the term *sour grapes*; from *The Two Bags*, they realize how easily they see the faults of others yet fail to see their own shortcomings. Children and adults love fables and naturally relate to them on various levels. For children, however, the fable provides a simple, interesting plot, situations with which they can identify, and a message that can be internalized.

Selecting and Evaluating Fables

The following criteria should be used in selecting and evaluating fables.

- ❏ 1. Is there a message or a moral, whether implied or stated?
- ❏ 2. Does the fable contain few characters, each reflecting one main quality?
- ❏ 3. Are any characters, animate or inanimate, personified?
- ❏ 4. Is there a brief, though interesting, plot?
- ❏ 5. Does the story reflect human strengths, weaknesses, and imperfections?

Activities to Use with Fables

1. Have students look through books of quotations, such as Bartlett's *Familiar Quotations,* and copy a quotation that would make a good moral for a story. Have them write a fable that will lead to the moral they have selected. Compile a class book of their fables.
2. Have students rewrite the morals of favorite fables, so that the wording is unfamiliar. Give the "new" moral to others in the class and ask them to identify the original version.
3. Have each student summarize and illustrate a favorite fable on poster paper and write its moral. Each week, select and display one of the posters and discuss the story and moral.
4. Involve students in a comparison of fables and parables. Can they create a fable from a parable, and vice versa?
5. Ask students to think of a time when their parents used a fable to make a point. Have them write a paragraph describing the situation.

Myths and Legends

In the beginning, humans told stories to explain what was then incomprehensible and to make sense out of the wonders they beheld. They told stories to reassure themselves that light would follow the darkness, that spring would follow winter, and that everything in life had its own special reason for being. These stories were passed orally from generation to generation and were shared by cultures who adapted them to reflect their own beliefs, values, and customs.

Yet, regardless of the culture and although the characters and names varied, the themes remained constant. They acquaint us with past times and yet help raise a consciousness concerning our own lives. They reflect the struggle between good and evil, as in Leonard Everett Fisher's version of *Theseus and the Minotaur*, which relates the story of the hero Theseus, who slew the cruel Minotaur to save the people of Athens. And they strengthen our conviction that goodness will be rewarded, as reflected in *Baucis and Philemon*, one of the many myths included in Edyth Hamilton's classic, *Mythology.* Creation myths relate to the origins of life. For example, Deborah Nourse Lattimore's *Why There Is No Arguing in Heaven*, a Mayan myth, relates the tale of Hunab Ku, the first Creator God of the Mayas, creator of the earth and all the animals, who challenges the other gods, "Whoever can create a being worthy of worshipping us will be the second greatest god after me." Nature myths explain the seasons, animals, and movements of the planets, providing a rationale for natural phenomena. Stories about Persephone and Demeter, for example, explain why we have four seasons, and the story of Pandora explains the evils of the world and the existence of hope. Gerald McDermott's *Musicians of the Sun*, the Aztec myth, explains how the Aztec god, the Lord of the Night, tired of the gray and joyless world he saw, brought music to the world.

Myths also help the reader understand common human traits and how these traits affect them. Myths relating the jealousy of Hera, the curiosity of Pandora, the vanity of Narcissus, the greed of King Midas, and the bravery of Hercules, for example, illustrate fundamental qualities with which we can all identify. In Deborah Nourse Lattimore's *The Prince and the Golden Ax,* a Minoan tale, the reader learns how a young hunter's boasting brought about the ruin of his island home. Furthermore, myths allow the reader to compare cultures and understand their customs. For example, *Isis and Osiris* explains why Egyptians embalmed their dead and put the bodies beneath towering pyramids.

It is interesting to note that almost every aspect of life has been affected by the mythology we read. Our language is filled with words and phrases with origins in mythology, such as *tantalize, narcissism,* and "opening Pandora's box." We can drive a Mercury or an Aries, we can visit a physician and see a caduceus, and we can look to the heavens and see planets named for gods and goddesses. For example, Mars, the Red Planet, was aptly named for the Roman god of war.

Legends differ from myths in several fundamental ways. Often legends have a more historical basis. King Arthur may have ruled Britain long ago, although the legend may be hyperbole. There may have been a Robin Hood, and most certainly there was a Sheriff of Nottingham! While the influence of the gods and goddesses may be felt in some legends, the main focus is on the hero and his or her adventures. Legends also provide background for incidents that might have happened, such as the Trojan War or the disappearance of Atlantis.

The heroes usually exemplify qualities cherished by the cultures in which they lived. The heroes of traditional literature represent countries in every corner of the globe and include such legendary characters as Odysseus of Greece, Aeneas of Rome, and El Cid of Spain. As legends were passed from generation to generation, their heroes' deeds became more astounding, their wisdom deeper, and their courage limitless. As a result of these legends, we tend to set standards by which we measure our own accomplishments and establish our own ideas and ideals.

Selecting and Evaluating Myths and Legends

The following criteria will aid in the selection and evaluation of myths and legends.

❒ 1. Does the tale reflect the customs, values, and beliefs of the culture from which it originated?

❒ 2. Is there an explanation for natural phenomena, the origins of life, or human behavior?

❒ 3. Are the origins of social or religious customs explained?

❒ 4. Does the tale contain action, suspense, and conflict?

❒ 5. Is the story entertaining without requiring a prior knowledge of mythological or legendary characters and events?

❒ 6. Is the setting appropriate for the plot?

❐ 7. Will the tale help the reader better understand human vulnerabilities and strengths?

❐ 8. Does the story provide lessons for life?

❐ 9. Does it stimulate the reader's imagination?

Activities to Use with Myths and Legends

(See pages 115–119 for a comprehensive mythology unit.)

1. Have students create a scrapbook of words and symbols used today that come from mythology. Ask them to include a brief explanation of the origin of each word or symbol.

2. Try to obtain tapes of the television show *This Is Your Life.* Have groups of students select mythological characters they would like to honor in a "This Is Your Life" show and plan programs such as "This Is Your Life . . . Zeus." Different gods, goddesses, heroes, and other characters can be introduced to tell anecdotes about their experiences with Zeus. If possible, videotape the programs.

3. Have students create a web for the word *hero.* As they read myths of different heroes and heroines have them add to this web. At the end of the unit, ask students to come up with their own definitions of *hero.*

4. Have students compare the hero of a legend with a hero of today by writing a diamonte (see page 64).

5. Have students change the setting of a myth or legend. For example, the story could focus on Robin Hood in New York City in the 1990s, or Sigurd, the Norse hero, could be transported to the Old West.

6. Have each student or group of students select a favorite mythological or legendary character. Ask them to identify the strengths, weaknesses, likes, dislikes, values, and so on of this character and introduce him or her to the world as a model or toy, in a modern-day skit, or in a literary work (poem, news article, etc.).

Extending Your Knowledge of Traditional Literature

1. Prepare a folk tale for storytelling. Obtain feedback from colleagues before presenting it to a group of children.

2. Create a chart listing various folk tales by motif (tales of talking beasts, tales of magical powers and the supernatural, cumulative tales, humorous tales, realistic tales, romantic tales, etc.).

3. Read several versions of the same folk tale, including as many versions as possible from different cultures. Prepare an annotated bibliography.

4. Locate various audiovisual materials to use along with the reading of folk tales. List available supplementary materials, including folk tale plays and puppet sets.

5. Read several tall tales and describe the elements common to this type of folk tale.
6. Read and summarize fables from several sources, such as Aesop, the *Panchatantra, Jatakas,* and *The Fables of La Fontaine.* Which collection do you find most appropriate for children? Which do you feel would be most appealing to children?
7. Locate myths/legends from different cultures. How are they alike? How are they different? What attitudes and ideas about the culture can you discover from their myths?
8. Read several of the *Just So Stories,* by Rudyard Kipling. Compare them to the *pourquoi* tales of various myths.
9. Read several myths, legends, folk tales, and fables. How would you define each literary form? What are the characteristic elements of each?

Poetry

In "Wind Song," Carl Sandburg describes poetry as "a series of explanations of life, fading off into horizons, too swift for explanations." Eve Merriam has said, "I feel that poetry is the essence of living . . . of course one must have the basic essentials. But I feel that poetry—and the music of language—are so close to that" (Cox, 1989). Poetry, with a magic all its own, has several very different characteristics from the other genres. For example, poetry includes a distinctive manipulation of words. The words must be carefully selected to convey beautiful sounds and images, as well as meaning. Well-written poetry appeals to the senses and the emotions. Poetry must be read and reread to children in order for them to hear and feel what the poet is saying and to gain the most from the genre.

Poems, like pictures, convey different meanings to different people. As Siddie Joe Johnson so aptly wrote:

> Poetry is a story, a song, a picture. Poetry is the first time you hold a firefly in your hand. . . . Poetry is magic. Poetry is what happens every day to everybody. Poetry is sunlight through a window with leaves moving just outside. . . . Poetry is remembering yesterday and looking ahead to tomorrow and tomorrow and tomorrow. Poetry is something your heart understands but sometimes your mind does not. . . . Poetry is you. And me. And all the people we know, all the people everywhere. Poetry is the nothingness of spider webs and seafoam. Poetry is everything! Yes everything!

Nursery rhymes are often children's introduction to poetry. Just as they enjoy the singing quality, melody, and movement of the word patterns in nursery rhymes, they will also enjoy these qualities in the poetry they read later. Poetry for children has particular elements that are appealing to them, such as rhythm, rhyme, sound patterns, imagery, figurative language, and repetition. Robert Louis Stevenson's "Windy Nights" conveys many of these elements:

Windy Nights

Whenever the moon and stars are set,
　　Whenever the wind is high,
All night long in the dark and wet,
　　A man goes riding by.
Late in the night when the fires are out,
Why does he gallop and gallop about?

Whenever the trees are crying aloud,
　　And ships are tossed at sea,
By, on the highway, low and loud,
　　By at the gallop goes he:
By at the gallop he goes, and then,
By he comes back at the gallop again.

As children read or hear "Windy Nights," they can feel the elements of rhythm or movement of the words. They can hear the rhyming words and sound patterns as they read phrases like "Late in the night when the fires are out/Why does he gallop and gallop about?" Repetition is another appealing element in this poem; note the phrase "at the gallop."

The images of sight, sound, smell, touch, or taste naturally occur as the lines of Robert Frost's "Stopping by Woods on a Snowy Evening" unfold:

The only other sound's the sweep
Of easy wind and downy flake
The woods are lovely, dark and deep
But I have promises to keep . . .

Figurative language is best described as a combination of simile and metaphor. A simile compares one thing with another, and a metaphor refers to an object or idea as if it were another object. Alfred Noyes's "The Highwayman" provides a good example of figurative language in the following lines:

The moon was a ghostly galleon tossed upon the cloudy sea.
The road was a ribbon of moonlight over the purple moor,
And the highwayman came riding—
Riding—riding.

Poems can be found to match any mood, any topic. Poems can be serious or humorous, rhyming or free verse. Poetry addresses the same subjects, concerns, and issues as other literary genres. The only thing all poems have in common is that they touch the reader or listener in some way. Poetry can fill children with wonder and inspire their imaginations. It can help children explore themselves and the world in which they live. When first introducing children to poetry, it is important to select poems that will encourage them to join in, repeating phrases, chants, and so on. Nursery rhymes, with their familiar rhythm and rhyme and singsonglike verses, are a perfect introduction to poetry. It is also important to surround children with poetry to which they can connect. The poems of Eloise Greenfield, Myra Cohn Livingston, Jack Prelutsky, Shel Silverstein, and Judith Viorst are especially popular with children. Their poetry seems to reflect what children think and feel and allows them to see the beauty as well as the humor in life. For example, Judith Viorst's book of verses, *If I Were in Charge of the World and Other Worries*, lets children know they are not alone. The title poem encourages children to imagine how they would change the world; many others encourage children to explore their own wishes and fears; still others speak to those who have ever had to keep a secret, had a broken heart, or missed a friend who moved away. Greenfield's poem "By Myself," from *Honey, I Love and Other Love Poems*, reflects the rich imagination of childhood and the vital need of children to recognize their own self-worth:

> *By Myself*
>
> When I'm by myself
> And I close my eyes
> I'm a twin
> I'm a dimple in a chin
> I'm a room full of toys
> I'm a squeaky noise
> I'm a gospel song
> I'm a gong
> I'm a leaf turning red
> I'm a loaf of brown bread
> I'm a whatever I want to be
> And anything I care to be
> And when I open my eyes
> What I care to be
> Is me.

Books of poetry should be an important part of any classroom library. Teachers should read poems daily and incorporate poetry into the curriculum. No matter what the occasion or curricular topic, a special poem can be found that fits. Poems can be found in general anthologies and special subject anthologies, such as *A Child's Treasury of Seaside Verses*, or *A Child's Treasury of Animal Verses*, compiled by Mark Daniel. In these books, the poems of such classic writers as Whitman, Wordsworth, Byron, Kipling, and Yeats are accompanied by rich and colorful illustrations. In *A Year in a River Valley/Nature Poems*, compiled by Josette Frank, paintings by Thomas Locker accompany poems that describe the changing face of nature during one year. Poems by Langston Hughes, Rachel Field, and Christina Rossetti, among others, capture the essence of the seasons. Single story poems include *Stopping by Woods on a Snowy Evening*, Robert Frost's poem illustrated by Susan Jeffers, and *A Visit to William Blake's Inn*, the first book of poetry to be awarded the Newbery Medal, written by Nancy Willard and illustrated by Alice and Martin Provensen. Concepts and ideas in the general curriculum gain additional dimension with the use of appropriate poetry. For example, a study of the Revolutionary War can be enhanced by reading Longfellow's "The Midnight Ride of Paul Revere," while a lesson on pioneers and America's West can be augmented through the readings of many of the poems included in *America Forever New,* compiled by Sara and John Brewton. A study of insects will never be the same as children choral read and move to the "joyful noises" of grasshoppers, whirligig beetles, house crickets, and other fascinating insects, thanks to the ingenuity of Paul Fleishman in his award-winning *Joyful Noise: Poems for Two Voices.* As children read the lines of his poems, the insect world comes alive with music. Resources such as *Children's Literature in the Elementary School* (Huck, Hepler, and Hickman, 1993) offer guides for connecting poetry and prose with subject areas and themes.

Too often, especially in the upper elementary grades, teachers' selection of poets is limited to the more traditional poems, rather than contemporary ones. Yet children relate well to the more contemporary poems, which seem better to reflect their experiences and interests. While children should be introduced to some of the more traditional poems and poets, if the poem is too difficult, too abstract, or too far removed from their background knowledge, they may lose interest.

Poetry must first, and most important, be enjoyed for the delight it brings and the feelings it evokes. Children should generally be encouraged to respond to the entire poem rather than take it apart through analysis. Once children are hooked on poetry, teachers, can help them explore poems to understand the elements that make them so effective. This often heightens their understanding, sensitivity, and appreciation of poetry. As a word of caution, however, be sure not to have them overanalyze. You may wish to focus on one device that is especially significant. The intermediate poetry unit on pages 119–124 details one way to achieve this while keeping at the forefront the main goals of holding children's interest and increasing their delight in poetry.

Poetry can also be used as a model for children's own writing. Children will enjoy being introduced to the scope of poetic forms—limericks, haiku, biopoems, clerihews, diamontes, and cinquains. These forms can be used as a model for children's own writing as they experiment to find their own voices.

Haiku is a poem with only three lines and 17 syllables; it usually depicts some aspect of nature:

Line 1: Five syllables
Line 2: Seven syllables
Line 3: Five syllables

A *cinquain* is a five-line poem, written in the following format:

Line 1: One word (which may be the title)
Line 2: Two words (describing the title)
Line 3: Three words (an action)

Line 4: Four words (a feeling)
Line 5: One word (referring to the title)

When completed, a *diamonte* is diamond-shaped. It is written in the following format:

Line 1: One word (a noun or pronoun)
Line 2: Two words (adjectives describing line 1)
Line 3: Three words ("ing" verbs showing action, related to line 1)
Line 4: Four words (nouns—the first two relate to line 1, the last two relate to line 7)
Line 5: Three words ("ing" verbs showing action, related to line 7)
Line 6: Two words (adjectives describing line 7)
Line 7: One word (a noun or pronoun, often the opposite of the word in line 1)

Clerihew poetry contains four lines with an *aabb* rhyme scheme. The poem is usually written about a well-known person, either living or dead, or a fictional character. The person's name becomes the first line of the poem.

A *biopoem* tells about a famous person, real or fictitious, written in the following format:

Line 1: First name
Line 2: Title
Line 3: Four words (that describe the person)
Line 4: Lover of (three or more things or ideas)
Line 5: Who believed (one or more ideas)
Line 6: Who wanted (three things)
Line 7: Who used (three things or methods)
Line 8: Who gave (three things)
Line 9: Who said (a quote)
Line 10: Last name

A *limerick*, popularized by Edward Lear, is a humorous poem with five lines. Lines 1, 2, and 5 rhyme and have a similar rhythm, lines 3 and 4 are shorter, have a similar rhythm pattern, and rhyme with each other.

Selecting and Evaluating Poetry

When selecting and evaluating poetry for children, it is important to choose poetry they can understand and appreciate. The previously mentioned elements of good poetry must also be considered. The following questions may serve as a guide when selecting and evaluating poetry for children.

☐ 1. Are sensory images of sight, smell, taste, hearing, and touch created?
☐ 2. Does the poem contain figurative and alliterative language?
☐ 3. Is there adequate and interesting repetition?
☐ 4. Does the poem flow in a natural and rhythmic manner?
☐ 5. Are the language and speech appropriate for the child's understanding?

Reflections of . . .
Lee Bennett Hopkins

Why should we bring poetry into children's lives? Simply because we must! Poetry works with any child, anywhere, no matter what rung they are standing upon on the reading ladder.

As a young elementary school teacher, I immediately became aware of the richness of poetry—the incredible impact it had on both my students and myself. Poems are usually short, the vocabulary usually simple, and so *much* can be said and felt in a mere 8 or 10 or 12 lines.

When is it time for poetry? All times! Weave it throughout the curriculum—from mathematics to social studies—science to physical education. Read it aloud for pleasure, to elicit feelings, to give children the rich heritage they deserve. Make it a part of every, single day.

What types of poems should you use with children? All kinds! Give them the words from the legacy of Mother Goose, the light verse of Shel Silverstein, Jack Prelutsky, and X. J. Kennedy; share the serious, sensitive sounds created by past masters such as Robert Frost, Langston Hughes, and Carl Sandburg, as well as contemporary masters, including Barbara Juster Esbensen, Aileen Fisher, Karla Kuskin, Myra Cohn Livingston, David McCord, Eve Merriam, Lilian Moore, and Valerie Worth.

Encourage children to dip into original volumes created by individual poets, general anthologies containing a multitude of subjects, and specific anthologies relating to one theme to show them that there are poems on nearly every subject they can think of—from summer to spaghetti, fall to foghorns, winter to whiskers, spring to secret places.

How do you find time for poetry? You must *make* time! Make it part of opening day activities. Read it before or after any lesson, at recess, before children leave the classroom at the close of the school day.

Through poetry children witness life's many faces and facets; they can laugh, cry, wonder, wander, wrap themselves up in emotions they never thought could be possible.

The poet Yuan Mei has written: "Only be willing to search for poetry, and there will be poetry."

Set students on the search. Pass the poetry—*please!*

❐ 6. Are the words manipulated in an appealing manner to contribute to the meaning of the poem?
❐ 7. Does the poem appeal appropriately to a child's emotions?
❐ 8. Does the poem appeal to a child's sense of humor?
❐ 9. Is there a quality of imagination, so a child perceives something in a new way?
❐ 10. Does the poem have a purpose?

Reflections of . . .

Myra Cohn Livingston

What's Happening to Poetry?

How strange that poetry, which has long been the stepchild of literature, has suddenly become somewhat of a spoiled, often undisciplined darling, fêted by both its creator and its adoring friends, encouraged to slouch all over the furniture, utter whatever comes into its mind in prose arranged as verse and, in short, gushed over by a number of overnight anthologists who, with little idea that a fine collection is meant to contain only the "flowers of poetry," often substitute handfuls of weeds.

Does this bode ill for the genre? It is too early to tell. In the rush to get books of verse into print, some publishers are grinding out a great many poor picture books in rhyme. Oftentimes they are encouraging versifiers who do well with rhythm and rhyme, but have nothing more to say than an ability to raise a quick guffaw by titiillating the baser emotions of the young. Sometimes, a revival of the magic word "multicultural" has opened the way for a great many who think they are writing poetry, when indeed, it is usually only aligned prose. Far too often the mention of nature sends writers off in a torrent of prose that is, because of its arty alignment, termed poetry. Thus, the books themselves seem more dedicated to how the illustrator and marketing can capture the public eye than to the words themselves.

There is more to poetry, or even verse, than instantaneous laughter, immediate success, the quick cooky-fix on the one hand, or dancing daffodils and a village blacksmith on the other. There was a time when poetry for children was always didactic; it was necessary that all verse instruct children, show them the right way to behave, study, and discipline themselves. Although this phase faded away in the latter part of the 19th century, many in the late 20th century tend to equate poetry with either some high-flown beauty, truth, wisdom or summoning of the lost rural past on the one hand—or racuous laughter on the other.

Somewhere between, it seems to me, lies the value of poetry and good verse for children, a way of looking at something, either metaphorically or realistically, which enriches the spirit and confronts and reflects the emotions of childhood honestly. Babette Deutsch once wrote that the great themes of poetry, love and death, are not understood by children. I would disagree; for even adults do not literally understand these themes. Both love and death can be handled in the terms which a child understands; the love of family, of friends, of pets, and consequently, a first apprehension of what it means to lose this love. When the poet can evoke in some fresh, startling image a new way of looking, of feeling, of responding to life, this becomes the poetry we should seek, cherish, and share with our children. They deserve nothing less.

Activities to Use with Poetry

(See pages 119–124 for a unit on poetry.)

1. Introduce children to the poetry of some of their favorite poets. For example, have a Shel Silverstein week or a Myra Cohn Livingston week during which you and the students read (chorally and independently) his or her poems and use this poetry as a model for students' own poems. Have the students create an illustrated anthology to reflect their favorite poems by this poet.

2. Have students keep poetry journals in which they write and draw pictures to reflect their feelings and reactions to various poems they read or listen to. Allow time for them to discuss specific poems with their classmates in small group and class discussions.

3. Introduce students to the poetry of Paul Fleischman in *Joyful Noise*. Divide students into groups and have each group choral read the poem and move as the rhythm and beat of the words suggest.

4. Involve students in a shared reading of poetry (see Chapter 5). Use the same rhyming pattern and repetition as a model for students' writing.

5. Have students create a poetry calendar by selecting a topic of interest, such as space, dinosaurs, or machines, and from various collections of poetry, choosing 12 favorite poems appropriate to the topic. Have them illustrate the poems and glue the poems and pictures onto calendar pages.

6. Encourage students to skim through books of poetry to find a poem that says something special to them. Ask students to research the poet and prepare a presentation to introduce the poet to the class. Each presentation should include a reading of the poem that initially stimulated the student to research the poet. Combine the selected poems into an illustrated anthology of classroom favorites.

7. Select a contemporary poem, such as one written by Judith Viorst, Shel Silverstein, or Jack Prelutsky, which involve children's concerns and relationships, and use it as a model for students' own poetry. For example, after they've read the title poem from Viorst's *If I Were in Charge of the World and Other Worries*, ask students to write their own verse to explain what they would do if they were in charge of the world.

8. Every culture has its own poetry. Read to students examples of poems from different cultures and discuss how they reflect their cultures. On a large world map, display favorite poems next to their countries of origin.

9. Have students suggest criteria for good poetry and list these on a chart. Have students assume the role of a literary critic for a journal. Read several reviews of poems from literary magazines to give students a feel for the kind of information that goes into a review. Select several poems for the students to review. Periodically print reviews in a classroom or school paper for others to read.

10. Play recordings of children's poetry. Have students make their own anthologies on cassette, selecting poems on specific topics or by specific poets.

11. Encourage students to react to a particular book, specific story element, or character through poetry. Poems can be created based on plot, setting, theme, or characters. Save the poems in an individual poetry or literature booklet. Students should become familiar with a variety of poetic forms—haiku, cinquain, diamonte, clerihew, biopoem, and limerick—(see pages 63–64) and read several examples before writing their poetry.

Extending Your Knowledge of Poetry

1. To make poetry part of the daily curriculum, locate poems that fit various classroom lessons. Make a chart listing various subject areas/topics and copy several poems that fit each.

2. Research the life of a favorite poet. Discuss how his or her life influenced his or her poetry.

3. Read the poetry of a selected cultural group in America. Create an annotated bibliography of these poems and be prepared to discuss how the poems reflect the culture. Develop activities or a thematic unit that incorporates these poems into the curriculum.

4. Conduct a survey to determine the favorite poems/poets of children in various grade levels. What did you discover?

5. After perusing books of poetry and poetry anthologies and speaking with children and their teachers about their favorite poems and poets, create a wish list of poetry books you would like to have as part of your classroom library.

6. Locate various recordings and film strips based on specific poems. How do these recordings affect the mood of the poem? How do children respond to them?

Informational Books

Children's natural curiosity is whetted and satisfied as they read informational books. Discoveries about our expanding world await children as they leaf through these books, through which they can explore on their own and search for answers to questions such as "What makes a clock tick? What do hamsters like to eat? Where did I come from? What makes popcorn pop?" Informational books play a crucial role in the total learning process. The right book at the right time has far-reaching consequences and can be a tremendous motivating force in a child's life.

Informational books represent one of the fastest-growing and demanding markets for children's books today. From simple concept books for young children to more complex books for adults, informational books provide the reader with accurate, up-to-date, significant facts on a variety of topics. This genre requires authors to be well versed in the subject and to express the information in a fresh, vivid, engrossing manner.

The scope of informational books is unlimited. There are books on crafts and careers, animals and aviation, space and the depths of the oceans. Informational books encourage readers to uncover the secrets of the universe. This genre of books is becoming increasingly popular as teachers incorporate them into the curriculum to extend and encourage learning. Informational books have recently received some of the honors and recognition previously reserved for outstanding literature of other genres. For example, Patricia Lauber's *Volcano: The Eruption and Healing of Mt. St. Helens* was named a Newbery honor book.

Informational books allow children to increase their knowledge about subjects they hear about on television or read about in the newspaper. After reading about a city's pollution problems, for example, children may choose to read *Lives at Stake: The Science and Politics of Environmental Health*, by Laurence Pringle, which deals with the many problems confronting and threatening our environment.

From learning how to cook to making a kite to taking care of a pet, informational books provide children with the instructions necessary to accomplish new tasks. *The Fun of Cooking*, by Jill Krementz, teaches children how to use a variety of cooking tools and equipment safely and how to select nutritional foods. The Practical Puffin series teaches how to make a kite. Alvin and Virginia Silverstein's *Hamsters: All About Them* tells what to feed a pet hamster. No matter what their interest, children can find an informational book to help satisfy their desire to learn.

Isaac Asimov's *The Birth of the United States 1763–1816* or John Loeper's *Going to School in 1876* can bring the school's curriculum to life. Children can experience and understand history through the artistry of authors who weave together events in a way that captivates their readers. Informational books cover topics and concepts in all areas of the curriculum, providing children with a resource that not only supplements basal texts, but also enhances and expands understanding.

Through informational books, children can develop higher-order thinking skills and critical reading abilities. As they read several books on the same subject but by different authors, they can compare the treatment of the subject as they contrast and evaluate the contents of the books. For example, they may compare Sara Stein's *About Dying* and Herbert Zim and Sonia Bleeker's *Life and Death* and discover that the authors approach death from different perspectives. This will encourage them to formulate their own perspectives about death. In addition, they may analyze the relevance, objectivity, and accuracy of the material. When children compare the contents of books on certain subjects, they must be aware of the importance of the copyright date. For example, comparing information in a book written in 1980 about space travel with a book written in 1990 would not be fair.

Through informational books, children become inspired as they read about the achievements of others. A budding young artist may be encouraged by reading Piero Ventura's *Great Painters.* Young girls see the limitless possibilities open to them as they explore career opportunities in such books as Gloria and Esther Goldreich's *What Can She Be? A Newscaster,* which portrays women in a variety of significant occupations. Books such as Gail Gibbons's, *Say Woof! The Day of a Country Veterinarian,* explores a special field of veterinary medicine. David Macaulay's books, such as *Cathedral, City,* and *Castle,* allow children to explore the marvels of architectural innovation. Students become pilots in *Fly the Hot Ones,* by Steven Lindblom. Their interest in flight can be encouraged by *Flight: Fliers and Flying Machines,* by David Jefferies. As they read about various careers and their contributions, children learn more about the realities of a profession so often obscured by television and movies.

Informational books can be a springboard for developing an interest or hobby. Miriam Cooper's *Snap! Photography* or Edward E. Davis's *In the Dark, a Beginner's Guide to Developing and Printing Black and White Negatives* are two of the many books that can encourage a child's interest in photography.

Trends in informational books include a variety of new ways of providing up-to-date, relevant information. Informational books are appropriate for all ages. Concept books, discussed earlier, are informational books for young children. Many picture books, such as Aliki's *How a Book Is Made,* are informational books as well. Some informational books take a quite serious tone while others are lighter in nature. Joanna Cole's Magic School Bus series combines informational text with fantasy as a miniaturized school bus filled with children enters and explores the solar system, the Earth, and the human body. Several informational books have been developed into pop-up books.

Trends in education are making informational books a popular genre for children to read as teachers include more of them in their lessons. As a result, learning specific concepts and exploring ideas becomes far more interesting, relevant, and comprehensive. Informational books are essential resources for children searching for facts, comparing perspectives, seeking new ideas, or developing theories. No matter what the topic, informational books are available to encourage children to broaden their knowledge and sustain their natural curiosity.

Selecting and Evaluating Informational Books

The following criteria should be considered when selecting and evaluating informational books.

☐ 1. Is accurate information presented?
☐ 2. Is the information up-to-date?

❏   3. Are the most relevant and significant facts being presented?
❏   4. Does the book reflect the work of an author who is qualified to write
        on the subject being presented?
❏   5. Is the information presented without relying on anthropomorphism?
❏   6. Does the book avoid stereotyping of race, ethnicity, and sex?
❏   7. Does the book distinguish between fact and theory?
❏   8. Are different points of view or controversial subjects presented when
        appropriate?
❏   9. Does the book encourage the reader to become involved, when appro-
        priate, by observing, collecting data, and experimenting?
❏ 10. Are the illustrations accurate, useful, and appealing?
❏ 11. Is the reader encouraged to pursue the subject further?
❏ 12. Is the text written in an interesting, compelling, and straightforward
        style?

Activities to Use with Informational Books

1. Prepare a scavenger hunt in which students locate certain informational
   books in the library.
2. Have students create and present a play that will introduce other students
   to the library and the Dewey Decimal System.
3. Have students develop a class museum with exhibits that change periodically. The exhibits should be varied and tied to the curriculum whenever
   possible. For example, an exhibit could focus on shell collections, insect
   collections, or a history of transportation. The students should prepare
   index cards describing the items exhibited and include any pertinent information found in informational books.
4. Have students use informational books to prepare and demonstrate "how
   to" speeches on various topics—how to make a quilt, how to build a
   model train, how to make a homemade camera, and so on.
5. Ask each student to write five "I wonder about" questions. Then have
   them research the questions, using informational books. Compile the
   questions and answers into a class "I Wonder About" book.
6. Have students research a topic about which there is still debate, such as
   UFOs, the Bermuda Triangle, or the reasons for the disappearance of dinosaurs. Have the students present their own conclusions, based on the informational books they've read, in a persuasive speech or through debate.
7. Help students learn how informational books can help in problem solving
   (see Chapter 9). Select a modern-day problem or community concern. Encourage students to research the problem by reading informational books,
   offer solutions to the problem, and suggest criteria on which to evaluate
   their solutions. When students have selected a solution, have them write
   (and, if possible, carry out) a plan of action for helping to alleviate the
   problem.

8. Based on a topic being studied, create a class book that younger children can read to learn pertinent information related to the subject. Have students review the criteria for informational books and be sure the pictures and text work well together.

9. K-W-L (Ogle, 1986) is a three-step framework to help students take an active role in the reading process and exhibit some control over what they learn through nonfiction text. K-W-L (What I *Know,* What I *Want* to Learn, What I *Learned*) has students assess their knowledge of a topic, determine what they would like to learn, and evaluate what they learned. Involve students in the K-W-L strategy based on a topic in a specific informational book they are reading. Have them follow the steps below, using the chart provided on page 73.

   a. Talk with students about what they already know about the topic of the text. This information should be freely volunteered and written on the chalkboard or in Section 1 *(K—What We Know)* of the chart. The chart can be duplicated and given to individuals or small groups, or developed into a transparency and projected for the entire class.

   b. Ask students to categorize the information they have volunteered. This can be done through various grouping strategies such as semantic webbing. These groupings can be recorded in Section 2 of the chart.

   c. Ask students to make predictions about the information the text will contain. These predictions should be based on students' background knowledge and the categories of information generated in Step 2. These can be discussed and recorded in Section 3 of the chart.

   d. Have students generate their own questions about the text. These can be discussed and recorded in the *W—What We Want To Find Out* section of the chart. (Section 4).

   e. Have students read the text and record any answers to their questions (in Section 5 on the chart). Students may wish to do this individually or in small groups.

   f. Upon completion of the text, give students an opportunity to discuss and record (Section 6 on the chart) the information learned and how the data relates to their prior knowledge. Talk about questions posed for which no information was found. Help students discover other sources for satisfying their inquiries.

Extending Your Knowledge of Informational Books

1. Read several informational books on a selected topic. Compare the books and their treatment of the subject. You may wish to focus on accuracy of facts, style, appropriateness for the audience, organization, reference aids, the author's qualifications, and the level of reader involvement.

2. Survey students in a classroom to learn their hobbies and interests. Compile a list or database of informational books that highlight several of these hobbies.

K-W-L Strategy Sheet		
1. K –What we know	4. W –What we want to find out	6. L –What we learned & still need to learn

2. Categories of information we expect to use:

A.   E.

B.   F.

C.   G.

D.   H.

3. Predictions of the information included in the text:

A.

B.

C.

D.

5. Answers to self-initiated questions discovered in the text:

SOURCE: Adapted from Ogle, D. "K–W–L: A Teaching Model That Develops Active Reading of Expository Text", *The Reading Teacher*, February 1986, pp. 564-570

3. Select several topics generally taught in the elementary curriculum. Create an annotated bibliography of books representative of a variety of genres, including informational books, that could be used in lessons on these topics.

4. Create a thematic unit (see Chapter 13) that encourages the use of informational books along with other literary genres.

5. Create several activities to encourage the reading of informational books. For example, have students create a "How Things Work" booklet, modeled after David Macaulay's *The Way Things Work*. The book can focus on specific items being studied, or focus on a variety of items that relate to a unit. For example, a unit on communication might result in a "how things work" book that includes television, telephone, computers, satellites, video, and animation, or in a unit on communication, could be a cornucopia of items.

6. Many companies have published series of informational books on specific subjects. Identify several of these series and discuss ideas for incorporating them into your curriculum.

Biographies

Children wonder! Children fantasize! Children pretend! Children *also* seek out truth and reality. By reading a biography, children can step into someone else's shoes and walk through their lives, sharing their accomplishments and failures, loves and hates, strengths and frailties, joys and sorrows. A good biography offers accurate, rich, and vivid details of another person's life and contributes to a better understanding of that person and his or her effect on society.

Until recently, biographies were written primarily about national heroes, mainly men. Today, however, the subject is no longer determined by race, gender, or social position. Today's biographies are concerned with people who have made significant contributions in a wide range of areas. For example, more biographies are being written about contemporary figures involved in areas from science to sports.

Authors of biographies have three main elements to consider. First, the author must "know" the subject well and offer substantial pertinent information. Books, interviews, letters, diaries, newspapers, and accounts of what the subject is credited with saying are just a few of the resources that can provide an accurate picture. Second, the author must consider history and the subject's place in history. The author must have a sense of how the subject affected and was affected by the time and place in which he or she lived or lives. An understanding of significant events that influenced the course of history is also vital. Third, the author must be able to combine the two elements described with good literature. To make an impact, the biography must bring the subject to life in an exciting fashion.

Biographies written for children have always been more fictionalized than those written for adults. Although the emphasis is on authentic facts, authors have the freedom to dramatize certain events to make the reading more interesting. Care is taken in fictionalized biographies to eliminate bias and accurately represent the subject and the period in which he or she lived. The elements of the story, such as dialogue, setting, and situations, can be embellished or invented by the author *only* if they do not violate the authenticity of the subject's life.

One of the greatest values of children's biographies is that by reading about other people, children are often inspired to set goals for their own lives. They gain insight into the qualities and dedication that lead to achievement and a perspective on how these achievements have influenced others. One of the best examples is Catherine Owen Peare's *The Helen Keller Story,* which dramatically demonstrates how a person can triumph over physical handicaps and inspire others through courage and tenacity. Russell Freedman's *The Wright Brothers: How They Invented the Airplane* illustrates the perserverance and courage that led to the human conquest of the skies.

Biographies also familiarize children with the lives and times of prominent world figures, past and present, and help them develop an understanding of the circumstances and events that may have contributed to their accomplishments. *The Life and Words of John F. Kennedy,* by James Wood and Gertrude Norman's *A Man Called Washington* provide detailed accounts of the historical forces that shaped the experiences and accomplishments of these men. Russell Freedman's *Lincoln: A Photobiography* uses photographs to enhance and extend children's understanding of the sixteenth president of the United States. This outstanding book was awarded the Newbery Medal in 1988, the first biography to do so. His biography, *Eleanor Roosevelt: A Life of Discovery* was a 1994 Newbery honor book.

In our world, there is much political unrest. George Sullivan's *Sadat: The Man Who Changed Mid-East History* provides an excellent portrait of the successful effort of two warring cultures, Israel and Egypt, to convert their swords to plows and attain a true peace. The reader is afforded an additional dimension to consider as he or she evaluates current problems and conflicts.

Biographies can provide insights into different cultures and races. Ed Clayton's *Martin Luther King: The Peaceful Warrior* helps children better understand the antagonism between races. It is hoped that as children come face to face with prejudice, they will grow in compassion and strive to shape a society in which differences are accepted and appreciated.

By reading biographies, children are exposed to a variety of careers, from astronaut to zoologist and everything in between. June Behrens's *Sally Ride, Astronaut: An American First* and Ernest Raboff's *Pablo Picasso* are two examples of books that provide children with accurate information concerning all aspects of a career and encourage further investigation.

Reading more contemporary biographies allows children to enjoy a sense that they are sharing the lives of popular celebrities. Reading Harold and Geraldine Woods's *Bill Cosby: Making America Laugh and Learn,* for example, will foster an appreciation for the way Bill Cosby overcame many setbacks to become a success in the entertainment world and a role model in his commitment to education. In addition to stars of the stage and screen, many children also relate to sports heroes. *Jose Canseco: Baseball's 40–40 Man,* by Nathan Aaseng, describes what it is like to be a star baseball player and gives shape to the dreams of Little Leaguers with similar aspirations.

Reflections of . . .
Milton Metzler

In starting work on a biography, I always ask first: How did the person whose story I'm to tell learn about the world he finds himself in? Who or what taught him what he knows?

I think children are eager to find out how other people live, because they want to know how to live themselves. Biography, like any form of literature, allows them to experience more fully, to imagine more fully, to live more fully.

But this doesn't mean I write life stories for the purpose of inspiration. I don't intend to make readers feel that if only they try hard enough they will be rewarded with success. For I don't believe our social system works that way. We can all name men and women who wield considerable power, who devote themselves chiefly to piling up material wealth and personal privilege, and who have little concern for what happens to those they call the "losers" in our society. It occurs to me that there ought to be biographies of such people too.

Such lives are worth writing about. Every life is. There is no such thing as an ordinary person. Obscure, yes, but not ordinary. Anyone's life is worth getting down truthfully. The truth about human character is desirable, no matter what that character is. Nothing is more fascinating—and useful—than to portray a human life in all its strength and frailty. As the young grow, they are enlarged and enriched by what they learn about past lives, whether lived yesterday or long ago.

The task of the biographer is to make the young reader believe your subject really walked the earth, spoke, and acted with all the contradictory impulses, doubts, fears, drives, hatreds, and loves we all share. Biography always challenges the writer to explain the mysteries and magic of human behavior. What kinds of experience feed growth? What kinds cripple it? Can the same kind have opposite effects on two different people? Not to grapple with these inconsistencies and contradictions is to risk contributing to myth.

After reading a great number of biographies and autobiographies and observing the lives around me, I can't believe that either our character or our fate is precast. Living is partly an act of creativity. At certain moments we make important choices—of a school, a mate, a career—that may be creative or destructive. It's as though we decide upon the story of our own lives. Of course, accident—which means only the thus-far unexplained—does occur and it may radically change the plot of our story.

On speaking dates around the country, I've found that teachers are making greater use of biography and autobiography in their work. They find life stories help young readers to learn about both personality and culture. Such books offer a special kind of knowledge about a society and the individuals shaped by it. And in contrast to the average textbook, the material is not dished out as raw data. It comes as interpreted personal experience that the reader finds moving and illuminating. It makes the reader aware of how social and intellectual forces play upon every life, offering alternatives. Boys and girls reading such personal history may discover that they, too, can create a pattern of life for themselves that can be original, independent, and free.

As more educators incorporate literature into the classroom curriculum, children become more interested in learning about the authors of their favorite books. Book series such as Meet the Author, published by Richard Owen, give children the opportunity to read books written by their favorite authors— Verna Aardema, Jean Fritz, Lee Bennett Hopkins, Jane Yolen, and others. Through these books, authors share their childhood, families, and inspiration with the reader. The result is an additional dimension to the books they write, because children have a greater understanding of where the author "is coming from." Other series focus on personalities from the past and present, representing a variety of career fields and areas. Aladdin Books, for example, has divided their biographies into such series as Sports, Advocates for Women's Freedom, and Politics. Through the books in these series the reader is given a look at the childhood of men and women who have made significant contributions. Chelsea House's American Women of Achievement series, allows children to explore the lives of women who have made a difference. Their Black Americans of Achievement series gives children the opportunity to learn about the triumphs of, as well as obstacles faced by such outstanding people as Scott Joplin and Martin Luther King. The HarperCollins Art for Children series, by Ernest Raboff, presents the works and lives of 16 of the world's most recognized artists, including Michelangelo, Matisse, and Picasso.

Biographies are a unique genre that provide something for everyone. A biography can be found to fit virtually any child's needs and interests. Biographies allow the reader to take part in historical events, witness great discoveries, and walk beside those men and women who have impacted the past, the present, and even the future. Their stories provide inspiration and confirm our own hopes, goals, and ideals.

Selecting and Evaluating Biographies

When selecting and evaluating biographies, consider the following criteria, as well as all the standards of good literature.

❐ 1. Are the person and setting depicted in an authentic and accurate manner?

❐ 2. Is a balance provided between the requirement for accuracy and the requirement to hold the reader's interest?

❐ 3. Do rich and vivid details about a *worthy* subject allow for a better understanding of that person's role or contribution(s) to humankind?

❐ 4. Is the information presented such that the subject seems alive and real?

❐ 5. Is the subject represented honestly, including shortcomings and virtues and avoiding unnecessary ridicule or acclaim?

❐ 6. Does the book omit significant information that may distort the subject's life?

❐ 7. Do the text and illustrations seem to have been researched?

❐ 8. Do the dialogue and quotations add depth to the reader's understanding of the subject?

❑ 9. Does the book provide a historical perspective?

❑ 10. Are experiences or information provided that expand the reader's awareness of the possibilities in his or her own life?

Activities to Use with Biographies

1. After reading the biography/autobiography of a favorite author have students read several books by him or her. Discuss with them how their knowledge of the author impacted the way they understood and reacted to the books.

2. Ask each student to select and read a biography. (When possible, choices should be correlated to the topics/curriculum area being studied.) Have the student create a characterization of the person by becoming familiar with such aspects of the person as appearance, personal traits, accomplishments, problems encountered, quotations attributed to him or her, and the period during which he or she lived. Have students role-play the character in one of the following ways:

   a. "What's My Line"—others in the class prepare questions to learn the identity of their special guest

   b. Talk show—using interview format, students share the knowledge they have gained by answering questions other students ask

   c. "Meeting of the Minds"—students who are characterizing people in related fields form a panel to discuss their contributions and the similarities and differences in their work, philosophy, and so on

3. After students have read some biographies, discuss the reasons a person might be selected as the subject of a biography. Using these reasons, ask them to list local men and women whom they feel would be excellent subjects for a biography. Have students write a biography of a selected community leader. As a class, generate questions that you will use to interview the subject.

4. Encourage students to see themselves as subjects for tomorrow's biographies. Have each student produce a caricature of himself or herself as a person who has made a difference. Have them generate a list of words that reflect their ideas about how they see themselves in the future and write these words on their caricatures. Ask students to think of quotations for which they would like to be remembered and write these quotations on their caricatures. Allow time for students to share their caricatures.

5. Have students pretend a biography is being written about them. In preparation for the biography, they have been asked to write an article reporting the pertinent facts about their lives, events leading up to their fame (as they envision it in the future), and their obstacles, successes, and failures as well as anecdotes about their experiences. Compile the articles into a class anthology, "Biographies of the Future."

6. After reading biographies of selected individuals, have students prepare monologues that relate one significant event in these peoples' lives. Have

each student introduce his or her monologue by giving a brief summary of the person and his or her contributions, then present the monologue as if he or she were that person.

7. After reading a biography, have students select a favorite quotation from the subject—one that best seems to reflect the subject's philosophy. Have them illustrate the quotation and compile a booklet of these quotations.

8. Have students create a biopoem based on the subject of a biography (see page 64 for the format).

9. After they're read a biography of a famous individual from the past, involve students in one of the following "What if" scenarios:
    a. What if that person were alive today? What might he or she be famous for accomplishing in today's world?
    b. What if you could go back in time and meet this person? What one question would you ask? Why is this important to you?
    c. What if this person were alive today? What might he or she say about our world or about the field to which he or she once made a contribution?
    d. What if you were to make a movie of this person's life? What would the title be? Who would play the leading roles?
    e. What if this person had never lived? How would our world be different?

10. After they've read a biography, have students research the field to which the subject of the biography contributed. This may include writing letters and speaking to people in the field to learn how the subject influenced others.

Extending Your Knowledge of Biographies

1. Read different biographies of the same individual. Be prepared to discuss your perceptions of the subject and the way the different books dealt with the subject. For example, which book seemed to present a more accurate portrait? Which seemed to present the time period in which the person lived most vividly? Which seemed to fictionalize the person most? What details most helped you understand the subject?

2. After reading a biography, read an informational book about the person and his or her times and compare this information with that in the biography. How accurate was the portrayal in the biography? Were the major events that led to the person's accomplishments discussed? Was the subject portrayed realistically or were only his or her good qualities discussed?

3. Make a list of various categories of endeavor, such as politics, invention, entertainment, literature, music, exploration, and philosophy. Using magazines, newspapers, and other sources, create a "Who's Who" for one of these categories. Identify biographies/autobiographies for the people you've listed in your "Who's Who."

4. Design a bulletin board entitled "_____ Hall of Fame" (fill in the blank with a specific time, or field, or group of people) and prepare a list of biographies from which students can choose. Prepare questions that will help them write a biographic sketch of the person they read about.
5. After reading several biographies, write an essay on the value of biographies for children.

Children's Literature

*Cited in text

Picture Books

Alphabet Books

*Anno, Mitsumasa. *Anno's Alphabet*. Thomas Y. Crowell, 1975.

Azarian, Mary. *A Farmer's Alphabet*. Godine, 1981.

*Base, Graeme. *Animalia*. Abrams, 1987.

Bayer, Jane. *My Name Is Alice*. Dial, 1984.

Bruna, Dick. *B Is for Bear*. Methuen, 1987.

Duke, Kate. *The Guinea Pig ABC*. Dutton, 1983.

*Ehlert, Lois. *Eating the Alphabet: Fruits and Vegetables from A to Z*. Harcourt, 1989.

Eichenberg, Fritz. *Ape in a Cape*. Harcourt Brace Jovanovich, 1980.

Elliot, David. *An Alphabet of Rotten Kids!* Illustrated by Oscar de Mejo. Philomel, 1991.

Ellis, Veronica Freeman. *Afro-Bets First Book about Africa*. Illustrated by George Ford. Just Us Books, 1990.

*Feelings, Muriel. *Jambo Means Hello: Swahili Alphabet Book*. Illustrated by Tom Feelings. Dial, 1974.

Harrison, Ted. *A Northern Alphabet*. Tundra, 1982.

Hoban, Tana. *A.B. See!* Greenwillow, 1982.

Isadora, Rachel. *City Seen from A to Z*. Greenwillow, 1983.

Jonas, Ann. *Aardvarks, Disembark!* Greenwillow, 1990.

Kellogg, Steven. *Aster Aardvark's Alphabet Adventures*. Morrow, 1987.

Kitchen, Bert. *Animal Alphabet*. Dial, 1988.

Lear, Edward. *An Edward Lear Alphabet*. Illustrated by Carol Newsom. Lothrop, 1983.

Lobel, Anita. *Alison's Zinnia*. Greenwillow, 1990.

*Lobel, Arnold. *On Market Street*. Illustrated by Anita Lobel. Greenwillow, 1981.

MacDonald, Suse. *Alphabatics*. Bradbury, 1986.

Martin, Bill Jr., and John Archambault. *Chicka Chicka Boom Boom*. Illustrated by Lois Ehlert. Simon & Schuster, 1989.

*Musgrove, Margaret. *Ashanti to Zulu: African Traditions*. Illustrated by Leo and Diane Dillon. Dial, 1976.

Oxenbury, Helen. *ABC of Things*. Watts, 1972.

Piers, Helen. *Puppy's ABC*. Oxford, 1987.

Provensen, Alice, and Martin Provensen. *A Peaceable Kingdom: The Shaker ABECEDARIUS*. Viking, 1978.

Ryden, Hope. *Wild Animals of America ABC*. Lodestar/Dutton, 1988.

Stock, Catherine. *Alexander's Midnight Snack: A Little Elephant's ABC*. Clarion, 1988.

Van Allsburg, Chris. *The Z Was Zapped*. Houghton Mifflin, 1987.

Wildsmith, Brian. *Brian Wildsmith's ABC.* Watts, 1962.

Wilks, Mike. *The Ultimate Alphabet.* Holt, Rinehart & Winston, 1987.

Counting Books (generally suitable for Pre-S–1)

Aker, Susan. *What Comes in 2's, 3's, and 4's?* Illustrated by Bernie Karlin. Simon & Schuster, 1990.

Anno, Mitsumasa. *Anno's Counting Book.* Thomas Y. Crowell, 1975.

*———. *Anno's Counting House.* Thomas Y. Crowell, 1983.

Bang, Molly. *Ten, Nine, Eight.* Greenwillow, 1983.

Carle, Eric. *My Very First Book of Numbers.* Thomas Y. Crowell, 1974.

———. *The Very Hungry Caterpillar.* Philomel, 1969.

Dunrea, Olivier. *Deep Down Underground.* Macmillan, 1989.

Ehlert, Lois. *Fish Eyes: A Book You Can Count On.* Harcourt, 1990.

Feelings, Muriel. *Moja Means One: Swahili Counting Book.* Illustrated by Tom Feelings. Dial, 1971.

*Gardner, Beau. *Can You Imagine . . . ? A Counting Book.* Dodd, Mead. 1987.

Harshman, Marc. *Only One.* Illustrated by Barbara Garrison. Cobblehill, 1993.

Hoban, Russell. *Ten What? A Mystery Counting Book.* Scribner's, 1974.

Hoban, Tana. *Count and See.* Greenwillow, 1985.

*———. *1, 2, 3.* Greenwillow, 1985.

*Hutchins, Pat. *The Doorbell Rang.* Greenwillow, 1986.

———. *I Hunter.* Greenwillow, 1982.

*Keats, Ezra. *Over in the Meadow.* Scholastic, 1971. (Based on original verse by Oliver A. Wadsworth.)

Lindbergh, Reeve. *Midnight Farm.* Illustrated by Susan Jeffers. Dial, 1987.

Manushkin, Fran. *Walt Disney's 101 Dalmatians: A Counting Book.* Illustrated by Russell Hicks. Disney, 1991.

McMillan, Bruce. *Counting Wildflowers.* Lothrop, 1986.

Oxenbury, Helen. *Numbers & Things.* Watts, 1983.

Peek, Merle. *The Balancing Act: A Counting Book.* Clarion, 1987.

Potter, Beatrix. *Peter Rabbit's 1 2 3.* Warner, 1988.

Sis, Peter. *Waving: A Counting Book.* Greenwillow, 1988.

Tafuri, Nancy. *Who's Counting?* Greenwillow, 1986.

Testa, Fulvio. *If You Take a Pencil.* Dial, 1983.

Wildsmith, Brian. *Brian Wildsmith's 1, 2, 3's.* Watts, 1988.

Mother Goose Rhyme Books (generally suitable for Pre-S–1)

Arnold, Ted. *Mother Goose's Words of Wit and Wisdom: A Book of Months.* Dial, 1990.

Aldersen, Brian. *Cakes & Custard.* Illustrated by Helen Oxenbury. Morrow, 1975.

Brooks, Leslie. *Ring O'Roses.* Warne, 1972.

Cousins, Lucy. *The Little Dog Laughed and Other Nursery Rhymes.* Dutton, 1990.

*dePaola, Tomie. *Hey Diddle Diddle.* Putnam, 1985.

———, *Tomie de Paola's Mother Goose.* Putnam, 1985.

Griego, Margot, et al. *Tortillitas Para Mama and Other Nursery Rhymes/Spanish and English.* Illustrated by Barbara Cooney. Holt, 1981.

Hague, Michael. *Mother Goose: A Collection of Classic Nursery Rhymes.* Holt, Rinehart & Winston, 1984.

Hale, Sarah Josepha. *Mary Had a Little Lamb.* Photographs by Bruce McMillan. Scholastic, 1990.

Lobel, Arnold. *The Random House Book of Mother Goose.* Random House, 1986.

————. *Whiskers & Rhymes*. Greenwillow, 1985.

Marshall, James. *James Marshall's Mother Goose*. Farrar, Straus & Giroux, 1979.

Opie, Iona, and Peter Opie. *I Saw Esau*. Illustrated by Maurice Sendak. Candlewick, 1992.

*————. *The Oxford Nursery Rhyme Book*. Oxford University Press, 1952.

*Spier, Peter. *London Bridge Is Falling Down*. Doubleday, 1967.

*Sutherland, Zena. *The Orchard Book of Nursery Rhymes*. Illustrated by Faith Jacques. Orchard, 1990.

Tudor, Tasha. *Mother Goose*. Walck, 1944.

Westcott, Nadine Bernard, adapt. *The Lady with the Alligator Purse*. Little, Brown, 1988.

Wildsmith, Brian. *Brian Wildsmith's Mother Goose*. Watts, 1965.

Wright, Blanche Fisher. *The Real Mother Goose*. Rand McNally, 1965.

Wyndham, Robert. *Chinese Mother Goose Rhymes*. Illustrated by Ed Young. Philomel, 1968.

Toy Books (generally suitable for Pre-S–1)

Anholt, Lawrence, and Catherine Anholt. *Can You Guess?* Puffin, 1993.

Anno, Mitsumasa. *Anno's Sundial*. Philomel, 1985.

Baker, Keith. *The Magic Fan*. Harcourt, 1989.

Beatrix Potter's Peter Rabbit: A Lift-the-Flap Rebus Book. Warner, 1991.

Bond, Michael. *Paddington's Pop-Up Book*. Illustrated by Igor Wood. Price, Stern, Sloan, 1977.

Burdett, Alice. *Nature's Savage Cats*. Dial, 1993.

*Carle, Eric. *The Very Busy Spider*. Philomel, 1984.

————. *The Very Hungry Caterpillar*. Philomel, 1969.

Carter, David A. *In a Dark, Dark Wood*. Simon & Schuster, 1991.

Crowther, Robert. *The Most Amazing Hide-and-Seek Alphabet Book*. Viking, 1978.

Goodall, John. *Paddy Finds a Job*. Atheneum, 1977.

Hellen, Nancy. *Old MacDonald Had a Farm*. Orchard, 1990.

Hill, Eric. *Where's Spot?* Putnam, 1980.

*Hurd, Clement. *The Goodnight Moon Room*. HarperCollins, 1984.

Hurd, Thatcher. *A Night in the Swamp*. Harper & Row, 1987.

*Kunhardt, Dorothy. *Pat the Bunny*. Golden, 1962.

McHenry, Ellen Johnston. *Inside a Freight Train*. Cobblehill, 1993.

Munari, Bruno. *Who's There? Open the Door*. Philomel, 1960.

Oxenbury, Helen. *Friends*. Simon & Schuster, 1981.

Pellem, David. *Sam's Sandwich*. Dutton, 1990.

Roddie, Shen. *Mrs. Wolf*. Illustrated by Korky Paul. Dial, 1993.

Roffey, Maureen. *Home Sweet Home*. Coward-McCann, 1983.

Spier, Peter. *The Pet Store*. Doubleday, 1973.

Stott, Dorothy. *Puppy and Me*. Dutton, 1993.

————. *Kitty and Me*. Dutton, 1993.

Tripp, Wallace. *The Bad Child's Pop-up Book of Beasts*. Putnam, 1986.

Yee, Patrick. *Little Buddy Goes Shopping*. Viking, 1993.

Zelinsky, Paul O. *The Wheels on the Bus*. Dutton, 1990.

Concept Books (generally suitable for Pre-S–K)

*Aliki. *My Feet*. Crowell, 1990.

*————. *My Hands*. Crowell, 1990.

Baer, Gene. *Thump, Thump, Rat-a-Tat-Tat*. Illustrated by Lois Ehlert. Harper, 1989.

Barton, Byron. *Dinosaurs, Dinosaurs*. Crowell, 1989.

Coleridge, Sara. *January Brings the Snow*. Illustrated by Jenni Oliver. Dial, 1986.

Crews, Donald. *Flying*. Greenwillow, 1986.

———. *Freight Train*. Greenwillow, 1978.

Ehlert, Lois. *Growing Vegetable Soup*. Harcourt, 1987.

Emberly, Rebecca. *Jungle Sounds*. Little, Brown, 1989.

*Fisher, Leonard. *Look Around! A Book about Shapes*. Viking, 1987.

Florian, Douglas. *A Summer Day*. Greenwillow, 1988.

———. *A Winter Day*. Greenwillow, 1987.

Fowler, Susi Gregg. *When Summer Ends*. Illustrated by Marisabina Russo. Greenwillow, 1989.

Gerstein, Mordicai. *The Sun's Day*. Harper, 1989.

Gillham, Bill, and Susan Hulme. *Let's Look for Opposites*. Illustrated by Jan Siegieda. Coward, 1984.

*———. *Let's Look for Shapes*. Illustrated by Jan Siegieda. Coward, 1984.

*Hoban, Tana. *Circles, Triangles and Squares*. Macmillan, 1974.

———. *Exactly the Opposite*. Greenwillow, 1990.

*———. *Is It Larger? Is It Smaller?* Greenwillow, 1978.

———. *Look! Look! Look!* Greenwillow, 1988.

*———. *Of Colors and Things*. Greenwillow, 1989.

*———. *Shapes and Things*. Macmillan, 1970.

———. *26 Letters & 99 Cents*. Greenwillow, 1987.

*Hughes, Shirley. *All Shapes and Sizes*. Lothrop, 1989.

———. *The Big Concrete Lorry*. Lothrop, 1990.

Kraus, Ruth. *A Hole Is to Dig By*. Illustrated by Maurice Sendak. Harper & Row, 1982.

Martin, Bill Jr., and John Archambault. *Here Are My Hands*. Holt, Rinehart & Winston, 1987.

McMillan, Bruce. *Growing Colors*. Lothrop, 1988.

———. *Super Super Superwords*. Lothrop, 1989.

Reiss, John. *Colors*. Bradbury, 1969.

*———. *Shapes*. Bradbury, 1974.

Rockwell, Harlow. *My Kitchen*. Greenwillow, 1980.

Schwartz, David M. *If You Made a Million*. Illustrated by Steven Kellogg. Photographs by George Ancona. Lothrop, 1989.

Spier, Peter. *Crash! Bang! Boom!* Doubleday, 1972.

*———. *Fast–Slow High–Low: A Book of Opposites*. Doubleday, 1972.

Tudor, Tasha. *First Delights*. Platt & Munk, 1988.

Turner, Gwenda. *Opposites*. Viking, 1993.

verDom, Bethea. *Moon Glows*. Illustrated by Thomas Graham. Arcade, 1990.

Walsh, Ellen Stoll. *Mouse Paint*. Harcourt, 1989.

Wordless Picture Books (generally suitable for Pre-S–1)

Anno, Mitsumasa. *Anno's Journey*. Philomel, 1980.

Day, Alexandra. *Carl Goes Shopping*. Farrar, Straus & Giroux, 1989.

DePaola, Tomie. *The Knight and the Dragon*. Putnam, 1980.

———. *Pancakes for Breakfast*. Harcourt Brace Jovanovich, 1978.

Handford, Martin. *Find Waldo Now*. Little, Brown, 1988.

———. *Where's Waldo?* Little, Brown, 1987.

Hutchins, Pat. *Changes, Changes*. Macmillan, 1971.

Keats, Ezra. *Kitten for a Day*. Watts, 1974.

Martin, Rafe. *Will's Mammoth*. Illustrated by Stephen Gammell. Putnam, 1989.

Mayer, Mercer. *One Frog Too Many*. Dial, 1975.

McCully, Emily Arnold. *First Snow*. Harper & Row, 1985.

———. *New Baby*. Harper, 1988.

Omerod, Jan. *Moonlight*. Lothrop, 1982.

———. *Picnic*. Harper & Row, 1984.

Spier, Peter. *Noah's Ark*. Doubleday, 1977.

———. *Peter Spier's Rain*. Doubleday, 1982.

Tafuri, Nancy. *Early Morning in the Barn*. Greenwillow, 1983.

———. *Follow Me!* Greenwillow, 1990.

Wiesner, David. *Free Fall*. Lothrop, 1988.

*———. *Tuesday*. Clarion, 1991.

Predictable Books (generally suitable for Pre-S–1)

Anholt, Catherine, and Laurence Anholt. *What I Like*. Putnam, 1991.

Baer, Gene. *Thump, Thump, Rat-a-Tat-Tat*. Illustrated by Lois Ehlert. Harper, 1989.

*Brown, Margaret Wise. *Goodnight Moon*. Harper, 1947.

Brown, Ruth. *A Dark Dark Tale*. Dial, 1981.

Carle, Eric. *The Grouchy Ladybug*. Crowell, 1977.

*———. *The Very Busy Spider*. Philomel. 1984.

———. *The Very Hungry Caterpillar*. HarperCollins, 1969.

———. *The Very Quiet Cricket*. Philomel, 1990.

Cuyler, Margery. *That's Good, That's Bad*. Illustrated by David Catrow. Holt, 1991.

Emberly, Barbara. *Drummer Hoff*. Illustrated by Ed Emberly. Prentice-Hall, 1967.

Fox, Mem. *Shores from Grandpa*. Orchard, 1990.

*Gag, Wanda. *Millions of Cats*. Coward-McCann, 1928.

Galdone, Paul. *The Gingerbread Boy*. Seabury, 1975.

———. *Henny Penny*. Scholastic, 1968.

*———. *The Little Red Hen*. Scholastic, 1973.

———. *The Teeny, Tiny Woman*. Clarion, 1984.

Ginsburg, Mirra. *Across the Stream*. Illustrated by Nancy Tafuri. Greenwillow, 1982.

———. *The Chick and the Duckling*. Illustrated by Jose and Ariane Aruego. Macmillan, 1972.

Goennel, Mordicai. *My Dog*. Orchard, 1990.

Greely, Valerie. *White Is the Moon*. Macmillan, 1990.

Guarino, Deborah. *Is Your Mama a Llama?* Illustrated by Steven Kellogg. Scholastic, 1989.

Hawkins, Colin, and Jacqui Hawkins. *I Know an Old Lady Who Swallowed a Fly*. Putnam, 1987.

Hayes, Sarah. *The Grampalump*. Clarion, 1990.

Hellen, Nancy. *The Bus Stop*. Orchard, 1990.

———. *Old MacDonald Had a Farm*. Orchard. 1990.

Hennessy, B. G. *Jake Baked the Cake*. Illustrated by Mary Morgan. Viking, 1990.

Hill, Eric. *Spot Goes to the Beach*. Putnam, 1985.

———. *Where's Spot?* Putnam, 1980.

Hutchins, Pat. *Rosie's Walk*. Macmillan, 1968.

———. *Titch*. Macmillan, 1971.

———. *What Shall We Play?* Greenwillow, 1990.

Jones, Carol. *Old MacDonald Had a Farm*. Houghton Mifflin, 1989.

Kraus, Robert. *Where Are You Going, Little Mouse?* Illustrated by Jose Aruego and Ariane Dewey. Greenwillow, 1986.

Langstaff, John. *Oh, A-Hunting We Will Go.* Illustrated by Nancy Winslow Parker. D.C. Heath, 1989.

Lyon, George Ella. *The Outside Inn.* Orchard, 1991.

*Martin, Bill Jr. *Brown Bear, Brown Bear, What Do You See?* Illustrated by Eric Carle. Holt, Rinehart & Winston, 1983.

———. *Chicka Chicka Boom Boom.* Illustrated by Lois Ehlert. Simon & Schuster, 1989.

*———. *Polar Bear, Polar Bear, What Do You Hear?* Illustrated by Eric Carle. Holt, 1990.

McMillan, Bruce. *Play Day: A Book of Terse Verse.* Holiday 1991.

Nerlove, Miriam. *I Meant to Clean My Room Today.* McElderry, 1988.

Numeroff, Laura J. *If You Gave a Mouse a Cookie.* Harper & Row, 1985.

Pizer, Abigail. *It's a Perfect Day.* Lippincott, 1990.

Roe, Eileen. *All I Am.* Illustrated by Helen Cogancherry. Bradbury, 1990.

Rosen, Michael, reteller. *We're Going on a Bear Hunt.* Illustrated by Helen Oxenbury. McElderry, 1989.

Roy, Ron. *Three Ducks Went Wandering.* Illustrated by Paul Galdone. Clarion, 1979.

Sendak, Maurice. *Chicken Soup with Rice.* Scholastic, 1962.

Shapiro, Arnold. *Who Says That?* Illustrated by Monica Wellington. Dutton, 1991.

Slate, Joseph. *Who is Coming to Our House?* Illustrated by Ashley Wolff. Putnam, 1988.

Sundgaard, Arnold. *The Lamb and the Butterfly.* Illustrated by Eric Carle. Orchard, 1988.

Tolstoy, Alexei. *The Great Enormous Turnip.* Illustrated by Helen Oxenbury. Watts, 1968.

Viorst, Judith. *Alexander and the Terrible, Horrible, No Good, Very Bad Day.* Illustrated by Ray Cruz. Atheneum, 1972.

Weiss, Nicki. *Where Does the Brown Bear Go?* Greenwillow, 1989.

Wildsmith, Brian. *The Cat Sat on the Mat.* Oxford, 1983.

———. *Toot Toot.* Oxford, 1984.

Wood, Audrey. *The Napping House.* Harcourt, 1984.

Easy-to-Read Books (generally suitable for K–2)

Adler, David A. *My Dog and the Birthday Mystery.* Illustrated by Dick Gackenbach. Holiday House, 1984.

Apablasa, Bill, and Thiesing, Lisa. *Rhymin' Simon and the Mystery of the Fake Snake.* Dutton, 1992.

Bulla, Clyde Robert. *The Child Box Kid.* Illustrated by Thomas B. Allen. Random House, 1987.

Byars, Betsy. *Hooray for the Golly Sisters!* Illustrated by Sue Truesdell. Harper, 1990.

Cherry, Lynne. *Who's Sick Today?* Dutton, 1988.

Cohen, Miriam. *It's George!* Illustrated by Lillian Hoban. Greenwillow, 1988.

Cole, Joanna, and Stephanie Calmenson, comps. *Ready . . . Set . . . Read!: The Beginning Reader's Treasury.* Illustrated by Ann Burgess and Chris Demarest. Doubleday, 1990.

de Brunhoff, Laurent. *Babar's Little Circus Star.* Random House, 1988.

Hoban, Lillian. *Arthur's Great Big Valentine.* Harper, 1989.

———. *Tidy Titch.* Greenwillow, 1991.

———. *What Game Shall We Play?* Greenwillow, 1990.

Hoff, Syd. *Sammy the Seal.* Harper & Row, 1959.

Lobel, Arnold. *Grasshopper on the Road.* Harper & Row, 1978.

McDonald, Megan. *Is This a House for Hermit Crab?* Illustrated by S. D. Schindler. Orchard, 1990.

Minarick, Else Homelund. *Little Bear.* Illustrated by Maurice Sendak. Harper & Row, 1957.

Moore, Lillian. *I'll Meet You at the Cucumbers.* Illustrated by Sharon Wooding. Atheneum, 1988.

Porte, Barbara Ann. *Harry in Trouble.* Illustrated by Yossi Aboladia. Greenwillow, 1989.

Rosen, Michael, reteller. *We're Going on a Bear Hunt.* Illustrated by Helen Oxenbury. Macmillan, 1989.

Rylant, Cynthia. *Henry and Mudge and the Happy Cat.* Illustrated by Sucie Stevenson. Bradbury, 1990.

*Seuss, Dr. (Theodor Geisel). *And to Think That I Saw It on Mulberry Street.* Vanguard, 1937.

*———. *The Cat in the Hat.* Beginner Books, 1957.

Shaw, Nancy. *Sheep on a Ship.* Illustrated by Margot Apple. Houghton, 1989.

Weiss, Nicki. *Where Does the Brown Bear Go?* Greenwillow, 1989.

Wellington, Monica. *All My Little Ducklings.* Dutton, 1989.

Williams, Sue. *I Went Walking.* Illustrated by Julies Vivas. Harcourt, 1990.

Picture Storybooks

*Aardema, Verna. *Why Mosquitoes Buzz in People's Ears.* Illustrated by Leo and Diane Dillon. Dial, 1975. (Grades K–4)

Ackerman, Karen. *Song and Dance Man.* Illustrated by Stephen Gammel. Knopf, 1988. (Grades 1–3)

Ahlberg, Janet, and Allen Ahlberg. *Each Peach Pear Plum.* Puffin, 1978.

———. *The Jolly Postman.* Little, Brown, 1986. (Grades 1–4)

Allard, Harry, and James Marshall. *Miss Nelson Has a Field Day.* Illustrated by James Marshall. Houghton, 1985. (Grades 1–3).

———. *Miss Nelson Is Missing!* Houghton Mifflin, 1977. (Grades 2–4)

Allen, Pamela. *Belinda.* Viking, 1993. (Grades Pre-S–3)

Babbit, Natalie. *Nellie: A Cat on Her Own.* Farrar, Straus & Giroux, 1989. (Grades 1–3)

Bang, Molly. *The Paper Crane.* Greenwillow, 1985. (Grades 2–4)

Barber, Antonia. *The Mousehole Cat.* Illustrated by Nicola Bayley. Macmillan, 1990. (Grades 1–3)

Barracca, Debra, and Sal Barracca. *The Adventures of Taxi Dog.* Illustrated by Mark Buehner. Dial, 1990. (Grades 1–3)

Brett, Jan. *Annie and the Wild Animals.* Lothrop, 1987. (Grades Pre-S–3)

———. *The Wild Christmas Reindeer.* Putnam, 1990. (Grades 1–3)

*Brinckloe, Julie. *Fireflies!* Aladdin, 1985. (Grades K–2)

Bunting, Eve. *The Wall.* Illustrated by Ronald Himler. Clarion, 1990. (Grades 1–3)

Calhoun, Mary. *Cross Country Cat.* Mulberry, 1986. (Grades 1–3)

Carlstrom, Nancy White. *Blow Me a Kiss, Miss Lilly.* Illustrated by Amy Schwartz. Harper, 1990. (Grades K–2)

Cherry, Lynne. *The Great Kapok Tree: A Tale of the Amazon Rainforest.* Harcourt, 1990. (Grades 1–4)

Chetwin, Grace. *Box and Cox.* Illustrated by David Small. Bradbury, 1990. (Grades 1–3)

*Cole, Joanna. *The Magic School Bus at the Waterworks.* Illustrated by Bruce Degen, Scholastic, 1986. (Grades 1–4)

*———. *The Magic School Bus Inside the Human Body.* Illustrated by Bruce Degen. Scholastic, 1989. (Pre-S–3)

*———. *The Magic School Bus Lost in the Solar System.* Illustrated by Bruce Degen. Scholastic, 1990. (Pre-S–3)

*———. *The Magic School Bus Inside the Earth.* Illustrated by Bruce Degen. Scholastic, 1987. (Grades K–3)

Cooney, Barbara. *Hattie and the Wild Waves: A Story from Brooklyn.* Viking, 1993. (Grades 1–3)

————. *Miss Rumphius.* Puffin, 1982. (Grades 1–3)

de Paola, Tomie. *Strega Nona.* Prentice-Hall, 1975. (Grades 1–3)

de Regniers, Beatrice Schenk. *May I Bring a Friend?* Illustrated by Beni Montresor. Atheneum, 1965. (Grades Pre-S–3)

*Dorros, Arthur. *Abuela.* Illustrated by Elisa Kleven. Dutton, 1991. (Pre-S–2)

Ets, Marie Hall. *Gilberto and the Wind.* Viking, 1963. (Grades 1–3)

Everitt, Betsy. *Frida the Wondercat.* Harcourt, 1990. (Grades 1–3)

Fleishman, Syd. *The Scarebird.* Greenwillow, 1988. (Grades 1–3)

Fox, Mem. *Shoes from Grandpa.* Illustrated by Patricia Mullins. Orchard, 1990. (Grades 1–3)

*Frost, Robert. *Stopping by Woods on a Snowy Evening.* Illustrated by Susan Jeffers. Dutton, 1978; (Grades 5+)

Galdone, Paul. *The Little Red Hen.* Seabury, 1973. (Grades Pre-S–2)

Garza, Carmen. *Family Pictures: Cuadros de Familia.* Children's Book Press, 1990. (Grades 1–7)

*Golenbock, Peter. *Teammates.* Illustrated by Paul Bacon. Harcourt Brace Jovanovich, 1990. (Grades 1–4)

Greenfield, Eloise. *Nathaniel Talking.* Illustrated by Jan Spivey Gilchrist. Writers and Readers, 1989. (Grades 1–3)

Henkes, Kevin. *Julius, the Baby of the World.* Greenwillow, 1990. (Grades K–2)

*Innocenti, Roberto. *Rose Blanche.* Stewart, Tabori and Chant, 1990. (Grades 3+)

Johnson, Angela. *When I Am Old with You.* Illustrated by David Soman. Orchard, 1990. (Grades 1–3)

Johnson, Tony. *The Quilt Story.* Illustrated by Tomie dePaola. Putnam, 1985. (Grades 1–3)

Joyce, William. *A Day with Wilbur Robinson.* Harper, 1990. (Grades 1–3)

*Jukes, Mavis. *I'll See You in My Dreams,* Illustrated by Stacey Schuett. Knopf, 1993. (Grades K–5)

Kalman, Maira. *Max Makes a Million.* Viking, 1990. (Grades 1–3)

*Keats, Ezra Jack. *The Snowy Day.* Viking, 1962. (Grades K–2)

*Kraus, Robert. *Leo the Late Bloomer.* Illustrated by Jose Aruego. Simon & Schuster, 1971. (Grades K–3)

Lindbergh, Reeve. *The Day the Goose Got Loose.* Illustrated by Steven Kellogg. Dial, 1990. (Grades K–2)

Lionni, Leo. *Swimmy.* Pantheon, 1963. (Grades K–3)

Lotz, Karen E. *Can't Sit Still.* Illustrated by Coleen Browning. Dutton, 1993. (Grades Pre-S–3)

Lyon, George Ella. *Come a Tide.* Illustrated by Stephen Gammell. Orchard, 1990. (Grades 1–3)

Mahy, Margaret. *The Great White Man-Eating Shark: A Cautionary Tale.* Illustrated by Jonathan Allen. Dial, 1990. (Grades 2–5)

Martin, Bill Jr., and John Archambault. *Knots on a Counting Rope.* Illustrated by Ted Rand. Holt, 1987. (Grades 1–3)

*McDermott, Gerald. *Arrow to the Sun.* Viking, 1974. (Grades 1+)

*Mosel, Arlen. *The Funny Little Woman.* Illustrated by Blair Lent. Dutton, 1972. (Pre-S–4)

Munsch, Robert. *Love You Forever.* Firefly, 1986. (Grades K–3)

Ness, Evaline. *Sam, Bangs, & Moonshine.* Holt, Rinehart & Winston, 1966.

Nobel, Trinka H. *Jimmy's Boa and the Big Splash Birthday Bash.* Illustrated by Steven Kellogg. Dial, 1989. (Grades 1–3)

Polacco, Patricia. *Babushka's Doll.* Simon & Schuster, 1990. (Grades 1–3)

————. *Thunder Cake.* Putnam, 1990. (Grades 1–3)

Pomerantz, Charlotte. *The Chalk Doll.* Illustrated by Frane Lessac. Harper, 1989. (Grades 1–3)

*Ringgold, Faith. *Tar Beach.* Crown, 1991. (Grades 2–5)

*Sendak, Maurice. *Where the Wild Things Are.* Harper & Row, 1963. (Grades K–3)

Seuss, Dr. [pseud.] (Theodor S. Geisel). *Oh, the Places You'll Go!* Random House, 1990. (Grades 1–3)

Siebert, Diane. *Sierre.* Illustrated by Wendell Minor. Harper, 1991. (Grades 2–5)

Steig, William. *Sylvester and the Magic Pebble.* Windmill/Simon, 1969. (Grades 1–3)

Steptoe, John. *Mufaro's Beautiful Daughter.* Lothrop, 1987. (Grades 1–3)

Swope, Sam. *The Araboolies of Liberty Street.* Illustrated by Barry Root. Clarkson N. Potter, 1989. (Grades 1–3)

Tompert, Ann. *Grandfather Tang's Story.* Illustrated by Robert Andrew Parker. Crown, 1990. (Grades 1–3)

*Van Allsburg, Chris. *Jamanji.* Houghton Mifflin, 1981. (Grades 1–3)

———. *Just a Dream.* Houghton Mifflin, 1985. (Pre-S+)

———. *The Mysteries of Harris Burdick.* Houghton Mifflin, 1984. (Grades 1–3)

———. *Polar Express.* Houghton Mifflin, 1985. (Grades 1–4)

*Viorst, Judith. *Alexander and the Terrible, Horrible, No Good, Very Bad Day.* Illustrated by Ray Cruz. Aladdin, 1972. (Grades K–4)

*———. *The Tenth Good Thing About Barney.* Illustrated by Erik Blegvad. Atheneum, 1971. (Grades K–4)

Ward, Lynd. *The Biggest Bear.* Houghton Mifflin, 1952. (Grades K–3)

Warne, Frederick. *The Tale of Tom Kitten and Jemina Puddle-Duck.* Viking, 1993. (Grades Pre-S–2)

Wild, Margaret. *The Very Best of Friends.* Illustrated by Julie Vivas. Harcourt, 1990. (Grades K–3)

Williams, Vera. *More, More, More, Said the Baby.* Greenwillow, 1990. (Grades K–3)

Williams, Vera B., and Jennifer Williams. *Stringbean's Trip to the Shining Sea.* Greenwillow, 1988. (Grades 1–3)

*Yolen, Jane. *Encounter.* Illustrated by D. Shannon. Harcourt Brace Jovanovich, 1991. (Grades K–4)

*———. *Owl Moon.* Philomel, 1987. (Grades 1–3)

Zelinsky, Paul O. *The Maid and the Mouse and the Odd-Shaped House.* Dutton, 1993. (Grades Pre-S–2).

Realistic Fiction

Alexander, Lloyd. *The El Dorado Adventure.* Dutton, 1987. (Grades 6+)

Armstrong, William. *Sounder.* Illustrated by James Barkley. Harper & Row, 1969. (Grades 5+)

*Blume, Judy. *Are You There, God? It's Me, Margaret.* Bradbury, 1970. (Grades 4–6)

*———. *Blubber.* Bradbury, 1974. (Grades 4–6)

———. *Freckle Juice.* Four Winds, 1971. (Grades 3–6)

———. *Superfudge.* Dutton, 1980. (Grades 3–5)

*Bunting, Eve. *How Many Days to America?* Illustrated by Beth Peck. Clarion/T & F, 1988. (Grades K–3)

Burch, Robert. *Christmas with Ida Early.* Viking, 1983. (Grades 4–6)

*Burnett, Frances Hodgson. *The Secret Garden.* Illustrated by Shirley Hughes. Viking, 1989 [1910]. (Grades 5–9)

*Byars, Betsy. *The Cybil War.* Illustrated by Gail Owens. Viking, 1981. (Grades 2–5)

*———. *The Not-Just-Anybody Family.* Illustrated by Jacqueline Rogers. Delacorte, 1986. (Grades 4–6)

*———. *The Pinballs.* Harper & Row, 1977. (Grades 4–7)

*———. *The Summer of the Swans.* Illustrated by Ted CoConis. Viking, 1970. (Grades 4+)

Cameron, Eleanor. *Julia's Magic.* Illustrated by Gail Owen. Dutton, 1984. (Grades 3–5)

Cebulash, Mel. *Ruth Marini, Dodger Ace.* Lerner, 1983. (Grades 4+)

*Cleary, Beverly. *Dear Mr. Henshaw.* Illustrated by Paul O. Zelinsky. Morrow, 1983. (Grades 3–6)

———. *Ramona Forever.* Illustrated by Alan Tiegreen. Morrow, 1984. (Grades 3–5)

———. *Strider.* Illustrated by Paul O. Zelinsky. Morrow, 1991. (Grades 4–8)

*Cleaver, Vera, and Bill Cleaver. *Where the Lilies Bloom.* Lippincott, 1969. (Grades 6+)

Clymer, Eleanor. *The Horse in the Attic.* Illustrated by Ted Lewin. Bradbury, 1983. (Grades 4–6)

Conrad, Pam. *My Daniel.* HarperCollins, 1989. (Grades 4–8)

*———. *Staying Nine.* Illustrated by Mike Wimmer. Harper, 1990. (Grades 2–5)

Danziger, Paula. *Divorce Express.* Delacorte, 1982. (Grades 7+)

*DeClements, Barthe. *Nothing's Fair in the Fifth Grade.* Puffin, 1990. (Grades 3–6)

*de Paola, Tomie. *Nana Upstairs, Nana Downstairs.* Putnam, 1983. (Grades K–3)

*———. *Now One Foot, Now the Other.* Putnam, 1984. (Grades K–3)

*de Regniers, Beatrice Schenk. *May I Bring a Friend?* Illustrated by Beni Montresor. Atheneum, 1964. (Grades K–3)

Ellis, Sarah. *Next-Door Neighbors.* Macmillan, 1990. (Grades 4–8)

*Estes, Eleanor. *The Hundred Dresses.* Illustrated by Louis Slobodkin. Harcourt Brace Jovanovich, 1944. (Grades 2–5)

*Farber, Norma. *How Does It Feel to Be Old?* Dutton, 1988. (Grades K–3)

*First, Julie. *Look Who's Beautiful!* Franklin Watts, 1980. (Grades 4–6)

*Fitzhugh, Louise. *Harriet the Spy.* Harper, 1964. (Grades 4–6)

*Fox, Paula. *Monkey Island.* Watts, 1991. (Grades 4–7)

———. *One-Eyed Cat.* Bradbury, 1984. (Grades 5–7)

*George, Jean Craighead. *Julie of the Wolves.* Harper & Row, 1972. (Grades 4+)

———. *The Talking Earth.* Harper & Row, 1983. (Grades 5+)

———. *Water Sky.* Harper & Row, 1987. (Grades 5+)

Giff, Patricia Reilly. *Kids of Polk Street Series.* 12 titles. Dell, 1985. (Grades K–1)

Gilson, Jamie. *Sticks and Stones and Skeleton Bones.* Illustrated by Dee deRosa. Lothrop, 1991. (Grades 3–6)

*Gould, Marilyn. *Golden Daffodils.* Addison Wesley, 1982. (Grades 4–6)

*Greene, Bette. *Get On Out of Here, Philip Hall.* Dial, 1981. (Grades 4–6)

Hamilton, Virginia. *Cousins.* Putnam, 1990. (Grades 4–8)

*———. *M.C. Higgins, the Great.* Macmillan, 1974. (Grades 5+)

———. *Zeely.* Illustrated by Symeon Shimin. Macmillan, 1967. (Grades 3–6)

Harper, Anita. *It's Not Fair.* Illustrated by Susan Hellard. Putnam, 1986. (Pre-S–K)

Hazen, Barbara Shook. *Tight Times.* Viking, 1979. (Grades K–3)

Hermes, Patricia. *Mama, Let's Dance.* Little, 1991. (Grades 5+)

*———. *You Shouldn't Have to Say Goodbye.* Harcourt Brace Jovanovich, 1982. (Grades 5+)

*Hinton, S. E. *The Outsiders.* Viking, 1967. (Grades 6+)

*Hurwitz, Johanna. *Aldo Applesauce.* Illustrated by John Wallner. Morrow, 1979. (Grades 4–6)

Jones, Rebecca C. *Germy in Charge.* Dutton, 1993. (Grades 3–6)

*Jukes, Mavis. *I'll See You in My Dreams.* Illustrated by Stacey Schuett. Knopf, 1993. (Grades 1–4)

*Keats, Ezra Jack. *Peter's Chair*. Harper & Row, 1967. (Grades K–3)

*Keith, Harold Verne. *The Runt of Rodgers School*. Lippincott, 1971. (Grades 4–7)

*Keller, Beverly. *Desdemona—Twelve Going on Desperate*. William Morrow, 1986. (Grades 4–7)

Kinsey-Warnock, Natalie. *The Canada Geese Quilt*. Illustrated by Leslie W. Bowman. Dutton, 1989. (Grades 3–7).

Klein, Robin. *Enemies*. Illustrated by Noela Young. Dutton, 1989. (Grades 4–7)

*Konigsburg, E. L. *About the B'nai Bagels*. 1969. (Grades 4–6)

*———. *From the Mixed-Up Files of Mrs. Basil E. Frankweiler*. Atheneum, 1967. (Grades 4+)

*Krumgold, Joseph. *. . . And Now Miguel*. Harper & Row, 1953. (Grades 6+)

———. *Onion John*. Harper & Row, 1959. (Grades 4–7)

*Little, Jean. *Mama's Going to Buy You a Mockingbird*. Viking, 1984. (Grades 3–6)

———. *Mine for Keeps*. Illustrated by Lewis Parker. Little, Brown, 1962. (Grades 4–7)

*Lord, Bette Bao. *In the Year of the Boar and Jackie Robinson*. HarperCollins, 1984. (Grades 1–4)

*Lowry, Lois. *Anastasia Krupnik*. Houghton, 1979. (Grades 3–6)

———. *Anastasia Has the Answers*. Houghton, 1986. (Grades 4–6)

———. *Anastasia on Her Own*. Houghton, 1985. (Grades 4–6)

———. *Rabble Starkey*. Houghton Mifflin, 1987. (Grades 5+)

———. *A Summer to Die*. Illustrated by Jenni Oliver and Diane de Groat. Dial, 1981. (Grades 4+)

*MacLachlan, Patricia. *Arthur, for the Very First Time*. Harper & Row, 1980. (Grades 3–6)

*———. *Baby*. Delacorte, 1993. (Grades 3–6).

———. *Journey*. Illustrated by Barry Moser. Delacorte, 1991. (Grades 5–9)

*———. *Through Grandpa's Eyes*. Illustrated by Deborah Ray. Harper, 1979. (Grades K–3)

*Manes, Stephen. *Be a Perfect Person in Just Three Days*. Clarion, 1982. (Grades 3–6)

Mark, Jan. *Handles*. Atheneum, 1985. (Grades 5–9)

Martin, Ann. *Kristy's Great Idea: The Baby-Sitters Club* (and other Baby-Sitters Club books). Scholastic, 1986. (Grades 2–5)

Martin, Bill Jr., and John Archambault. *Knots on a Counting Rope*. Illustrated by Ted Rand. Holt, Rinehart & Winston, 1987. (Grades K–3)

*Mathis, Sharon Bell. *The Hundred Penny Box*. Illustrated by Leo and Diane Dillon. Viking, 1975. (Grades 2–6)

*Miles, Miska. *Annie and the Old One*. Illustrated by Peter Parnell. Little, Brown, 1971. (Grades K–4)

*Mohr, Nicolasa. *Felita*. Illustrated by Ray Cruz. Dial, 1979. (Grades 3–6)

*Myers, Walter Dean. *Scorpions*. HarperCollins, 1988. (Grades 5+)

*Naidoo, Beverley. *Journey to Jo'berg*. Illustrated by Eric Velasquez. Lippincott, 1990. (Grades 3–6)

Naylor, Phyllis Reynolds. *Reluctantly Alice*. Atheneum, 1991. (Grades 3–6)

*Parish, Peggy. *Play Ball, Amelia Bedelia*. Harper & Row, 1977. (Grades K–3)

*Paterson, Katherine. *Bridge to Terabithia*. Illustrated by Donna Diamond. Thomas Y. Crowell, 1977. (Grades 4–7)

*———. *The Great Gilly Hopkins*. Thomas Y. Crowell, 1978. (Grades 5+)

*———. *Jacob Have I Loved*. Harper & Row, 1980. (Grades 6+)

———. *Park's Quest*. Lodestar, 1988. (Grades 5+)

*Paulsen, Gary. *Hatchet*. Bradbury, 1987. (Grades 5+)

Pittman, Helena Clare. *The Gift of the Willows*. Pittman, 1988. (Grades K–4)

Reuter, Bjarne. *Buster's World*. Translated from Danish by Anthea Bell. Dutton, 1989. (Grades 4–7).

———. *The Sheik of Hope Street.* Dutton, 1991. (Grades 4–7)

*Rockwell, Thomas. *How to Eat Fried Worms.* Watts, 1973. (Grades 5+)

Rylant, Cynthia. *Missing May.* Jackson/Orchard, 1992. (Grades 4–6)

Sachs, Marilyn. *Thirteen Going on Seven.* Dutton, 1993. (Grades 4–7)

*Schick, Eleanor. *City in the Winter.* Macmillan, 1982. (Grades 3–5)

*Screen, Robert Martin. *With My Face to the Rising Sun.* Harcourt Brace Jovanovich, 1977. (Grades 4+)

Shreve, Susan. *The Gift of the Girl Who Couldn't Hear.* Morrow, 1991. (Grades 5–8)

*Shyer, Marlene. *Welcome Home, Jellybean.* Scribner's, 1978. (Grades 4–6)

*Slepian, Jan. *The Alfred Summer.* Macmillan, 1980. (Grades 4–6)

Slote, Alfred. *The Trading Game.* Lippincott, 1990. (Grades 4–7)

Smith, Doris Buchanan. *The Pennywhistle Tree.* Putnam, 1991. (Grades 4–7)

Smith, Janice Lee. *The Show and Tell War and Other Sources About Adam Joshua.* Illustrated by Dick Gackenbach. Harper & Row, 1988. (Grades 1–4)

Smith, Robert Kimmel. *Bobby Baseball.* Illustrated by Allen Tiegreen. Delacorte, 1989. (Grades 3–6)

*———. *The War with Grandpa.* Dell, 1984. (Grades 4–6)

*Speare, Elizabeth George. *The Sign of the Beaver.* Dell, 1983. (Grades 4+)

*Sperry, Armstrong. *Call It Courage.* Macmillan, 1960. (Grades 4–7)

*Spinelli, Jerry. *Maniac Magee.* Little, Brown, 1990. (Grades 4–7)

*Steptoe, John. *Stevie.* Harper, 1969. (Grades 1–3)

Stoltz, Mary. *The Explorer of Barkham Street.* Illustrated by Emily A. McCully. Harper & Row, 1985. (Grades 5–7)

Viorst, Judith. *Alexander and the Terrible, Horrible, No Good, Very Bad Day.* Illustrated by Ray Cruz. Atheneum, 1972. (Grades K–3)

*———. *Rosie and Michael.* Macmillan, 1974. (Grades K–3)

*———. *The Tenth Good Thing About Barney.* Illustrated by Erik Blegvad. Atheneum, 1971 (Grades K–3)

*Voigt, Cynthia. *Dicey's Song.* Atheneum, 1983. (Grades 6+)

Walter, Mildred Pitts. *Have a Happy . . .* Illustrated by Carole Byard. Lothrop, 1989. (Grades 4–7)

*———. *Justin and the Best Biscuits in the World.* Illustrated by Catherine Stock. Knopf, 1986. (Grades 3–7)

*White, E. B. *Trumpet of the Swans.* Harper & Row, 1970. (Grades 4–6)

*Williams, Vera B. *A Chair for My Mother.* Greenwillow, 1982. (Grades K–3)

*Wojciechowska, Maia. *Shadow of a Bull.* Illustrated by Alvin Smith. Atheneum, 1964. (Grades 4–7)

*Yashima, Taro. *Crow Boy.* Viking, 1955. (Grades 3–5)

*Yep, Laurence. *Child of the Owl.* Harper, 1977. (Grades 5+)

*———. *Sea Glass.* Harper, 1979. (Grades 4+)

Zolotow, Charlotte. *The Hating Book.* Illustrated by Ben Shecter. Harper & Row, 1971. (Grades K–3)

Historical Fiction

Aiken, Joan. *The Teeth of the Gale.* Harper, 1988. (Grades 4+)

Antle, Nancy. *Hard Times: A Story of the Great Depression.* Illustrated by James Watling. Viking, 1993. (Grades 2–5)

Avi. *The True Confessions of Charlotte Doyle.* Orchard, 1990. (Grades 3–7)

Bawden, Nina. *Henry.* Illustrated by Joyce Powzyk. Lothrop, 1988. (Grades 4–7)

Beatty, Patricia. *Charley Skedaddle.* Morrow, 1987. (Grades 6–9)

————. *Jayhawker*. Morrow, 1991. (Grades 5–9)

Bergman, Tamar *The Boy from Over There*. Translated by Hillel Holkin. Houghton Mifflin, 1988. (Grades 3–7)

Blos, Joan. *A Gathering of Days: A New England Girl's Journal 1830–1832*. Scribner's, 1979. (Grades 5–7)

Brett, Jan. *First Dog*. Harcourt Brace Jovanovich, 1988. (Pre-S–3)

Brink, Carol Ryrie. *Caddie Woodlawn*. Illustrated by Trina Schart Hyman. Macmillan, 1935. (Grades 4–7)

*Bulla, Clyde. *A Lion to Guard Us*. Illustrated by Michele Chessare. Crowell, 1981. (Grades 2–4)

Chang, Margaret, and Raymond Chang. *In the Eye of the War*. Macmillan, 1990. (Grades 5–7)

*Clapp, Patricia. *Constance: A Story of Early Plymouth*. Lothrop, 1968. (Grades 6+)

*————. *I'm Deborah Simpson: A Soldier in the War of the Revolution*. Lothrop, 1977. (Grades 4–7)

*Coerr, Eleanor. *The Josefina Story Quilt*. Illustrated by Bruce Degen. Harper, 1986. (Grades 1–3)

*————. *Sadako and the Thousand Paper Cranes*. Putnam, 1977. (Grades 2–5)

Collier, James, and Collier, Christopher. *My Brother Sam Is Dead*. Four Winds, 1974. (Grades 5+)

*Conrad, Pam. *Prairie Songs*. Harper & Row, 1985. (Grades 4–6)

*Dalgliesh, Alice. *The Courage of Sarah Noble*. Illustrated by Leonard Weisgard. Scribner's, 1954. (Grades 2–5)

DeAngeli, Marguerite. *The Door in the Wall*. Doubleday, 1949. (Grades 5+)

De Felice, Cynthia. *Weasel*. Macmillan, 1990. (Grades 4–7)

Fleischman, Paul. *The Borning Room*. Harper, 1991. (Grades 6+)

*Forbes, Esther. *Johnny Tremain*. Illustrated by Lynd Ward. Houghton Mifflin, 1943. (Grades 6+)

*Fox, Paula. *The Slave Dancer*. Illustrated by Eros Keith. Bradbury, 1973. (Grades 6+)

*Fritz, Jean. *Early Thunder*. Illustrated by Lynd Ward. Coward, 1967. (Grades 4+)

*————. *Shh! We're Writing the Constitution*. Illustrated by Tomie de Paola. Scholastic, 1987. (Grades 4–7)

*Griffin, Judith Berry. *Phoebe and the General*. Dutton, 1981. (Grades 3–6)

Hahn, Mary Downing. *Stepping on the Cracks*. Clarion, 1991. (Grades 5+)

*Hall, Anna Gertrude. *Cyrus Holt and the Civil War*. Illustrated by Dorothy Morse. Viking, 1964. (Grades 3–5)

*Hamilton, Virginia. *The House of Dies Drear*. Macmillan, 1968. (Grades 5+)

Hendershot, Judith. *In Coal Country*. Illustrated by Thomas B. Allen. Knopf, 1987. (Pre-S–5)

*Innocenti, Roberto. *Rose Blanche*. Stewarata, Tabori & Chang, 1985. (Grades 1–6)

Johnson, Tony. *Yonder*. Illustrated by Lloyd Bloom. Dial, 1988. (Grades K-3)

Kudlinski, Kathleen V. *Earthquake! A Story of Old San Francisco*. Illustrated by Ronald Himler. Viking, 1993. (Grades 2–5)

————. *Pearl Harbor Is Burning: A Story of World War II*. Viking, 1991. (Grades 2–6)

Lasky, Kathryn. *The Bone Wars*. Morrow, 1988. (Grades 6+)

*Lowry, Lois. *Number the Stars*. Houghton Mifflin, 1989. (Grades 4–7)

*MacLachlan, Patricia. *Sarah, Plain and Tall*. Harper & Row, 1985. (Grades 3–5)

Matas, Carol. *Lisa's War*. Scribner's, 1989. (Grades 5–8)

*Moeri, Louise. *Save Queen of Sheba*. Dutton, 1981. (Grades 4–6)

Morpurgo, Michael. *Waiting for Anya*. Viking, 1991. (Grades 5–9)

*O'Dell, Scott. *Sarah Bishop*. Houghton Mifflin, 1980. (Grades 6+)

———. *Island of the Blue Dolphin*. Houghton Mifflin, 1960. (Grades 5+)

Osborne, Chester G. *The Memory String*. Atheneum, 1984. (Grades 4–8)

Paterson, K. *Lyddie*. Puffin, 1991. (Grades 6+)

Paulsen, Gary. *The Cookcamp*. Orchard, 1991. (Grades 5–8)

Pelgrom, Els. *The Winter When Time Was Frozen*. Rudnik, 1980. (Grades 2–6)

Rappaport, Doreen. *Trouble at the Mines*. Illustrated by Joan Sandin. Thomas Y. Crowell, 1987. (Grades 2–6)

*Ringgold, Faith. *Aunt Harriet's Underground Railroad in the Sky*. Crown, 1992. (Grades K–5)

Sebestyen, Ouida. *On Fire*. Atlantic, 1985. (Grades 6+)

Slepian, Jan. *Risk 'n Roses*. Putnam, 1990. (Grades 6–9)

*Speare, Elizabeth George. *The Bronze Bow*. Houghton, 1961. (Grades 5+)

*———. *Calico Captive*. Illustrated by W. T. Mars. Houghton Mifflin, 1961. (Grades 5+)

*———. *The Sign of the Beaver*. Houghton Mifflin, 1983. (Grades 5+)

*———. *The Witch of Blackbird Pond*. Houghton Mifflin, 1958. (Grades 5+)

Talbert, Marc. *The Purple Heart*. HarperCollins, 1992. (Grades 5–8)

*Taylor, Mildred. *Roll of Thunder, Hear My Cry*. Illustrated by Jerry Pickney. Dial, 1976. (Grades 5+)

Turner, Ann. *Dakota Dugout*. Illustrated by Ronald Himler. Macmillan, 1985. (Grades K–3)

von Tscharner, Renata, and Ronald Lee Fleming. *New Providence*. Illustrated by Denis Orloff. Gulliver/Harcourt Brace Jovanovich, 1987. (Pre-S+)

Vos, Ida. *Hide and Seek*. Translated from Dutch by Terese Edelstein and Inez Smidt. Houghton, 1991. (Grades 4–8)

Westall, Robert. *The Kingdom by the Sea*. Farrar, Straus & Giroux, 1991. (Grades 5–8)

White, Ruth. *Sweet Creek Holler*. Farrar, Straus & Giroux, 1988. (Grades 5+)

*Wilder, Laura Ingalls. *Little House in the Big Woods*. Illustrated by Garth Williams. Harper & Row, 1932. (Grades 4–6)

*———. *Little House* series. Harper & Row. (Grades 4–6)

*Yep, Laurence. *Dragonwings*. HarperCollins, 1975 (Grades 5+)

———. *Mountain Light*. Harper & Row, 1985. (Grades 5+)

Yolen, Jane. *Children of the Wolf*. Viking, 1984. (Grades 7+)

———. *The Devil's Arithmetic*. Viking Penguin, 1990. (Grades 5+)

*———. *Encounter*. Illustrated by David Shannon. Harcourt Brace Jovanovich, 1992. (Grades 2–5)

Fantasy/Science Fiction

Fantasy

Alexander, Lloyd. *The Beggar Queen*. Dutton, 1984. (Grades 5–8)

———. *Westmark*. Dutton, 1981. (Grades 5+)

*Andersen, Hans Christian. *The Emperor's New Clothes*. Retold by Anne Rockwell. Harper & Row, 1982. (Grades 1–4)

*———. *The Ugly Duckling*. Illustrated by Alan Marks. Translated by Anthea Bell. Picture Book Studio, 1989. (Grades 1–4)

Babbitt, Natalie. *The Devil's Other Storybook*. Farrar, Straus & Giroux, 1987. (Grades 3–6)

*———. *Tuck Everlasting*. Farrar, Straus & Giroux, 1970. (Grades 5–7)

Baum, L. Frank. *The Wizard of Oz*. Illustrated by W. W. Denslow. Reilly, 1956. (Grades 3–6)

Bond, Michael. *A Bear Called Paddington.* Illustrated by Peggy Fortnum. Houghton Mifflin, 1960. (Grades 3–5)

Carroll, Lewis. *Alice's Adventures in Wonderland.* Illustrated by John Tenniel. Macmillan, 1963. (Grades 5+)

Cassedy, Sylvia. *Lucie Babbidge's House.* Crowell, 1989. (Grades 4–7)

Conrad, Pam. *Stonewords: A Ghost Story.* Harper, 1990. (Grades 3–7)

Cooper, Susan. *The Grey King.* Atheneum, 1975. (Grades 3–7)

———. *Silver on the Tree.* Atheneum, 1977. (Grades 5–7)

Dahl, Roald. *Charlie and the Chocolate Factory.* Illustrated by Joseph Schindelman. Knopf, 1973. (Grades 4–6)

———. *James and the Giant Peach.* Illustrated by Nancy Burdert. Knopf, 1961. (Grades 4+)

Ernst, Lisa Campbell. *When Bluebell Sang.* Bradbury, 1989. (Grades K–3)

Everett, Percival. *The One That Got Away.* Illustrated by Dick Zimmer. Clarion, 1992. (Grades 2–4)

Garden, Graeme. *The Skylighters.* Illustrated by Neil Canning. Oxford, 1988. (Grades 6+)

Grahame, Kenneth. *The Wind in the Willows.* Illustrated by E. H. Shepard. Scribner's, 1908. (Grades 5–7)

Hahn, Mary Downing. *The Doll in the Garden: A Ghost Story.* Clarion, 1989. (Grades 4–7)

Hilgartner, Beth. *The Feast of the Trickster.* Houghton, 1991. (Grades 6+).

*Hunter, Mollie. *The Mermaid Summer.* HarperTrophy, 1988. (Grades 5–8)

Kesey, Ken. *Little Tricker the Squirrel Meets Big Double the Bear.* Illustrated by Barry Moser. Viking, 1990. (Grades 3–6)

King-Smith, Dick. *Ace: The Very Important Pig.* Illustrated by Lynette Hemmant. Crown, 1990. (Grades 2–6)

Kipling, Rudyard. *Just So Stories.* Doubleday, 1952. (Grades 4–6)

LeGuin, Ursula K. *Catwings Return.* Illustrated by S. D. Schindler. Orchard, 1989. (Grades 2–5)

———. *The Farthest Shore.* Illustrated by Gail Garraty. Atheneum, 1972. (Grades 6+)

———. *The Tombs of Atuan.* Illustrated by Gail Garraty. Atheneum, 1971. (Grades 6+)

*Lewis, C. S. *The Lion, the Witch, and the Wardrobe.* Illustrated by Pauline Baynes. Macmillan, 1950. (Grades 4–8)

Lillegard, Dee. *My Yellow Ball.* Illustrated by Sarah Chamberlain. Dutton, 1993. (Grades K–3)

Lisle, Janet Taylor. *The Lampfish of Twill.* Illustrated by Wendy Anderson Halperin. Orchard, 1991. (Grades 4–8)

Lowry, Lois. *The Giver.* Bantham Doubleday Dell, 1993. (Grades 5+)

Mahy, Margaret. *Dangerous Spaces.* Viking, 1991. (Grades 3–7)

Marshall, James. *Rats on the Roof and Other Stories.* Dial, 1991. (Grades 1–4)

McBratney, Sam. *The Ghosts of Hungryhouse Lane.* Holt, 1989. (Grades 2–5)

McCaffrey, Anne. *Dragondrums.* Illustrated by Fred Marcellino. Atheneum, 1979. (Grades 6+)

———. *Dragonsinger.* Atheneum, 1977. (Grades 6–8)

———. *Dragonsong.* Illustrated by Laura Lydecker. Atheneum, 1976. (Grades 6–8)

McGilvray, Richard. *Don't Climb Out the Window Tonight.* Illustrated by Alan Snow. Dial, 1993. (Grades Pre-S–2)

McPhail, David. *Emma's Vacation.* Dutton, 1987. (Grades K–2)

*Milne, A. A. *Winnie the Pooh.* Illustrated by Ernest H. Shepard. Dutton, 1954. (Grades 2–5)

*Norton, Mary. *The Borrowers.* Illustrated by Beth and Joe Krush. Harcourt Brace Jovanovich, 1953. (Grades 3–6)

Peters, Julie Anne. *The Stinky Sneakers Contest*. Illustrated by Cat Bowman Smith. Joy Street/Little, Brown, 1992. (Grades 2–5)

Scieszka, Jon. *Knights of the Kitchen Table*. Puffin, 1991. (Grades 2–6)

Sendak, Maurice. *Outside Over There*. HarperCollins, 1981. (Grades 1–3)

*———. *Where the Wild Things Are*. Harper, 1963. (Grades 1–3)

Sherman, Josepha. *Child of Faerie, Child of Earth*. Walker, 1992. (Grades 6+)

Tolkien, J. R. R. *The Hobbit*. Houghton Mifflin, 1938. (Grades 5+)

Travers, Pamela L. *Mary Poppins*. Illustrated by Mary Shepard. Harcourt Brace Jovanovich, 1962. (Grades 3–6)

*White, E. B. *Charlotte's Web*. Illustrated by Garth Williams. Harper & Row, 1952. (Grades 3+)

Wiesner, David. *Free Fall*. Lothrop, 1989. (Grades 1–4)

———. *Tuesday*. Clarion, 1992. (Grades 2–4)

*Williams, Margery. *The Velveteen Rabbit*. Illustrated by Ilse Plume. Godine, 1982. (Grades 2–5)

Winthrop, Elizabeth. *The Castle in the Attic*. Holiday House, 1985. (Grades 3–7)

Wrede, Patricia C. *Dealing with Dragons*. Harcourt Brace Jovanovich, 1990. (Grades 4–7)

Yep, Laurence. *Dragon of the Lost Sea*. Harper, 1982. (Grades 5+)

———. *Dragon Steel*. Harper, 1985. (Grades 5+)

*Yolen, Jane. *The Devil's Arithmetic*. Viking, 1988. (Grades 5+)

*———. *The Girl Who Loved the Wind*. Illustrated by Ed Young. Crowell, 1972. (Grades 3–6)

Yorinks, Arthur. *Hey, Al*. Illustrated by Richard Egielski. Farrar, Straus & Giroux, 1987. (Grades 1–5)

Science Fiction

Asimov, Isaac. *Fantastic Voyage II: Destination Brain*. Doubleday, 1987. (Grades 7+)

Beatty, Jerome Jr. *Matthew Looney and the Space Pirates*. Illustrated by Gahan Wilson. Young Scott, 1972. (Grades 2–4)

Bradbury, Ray. *The Martian Chronicle*. Dell, 1946. (Grades 6+)

Cameron, Eleanor. *The Court of the Stone Children*. Dutton, 1973. (Grades 4+)

———. *The Wonderful Flight to the Mushroom Planet*. Illustrated by Robert Henneberger. Little, Brown, 1954. (Grades 4–6)

Christopher, John. *The City of Gold and Lead*. Macmillan, 1967. (Grades 5+)

Engdahl, Sylvia Louise. *Enchantress from the Stars*. Illustrated by Rodney Shackell. Atheneum, 1970. (Grades 6+)

Etra, Jonathon, and Stephanie Spinner. *Aliens for Breakfast*. Illustrated by Steve Bjorkmann. Random House, 1988. (Grades 2–4)

*Harding, Lee. *The Fallen Spaceman*. Illustrations by John and Ian Schoenherr. Harper & Row, 1980. (Grades 2–6)

Hoover, H. M. *Away Is a Strange Place to Be*. Dutton, 1989. (Grades 4–7)

*———. *This Time of Darkness*. Viking, 1980. (Grades 7+)

Hughes, Monica. *The Dream Catcher*. Atheneum, 1987. (Grades 4+)

Key, Alexander. *The Forgotten Door*. Westminster, 1965. (Grades 4–7)

L'Engle, Madeleine. *A Swiftly Tilting Planet*. Farrar, Straus & Giroux, 1978. (Grades 5+)

———. *A Wrinkle in Time*. Farrar, Straus & Giroux, 1962. (Grades 5+)

MacGregor, Ellen. *Miss Pickerell Goes to Mars*. Illustrated by Paul Galdone. McGraw-Hill, 1951. (Grades 2–6)

*Norton, André, and Dorothy Madlee. *Stat Ka'at*. Walker, 1976. (Grades 2–6)

Nostlinger, Christine. *Konrad.* Watts, 1977. (Grades 4–6)

Rubenstein, Gillian. *Space Demons.* Dial, 1988. (Grades 5+)

Rubinstein, Gillian. *Beyond the Labyrinth.* Watts, 1990. (Grades 6+)

Service, Pamela F. *Stinker from Space.* Scribner's, 1988. (Grades 4–7)

Slobodkin, Louis. *The Space Ship Under the Apple Tree.* Macmillan, 1952. (Grades 3–7)

Slote, Alfred. *My Robot Buddy.* Lippincott, 1975. (Grades 4–6)

———. *My Trip to Alpha 1,* Harper, 1978. (Grades 4–6)

*Walsh, Jill Paton. *The Green Book.* Illustrated by Lloyd Bloom. Farrar, Straus & Giroux, 1982. (Grades 4–7)

Williams, Jay, and Raymond Abrashkin. *Danny Dunn and the Anti-Gravity Paint.* Illustrated by Ezra Jack Keats. McGraw-Hill, 1964. (Grades 4–6)

Traditional Literature

Folk Tales

*Aardema, Verna. *Why Mosquitoes Buzz in People's Ears.* Illustrated by Leo and Diane Dillon. Dial, 1975. (Grades K–3)

Ada, Alma Flor. *The Rooster Who Went to His Uncle's Wedding: A Latin American Folktale.* Illustrated by Kathleen Kuchera. Putnam, 1993. (Grades K–3)

Aiken, Joan. *Past Eight O'Clock.* Illustrated by Jan Pienkowski. Viking Kestrel, 1987. (Grades 2–6)

*Aliki. *The Story of Johnny Appleseed.* Prentice-Hall, 1987. (Pre-S–2)

*Andersen, Hans Christian. *The Complete Book of Fairy Tales and Stories.* Translated by Erik Christian Haugaard. Doubleday, 1974. (Grades 3+)

Armstrong, Jennifer. *Chin Yu Min and the Ginger Cat.* Crown, 1993. (Pre-S–4)

Bierhorst, John, ed. *The Naked Bear.* Illustrated by Dirk Zimmer. Morrow, 1987. (Grades 3+)

Brett, Jan. *Goldilocks and the Three Bears.* Dodd, Mead, 1987. (Grades K–3)

———. *The Mitten.* Putnam, 1989. (Grades K–3)

Brittain, Bill. *Dr. Dredd's Wagon of Wonders.* Drawings by Andrew Glass. Harper & Row, 1987. (Grades 3–7)

Brown, Marcia. *Stone Soup.* Scribner's, 1947. (Grades 1–4)

*Cauley, Lorinda Bryan. *Jack and the Beanstalk.* Putnam, 1983. (Grades K–3)

*Climo, Shirley. *The Egyptian Cinderella.* Illustrated by Ruth Heller. HarperCollins, 1989. (Grades K–3)

Cooper, Susan. *The Silver Cow.* Illustrated by Warwick Hutton. Atheneum, 1983. (Grades K–4)

———, reteller. *Tam Lin.* Illustrated by Warwick Hutton. McElderry, 1991. (Grades 3–5)

d'Aulaire, Ingri, and Edgar d'Aulaire, ed. and illus. *East of the Sun and West of the Moon.* Viking, 1969. (Grades 4–6)

DeArmond, Dale. *The Seal Oil Lamp.* Little, Brown, 1988. (Grades K–4)

*Dewey, Ariane. *The Narrow Escapes of Davy Crockett.* Greenwillow, 1990. (Grades 1+)

*Galdone, Paul. *Henny Penny.* Seabury, 1968. (Grades K–3)

———. *The Little Red Hen.* Seabury, 1974. (Grades K–2)

———. *The Three Little Pigs.* Seabury, 1970. (Grades K–3)

*Grimm Brothers. *The Fisherman and His Wife.* Illustrated by Margot Zemach. Farrar, Straus & Giroux, 1980. (Grades K–3)

———. *Grimms' Fairy Tales.* Illustrated by Fritz Kredel. Grosset & Dunlap, 1945. (Grades K+)

———. *Hansel and Gretel.* Translated by Charles Scribner, Jr. Illustrated by Adrienne Adams. Scribner's, 1975. (Grades K–3)

———. *Little Red Riding Hood.* Illustrated by Trina Schart Hyman. Holiday House, 1983. (Grades K–3)

*Hamilton, Virginia. *The People Could Fly: American Black Folktales.* Illustrated by Leo and Diane Dillon. Knopf, 1985. (Grades 4–7)

Huck, Charlotte. *Princess Furball.* Illustrated by Anita Lobel. Greenwillow, 1989. (Grades 1–3)

Jones, Terry. *Terry Jones' Fantastic Stories.* Illustrated by Michael Foreman. Viking, 1993. (All ages)

*Kellogg, Steven. *Johnny Appleseed.* Morrow, 1988. (Grades K–3)

*———. *Paul Bunyan.* Morrow, 1984. (Grades K–3)

*———. *Pecos Bill.* Morrow, 1986. (Grades K–3)

Kimmel, Eric. *Hershel and the Hanukkah Goblin.* Illustrated by Trina Schart Hyman. Holiday, 1990. (Grades 1–4)

*Kipling, Rudyard. *Just So Stories.* Woodcuts by David Frampton. HarperCollins, 1991. (Grades 3–7)

Lester, Julius, reteller. *The Tales of Uncle Remus.* Illustrated by Jerry Pinkney. Dial, 1987. (Grades 5–7)

*Lindbergh, Reeve. *Johnny Appleseed.* Illustrated by Kathy Jakobsen. Little, Brown, 1990. (Grades 1–3)

*Louie, Ai-Ling. *Yeh-Shen: A Cinderella Story from China.* Illustrated by Ed Young. Philomel, 1982. (Grades 3–6)

Marshall, James, reteller. *Goldilocks and the Three Bears.* Dial, 1988. (Grades K–3)

Martin, Rafe. *The Rough-Face Girl.* Illustrated by David Shannon. Putnam, 1992. (Grades 2–8)

McKissack, Patricia. *Mirandy and Brother Wind.* Dial, 1989. (Grades 1–3)

*Ness, Evaline. *Tom Tit Tot.* Scribner's, 1965. (Grades K–3)

Nimmo, Jenny. *The Starlight Cloak.* Illustrated by Justin Todd. Dial, 1993. (Grades Pre-S–3)

Nygren, Tord. *The Fiddler and His Brothers.* Morrow, 1987. (Grades 4–5)

Opie, Iona, and Peter Opie. *The Classic Fairy Tales.* Oxford, 1974. (Grades 3+)

*Perrault, Charles. *Cinderella.* Illustrated by Marcia Brown. Scribner's, 1954. (Grades K–4)

———. *Puss in Boots.* Illustrated by Fred Marcellino. Farrar, 1991. (Grades K–2)

San Souci, Robert D. *The Talking Eggs.* Illustrated by Jerry Pinkney. Dial, 1990. (Grades K–3)

Scieszka, Jon. *The Stinky Cheese Man and Other Fairly Stupid Tales.* Viking, 1992. (Grades 3+)

* ———. *The True Story of the Three Little Pigs.* Viking, 1989. (Grades 1–6)

*Singer, Isaac Bashevis. *Zlateh the Goat and Other Stories.* Harper, 1966. (Grades 5–7)

Stamm, Claus. *Three Strong Women: A Tale from Japan.* Illustrated by Jean and Mon-sien Tseng. Viking, 1990. (Grades 1–3)

*Steptoe, John. *Mufaro's Beautiful Daughters: An African Tale.* Lothrop, 1987. (Grades K–4)

Stobbs, William. *The House that Jack Built.* Oxford, 1983. (Grades 4–6)

Tejima. *Ho-Limlim: A Rabbit Tale from Japan.* Philomel, 1990. (Grades 1–3)

*Vuong, Lynette Dyer. *The Brocaded Slipper and Other Vietnamese Tales.* Illustrated by Vo-Dinh Mai. HarperCollins, 1991. (Grades 2–6)

Yacowitz, Caryn. *The Jade Stone: A Chinese Folktale.* Illustrated by Ju-Hong Chen. Holiday, 1992. (Grades K–4)

*Yep, Laurence. *The Rainbow People.* HarperCollins, 1989. (Grades 5+)

*Yorinks, A. *Ugh.* Farrar, Straus & Giroux, 1990. (Pre-S–3)

*Young, Ed. *Lon Po Po: A Red Riding Hood Story from China.* Philomel, 1989. (Grades 2–4)

*Zemach, Harve. *Duffy and the Devil.* Illustrated by Margot Zemach. Farrar, Straus & Giroux, 1973. (Grades K–3)

———. *Too Much Noise, An Italian Tale.* Illustrated by Margot Zemach. Holt, Rinehart & Winston, 1967. (Grades 4–6)

Zemach, Margot. *The Three Little Pigs.* Farrar, Straus & Giroux, 1988. (Grades K–3)

Fables

*Aesop. *Aesop's Fables.* Illustrated by Heidi Holder. Viking, 1981. (Grades 4–7)

*———. *The Lion and the Mouse.* Illustrated by Ed Young. Doubleday, 1980. (Grades K–3)

Brown, Marcia. *Once a Mouse.* Scribner's, 1961. (Pre-S–3)

*De Roin, Nancy, ed. *Jataka Tales.* Illustrated by Ellen Lanyon. Houghton Mifflin, 1975. (Grades 3–5)

*Gaer, Joseph. *The Fables of India.* Illustrated by Randy Monk. Little, Brown, 1955. (Grades 5+)

Galdone, Paul. *Androcles and the Lion.* McGraw-Hill, 1970.

Hague, Michael. *Aesop's Fables.* Holt, Rinehart & Winston, 1985. (Pre-S–2)

*La Fontaine, Jean. *The Fables of La Fontaine.* Adapted and illustrated by Richard Scarry. Doubleday, 1963. (Grades 2–6)

Lionni, Leo. *Frederick.* Pantheon, 1967. (Pre-S–3)

McGovern, Ann. *Hee Haw.* Illustrated by Eric von Schmidt. Houghton Mifflin, 1969. (Grades 2–3)

*Paxton, Tom, reteller. *Aesop's Fables.* Illustrated by Robert Rayevosky. Morrow, 1988. (Pre-S+)

*Rackham, Arthur. *Aesop's Fables.* Watts, 1968. (Grades 4–7)

Myths and Legends

Asimov, Isaac. *Words from Myths.* Illustrated by William Barss. Houghton Mifflin, 1961. (Grades 5–10)

Bartah, Edna. *Cupid and Psyche, A Love Story.* Clarion, 1976. (Grades 4–6)

Bierhorst, John. *The Hungry Woman: Myths and Legends of the Aztecs.* Morrow, 1984. (Grades 5+)

———. *The Mythology of Mexico and Central America.* Morrow, 1990. (Grades 7+)

———. *The Mythology of North America.* Morrow, 1985. (Grades 7+)

———. *The Mythology of South America.* Morrow, 1988. (Grades 7+)

Chant, Joy. *The High Kings.* Illustrated by George Sharp. Bantam, 1983. (Grades 3–5)

Colum, Padraic. *The Children's Homer: The Adventures of Odysseus and the Tale of Troy.* Illustrated by Willy Pogany. Macmillan, 1962. (Grades 5+)

*Creswick, Paul. *Robin Hood.* Illustrated by N. C. Wyeth. Scribner's, 1984. (Grades 6+)

d'Aulaire, Ingri, and Edgar d'Aulaire. *Book of Greek Myths.* Doubleday, 1962. (Grades 3–6)

*———. *Norse Gods and Giants.* Doubleday, 1967. (Grades 3–6)

de Paola, Tomie. *The Legend of the Indian Paintbrush.* Putnam, 1988. (Pre-S–2)

Farmer, Penelope. *Daedalus and Icarus.* Illustrated by Chris Conner. Harcourt Brace Jovanovich, 1972. (Grades 4–6)

*Fisher, Leonard Everett. *Theseus and the Minotaur.* Holiday, 1988. (Grades 4–6)

Gates, Doris. *The Golden God: Apollo.* Illustrated by Constantinos CoConis. Viking, 1973. (Grades 4–6)

Goble, Paul. *Her Seven Brothers.* Bradbury, 1988. (Pre-S–2)

Green, Roger Lancelyn. *A Book of Myths.* Illustrated by Joan Kiddell-Monroe. Dutton, 1965. (Grades 4–6)

*Hamilton, Edith. *Mythology.* Little, Brown, 1942. (Grades 6+)

Hamilton, Virginia. *In the Beginning: Creation Stories from Around the World.* Illustrated by Barry Moser. Harcourt Brace Jovanovich, 1988. (Grades 6+)

Hazeltine, Alice. *Hero Tales from Many Lands.* Abingdon, 1961. (Grades 4–6)

Hodges, Margaret. *The Arrow and the Lamp: The Story of Psyche.* Illustrated by Donna Diamond. Little, Brown, 1989. (Grades 4–8)

Hoover, H. M. *The Dawn Palace: The Story of Medea.* Dutton, 1988. (Grades 7+)

*Lattimore, Deborah Nourse. *The Prince and the Golden Ax.* Harper, 1982. (Grades 2–5)

*———. *Why There Is No Arguing in Heaven: A Mayan Myth.* Harper, 1989. (Grades 2–5)

*McDermott, Gerald. *Daughter of the Earth: A Roman Myth.* Delacorte, 1984. (Grades 2–5)

*———. *Musicians of the Sun: A Myth of Ancient Mexico.* Delacorte, 1988. (Grades 2–6)

Melling, O. R. *The Singing Song.* Viking Kestrel, 1987. (Grades 5–9)

Osborne, Mary Pope. *Favorite Greek Myths.* Illustration by Troy Howell. Scholastic, 1989. (Grades 2–6)

Switzer, Ellen, and Costas. *Greek Myths: Gods, Heroes, and Monsters.* Photographs by Costas. Atheneum, 1988 (Grades 6+)

Talbott, Hudson. *King Arthur: The Sword in the Stone.* Morrow, 1991. (Grades 5+)

Poetry

Adoff, Arnold. *Chocolate Dreams.* Illustrated by Turi MacCombie. Lothrop, 1989.

———, ed. *The Poetry of Black America: Anthology of the 20th Century.* HarperCollins, 1973.

———. *Sports Pages.* Illustrated by Steve Kuzma. Lippincott, 1986.

Atwood, Ann. *Haiku: The Mood of the Earth.* Scribner's, 1971.

Behn, Harry, trans. *More Cricket Songs: Japanese Haiku.* Harcourt Brace Jovanovich, 1971.

*Brewton, John, and Brewton, Sara, eds. *America Forever New.* Illustrated by Ann Grifalconi. Crowell, 1968.

Carle, E. *Animals Animals.* Philomel, 1989.

Carroll, Lewis. *Jabberwocky.* Illustrated by Graeme Base. Abrams, 1989.

Carter, Anne, comp. *Birds, Beasts, and Fishes: A Selection of Animal Poems.* Illustrated by Reg Cartwright. Macmillan, 1991.

Cassedy, Sylvia, and Suetake, Kunihiro. *Bed Dragonfly on My Shoulder.* Illustrated by Molly Bang. HarperCollins, 1992.

Ciardi, John. *The Hopeful Trout and Other Limericks.* Illustrated by Susan Meddaugh. Houghton, 1989.

Coatsworth, Elizabeth. *Poems.* Illustrated by Vee Guthrie. Macmillan, 1958.

*Daniel, Mark, ed. *A Child's Treasury of Animal Verses.* Dial, 1989.

*———, ed. *A Child's Treasury of Seaside Verses.* Dial, 1991.

dePaola, Tomie. *Tomie dePaola's Book of Poems.* Putnam, 1988.

deRegniers, B. S. *Sing a Song of Popcorn.* Scholastic, 1988.

*deRegniers, Beatrice Schenk, et al., eds. *Sing a Song of Popcorn.* Scholastic, 1988.

Esbensen, B. *Who Shrank My Grandmother's House?* HarperCollins, 1992.

Farjeon, Eleanor. *Eleanor Farjeon's Poems for Children.* Lippincott, 1985.

Fatchen, Max. *The Country Mail Is Coming: Poems from Down Under.* Little, Brown, 1990.

Field, Rachel. *Poems.* Macmillan, 1964.

Fisher, Aileen. *Always Wondering: Some Favorite Poems.* Harper & Row, 1991.

———. *Feathered Ones and Furry.* Illustrated by Eric Carle. Thomas Y. Crowell, 1971.

*Fleischman, Paul. *I Am Phoenix: Poems for Two Voices.* Illustrated by Ken Nurt. Harper, 1985.

*———. *Joyful Noise: Poems for Two Voices.* Illustrated by Eric Beddows. Harper, 1988.

*Frank, Josette, ed. *A Year in a River Valley/Nature Poems.* Paintings by Thomas Locker. Dial, 1990.

*Frost, Robert. *Stopping by Woods on a Snowy Evening.* Illustrated by Susan Jeffers. Dutton, 1978.

———. *Birches.* Illustrated by Ed Young. Holt, 1988.

Gordon, Ruth, comp. *Time Is the Longest Distance: An Anthology of Poems.* HarperCollins, 1991.

*Greenfield, Eloise. *Honey, I Love and Other Love Poems.* Illustrated by Diane and Leo Dillon. HarperCollins, 1978.

———. *Night on Neighborhood Street.* Dial, 1991.

———. *Under the Sunday Tree.* Illustrated by Amos Ferguson. Harper, 1988.

Hopkins, Lee Bennett. *Pass the Poetry, Please!* Harper & Row, 1987.

———, ed. *Rainbows Are Made.* Harcourt Brace Jovanovich, 1992.

———. *Through Our Eyes: Poems and Pictures About Growing Up.* Little, Brown, 1992.

———. *Voyages.* Harcourt Brace Jovanovich, 1988.

Hudson, Wade, ed. *Pass It On: African-American Poetry for Children.* Illustrated by Floyd Cooper. Scholastic, 1993.

*Hughes, Langston. *Don't You Turn Back.* Illustrated by Ann Grifalconi. Knopf, 1969.

Hughes, Shirley. *Out and About.* Lothrop, 1988.

Johnson James W. *Lift Every Voice.* Illustrated by Elizabeth Catlett. Walker, 1993.

*Johnson, Siddie Joe. *Poetry Is.* Atheneum, 1967.

Jones, Hettie. *The Trees Stand Shining: Poetry of the North American Indians.* Paintings by Robert Andrew Parker. Dial, 1993.

Kuskin, K. *Soap Soup and Other Verses.* HarperCollins, 1992.

Larrick, Nancy, ed. *Bring Me All Your Dreams.* Photographs by Larry Mulvehill. M. Evans, 1980.

———. *Cats Are Cats.* Illustrated by Ed Young. Philomel, 1988.

———, comp. *Mice Are Nice.* Illustrated by Ed Young. Philomel, 1990.

———. *To the Moon and Back: A Collection of Poems.* Illustrated by Catherine O'Neill. Delacorte, 1991.

Lear, Edward. *The Complete Nonsense Book.* Dodd, Mead, 1946.

———. *Of Pelicans and Pussycats: Poems and Limericks.* Illustrated by Jill Newton. Dial, 1990.

———. *The Nonsense Poems of Edward Lear.* Illustrated by Leslie Brooke. Clarion, 1991.

Lenski, Lois. *Sing a Song of People.* Illustrated by Giles Laroche. Little, Brown, 1987.

Levy, Constance. *I'm Going to Pet a Worm Today and Other Poems.* McElderry/Macmillan, 1991.

Lewis, J. P. *Earth Verse and Water Rhymes.* Atheneum, 1991.

———. *Two-legged, Four-legged, No-legged Rhymes.* Knopf, 1991.

Livingston, Myra Cohn. *If the Owl Calls Again: A Collection of Owl Poems.* McElderry/Macmillan, 1990.

———. *I Like You, If You Like Me.* McElderry, 1987.

———. *I Never Told.* McElderry, 1992.

———. *My Head Is Red and Other Riddle Rhymes.* Illustrated by Tere LoPrete. Holiday, 1990.

————. *Remembering and Other Poems.* McElderry/Macmillan, 1989.

Longfellow, Henry Wadsworth. *Hiawatha.* Illustrated by Susan Jeffers. Dial, 1983.

————. *Paul Revere's Ride.* Illustrated by Ted Rand. Dutton, 1990.

McCord, D. *All Day Long: Fifty Rhymes of the Never Was and Always Is.* Little, Brown, 1992.

————. *Far and Few: Rhymes of the Never Was and Always Is.* Illustrated by Henry B. Kane. Little, Brown, 1952.

*Merriam, E. *The Singing Green: New and Selected Poems for All Seasons.* Morrow, 1992.

————. *You Could Be Good and I'll Be Night.* Illustrated by Karen Lee Schmidt. Morrow, 1988.

Mitchel, Adrian. *Strawberry Drums.* Illustrated by Frances Lloyd. Delacorte, 1989.

Moore, L. *Adam Mouse's Book of Poems.* Atheneum, 1992.

Morrison, Lillian, ed. *Rhythm Road: Poems to Move To.* Lothrop, 1988.

*Noyes, Alfred. *The Highwayman.* Illustrated by Charles Keeping. Oxford, 1981.

Prelutsky, Jack. *The Dragons Are Singing Tonight.* Illustrated by Peter Sis. Greenwillow, 1993.

————. *The New Kid on the Block.* Illustrated by James Stevenson. Greenwillow, 1984.

————. *Something Big Has Been Here.* Illustrated by James Stevenson. Greenwillow, 1990.

Ryder, Joanne. *Hello, Tree!* Illustrated by M. Hays. Dutton, 1991.

————. *Mockingbird Morning.* Illustrated by D. Nolan. Four Winds, 1989.

————. *Under Your Feet.* Illustrated by D. Nolan. Four Winds, 1990.

*Silverstein, Shel. *A Light in the Attic.* Harper & Row, 1981.

————. *Where the Sidewalk Ends: Poems and Drawings.* Harper & Row, 1974.

Slier, D., ed. *Make a Joyful Sound: Poems for Children by African-American Poets.* Checkerboard, 1991.

Smith, W. J. *Laughing Time: Collected Nonsense.* Farrar, Straus & Giroux, 1990.

Sneve, Virginia Driving Hawk, selector. *Dancing Teepees: Poems of American Indian Youth.* Illustrated by Stephen Gammell. Holiday, 1989.

Stevenson, Robert Louis. *A Child's Garden of Verses.* Illustrated by Brian Wildsmith. Oxford, 1966.

————. *A Child's Garden of Verses.* Illustrated by Henriette Willebeek Mair. Philomel, 1991.

————. *My Shadow.* Illustrated by Ted Rand. Putnam, 1990.

Sutherland, Zena. *The Orchard Book of Nursery Rhymes.* Illustrated by Faith Jacques. Orchard, 1990.

*Viorst, Judith. *If I Were in Charge of the World and Other Worries.* Illustrated by Lynne Cherry. Macmillan, 1981.

Whipple, Laura, comp. *Eric Carle's Dragons Dragons and Other Creatures That Never Were.* Illustrated by Eric Carle. Philomel, 1991.

*Willart, Nancy. *A Visit to William Blake's Inn.* Illustrated by Alice and Martin Provensen. Harcourt, 1981.

Woogler, David, ed. *Who Do You Think You Are? Poems About People.* Oxford, 1990.

Worth, V. *At Christmastime.* HarperCollins, 1992.

Yolen, J. *Birdwatch: A Book of Poetry.* Philomel, 1990.

————. *Weather Report.* Illustrated by Annie Gusman. Wordsong/Boyds, 1993

Informational Books

Aaseng, Nate. *Meat Eating Animals.* Illustrated by Alcuin C. Dornisch. Lerner, 1987. (Grades K–3)

Aliki. *How a Book Is Made.* Crowell, 1986. (Grades 1–4)

Ancona, George. *My Camera.* Crown, 1992. (Grades 2–7)

———. *Turtle Watch.* Macmillan, 1987. (Grades 1–5)

Arnold, Caroline. *Dinosaurs Down Under: And Other Fossils from Australia.* Photographs by Richard Hewett. Clarion, 1990. (Grades 3–5)

———. *Walk on the Great Barrier Reef.* Photographs by Arthur Arnold. Carolrhoda, 1988. (Grades 2–5)

———. *Koala.* Photographs by Richard Hewett. Morrow, 1987. (Grades 2–5)

———. *Trapped in Tar: Fossils from the Ice Age.* Photographs by Richard Hewett. Clarion, 1987. (Grades 3–6)

Asimov, Issac. *The Birth of the United States 1763–1816.* Houghton Mifflin, 1974. (Grades 5+)

Baird, Anne. *Space Camp: The Great Adventure for NASA Hopefuls.* Photographs by Robert Koropp. Morrow, 1992. (Grades 3+)

Banks, Ann. *It's My Money: A Kid's Guide to the Green Stuff.* Illustrated by Susanna Natti. Puffin, 1993. (Grades 2–5)

Barboza, Steven. *I Feel Like Dancing: A Year with Jacques d'Amboise and the National Dance Institute.* Illustrated by Carolyn George d'Amboise. Crown, 1992. (Grades 2–5)

Barrett, Norman S. *Pandas.* Watts, 1988. (Grades 2–5)

Boyne, Walter. *The Smithsonian Book of Flight for Young People.* Atheneum, 1988. (Grades 3–7)

Brown, Laurene Krasny, and Marc Brown. *Dinosaurs Alive and Well! A Guide to Good Health.* Little, Brown, 1990. (Grades 1–3)

Casey, Denise. *Big Birds.* Photographs by Jackie Gilmore. Cobblehill, 1993. (Grades 1–5)

Cole, Joanna. *Evolution.* Illustrated by Aliki. Crowell, 1990. (Grades 1–3)

*———. *The Magic School Bus at the Waterworks.* Illustrated by Bruce Degen. Scholastic, 1988. (Grades 2–4)

*———. *The Magic School Bus Inside the Earth.* Illustrated by Bruce Degen. Scholastic, 1987. (Grades 2–4)

*———. *The Magic School Bus Inside the Human Body.* Illustrated by Bruce Degen. Scholastic, 1989. (Grades 2–4)

*———. *The Magic School Bus Lost in the Solar System.* Illustrated by Bruce Degen. Scholastic, 1990. (Grades 2–4)

———. *My Puppy Is Born.* Photographs by Jerome Wexler. Morrow, 1973 (revised and expanded, 1991). (Grades 1–3)

Cone, Molly. *Come Back Salmon: How a Group of Dedicated Kids Adopted Pigeon Creek and Brought It Back to Life.* Photographs by Sidnee Wheelwright. Sierra Club, 1992. (Grades 2–6)

*Cooper, Miriam. *Snap! Photography.* Messner, 1981. (Grades 2–5)

Cummings, Pat. *Talking with Artists.* Bradbury, 1992. (Grades 4+)

*Davis, Edward E. *Into the Dark, a Beginner's Guide to Developing and Printing Black and White Negatives.* Atheneum, 1979. (Grades 2–5)

Ellis, Veronica Freeman. *Afro-Bets First Book About Africa.* Illustrated by George Ford. Just Us Books, 1990. (Grades K–1)

Esbensen, Barbara Juster. *Great Northern Diver: The Loon.* Illustrated by Mary Barrett Brown. Little, Brown, 1990. (Grades 3–5)

Fisher, Leonard Everett. *Calendar Art.* Four Winds, 1979. (Grades 3–5)

———. *The Wailing Wall.* Macmillan, 1989. (Grades 4–7)

Flacklam, Margery. *And Then There Was One: The Mysteries of Extinction.* Illustrated by Pamela Johnson. Little, Brown, 1990. (Grades 3–7)

George, Jean C. *One Day in the Woods.* Illustrated by Gary Allen. Crowell, 1988. (Grades 2–4)

Gherman, Beverly. *Sandra Day O'Conner: Justice for All.* Illustrated by Robert Masheris. Puffin, 1993. (Grades 2–5)

*Gibbons, Gail. *Say Woof! The Day of a Country Veterinarian.* Macmillan, 1992. (Grades 1–5)

———. *Weather Words and What They Mean.* Holiday, 1990. (Grades 1–3)

Giblin, James Cross. *Let There Be Light.* Thomas Y. Crowell, 1988. (Grades 3–7)

*Goldreich, Gloria, and Esther Goldreich. *What Can She Be? A Newscaster.* Photographs by Robert Ipcar. Lothrop, 1973. (Grades 3–6)

Hackwell, W. John. *Signs, Letters, Words.* Scribner's, 1987. (Grades 7+)

Hausherr, Rosemarie. *What Instrument Is This?* Clarion, 1992. (Grades 2–4)

Heller, Ruth. *Animals Born Alive and Well.* Grosset & Dunlap, 1982. (Grades K–2)

Hirschi, Ron. *Who Lives in the Forest?* Photographs by Galen Burrell. Dodd, Mead, 1987. (Pre-S–2)

Horner, John, and Don Lessem. *Digging Up Tyrannosaurus Rex.* Crown, 1992. (Grades 2–6)

Hoyt-Goldsmith, Diane. *Arctic Hunter.* Illustrated by Lawrence Migdale. Holiday, 1992. (Grades 3–7)

———. *Totem Pole.* Photographs by Lawrence Migdale. Holiday, 1990. (Grades 2–4)

Jasperson, William. *Cranberries.* Houghton, 1991. (Grades 3–5)

*Jefferis, David. *Flight: Fliers and Flying Machines.* Watts, 1991. (Grades 4+)

———. *The Jet Age: From the First Jet Fighters to Swing-Wing Bombers.* Illustrated by Terry Hadler, Ron Jobson, and Michael Roffe. Watts, 1988. (Grades 3–7)

———. *Trains: The History of Railroads.* Watts, 1991. (Grades 3–6)

Jenness, Aylette. *Families: A Celebration of Diversity, Commitment, and Love.* Houghton Mifflin, 1990. (Grades 3–5)

Kendall, Russ. *Eskimo Boy: Life in an Inupiaq Eskimo Village.* Scholastic, 1992. (Grades 3–5)

King, Elizabeth. *Backyard Sunflower.* Dutton, 1993. (Grades Pre-S–3)

*Krementz, Jill. *The Fun of Cooking.* Knopf, 1985. (Grades 5–9)

Lampton, Christopher. *Stars and Planets.* Illustrated by Ron Miller. Doubleday, 1988. (Grades 1–7)

Landau, Elaine. *Rabies.* Lodestar, 1993. (Grades 2–5)

Lasky, Kathryn. *Dinosaur Dig.* Illustrated by Christopher Knight Morrow. Morrow, 1990. (Grades 3–5)

———. *Think Like an Eagle: At Work with a Wildlife Photographer.* Photographs by Christopher G. Knight and Jack Swedberg. Little, Brown/Joy Street, 1992. (Grades 3+)

*Lauber, Patricia. *Volcano: The Eruption and Healing of Mt. St. Helens.* Bradbury, 1986. (Grades 4–7)

*Lindblom, Steven. *Fly the Hot Ones.* Houghton Mifflin, 1991. (Grades 5+)

*Loeper, John J. *Going to School in 1876.* Atheneum, 1984. (Grades 4–7)

*Macaulay, David. *Castle.* Houghton Mifflin, 1977. (Grades 5+)

*———. *Cathedral: The Story of Its Construction.* Houghton Mifflin, 1973.

*———. *City: A Story of Roman Planning and Construction.* Houghton Mifflin, 1974. (Grades 5+)

*———. *The Way Things Work.* Houghton Mifflin, 1976. (Grades 5+)

Margolies, Barbara. *Kanu of Kathmandu: A Journey in Nepal.* Four Winds, 1992. (Grades 6–9)

McMillan, Bruce. *Going on a Whale Watch.* Scholastic, 1992. (Grades K+)

Miller, Jonathan. *The Human Body.* Designed by David Pelham. Viking, 1983. (Grades 4–7)

Morris, Ann. *Bread, Bread, Bread.* Photographs by Ken Heyman. Lothrop, 1989. (Grades 3–5)

Newnham, Jack. *Kites.* Penguin, Practical Puffin Series, 1977. (Grades 4–7)

Norsgaard, E. Jaediker. *How to Raise Butterflies.* Photographs by Campbell Norsgaard. Dodd, Mead, 1988. (Grades 2–5)

Patent, Dorothy. *Farm Animals.* Photographs by William Munoz. Holiday, 1984. (Grades 1–4)

———. *Whales, Giants of the Deep.* Holiday, 1987. (Grades 3–7)

———. *Spider Magic.* Holiday, 1982. (Grades 5+)

Patterson, Francine. *Koko's Kitten.* Photographs by Ronald H. Cohn. Scholastic, 1985. (Grades K+)

Pringle, Laurence. *Global Warming: Assessing the Greenhouse Threat.* Arcade, 1990. (Grades 2–4)

*———. *Lives at Stake: The Science and Politics of Environmental Health.* Macmillan, 1980. (Grades 3–6)

Raboff, Ernest. *Art for Children Series.* HarperCollins, 1987. (Grades 3+)

Ride, Sally. *To Space and Back.* Lothrop, 1986. (Grades 1–3)

Rogasky, Barbara. *Smoke and Ashes: The Story of the Holocaust.* Holiday, 1988. (Grades 5+)

Rogers, Jean. *The Secret Moose.* Illustrated by Jim Fowler. Greenwillow, 1985. (Grades 3–5)

Rosenberg, Maxine B. *Brothers and Sisters.* Photographs by George Ancona. Clarion, 1991. (Grades 1–3)

Ruschak, Lynette, and Beth B. Norden. *Magnification.* Lodestar, 1993. (Grades 2–5)

Sattler, Helen Roney. *Stegosaurus: The Solar-Powered Dinosaurs.* Illustrated by Turi Mac-Combie. Lothrop, 1992. (Grades 1+)

Schwartz, David. *How Much Is a Million?* Scholastic, 1985. (Grades K–3)

*Silverstein, Alvin, and Virginia B. Silverstein. *Hamsters: All About Them.* Photographs by Frederick Breda. Lippincott, 1976. (Grades 4+)

Simon, Seymour. *Icebergs and Glaciers.* Morrow, 1987. (Pre-S–3)

———. *Storms.* Morrow, 1989. (Grades 3–5)

Smallman, Claire. *Outside-In.* Barron's, 1986. (Pre-S–2)

Stanley, Diane, and Peter Vennema. *Bard of Avon: The Story of William Shakespeare.* Illustrated by Diane Stanley. Morrow, 1992. (Grades 2+)

*Stein, Sara Bonnett. *About Dying.* Photographs by Dick Frank. Walker, 1974. (Pre-S–8)

Sullivan, George. *In-Line Skating: A Complete Guide for Beginners.* Cobblehill, 1993. (Grades 4+)

*Ventura, Piero. *Great Painters.* Putnam, 1984. (Grades 5+)

Wharton, Anthony. *Discovering Seabirds.* Watts, 1987. (Grades 1+)

*Zim, Herbert, and Sonia Bleeker. *Life and Death.* Illustrated by Rene Martin. Morrow, 1974. (Grades 3–5)

Biography

*Aardema, Verna. *A Bookworm Who Hatched.* Richard C. Owen, 1992. (Grades 2–6)

*Aaseng, Nathan. *Jose Canseco: Baseball's 40–40 Man.* Lerner, 1989. (Grades 4–9)

*Aliki (Brandenberg). *The Many Lives of Benjamin Franklin.* Prentice-Hall, 1977. (Pre-S–3)

Behrens, June. *Barbara Bush: First Lady of Literacy.* Children's Press, 1990. (Grades 2–5)

*———. *Sally Ride, Astronaut: An American First.* Children's Press, 1984. (Grades 2–5)

Burchard, Marshall. *Sports Hero: Ron Guidry.* Putnam, 1981. (Grades 4–6)

Burleigh, Robert. *Flight: The Journey of Charles Lindbergh.* Illustrated by Mike Wimmer. Philomel, 1991. (Grades 1–5)

*Clayton, Ed. *Martin Luther King: The Peaceful Warrior,* 3rd ed. Illustrated by David Hodges. Prentice-Hall, 1968. (Grades 3–6)

Cleary, Beverly. *A Girl from Yamhill: A Memoir.* Morrow, 1988. (Grades 3–5)

Cone, Molly. *Leonard Bernstein.* Illustrated by Robert Glaster. Thomas Y. Crowell, 1970. (Grades 4–6)

Crisman, Ruth. *Thomas Jefferson: Man and a Vision.* Scholastic, 1992. (Grades 3–6)

de Paola, Tomie. *The Art Lesson.* Putnam, 1989. (Pre-S–3)

Faber, Doris. *Eleanor Roosevelt, First Lady of the World.* Illustrated by Donna Ruff. Viking Kestrel, 1985. (Grades 2–6)

*Freedman, Russell. *Eleanor Roosevelt: A Life of Discovery.* Clarion, 1993. (Ages 9+)

*———. *Franklin Delano Roosevelt.* Clarion, 1990. (Grades 4–7)

———. *Indian Chiefs.* Holiday, 1987. (Grades 4–7)

*———. *Lincoln: A Photobiography.* Clarion, 1987. (Grades 4–7)

*———. *The Wright Brothers: How They Invented the Airplane.* Holiday, 1991. (Ages 10+)

Fritz, Jean. *And Then What Happened, Paul Revere?* Illustrated by Margot Tomes. Coward-McCann, 1973. (Grades 2–6)

———. *Bully for You, Teddy Roosevelt!* Putnam, 1991. (Grades 3–5)

———. *The Great Little Madison.* Putnam, 1989. (Grades 4–7)

*———. *Surprising Myself.* Richard C. Owen, 1992. (Grades 2–6)

———. *Traitor: The Case of Benedict Arnold.* Putnam, 1981. (Grades 3–7)

Golenbock, Peter. *Teammates.* Illustrated by Paul Bacon. Harcourt Brace Jovanovich, 1990. (Grades 2–4)

*Hopkins, Lee Bennett. *The Writing Bug.* Richard C. Owen, 1992. (Grades 2–6)

Jones, Hettie. *Big Star Fallin' Mama: Five Women in Black Music.* Viking, 1974. (Grades 3–6)

Kellogg, Steven. *Johnny Appleseed.* Morrow, 1988. (Grades 1–3)

Lauber, Patricia. *Lost Star: The Story of Amelia Earhart.* Scholastic, 1988. (Grades 4–7)

Lindbergh, Reeve. *Johnny Appleseed.* Illustrated by Kathy Jacobsen. Little, Brown, 1990. (Grades 1–3)

Myers, Walter Dean. *Malcolm X.* Scholastic, 1993. (Grades 6+)

*Norman, Gertrude. *A Man Called Washington.* Illustrated by James Caraway. Putnam, 1960. (Grades 5–7)

Peare, Catherine Owen. *The Helen Keller Story.* Thomas Y. Crowell, 1965. (Grades 5+)

Petrillo, David. *Robert F. Kennedy.* Chelsea House, 1988. (Grades 3+)

*Preston, Katherine. *Scott Joplin.* Chelsea House, 1988. (Grades 5+)

*Raboff, Ernest. *Pablo Picasso.* Doubleday, 1968. (Grades 3+)

Say, Allen. *El Chino.* Houghton, 1990. (Grades 3–5)

Shore, Nancy. *Amelia Earhart.* Chelsea House, 1987. (Grades 7–10)

*Shuker, Nancy. *Martin Luther King.* Chelsea House, 1985. (Grades 7–10)

Sills, Leslie. *Inspirations: Stories about Women Artists.* Whitman, 1989. (Grades 2–8)

Stanley, Diane, and Peter Vennema. *Good Queen Bess: The Story of Elizabeth I of England.* Four Winds, 1990. (Grades 3–5)

———. *Shaka: King of the Zulus.* Illustrated by Diane Stanley. Morrow, 1988. (Grades 1–4)

*Sullivan, George. *Sadat: The Man Who Changed Mid-East History.* Walker, 1981. (Grades 6+)

*Wood, James Playstead. *The Life and Words of John F. Kennedy.* Scholastic, 1966. (Grades 3–5)

*Woods, Harold, and Geraldine Woods. *Bill Cosby: Making America Laugh and Learn.* Dillan, 1983. (Grades 3–5)

*Yolen, Jane. *A Letter from Phoenix Farm.* Richard C. Owen, 1992. (Grades 2–6)

Professional Resources

*Alexander, Lloyd. "Fantasy and the Human Condition." *New Advocate,* 1: 75, 1988.

*Bartlett, John. *Familiar Quotations.* Little, Brown, 1982.

Benedict, S. and Carlisle, L. *Beyond Words: Picture Books for Older Readers and Writers.* Heinemann, 1992.

Bettelheim, Bruno. *The Uses of Enchantment: The Meaning and Importance of Fairy Tales.* Knopf, 1977.

Carr, Jo, comp. *Beyond Fact: Nonfiction for Children and Young People.* American Library Association, 1982.

*Commire, Anne, ed. *Yesterday's Authors of Books for Children.* Gale Research, 1977.

*Cox, Susan Taylor. "A Word or Two with Eve Merriam: Talking About Poetry." *The New Advocate* 2: 138, 1989.

*Dreyer, Sharon Spredemann. *The Bookfinder.* American Guidance Service, 1985.

Fredericks, Anthony D. *Frantic Frogs & Other Frankly Fractured Folktales for Readers Theatre.* Teacher Ideas Press, 1993.

Freeman, Evelyn, and Diane Goetz Person, eds. *Using Nonfiction Trade Books in the Elementary Classroom: From Ants to Zeppelins.* NCTE (National Council for Teachers of English), 1992.

*Gillespie John, and Christine Gilbert. *Best Books for Children: Preschool through the Middle Grades.* American Library Association, 1985.

Harris, Jeanne McLain and Lucille Lettow. "Recent Poetry for Children." *Reading Teacher,* Vol. 45, No. 4, Dec. 1991, p. 274.

Head, Georgia. *For the Good of the Earth and the Sun: Teaching Poetry.* Heinemann, 1989.

*Huck, Charlotte, Susan Hepler, and Janet Hickman. *Children's Literature in the Elementary School,* 5th ed. Harcourt Brace Jovanovich, 1993.

*Johnson, Siddie Joe. *Poetry Is.* Atheneum, 1967.

Kobrin, Beverly. *Eyeopeners: How to Choose and Use Children's Books about Real People, Places and Things.* Viking, 1988.

Lukens, Rebecca. *A Critical Handbook of Children's Literature,* 5th ed. Harper, 1990.

*MacDonald, Margaret Read. *The Storyteller's Sourcebook: A Subject, Title, and Motif Index to Folklore Collections for Children.* Gale Research, 1982.

McClure, Amy A., with Peggy Harrison. *Sunrises and Songs: Reading and Writing Poetry in an Elementary Classroom.* Heinemann, 1990.

*National Council for the Social Studies. *Notable Children's Trade Books in the Field of Social Studies.* 1991.

National Science Teachers Association. *Outstanding Science Trade Books for Children.* Annual annotated bibliography.

*Norton, Donna E. *Through the Eyes of a Child: An Introduction to Children's Literature.* Merrill, 1991.

Ogle, Donna. "KWL: A Teaching Model That Develops Active Reading of Expository Text." *The Reading Teacher,* 564–570, Feb. 1986.

Rap Tale Series. Scholastic.

A Reference Guide to Historical Fiction for Children and Young Adults. Greenwood, 1987.

*Sipe, Laurence R. "Using Transformations of Traditional Stories: Making the Reading–Writing Connection." *The Reading Teacher* 47: 18, 1993.

Something about the Author: Facts and Pictures about Authors and Illustrators of Books for Young Children. Gale Research, annual.

*Sutherland, Zena and May Hill Arbuthnot. *Children and Books,* 8th ed. HarperCollins, 1991.

*VanMeter, Vandalia. *American History for Children and Young Adults: An Annotated Bibliographic Index.* Libraries Unlimited, 1990.

Zarnowsi, Myra. *Learning about Biographies: A Reading and Writing Approach for Children.* NCTE/NCSS, 1990.

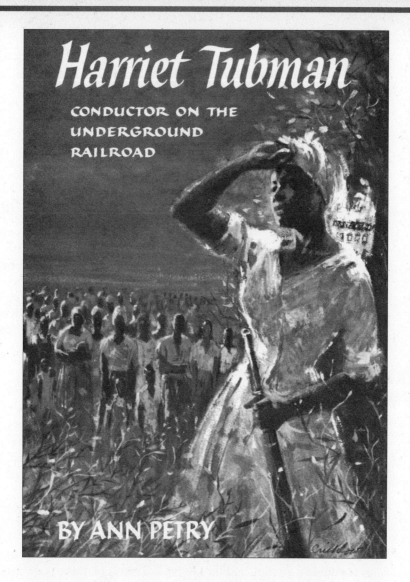

Harriet Tubman
CONDUCTOR ON THE UNDERGROUND RAILROAD

BY ANN PETRY

CHAPTER 2

Selecting a Variety of Genres

Children and adults can get into a reading rut by selecting books from one or two genres and neglecting the offerings of other genres. Often, they select books out of habit rather than by conscious choice. A concerted effort must be made to familiarize students with a variety of genres. The activities offered in this section encourage students to read books that represent different genres. Once they are familiar with every genre, we hope they will be motivated to choose from the many literary offerings available and expand their horizons.

Interest Inventories

It is important to understand why children read and what they read in order to select materials that will motivate them to want to read. Research indicates that children and adults read for two major reasons: to gather information and for enjoyment. First, however, the person must be motivated to read. For some, this motivation occurs naturally. Motivation to read a particular book usually stems from an interest in the subject matter.

In the past, there was much concern over matching student reading levels with the readability level of books, as determined by formulas such as those developed by Dale and Chall (1948), Spache (1966), or Fry (1977). However, research has found that many other factors, including interest and maturation, determined a student's ability to read. Therefore, there is no need to be overly concerned with readability because students will select the books they can and want to read. Instead, the emphasis should be on providing students with as many opportunities as possible to be involved with books.

Although some generalities can be drawn from the research, such as the types of books a child of a particular age might like better or the types of books girls might prefer, it is important to determine what subjects most interest individual students. Without considering individual interests, a teacher may overlook the fact that a first-grade girl is interested in baseball—a topic that research indicates is generally of interest to older boys. In addition, with an awareness of the subjects that most interest the students, the teacher can more effectively select books for read-aloud and silent reading programs and assist individual students who seem reluctant to select books on their own.

There are several ways to determine the students' reading interests. The simplest way is to ask questions: "What do you like to read about?" "Do you have any hobbies?" When working with a number of children, however, usually some way of recording the information, such as the Interest Inventory on page 112, is needed. On this form, students answer questions about their favorite television shows, hobbies, sports, and so on. Older students can write in their own answers, and adults can help younger children read the form and fill in the answers.

Monthly Topics

Each month, explore a particular topic of interest to the students. Have all students read at least one selection based on that topic from a book that is representative of an assigned genre. For example, if the topic is baseball, students might read the following:

Poetry: *Casey at the Bat*, by Ernest L. Thayer
Realistic fiction: *Here Comes the Strikeout*, by Leonard Kessler
Biography: *Hank Aaron*, by Bill Gertman
Informational: *Basic Baseball Strategy*, by S. H. Freeman

At the end of the month, allow time for the students to react to the selection they read, and compile a "baseball anthology."

Current Events

This activity is similar to the monthly topic activity described earlier, but the topic selection is based on current events. Allow time for the students to discuss major issues facing their city or state or the world. Have them vote on the topic they would most like to learn about. Once students have completed their readings on the selected topic, conduct a discussion in which they debate the merits of the type of genre they used in learning about the topic.

Author, Author

Many well-known authors have written books in several genres. Divide the students into groups and have each group select an author from a list of those who have written across the genres, such as Isaac Asimov, Judith Viorst, or Herbert Zim. Have groups read and discuss several of the author's books. (Make sure that the books chosen are not all in the same genre.) Encourage students to discuss their opinions and reactions to the books, which ones they preferred, and why. Then have each group plan a short skit in which the author and some of his or her works are introduced to the class. Chapter 12 contains activities for an author unit.

INTEREST INVENTORY

1. My name is _____

2. My address is _____

3. My phone number is _____

4. I have _____ sisters and _____ brothers.

5. I like to read books about _____

6. The best book I have ever read is _____

7. I would like to know more about _____

8. I already know a lot about _____

9. Some interesting places I have visited are _____

10. Places that I would like to visit are _____

11. I like to collect _____

12. My favorite TV show is _____

13. When I have free time, I like to _____

14. My favorite sport is _____

15. The person I most admire is _____

16. When I grow up, I want to be a _____

17. The thing I worry about most is _____

18. The thing I do best is _____

19. The area in which I need the most help is _____

20. My favorite animal is _____

Circle *Yes* or *No.*
I enjoy reading. Yes No
I have a library card. Yes No
I like for someone to read to me. Yes No
I get books from the school library. Yes No
I like to get books as gifts. Yes No
I read a newspaper every day. Yes No
I subscribe to at least one magazine. Yes No

Calendar of Genres

Divide the class into eight groups, one for each genre: realistic fiction, historical fiction, fantasy/science fiction, traditional literature (folk tales, fables, myths, and legends), poetry, informational books, biographies, and picture books. Have each group develop activities for one month that involve the class in that group's genre. For example, October might be "fantasy month" and December might be "poetry month." Activities should include decorating the room or bulletin board, providing the class library with books representative of the genre, planning the month's read-aloud program, preparing an annotated bibliography of the group's favorite selections, and preparing a culminating activity that will familiarize the class with favorite selections from the genre. This last activity can take any form. Try monologues from various selections, role-playing of scenes from different selections, or a game show.

Genre Units

Develop units in which students read a variety of selections within a genre. Then design activities to foster an appreciation for and enjoyment of the genre and to help students understand the elements and characteristics specific to that genre. Examples of unit plans—traditional literature (folk tales), traditional literature (mythology), and poetry—are given below. For variety, the format and resulting products of each unit are quite different. In addition to fostering growth in reading, these activities will further objectives in other content areas, such as writing, social studies, and the arts. This activity is most appropriate for students in the intermediate grades, although students in the primary grades may be introduced to the genres and their elements.

Traditional Literature—Folk Tales Unit

Objectives
On completion of this unit, students will:

- list the characteristics of a folk tale in terms of characterization, plot, setting, and point of view
- analyze folk tales for other commonalities
- create a folk tale based on their knowledge of the genre's ingredients

Procedure
1. Assign each student a different folk tale.
2. Distribute the Folk Tales worksheet on page 114; allow sufficient time for students to read their story and complete the worksheet. Note: With lower-level students, read aloud several of the folk tales and discuss the questions from the worksheet.
3. Put the following elements on the chalkboard, and discuss each one according to the tales the students have read and analyzed:

FOLK TALES

Title of folk tale: _____

1. List the main character in the story and describe his or
   her physical appearance.

   _____

2. Describe the main character's personality and other
   qualities that can't be seen in a picture.

   _____

   _____

3. When did the story take place?

   _____

4. Where did the story take place?

   _____

5. Briefly explain the plot of the story.

   _____

   _____

6. What message do you think the story is trying to give?

   _____

   _____

7. From whose point of view is the story being told?

   _____

8. What magical happenings, chants, etc., were described?

   _____

   _____

9. What was the first line of the story? Copy it.

   _____

   _____

10. How did the story end (happily, sadly, etc.)? Explain.

    _____

    _____

11. In your opinion, why has this story continued to be a
    favorite of children for over a hundred years?

    _____

    _____

    a. Setting—where and when
    b. Characters/characterization
    c. Plot
    d. Purpose of the tale
    e. Point of view
    f. Common features

4. Once every student has had an opportunity to share his or her selection, encourage the class to form generalizations regarding the elements of folk tales. The following generalizations might be elicited.

    a. Setting—Where: In a land far, far away; a land that is part of the real world, no matter how strange. When: Once upon a time, long, long ago.

    b. Characters/characterization: Characters usually are good or evil, rich or poor (and the poor often become rich). Characters have human faults and desires and often exhibit qualities similar to our own and to those of people we know.

    c. Plot: The plot is more important than the characters. It is filled with action and holds the reader's interest.

    d. Point of view: Told in the third person, the teller is omniscient.

    e. Commonalities: Things happen in threes—three wishes, three chances. Often include elements of magic: a magical chant, a magical character, magical objects.

5. Encourage students, either individually or in groups, to create their own folk tales. Review the formula that has made folk tales such popular, well-loved stories. The tale can be an updated version of an older tale (Space-Age Cinderella), can feature a new plot with characters from older tales, or can be an entirely new tale. Read several transformations of folk tales, such as Jon Scieszka's *The Frog Prince Continued* or Jane Yolen's *Sleeping Ugly*.

Traditional Literature—Mythology Unit

Objectives

On completion of this unit, students will:

- understand the way mythological characters share characteristics of people everywhere
- be able to evaluate the influence of mythology on their lives
- be aware of the elements of mythological stories and the purposes for which they were written
- create a myth based on knowledge of the elements of mythological stories

Procedure

Have students compile the activities they complete into a mythological booklet for future reference.

1. Before students can analyze mythological characters, they must first be able to identify them. Have students fill in a chart similar to the Gods and Goddesses chart with the names of the major and some minor Greek or Roman gods and goddesses, along with their "titles." You may wish to extend the activity to include the identification of mythological characters from other countries and other Greek or Roman mythological characters and deities.

GODS AND GODDESSES

Greek Name	Roman Name	Title
Zeus	Jupiter	King of all the gods
Poseidon	Neptune	God of the seas

2. Read several myths aloud. List the main characters in each myth on the chalkboard. Ask students to suggest words that best describe the characters listed. Involve students in a discussion comparing the characters in mythology with people they know today.

3. Have students write a paper defending the statement: "Zeus was at times extreme in both his punishments and rewards." Encourage them to cite specific examples. Have each student choose one additional mythological character. Ask them to list the character's main qualities and then cite specific examples that led them to their conclusions.

4. Read the following myths aloud. Involve students in a discussion that allows them to react to the stories. Discussion can also focus on the questions included:

   a. "Daedalus and Icarus"
      Why was Daedalus imprisoned?
      What inspired Daedalus's escape plan?
      What does this story tell you about the desire to fly?
      Look at a map of Europe. What body of water was named for one of the characters in this story?

   b. "Pandora"
      What was Pandora's main fault?

What happenings in life does this myth help explain?
Do you agree that "hope" is the most wonderful gift of all? Explain.
What does the phrase "You've opened a Pandora's box" mean?
Tell about the time you or someone you know opened a "Pandora's box."

c. "Phaëton and the Chariot of the Sun"
How did the ancients explain day and night?
What landforms does this myth help to explain?
What quality did Phaëton possess that almost destroyed the earth?
What other qualities are equally destructive? Why?

5. Have students read at least two myths. Ask them to summarize each myth and determine its purpose. Was the purpose to explain a natural phenomenon? human qualities?

6. Have students read the following stories (or read them aloud to the class). After reading each pair of stories, discuss the questions that follow:

a. "Odin and Mimir" and "King Midas"
What does the story of Odin and Mimir tell us about the importance of wisdom?
Is wisdom easily achieved? Explain.
Which do you think is more important—wealth or wisdom? Why?
How would you describe King Midas at the beginning of the story? at the end of the story? What caused him to change?
What do you think was the main message he learned?
What is your definition of *wisdom?*

b. "Arachne" and "Prometheus"
What was Arachne's main fault?
Do you agree with her punishment? Why or why not?
If you were Athena, how would you have punished her?
Why was Prometheus punished?
Do you agree with his punishment? Why or why not?
Of Arachne and Prometheus, whose actions can you defend more easily? Explain.

7. Nowhere in our culture is mythology's influence more greatly felt than in our language.

a. Have students copy the following list of mythological characters and the derived words that appear in our language today (shown in parentheses beside the character's name).

Arachne (arachnid)	Furies (fury, furious)
Atlas (an atlas)	Gaea (geography, geology)
Brontes (brontosaurus)	Hydra (hydrant)
Ceres (cereal)	Hygeia (hygiene)
Chaos (chaos, chaotic)	Iris (iridescent, iris)

Janus (January)   Narcissus (narcissism)
Mars (martial)   Pan (panacea, panic)
Midas (the Midas touch)   Tantalus (tantalize)
Muses (museum)   Titans (titanic)

b. Ask the students to tell a little about the mythological character and then define the word in parentheses. Make sure that they are able to make a connection between the word and the character. For example:

Arachne was a proud Greek girl who was foolish and challenged the goddess Athena to a weaving contest. Because of Arachne's pride, Athena turned her into a spider so that she could weave forever.

An *arachnid* is a classification of arthropods. Spiders are included in this classification.

8. Have students create their own myths by completing the chart below.

BE A MYTH MAKER!

1. Select two myths. List the main characters of each myth, and below the names include one or two words that best describe the character. Decide what the purpose of each myth might be (e.g., to explain a happening in nature).

Title: _____

Main characters: _____

Qualities: _____

Purpose: _____

Title: _____

Main characters: _____

Qualities: _____

Purpose: _____

2. List ten happenings in nature that you would like to explain. (For example: Why are there hurricanes? Why do stars shine? Why do rainbows disappear?)

_____   _____

_____   _____

_____   _____

_____   _____

_____   _____

(continued)

3. Choose one happening from the list as the basis for your own myth. Decide how the ancients might have explained this happening and write a short summary below.

_____

_____

_____

_____

4. Based on your knowledge of their talents and qualities, what mythological characters would best fit into this story? List the characters with a brief explanation or their part in the myth.

_____

_____

_____

What additional characters would you create? What talents or qualities would they possess?

_____

_____

5. Write your own myth to explain the happening you selected.

6. Illustrate your myth and share it with others.

Poetry Unit

A unit such as this comes well after students have been listening to and reading poetry for the sheer joy of it. Poetry should be a part of every day's curriculum. The inclusion of activities incorporated into this unit and geared for upper intermediate students should add another dimension to their understanding of poetry and the poetic devices that make it so rich and appealing.

Objectives:

On completion of this unit, students will:

- gain an appreciation for and enjoyment of both traditional and contemporary poetry
- distinguish the various devices used in poetry
- understand the purposes behind many poems
- use quality poetry as models for their own poems
- be familiar with many traditional and contemporary poets

Materials:

The following poems are suggested, but based on availability, student interest, and teacher discretion, other poems can easily be substituted to meet the unit's objectives.

Traditional Poems

"Father William," by Lewis Carroll
"Jabberwocky" by Lewis Carroll
"Silver," by Walter De la Mare
"The Road Not Taken," by Robert Frost
"Stopping by Woods on a Snowy Evening," by Robert Frost
"If," by Rudyard Kipling
"The New Colossus," by Emma Lazarus
"The Arrow and the Song," by Henry Wadsworth Longfellow
"The Midnight Ride of Paul Revere," by Henry Wadsworth Longfellow
"Sea Fever," by John Masefield
"Annabel Lee," by Edgar Allan Poe
"Wind Song," by Carl Sandburg
"Casey at the Bat," by Ernest L. Thayer
"O Captain! My Captain!" by Walt Whitman

Contemporary Poems

"When I Tell You I'm Scared," by Beatrice Schenk de Regniers
"Cicadas," by Paul Fleischman
"Fireflies," by Paul Fleischman
"By Myself," by Eloise Greenfield
"A Dream Deferred," by Langston Hughes
"I'm Sorry Says the Machine," by Eve Merriam
"The Cherries' Garden Gala," by Jack Prelutsky
"When Tillie Ate the Chili," by Jack Prelutsky
"The Homework Machine," by Shel Silverstein
"Listen to the Mustn'ts," by Shel Silverstein
"The Yipiyuk," by Shel Silverstein
"Fifteen, Maybe Sixteen, Things to Worry About," by Judith Viorst
"If I Were in Charge of the World," by Judith Viorst

Procedure

1. Introduction

   a. Choral read a variety of poems, including the sublime as well as the ridiculous (e.g., "If," "Father William," "By Myself," "Jabberwocky" and "The Homework Machine").

   b. Discuss the question: "Which of these can be considered poems?" Students should come to understand that all of the selections are poems, although they cover a wide spectrum of content, styles, and moods.

   c. In "Wind Song," Carl Sandberg described poetry as "a series of explanations of life, fading off into horizons, too swift for explanations." Have students discuss this quote and write and share their own definitions of *poem*.

2. Students can better understand, appreciate, and write their own poetry if they recognize the devices poets use to convey their thoughts and feelings.

   a. Many poets use the devices described on page 122. Periodically, you may wish to select poems that use one or more of these devices.

   b. Choral read poems that reflect the device you are focusing on. Discuss with students the device(s) used in each and how it enhances the poem. For example, a study of alliteration might include "Sea Fever" and "Fireflies." A study of rhyme might focus on "The Yipiyuk" or "When Tillie Ate the Chili." "The Cherries' Garden Gala" and "Silver" contain examples of personification.

   c. Use various poems as a model for children's own poetry as they experiment with using various poetic devices.

3. Purposes of poetry

   a. Discuss the question: "Why are poems written?" Possible responses include: to tell a story; to offer insight; to create a feeling; to capture a mood or a moment; to entertain.

   b. Choral read and discuss the purposes of poems such as "The Arrow and the Song," "Casey at the Bat," "Fifteen, Maybe Sixteen, Things to Worry About," "A Dream Deferred," and "I'm Sorry Says the Machine."

   c. Have students write reactions to the poem(s) in their journals and share them. When appropriate, encourage them to use the verses as a model for their own poems, using the same type of pattern and repetition. "Fifteen, Maybe Sixteen, Things to Worry About" and "I'm Sorry Says the Machine" lend themselves well to this type of activity.

   d. When possible, select poems that correlate with the curriculum. For example, when studying Abraham Lincoln and the Civil War, you may wish to include "O Captain! My Captain!" A study of the Revolutionary War could include "The Midnight Ride of Paul Revere." "The New Colossus" is a perfect choice when studying U.S. immigration.

DEVICES USED IN POETRY

1. Rhythm—Regular patterning of sounds
2. Alliteration—Repetition of the same first letter or consonant sound, such as "snowy summits old in story"
3. Euphony—Succession of light harmonious syllables that have a pleasing sound, such as "the splendor falls on castle walls"
4. Blank or free verse—Lines that do not rhyme
5. Simile—Comparison of two unlike objects or ideas, using the words *like* or *as;* for example, "couched in his kennel, like a log, with paws of silver, sleeps the dog"
6. Metaphor—Comparison of two unlike objects or ideas, without using the words *like* or *as,* such as "The road was a ribbon of moonlight"
7. Personification—Giving human characteristics to objects or ideas that are not human; for example, "Slowly, silently, now the moon Walks the night in her silver shoon"
8. Rhyme—When the endings of words are alike in sound; poems may have end rhyme, in which the last words of lines rhyme, or internal rhyme, in which a word in the middle of the line rhymes with a word at the end of the line
9. Repetition—Deliberate repeating of a key word
10. Onomatopoeia—Forming or putting together words to resemble the sounds made by the thing signified

A good poem:

- sounds good rhythmically
- uses devices such as alliteration and onomatopoeia effectively
- employs vivid images by using devices such as metaphors, similies, and personification
- offers insights into meaningful ideas
- is imaginative
- draws the reader back again and again

4. Experiencing mood from poetry

   a. Depending on the poem and the reader's interpretation, poems can leave the reader with a variety of feelings that cover the entire scope of emotions. Allow students time to read one or more of the following poems: "Stopping by Woods on a Snowy Evening," "Annabel Lee," "Listen to the Mustn'ts," or "If I Were in Charge of the World."

   b. Have students relate, either verbally or in journals, how each poem affected them.

5. Poems tell a story and more. Occasionally, you may wish to have students look at a poem more carefully. While we don't want students to take poems apart line by line or word by word, it is important that they be encouraged to look beyond the literal word, beyond the obvious, to gain additional insights. Allow time for students to discuss their reactions and interpretations of poems read. Several well-planned questions can augment the discussion. "The Road Not Taken" is an excellent choice for helping children expand their understanding of a poem. The activity below, based on this poem, will generate a good deal of discussion and give students a deeper sense of meaning:

   a. Choral read the poem and discuss any vocabulary students may not understand.

   b. Discuss why Frost might have written the poem. To what might he have been referring when he wrote, "Two roads diverged in a wood, and I—I took the one less traveled by, And that has made all the difference"?

   c. Ask students to relate a time when they had to make a choice. How did they feel about the choices they made? How did the person in the poem feel about his choice?

   d. Discuss how the poem made the students feel. Encourage them to identify what most prompted this feeling.

   e. Choral read the poem once again.

6. Who are the men and women behind the lines of verse that cause us to laugh, cry, wonder, and dream? Allow students time to peruse a wide variety of poetry books representing both contemporary and traditional poems. Ask them to skim the books until each finds a poem that says something special to him or her. Page 124 lists collections of contemporary and traditional poets whose work you may wish to make available. Then:

   a. Have the students copy the poem selected.

   b. Have students, individually or in groups, research the poet.

   c. Have students prepare presentations to introduce these poets to the class. Each presentation should include a reading of the poem that initially stimulated the student to research the poet.

   d. Combine the poems selected into an anthology of classroom favorites.

POETS OF THE PAST AND PRESENT

Traditional Poets
(prior to the 1960s)

Rosemary and Stephen Binet
Lewis Carroll
Elizabeth Coatsworth
Samuel Taylor Coleridge
e.e.cummings
Walter De la Mare
Emily Dickinson
T. S. Eliot
Ralph Waldo Emerson
Eugene Field
Robert Frost
Oliver Wendell Holmes
Langston Hughes
Rudyard Kipling
Emma Lazarus
Vachel Lindsay
Henry Wadsworth Longfellow
John Masefield
Edna St. Vincent Millay
A. A. Milne
Ogden Nash
Alfred Noyes
Edgar Allan Poe
James W. Riley
Carl Sandburg
Robert Louis Stevenson
Sara Teasdale
Alfred Lord Tennyson
Ernest L. Thayer
Walt Whitman
William Wordsworth

Contemporary Poets
(1960 to the present)

Arnold Adoff
N. M. Bodecker
Beatrice Schenck de Regniers
Barbara Juster Esbensen
Norma Farber
Aileen Fisher
Paul Fleischman
Eloise Greenfield
Lee Bennett Hopkins
Denise Lee
Constance Levy
Myra Cohn Livingston
David McCord
Eve Merriam
Lillian Moore
Lillian Morrison
Jack Prelutsky
Joanne Ryder
Cynthia Rylant
Diane Siebert
Shel Silverstein
Judith Viorst
Nancy Willard
Valerie Worth
Jane Yolen

Children's Literature

*Cited in text.
*Freeman, S. H. *Basic Baseball Strategy.* Illustrated by Leonard Kessler. Doubleday, 1965.
*Gertman, Bill. *Hank Aaron.* Grosset, 1973.
*Kessler, Leonard. *Here Comes the Strikeout.* HarperCollins, 1965.
*Scieszka, Jon. *The Frog Prince Continued.* Viking, 1991. (Grades 3–4)
*Thayer, Ernest L. *Casey at the Bat.* Illustrated by Patricia Polacco. Putnam, 1988.
*Yolen, Jane. *Sleeping Ugly.* Coward, 1981.

Professional Resources

*Dale, Edgar, and Jeanne S. Chall. "A Formula for Predicting Readability: Instructions."
    Educational Research Bulletin, 27: 37, 1948.
*Fry, Edward. "Fry's Readability Graph: Clarifications, Validity, and Extension to Level
    17." *Journal of Reading,* 21: 249, 1977.
*Spache, George. *Good Reading for Poor Readers,* 6th ed. Garrard Press, 1966.

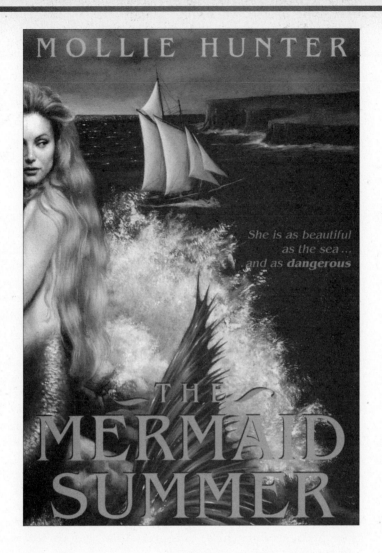

CHAPTER 3

Exploring Literary Elements

Rebecca Lukens (1990, p. 9) defines literature as "a significant truth expressed in appropriate elements and memorable language." As children select their own reading material, they must develop an understanding of the elements of good literature. In the process, they will become more adept at evaluating and selecting the best possible children's literature. This chapter describes the elements that constitute good literature: characterization, plot, setting, theme, point of view, style, and tone.

An integral part of a literature-based reading program, (Chap. 12) is the strategy lesson, in which the teacher works with the entire class or small groups to introduce a book or concept, teach a specific skill, focus on a literary genre, or explore one of its elements. Following the discussion of each element in this chapter are activities that can be used as part of a strategy lesson to help augment an awareness of, understanding of, and appreciation for good literature and the elements that combine to create quality literature. These activities, some more appropriate for or applicable to certain genres, will give children an opportunity to suggest alternatives, analyze motivation, question outcomes, gain new meaning and insights, make connections with their own lives, recognize the interdependence of elements, and explore perspectives. They can also be adapted to create a unit on individual elements or used as a springboard for book talks, literature circles or conversations, literary letters, journal writing, and other strategies (see Chap. 9).

Characterization

Developing strong, believable characters is an important element of good literature. Authors build and reveal their characters in many ways: through the character's thoughts, conversations, actions, and behaviors; through narration; and through other characters' thoughts.

Characters should be as lifelike as possible. Whether human or personified, as is Charlotte in E. B. White's *Charlotte's Web*, the characters should have qualities to which children can relate. Children can easily identify with and understand Frances the badger in Russell Hoban's *Bedtime for Frances*, as she goes through the typical ritual of postponing the final good night to her parents.

Children will remember Frances as they go through their own good night escapades. Many fantasy characters are memorable because of their unusual behavior or because they live in unique worlds. Charlotte the loyal spider and Wilbur the wonderful pig in *Charlotte's Web* are vividly portrayed, and they remain in the reader's memory long after the specifics of the story are forgotten.

The characters' actions should be appropriate for their age and culture, such as Alexander's behavior in Judith Viorst's *Alexander and the Terrible, Horrible, No Good, Very Bad Day.* Alexander is upset because he doesn't get a surprise in his breakfast cereal and because he can't get the colorful sneakers he wants. This behavior would be inappropriate, however, for Tom Sawyer in Mark Twain's *The Adventures of Tom Sawyer.*

Characters generally should be dynamic and multifaceted, just as people are. Winnie in Natalie Babbitt's *Tuck Everlasting* develops from a girl afraid to venture out of her yard to a mature, adventuresome young lady capable of facing life's choices and challenges. Gilly in Katherine Paterson's *The Great Gilly Hopkins,* changes from a difficult, angry person to one who gradually learns to respect and admire her foster mother.

Whether or not they are human, the characters should be memorable. The title character in Jerry Spinelli's *Maniac Magee* takes on heroic proportions. Once children get to know Maniac, they will never forget him.

Activities

The following activities help children explore characterization as an element of good literature.

1. Discuss what is meant by *physical characteristics.* Select a book that is familiar to all your students and ask them to generate a list of physical characteristics for one of the main characters. Encourage them to imagine what this character might look like if each characteristic were exaggerated in some way. Explain that a *caricature* is a picture in which specific details are exaggerated and which frequently highlights the subject's likes, interests, and hobbies. Have students create their own caricatures for this book and others that they read independently. Allow enough time for students to share and compare their drawings and to discuss ways the author helped them "see" the characters.

2. Too often, readers focus on a character's physical attributes, ignoring the qualities below the skin that shape his or her attitudes and actions. To help students gain a deeper understanding of a character, introduce the concept of a continuum. This will encourage students to analyze the character's inner qualities as they determine where on the continuum their character would fall. Use the following Character Continuum or let students create their own. It is important for students to realize that most people fall somewhere between the two extremes; this middle area results

CHARACTER CONTINUUM

Title of book _____

Name of character _____

friendly	———————————————	unfriendly
happy	———————————————	sad
popular	———————————————	unpopular
wise	———————————————	foolish
content	———————————————	discontent
outgoing	———————————————	shy
unselfish	———————————————	selfish
sociable	———————————————	unsociable
ambitious	———————————————	lazy
neat	———————————————	untidy
mature	———————————————	immature
honest	———————————————	dishonest
brave	———————————————	cowardly
kind	———————————————	cruel

in our humanness and individuality. Characters in books should emulate people, and except in certain genres, such as folk tales, they should be as multifaceted as the people we meet each day.

3. Characters are revealed in many ways, through their actions and conversations, the author's narration, and the other characters' comments. To familiarize students with these techniques, have them analyze a character in a selected book and find examples of how each technique enhanced their understanding of the character. The following Character Analysis chart can be used in this analysis. Ask students to list various qualities of the character and provide examples of those techniques that helped them understand the character.

CHARACTER ANALYSIS

Title of book: _____The Story of Ferdinand_____

Author: _____Munro Leaf_____

Name of character: _____Ferdinand_____

Qualities	Actions	Conversations	Narration	Comments of Others
subdued	sat and smelled flowers	Ferdinand said, "I like it better here where I can sit quietly and smell the flowers."	He liked to just sit quietly and smell the flowers.	Mother said, "Why don't you run and play with the other bulls and skip and butt your head."
big and strong			As the years went by, Ferdinand grew until he was big and strong.	Five men saw him and they all shouted with joy. Here was the largest and fiercest bull of all.

As an alternative, have students list the name of a major character in a large circle in the middle of a page. Ask them to list characteristics or qualities of this character in smaller circles and draw lines from the larger circle to the smaller ones. Next to each quality, on the lines they have just drawn, have the students give examples of an action, conversation, narration, or comment that helped determine that quality. Have students identify which technique was used and place it in parentheses above the circle. For example, based on Harry Allard and James Marshal's *Miss Nelson Is Missing:*

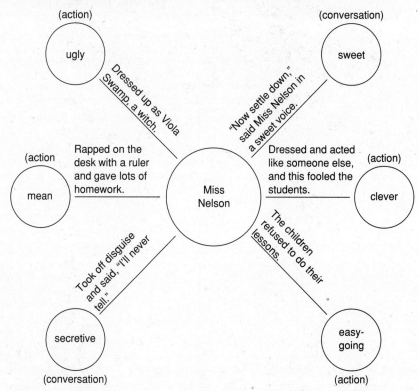

4. People's perceptions of one another are based on many factors. One important determinant is the way a person relates to others and the relationships he or she forms. Sociograms have been used to understand these relationships better. (A sociogram is a chart used to plot the structure of interpersonal relationships in a group situation.) Sociograms can also help readers better understand the characters in books.

Have students create a sociogram for the book they are reading. In one type of sociogram the name of the main character is placed in a large circle in the center of a page. Smaller circles are placed around the larger circle to represent other characters in the book. Arrows drawn from the larger circle to the smaller ones contain the main character's perceptions of the other characters. Arrows drawn from the smaller circles back to the larger circle contain the other characters' perceptions of the main character. For example, see the sociogram on page 133 that is based on Frances Burnett's *The Secret Garden.*

Another type of sociogram focuses on the various types of relationships between the main character and the other characters. The name of

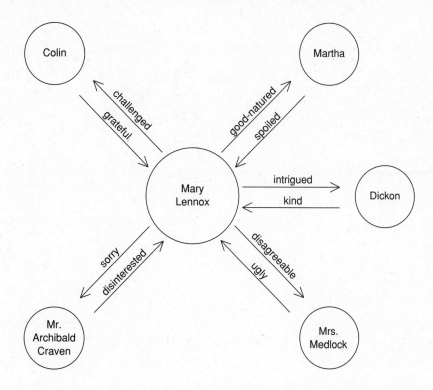

the main character is placed in a large circle in the center of a page. Smaller circles, containing the names of the other characters, are drawn around the larger one. One line is drawn from the larger circle to each of the smaller circles. This line contains a description of the relationship between the two characters. See example on page 134 that is based on Laura Ingalls Wilder's *Little House in the Big Woods.*

5. An interview technique can help students gain better insights into a character. Ask each student to identify a specific character in a selected book and create a list of questions to ask him or her. These questions can explore the character's motivation, actions, feelings, and attitudes. For example, if Charlotte from *Charlotte's Web* were to be interviewed, she might be asked: "How did you get the idea for the words you wrote on the web?" "What other ideas did you have for saving Wilbur?" "What are your feelings about Templeton?"

Ask one student to assume the role of interviewer and the student who wrote the questions to become the character and answer them. If two (or more) students read the same book, one of them may "become" the character being interviewed while the other prepares and conducts the interview. This activity will compel students to analyze the character in order to answer the questions insightfully.

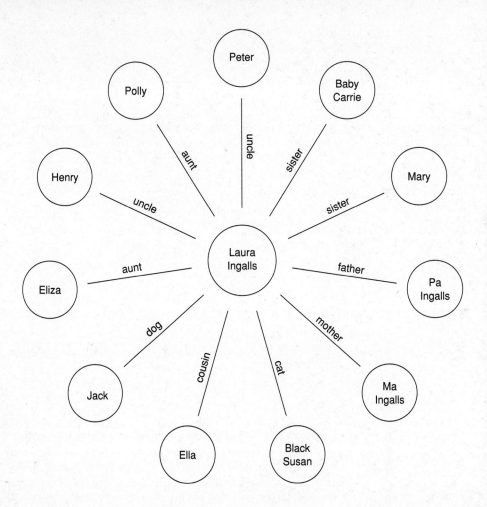

6. Students can better identify with the characters in a story by engaging in discussions that focus on such questions as: "Who do you know that is like this person?" "Which character would you select as a friend?" "Which character is most like you?" "Which character do you most admire?" "Did your feelings about the character change at any time? What might have caused this?" Ask students to explain their responses.

7. Involve students in a "What if" exercise that asks what might happen if a character from one book visited the character(s) in another. For example, "What if Maniac Magee visited Cassie's town in *Roll of Thunder, Hear My Cry*?"

8. Often an author will not only tell about a character, but show what the character is like. Introduce students to various examples of writing in which the author shows the character through conversation, description, action, and so on. Ask them to write a "showing" paragraph that will

introduce the reader to an unforgettable character they have met. Ask them also to show this character through dramatic interpretation.

9. Encourage students to make inferences about a character and then check their inferences as they read. For example, on the first page of *The Great Gilly Hopkins* we learn that Gilly has been in three homes in less than three years. Students can predict why this has happened and its effect on Gilly's attitudes and temperament. As students read, have them address their inferences and make others based on new information.

10. Have students compare a character from a historical novel with one from a more contemporary book or compare a character from a classic with a character from contemporary fiction. Ask them to create a Venn diagram to illustrate this comparison. For example:

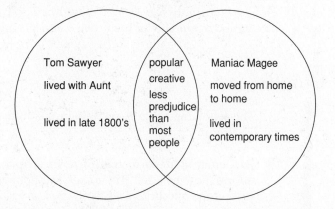

11. Events that involve us as well as interactions with other people often affect the way we look at ourselves and our lives. Have students prepare a "This is Your Life" program in which one person becomes the main character from a book who is being honored. Other students become the people and events that have been significant in this character's life and greet the main character with a brief explanation of their importance to the character.

12. After reading a book of fantasy in which the main character is a personified animal or object, list the ways the author made the character believable. Use the book as a model for students' own short stories about a favorite toy/animal that is personified.

Plot

When evaluating any book, a major factor is whether it tells a good story. In other words, does the book have a good plot? If the plot is well developed, the reader will have a difficult time putting the book down; if not, the reader will lose interest. The plot is what keeps the reader involved.

The plot involves developing a plan of action, which usually follows a certain sequence of events. Children's books are usually presented in a linear manner, because children have difficulty following more than one plot at a time. Plots may be simple or complex. Younger children are satisfied with simple plots, whereas more mature children enjoy more complex plots.

Good children's books usually have fast-moving, exciting plots. The climax is usually easy to identify and followed by a quick conclusion. Usually the excitement occurs when there is some type of conflict or struggle. The conflict may seem real to many children because they may be encountering similar problems in their own lives. For example, Sam in Evaline Ness's *Sam, Bangs and Moonshine* does not intend to cause any problems with her fibs and lies, but they do cause problems and almost cost a friend's life. Children who read this story will probably carry away something about the hazards of not telling the truth. Thus, when children read stories with well-developed conflicts, they may be able to understand better their own conflicts and problems.

Activities

The following activities will help children explore plot as an element of good literature.

1. Encourage students to analyze a newspaper article to identify the type of information included. Their analysis should uncover the fact that articles answer the questions *who, what, where, when, why,* and *how.* Encourage them to analyze the plot of a story in a similar fashion. Using this information, they can create a literary newspaper by writing articles based on the plots of their favorite stories. They can create a catchy headline, such as "Fountain of Youth Discovered" (*Tuck Everlasting*), draw or photograph illustrations, and write captions for pictures.

2. From a book the entire class has read, select specific incidents or parts of the plot. Write the incidents on separate index cards and distribute one card to each student. Ask each student to read his or her card aloud. Then ask the students to put the cards in the correct chronological order. As the plot unfolds, be prepared for a heated debate!

   As an alternative, have students create a time line. Ask each student to select a specific incident from a book everyone has read and summarize the incident in words and/or illustrations on a piece of construction paper. Allow time for them to share their work, and then have them determine the correct sequence of events. Display the time line. If several students select the same incident, simply cluster their work on the time line.

3. The conflicts in a book and how they are dealt with or solved are crucial to the plot. In literature, there are four main types of conflict: person versus

nature, person versus self, person versus society, and person versus person. Select a book and have a class discussion of the type(s) of conflict in it. It is not unusual for several types of conflict to be included in one selection.

4. Select one of the conflicts in a story and have students prepare and present a monologue to express their feelings as if they were the character involved. This monologue should include their thoughts as they decided how to deal with the situation(s). Have younger children tape their monologues rather than write them.

5. Have students select a conflict in their lives that parallels a conflict from one of the books they have read. Lead students in the steps of creative problem solving (see Chap. 9) to select and plan a solution to the conflict.

6. The sequence of events in a story—the plot—follows different patterns. At some point, usually toward the end of the story, the action reaches a climax. Some stories do not have a climax; instead, the events follow one another in an interesting way and increasingly involve the reader with the characters. Have students plot the events of a story to see where, or if, the story has a definite climax. The figure below illustrates this kind of event plotting, based on *Charlotte's Web:*

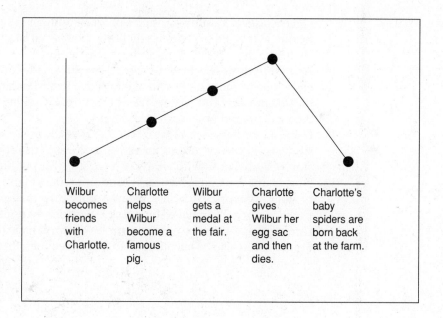

| Wilbur becomes friends with Charlotte. | Charlotte helps Wilbur become a famous pig. | Wilbur gets a medal at the fair. | Charlotte gives Wilbur her egg sac and then dies. | Charlotte's baby spiders are born back at the farm. |

7. Discuss how just one happening in life can completely change the course of events. Make this relevant to content being studied. For example, what if the Pilgrims had landed on the west coast of North America instead of

on the east coast, what in the United States or our lives might be different? After this discussion, ask students to read a story and select a specific plot line or incident that they would like to change. Have them write a synopsis of the change and an explanation of how this would affect the entire outcome of the story. For example, what if the Ugly Duckling had not grown into a beautiful swan but had remained "ugly"?

8. Discuss the type of conflict(s) in a book. Have students create a poster advertising and describing this conflict as if it were the "fight of the century." For example, "Karana vs. the Wild Dogs" from Scott O'Dell's *Island of the Blue Dolphins*, Mafato vs. the Hurricane" from Armstrong Sperry's *Call It Courage*, or "Gilly vs. Gilly" from Katherine Paterson's *The Great Gilly Hopkins*.

9. Discuss the concept of foreshadowing. Cite several examples from books the students have read, such as the following from Natalie Babbitt's *Tuck Everlasting:*

> The people would have noticed the giant ash tree at the center of the wood, and then, in time, they'd have noticed the little spring bubbling up among its roots in spite of the pebbles piled there to conceal it. And that would have been a disaster so immense that this weary old earth, owned or not to its fiery core, would have trembled on its axis like a beetle on a pin.

Have students identify examples of foreshadowing in the book(s) they are reading. Have them share predictions about what might happen, and challenge these predictions as the story unfolds.

10. Ask students to select from a story a specific incident that greatly influenced one or more of the characters. Have them imagine they are one of these characters and write a "Dear Diary" entry telling their reaction to the incident and how it affected them.

11. Using a wordless picture book, such as *Tuesday,* by David Wiesner, have students, in groups, use picture clues to develop their own text for the story. Create books with words or have students put the story onto cassette.

12. Story maps can take many forms and can reflect many different elements of a literary work. As a class, create a story map that reflects the plot of a popular story. Then have students create story maps of books they are reading. Page 139 shows two examples of story maps that focus on plot. Students can also be encouraged to illustrate their story maps.

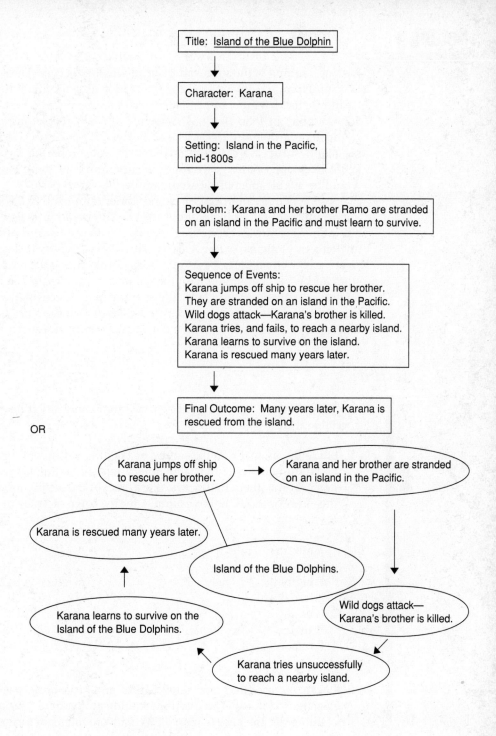

Setting

A story's setting is the time and place in which it occurs. The setting is important in helping create a mood for the reader. If a specific time or geographic location is used, it must be presented accurately, especially for historical fiction. For example, in Joan Blos's *A Gathering of Days*, the setting is a small New Hampshire farm in the 1830s. The author vividly portrays collecting nuts, tasting maple syrup tapped from maple trees, and preparing a cold remedy in a kettle over open flames. Without the description of these events, the reader would be unable to envision an unfamiliar historical period.

Setting is more important in some stories than in others. Sometimes it is so important that neither the plot nor the characters can fully be developed without it. In other stories the setting simply provides a background. For example, in Kenneth Grahame's *The Wind in the Willows*, the vivid descriptions of the river and the changing seasons play a major role giving the reader a sense of the story and what is going on with the animals. However, in *The Three Billy Goats Gruff* and many other fairy tales, the opening line, "Once upon a time . . ." establishes the background. The reader understands that the story happened somewhere, sometime, usually long ago in some faraway never-never land.

Activities

The following activities will help children analyze setting as an element of good literature.

1. Students can focus on the setting by creating a different type of acrostic. Have students write the name or location of a setting from a selected book or story. Ask them to describe one aspect of the setting for each letter of the name or location. For example, for the town of Treegap from *Tuck Everlasting:*

   T ranquil
   R emote
   E nigmatic
   E ternal
   G entle
   A ustere
   P rivate

2. Locate pictures that represent the time and place of a selected story and use them to stimulate a discussion of life at that time: "What types of clothing did the people wear?" "What were the main forms of transporta-

tion?" "What do the expressions on the people's faces tell you about the times?" "How did children spend their time?" Following this discussion, have students compare, in written, oral, or artistic form, life today with life at that time. You can extend this activity by having students research the specific time and place to discover how accurate or inaccurate their perceptions were.

3. Good literature is like good art, in that it affects the reader in a personal way. Have students create a collage or poem to express the mood a specific book conveyed to them. If students select the same book, it will be interesting to discuss how different individuals were affected by the story and the reasons their interpretations of the mood established are different.

4. Illustrations can be very important to a story because they often extend the text by adding an extra dimension to the mood established. Select a story that includes vivid description as well as illustrations. Read aloud a specific segment of the story and ask students to name the story clues that most encouraged a mental picture. Have them illustrate the same scene based on the clues mentioned. Allow time for students to compare their illustrations with one another as well as with the illustrations in the book.

5. Book illustrators use a variety of media to convey their impressions— woodcuts, collages, watercolors, crayons, ink, and so on. Display examples of each medium to give students the background they need to compare artistic media. Select several versions of the same story. Folk tales are especially appropriate, since so many versions of the same stories have been written. Allow students to study the illustrations from the different versions. Ask them to give a one- or two-word reaction to each medium used and encourage them to give reflective responses, such as "detailed," "delicate," "realistic." Then ask questions such as: "Which illustrations did you prefer? Why?" "Which illustrations seemed best to convey the mood of the story?" "Which illustrations added dimension to the story? Explain." "How do illustrations contribute to the mood of a story?" "How do the various media affect mood?" Allow time for students to experiment with the media as they illustrate scenes from a favorite story or from a story they have written.

6. Compare the setting from several versions of the same story. Discuss students' preferences and reasons for these preferences. (Folk tales work well with this activity.)

7. In good literature, the author selects a time period and makes the details of the story accurate and consistent with that period. Select a story set in an earlier time. Have students select a specific event from the story and rewrite it as if the story were taking place in a very different time and location. For example, what if the setting of Carol Ryrie Brink's *Caddie Woodlawn* were New York City in the 1960s instead of the Wisconsin wilderness in the 1860s: "What dangers might she face rather than Indian raids?"

"What leisure activity might she take part in?" "In what ways would Caddie be different if she lived in a different time?" Remind students of the importance of language usage and vocabulary in keeping with the setting.

8. Create a literary time line by stringing a clothesline across the room. As students complete a story, have them fill out the Literary Time Line Card below. The first completed card can be placed anywhere on the line. Additional cards should be placed in appropriate locations in relation to the times indicated on the other cards. This will allow students to become familiar with and gain insight into the past and present and help them formulate their own impressions of life in the future.

LITERARY TIME LINE CARD

Title: _____

Author: _____

Setting: Time _____ Place_____   _____

Impressions (brief explanation of what life is like at that

time and place): _____

_____

_____

_____

_____

Illustration (photograph, picture, or your own drawing to

illustrate the setting):

9. Read various transformations of folk takes in which the setting has been altered. Discuss how the story was changed. Have students rewrite a favorite folk tale using a setting from the present or future.
10. Compare the setting and mood established after reading books on a similar theme or about a similar time. For example, students can compare two books that deal with the Holocaust, Lois Lowry's *Number the Stars* and Jane Yolen's *The Devil's Arithmetic.*
11. After reading a book set in another country, have students create a word cluster, including words and phrases that reflect their perceptions of the country. Set up a center in the room with books, pamphlets, maps, and so on about the country so they can learn more about the area.
12. After reading a book of fantasy that takes place in a strange new world, have students discuss the setting and how it became believable. Have them create a map of this new world, based on the description in the story.

Theme

The story's theme ties together the plot, characters, and setting. A story's theme is its message. It is a feeling, an idea, a meaning the author wants to convey about life, values, beliefs, society, or human behavior. Often, themes deal with understanding oneself and others. Elizabeth Speare's *The Witch of Blackbird Pond* deals with prejudice and the determination of two children to listen to their own hearts rather than the preconceived and misguided notions of the adults around them. *Call It Courage,* by Armstrong Sperry, in which Mafatu's search for courage leads him to danger and the unknown, is an excellent example of a theme that focuses on dealing with a problem, regardless of the difficulty.

Some themes are timeless, like the friendship in *Charlotte's Web,* and their messages are as appropriate now as they were when the stories were written. Other themes are more contemporary. Often, the theme is stated directly; other times, it is implied, and the reader must interpret the message based on his or her frame of reference. Implied theme is generally more effective and makes a more lasting impression. Stories for young children contain themes, just as stories for older children illustrate specific ideas. Often a theme will touch a nerve in the reader, causing him or her to question, analyze, and reevaluate his or her values. Perhaps the message readers take with them will help them become more caring individuals who are capable of improving the quality of their own lives and those of others.

Reflections of . . .

Rebecca Lukens

If we ever wonder whether it matters what children read, if stories have impact on readers or change their attitudes, it's useful to look back on our own experiences. An elementary teacher in my children's literature class once told about the intense interest of her second-graders as each day she read another chapter or two of that classic, *Charlotte's Web.* The children worried about Wilbur's escaping a ham-and-bacon fate, giggled at Templeton's self-interest so like their own, and loved, just loved, Charlotte, the perfectly patient mother who sacrificed her own comfort and convenience for Wilbur's sake.

Then one day, trying hard to focus class interest on numbers instead of words, the teacher noticed that all eyes were straining to see something in midair. She walked to the center of the room and there saw hanging from an invisible thread a fat spider. Thoughtlessly, she made a swipe with her open hand. Then, wanting to get back to numbers, she squished with the toe of her shoe the spider that had dropped to the floor.

A din arose. Groans and gasps and cries.
"Why'd you *do* that?"
"That was Charlotte!"
"You killed her!"

And that teacher had some mighty explaining to do. She had not just destroyed a nameless spider, but for the moment had challenged their fantasy that loving mothers were invulnerable. Charlotte, the patient nurturer they loved, remained, however, in their memories and in their visions of the ideal mother.

At another time I was teaching a freshman class of veterans newly returned from the Vietnam War, a group hoping through the GI Bill to find some compensation for their months and years of disillusionment at the cause they had gone to fight for and at the lack of appreciation that greeted their return. Profoundly changed by their experiences, they had returned to a society that seemed totally preoccupied with interest in its own pursuits, a society that knew nothing of living in abject poverty and privation, or at the edge of death. Understandably, they believed no one understood. One of these young men confessed to the class and to me that he had never read a book and he never intended to. Writers "just don't know what it's like."

The next Tuesday, suggesting to the veteran that he might find this book worth reading, I handed him a copy of *Catcher in the Rye.* The following week he returned with a simple statement: "I couldn't put it down. Are there any more like this?"

Holden Caulfield's struggle to keep his own values and yet to accept the flaws in other people, to understand and even to forgive their "phoniness," to make sense of imperfect human beings living in an imperfect society, had struck this mature veteran as "telling it like it is." I hope Holden made a reader of him, but perhaps not. In any event, he had read an entire book, and it had made an impression, a profound impression.

Activities

The following activities will help children explore theme as an element of good literature.

1. Often, the theme of a story is stated directly, as in Aesop's Fables. Read several of these fables to the class and discuss the themes of each. Have each student select one theme and relate, through written, oral, or artistic expression, a time when this theme had significance in his or her life. For example, after reading *The Tortoise and the Hare* and discussing the themes of "overconfidence" and "persistence can be more important than speed," a student might relate a time when she didn't think she had a chance of achieving a certain goal, yet she kept at it and ultimately found success.

2. Authors write for many purposes: to persuade or change perceptions; to relate an incident in their own lives; to provide insight into human behaviors, virtues, and faults; to share a philosophy. At the same time, they entertain us through the events and characters they create. Hans Christian Andersen's tales are excellent sources for examining the author's purpose and his message.

    Ask students, either individually or in groups, to read selected tales by Andersen. *The Ugly Duckling* and *The Tinder Box* are examples of his biographical stories. *The Emperor's New Clothes* and *The Red Shoes* illustrate human behavior. Andersen shares his philosophies in *The Fir Tree* and *The Little Match Girl*. As students read these and other Andersen stories, have them identify and discuss the main theme. Ask them to find one quote in the story that best sums up the theme. Then have them illustrate the quote. Display the pictures in the classroom (see illustration on page 146).

3. Gather lyrics of folk songs, especially those made popular in the 1960s, such as "If I Had a Hammer" or "Blowing in the Wind." Choral read the lyrics with students and discuss the theme of each song. Have students identify stories that might contain similar themes.

4. Select a specific theme and, depending on their reading level, either read them selected books or assign specific books that deal with this theme. Have them compare the way different books deal with the theme.

5. Allow students to make an anthropomorphic connection as they become the theme of a story. For example, after reading a book that deals with pioneer life, such as *Prairie Songs,* by Pam Conrad, *Sarah, Plain and Tall,* by Patricia MacLachlan, or any of the Little House books, by Laura Ingalls Wilder, ask students to look at "the pioneer spirit" from a different perspective, as they *become* the pioneer spirit. Have them describe how the pioneer spirit might look (its form and color), feel, smell, or taste. Have them write about their lives as the pioneer spirit. Encourage them to use the story and the feelings it evokes to help them with this activity. The use

"It does not matter that one has been born in the hen yard as long as one has lain in a swan's egg."

of webbing and/or clustering (see Chap. 9) will help them generate responses.

6. The theme of a book often illustrates "a significant truth" (Lukens, 1990, p. 88). For example, in Jerry Spinelli's *Maniac Magee* we witness the ability of kindness and understanding to lessen the gap between people; in Laurence Yep's *Dragonwings* we learn that we must all follow our dreams and how vital hope is. Guide students in a discussion of the significant truths they gained through reading a specific book.

7. After students have read books relating to a similar theme, have them adopt the persona of one of the main characters in each book. Hold a "meeting of the minds" in which the characters discuss questions posed by the "audience." The students should answer the questions as their characters would. Try to have characters from books representative of classical and contemporary fiction and representative of a variety of genres.

Point of View

The interpretation of an event or experience can vary drastically when described by different people, because their points of view vary due to their different values, cultures, experiences, and perspectives. Consider how Beverly

Cleary's *Ramona Quimby, Age 8* might change if the story were told from an adult's point of view rather than that of a 7- or 8-year-old child.

An author has several options when deciding on the story's point of view: a first or third person's point of view; an objective point of view, in which the actions speak for themselves; or a limited omniscient point of view, in which the experience of one character is highlighted but the author may be all-knowing about the other characters. Although there doesn't seem to be a preference in children's literature regarding the author's choice of point of view, certain genres appear to favor one viewpoint over another. For example, realistic fiction tends to favor first person because it allows children easily to empathize or identify with characters.

Activities

The following activities will help children explore point of view as an element of good literature.

1. A story's point of view is responsible for the way the reader sees the characters, events, and theme. Have students read a book written in first or third person. Then ask them to select one of the characters and determine how they would be affected if the book were written from that character's point of view. Have students choose one small event and rewrite it from this new point of view. For example, if *Cinderella* were written from the viewpoint of one of the stepsisters, it might read as follows:

    > Everyone always felt sorry for Cinderella. She looked so lovely and so angelic people thought she could do no wrong. But the Cinderella the public saw was very different from the way she actually was. When our mother married Cinderella's father, we tried to be nice to her. We wanted to help her with the chores, but every time we tried to help she played tricks on us and teased us until we cried. After years of taking this abuse, we decided that it was time to teach Cinderella a lesson. . . .

2. Involve students in a discussion based on questions dealing with point of view. The questions are speculative; there should be no right or wrong answers. Students should be able to cite specific portions of the selection to defend their responses: For example, if Natalie Babbitt's *Tuck Everlasting* were written from the stranger's point of view, how would he or she describe the value of the spring? If E. B. White's *Charlotte's Web* were written from Templeton's point of view, what would he suggest they do to save Wilbur's life?

3. Encourage students to select a specific incident that is perceived as negative by character. Have them discuss how the situation can be looked at in a more positive way. For example, in Judith Viorst's *Alexander and the Terrible, Horrible, No Good, Very Bad Day*, Alexander realizes his mother forgot to pack a dessert with his lunch. Perhaps a different character would see

this as a positive occurrence: it might prevent Alexander from getting a cavity and gaining weight!

4. Select a book the entire class has read. Have the class decide on a specific incident. Then have each student write a "Dear Diary" entry from the point of view of one of the characters. Allow time for students to compare their diary entries, and then discuss the way point of view changes their perceptions of certain characters and even of the story's theme.

5. Have students create a comic that illustrates the way two different characters from the same story perceive a certain situation. For example, in William Steig's *Sylvester and the Magic Pebble,* Sylvester is turned into a rock. This event greatly saddens both the lion who is about to pounce on Sylvester and Sylvester's parents because they lost someone they love.

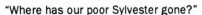

"Where has our poor Sylvester gone?"　　　　　"I'm hungry."

6. Discuss the various points of view an author can use to tell a story. After reading a selected book, have students rewrite several paragraphs using a different point of view. For example, they may experiment with omniscient or third person perspective with a book such as Scott O'Dell's *Island of the Blue Dolphin* that is written in first person.

7. Ask each student to write a "Dear Abby"-type letter as if he or she were the main character of a book they have read. Place these letters in a special box and periodically select one and have the class respond from their own points of view.

Style and Tone

Style refers to how an author conveys the story—the mood. It refers to the language, syntax, and tone. Often the style matches the setting, characters, or conflict. Every writer has a style of his or her own; recognizing this, children often select books by the same author.

Perhaps the most obvious stylistic device is figurative language—the similes, metaphors, personification, and hyperbole used to describe a person, place, or thing. In *Tuck Everlasting*, Natalie Babbitt uses many similes and metaphors, beginning with the first line of the story: "The first week of August hangs at the very top of the summer, the top of the live-long year, like the highest seat of a Ferris wheel when it pauses in its turning." In *The Talking Earth*, Jean C. George uses similes to bring the Everglades to life: "grass blades glistened like a copper spear in the hot June sun" and "trees looked like dead men standing in their graves." Symbolic language and imagery (the appeal to the senses) are devices that work together to enrich style and bring the story to life, enabling the reader to see, feel, taste, and touch that which is described.

Poetry and prose often share similar devices, especially the devices of sound. Alliteration, rhythm, and onomatopoeia, for example, can be found in both. Often prose reads like a song or a poem, as evidenced in Jane Yolen's *Owl Moon*:

> When you go owling
> you don't need words
> or warm
> or anything but hope.
> That's what Pa says.
> The kind of hope that flies on silent wings
> under a shining
> Owl Moon.

Tone is the author's attitude toward the character, plot, or other elements. The tone is determined by the style, which, in turn, is determined by the author's choice of words, sentence structure, language, and so forth. The tone, according to Lukens (1990, p. 158), is "the author's attitude toward story and readers. By the writer's choice of materials, the writer almost inevitably reveals something about his or her own personality." The tone can be ironic, filled with wonder, humorous, or serious. It can reflect pathos and sympathy, acceptance, or doubt. Tone can give the reader hope and optimism, as does the title character in *M.C. Higgins the Great*, by Virginia Hamilton, who views life from the top of a 40-foot pole, or can evince longing and despair, as in *The Ugly Duckling*. Just as characters and plot change, so, too, does tone. As Gilly Hopkins's (*The Great Gilly Hopkins*, by Katherine Paterson) perceptions of her life and the people around her change, the tone moves from a sense of irony to one of compassion and love. At the beginning, the author's tone causes a skeptical feeling toward Gilly, which changes later to sympathy and finally to empathy.

Activities

The following activities will help children explore style and tone as elements of good literature.

1. Select several versions of the same folk tales that originated in different cultures. For example, *Lon Po Po*, by Ed Young, is a Chinese version of *Little Red Riding Hood*. Have students discuss and compare the style and tone of the stories to see what generalizations they can make. Ask them whether they believe the style and tone of a story reflect the culture from which it originated. Ask them to support their responses with citations from the stories.
2. After reading a story in which an animal is personified, ask children to read a variety of genres dealing with a similar animal. Compare the styles evident in the various genres.
3. Hyperbole and understatement are devices used by many authors. Have students locate an example of hyperbole in a selected piece of literature and rewrite the paragraph as an understatement, or vice versa. Discuss how this changes the story.
4. Locate several examples of simile or metaphor in a selected literary work. Ask students to use the piece as a model for writing and illustrating their own similes and metaphors. For example, what other comparisons can they make to describe the trees described in Jane Yoren's *Owl Moon* as standing "still as giant statues"?
5. Authors of poetry and prose alike often use alliteration. Involve students in a lesson on alliteration using *Anamalia*, by Graeme Base. Have them select a theme such as transportation ("Transportalia") or communication ("Communicalia") for a new book of alliteration. Ask each group to write a page of text that focuses on the assigned letter(s), using *Anamalia* as a model.
6. Choose a specific incident from a book being read and have students write those paragraphs so the tone is changed. For example, if they are reading an informational book on nutrition they could write a humorous piece called "How to Eat Like a Child."
7. Before reading a specific selection, provide children with books, articles, and so on to give them background on the author's life. After reading the book, involve students in a discussion that focuses on how the author's own attitudes and values are evident in the story.
8. Ask students to find and read aloud examples from other literary works that reflect the same tone as that in a selected book. After each reading, discuss what the author did to establish the tone.

Evaluating Genres and Their Elements: A Synthesis

Once students are familiar with the various genres and literary elements that constitute good literature, they should be given activities that will cause them to synthesize and apply these understandings. Synthesis activities require students to evaluate selected works based on their knowledge of the elements of literature, their understanding of the different genres, and their ability to discern and apply the criteria for selecting good literature. These activities will help them become educated readers who are more adroit at selecting books that represent the best in children's literature.

Activities

1. Have students become the evaluators as they "grade" books they have read. Their evaluation can be based on the way the specific literary elements were used to develop the story. Encourage them to use the criteria checklists given in Chapter 1. A literary evaluation can take different forms; see page 152.

2. Have the class think of a name for the prize for a special book competition. Books will be competing for Best Realistic Fiction, Best Picture Book, Best Biography, and so on. Use the following steps.

   a. Set aside a day at the end of the year for the awards. Allow students to design a special plaque or trophy that will be awarded to the winning selections.

   b. Throughout the year, have students nominate their favorite selection in each genre. To nominate a book, the student must complete a Nomination Form (see page 153) to explain why the selection is an outstanding contribution to the genre and to children's literature.

   c. Set a date by which all nominations must be made (approximately four weeks before the awards assembly). Read all nomination forms to the class and compile lists of the nominees by genre.

   d. Allow time for a class discussion in which students discuss the merits of each nominee.

   e. Conduct an election in which students vote, by secret ballot, for the books (one per genre) of their choice.

   f. Select a student to be the Master of Ceremony and choose the students who best championed each winner to accept the award.

   g. Display winning books and their awards, as well as the other nominated books, in the classroom so students have an opportunity to read these outstanding selections.

LITERARY EVALUATION

Date of evaluation: _____

Title being evaluated: _____

Author: _____

Genre: _____

Literary Element	Grade	Comments
Characterization:	☐	_____
Plot:	☐	_____
Theme:	☐	_____
Setting:	☐	_____
Point of view:	☐	_____
Style:	☐	_____
Tone:	☐	_____
Overall evaluation:	☐	_____

Name of evaluator: _____

— —

Evaluation Guide

5 = Outstanding   4 = Good   3 = Fair

2 = Needs improvement   1 = Poor (a waste)

Censorship and Children's Literature

In recent years, more and more pressure has been exerted by individuals and groups seeking to influence the content of children's literature. Those who seek to control children's literary choices find the central issues and ideas of many

NOMINATION FORM

Title: _____

Author: _____

Genre: _____

In fifty words or less, explain how this book is an outstanding

example of its genre: _____

_____

_____

_____

_____

_____

_____

_____

What one thing about this book impresses you most?

_____

_____

Student's name: _____ Date: _____

books inappropriate for children or find the language of some books offensive. Those who oppose censorship of literature are concerned with "the principle of intellectual freedom." They believe that literature is a reflection of life and that children must have the opportunity to learn how to select good literature, how to read critically, and how to interact with books. They believe that as children read about other people, explore new ideas, learn about diverse viewpoints, and analyze the way in which others solve problems similar to their own, they will be more prepared to choose their own options, find their own solutions to problems, and affirm their own values.

In addition to the activities in this book that were developed to bring children and books together, children need to become involved in activities that promote an understanding of censorship, especially as it relates to the books they read. You may wish to incorporate some of the activities described below into your curriculum to help students become aware of the causes and effects of censorship and the way in which our country works to defend individual rights. You and your students may wish to contact the American Library Association's Office for Intellectual Freedom for current information on censorship of Children's Literature (312-280-4223).

Activities

1. What is censorship? Allow time for students to research the term *censorship*. Try to obtain a group consensus as to the definition of the term. (This is most easily done by first having individuals write their own definitions, then work together in small groups to arrive at a group definition, and finally share group definitions to arrive at a class definition.)
2. Have students make a word cluster about the term *censorship* to see what feelings, images, or ideas the term represents to them.
3. Provide students with copies of the Bill of Rights. Discuss how the First Amendment of the Bill of Rights relates to the issue of censorship.
4. Find information about the three Supreme Court cases in which the Court rendered decisions affecting young people's First Amendment rights: *Barnett v. West Virginia* (1943), *Tinker v. Des Moines Independent School District* (1969), and *Hazelwood School District v. Kuhlmeier* (1988).

   Divide students into three groups and allow each group to study one of the cases. Have the students in the group prepare a persuasive speech as if they were a Supreme Court justice rendering the Court's verdict and citing reasons for the decision. After each speech has been delivered, encourage students to discuss the case and the implications of the verdict.
5. Find information about recent cases of censorship of literature in your own state. Have students write letters to the editor of a local newspaper or letters to the local school board stating their views on the subject of this censorship.
6. Select a book that has frequently been censored, such as Maurice Sendak's *In the Night Kitchen*, Mark Twain's *The Adventures of Huckleberry Finn*, or Judy Blume's *Are You There, God? It's Me, Margaret*. Read the book aloud or have students read the book independently. Then have students prepare a mock trial in which the book itself is tried for the reason cited by those who want to censor it. The case could be called _____ (name of book) *v.* the School Board of _____ (name of county).
7. Debate literary censorship. Divide students into three groups and then divide each group into two smaller groups, each one taking the opposite position. Have each group debate whether or not censorship is justified by the Bill of Rights of the U.S. Constitution. After all the groups have completed preparations, allow each large group to present its debate. When all groups have completed their debates, have students compare the argu-

ments cited by the different groups to determine which arguments were most effective and why.

8. Encourage students to look at censorship in a different way by completing the following analogies. Once they have completed the exercise, have them draw their own interpretive illustration of censorship.
   Censorship is like (name of an animal) because _____
   Censorship is like (name of a season) because _____
   Censorship is like (a number) because _____
   Censorship is like (an object) because _____
   Censorship is like (a food) because _____

9. Invite speakers from organizations such as the American Civil Liberties Union that provide information on fighting censorship and that help individuals defend themselves in censorship cases. If you cannot get a guest speaker to come to the classroom, have students write to these organizations to obtain their literature. Guide students in the preparation of questions to ask the speaker or to include in the letters they write. These questions should attempt to elicit more information about censorship, what is being done to fight censorship, what books are being censored, reasons for this censorship, and so on.

10. Use the following questions as the basis for a discussion of censorship:
    What types of censorship exist (moral, military, political, religious)?
    How does censorship affect your parents' lives? Your own life?
    Why do some people feel censorship is important?
    Why do some people feel censorship is never justified?
    Should censorship be allowed? If so, in what situations?
    Should anyone have the right to determine what is and what is not allowed? If so, who?

11. Read students "Mrs. Bennett's Dilemma," on page 156, and, using the following steps, guide them through a discussion of moral dilemmas.

Steps in the Discussion of Moral Dilemmas

1. Present the dilemma. Read it aloud or have students read it silently.
2. Clarification of facts. Encourage students to list the facts of the situation. Discuss the events, people involved, and alternatives.
3. Students choose an alternative. Students independently decide which alternative the main character should take and write three reasons to explain their choice.
4. Small-group discussion. By a show of hands, find out which alternatives students selected. If the class is fairly split on the issues, divide them into groups depending on their position. If a majority of the class selects the same position, place some students in the group that took an alternative position, or place them in groups depending on their reasons for their position. (Those students who have a similar reason can be placed

MRS. BENNETT'S DILEMMA

Lucy Bennett has been an elementary school teacher for almost thirty years. During those years she has had the freedom to select the books her students read in class. Mrs. Bennett has a tremendous love for both classic and contemporary literature and has been extremely successful in motivating her students to read. Her former students credit Mrs. Bennett with helping them develop a love of literature.

This past year, certain interest groups decided that most of the books in Mrs. Bennett's curriculum are unsuitable for children and pressured the school board into removing these materials and adopting other materials that met with their approval. Mrs. Bennett went to court seeking to have the court deny the school board the right to remove materials. Mrs. Bennett lost her case when the Federal District Court upheld the right of the school board to remove any materials they felt were unsuitable.

Mrs. Bennett feels strongly about the right to educate children using the literature she has used so successfully for so long. She knows that this material provides her students with important experiences and believes the books cause them to think and form their own philosophies and conclusions. She also knows that the material approved by the board is boring, unimaginative, unrealistic, and totally unappealing to children.

Mrs. Bennett has been warned that if she goes against the court's ruling she will automatically be dismissed from her teaching position and lose all retirement benefits. Mrs. Bennett is a widow with very little savings. She has two years left until she can retire with full benefits. What should she do?

together.) Once in groups, have students discuss the position they took and focus on the most important reasons for taking the position.

5. Class discussion. Seat students in a circle to best promote group interaction. Allow time for students to discuss their positions and their reasons for taking them. Initiate discussion by having each group summarize their position and reasons for it, or a general discussion can follow your questions: "What should the character do? Why?

   During this discussion, it is important to be nonjudgmental and to encourage all students to participate and interact with one another. Help students clarify their own reasons and perceptions of the issue with questions.

6. Students reevaluate their positions. Encourage students to think about the facts, issues, and reasons discussed, and then individually record what

they think the main character should do and the most important reason for taking this position. If the students did change their original positions, encourage them to write about what caused them to look at the issue differently. Do not attempt to reach a class consensus.

When students have completed their papers, compare responses to their earlier responses to see if any ideas changed.

Children's Literature

*Cited in text

*Allard, Harry, and James Marshal. *Miss Nelson Is Missing*. Illustrated by James Marshal. Houghton Mifflin, 1977.

*Andersen, Hans Christian. *The Complete Book of Fairy Tales and Stories*. Illustrated by Erik Haugaard. Doubleday, 1974.

*Aesop. *Aesop's Fables*. Illustrated by Heidi Holder. Viking, 1981.

*Babbitt, Natalie. *Tuck Everlasting*. Farrar, Straus & Giroux, 1975.

Base, Graeme. *Animalia*. Abrams, 1987.

*Blos, Joan. *A Gathering of Days: A New England Girl's Journal, 1830–32*. Scribner's, 1979.

*Brink, Carol Ryrie. *Caddie Woodlawn*. Illustrated by Kate Seredy. Macmillan, 1936.

*Burnett, Frances H. *The Secret Garden*. Illustrated by Tasha Tudor. Lippincott, 1936.

*Cleary, Beverly. *Ramona Quimby, Age 8*. Illustrated by Alan Tiegreen. Morrow, 1981.

Conrad, Pam. *Prairie Songs*. Harper & Row, 1985.

*Galdone, Paul. *The Three Billy Goats Gruff*. Clarion, 1973.

George, Jean C. *The Talking Earth*. Harper, 1983.

*Grahame, Kenneth. *The Wind in the Willows*. Illustrated by E. H. Shepard. Scribner's, 1940.

Hamilton, Virginia. *M. C. Higgins, The Great*. Macmillan, 1974.

*Hoban, Russell. *Bedtime for Frances*. Illustrated by Garth Williams. Harper & Row, 1960.

*Leaf, Munro. *The Story of Ferdinand*. Illustrated by Robert Lawson. Puffin, 1977.

Lowry, Lois. *Number the Stars*. Houghton, 1989.

MacLachlan, Patricia. *Sarah, Plain and Tall*. Harper & Row, 1987.

*Ness, Evaline. *Sam, Bangs & Moonshine*. Holt, Rinehart & Winston, 1966.

O'Dell, Scott. *Island of the Blue Dolphins*. Dell, 1960.

Paterson, Katherine. *The Great Gilly Hopkins*. Harper, 1978.

*Speare, Elizabeth. *The Witch of Blackbird Pond*. Houghton Mifflin, 1958.

*Sperry, Armstrong. *Call It Courage*. Macmillan, 1968.

Spinelli, Jerry. *Maniac Magee*. HarperCollins, 1990.

*Steig, William. *Sylvester and the Magic Pebble*. Windmill, 1969.

Taylor, Mildred. *Roll of Thunder, Hear My Cry*. Illustrated by Jerry Pinkney. Dial, 1976.

*Twain, Mark (pseud. Samuel Clemens). *The Adventures of Tom Sawyer*. Harper & Row, 1876.

*Viorst, Judith. *Alexander and the Terrible, Horrible, No Good, Very Bad Day*. Illustrated by Ray Cruz. Atheneum, 1972.

*White, E. B. *Charlotte's Web*. Illustrated by Garth Williams. Windmill, 1969.

Wiesner, David. *Tuesday*. Clarion, 1991.

*Wilder, Laura Ingalls. *Little House* series. Illustrated by Garth Williams. Harper & Row, 1953.

*———. *Little House in the Big Woods*. Illustrated by Garth Williams. Harper & Row, 1932.

Yep, Laurence. *Dragonwings.* HarperCollins, 1975.
Yolen, Jane. *The Devil's Arithmetic.* Viking, 1990.
————. *Owl Moon.* Illustrated by John Schoenherr. Philomel, 1987.
Young, Ed. *Lon Po Po: A Red Riding Hood Story from China.* Philomel, 1989.

Professional Resources

*Lukens, Rebecca. *A Critical Handbook of Children's Literature,* 4th ed. Scott, Foresman,
     1990.
Parnes, Sidney J. "Guiding Creative Action." *The Gifted Child Quarterly,* 21:460–472, 1977.
Sutherland, Zena, and May Hill Arbuthnot. *Children and Books,* 7th ed. Scott, Foresman,
     1986.

PART II

The World Through Books: Bringing Together Children and Books

CHAPTER 4 • **The Read-Aloud Program**

CHAPTER 5 • **The Shared Reading Experience**

CHAPTER 6 • **Independent Reading**

CHAPTER 7 • **Storytelling**

CHAPTER 8 • **Diversity and Children's Books: Finding the Right Book**

All good books are alike in that they are truer than if they had really happened and after you are finished reading one you will feel that all that happened to you and afterwards it all belongs to you: the good and the bad, the ecstasy, the remorse and sorrow, the people and the places and how the weather was. If you can get so that you can give that to people, then you are a writer.

Ernest Hemingway
1899–1961

Most children begin their school life with high expectations. Children, especially those who have been exposed to books at home, anxiously await the moment when a book is placed in their hands. They open it and read! All too often, their hopes and expectations are dashed when they are given their first preprimer in reading class. What happened to the magic? What happened to the joy of reading?

Bringing children and books together is one of the most important, rewarding, and, perhaps, frustrating outcomes of teaching. Teachers often lament their inability to motivate students to read for the sheer pleasure of reading. Often, they are trying to motivate children who wanted desperately to read in the early grades.

There is no magic formula to develop interest in reading, and no amount of begging will change children's perceptions of reading. The solution is quite simple and has been in our libraries and classrooms for centuries—books, real works of literature brimming with the knowledge of ages past and yet to come, just waiting to excite the imagination and nourish the soul.

Children need to be surrounded by good books. They need to be introduced to and involved with quality works of literature. Many approaches have been successful in bridging the gap between children and books. The second part of *Legacies* focuses on four of these approaches: the read-aloud program (Chapter 4), shared reading experience (Chapter 5), independent reading (Chapter 6), and storytelling (Chapter 7). Each approach is described in detail, guidelines for establishing the classroom climate and techniques for developing the approach are offered, and books that meet the criteria for each approach are suggested. In addition, activities that extend the use and impact of each approach are described.

One of the most incredible aspects of children's literature is that there is virtually something for everyone. There are books that present an understanding of people from every corner of the world and from every walk of life. There are also books that deal with our special children, those who are differently enabled or learning disabled, and those for whom English is a second language. Chapter 8 will help you discover books and resources to find the book or verse that will speak directly to each child and give a sense of self and others. The chapter also offers activities to encourage children's reactions and interactions with these works.

CHAPTER 4

The Read-Aloud Program

The Importance of Reading Aloud

A great deal of evidence indicates that a person's success in reading depends largely on his or her experiences with literature and reading during the early years at home and the first few years in school. Much evidence indicates that some children can read when they begin school. It is consistently found that children who were read to at home are better readers (Durkin, 1966; Noyce and Christine, 1987; Sakamato, 1977; Wells, 1986). Reading aloud to children improves their listening, verbal, and written skills and fosters a lifetime love of books and reading. Children tend to imitate and model after adults. If children see adults reading or if they are read to by adults, they are more likely to want to read themselves (Elkind, 1974; Gordon, 1976; Martinez and Teale, 1988).

Reading aloud, however, should not be confined to the home. A read-aloud program should be an integral part of the daily classroom curriculum for all students. In fact, reading aloud is just as important for older children as it is for younger ones (Tiedt, 1989). Studies of school-age children show that children who had been read to by their teachers were significantly ahead of those who had not been given such opportunities in reading, vocabulary development, and comprehension (Cohen, 1968; Cullinan, Jagger, and Strickland, 1974). Sulzby (1985) strongly suggests that children typically transfer oral language skills to the act of reading and that, as a result of being read to, progress more quickly through the stages of language development.

Research has demonstrated that reading to children not only helps them learn to read but also results in benefits such as establishing a mutual bond among listeners. The warmth of the oral reading period and the generally effective climate created during the reading time help support the child's emotional well-being, helping to build their self-confidence.

Through the read-aloud process, children learn much about books and gain basic understandings about the reading process itself (Durkin, 1970; Rosen, 1987; Trelease, 1989). For example, children learn that print is read from left to right, that books have a top and a bottom and a beginning and an end, and that adults read what is printed in the books.

Language is developed through read-aloud sessions (Durkin, 1970; Elley, 1983, 1989; Flood, 1977; Olson, 1979; Smith, 1977). During the actual reading of the story and the follow-up discussions, children hear many words, many of which will become part of their listening and speaking vocabularies and, later, their reading and writing vocabularies. Reading books aloud can provide a support for language acquisition of English-as-a-second-language students (Allen, 1989).

There is also a connection between being read to and writing performance (Calkins, 1991; Clay, 1975; Graves, 1983). Reading to children sparks their imagination, giving them ideas to write about. Often what is read today will be written about tomorrow.

First-hand experiences are important when children are developing the concepts, knowledge, and thinking skills that are vital to the process of reading; however, many children have limited opportunities to acquire these essential experiences. When first-hand experiences are not feasible, one of the next best approaches is to offer them vicariously through reading aloud.

It is important to introduce children to high-quality multicultural literature. By reading books from a variety of cultures, teachers and parents can help children understand and appreciate their own culture as well as those of others (Harris, 1992).

When teachers select a variety of genres to read aloud to children, they help them develop a love and appreciation of books. It is not unusual for children to want to read a book that has been read to them, and often they choose to read it over and over again. As read-aloud books are made available to children, they can improve their reading skills by rereading familiar books.

Reading to children provides them with an enjoyable and pleasurable activity. It is not surprising that long after they forget the worksheets and textbooks, they still remember a favorite story that was read to them. Reading aloud often whets children's appetite for more reading and exposes them to literature they would otherwise not be able to experience.

Preparing a Read-Aloud Program

A successful read-aloud program requires preparation. You must set the proper classroom climate, select appropriate read-aloud materials, and use techniques that will help develop the program's objectives.

Setting the Climate

A message is sent to children when they realize their teacher believes reading is important and takes time daily to read to them. Students will begin to look forward to the read-aloud time and savor the moment when their teacher sits down, opens the book, and brings the words and story to life.

Too often, children are credited with being able to choose the best books for themselves. Unfortunately, frequently they select books from the same genre and do not choose books that exemplify good literature. A read-aloud program can introduce children to a wide range of outstanding books. After hearing a book read aloud, children often scramble to locate a copy for themselves to read

in their free time. How rewarding to know that reading aloud heightens children's awareness, understanding, and sensitivity to good literature!

It is especially important to set aside a specific time for reading aloud, rather than trying to fit it into the schedule haphazardly. The rationalization that there isn't enough time is simply an excuse. Making the time for read-aloud sessions should be high on the list of priorities for all teachers. Certainly 15 minutes a day can be dedicated to enriching students' lives and unlocking the door to the unique and unlimited possibilities that literature holds.

Teachers' flexibility and creativity will ensure that they find time to read aloud. Many teachers have found that in the morning, right after the bell has rung, is an especially good time to read aloud. Children quickly settle down for this special time, and it sets the tone for the entire day. Immediately after lunch or just before dismissal are also excellent times to read aloud. Taking just 2–3 minutes from the class times allotted to other subjects and combining them into a 15-minute period can provide the needed time for reading aloud. As a word of caution, avoid beginning the read-aloud session when you only have a minute or two. Little can be accomplished in so short a time, and children may lose interest.

Attention span is important to consider when determining the length of read-aloud sessions. Teachers of young children might wish to schedule two or three shorter read-aloud times, since their students' attention span is shorter. Generally, stories for children younger than 7 should be short enough to complete during a single session. Older children enjoy longer stories that may be completed over a longer period. Teachers may schedule one longer period for the read-aloud session, rather than several shorter ones. If children are not accustomed to being read to, read-aloud sessions should be kept rather short. As they develop skill in listening and interest in the readings, the sessions can be lengthened.

In addition to setting aside specific times for reading aloud, consider spontaneous reading. Various lessons might lend themselves to a specific story or poem. For example, Henry Wadsworth Longfellow's "The Midnight Ride of Paul Revere" or *And Then What Happened Paul Revere?*, by Jean Fritz, might be appropriate during a lesson on the Revolutionary War. A lesson on World War II would be enhanced by reading *Anne Frank: Beyond the Diary* by Ruud van der Rol and Rian Verhoeven.

Selecting Read-Aloud Books

With thousands of books available, knowing how to select the best books for reading aloud is critical. You must be aware of good children's literature and keep up with the newest additions. Perhaps the most important criterion for a read-aloud selection is how you feel about the book, since this feeling is immediately transmitted to the students. It is crucial that teachers select books that affect them, books that cause them to react in some way, challenge their imagination or inspire their dreams, make them laugh, cry, or beg for more. Enthusiasm is contagious. A teacher who is excited about reading will have equally motivated students.

The following criteria should be considered when selecting books to read aloud.

1. Select well-written books. By first grade, students have expectations of what a story should be and can differentiate between literature that has merit and literature that does not. Children especially enjoy stories that have a strong, fast-paced plot and interesting, well-delineated, memorable characters with whom they can identify. Children need literature that they can become totally immersed in. *Song and Dance Man,* by Karen Akerman, is a beautifully illustrated Caldecott Award-winning book that allows children to turn back the hands of time to experience the days of vaudeville. Children also can identify with or feel what it would be like to enjoy time with grandparents. Natalie Babbitt's *Tuck Everlasting* is a haunting tale that causes readers and listeners to reflect on their mortality. It stays with them long after the last word is read. Its words are stirring and challenging, taking its readers beyond the daily routines of life.

2. Select books that reflect your students' interests. Use interest inventories. Talk to your students—find out what makes them tick, what they love, what they hate, and what they fear. Books become even more appealing when they relate to specific interests or when students can identify with the characters, learning how others deal with situations and problems similar to their own. Children having difficulty developing and maintaining friendships might relate to Mildred Taylor's *The Friendship*, which reflects the renunciation of friendship, or Margaret Wild's *The Very Best Friends*, which describes the loving friendships between James and Jessie and between James and his cat, William. Children who lack a sense of belonging might identify with Hans Christian Andersen's *The Ugly Duckling* or with Wanda in Eleanor Este's *The Hundred Dresses*, who longs for acceptance from her peers.

3. Select books that will stimulate students' imaginations. One of the most rewarding outcomes of reading is that it gives vent to the imagination. It lets the reader dare to dream, to journey to far-off places, to break away from earthly boundaries and take part in wonderful adventures. Laura Ingalls Wilder's Little House series allows children to experience life in a different time and share in the excitement, adventure, danger, and happiness of pioneer life. In *The Great Kapok Tree: A Tale of the Amazon Rain Forest*, Lynn Cherry, with her lush paintings of the Amazon rainforest, has created a magical tale with a conservation message for all children.

4. Select books from a variety of genres. Choosing a wide variety of read-aloud books will broaden your students' interests as well as their own selection of books. Fiction books (realistic fiction, historical fiction, fantasy, folklore) provide children with characters and emotions with which they can identify and establish settings and themes that captivate their imaginations and explore the human condition. Fiction also helps children understand themselves and others.

Poetry should play an important part in the read-aloud program as well. Poems express human feelings and motivation, and students can readily identify with the characters and themes in both contemporary and traditional poetry. Poems also provide a natural outlet through which students can express their own feelings, even though students enjoy writing free verse. In general, elementary school children prefer poetry with a clear rhyme and rhythm, since they have not yet developed the sophistication and skill to become interested in and to understand poems that are abstract or that rely heavily on imagery. Younger children delight in the same nursery rhymes we all recited as children, and as they mature they can identify with the poetry of Dickinson, Merriam, Livingston, Greenfield, Poe, Stevenson, Whitman, Longfellow, and Frost, to name a few. For example, the alliteration and repetition in "Diddle diddle dumpling, my son John," can later be enjoyed in poems such as Lord Tennyson's "Blow, Bugle, Blow":

The splendour falls on castle walls
And snowy summits old in story:

The long light shakes across the lakes,
  And the wild cateract leaps in glory.
Blow, bugle, blow, set the wild echoes flying,
Blow, bugle; answer, echoes, dying, dying, dying . . .

Nonfiction books (informational books and biographies) provide students with a wide range of information. Nonfiction arms students with the facts and background they will need to connect new concepts and knowledge. For example, *Harriet Tubman: Conductor on the Underground Railroad,* by Ann Petry, adds another dimension to students' understanding of the Civil War and its consequences. *Franklin Delano Roosevelt,* by Russell Freedman, and *A Picture Book of Eleanor Roosevelt,* by David Adler, add another dimension to students' understanding of the lives of a president of the United States and his wife during a difficult time in history.

5. Select books from both traditional and modern literature. Modern literature reflects contemporary settings, language, and characters, but the themes may be contemporary or universal. Traditional literature provides links with the past and carries the reader to another place and time. Traditional literature contains timeless, universal themes that are as relevant today as they were at the time the story was written.

6. Select several books by the same author to help your students gain an appreciation for that author's particular style and work. For example, read several of Ezra Keats's books to your students and involve them in a comparison of the books: How are *The Snowy Day, Peter's Chair*, and *Hi Cat!* similar? Compare the characters in each. How would you describe books by Ezra Keats? What quality do all of his books seem to have? Compare the illustrations in each. Eric Carle's *Have You Seen My Cat?, The Very Busy Spider*, and *The Very Quiet Cricket* would also provide an interesting comparison and contrast of an author's style.

7. Select books that cover a specific theme or concept being developed in class. This will further students' understanding of the concept and add a new dimension. "Arithmetic," by Carl Sandburg, or "The Homework Machine," by Shel Silverstein, can really enliven a mathematics lesson.

8. Select books that are models for good writing and that are rich in language. Listening to the language of literature affects students' oral and written communication skills. They learn to write not only through the process of writing but also by reading the works of others (Smith, 1982). For example, have students employ the pattern, rhythm, and rhyme of Robert Frost's "Stopping by Woods on a Snowy Evening" in writing a poem of their own. "Whose woods these are I think I know . . ." may become "Whose dreams these are, . . ."

9. Select books that are appropriate to your students' intellectual and emotional levels. No matter how outstanding a book may be, if its subject matter or vocabulary is too sophisticated, students will lose interest. A distinction must be made between the students' listening level and their reading

level. For example, first-graders have a reading vocabulary of approximately 350 words, while their listening vocabulary is greater than 10,000 words.

10. Allow students to help select books to read aloud. You might display a folder of Suggestions for Reading Aloud forms (see below), which students can use to suggest books or poems they would like to have included in the read-aloud program. When a student's book or poem is selected, allow him or her to introduce the selection to the class. Sources such as *The New Advocate* (Boston, MA: Christopher-Gordon), *The Reading Teacher* (Newark, DE: International Reading Association), *Hornbook* (14 Beacon Street, Boston, MA), *School Library Journal* (P.O. Box 1978, Marion, OH), and *Booklinks* (Chicago, IL: American Library Association) review new children's books.

SUGGESTIONS FOR READING ALOUD

Student's name _____

Suggested read aloud title _____

Author _____

Why I like this book _____

_____

_____

Guidelines for Reading Aloud

Certain techniques can help make the read-aloud sessions more successful. The following guidelines describe points to consider when establishing a read-aloud program:

1. Begin reading to students on their first day in class. Sharing a good book provides a wonderful opportunity for you and your students to share a warm, pleasurable moment, establishes the climate for the rest of the year, and establishes a close bond.

2. Before reading a story or poem aloud, be familiar with the material. You will know what parts to emphasize, what words or concepts to introduce prior to the reading to help avoid confusion, what mood to set, and what

tone and pace the reading should take. Practice reading the story aloud to yourself, on a tape recorder, or to a friend or colleague before reading it to the class. Reading aloud is an art that is very important to master. Some teachers have established after-school workshops for developing reading-aloud strategies. They pair off and read aloud to each other, giving necessary feedback. This also allows teachers to become familiar with a vast amount of good read-aloud literature. Do not feel as if you have to read every single word of the text. Often long, overly descriptive passages should be shortened for certain groups. For the reading to flow more smoothly, practice reading a story or parts of a story aloud before reading it to children.

3. Hold prereading discussions to establish interest in the book. Children love learning anecdotes about the author or illustrator, and this information brings them even closer to the story or poem. Students may be interested to learn that Robert Louis Stevenson amused his stepson with tales about pirates and buried treasure and that these tales grew into *Treasure Island.* Knowing that Stevenson fought illness constantly, writing many of his best books and poems from a sickbed, may make children feel more deeply about the poetry of this great writer. Students might be fascinated to know that Robert McCloskey kept ducks in his bathtub to study while writing *Make Way for Ducklings.*

    The following questions can be used in a prereading discussion with any form of literature: Look at the title (or cover). What do you think the book might be about? Who is the author? Have you heard of the author before? What other books did this author write? Who is the illustrator? What other books did this illustrator illustrate? How would you describe this illustrator's style?

4. Have children sit comfortably in a semicircle around you and try to eliminate all distractions. Establish eye contact with students throughout the reading. Do not allow the students to do other activities during read-aloud time.

5. Sit on a low chair close to the students and hold the book so they can see the illustrations. Illustrations are of particular importance in books for young children. Allow time for students to examine the illustrations and develop their powers of observation. Illustrations for older students might be shown at the end of certain chapters, allowing them to form mental images before they see the accompanying illustrations. Mention what type of illustrations are used (e.g., pen-and-ink, collage, photographs).

6. Become immersed in the story or poem, express the emotions evoked, and bring the literature to life with gestures, sound effects, and voice inflections. You need not be an actor, but a flair for the dramatic can be a plus. Attempt to be as authentic as possible when reading dialogue. As the reader becomes involved, so do the listeners.

7. Encourage children to participate in the reading when appropriate. For example, they might take part in reciting a repeated word, line, or chorus. Allow them to ask questions and respond to them.

8. Periodically ask questions to enhance comprehension and interest. The main objective of reading aloud is to provide an opportunity for students to relax and enjoy the magic that is good literature, so do not ask questions constantly, therefore turning the session into a test. You might reread certain passages and ask students to give their interpretation of what is happening. Students might sometimes be asked to predict the outcome. This heightens interest as they listen to determine whether their predictions were accurate. Rather than interrupt the continuity of the story, discussion should usually be saved until the end of the session.

9. If it is not possible to complete an entire book or chapter in one reading, try to stop at a cliffhanger. Leave the students on the edge of their seats, anxious to know what happens next. But don't give the ending away! Spend a few minutes brainstorming about what might come next. Write student responses, accompanied by the student's initials, on the board or a chart. In subsequent sessions, see how accurate the responses were.

10. At the completion of a story or poem, allow time for the students silently to contemplate what they have heard, explore their own feelings, and internalize the work. Students may wish to write in their journals at this time as well. Chapter 9 includes suggestions for connecting literature and writing.

11. Once the story or poem is completed, allow time for the students to express freely their feelings, opinions, and conclusions. They usually have a need to respond in some way to what has been read. Their responses may be artistic (illustrating a favorite scene, drawing a picture to represent their feelings about a certain part of the story) or dramatic (puppetry, role playing, miming a scene) rather than verbal.

12. Encourage students to express their feelings, attitudes, and opinions about the story or poem. Often, you may have to stimulate the discussion to aid more in-depth exploration. For example, after reading *Class President*, by Johanna Hurwitz, you might ask the students what they liked best about the story. A common reply is, "Julio." Ask what about Julio they liked. To aid children in exploring and expressing their own ideas, you might also ask the questions below, or similar questions that focus on other elements of the story.

    a. Why did the character act the way he or she did?
    b. What would you have done differently?
    c. How is the character similar to someone you know?
    d. How is the character similar to (or different from) _____ (a character in a book read recently)?

13. If a book selected for a session does not hold a majority of the students' attention, do not continue reading it. Instead, suggest that those students who are interested in the book read it independently and then select another book for the read-aloud session.

14. Include copies of books that have been read aloud (and other books by the same author) in the classroom library. This provides children with the op-

portunity to read and reread their favorites, as well as others in a series (e.g., the Little House series).

15. To evaluate student participation and interest in read-aloud stories, consult the Shared Reading Observation Sheet (p. 192). Most of the questions are appropriate for evaluating the success of read-aloud sessions.

Activities for Reading Aloud

The following activities can extend the use and impact of a read-aloud program.

1. Allow children to help prepare their own class lists of recommended books for the read-aloud program. The books should meet specific criteria that you and the students have discussed. These criteria can be based on the list given in Selecting Read-Aloud Books.
2. Set up a program for older students to create a read-aloud program for younger students at the school. Before implementing the program, introduce students to the guidelines for reading aloud discussed in the previous section and give them an opportunity to practice reading aloud the selections they want to read to the younger students.
3. Beyond the traditional approach to reading aloud, you might incorporate other strategies into the classroom discussion. For example:

- Tape relevant and strong sections on cassettes for groups or individuals to enjoy.
- Pair students so that a more powerful reader and a weaker one take turns reading a section to each other.
- Allow students to time themselves as they read a specific portion of a book. Have them time themselves at different sessions and record their progress.

4. Hold a class discussion in which each student discusses his or her favorite scene. Divide the class into groups according to their favorite part. Create a class mural on which each group draws a picture showing the part of the story they selected. The scenes should be drawn sequentially according to the plot so the completed mural is a pictorial representation of the book.
5. Ask the students to develop creative "what if" questions and to suggest read-aloud books to help answer the questions. For example, "What if you could be any animal for a week, what animal would you be?" Suggested read-aloud books might include *Just So Stories* or *The Jungle Book,* by Rudyard Kipling, Jan Brett's *The Mitten,* or Patrick J. Lewis's *A Hippopotamusn't.*
6. Audio tape or video tape stories that are read aloud to enable students who are absent to share the story. A classroom library of read-aloud tapes could be developed for students to check out.

Assessing the Read-Aloud Program

To determine the effectiveness or enjoyment level of your read-aloud program ask yourself the following questions.

1. Given a choice of activities, do students select reading aloud?
2. As an audience, do they appear interested?
3. When students read aloud, do they model good read-aloud techniques?
4. Are the students able to discuss and interact with the read-aloud selections?
5. Are students motivated to reread selections that are read aloud?
6. Do students seem interested in recommending books for reading aloud?
7. When given the opportunity, do students want to read aloud to other classes or their own class?

Ask students to list the five (in priority) reading-type activities done at school that they enjoy most. Check to see how many students include read-aloud in the list.

Students can also periodically complete the Read-Aloud Evaluation Form on page 175 after a read-aloud session. This form is short enough that it is not seen as another book report.

Suggested Read-Aloud Books

The bibliography to this chapter lists suggested read-aloud books from each genre. Many of these books were selected because they are children's classics and students continually enjoy them. Others were selected because they appeared on such lists as "Children's Choices: Teaching with Books Children Like," published annually in *The Reading Teacher* by the International Reading Association. Others appear because they are award-winning books. Finally, careful consideration was given to including multicultural books.

Children's Literature

*Cited in text

Picture Books

Adler, David A. *A Picture Book of Hanukkah.* Illustrated by Linda Heller. Holiday, 1982. (Grades K–2)

Ahlberg, Janet, and Allan Ahlberg. *The Jolly Postman.* Little, Brown, 1989. (Grades K–3)

*Akerman, Karen. *Song and Dance Man.* Illustrated by Stephen Gammell. Knopf, 1991. (Grades 1–3)

Alexander, Lloyd. *The Fortune-Tellers.* Illustrated by Trina Schart Hyman. Dutton, 1992. (Grades pre-K–3)

Aliki. *My Hands.* Crowell, 1990. (Grades K–1)

READ-ALOUD EVALUATION FORM

Student's name: _____

Date: _____

Title: _____

Author: _____

The part I enjoyed most was when _____

_____

_____

_____

_____

The part I enjoyed least was when _____

_____

_____

_____

_____

On a scale of 1 to 5 (5 meaning you loved it and 1 meaning you

didn't enjoy it at all), I would rate the selection a _____ .

Allard, Harry. *Miss Nelson Is Missing!* Illustrated by James Marshall. Houghton Mifflin, 1977. (Grades 2–5)

*Andersen, Hans Christian. *The Ugly Duckling.* Illustrated by Alan Mark. Translated by Anthea Bell. Picture Book Studios, 1989. (Grades 1–4)

Arnold, Tedd. *The Signmaker's Assistant.* Dial, 1992. (Grades K–3)

Ashforth, Camilla. *Horatio's Bed.* Candlewick, 1992. (Grades pre-K+)

Aylesworth, Jim. *Old Black Fly.* Illustrated by Stephen Gammell. Holt, 1992. (Grades pre-K–2)

Bemmelmans, Ludwig. *Madeline.* Viking, 1962. (Grades K–3)

*Brett, Jan. *The Mitten.* Putnam, 1989. (Grades pre-K–1)

———. *Trouble with Trolls.* Putnam, 1992. (Grades pre-K–3)

Bunting, Eve. *Fly Away Home.* Illustrated by Ronald Himler. Clarion, 1991. (Grades pre-K–2)

Butler, Stephen. *Henny Penny.* Tambourine, 1991. (Grades K–3)

Calmenson, Stephanie. *The Principal's New Clothes.* Illustrated by Denise Brunkus. Scholastic, 1989. (Grades K–4)

*Carle, Eric. *Have You Seen My Cat?* Picture Book Studio, 1987. (Grades K–3)

*———. *The Very Busy Spider.* Philomel, 1984 (Grades K–3)

———. *The Very Hungry Caterpillar.* World, 1968. (Grades K–2)

*———. *The Very Quiet Cricket.* Philomel, 1990. (Grades K–3)

Carlstrom, Nancy White. *Blow Me a Kiss, Miss Lily.* Illustrated by Amy Schwartz. Harper, 1990. (Grades K–2)

*Cherry, Lynn. *The Great Kapok Tree: A Tale of the Amazon Rain Forest.* Harcourt, 1990. (Grades 1–5)

Christiansen, Candace. *Calico and Tin Horns.* Illustrated by Thomas Locker. Dial, 1992. (Grades 1–3)

Cooney, Barbara. *Hattie and the Wild Waves.* Puffin, 1993. (Grades K–3)

———. *Miss Rumphius.* Puffin, 1985. (Grades K–3)

Cooper, Helen. *The Bear under the Stairs.* Dial, 1993. (Grades pre-S–2)

Crews, Donald. *Short Cut.* Greenwillow, 1993. (Grades K–3)

de Paola, Tomie. *Jamie O'Rourke and the Big Potato.* Putnam/Whitebird, 1992. (Grades pre-K–3)

———. *Nana Upstairs, Nana Downstairs.* Penguin, 1978. (Grades 2–4)

de Regniers, Beatrice S. *May I Bring A Friend?* Illustrated by Beni Montresor. Atheneum, 1964. (Grades K–3)

Dooley, Noah. *Everybody Cooks Rice.* Illustrated by Peter J. Thornton. Carolrhoda, 1991. (Grades K–3)

Dorros, Arthur. *Abuela.* Illustrated by Elisa Kleven. Dutton, 1991. (Grades K–3)

Drescher, Joan. *The Birth-Order Blues.* Viking, 1993. (Grades pre-S–3)

Flack, Marjorie. *Ask Mr. Bear.* Macmillan, 1968. (Grades K–1)

Fleming, Denise. *Lunch.* Holt, 1992. (Grades pre-K–2)

Foreman, Michael. *Jack's Fantastic Voyage.* Harcourt Brace Jovanovich, 1992. (Grades K–3)

Freeman, Don. *Corduroy.* Viking, 1968. (Grades K–2)

———. *Dandelion.* Viking, 1964. (Grades K–2)

Fox, Mem. *Possum Magic.* Illustrated by Julie Uwas. Harcourt, 1990. (Grades 1–3)

Gag, Wanda. *Millions of Cats.* Coward-McCann, 1928. (Grades K–2)

Geisert, Arthur. *Pigs from 1 to 10.* Houghton, 1992. (Grades K–2)

Greene, Carol. *The Old Ladies Who Liked Cats.* Illustrated by Loretta Krupinski. Harper-Collins. (Grades K–3)

Greenfield, Eloise. *Nathaniel Talking.* Illustrated by Jan Spivey Gilchrist. Black Butterfly, 1989. (Grades 1–4)

Hall, Donald. *Ox-Cart Man.* Illustrated by Barbara Cooney. Viking, 1979. (Grades 2–4)

Hamilton, Virginia. *The All Jadhu Storybook.* Illustrated by Barry Moser. Harcourt, 1991. (Grades 2–4)

Hirschi, Ron. *Hungry Little Frog.* Photos by Dwight Kuhn. Cobblehill, 1992. (Grades pre-K–2)

Houston, Gloria. *My Great-Aunt Arizona.* Illustrated by Susan Condie Lamb. Harper-Collins, 1992. (Grades 1–4)

Johnston, Tony, and Warren Ludwig. *The Cowboy and the Black-Eyed Pea.* Putnam, 1992. (Grades pre-K–3)

Kalman, Maira. *Max Makes a Million.* Viking, 1990. (Grades 2–4)

Kantrowitz, Mildred. *Maxie.* Illustrated by Emily A. McCully. Parents, 1970. (Grades 2–4)

*Keats, Ezra Jack. *Hi Cat!* Macmillan, 1969. (Grades 1–3)

*———. *Peter's Chair.* Harper, 1967. (Grades 1–3)

*———. *The Snowy Day*. Viking, 1962. (Grades K–1)

*Kipling, Rudyard. *The Jungle Book*. Illustrated by Fritz Eichenberg. Grosset, 1950. (Grades K–3)

*———. *Just So Stories*. Woodcuts by David Frampton. HarperCollins, 1991. (K–6)

Kraus, Robert. *Leo the Late Bloomer*. Illustrated by Jose and Ariane Aruego. Thomas Y. Crowell, 1971. (Grades 2–4)

Kroll, Virginia. *Masai and I*. Illustrated by Nancy Carpenter. Four Winds, 1992. (Grades K–2)

Marshall, James. *The Cut-Ups Carry On*. Puffin, 1993. (Grades pre-S–3)

———. *The Cut-Ups Crack Up*. Viking, 1992. (Grades pre-K–3)

Martin, Bill Jr. *Brown Bear, Brown Bear*. Holt, Rinehart & Winston, 1983. (Grades K–2)

*McCloskey, Robert. *Make Way for Ducklings*. Viking, 1941. (Grades K–6)

McCully, Emily Arnold. *Mirette on the High Wire*. Putnam, 1992. (Grades pre-K–3)

McKissack, Pat. *A Million Fish . . . More or Less*. Illustrated by Dena Schutzer. Knopf, 1992. (Grades pre-K–3)

Moore, Elaine. *Grandma's House*. Illustrated by Elsie Primavera. Lothrop, 1985. (Grades K–3)

Mora, Pat. *A Birthday Basket for Tia*. Illustrated by Cecily Lang. Macmillan, 1992. (Grades pre-K–1)

Moss, Marissa. *After-School Monster*. Puffin, 1993. (Grades pre-S–3)

Musgrove, Margaret. *Ashanti to Zulu: African Traditions*. Illustrated by Leo and Diane Dillon. Dial, 1976. (Grades 3–6)

Ness, Evaline. *Sam, Bangs and Moonshine*. Holt, Rinehart & Winston, 1966. (Grades 2–4)

Novak, Matt. *Elmer Blunt's Open House*. Orchard, 1992. (Grades pre-K–1)

Numeroff, Laura. *If You Give a Mouse a Cookie*. Illustrated by Felicia Bond. Harper, 1985. (Grades K–2)

———. *If You Give a Moose a Muffin*. Illustrated by Felicia Bond. HarperCollins, 1991. (Grades K–2)

Paulsen, Gary. *The Haymeadow*. Illustrated by Ruth Wright Paulsen. Delacorte, 1992. (Grades 5–8)

Polacco, Patricia. *Picnic at Mudsock Meadow*. Putnam, 1992. (Grades pre-K–3)

Ringgold, Faith. *Tar Beach*. Crown, 1991. (Grades K–3)

Scieszka, Jon, and Lane Smith. *Stinky Cheese Man and Other Fairly Stupid Tales*. Viking, 1992. (Grades 1–3)

Seattle, Chief. *Brother Eagle, Sister Sky*. Illustrated by Susan Jeffers. Dial, 1991. (Grades K–4)

Seuss, Dr. [Theodor S. Geisel, pseud.]. *The Cat in the Hat*. Random House, 1957. (Grades K–3)

Sierra, Judy. *The Elephant's Wrestling Match*. Illustrated by Brian Pinkney. Lodestar, 1992. (Grades K–3)

Steig, William. *Doctor De Soto*. Farrar, Straus & Giroux, 1980. (Grades 1–3)

Stevenson, James. *That Dreadful Day*. Greenwillow, 1985. (Grades 1–3)

Stow, Jenny. *The House that Jack Built*. Puffin, 1993. (Grades pre-S–2)

Van Allsburg, Chris. *The Polar Express*. Houghton Mifflin, 1985. (Grades K+)

———. *The Widow's Broom*. Houghton Mifflin, 1992. (Grades K–3)

Viorst, Judith. *Alexander and the Terrible, Horrible, No Good, Very Bad Day*. Illustrated by Ray Cruz. Atheneum, 1972. (Grades 1–6)

Waber, Bernard. *Ira Sleeps Over*. Houghton Mifflin, 1972. (Grades 1–3)

Waddell, Martin. *Can't You Sleep, Little Bear?* Illustrated by Barbara Firth. Candlewick, 1992. (Grades pre-K+)

————. *Farmer Duck.* Illustrated by Helen Oxenbury. Candlewick, 1992. (Grades pre-K–2)

————. *Owl Babies.* Illustrated by Patrick Benson. Candlewick, 1992. (Grades pre-K+)

Wells, Rosemary. *Watch Where You Go.* Greenwillow, 1990. (Grades K–1)

*Wild, Margaret. *The Very Best of Friends.* Illustrated by Julie Vivas. Harcourt, 1990. (Grades K–2)

Williams, Margery. *The Velveteen Rabbit.* Illustrated by William Nicholson. Doubleday, 1958. (Grades 2–4)

Wood, Rosemary. *The Napping House.* Illustrated by Don Wood. Harcourt, 1984. (Grades K–2)

Yacowitz, Caryn. *The Jade Stone.* Illustrated by Ju-Hong Chen. Holiday, 1992. (Grades pre-K–3)

Yolen, Jane. *Owl Moon.* Illustrated by John Schoenheir. Philomel, 1987. (Grades 1–3)

Young, Ed. *Seven Blind Mice.* Philomel, 1992. (Grades pre-K–6)

Zion, Gene. *Harry, the Dirty Dog.* Illustrated by Margaret Bloy Graham. Harper & Row, 1956. (Grades K–3)

Zolotow, Charlotte. *Mr. Rabbit and the Lovely Present.* Illustrated by Maurice Sendak. Harper & Row, 1962. (Grades K–3)

————. *My Grandson Lew.* Illustrated by William Pene du Bois. Harper & Row, 1972. (Grades K–3)

Realistic Fiction

Burch, Robert. *Queeny Peavy.* Illustrated by Jerry Lazare. Viking, 1966. (Grades 5–6)

Byars, Betsy C. *The Summer of the Swans.* Illustrated by Ted CoConis. Viking, 1970. (Grades 5–6)

Cleary, Beverly. *Dear Mr. Henshaw.* Illustrated by Paul O. Zelensky. Morrow, 1983. (Grades 5–6)

Cohen, Barbara. *Thank You, Jackie Robinson.* Illustrated by Richard Caffari. Lothrop, 1974. (Grades 4–6)

Cooper, Ilene. *Seeing Red.* Puffin, 1993. (Grades 3–6)

*Estes, Eleanor. *The Hundred Dresses.* Illustrated by Louis Slobodkin. Harcourt Brace Jovanovich, 1942. (Grades 3–6)

*Hurwitz, Johanna. *Class President.* Scholastic, 1990. (Grades 3–5)

————. *Russell and Elisa.* Morrow, 1989. (Grades 1–4)

Levinson, Nancy Smiler. *Sweet Notes, Sour Notes.* Illustrated by Beth Peck. Lodestar, 1993. (Grades 2–5)

Lowry, Lois. *Attaboy, Sam!* Illustrated by Diane de Groat. Houghton, 1992. (Grades 2–6)

Manes, Stephen. *Make Four Million Dollar$ by Next Thur$day!* Illustrated by George Ulrich. Bantam, 1991. (Grades 3–6)

Naylor, Phyllis Reynolds. *Shiloh.* Atheneum, 1991. (Grades 3–6)

Paterson, Katherine. *Bridge to Terabithia.* Illustrated by Donna Diamond. Thomas Y. Crowell, 1977. (Grades 5–6)

Peters, Julie Anne. *The Stinky Sneakers Contest.* Illustrated by Cat Bowman Smith. Joy Street/Little, Brown, 1992. (Grades 2–5)

Rawls, Wilson. *Where the Red Fern Grows.* Doubleday, 1961. (Grades 4–6)

Saint-Exupery, Antoine. *The Little Prince.* Translated by Katherine Woods. Harcourt Brace Jovanovich, 1943. (Grades 2–4)

Snyder, Zilpha K. *Libby on Wednesday.* Delacorte, 1990. (Grades 4–6)

Sperry, Armstrong. *Call It Courage.* Macmillan, 1968. (Grades 4–6)

*Stevenson, Robert Louis. *Treasure Island.* Illustrated by N. C. Wyeth. Scribner's, 1981 (1883). (Grades 3–5)

Walter, Mildred Pitts. *Justin and the Best Biscuits in the World.* Illustrated by Catherine Stock. Lothrop, 1986. (Grades 3–6)

Yep, Laurence. *Child of the Owl.* Harper & Row, 1971. (Grades K–3)

Historical Fiction

Baylis-White, Mary. *Sheltering Rebecca.* Lodestar, 1993. (Grades 3–6)

Benchley, Nathaniel. *Sam the Minuteman.* Harper & Row, 1972. (Grades 4–5)

Brink, Carol R. *Caddie Woodlawn.* Illustrated by Kate Seredy. Macmillan, 1936. (Grades 3–6)

Dalgliesh, Alice. *The Courage of Sarah Noble.* Illustrated by Leonard Weisgard. Scribner's, 1954. (Grades 2–4)

Forbes, Esther. *Johnny Tremain.* Illustrated by Lynn Ward. Houghton Mifflin, 1946. (Grades 4–8)

Fox, Paula. *Slave Dancer.* Illustrated by Eros Keith. Bradbury, 1973. (Grades 2–4)

Hamilton, Virginia. *The Bells of Christmas.* Illustrated by Lambert Davis. Harcourt, 1989. (Grades 3–6)

Harvey, Brett. *Cassie's Journey: Going West in the 1860s.* Illustrated by Deborah Kogan Ray. Holiday, 1988. (Grades 2–4)

Holling, Holling C. *Paddle-to-the-Sea.* Houghton Mifflin, 1941. (Grades 5–6)

Lobel, Arnold. *On the Day Peter Stuyvesant Sailed to Town.* Harper & Row, 1981. (Grades 1–4)

Lowry, Lois. *Number the Stars.* Houghton, 1989. (Grades 3–7)

MacLachlan, Patricia. *Sarah, Plain and Tall.* Harper & Row, 1985. (Grades 4–6)

O'Dell, Scott. *Island of the Blue Dolphins.* Houghton Mifflin, 1960. (Grades 5–6)

*Petry, Ann. *Harriet Tubman: Conductor on the Underground Railroad.* Thomas Y. Crowell, 1955. (Grades 6–10)

Reeder, Carolyn. *Shades of Gray.* Macmillan, 1989. (Grades 4–7)

*Taylor, Mildred. *The Friendship.* Illustrated by Max Ginsburg. Dial, 1987. (Grades 3–5)

*Wilder, Laura Ingalls. *Little House in the Big Woods.* Illustrated by Garth Williams. Harper & Row, 1953. (Grades 2–4)

Wisler, Clifton G. *Jericho's Journey.* Lodestar, 1993. (Grades 5–9)

Fantasy/Science Fiction

Alexander, Lloyd. *The Remarkable Journey of Prince Jen.* Dutton, 1991. (Grades 5+)

Andersen, Hans Christian. *The Emperor's New Clothes.* Illustrated by Virginia Lee Burton. Houghton Mifflin, 1949. (Grades 3–6)

*Babbitt, Natalie. *Tuck Everlasting.* Farrar, Straus & Giroux, 1975. (Grades 5–6)

Carroll, Lewis. *Alice's Adventures in Wonderland.* Macmillan, 1963. (Grades K–6)

Dahl, Roald. *Matilda.* Illustrated by Quentin Blake. Viking, 1988. (Grades 3–6)

Fleischman, Sid. *The Midnight Horse.* Illustrated by Peter Sis. Greenwillow, 1990. (Grades 3–6)

Grahame, Kenneth. *The Wind in the Willows.* Illustrated by Beverly Gooding. Scribner's, 1982. (Grades 4–6)

*Kipling, Rudyard. *Just So Stories.* Illustrated by Etienne Delessert. Doubleday, 1972. (Grades K–6)

Lawson, Robert. *Rabbit Hill.* Viking, 1944. (Grades K–3)

L'Engle, Madeline. *A Wrinkle in Time.* Farrar, Straus & Giroux, 1962. (Grades 4–6)

Lewis, C. S. *The Lion, the Witch, and the Wardrobe.* Illustrated by Pauline Baynes. Macmillan, 1961. (Grades 4–6)

London, Jonathan. *Into This Night We Are Rising.* Illustrated by G. Brian Karas. Viking, 1993. (Grades pre-S–3)

McGowen, Tom. *A Question of Magic.* Lodestar, 1993. (Grades 5–9)

Milne, A. A. *Winnie the Pooh.* Illustrated by Earnest Shepard. Dutton, 1926. (Grades K–4)

Norton, Mary. *The Borrowers.* Illustrated by Beth and Joe Krush. Harcourt Brace Jovanovich, 1963. (Grades 4–6)

Scieszka, Jon. *The Not-So-Jolly Roger.* Puffin, 1993. (Grades 2–5)

Tolkien, J. R. R. *The Hobbit.* Houghton Mifflin, 1938. (Grades 1–3)

White, E. B. *Charlotte's Web.* Illustrated by Garth Williams. Harper & Row, 1952. (Grades 2–6)

Folklore

Aardema, Verna, reteller. *Traveling to Tondo: A Tale of the Nkundo of Zaire.* Illustrated by Will Hillenbrand. Knopf, 1990. (Grades 2–4)

———. *Why Mosquitos Buzz in People's Ears: A West African Tale.* Illustrated by Leo and Diane Dillon. Dial, 1975. (Grades K–3)

Aesop. *Aesop's Fables.* Illustrated by Heide Holder. Viking, 1981. (Grades 2–6)

Asbjornsen, Peter Christian, and Jorgen E. Moe. *East of the Sun and West of the Moon and Other Tales.* Illustrated by Tom Vromay. Macmillan, 1963. (Grades 3–5)

Brown, Marcia. *Stone Soup.* Scribner's, 1947. (Grades 1–4)

D'Aulaire, Ingri, and Edgar P. D'Aulaire. *Norse Gods and Giants.* Doubleday, 1967. (Grades 3–5)

Gag, Wanda. *Tales from Grimm.* Coward-McCann, 1978. (Grades 4–6)

Galdone, Paul. *Henny Penny.* Seabury, 1968. (Grades 1–4)

———. *The Little Red Hen.* Seabury, 1974. (Grades K–2)

Grimm, Jacob, and Wilhelm Grimm. *Rapunzel.* Illustrated by Trina S. Hyman. Holiday, 1982. (Grades 2–5)

Hooks, William H. *The Ballad of Belle Dorcas.* Illustrated by Brian Pinkney. Knopf, 1990. (Grades 3–5)

Ivimey, John W. *Three Blind Mice.* Illustrated by Victoria Chess. Little, Brown, 1990. (Grades 2–4)

Mahy, Margaret. *The Seven Chinese Brothers.* Illustrated by Jean and Mon-Sien Tseng. Scholastic, 1990. (Grades 1–3)

Martin, Rafe. *The Rough-Faced Girl.* Illustrated by David Shannon. Putnam, 1992. (Grades 1–3)

Paterson, Katherine. *The Tale of the Mandarin Ducks.* Illustrated by Leo and Diane Dillon. Lodestar, 1990. (Grades 2–4)

Perrault, Charles. *Cinderella.* Illustrated by Marcia Brown. Scribner's, 1954. (Grades 1–4)

———. *Little Red Riding Hood.* Illustrated by Beni Montresor. Doubleday, 1991. (Grades 3–5)

Ross, Tony. *The Three Pigs.* Pantheon, 1983. (Grades K–2)

Stoutenburg, Adrien. *American Tall Tales.* Illustrated by Richard M. Powers. Viking, 1966. (Grades 4–6)

Wahl, Jan, reteller. *Tailypso!* Illustrated by Wil Cay. Holt, 1991. (Grades K–3)

Yacowitz, Caryn. *The Jade Stone: A Chinese Folktale.* Illustrated by Ju-Hong Chen. Holiday, 1992, (Grades K–4)

Yagawa, Sumiko. *The Crane Wife.* Translated by Katherine Paterson. Illustrated by Suekichi Akaba. Morrow, 1981. (Grades 3–5)

Young, Ed. *Lon Po Po: A Red Riding-Hood Story from China.* Philomel, 1990. (Grades K–2)

Poetry

Adoff, Arnold. *Flamboyan.* Illustrated by Karen Barbour. Harcourt, 1988. (Grades 1–6)

Benet, Rosemary, and Stephen Benet, eds. *A Book of Americans.* Holt, Rinehart & Winston, 1987. (Grades 3–6)

Booth, David, ed. *Voices on the Wind: Poems for All Seasons.* Illustrated by Michele Lemieux. Morrow, 1990. (Grades 1–6)

Brewton, Sara, and John Brewton, eds. *America Forever New: A Book of Poems.* Thomas Y. Crowell, 1968. (Grades 2–6)

Bryan, Ashley. *Turtle Knows Your Nose.* Atheneum, 1989. (Grades 1–6)

Chandra, Deborah. *Balloons and Other Poems.* Farrar, Straus & Giroux, 1990. (Grades K–3)

Clark, E. C. *I Never Saw a Purple Cow.* Little, Brown, 1991. (Grades K–3)

Cole, William. *A Book of Animal Poems.* Illustrated by Robert Andrew Parker. Viking, 1973. (Grades 2–6)

Dickinson, Emily. *I'm Nobody! Who Are You? The Poems of Emily Dickinson.* Stemmer, 1978. (Grades 5–6)

Dunning, Stephen, Edward Lueders, and Hugh Smith. *Reflections on a Gift of Watermelon Pickle and Other Modern Verses.* Scott, Foresman, 1966. (Grades 4–9)

Fisher, Aileen. *Out in the Dark and Daylight.* Illustrated by Gail Owens. Harper & Row, 1980. (Grades 2–6)

Fleischman, Paul. *Joyful Noise.* Illustrated by Eric Beddows (Charlotte Zolotow). Harper & Row, 1988. (Grades K–6)

Frank, Josette, sel. *Snow Toward Evening: A Year in a River Valley/Nature Poems.* Illustrated by Thomas Locker. Dial, 1990. (Grades 2–5)

Froman, Robert. *Seeing Things: A Book of Poems.* Thomas Y. Crowell, 1974. (Grades 4–6)

Frost, Robert, comp. *How Pleasant to Know Mr. Lear!* Holiday, 1982. (Grades 4–6)

———. *Stopping by Woods on a Snowy Evening.* Illustrated by Susan Jeffers. Dutton, 1978. (Grades 5–7)

Greenfield, Eloise. *Honey, I Love, and Other Love Poems.* Illustrated by Diane and Leo Dillon. Crowell, 1978. (Grades 1–6)

Hoberman, M. A. *Fathers, Mothers, Sisters, Brothers: A Collection of Family Poems.* Little, Brown, 1991. (Grades 1–6)

Kennedy, X. J. *Fresh Brats.* Illustrated by James Watts. Macmillan, 1990. (Grades 3–6)

Lee, Dennis. *The Ice Cream Store.* Illustrated by David McPhail. Scholastic, 1991. (Grades 1–6)

*Lewis, J. P. *A Hippopotamusn't and Other Animal Verses.* Illustrated by Victoria Chess. Dial, 1990. (Grades K–3)

Merriam, Eve. *Independent Voices.* Illustrated by Arvis Stewart. Atheneum, 1968. (Grades 1–3)

Prelutsky, Jack, ed. *For Laughing Out Loud: Poems to Tickle Your Funnybone.* Illustrated by Marjorie Priceman. Knopf, 1991. (Grades 1–6)

———. *New Kid on the Block.* Illustrated by James Stevenson. Greenwillow, 1984. (Grades 3–6)

Silverstein, Shel. *A Light in the Attic.* Harper & Row, 1991. (Grades 2–6)

———. *Where the Sidewalk Ends: Poems and Drawings.* Harper & Row, 1974. (Grades 1–6)

Sutherland, Zena, and Myra Livingston. *The Scott, Foresman Anthology of Children's Literature.* Scott, Foresman, 1987. (Grades 2–6)

Thayer, Ernest L. *Casey at the Bat.* Illustrated by Patricia Polacco. Putnam, 1988. (Grades 2–6)

Informational

Aliki. *Dinosaur Bones.* Thomas Y. Crowell, 1988. (Grades 1–3)

———. *Dinosaurs Are Different.* Thomas Y. Crowell, 1985. (Grades 1–3)

Ancona, George, and Mary Beth Ancona. *Handtalk Zoo.* Photographs by George Ancona. Four Winds, 1989. (Grades 2–4)

Anderson, LaVere. *The Story of Johnny Appleseed.* Garrard, 1974. (Grades 2–4)

Arnosky, Jim. *Secrets of a Wildlife Watcher.* Lothrop, 1983. (Grades 3–6)

Baer, Edith. *This Is the Way We Go to School: A Book About Children Around the World.* Illustrated by Steve Bjorkman. Scholastic, 1990. (Grades 1–5)

Bash, Barbara. *Tree of Life: The World of the African Baobab.* Little, Brown, 1989. (Grades 2–4)

Black, Wallace B., and Jean F. Blashfield. *Pearl Harbor!* Crestwood, 1991. (Grades 3–6)

Bunting, Eve. *The Wall.* Illustrated by Ronald Himler. Clarion, 1990. (Grades 1–3)

Cole, Joanna. *The Magic School Bus on the Ocean Floor.* Illustrated by Bruce Degen. Scholastic, 1992. (Grades 1–4)

de Paola, Tomie. *The Quicksand Book.* Holiday, 1977. (Grades 2–5)

Gibbons, Gail. *Whales.* Holiday, 1991. (Grades 1–3)

Hewett, Joan. *Hector Lives in the US Now: The Story of a Mexican American Child.* Photographs by Richard Hewett. HarperCollins, 1990. (Grades 2–5)

Isenbart, Hans-Heinrich. *A Duckling Is Born.* Photographs by Othmar Baumli. Putnam, 1981. (Grades 2–4)

Kushkin, Karla. *The Philharmonic Gets Dressed.* Illustrated by Marc Simont. Harper & Row, 1982. (Grades 2–5)

Lauber, Patricia. *Seeds: Pop Stick Glide.* Photographs by Jerome Wexler. Crown, 1981. (Grades K–3)

Paterson, Francine. *Koko's Kitten.* Photographs by Ronald H. Cohn. Scholastic, 1985. (Grades 1–3)

Sattler, Helen R. *Dinosaurs of North America.* Illustrated by Anthony Rao. Lothrop, 1984. (Grades 3–6)

Selsam, Millicent E. *Cotton.* Photographs by Jerome Wexler. Morrow, 1982. (Grades 3–5)

———. *See Through the Forest.* Harper & Row, 1956. (Grades 2–4)

Biography

*Adler, David A. *A Picture Book of Eleanor Roosevelt.* Holiday, 1991. (Grades 1–3)

Aliki. (Brandenberg). *The Many Lives of Benjamin Franklin.* Prentice-Hall, 1977. (Grades 1–3)

Anderson, Catherine Corley. *John F. Kennedy: Young People's President.* Lerner, 1991. (Grades 1–3)

Clayton, Edward. *Martin Luther King: The Peaceful Warrior,* 3rd ed. Illustrated by David Hodges. Prentice-Hall, 1968. (Grades 4–6)

Faber, Doris. *Eleanor Roosevelt: First Lady of the World.* Illustrated by Donna Ruff. Viking, 1985. (Grades 3–6)

Feinberg, Barbara S. *Franklin D. Roosevelt: Gallant President.* Lothrop, 1981. (Grades 5–6)

*Freedman, Russell. *Franklin Delano Roosevelt.* Clarion, 1990. (Grades 4–6)

———. *The Wright Brothers: How They Invented the Airplane.* Holiday, 1991. (Grades 4–7)

*Fritz, Jean. *And Then What Happened Paul Revere?* Illustrated by Margot Tomes. Coward-McCann, 1973. (Grades 3–6)

McGovern, Ann. *The Secret Soldier: The Story of Deborah Sampson.* Illustrated by Ann Grifalconi. Four Winds, 1975. (Grades 4–6)

Parks, Rosa, with James Haskins. *Rosa Parks: My Story.* Dial, 1991. (Grades 5–8)

Peet, Bill. *Bill Peet: An Autobiography.* Houghton Mifflin, 1990. (Grades 3–5)

*Petry, Ann. *Harriet Tubman: Conductor on the Underground Railroad.* Thomas Y. Crowell, 1955. (Grades 2–4)

Stanley, Fay. *The Last Princess: The Story of Princess Ka'iulani of Hawaii.* Illustrated by Diane Stanley. Four Winds, 1991. (Grades 1–4)

Syme, Ronald. *Magellan: First Around the World.* Burdett, 1983. (Grades 4–6)

van der Rol, Ruud and Rian Verhoeven. *Anne Frank: Beyond the Diary: A Photographic Remembrance.* Viking, 1993. (Grades 4–7)

Professional Resources

*Cited in text

*Allen, V. G. "Literature as a Support to Language Acquisition." In P. Rigg and V. G. Allen, eds. *When They Don't All Speak English.* National Council of Teachers of English, 1989, pp. 55–64.

*Calkins, L. M. *Living Between the Lines.* Heinemann, 1991.

*Clay, Marie. *What Did I Write?* Heinemann Educational, 1975.

*Cohen, Dorothy. "The Effect of Literature on Vocabulary and Reading Achievement." *Elementary English,* 45:209–213, 217, 1968.

*Cullinan, Bernice E., Angela Jagger, and Dorothy Strickland. "Language Expansion for Black Children in the Primary Grades: A Research Report." *Young Children,* Volume 29, 98–112, 1974.

*Durkin, Dolores. *Children Who Read Early.* Teachers' College Press, 1966.

*———. *Teaching Them to Read.* Boston: Allyn & Bacon, 1970.

*Elkind, David. "Cognitive Development and Reading." *Claremont Reading Conference Yearbook,* 38: 10–20, 1974.

*Elley, W. "Vocabulary Acquisition from Listening to Stories." *Reading Research Quarterly,* 14: 174–188, 1989.

*Elley, W. B., and F. Mangubhai. "The Impact of Reading on Second Language Learning." *Reading Research Quarterly,* 19: 53–67, 1983.

*Flood, James. "Parental Styles in Reading Episodes with Young Children." *The Reading Teacher,* 35: 864–867, 1977.

*Gordon, Ira. "Parenting, Teaching, and Child Development." *Young Children,* 31: 173–183, 1976.

*Graves, Donald. *Writing: Teachers and Children at Work.* Heinemann Educational Books, 1983.

*Harris, V. J., ed. *Teaching Multicultural Literature in Grades K–8.* Christopher-Gordon, 1992.

*Kozol, Jonathon. "Illiterate America." *Marketing News,* May 1983, p. 18.

*Martinez, M., and W. H. Teale. "Reading in a Kindergarten Classroom Library." *The Reading Teacher*, 41: 568–572, 1988.

*Noyce, R. M., and J. F. Christine. *Integrating Reading and Writing Instruction*. Allyn & Bacon, 1989.

*Olson, D. "From Utterance to Text: The Bias of Language in Speech and Writing." *Harvard Educational Review*, 47: 257–281, 1977.

*Rosen, Nancy L. "Research Currents: Rethinking Literature and Literacy." *Language Arts*, 64: 90–107, 1987.

*Sakamoto, T. "Beginning Reading in Japan." Paper presented at the annual meeting of the International Reading Association, Miami, May 1977.

*Smith, Frank. "Making Sense of Reading and Reading Instruction." *Harvard Educational Review*, 47: 386–395, 1977.

*———. *Writing and the Writer*. Holt, 1982.

*Sulzby, Elizabeth. "Children's Emergent Reading of Favorite Story Books." *Reading Research Quarterly*, 20: 458–481, 1985.

*Tiedt, I. *Reading/Thinking/Writing: A Holistic Language and Literacy Program for the K–8 Classroom*. Allyn & Bacon, 1989.

*Trelease, Jim. *The New Read Aloud Handbook*. Penguin, 1989.

*Wells, Gordon. *The Mean Maker: Children Learning Language and Using Language to Learn*. Heinemann, 1986.

CHAPTER 5

The Shared Reading Experience

Very closely related to the read-aloud program is a classroom version of the bedtime story, called the shared reading experience. Just as a parent shares a book with a child at bedtime, a teacher shares a book with a group of children. This technique is as effective with older children as it is with primary-aged children. In shared reading, the teacher and children share in the reading and rereading of books that include favorite stories, rhymes, songs, chants, and poems.

The Importance of the Shared Reading Experience

Shared reading is a social activity in which children, both young and old, share well-written books and poetry with other readers or listeners. Holdaway (1979, 1982) is credited with discovering the effectiveness of the shared reading experience as a result of his investigation into the alarming increase of illiteracy in New Zealand. Instead of looking at what caused readers to fail, Holdaway and a team of teachers began to look at what was different about successful readers. They found that the most successful readers came from homes in which books, reading, and bedtime stories were part of their everyday lives. Holdaway's team studied the bedtime story setting to find out what gave these children such an advantage. They found that during the bedtime story, the reader usually snuggled close to the child as the story was being read. When the story was completed, the child typically asked the reader to read it again. As the reader read the same story over and over again, night after night, the child learned what the story said. When the reader skipped a few pages, the child insisted that the reader read the whole story exactly as written. As the reader read the story, the child often turned the pages, becoming familiar with the illustrations and learning that the book had a top and a bottom, that words were read from left to right, and that print represented what was being read. Often, as the reader pointed to the words being read, the child repeated the words he or she recognized. From these investigations, Holdaway's team found that many children actually learned to read during the bedtime story time, even though the reader made no conscious effort to teach reading. In fact, the reader was usually not trained in methods of teaching reading. The child learned to read naturally.

Research from several countries supports the belief that children can learn to read naturally through a literature-based language arts program. Doake (1979), Durkin (1966), and Smith (1971) found that preschool children learned to read without formalized reading instruction, by being read to. Clay (1977) and Sulzby (1985) found that strategies used in the shared reading experience that were effective in teaching reading to preschoolers were also valuable for classroom use. Butler (1985) reported that children in Australia and New Zealand have been taught to read using big books through shared reading. Thus, the use of big books for shared reading is increasing. This approach is especially effective with young children.

Shared reading is helpful for all readers, but it is particularly helpful for the emergent readers, those learning English as a second language, and less able readers, because it shows them how to read. Shared reading should be an enjoyable, relaxed, cooperative activity that takes place in a nonthreatening, supportive atmosphere where it is okay to make a mistake and take risks (Morrow, 1989).

It is no surprise that children learn to read when the shared reading experience is used, since many important beginning reading skills are introduced during the process. Children learn that there is a connection between the written and spoken forms of language. Because they repeatedly hear the words and see the print, they begin to associate letters and sounds. Many children figure out the code by themselves. In addition, they learn that reading is a pleasurable and enjoyable activity, the ultimate goal of any reading program.

Approaches to Shared Reading

There are different approaches to shared reading: shared book experience, shared poetry reading, paired/buddy reading, and literature circles. One of the most popular approaches is the shared book experience, in which a big book is often used. This chapter deals primarily with the shared book experience and shared poetry reading, although many of the guidelines and activities can be adapted to other approaches to shared reading. Paired reading and literature circles are discussed in Chapters 6 and 9, respectively.

The Shared Book Experience

Selecting Books for the Shared Book Experience

Choosing the right book for the shared book experience is crucial. It is much easier to select a book for a bedtime story, when you can easily cater to the in-

dividual child's preference, than for a classroom shared book experience, when you have to select a book that appeals to every child.

Books for the shared book experience are selected in much the same manner as for reading aloud, but there are a few aspects of a story that are particularly important for a successful shared book experience:

1. Select books that are predictable, whose outcome can be imagined very easily from the reading. This allows children, after reading a few pages, to tell what they think will happen next or how the story will end. For example, in *Oh, A-Hunting We Will Go,* after you have read "Oh, a-hunting we will go, a-hunting we will go; we'll catch a snake and put him in a cake," the children are ready to call out "house" when you read, "Oh, a-hunting we will go, a-hunting we will go; we'll catch a mouse and put him in a _____." A similar technique can be used with the book *Danger.* After you have read a few pages, such as "Look out for the chairs. They are full of bears. Look out for the cakes. They are full of snakes," the children are ready to call out "witches" when you read, "Look out for ditches. They are full of _____." In both situations, the children use meaning clues as well as rhyming clues to predict words and happenings.

2. Select books that are repetitious, whose patterns repeat over and over again. Repetition allows children to participate actively by joining in a chant or chorus that repeats itself frequently. For example, in *The Very Busy Spider,* the sentence pattern "The spider didn't answer. She was very busy spinning her web" is repeated on nearly every other page. Therefore, when you come to this repeated phrase, the children join in. This kind of repetition is important when learning to read, because words need to be repeated many times before they actually become part of a child's reading vocabulary. Repeating the words in a shared reading experience is much more interesting and fun than learning them from a list on the chalkboard.

3. Select books that contain rich, descriptive, and memorable language with lots of rhythm and rhyme. For example, in *The Night Train,* the words sound like a train making its way along the track: "They go along the hallway, Ticketty-tat, Ticketty-tat. They go along the hallway, Tania and Jessie and Cat."

4. Select books that reflect warmth, humor, and fun. Children enjoy *A Monster Sandwich* because it is fun to see the huge amounts of things being put on the sandwich. For example, whole heads of lettuce are used instead of a single piece of lettuce. Children have fun imagining what a big sandwich like this would look like.

5. Children love nonsensical words and lines, such as those in *Mrs. Wishy-Washy.* They love repeating "In the tub you go . . . wishy-washy, wishy-washy."

6. Select books with attractive, appropriate illustrations that enhance the text. For example, in *The Enormous Watermelon,* two full pages reveal an *enormous* watermelon. Children squeal with delight at the sight of this enormous watermelon. What a wonderful way to exhibit what *enormous* means!

7. Select books that have characters and situations with which children can identify. As *In a Dark, Dark Woods* is read, children often identify with darkness and their own scary fantasies and dreams, the darkness of their rooms, and the darkness of outside. Therefore, the children can especially relate to the last line of the book, "And in the dark, dark box, THERE WAS A GHOST."

8. Select books that have an active story line. For example, in *Three Little Ducks* the ducks "paddle, paddle, paddle," "waddle, waddle, waddle," and "gobble, gobble, gobble." All of these actions are enjoyable to read about or act out.

Guidelines for Using Big Books

According to Butler (1987), the secret to success with the shared book experiences is creating the right environment, one in which a trusting, exciting, and secure feeling is established. The environment must be free of competition, criticism, and constant correction. The children and teacher usually develop a feeling of intimacy much like that established during bedtime stories. Therefore, when conducting a shared book experience in a classroom setting, it is important to consider the following guidelines:

1. Seat the children on the floor as close to you as possible so that everyone can see the illustrations and text. It is best if the big book is placed on an easel so you can conveniently turn the pages and point to the words as it is read. It may be desirable to have a student turn the pages.

2. Introduce the story by discussing the front cover illustration, the title, any connections with past experiences, and so on. The introduction should be brief. For example, to introduce Ezra Jack Keats's *The Snowy Day*, you

might ask: What is snow like? How does it feel? Have you ever played in the snow? If not, what do you think it would be like to play in the snow? The aim of the introduction is to whet the listeners' appetite so they are interested in hearing what the story is about.

3. Read the story. The first time, read the story for pure enjoyment and pleasure; subsequent readings should provide a means for learning to read. Since many teachers find it difficult to point to the words while reading with expression, that can come with future readings. You may want to use a pointer so the children can see exactly what is being read. As you reread the big book, point to the words and invite the children to participate. They can repeat a familiar refrain or chant or make simple hand actions or appropriate sound effects. As you point to the words, they see that print follows certain conventions, and they begin to recognize sound–symbol relationships and words.

4. Following the initial reading, discuss the illustrations, characters, or favorite part of the book. At this point the discussion should flow naturally. Making connections with the author's intended meaning or testing for comprehension is inappropriate. You will return to this story many times; therefore, this initial discussion should be brief, ending before the children lose interest.

5. After the initial or subsequent rereadings of the big book, conduct appropriate follow-up activities. These activities may include independent reading of the story, dramatization, art, music, and writing. Of all the follow-up activities, independent reading is most important, because it allows the children to become part of a reading community. Small versions of big books are available for independent reading. These should be made readily available to the children so they can reread their favorite books as often as possible. The ultimate goal of independent reading is for the children to learn to read by reading.

6. During and after the shared book experience, evaluate each student's progress. Once a student has accomplished a particular skill, record it on the Shared Reading Observation Sheet (see page 192).

Activities for the Shared Book Experience

There are many stimulating and useful follow-up activities to extend the shared book experience, either using existing text or creating new big books. You may need to provide both independent and group activities, depending on the students' needs.

The following activities use existing text to teach reading skills.

1. After you have read the text to the students at least two or three times, use the popular cloze technique to develop word recognition skills. Place blank pieces of paper over key words in the selection. Then reread the text, stopping at each blank and allowing the children to supply the missing word.

SHARED READING OBSERVATION SHEET

Name of Students

Does the student . . .

1. Show interest in the story?

2. Become actively involved?

3. Participate in responses to key words or phrases?

4. Participate in predicting happenings?

5. React appropriately to the emotions conveyed?

6. Demonstrate curiosity about the story's characters and plot?

7. Take part in discussions before or after the story is read?

8. Show interest in reading the book independently?

9. Show a desire to read and reread the book?

10. Transfer ideas from the story to his or her own writing?

Another way to use the cloze technique is to write the words from a page of the text on individual cards. For example, using *Bedtime for Francis*, write the following words on the cards:

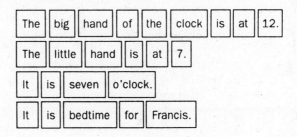

Tape the word cards on the chalkboard, omitting some of the words, as follows:

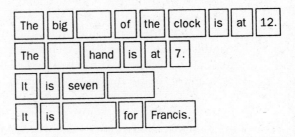

Have the students read the paragraph, supplying the missing words as they read. The missing words can then be taped to the chalkboard and the paragraph reread.

2. Make up new stories by replacing characters and actions in a book you have read. For example, *Woosh* reads "I had a little dog. His name was Dandy. His tail was long. And his legs were bandy." Help the students make innovations in the text that may read something like: "I had a little cat. His name was Tingle. He had a bell around his neck. It went jingle, jingle." This is fun to do and extends the use of available books. In addition, children are being creative as they develop skills necessary to learn to read.

3. Using the vocabulary words from a big book story, make word cards on 5×8-inch index cards. Line up the cards along the chalkboard tray. Display the big book pages so everyone can see them. Direct a student to select a word from the tray and then find the same word in the story. This activity can be used as a readiness activity to reinforce visual discrimination skills or with beginning readers to reinforce word recognition. Students can also make their own word cards to create individual word banks.

4. Discuss sentences by pointing out that sentences begin with capital letters and have punctuation marks at the end. Discuss the different punctuation marks, explaining the purpose of each. While you read the text aloud and the students follow along, they have an opportunity to observe that punctuation marks help guide reading. As you draw attention to the functions of the punctuation marks, the students will begin to make the connection between reading and writing. This will help guide them in their reading and help them with their writing. For example, in *The Big Toe*, when you read the line, "Then something by the gate said, 'Who's got my big toe?'" you can point out that the line "Who's got my big toe?" is in quotation marks to indicate that someone is speaking. As a result, students may transfer this knowledge to the works they write.

5. Present a play based on a story. This is excellent motivation for getting students to read and reread a story. They can make costumes, masks, and props. *The Farm Concert* is an excellent book to act out. Have the students help make masks for a farmer, dog, duck, frog, pig, and sheep. Choose a student to be the farmer and other students or groups of students to represent the animals. You and the remaining students can read the story as each animal character joins in as the text is being read. For example, when the character of the cow says "Moo-moo," the group reads "went the cow."

6. Invite the students to identify repetitive lines and indicate which words are the same. Discuss how some words sound the same but look different, such as *heard* and *herd* or *hear* and *here.* Discuss the concept of rhyming words. Select from the story words that rhyme. Encourage the students to think of other words to rhyme with these words.

7. Once the students are familiar with the story, select a page or two and copy them, leaving spaces where they can add their own words, phrases, or lines. Read the story substituting the words, phrases, or lines suggested by the students. Discuss the differences and similarities between their version of the story and the original version.

8. Using a big book such as *Bedtime for Francis,* discuss the idea of selecting symbols to represent each of the characters. For example, Francis may be a circle, Mother Bear may be a triangle, and Father Bear may be a square. Allow the students to create the symbols from flannel and then retell the story on a flannel board using these symbols. This activity will also aid in the development of abstract thinking skills.

9. Introduce the students to word attack skills. It is important that they know how to approach an unfamiliar word. They can be introduced to the use of context clues, phonic analysis, structural analysis, and syllabication. For example, *caterpillar* can be divided into smaller units (syllables). Once the word is divided into syllables, the reader can pronounce each small unit and then finally put it together to pronounce the whole word.

Shared Poetry Reading

The shared poetry reading is very similar to the shared book experience with regard to the importance and effectiveness of exposing children to the written word. Most of the guidelines for selecting books for the shared book experience apply to selecting poetry for shared poetry reading. Poems selected should be appropriate for the students' age, interests, and experiences. They should include the elements of good poetry, such as rhythm, rhyme, imagery, and figurative language.

Poetry is particularly effective for shared reading because the language is very descriptive and the rhythmic sounds and patterns make poems perfect for chanting. Imagine children's joy as they share the reading of Rhoda Bacmeister's "Galoshes" or Eloise Greenfield's "Rope Rhyme."

Poetry is also highly desirable for shared reading because the selections are usually relatively short and can be easily enlarged or duplicated for individual copies. Poetry can be used without investing in expensive commercial materials.

Using poetry for shared reading also provides an exciting, interesting way to introduce students to a variety of poems. They will become engaged in a language-rich experience that can be highly motivating and can increase their desire to read poetry.

Creating Big Books

Big books, as well as smaller versions, are commercially available, but the lack of availability of specific titles and the cost may induce you to make your own big books. Students can help in the production process. This involvement stimulates interest in reading and fosters a feeling of ownership and pride in the product. There are several different ways to make big books. *Making and Using Big Books,* by Gail Herald-Taylor, may be a useful resource.

The first step is to select a favorite story, perhaps one students have rated highly in read-aloud sessions. Copy each page of the text onto blank pieces of paper approximately 25×15 inches. An older student can help with this. The text must be duplicated exactly and the print must be large enough for a group of children to see. Once the text is copied, reread the story and discuss possible illustrations. Give each student (or pair of students) one page of the text to illustrate. Circulate while the illustrations are being created and ask relevant questions to ensure that the pictures adequately illustrate the text. When the illustrations are completed, bring the children together as a group and display the pages of illustrated text. As a group, decide on the correct sequence of the pages. Once the sequence coincides with the order of the original text, display the pages along the chalkboard, bulletin board, or a clothesline for a time. This gives the children an opportunity to read and reread the story. Add a cover and title page and bind the pages, using a heavy-duty stapler, metal rings, or heavy stitching (dental floss works well). You may want to reinforce the spine of the book with heavy book-binding tape. A nice addition to a student-created big book is a book information page that lists the names of the illustrators, a photograph of the class, the date of publication, and the name of a make-believe publishing company. It is a good idea to laminate the covers. Then place a loan pocket on the inside of the back cover so children can check out the book.

Another way to make a big book is to follow the procedures above, but use the illustrations from the original book. Enlarge the originals using a photocopier or an opaque projector, and then color the illustrations. Finally, adhere the illustrations to the large sheets of paper and put them in sequence.

A third way to produce big books is to encourage children to write and illustrate their own books. This can be done by following the guidelines for the writing process (Chapter 9) but using large sheets of paper. Illustrations can include original photographs or pictures from magazines.

Commercial Big Books

Most children's book publishers recognize the need for commercial big books; as a result, there is a large array of big books available. However, they are usually expensive. Teachers need to compare the cost of commercial books with the number of regular-sized trade books that could be purchased with the same amount of money. The best commercial big books are those that replicate good trade books exactly, such as *Rosie's Walk*, by Pat Hutchens (Huck, Hepler, and Hickman, 1993). If the big book doesn't replicate the trade book, the teacher needs to be sure the big book version is appropriate for the children.

Suggested Big Books

*Cited in text

The following big books are available from Rigby Education, 4545 Virginia Street, Crystal Lake, IL 60014.

The Bean Bag Mom Made	**A Monster Sandwich*
Breakfast in Bed/Green Bananas	*Munching Mark*
*Danger	**The Night Train*
Debra's Dog	*Oh No!*
*The Enormous Watermelon	*The Three Billy Goats Gruff*
Excuses, Excuses	*The Three Little Pigs*
The Gingerbread Man	*Tricking Tracy*
Gobble, Gobble, Glup, Gulp	*The Trolley Ride*
The Greedy Gray Octopus	*The Ugly Duckling*
The Horrible Black Bug/	*When Goldilocks Went to*
On a Cold, Cold Day	*the House of the Three Bears*
Interruptions	*When Lana Was Absent*

Jack and the Beanstalk   Who's in the Shed?
The Little Red Hen

The following big books are available from Wright Group, 10949 Technology Place, San
Diego, CA 92127.

*The Big Toe   Obadiah
Boo-hoo   One Cold, Wet Night
Cooking Pot   Poor Old Polly
Dan, the Flying Man   Ratty-tatty
*The Farm Concert   The Red Rose
Grandpa, Grandpa   Sing a Song
Harry Bears   Smarty Pants
The Hungry Giant   *Three Little Ducks
*In a Dark, Dark Woods   To Market, To Market
The Jigaree   To Town
Just Like Me   Who Will Be My Mother?
Lazy Mary   *Woosh
The Monsters' Party   Yes Ma'am
*Mrs. Wishy-Washy

The following big books are available from Scholastic, P.O. Box 7501, 2931 East McCarty
Street, Jefferson City, MO 65102.

All the Pretty Horses   The Little Red Hen
*Bedtime for Francis   Madeline
Boss for a Week   More Spaghetti, I Say?
Bunches and Bunches of Bunnies   The New Baby Calf
Caps for Sale   Noisy Nora
Cats and Mice   On Market Street
Chicken Soup and Rice   The Owl and the Pussy Cat
Clifford's Family   Sing a Song of Mother Goose
Farmer Joe's Hot Day   *The Snowy Day
Have You Seen Birds?   The Three Billy Goats Gruff
A House Is a House for Me   What Do You Do with a Kangaroo?
How Much Is a Million?   Have You Been?
I Said to Sam   Why Can't I Fly?
Jump, Frog, Jump   Wynken, Blynken and Nod
The King's Cat

The following big books are available from Sundance, P.O. Box 1326, Newtown Road,
Littleton, MA 01460.

Alison's Zinnia   I Looked in the Mirror
The Alphabet Book/El Abecedario   Lisa's Daddy and Daughter Day
Animals on Parade   Lizard in the Sun
Bright Eyes/Brown Skin   Mei Ling's Tiger
The Calypso Alphabet   One of Three

Celebration   *Shoes from Grandpa*
Eat Up, Gemma   *The Sombrero of Luis Lucero*
Eyes   *Ten Little Rabbits*
Hands   *Tortilla for Emilia*
I Have a Dream   *What Game Shall We Play?*
Sadie, Remember   *What Is Orange?*

The following big books are available from Gryphon House, Early Childhood Book Collection, P.O. Box 275, Mt. Ranier, MD 20712.

A Dark Dark Tale   *Mouse Paint*
Big Red Barn   *My Five Senses*
Chicken Soup with Rice   *The Napping House*
Dinosaurs, Dinosaurs   **Oh, A-Hunting We Will Go*
Growing Vegetable Soup   *Over in the Meadow*
Hattie and the Fox   *Planting a Rainbow*
I Went Walking   *PolarBear, Polar Bear*
It Looked Like Split Milk   *There's a Nightmare in My Closet*
Is Your Mama a Llama?   *Tikki Tikki Tembo*
Jamberry   *Where's Waldo? The Magnificent Poster*
Make Way for Ducklings   *Book*

The following big books are available from The Trumpet Club, P.O. Box 605, Holmes, PA 19043-9865, 1-800-826-0110.

Another Mouse to Feed   *Old Mother Hubbard and Her Wonderful*
The Art Lesson   *Dog*
Arthur's Teacher Trouble   *Peanut Butter and Jelly: A Play Rhyme*
Demi's Find the Animal ABC   *People*
Five Little Monkeys Jumping on   *The Story of Johnny Appleseed*
  the Bed   *Sylvester and the Magic Pebble*
Hey Diddle Diddle & Other Mother   *Teeny Tiny*
  Goose Rhymes   *The Wheels on the Bus*
Little Rabbit Foo Foo
Mary Wore Her Red Dress and Henry
  Wore His Green Sneakers

The following big books are available from Harcourt Brace Jovanovich, Children's Books Division, 1250 Sixth Avenue, San Diego, CA 92101.

A Chair for My Mother   *Little Nino's Pizzeria*
The Cow That Went OINK   *Little Red Riding Hood*
Effie   *Mole's New Cap*
The Enormous Turnip   *Mouse Paint*
Feathers for Lunch   *Napping House*
Growing Vegetable Soup   *Night Noises*
The Happy Hippopotami   *Over in the Meadow*
Henry Goes West   *Planting a Rainbow*

How the Elephant Got Its Trunk`	*Planting a Rainbow*
How the Guinea Fowl Got Her Spots	*Rain Talk*
How to Catch a Ghost	*SanCake*
I Love You, Mouse	*Sterling: The Rescue of a Baby*
I Went Walking	*Harbor Seal*
If The Dinosaurs Came Back	*The Tale of Reddy Robot*
Jack and the Beanstalk	*Ten Little Mice*
King Bidgood's in the Bathtub	*The Three Bears*
The Lion and the Mouse	*The Three Little Pigs*
Little Duck Learns to Swim	*Where Can Raccoon Rest?*

The following big books are available from Penguin USA, Children's Book Marketing Department, 375 Hudson Street, New York, NY 10014.

A Dark Dark Tale	*Rosemary Wells Read-Aloud Set*
The Day Jimmy's Boa Ate the Wash	*Shy Charles*
Fix-It	*Sitting in My Box*
Fix-It (4-copy Display Unit)	*Sitting in My Box (4-copy Display*
Hazel's Amazing Mother	*Unit)*
Hazel's Amazing Mother Read-	*The Tale of Peter Rabbit*
Aloud Set	*The Tale of Peter Rabbit (4-copy*
I Like Me!	*Display Unit)*
Madeline	*There's a Nightmare in My Closet*
Madeline (4-copy Display Unit)	*The Unicorn and the Lake*
Make Way for Ducklings	*What Next, Baby Bear!*
Morris's Disappearing Bag	*What Next, Baby Bear! Read-Aloud*
The Mysterious Tadpole	*Set*
Peanut Butter and Jelly	*Why Mosquitoes Buzz in People's*
Pinkerton, Behave!	*Ears*

The following big books are available from Perfection Learning Corporation, 100 North Second Avenue, Logan, IA 51546-1099.

Anno's Counting Book	*Moongame*
Caps, Hats, Socks, and Mittens	*Morris's Disappearing Bag*
Chicken Soup with Rice	*My Five Senses*
Clifford's Puppy Days	*The Mysterious Tadpole*
A Dark Dark Tale	*Pinkerton, Behave!*
The Day Jimmy's Boa Ate the Wash	*Planting a Rainbow*
Franklin in the Dark	*Rosie's Walk*
Growing Vegetable Soup	*Shy Charles*
The Happy Hippopotami	*Strega Nona*
If the Dinosaurs Came Back	*There's a Nightmare in My Closet*
Is Your Mama a Llama?	*Thump, Thump, Rat-a-Tat-Tat*
It Looked Like Spilt Milk	*Tikki Tikki Tembo*
Jamberry	*Tommy at the Grocery Store*

Little Nino's Pizzeria   *The Very Busy Spider
Make Way for Ducklings

The following big books are available from The Book Vine, 304 Lincoln Avenue, Fox River, IL 60021.

Big Red Barn *The Napping House*
Dinosaurs, Dinosaurs *Over in the Meadow*
Good-Night Owl *Planting a Rainbow*
Growing Vegetable Soup *Polar Bear, Polar Bear, What Do You*
Hattie and the Fox   *Hear?*
I Went Walking *There's a Nightmare in My Closet*
It Looked Like Spilt Milk *Tikki Tikki Tembo*
My Five Senses *Who Said Red?*

The following big books are available from Children's Press, 5440 North Cumberland, Chicago, IL 60656.

Apple Tree! Apple Tree! *It's Best to Leave a Snake Alone*
Baby Koala Finds a Home *It's a Good Thing There Are Insects*
The Best Dressed Bear *Joshua James Likes Trucks*
A Big Fish Story *Just Like Me*
The Biggest Animal Ever *Katie Did It*
Bobby's Zoo *Listen to Me*
Bugs! *Messy Bessey*
Cubs and Colts and Calves and *Paul the Pitcher*
  Kittens *Please Don't Feed the Bears*
Eat Your Peas, Louise! *Purple Is Part of a Rainbow*
Fast Draw Freddie *Rub-a-dub-dub—What's in the Tub?*
Feeling Things *Seeing Things*
A Fishy Color Story *Smelling Things*
Frogs and Toads and Tadpoles Too! *Sneaky Pete*
Hearing Things *So That's How the Moon Changes*
Horses, Horses, Horses   *Shape*
Hot Rod Harry *Sometimes Things Change*
How Do You Know It's Fall? *The Sun Is Always Shining*
How Do You Know It's Spring?   *Somewhere*
How Do You Know It's Summer? *The Sun's Family of Planets*
How Do You Know It's Winter? *Sweet Dreams*
I Am *Tasting Things*
I Am an Explorer *Thanks to Cows*
I Love Cats *Turtles Take Their Time*
It Could Still Be a Bird *We Love Fruit*
It Could Still Be a Fish *What's the Weather Today?*
It Could Still Be a Mammal *What's Your Favorite Flower?*
It Could Still Be a Tree *A Whisper Is Quiet*
It Could Still Be Water *Who Is Coming?*

The following big books are available from HarperCollins Children's Books, 10 East 53 Street, New York, NY 10022.

Anno's Counting Book	*My Five Senses*
Big Red Barn	*Peter's Chair*
Bread and Jam for Frances	*The Right Number of Elephants Shoes*
Dinosaurs, Dinosaurs	*Thump, Thump, Rat-A-Tat-Tat*
It Looked Like Spilt Milk	*Tommy at the Grocery Store*
Jamberry	

For additional books to use for the shared book experience see the listing of predictable books (Chapter 1).

Professional Resources

*Cited in text

*Butler, Andrea. *Shared Book Experience: An Introduction.* Rigby Education, 1985.

*———. *The Story Box in the Classroom Stage 1.* Rigby Education, 1987.

*Clay, Marie. *Reading: The Patterning of Complex Behaviour.* Heinemann, 1977.

*Doake, David. "Book Experience and Emergent Reading Behaviour." Paper presented at Preconvention Institute No. 24, Research on Written Language Development, International Reading Association Annual Convention, Atlanta, April 1979.

*Durkin, Dolores. *Children Who Read Early.* Teachers' College Press, 1966.

*Herald-Taylor, Gail. *Making and Using Big Books.* Shirley Lewis Information Services, 1985.

*Holdaway, Don. *The Foundations of Literacy.* Ashton Scholastic, 1979.

*———. "Shared Book Experience: Teaching Reading Using Favorite Books." *Theory Into Practice,* 21: 293–300, 1982.

*Huck, C. S., Hepler, S., Hickman, J. *Children's Literature in the Elementary School,* 5th ed. Harcourt Brace Jovanovich, 1993.

*Morrow, L. M. *Literacy Development in the Early Years: Helping Children Read and Write.* Prentice-Hall, 1989.

*Smith, Frank. *Understanding Reading.* Holt, Rinehart & Winston, 1971.

*Sulzby, Elizabeth. "Children's Emergent Reading of Favourite Story Books." *Reading Research Quarterly,* 20: 458–481, 1985.

CHAPTER 6

Independent Reading

The ultimate goal of any reading program should be to turn students into readers who, by their own choice, read good books for enjoyment, information, and appreciation. To encourage students to become independent, lifelong readers it is important that parents and teachers set aside time each day for independent reading. The amount of time spent reading independently will depend mainly on the student's reading attention span. Young children (kindergarten and first grade) may spend only five or ten minutes reading independently, whereas fourth and fifth graders may spend up to an hour reading independently.

The Importance of Independent Reading

What is referred to here as independent reading is also called silent reading, sustained silent reading, uninterrupted sustained silent reading, and student quiet uninterrupted reading time. In recent years, independent reading has attracted more attention because of claims that reading is overtaught and underpracticed. Too many teachers give students little time to practice the word recognition and comprehension skills they teach. This is like learning the names of the notes on a piano and then not playing the piano. In many classrooms, a disproportionate amount of time is spent on skill-building activities, such as completing workbook pages or filling in the blanks. Reading is a skill; like all other skills, the more you use it the better you become. Anderson et al. (1985) substantiated the importance of practicing reading, recognizing that the best readers are those who read most. Other researchers (Barnett and Seefeldt, 1987; Bromage and Mayer, 1986; Mayer, 1986; Martinez and Rosen, 1985) have found that repeated readings, both orally and independently, is a successful technique for improving reading ability.

Researchers agree that the amount of reading done outside school relates consistently to achievement gains (Taylor, Frye, & Maruyama, 1990). Mork (1972) went so far as to suggest that the ratio of reading practice to reading instruction should be as high as 80 to 20. However, when Goodlad (1984) studied schools in America, he found that only 6 percent of classroom time in the elementary schools was spent reading.

In addition to providing the opportunity for transferring and applying reading skills to actual reading, independent reading may help create an interest in reading and thus develop lifelong readers. Today, more than ever before, producing lifelong readers seems to be a very worthwhile goal of the program. Research indicates a decline in the amount of reading and the number of people who read. Long and Henderson (1973) reported that during a two-week period, a group of fifth-grade students spent an average of only 3 hours reading, compared to 30 hours watching television. Other studies (Anderson et al., 1985) have revealed similar findings. Thus, it appears essential for schools to provide an independent, silent time for reading.

Selecting Independent Reading Materials

One of the most important considerations for establishing an independent reading program is providing a variety of reading materials. Although students select their own material, your responsibility is to make available a wide assortment of materials. Independent reading time is a time for reading enjoyment, and the materials provided should promote reading for the sheer pleasure of it. These materials should represent all of the various genres, reflect the vast interests of the students, and meet a wide range of independent reading abilities.

It is especially important to give beginning readers an opportunity to select from familiar books, such as display books that have been used in the read-aloud program or books they have listened to at home. Their knowledge of the story, coupled with their interest and use of context clues and decoding skills, will have them "reading the story" and feeling quite proud of their accomplishment.

For the nonreader, provide a selection of wordless picture books carefully chosen for their ability to adequately relate the story through the pictures. As children "read" wordless books, they develop independence and enjoy a sense of reading. Many reading readiness skills are fostered as children read their picture books. They learn to turn pages, practice "reading" from left to right, and love and respect books.

For independent reading to be successful, you must have a well-stocked classroom library! When books are easily accessible, children are much more likely to reach out for one. Periodicals, newspapers, and reference books, as well as quantities of books from the various genres, should be included. Chapter 12 discusses in detail the design, planning, organization, and implementation of a classroom library.

In addition to the classroom library, give students ample opportunity to use the school library. Arrange for the school librarian to give students a guided tour, pointing out the locations of various genres and explaining the procedures for locating and checking out materials, the rules of the library, and so on. Chapter 15 describes activities to acquaint students with the library. Encourage students to visit local public libraries and to become acquainted with the materials and services offered there.

Newspapers are a valuable classroom resource. Arrange for a local newspaper to be delivered daily or at least twice a week. This will help keep students abreast of current events. To help intermediate students become aware of different viewpoints, arrange to have at least two different papers delivered. Introduce students to the features of the newspaper—editorials, international news, national news, local news, advice columns, and weather reports—before the independent reading time and involve them in activities that will foster their understanding of the publication and its organization. Many local newspapers provide educational consultants who conduct sessions on using the newspaper. In addition to subscribing to local newspapers, subscribe to weekly classroom newspapers, such as *Scholastic, News Ranger,* or *Weekly Reader.*

Children's periodicals are also valuable sources of reading materials. These include *Highlights, Ranger Rick,* and *Cricket.* For a list of children's magazines and newspapers, see Appendix D.

Students, especially in the intermediate grades, enjoy reading reference books. For example, *The Guinness Book of World Records* contains many interesting facts. Students are fascinated by the world's largest roller coaster, the most difficult tongue twister, or records set in their favorite sports. The encyclopedia should also be available during independent reading time. Often students like to browse through an encyclopedia, reading articles that pique their interest and curiosity. Other reference books to display include *Famous First Facts, Familiar Quotations,* almanacs, and biographical dictionaries.

Often, teachers find it difficult to interest students in reading a variety of books. The following suggestions may help motivate students to select various reading materials for independent reading.

1. Provide a time for students to share books and magazines or newspaper articles. Encourage them to read or tell about a particularly interesting part of their selection.
2. Borrow a cart from the school library to use for a "Book Show on Wheels." Display books, magazines, and newspapers you have collected from the library and briefly introduce each selection. The introductions should be stimulating and provide just enough information to whet the students' appetites so that they can't wait to get their hands on the materials and read! You must be quite knowledgeable about the content of the materials for this type of presentation.
3. Allow a group of students to prepare their own "Book Show on Wheels." They may collect books relating to a specific theme or may base selections on their individual leanings. Provide time for students to share their selections with the rest of the class.
4. Conduct a "Literary Rap Session," in which each student has an opportunity to discuss a special interest. Encourage others in the class to suggest related reading materials the student might enjoy.

5. Recommend books based on or used as the motivation for popular movies or television programs. Encourage students to write short scripts, scenes, and story narratives.
6. Organize a paperback bookstore in your class or involve the school's parent association in such an endeavor. The bookstore could be operated before class in the morning, during lunch, or after school and could promote both new and used books. Encourage students to bring in books they have already read and trade them for other used books or apply their credit to newer books. Students may even take turns being the store's manager or salesperson.
7. Invite an author to come for a school visit to talk about his or her book(s). If this is not feasible, many authors have filmstrips or videos that describe their books and how they were motivated to write and/or illustrate them. This can be an effective way to interest students in books.

Establishing an Independent Reading Period

Establishing an independent reading period is relatively simple and requires little preparation; however, certain procedures should be followed to ensure a successful program. To establish and nurture the habit of independent reading of self-selected materials, acquaint students with the purpose of the independent reading period and the rules that must be followed. It is important that students recognize that the only thing they are expected to do is read. This is a time for free, uninterrupted reading.

A few rules need to be established, as follows. Do not permit talking, and do not allow students to roam about the room or reading area. To prevent students from constantly searching for new reading materials during the independent reading period, each student should have at least two items of reading material at his or her desk. Then if a book proves to be uninteresting or too difficult, another selection is readily available. During class time, either before or after the independent reading period, give students the opportunity to replenish their stock of reading materials. Encourage students to suggest books for the read-aloud program that they are interested in but that proved too difficult for independent reading.

The most basic rule for the independent reading period is that the only activity going on is reading. *No one* is exempt, not even the teacher. As the teacher becomes involved in independent reading, he or she provides an excellent role model. Sadly, the teacher may be the first adult students have seen who is involved in reading for pleasure, and therefore it is imperative that the teacher read and not be allowed to get sidetracked by daily classroom tasks. They can wait! In many schools, independent reading programs, such as sustained silent reading, are implemented as a schoolwide effort. Everyone, from the principal to the custodial staff, reads at the appointed time!

Discussion of the independent reading period and its rules should take place several days before it is implemented. You may want to brainstorm the rules with your students. Once the rules have been established, they should be prominently displayed. If a rule is broken, the infraction should simply be pointed out to the student and independent reading should continue. At the onset, students will be more likely to interrupt their reading. However, as they become more familiar with the process and as the independent reading habit is established, there will be fewer problems.

RULES FOR INDEPENDENT READING

Select at least two books you will enjoy reading.
Do not talk or move about the room.
Think about something you have read that you might like to share.

Independent reading should be scheduled for the same time each day or every other day. You may want to alternate independent reading with the paired reading program (see pages 210–213). Students should look forward to the independent reading period and be able to expect it as a permanent part of their routine. As you first implement independent reading, begin with shorter periods and gradually increase the time. The following chart provides guidelines, but your own experiences will be the best guide. Experiment to find the time frame that works best for your students. Often for younger children whose attention span is short, it is advantageous to plan two shorter independent reading periods rather than one longer one. As a rule of thumb, it is always better to schedule too short a time rather than too long a time. In that way, children will anxiously be awaiting the next independent reading period.

INDEPENDENT READING TIME GUIDE

Grade Level	Minimum Time	Maximum Time
K–1	3–5 minutes	10–15 minutes
2–3	5–10 minutes	15–20 minutes
4–6	10–15 minutes	20–30 minutes

Since the purpose of independent reading is to make reading an enjoyable part of the student's world, make the independent reading period as comfortable as possible. As adults, we usually do not sit in an upright position when we read for enjoyment; therefore, students shouldn't be required to sit at their desks to read. Allow them to find their own niche or corner of the room. They may wish to decorate it with a banner or poster and bring in pillows, towels, or cushions to sit on. If the weather permits, take them outside to read. Let them find a tree, lean against its trunk, and start to read.

Extended Activities for Independent Reading

Independent reading is not to be used as a prerequisite for a book report. Essential to the success of the program is the students' realization that the independent reading period has been established to give them an opportunity to read whatever they choose. Reserve some time at the end of the period for students to share something special from their readings if they desire. You may want to share as well, but begin this sharing time only after the program is well established.

Sharing can take many forms. Students can share their readings in small discussion groups where one student presents what he or she has read and other students can ask questions, discuss, react, and interact with the presentation. Students may also share their reading by working in pairs or small groups to do extension activities based on one book. For example, if the students have read *A River Ran Wild*, by Lynn Cherry, they may work as a group to collect and read other books related to water pollution or organize a community project to help preserve rivers and streams. They may even develop a thematic unit related to the environment.

To vary sharing sessions, you might also ask students to share specific portions of their readings. Again, student participation should be encouraged, not forced. You might ask the students to read or share a part that felt good, a part that made them wish they were somewhere else, the part they liked best, or a part that made them feel happy, uneasy, or surprised.

Suggest to the students that they keep a reading journal where they record their feelings, images, observations, and memories as they read independently. These notes can be used for later reference in discussion or other follow-up activities. A good alternative to reading journals, if the students own their own books, is to have them annotate their thoughts in the margins or underline or highlight important information as they read. In addition to providing a source of information during group discussions and conferences, reading journals can provide ideas for writing.

Students should be encouraged to keep a log of the books they read during independent reading and during other parts of the day. Younger students will need help in keeping their records; perhaps a class record would be more appropriate. You may want to reproduce the Independent Reading Log (page 211) for more mature students and allow them to keep a copy at their desk to fill in whenever they finish a book.

As an alternative to a log, create a booklet in which students can record their readings. Fold a sheet of $8\frac{1}{2} \times 11$-inch paper into book form. On the cover, write "Reading for Pleasure," and draw lines for the student's name and grade. On the inside and back cover put numbered lines where the student can list the title and author of each book he or she has read. At the end of the year, students should have a fairly impressive list of the books they have read just for the fun of it!

Paired Reading

Paired reading is a technique that allows children (tutees) who are less able readers to be paired with other children (tutors) who are more able readers, thus allowing the less able reader to read texts of higher readability level. This

---

INDEPENDENT READING LOG

Student's name: _____

Books I have read . . .

Date   Title   Author

_____

_____

_____

_____

_____

_____

_____

_____

_____

_____

_____

_____

_____

_____

---

technique was originally developed for parents and their children to use at home (Topping, 1987).

Today, paired reading is used in many different classroom settings and with a variety of age groups, including adults (Scoble, Topping, and Wiggleworth, 1988). Morris and Simmons (1991) implemented a whole-language buddies program in which primary and intermediate grade children were paired. These children became successfully involved in reading and writing creatively as they participated in activities using big books.

Regardless of the age group or setting, the following guidelines will assist in making paired reading successful:

1. Careful selection and matching of the participants is important. Cross-age pairing has advantages, but pairing students at one grade level is usually easier to organize. Some teachers rank all of the students in the class by reading ability and then split the list in half. They then match one student from the higher-ability group with one from the lower-ability group (Topping, 1989).

2. Some students should be designated as standby tutors in case a tutor is absent or drops out.

3. Well-chosen literature is critical to the success of the program. The books selected should not be too easy or too difficult for either the tutee or tutor.

4. It is essential to monitor the paired reading sessions to ensure that there are no problems in technique, choice of book, difficult words, interpersonal relationships, and so forth.

5. An evaluation and recording system may be developed to record the students' progress in terms of material read, behavior, and so forth.

6. Participants should have time periodically to review and evaluate the paired reading program and provide feedback.

7. Paired reading should be at a regularly scheduled time. It may be alternated with independent reading periods or, if space is available and the noise level can be kept at a minimum, can be scheduled concurrently with independent reading.

8. The area designated for paired reading should be comfortable, well-lighted, and quiet. The noise level must be kept to a minimum.
9. Children must be trained in paired reading. For example, they need to learn that when the text is difficult they should read out loud together. When the tutee makes an error, the tutor should say the word correctly and the tutee should repeat it. When the text is easier the tutee should read out loud; the tutor should assist when needed.

No literature program (independent reading or paired reading) can be successful without the support of school administrators and parents. One way to get their support of the program is to involve them in it. Increasingly, curriculum coordinators, principals, assistant principals, grandparents, and parents are rewarding children for reading books. Rewards may include such things as organizing clubs or distributing reading certificates, buttons, pencils, or notes of recognition. More important than the reward is the fact that students see that others are interested in them and their reading.

Professional Resources

*Cited in text

*Anderson, Richard C., Elfieda H. Hicbert, Judith A. Scott, and Ian A. G. Wilkinson. "Becoming a Nation of Readers: The Report of the Commission on Reading." National Institute of Education, 1985.

*Barnett, Jerrold E., and Richard W. Seefeldt. "Read Something Once, Why Read It Again?" Paper presented at the American Educational Research Association Annual Meeting, Washington, D.C., April, 1987.

*Bromage, Bruce K., and Richard E. Mayer. "Quantitative and Qualitative Effects of Repetition on Learning from Technical Text." *Journal of Educational Psychology*, 78: 271–278, 1986.

*Goodlad, John I. *A Place Called School.* McGraw-Hill, 1984.

*Long, Barbara H., and Edmund H. Henderson. "Children's Use of Time: Some Personal and Social Correlates." *The Elementary School Journal*, 73: 193–199, 1973.

*Martinez, Miriam, and Nancy Rosen. "Read It Again: The Value of Repeated Readings During Storytime." *The Reading Teacher*, 38: 782–786, 1985.

*Mayer, Richard E. "Can't You Repeat That? Qualitative Effects of Repetition and Advance Organizers from Science Prose." *Journal of Educational Psychology*, 75: 40–49, 1983.

*Mork, Theodore A. "Sustained Silent Reading in the Classrooms." *The Reading Teacher*, 25: 438–441, 1972.

*Morrice, Connie, and Maureen Simmons. "Beyond Reading Buddies: A Whole Language Cross-Age Program." *The Reading Teacher*, 44: 572–577, 1991.

*Scoble, John, Keith Topping, and Colin Wiggleworth. "Training Family and Friends as Adult Literacy Tutors." *Journal of Reading*, 31: 410–417, 1988.

*Topping, Keith. "Paired Reading: A Powerful Technique for Parent Use." *The Reading Teacher*, 40: 604–614, 1987.

*———. "Peer Tutoring and Paired Reading: Combining Two Powerful Techniques." *The Reading Teacher*, 42: 488–494, 1989.

*Taylor, B. M., B. J. Frye, and G. Maruyama. "Time Spent Reading and Reading Growth." *American Educational Research Journal*, 27: 351–362, 1990.

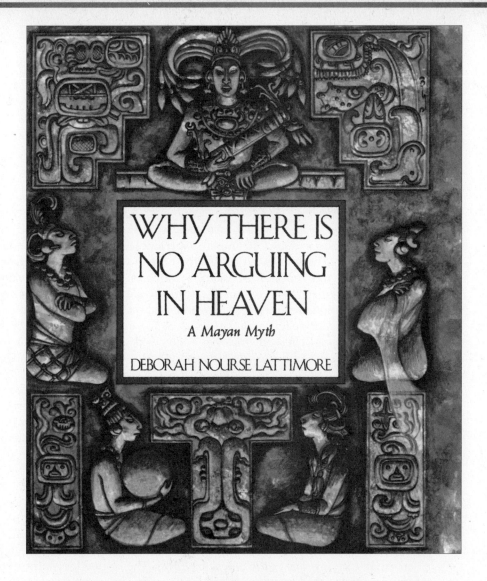

WHY THERE IS
NO ARGUING
IN HEAVEN

A Mayan Myth

DEBORAH NOURSE LATTIMORE

CHAPTER 7

STORYTELLING

Storytelling began thousands of years before written language existed, as early people spun tales to depict the human experience and to attempt to understand the unknown. These tales expressed the human qualities of hope, fear, love, and jealousy and represented interpretations of phenomena that confused, awed, and terrified their creators. As stories were passed orally from generation to generation, details were changed based on the times, the style and creativity of the storyteller, and the needs of the audience, yet the themes remained constant. These themes have survived over the ages due to their universal appeal, and the stories are the myths, legends, and folk tales we enjoy today.

As people traveled from country to country and continent to continent, they brought with them their culture and heritage, in the form of stories. Most myths and legends, whether Greek, Roman, or Norse, contain similar plots, characters, and themes. Likewise, popular folk tales retain those elements basic to understanding human motivation, and they reflect the values of good versus evil and right over might. Although each culture has its own tales that mirror the values of its people, such as the American tall tale that reflects the vast open spaces of the American West and the sense of "bigness," the themes transcend time and place.

One of the main reasons for the popularity and longevity of these tales is the talent and skill of the storyteller who breathes life into them. Storytelling is an art; in fact, it is one of the oldest art forms. The storyteller captures images, recreates the story, and captivates the audience. The storyteller *tells* the story, rather than reads it. A good storyteller must not only be able to communicate the plot but must also convey the mood, the sense of being there.

The Importance of Storytelling

The classroom is a perfect setting for storytelling—a strategy that is too often overlooked. Storytelling fulfills two main purposes: to entertain and to inform. A teacher can make the past come alive for his or her students and help them understand their own culture as well as those of other places and times. As they are transported through time, children gain an appreciation for the values that have shaped our lives. Storytelling can also bring much of the classroom curriculum to life. A lesson in electricity will be much more meaningful, for example, if students first listen to a story about the life of Edison and his successes, failures, and, especially, perseverance.

Through storytelling, students find that they are not alone. They experience the story together and realize that others share their feelings, insights, and understandings and the impact of the story on their lives. When children share a story, they enjoy it more. They laugh harder, feel more deeply, and become part of a bonding process that includes their classmates and the storyteller. As Baker and Greene (1977) wrote, "storytelling at best is cocreation."

Storytelling is a perfect strategy for improving communication skills—listening, writing, and speaking. With the teacher as storyteller, children must focus on the story, the action, and the dialogue to capture the meaning. They are better able to draw inferences when they listen rather than read. As this skill is developed through strategies such as storytelling, students become better equipped to draw inferences when reading independently.

Storytelling encourages children to appreciate and respect language. When students tell stories, they have an opportunity to practice using oral language, enrich their vocabulary, and develop their ability to organize thoughts and ideas. Storytelling is not only an effective technique for developing oral language; its benefits extend to written language as well. In addition, storytelling enhances students' sense of story structure. Storytelling is effective with exceptional student populations as well, because it is success-oriented, enhances self-esteem, and is fun.

Finally, through storytelling, the teacher can foster a love of literature. Introducing students to the various genres encourages them to seek similar books for their independent reading. Storytelling gives vent to their emotional needs, allows their imaginations to soar, and gives them an opportunity to share in the experiences that have shaped our world.

Selecting the Story

One of the most important criteria for selecting material for storytelling, as when choosing read-aloud materials, is the way the book or poem affects the storyteller. Since the storyteller has an intimate relationship with the audience, his or her feelings toward the story will be transferred to them.

Folklore, which includes myths, legends, fairy tales, and fables, is perhaps the most popular genre for storytelling. Children love these stories, and they contain elements that children relate well to, such as a fast-moving plot, realistic and convincing characters, little unnecessary detail, and universal themes. The message is transmitted in an appealing and easy-to-understand manner, never in a didactic, pedantic tone. And the tales affect young and old alike.

Even as adults, we cherish the belief that good will triumph over evil, that each ugly duckling will one day awaken to find that he or she has been transformed into a graceful and glorious creature.

Poetry also lends itself well to storytelling. Children soon learn to appreciate the beauty of poetry, its rhythm, rhyme, and verse. Through nursery rhymes, young children become familiar with alliteration. They look forward to the repetition that involves them in the storytelling. Older children also enjoy the ballads and narrative poems, whose verses tell of life, at times tragic and frustrating, but always exciting.

Realistic stories and biographies are also easily adapted for storytelling. Children thrill to those stories that satisfy their own needs for love, security, and adventure. These genres allow students to identify with the plot and character, depicting life the way it is—good and bad.

When choosing materials for storytelling, consider the following criteria.

1. Choose books for a variety of purposes. Storytelling can inform and entertain. Match the stories to the students' needs. The right materials can help students better understand themselves and others, gain insight into specific problems, become aware of past cultures as well as their own, and learn to appreciate the various genres.
2. Make sure the story fits your own style, talents, and personality. For example, if a book requires the use of dialects, you may find it difficult to reproduce the needed dialect effectively.
3. Select materials in which there is sufficient action and dialogue. You may often need to add dialogue when adapting a story; however, stories that rely on dialogue, exact wording, or illustrations are usually better selections for reading aloud. For example, because the illustrations in *The Very Hungry Caterpillar* are so realistic, colorful, and alive, they play a significant part in the story, helping children understand the metamorphosis of a butterfly. Because this concept would be more difficult to demonstrate through storytelling, the book is far more appropriate for reading aloud.
4. As you build a repertoire of materials for storytelling, select materials that reflect a variety of genres. It is helpful to establish a separate file for each story you learn and then keep all pertinent information and needed materials in it (see Steps for Preparing Storytelling on page 219). On the outside of the folder, list the name of the story or poem, author, and genre. Check your files to be sure each genre is represented.
5. Base your selections on your knowledge of the audience and their age, interests, and maturity. Be sure the vocabulary used fits the listening level, rather than the reading level, of your audience. Students can understand stories far beyond their reading level. A story written at a lower reading level with a theme of interest to older children could easily be adapted for storytelling. Listening levels can be determined by using instruments such as informal classroom reading inventories, available from many publishers.

Preparing the Story

A cardinal rule regarding storytelling is *don't memorize the story*. Each time a story is told, it should take on a personality of its own, reflecting an understanding of the audience, their needs, interests, maturity level, and listening level. It is crucial that the storyteller establish a rapport with the audience. Memorization usually hampers this, preventing the storyteller from being natural and responding to the audience's feedback.

Good storytelling does not come without effort. Just as an actor must rehearse lines, reaching into his or her soul for the right blend of honesty and emotion, so must the storyteller. To be an effective storyteller, you must know the story and become part of it. You must understand the motivations and conflicts of the characters, feel what they must feel, and be sensitive to the images and mood created by the author. There is no magic recipe for becoming a good storyteller. Preparation, practice, and experience are the main ingredients; only through trial and error will you become successful. The steps below will help you prepare stories for storytelling.

Steps for Preparing Storytelling

1. Read the story several times.
2. Analyze the plot to identify the introduction, conclusion, and various scenes.
3. Analyze the story to determine the action, conflict, and climax. These will merit emphasis during storytelling.
4. Notice the repetition of words and phrases.
5. Visualize the characters in order to bring them to life for the audience.
6. Visualize the setting and determine the mood of the story.
7. Consider what gestures, facial expressions, and voice tones would be most appropriate to establish the mood of the story.
8. Outline the story. Your outline should include the introduction, main scenes, climax, and conclusion. In folklore (folk tales, myths, legends, and fables), memorize a few sentences of the introduction and conclusion, since they immediately set the stage for the story and envelop students in their magic. Include any specific words or phrases that are repeated throughout the story so you can repeat them accurately and use them to involve students in the storytelling. The sample outline on page 220 may serve as a guide.
9. Practice telling the story in front of a mirror, using gestures, facial expressions, and proper voice inflections and tone. Practice the story until it becomes second nature, until you have become part of the story yourself. Use vocabulary that will captivate the audience and carry the story.
10. If possible, tape yourself (video or cassette). Be objective in your critique. Did you capture the mood of the story? Did you use rich language? Did you pace the story well? Was your diction clear? Did you use expressions and gestures to convey the mood and plot? Were you successful in transporting the audience to another place and time? Did you lose your own

identity and become part of the story? Make any necessary changes based on your analysis.

11. Save your outline for future reference. In this way, you will build a repertoire and be in constant demand as a storyteller.

The National Association for the Preservation and Perpetuation of Storytelling is a valuable resource for those wishing to learn more about storytelling.

RUMPELSTILTSKIN

I. Introduction

"There was once a miller who was very poor, but he had a beautiful daughter. Now it once happened that he had occasion to speak with the king, and in order to give himself an air of importance, he said, 'I have a daughter who can spin gold out of straw.'"

II. Scenes

A. King puts girl into chamber filled with straw, a reel, and a spinning wheel and tells her that unless she can spin all the straw into gold she will be killed. As girl cries, she is visited by a strange little man. "What will you give me if I spin it for you?" She gives him her necklace.

B. Scene is repeated, but this time she is put into a larger room filled with straw. She is visited again by the strange man. "What will you give me if I spin it for you?" She gives him her ring.

C. The third time, she is put into a still larger room and again visited by the strange man. "What will you give me if I spin it for you?" This time she has nothing and offers him her first-born child.

D. The girl becomes queen and a year later a child is born. The strange little man comes to claim the child. The queen begs him to give up his claim, and he says he will if, within three days, she can guess his name.

E. Queen sends messengers all over the land. First two times the strange man appears she tries all types of names. After each he says, "No, no, that's not my name."

F. Finally, a messenger in the woods hears:
"Today I bake; tomorrow I brew my beer;
The next day I will bring the Queen's child here.
Ah! lucky 'tis that not a soul doth know
That Rumpelstiltskin is my name. Ho! Ho!"

III. Climax

The queen guesses Rumpelstiltskin's name.

IV. Conclusion

After the queen guesses his name, Rumpelstiltskin becomes enraged: "In his rage, he stamped his right foot into the ground so deep that he sank up to his waist. Then in his rage he seized his left leg with both hands and tore himself asunder in the middle."

Its publications include magazines and newsletters with how-to information and a national directory with listings of storytellers, organizations, and events.

Guidelines for Good Storytelling

A good storyteller can capture the hearts and minds of his or her listeners. This ability is developed through careful preparation and a great deal of practice. In addition, the following guidelines will help you become a good storyteller:

1. Before beginning the storytelling session, establish a purpose for the story. This preintroduction can be short, but it should cause the audience to sit up and take notice. For example, before telling *The Ugly Duckling,* you might say, "Did you know that one of Hans Christian Andersen's fairy tales was a lot like his life?" Before reading *Rumpelstiltskin,* you might ask, "Have you ever made a promise that you knew you couldn't keep? What would cause you to make such a promise? I'm going to tell you a story about how a promise got a queen into a lot of trouble."

2. Watch for the audience's reactions. Be receptive to verbal and nonverbal indicators. Watch the students' faces. Do they seem to be feeling the emotions you are attempting to convey, or do they appear confused? Are they interested or restless? Are they involved, or are you losing their attention? Are you speaking too quickly or too slowly? Are they taking part in word or phrase repetition? Be prepared to change your style and technique based on the audience's reactions.

3. If possible, set aside a special area of the classroom for storytelling. You may even decorate the area to resemble a theater.

4. Have the students sit in low chairs or on cushions, carpet, foam, or towels. It is important that they sit close to one another, since this helps create a close, warm environment and contributes to the group's feelings of oneness.

5. Prepare any props in advance, and have them easily accessible. You don't want to interrupt the continuity and flow of the story by having to search for needed materials.

6. Many storytellers believe sound effects detract from the overall effect. Modulate the pitch and tone of your voice to convey the mood or feeling. For example, rather than emulate the sound of galloping horses, project the mood with the rhythm of the words you are using.

7. Do not quiz the audience after storytelling. Allow discussions to flow naturally, based on the students' questions and comments. You may want to ask a few thought-provoking questions to help foster meaningful dialogue among members of the audience. For example, you could ask, "Based on *The Ugly Duckling,* what do you think Hans Christian Andersen's life might have been like?" or "Was Rumpelstiltskin evil or good? What makes you believe this?" Encourage students to support their answers with specifics from the story.

8. Modify the storytelling for the individual audience. Take into account their maturity level, listening level, interests, and needs. Never talk down to your

audience. You can modify almost any story to fit the audience by selecting appropriate language and degree of sophistication.

9. Establish eye contact and attempt to involve members of the audience in the story. Encouraging children to take part in the repetition of words and phrases is one way of involving them. For example, repeat the chant Rumpelstiltskin sang and have students sing it together. Personalize the story, mentioning names of members of the audience when appropriate, such as, "Alan, can you guess what happens next?" or "Amanda, will you help Ali Baba repeat the magic words?"

10. Prepare a performance evaluation form and complete it after every storytelling session. The chart below will provide the feedback you will need to help prepare for your next storytelling session. Keep this chart for future reference.

STORYTELLING SELF-EVALUATION FORM

Title of story: _____

Date presented: _____

Age of group: _____

Props used: _____

Modifications made for specific audience prior to

presentation: _____

_____

Part of story that seemed most effective: _____

_____

Part of story that seemed least effective: _____

_____

Reactions of audience: _____

_____

What I should do differently next time: _____

_____

Questions that initiated meaningful discussion: _____

_____

Additional comments: _____

_____

11. Encourage students to use storytelling as a catalyst for classroom learning experience stories as well as their own experience stories.
12. Prepare a form on which the audience can evaluate the storytelling session. You may want to duplicate the following Audience Evaluation Form. This form is particularly useful with intermediate grades.

AUDIENCE EVALUATION FORM FOR STORYTELLING

Title: _____

Was rapport established?	1	2	3	4	5*
Was there eye contact?	1	2	3	4	5
Was storytelling dramatic?	1	2	3	4	5
Was voice level appropriate?	1	2	3	4	5
Did the storyteller appear to know the story well?	1	2	3	4	5
Did the storyteller hold your attention?	1	2	3	4	5

Total Points _____

Comments: _____
_____
_____

Name of evaluator: _____

Date: _____

*Note: 5 is the highest point score; 1 is the lowest.

Choosing Appropriate Props or Media

Often, storytelling authorities advise against the use of props or other types of media. They suggest relying instead on the storyteller's talents to create and enhance the plot and mood. However, those working with small children may want to use such media as flannel boards, puppets, and music to add a further dimension to the story.

Flannel characters can be made from flannel or Pellon, a fabric used to stiffen collars. Pellon is easy to see through and can be used to trace illustrations from any source. Paper cutouts can also be used with a flannel board by gluing small pieces of sandpaper to the back of the cutout. Children can then decorate and color their cutouts. Flannel boards can be purchased but also can be made by covering a sheet of cardboard with a piece of flannel. Ready-made flannel board stories are available for the primary grades. Each kit contains a summary of the story and large cutouts of the characters. *Flannelboard Stories for the Primary Grades,* by Paul Anderson, is one example of commercial materials available to aid in developing flannel board characters. It offers a variety of titles.

Flannel board stories lend variety to storytelling and provide material that allows students to reenact the story as reinforcement. As the story is told, the flannel characters are placed on the board and moved about as the story dictates. Stories with only a few characters and a rather simple plot are more adaptable to flannel boards. Stories in which new characters or events are added (cumulative stories), such as Marjorie Flack's *Ask Mr. Bear,* are especially effective, allowing children to watch as the plot unfolds. Once a flannel board story is told, allow it to remain in the classroom so children have an opportunity to retell the story and manipulate the figures. File flannel board characters for future reference.

Easy-to-make puppets—paper bag, stick, or sock—lend variety to storytelling. They can be used to tell the story, introduce the story, or, at the end, prompt discussion. Puppets can represent animate and inanimate story characters.

Often, a storyteller will use several props. These props can simply symbolize the character. For example, an egg might introduce *The Ugly Duckling,* or a rock might introduce *Sylvester and the Magic Pebble.*

Finally, music can enhance the atmosphere before the story is presented. The choice of music is important to establish the right mood. A lively, toe-tapping number might be perfect for *Mama Don't Allow,* but would be inappropriate for *Goodnight Moon,* for which a more serene selection would enhance the feeling of peace and contentment.

Organizing a Storytelling Festival at School

In 1973, in the heart of the southern Appalachian Mountains, an annual tradition was born—the National Storytelling Festival. It grew from an attendance in the hundreds to more than 6000 and has helped foster a love and appreciation for the art of storytelling. Start a tradition of your own, by organizing a storytelling festival for your school. A storytelling festival will benefit students by developing an appreciation of the art of storytelling, teaching them techniques and skills in storytelling, introducing various tales, and developing students' self-confidence and poise.

The storytelling festival can include many components. For example, you might consider the following:

1. Invite local professional storytellers who can share a potpourri of tales from near and far.
2. Invite parents and grandparents to take part in a "Family Showcase" in which they share tales of their childhood and region.
3. Hold a "Children's Hour," in which students present their favorite tales through storytelling.
4. Hold a "Meet the Storyteller" session, in which selected storytellers share their insights.
5. Involve students and professional storytellers in a "Storytellers Workshop," where skills and storytelling techniques are shared and performances are videotaped.
6. Provide a lunch that offers foods representative of many of the tales and cultures they represent. (Students can volunteer to prepare different foods.)

General Preparation

1. Find out whether other teachers would like their students to participate. Since it may be impossible for all students to present their stories at the

festival, be sure they all have an opportunity to do so to their own classes and selected other classrooms.

2. Form a festival committee of other teachers, parents, and students that is responsible for planning, including the following:
   - Select a day and location for the festival.
   - Locate professional storytellers to take part in the festival and/or introduce students to the art of storytelling.
   - Arrange for parents to be trained as coaches to help children prepare and present their stories.
   - Arrange for parents to prepare foods for the festival.
   - Send information to local news media so they can cover the festival.
   - Arrange for parent volunteers to facilitate the events and introduce storytellers.
   - Make certificates of appreciation to award each storyteller.
   - Prepare a program to hand out at the festival that outlines the day's events and activities. Include a map that clearly shows the location of each event. Have students illustrate the program.
   - Arrange each area appropriately for the event that will be held there. Make sure signs clearly identify the area for visitors.
   - Arrange for a group of judges to determine which students will present at the festival if it is not possible for all students to present. Be sure the judges are familiar with the criteria for evaluating storytelling
   - Ask parent volunteers to take photographs and/or videotape the day's events.

Classroom Preparation

1. Introduce the art of storytelling.
   a. Following the strategies presented earlier in this chapter, introduce children to storytelling and present a collection of tales representative of a variety of genres and cultures. Allow time for children to discuss the stories and presentations. What did they especially like about the storytelling? What gestures, voice tones, and other techniques were effective? You may wish to use storytelling tapes such as those by Childrens Press (5440 North Cumberland Avenue, Chicago, Illinois 60656; 1-800-621-1115).
   b. Select a fairly simple story and tell it to the class. Have students identify the parts of the story (beginning, sequence of events, ending), repetitions or chants, and so on. Together, prepare a story outline as described earlier in the chapter.
   c. Have pairs of students tell the story to one another. Have them experiment with gestures, eye contact, voice changes, pauses, and so on.
   d. Ask the librarian for help in selecting a wide variety of tales that lend themselves well to storytelling (see also Professional Resources). Have the students choose a story they would like to tell at the festival and

follow the strategies discussed earlier to plan their outline and practice their storytelling.

   e. Establish time guidelines for the storytelling presentations.

   f. Be sure you have worked with each student so their presentations will be smooth and successful. Try to elicit help from local storytellers and/or trained parent coaches.

2. Have students create invitations for the festival and send them to family, friends, school faculty, and students.
3. Have students prepare posters advertising the festival, to generate excitement.
4. Have a dress rehearsal so each student knows his or her responsibilities.

After the Festival

The following activities will bring closure to the festival and facilitate planning the next year's festival.

1. Have students write thank you notes to all guests, storytellers, parent volunteers, and others who helped organize and oversee the festival.
2. Create a bulletin board with photo highlights of the festival. Later put these in a special album.
3. Arrange for students to watch the videotape of the festival.
4. Make a list of the names and numbers of participants and assistants so that it is available for the next year.
5. Make a list of organizational strategies and a suggested time frame.
6. Ask students and teachers to evaluate the festival. What did they especially like? What additions would they like to see next year? What activities can be improved? How?
7. Keep copies of the program, newspaper articles, and the evaluation information in a file.

Children's Literature

*Cited in text

*Andersen, Hans Christian. *The Complete Fairy Tales and Stories.* Doubleday/Anchor, 1983.

*———. *The Ugly Duckling.* Illustrated and retold by Lorinda Bryan Cauley. Harcourt Brace Jovanovich, 1979.

*Brothers Grimm. *Grimms' Fairy Tales.* Grossett & Dunlap, 1945.

*Brown, Margaret Wise. *Goodnight Moon.* Illustrated by Clermont Hurd. Harper, 1947.

Bryant, Al. *Stories to Tell Boys and Girls.* Zonderman, 1952.

Bulfinch, Thomas. *A Book of Myths.* Macmillan, 1970.

*Carle, Eric. *The Very Hungry Caterpillar.* Philomel. 1969.

D'Aulaire, Ingrid, and Edgar D'Aulaire. *Book of Greek Myths.* Doubleday, 1962.

———. *Norse Gods and Giants.* Doubleday, 1967.

*Flack, Marjorie. *Ask Mr. Bear.* Macmillan, 1968.

Green, Roger L. *A Book of Myths.* Dutton, 1965.

*Hurd, Thacher. *Mama Don't Allow.* Thacher Hurd, 1984.

Jacobi, Frederick, Jr. *Tales of Grimm and Andersen.* Modern Library, 1952.

Lyttle, Kirk. *Pleasant Journeys: Twenty-Two Tales from Around the World.* Writing Works, 1979.

Mathon, Laura E., and Thusnelda Schmidt. *Treasured Tales.* Abingdon, 1960.

McDermott, Gerald. *Daughter of Earth: A Roman Myth.* Delacorte, 1984.

*Steig, William. *Sylvester and the Magic Pebble.* Windmill, 1969.

Untermeyer, Louis. *The World's Great Stories: 55 Legends that Live Forever.* Lippincott, 1964.

White, Anne Terry. *The Golden Treasury of Myths and Legends.* Illustrated by Alice and Martin Provensen. Golden, 1959.

Professional Resources

Anderson, Paul S. *Flannelboard Stories for the Primary Grades.* Dennison, 1962.

———. *Language Skills in Elementary Education.* Macmillan, 1964.

Baker, Augusta, and Ellin Greene. *Storytelling: Art and Technique,* 2nd ed. Bowker, 1977.

Bauer, Caroline. *Handbook for Storytellers.* American Library Association, 1977.

Briggs, Nancy E., and Joseph A. Wagner. *Children's Literature Through Storytelling and Drama.* William C. Brown, 1970.

Cathon, Laura, et al., eds. *Stories to Tell to Children: A Selected List.* University of Pittsburgh Press, 1974.

Coody, Bernice, ed. *Children's Literature in the Reading Program.* IRA, 1987.

Huck, Charlotte S., and Doris Young Kuhn. *Children's Literature in the Elementary School.* Holt, Rinehart & Winston, 1968.

Johnson, Terry D., and Daphne R. Louis. *Literacy Through Literature.* Heinemann, 1987.

Livo, Norma J., and Sandra Reitz. *Storytelling: Process and Practice.* Libraries Unlimited, 1986.

MacDonald, Margaret Read. *The Storyteller's Sourcebook: A Subject, Title and Motif Index to Folklore Collections for Children.* Gale, 1982.

———. *Twenty Tellable Tales: Audience Participation Folktales for the Beginning Storyteller.* Wilson, 1986.

Ross, Ramon R. *Storytelling,* 2nd ed. Merrill, 1980.

Schimmel, Nancy. *Just Enough to Make a Story: A Sourcebook for Storytelling.* Sisters' Choice, 1978.

Smith, Jimmy Neil, ed. *Homespun: Tales from Americans' Favorite Storytellers.* Crown, 1988.

Sutherland, Zena, and May Hill Arbuthnot. *Children and Books,* 8th ed. HarperCollins, 1991.

Sutherland, Zena, and Myra Cohn Livingston. *The Scott, Foresman Anthology of Children's Literature.* Scott, Foresman, 1984.

Tooze, Ruth. *Storytelling.* Prentice-Hall, 1976.

Video/Cassette Tapes

"A Master Class in Storytelling." Describes storytelling techniques. Vineyard Video Productions, 1983. (Video)

"Adventures in Storytelling." Series of audiocassettes featuring a storyteller who brings the tale to life. Childrens Press, 1991–1992. (Cassette)

Storyland Theater. Master storytellers telling tales of heroes and faraway places. Family Circle Paperback Visual Publishing, 1987. (Video)

Associations

National Association for the Preservation and Perpetuation of Storytelling (NAPPS), P.O. Box 309, Jonesborough, TN 37659, phone number: (800) 525-4514

National Story League (NSL), 3508 Russell, #6, St. Louis, MO 63104

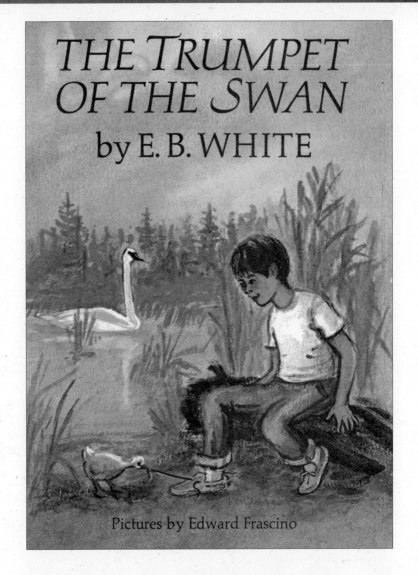

THE TRUMPET OF THE SWAN

by E. B. WHITE

Pictures by Edward Frascino

CHAPTER 8

Diversity and Children's Books: Finding the Right Book

One of the strengths of the United States is in the differences among its people. Nowhere is the tremendous diversity of cultures and student abilities more evident than in the classroom. Since literature speaks to us in such personal ways, it is important that teachers be aware of the tremendous scope of literary works that will speak to children of varying special needs, books with which they can identify and that will nurture their spirit, give them hope, and help them gather the courage and confidence needed to develop and grow. The literature introduced in this chapter used is important to all children, for it gives them insights into the special needs of others.

This chapter deals with cultural diversity and creating a multicultural classroom community—a classroom where all people, regardless of color, feel equal. Students need to feel pride in their heritage, for their self-concept is largely responsible for how they learn, how they treat themselves and others. There is a wealth of literature that focuses on the many cultures in the United States. Reading this literature and participating in the activities suggested will give students additional perspective on the richness of each culture. Multicultural literature should not be limited to a specific unit or month of the year. Books whose characters are representative of different backgrounds and cultures should be infused into the study of all topics throughout the year.

The main goal of this chapter is to help children better understand themselves and others, with the hope of fostering not only acceptance but genuine respect and caring.

Students with Special Learning Needs

Most of us are special or different in some way—we are all unique individuals. We do some things well and some not so well. The same is true of our students, who have a wide range of differences—those who are cognitively challenged (mental retardation), sensory impaired (hearing and vision), physically disabled, and those students who have behavioral and emotional disorders. It is the teacher's responsibility to provide opportunities that will increase the awareness and acceptance of *all children* with special learning needs.

Integration of students with special learning needs is a mainstay of education. Students with learning, behavioral, and physical disabilities are no longer excluded from general education classrooms but are part of the general education classroom for at least part of the day. This has been referred to as *mainstreaming*. Today there is a widespread call for *inclusion*, the education of children with disabilities in schools with nondisabled children. This includes partial or complete placement of children with disabilities in general education classrooms.

Guidelines for Inclusion of Students with Disabilities in the General Education Classroom

Teachers play an important role in making inclusion successful and in enhancing learning and social opportunities for all students. Teachers set the tone for acceptance through their own behaviors and attitudes. Following are some points to consider as you establish an educational community in your classroom that includes all students (Vaughn and Rothlein, 1994).

1. Children with disabilities are children first. Disabled students are more like their nondisabled classmates than they are like each other. They are children who have all the same needs for love, encouragement, acceptance, and concern that every other child has. Teachers need not worry about how to "treat" a disabled student. Most important is to treat him or her like a child. This message should be communicated both directly and indirectly to other students in the classroom.

2. Use the language of acceptance. Teachers have subtle and not so subtle ways of demonstrating that they accept their students. Students are significantly influenced by what their teachers think and can detect who their teachers like and dislike even when teachers do not intend for this to be apparent. Students are influenced by the teacher's attitude and perceptions of all students, including those with disabilities. Mrs. Wild, a second-grade teacher in an inclusion classroom stated, "I treat all students with respect and concern. I do not want any student in the classroom to feel as though I do not respect them as individuals first and foremost."

3. Provide encouragement and support, not sympathy, for students with disabilities. Students with disabilities do not need others to feel sorry for them or consider them less than any other child. When teachers feel sympathy for students with disabilities they project a disabling attitude that places the disabled student in an inferior position. Mr. Callwood, a sixth-grade teacher whose students represent a variety of exceptionalities, put it this way, "I tell Beverly that she will have to work harder because she has a learning disability and I'm willing to help her. I know it isn't 'fair' that she has to study harder for a test, but that's the way it is and I encourage and support her to do that." Communicate encouragement and support. Let the student know you are aware they have to work harder to succeed, but that you have confidence in them.

4. Be aware of all students' abilities as well as disabilities. All students have something to teach us. Every student is unique in some way that other students and the teacher can learn from. Be sure to discover each student's unique and wonderful qualities, particularly those of disabled students, and make these known to other students.

5. Include all students in the classroom community. Disabled students are sometimes *in* the classroom but not *part of* the classroom. Robert was a student with mental retardation who spent most of his time in Mr. Brett's first-grade class. When Robert was in the classroom he had his own special folder of activities, sat in a desk close to Mr. Brett's and away from other students, and was rarely included in group activities. It was clear to Robert and the other students that he was not part of their community. Ms. Mayo, on the other hand, assured all students they were part of the classroom process. She often provided opportunities for students to work in pairs and small groups so all students could be involved in different ways.

6. Inform students that some disabilities are "hidden." Ms. Borthwick asks her third-grade students to identify what they do well and what they do poorly. She then asks them to identify the things they do poorly that someone would not recognize when they met them. Through this process she informs students that not all of our difficulties are obvious and that often we have problems that interfere with our success that are not apparent to others. She then talks about children who have hearing, vision, health, and learning difficulties that interfere with their success but are not obvious to others.

Applying these principles will assure that all students perceive those with disabilities as valuable members of their classroom community. A checklist for creating an inclusive environment is given on p. 235.

Special Needs Children's Literature for the Inclusive Environment

Since first grade, Amanda knew she wanted to be a teacher. Although her parents tried to encourage her to pursue other areas, she never gave up on her idea to be a teacher. When the day arrived and she had finally achieved her goal, she realized she was not prepared to meet the challenge confronting her. She was assigned a group of second graders whose reading levels ranged from preprimer to sixth grade. She had four students who were identified as learning disabled, ten students who spoke a language other than English at home, and one visually and one physically impaired student. Although she had taken courses that informed her of the diversity she might find in a classroom, she was not sure what to do. She realized she would learn a lot this year. She knew the first thing she needed to do was to help the children to accept each other and learn to work as a community. They all needed to learn that *all* children are fundamentally alike in that they want to be accepted. With this in mind, she remembered her children's literature course and the wonderful children's

CHECKLIST FOR AN INCLUSIVE ENVIRONMENT

Children's Books

In selecting books, do you:

Yes   No

____ ____ Review the pictures for nonstereotypic portrayals of:

____ ____   Sex roles (e.g., show women and girls in assertive roles, men and boys in nurturing roles)?

____ ____   Race (e.g., show people of color in leadership roles)?

____ ____   Disability (e.g., show people with disabilities in active and interactive roles)?

____ ____ Review the text for offensive language (e.g., handicapped, crippled, and the generic "he")?

____ ____ Choose some books that have a female, a person of color, or a person who is disabled as the main character?

____ ____ Choose some books that have a disabled person as the main character?

____ ____ Choose books that depict people with disabilities expressing feelings and being independent and active?

____ ____ Select stories that stress similarities rather than differences between disabled and nondisabled people?

Pictures and Posters

Do the pictures on the walls in your classroom:

Yes   No

____ ____ Include a representative number of adults and children with disabilities?

____ ____ Depict people with a variety of disabilities?

____ ____ Show adults who are disabled in a variety of roles, such as parents, business owners, community workers or leaders, and teachers?

____ ____ Show adults and children with disabilities interacting with others who are not disabled?

____ ____ Show a variety of people from different racial/ethnic and socioeconomic backgrounds?

____ ____ Include women and men involved in nontraditional occupations?

____ ____ Show girls being active and boys expressing feelings?

Trips and Visitors

When planning trips and visits do you:

Yes   No

____ ____ Invite adults with disabilities to visit your class to talk about their work?

____ ____ Invite diverse people who will provide children with a variety of nontraditional role models?

____ ____ Include visiting a person who is disabled at her or his worksite?

____ ____ Plan class trips about accessibility to include pointing out curb cuts, ramps, or elevators with Braille buttons?

____ ____ Provide children with varied ways to experience their environment (e.g., touch, smell, sound, taste)?

General

Yes   No

____ ____ Do you find ways to incorporate disability into classroom activities?

____ ____ Do you take into account the varying skill levels of every child and plan so all children can equally participate in the activities?

____ ____ Do you select classroom materials to provide children with positive role models of women, people of color, and people with disabilities?

____ ____ Can the materials in the classroom be used by all children? If not, can the materials be adapted so all children will have equal access to them?

____ ____ Does the classroom environment provide children with a positive view of themselves and others?

____ ____ Does the dramatic play area offer opportunities to explore a variety of experiences with disability (e.g., child-size crutches, eyeglass frames, hearing aids)?

____ ____ Can the dramatic play area be changed to simulate a school, a store, an office, or other work site?

____ ____ Are you careful to use language that does not convey stereotypes of sex, race, or disability?

____ ____ Do you address children's biases and misconceptions in a sensitive and meaningful way?

____ ____ Are all children in the class represented in some way in the classroom environment?

Reprinted from *Including All of Us: An Early Childhood Curriculum about Disability* written by Merle Froschl, Linda Colon, Ellen Rubin, and Barbara Sprung. Educational Equity Concepts, Inc., 114 E. 32 Street, NY, NY 10025. With permission.

books that dealt with special needs children. "This is the beginning," she thought, as she walked into the library.

She was not surprised at what she found. Her library included only two books that dealt with children with special needs, *Shelley the Hyperactive Turtle*, by Deborah Moss and *Lisa and Her Soundless World*, by Edna Levine. She knew from her children's literature class that there were not many books available on special needs children. She checked out both books. This was her beginning in meeting the challenge of producing a community of learners who would learn about children who are special.

She found that *Shelley the Hyperactive Turtle*, allowed students to identify with Shelley, a little turtle who could not sit still. Shelley's mother becomes concerned because Shelley has such a difficult time staying still. Shelley always feels jumpy and wiggly inside, so his mother takes him to the doctor and they begin to understand why he is different from other turtles. This book provides a subtle introduction to being hyperactive. It helps children feel comfortable and talk about differences in their own and others' behaviors.

Lisa and Her Soundless World gave the students insight into how an 8-year-old's deafness is diagnosed and how it affects her life. This unique book fulfills a need for creating understanding attitudes toward deafness.

As Amanda continued to search for books about children with special needs, the librarian suggested she consult *Children's Books in Print*, where she could look for a subject, author, or title. For example, there are several good books available to introduce the topic of individuals with special needs, such as *About Handicaps: An Open Family Book for Parents and Children Together*, by Sara Bonnet Stein, and *Someone Special, Just Like You*, by Tricia Brown. Although *About Handicaps* focuses mainly on individuals with physical disabilities, it also provides a realistic representation of how young children feel when they encounter persons with a broader group of exceptionalities (e.g., cerebral palsy, missing arm). *Someone Special, Just Like You* contains wonderful photographs of disabled children doing the things children like to do best. The story demonstrates that although children may not hear, see, walk, or talk the way others do, they are not different in their need to experience life completely.

He's My Brother, by Joe Lasker, is a more direct book. It identifies Jamie as a learning disabled child. His older brother describes how things are for Jamie at home and at school. *Alex Is My Friend*, by Marisabina Russo, and Nancy Carlson's *Arnie and the New Kid* provide the reader with an insight and understanding of what it is like to be physically impaired. In *Alex Is My Friend*, Alex is much smaller and is less able to walk and run, even though he is older than his friend. The boys retain a beautiful friendship even though Alex has an operation, sometimes needs a wheelchair, and progressively becomes less physically able. Arnie in *Arnie and the New Kid* begins to see life from a different perspective when he becomes disabled because of a fall at school. As a result, he is able to accept and become friends with Phillip, a new kid (cat) at school who was in a wheelchair. Barbara Booth's beautifully illustrated *Mandy* is a sensitive story about Mandy, a hearing impaired girl, and how she and her grandmother enjoy doing many things (baking cookies, dancing, taking walks) together.

Many teachers, as well as students, have difficulty understanding and coping with unexpected behaviors. Tony Bradman's delightful *Michael* provides an enlightening message. Although Michael is different from all the other students, being late and frequently in trouble, in the end he surprises everyone with his brilliance. In *But Not Kate,* by Marissa Moss, Kate realizes that although she always thought everyone else had something special or was something special, she is special too.

Mental disabilities are dealt with sensitively in *My Sister Is Different,* by Betty Ren Wright, and *Our Brother Has Down's Syndrome,* by Shelly, Jasmine, and Tara Cairo. In both books, siblings struggle with a brother or sister who is mentally disabled only to find out how very special they are and how much in common they have with all other brothers and sisters in the world.

Spectacles, by Ellen Raskin, is a humorous story about Iris, a little girl who needs glasses. After some resistance, Iris realizes she can see better with glasses and enjoys them. In *Suzy,* by Elizabeth Chapman, a partially sighted child reads large-type books and needs to use a magnifying glass to see words and letters.

More and more, books that deal with health impairments are becoming available. For example, Margaret Merrifield's *Come Sit by Me* is a beautifully illustrated, sensitive, and realistic story about a young girl who learns that one of her schoolmates has AIDS.

The theme of all of these books is that while all children are exceptional or special in some way, some have disabilities that make their exceptional characteristics more obvious. The more we know about disabilities the more likely we are to "accept" and "integrate" individuals with disabilities into our classrooms.

Activities for Inclusion of Students with Special Learning Needs in the General Education Classroom

1. Read aloud or ask the students to read books about people who have physical disabilities, such as *My Brother, Matthew,* by Mary Thompson, or *Emmy,* by Connie Jordan Green. Then invite an adult with a physical disability to come to the class and explain why he or she has a physical disability and how he or she learned to use a compensating device. Allow students to ask questions.

2. Sometimes it is difficult to know when you can "catch something" from someone. For example, ask the students, can you catch a cold? a broken leg? Discuss these and other diseases and conditions to illustrate what you can and cannot catch from others. This is a good time to read *Come Sit by Me,* by Margaret Merrifield, which discusses how AIDS cannot be caught. Explain

that *contagious* refers to things you can "catch" from others and ask them to name a time they were sick with something that was contagious. Ask them to name a time when they or someone else had something wrong with them and it was not contagious.

3. Provide the students with an opportunity to walk as if they had cerebral palsy, like Joe in *About Handicaps*. Ask them how they would feel if they couldn't straighten their legs. What if someone teased them by imitating them?

4. Read aloud or ask the students to read one of Franklin D. Roosevelt's biographies. Ask if they knew one of our presidents was in a wheelchair. As a class, make a list of all the occupations persons with physical disabilities can have. Discuss the fact that there are very few careers those with physical disabilities cannot pursue.

5. Read a book about someone in a wheelchair, such as *Arnie and the New Kid*, by Nancy Carlson. Then bring in a wheelchair and show it to the students. Let them sit in it and push it. Ask them to make a list of things that are difficult to do in a wheelchair and another list of things that can be done easily in a wheelchair. Using the language experience approach, write a story about a child who is in a wheelchair or in some way physically impaired. Ask the students to illustrate the story.

6. Discuss how everyone is special in some way. Tell the students ways you think you are special. Ask them to tell you ways they think they are special. Read books about being special, such as *But Not Kate*, by Marissa Moss, or *Someone Special, Just Like You*, by Tricia Brown. Pair the students and ask them to identify something special about their partner. Ask each child to introduce his or her partner by saying, "This is John. He is special because he . . ."

7. Discuss how students do not all learn at the same rate and do things equally well. Read books such as *Leo the Late Bloomer*, by Robert Kraus, or *He's My Brother*, by Joe Lasker. Ask the students to list three things they do really well and three things that are hard for them to do. Talk about the differences in how they feel about doing things that are easy compared with those that are difficult.

8. In stories such as *Lisa and Her Soundless World*, by Edna S. Levine, and *Mandy*, by Barbara Booth, students read about what it is like not to be able to hear. Allow time for the students to sit quietly indoors or outdoors and listen for sounds. After a few minutes, make a list of sounds they heard. Ask them how their world would be different if they couldn't hear these sounds.

9. Make available sign language books, such as *Sesame Street Sign Language Fun*, by the Sesame Street Staff, or *Words in Our Hands*, by Ada B. Litchfield. Help the students learn some sign language.

10. Read books such as *Spectacles*, by Ellen Raskin, or *A Cane in Her Hand*, by Ada B. Litchfield, about needing glasses to see or a cane to move about.

Invite an optometrist or ophthalmologist to class to discuss the importance of taking proper care of their eyes. Ask him or her to bring brochures for the students.

English as a Second Language Students

There is a growing number of students in U.S. public schools who speak languages other than English. According to a recent U.S. Department of Education report (1991), more than 2.2 million students in U.S. schools have limited English proficiency. The Hispanic population has increased by 53 percent and the Asian/Pacific Islander population 107.8 percent from 1980–1990 levels (Forum, 1991). Many of these students are not receiving the type of instruction that best meets their needs, because schools are unable to provide bilingual teachers and other resources (books, magazines) for primary language literacy development (Freeman and Freeman, 1993).

There are at least four distinctly different methods of teaching English as a second language (ESL) being implemented across the United States. In pull-out ESL programs, Limited English Proficiency (LEP) students attend small-group classes taught by special teachers for a specific period of time. Usually no instruction in the student's primary language is provided. In two-way bilingual programs, students receive part of their instruction in English and part in their primary language. In content ESL programs, specially trained teachers provide content area instruction in English, modifying their methods and language so LEP students can understand. In transitional bilingual programs, students are provided a strong foundation in their primary language before English instruction is started. The content areas may be taught in the primary language for two or three years while English is also taught. There are advantages and disadvantages to each of these methods, but a significant amount of research supports the notion that the most effective way for ESL students to develop both English language proficiency and academic concepts is through their first language (Collier, 1989; Crawford, 1989; Cummins, 1989; Freeman and Freeman, 1992a, 1992b; Hudelson, 1987; Krashen, 1985; Krashen and Biber, 1988; Olsen and Mullen, 1990; Ramirez, 1991).

Parental involvement is very important in any type of ESL program. Researchers report that parents of ESL students are interested in their education and willing to work with the school to support their children's literacy learning (Delgado-Gaitan, 1990; Goldenberg, 1987). There is strong evidence that suggests that parents of children from diverse backgrounds will make a consistent effort to help their children with homework and are willing to work hard to foster their children's reading and writing (Goldenberg, 1987). Yet many teachers report what they sense as a lack of interest from parents of children from diverse backgrounds. Although parents of ESL students may not always come forward and volunteer to become involved with the schools in the education of their children, sufficient research supports their interest. One reason they do not come forward may be their unfamiliarity with the mainstream culture of the school; also, they may feel their limited abilities in English will make it difficult to communicate with the teacher (Delgado-Gaitan and Trueba, 1991). Teachers must do whatever they can to make these parents feel comfortable and a part of the school and classroom community.

It is important for teachers to be aware that many children of diverse backgrounds are part of extended families who help them. Therefore, communication with the home via newsletters, notes, and so on should be carefully worded to accommodate this. Inviting other members of the family to parent conferences, meetings, and other school activities can encourage additional participation (see Chap. 15).

Guidelines for Inclusion of English as Second Language Students in the General Education Classroom

Many ESL students who have reading and other academic problems are placed in special reading and/or language programs or special education resource rooms. Regardless of the method used for teaching ESL students, the following strategies need to be developed by general education teachers who work with these students, because they play an important role in helping ESL students learn English.

1. Make available books, magazines, and other resources written in the students' primary language. This sends a strong message to the students that you and the school value diversity in language and culture. For example, *Family Pictures/Cuadros de familia,* by Carmen Lomas Garza, not only is an easy-to-read bilingual (English/Spanish) text but also allows readers to identify with the Mexican American culture as they savor the fiestas, holidays, and religious activities of a close-knit Mexican American family. Lois Ehlert's bilingual (English/Spanish) *Moon Rope,* with striking graphic design, allows its Spanish-speaking readers to read the Peruvian folk tale in their primary language. Freeman and Cervantes (1991) have compiled an annotated bibliography of more than 300 children's books written in Spanish.
2. Serve as a speech model. For many children, the major contact with English is at school, and they need a good speech model to imitate. This is important because many ESL children converse in their native language at home and in their neighborhoods.
3. Demonstrate and communicate an appreciation of and respect for the culture and language of speakers of other languages. Read stories that share others' culture. There is a fast-growing list of excellent multicultural literature from which to select. For example, *Aunt Flossie's Hats,* by Elizabeth Howard, *When I Am Old With You,* by Angela Johnson, and *My Doll Keisha,*

by Eloise Greenfield, allow the reader to experience the everyday experiences of African American families. *The Lotus Seed,* by Sherry Garland, presents a vivid picture of Vietnamese culture and a girl's loyalty to her homeland. Authors such as José Aruego, Laurence Yep, and Yoshiko Uchida write excellent Asian/Pacific American literature. *Tonweya and the Eagles and Other Lakota Indian Tales,* by Rosebud Yellow Robe, *Big Thunder Magic,* by Craig Kee Strete, and *Hawk, I'm Your Brother,* by Byrd Baylor, provide insights into Native American culture.

4. Celebrate holidays of other cultures. Books such as *The Whole Earth Holiday Book,* by Linda Polin and Aileen Cantwell, *Family Pictures/Cuadros de familia,* by Carmen Lomas Garza, and *Nine Days to Christmas,* by Marie Hall Ets and Aurora Labastida, provide a sense of what holidays and celebrations are like in other countries.

5. Cook and serve foods from various cultures. Children's cookbooks, such as Carole Allyn and Lois Webb's *The Multicultural Cookbook for Students* and Norah Dooley's *Everybody Cooks Rice,* allow children to experiment with foods from various cultures.

6. Invite resource people from other cultures to share their culture with the class.

7. Use the students' primary language to enrich the print in the classroom. For example, write color words, number words, helpers, signs, and messages in multiple languages. Books such as Muriel Feelings's *Jambo Means Hello: Swahili Alphabet Book* and *Mojo Means One: Swahili Counting Book* provide good reinforcement.

8. Solicit help from bilingual parents, aides, and other students in reading and writing with students in their primary language.

9. Be aware that the students' first language differs from English not only in vocabulary but also in basic sentence patterns, intonation patterns, and phonemes that make up words.

10. Focus on and work with the students' oral language base. For example, after reading *The Trouble with Elephants,* by Chris Riddell, give students a chance to respond to the open statement "The trouble with elephants is . . ." Write the responses on the chalkboard and then choral read with the class.

11. Create a whole language learning environment that provides many direct experiences as well as books and media. Use easy-to-read books with predictable, repetitive, patterned stories.

12. Wait until students are literate in English to teach formal grammar.

13. Pair an ESL student with an English-speaking child. This helps the ESL student with language as well as adjustment to school.

14. Involve parents in providing support. Parents need to realize that the quality of home language interaction is vitally important, whether or not they speak English. It is important that they provide the multicultural link to the classroom, in terms of both social and emotional support. They can also provide factual information about language and culture.

Teachers should not get discouraged when working with ESL students; researchers cite evidence that most children require four to six years of instruction to achieve the level of proficiency in a second language needed to participate fully in school.

15. Invite bilingual students to publish and share their own stories written in other languages.

Children's Literature for English as a Second Language Students

A common strategy suggested for teachers working with ESL students is to create an environment that provides books with easy-to-read, predictable, repetitive, and patterned stories.

Hough et al. (1986) reported that frequent reading of stories to small groups of ESL students helps them acquire language and motivates them to want to read in English. They suggest the following guidelines for a read-aloud program:

1. Read often—at least once a day.
2. Focus on meaning while reading.
3. Involve the students in the story by asking thought-provoking questions at their level of proficiency.
4. Use predictable books and encourage the students to repeat the refrain.
5. Select books with good illustrations that are tied closely to the text.
6. Read and reread favorite books.
7. Have students listen to tapes or records of books as they follow along in the book.
8. Provide follow-up activities—dramatization, retelling the story in their own words, puppet shows, flannel board stories, and so on.

Stories or poetry can also be used to present new vocabulary and language structures. Students can join the reader when they are familiar with story, producing language on their own as well as benefitting by repetition of words and phrases.

Illustrations in books can be used to teach concepts. For example, in *Airport*, by Bryon Barton, students can learn the names of different parts of the plane as well as general procedures for traveling in an airplane.

Listening to stories helps ESL students learn story grammar, making it possible for them to express themselves through writing.

English as a second language students need to talk, read, and write about things within their own experience. Books can help provide the necessary background, using the guidelines below and the activities on pages 244–246. To begin, select a book appropriate for your students. The list that follows uses *The Gold Coin*, by Alma Flor Ada as an example.

1. **Initiating Activity.** Seat the children in a comfortable circle around you so everyone can see the illustrations. Show them the book. Point to the title as

you read it aloud. Read the summary of the book on the book jacket. Ask the students to predict what the story is about.

2. **Vocabulary Introduction.** Introduce key vocabulary words by writing them on the chalkboard and choral reading. Put up line drawings and picture clues to represent the key words.

3. **Reading Aloud.** Before reading the story, become familiar with the text. Be sure the students are comfortable and can see the illustrations. Eliminate all noise and distractions.

   Read with expression and maintain eye contract with the students throughout the reading. You need not read every single word. Especially for ESL students, long, overdescriptive passages often should be shortened. Allow time for the students to examine the illustrations. Encourage them to participate by periodically asking for predictions about what might happen next or questions that will enhance their comprehension and interest.

4. **Discussion Questions.** Ask that questions generate discussion. For example, ask students to describe what kind of person Juan is at the beginning of the story and at the end of the story. Why was Juan's skin so pale and sickly looking? What would have happened if Juan had stolen the gold coin from the woman the first night he saw it? Why was Dona Josefa called the healer? Is that a good name for her? Why or why not? The story said Juan had neither friend nor relative. Why was this the case? What happened that made Juan a nicer and happier person? Did Dona Josefa know Juan was a robber when he asked for the gold coin? What will Juan be after he fixes Dona Josefa's roof? Will he continue to steal from other people?

5. **Journal Writing Activity.** Remind the students that the book jacket said *The Gold Coin* is an original tale with a Central American setting that shows "there are other, human kinds of treasure waiting to be discovered." Ask them to write a journal entry explaining what they think that statement means.

6. **Follow-up Activities.**
   a. Write Dona Josefa's name vertically on the chalkboard. As a class, write words that begin with the letters in her name that describe the kind of person she is. For example:
      D   Dear
      O
      N
      A
      J
      O
      S
      E
      F
      A

b. Show the students the picture of Dona Josefa's hut and point out its thatched roof. Explain that thatched roofs are made of plant materials, such as straw, reeds, or palm fronds. Give the students a sheet of construction paper and ask them to draw Dona Josefa's hut. Have them use straw, grass, or other available plant materials to create a thatched roof. Discuss the pros and cons of having a thatched roof. Ask them if they have ever seen or lived in a house with a thatched roof.

c. Discuss why some people steal from other people and some ways to help stop people from stealing and/or to protect themselves from robbers. Ask a police officer to speak to the class about robberies and their consequences.

d. Discuss the meaning and purposes of book dedications. Read the dedication of the book and ask the students what they think the author meant by it. Have them create other dedications they think would be appropriate for the book.

e. Allow time for the students to look at the illustrations. Ask them to select their favorite character or part of the story and create an illustration for it.

f. Ask the students to think about how Juan looks at the beginning of the story and how he looks at the end. What differences do they see in his eyes and mouth? Have them draw, on the left side of a piece of paper, how Juan looks at the beginning of the story and, on the right, how he looks at the end. When they have completed their drawings, discuss what they think caused the difference in the way Juan looks.

g. In *The Gold Coin*, Dona Josefa cared for many people and offered them her gold coins. Ask the students to think of good things they have done for other people. Give them gold or yellow paper and ask them to cut out a large circle to represent a gold coin. Have them write on their coin one good deed they have done. Put the caption "Our Gold Coins" on the bulletin board and attach the children's good deed gold coins.

Activities for ESL Students

1. Have the students tell or write an original new ending to a story that is read to them.
2. Have students make illustrations of a story that has been read in the sequence in which it happened. Using these illustrations, ask them to retell the story in their own words.
3. Have students do a spontaneous dramatization of a story read to them.
4. Have students pantomime a character from a story that has been read to them. Ask other students to guess the character.
5. Ask students to create text to accompany the illustrations in a picture book. Write their story on the chalkboard and choral read it.
6. Have students listen to recordings of their favorite stories. You can produce these yourself.

7. Have students retell a favorite story using flannel board characters or puppets as props.

8. Have students create new lines for stories with repetitive lines. For example, in *The Mixed-Up Chameleon*, by Eric Carle, many of the sentences begin with, "I wish I could." Let the children create endings to this sentence. Write them on the chalkboard and choral read their suggestions. Students can copy the completed statements and illustrate them. These can be compiled into a book for the class library.

9. Read stories that emphasize pronouns and prepositions. (Hispanic students often have difficulty with pronouns and prepositions.)

10. Assign each student one page or section of a book to read and write one or two sentences about it. They can combine their contributions to make the story complete.

11. Use capsule vocabulary strategy (Crist, 1975).
    a. Prepare a capsule. Review or have students review a wordless picture book and select 10–15 words that seem necessary and important to tell the story.
    b. Introduce the capsule. Have a 5–15-minute discussion about the book, using the new vocabulary words. As each word is used, write it on the chalkboard and discuss it.
    c. Reinforce speaking vocabulary. Assign students to small groups to reinforce further standard English speaking skills and to learn the new vocabulary words. The students should try to use as many of the vocabulary words as possible. The discussion should last approximately ten minutes.
    d. Reinforce writing vocabulary. Have students write short paragraphs or stories using the new vocabulary words.

12. For each student, staple together 27 sheets of lined paper. On the cover, write the student's name. Write the letters of the alphabet at the top of each page (one per page). As students learn new vocabulary words, have them write them on the appropriate pages in their dictionary. Encourage them to write the words in English as well as in their primary language. Their dictionary will be filled quickly.

13. Have students prepare a sales pitch for a book they have listened to or read. Have them take their sales pitch, along with the book, to another classroom to tell the class about the book and why they should read it.

14. Make bingo cards with vocabulary words and play bingo.

15. Have students draw copies of book covers, being sure the title and author are visible. Mount them on a wall.

16. Have students keep a log of all the books they have read or listened to at home or in school. They could include summaries of each and add what they liked and disliked.

17. Ask students to read recipes to you as you prepare some simple dishes. The following cookbooks are good sources: *Everybody Cooks Rice*, by Norah Dooley, *Cooking the Mexican Way*, by Rosa Coronado, and *The Multicultural Cookbook for Students*, by Carole L. Allyn and Lois Webb.

18. Ask students to compare and contrast all of the books one author has written. For example, after reading *Flossie and the Fox*, *Mirandy and Brother Wind*, and *A Million Fish—More or Less*, by Patricia McKissack, discuss which book they liked most and which they liked least, and why.

19. Select an illustration and have students describe who is in the illustration, what is happening, and so forth. Ask them to tell a brief story about the illustration. *Tar Beach*, by Faith Ringgold, is an interesting book to use for this activity.

20. Provide a selection of bilingual books for the children to read (see Children's Literature at end of the chapter).

Cultural Diversity in a Literature-Based Classroom

The United States is becoming increasingly diverse. The 1990 U.S. Census reports that the United States has the largest foreign-born population in its history, with 19.7 million persons, or just under 8 percent of the population, born in another country. Many of these immigrants are Asian and Hispanic, the two fastest growing immigrant populations. Minority students outnumber whites in public schools in 23 of the 25 largest cities (Martin, 1988). Today, 12 percent of the U.S. population is African American, 9 percent is Hispanic, 3 percent Asian American, and 76 percent Anglo-American. It is projected that by the year 2050, only 52 percent of the United States will be Anglo-American. Nearly 32 million persons speak a language other than English at home. Felicity Barringer (1991) reports, "The racial complexion of the American population changed more dramatically in the past decade than at any time in the 20th century, with nearly one in every four Americans (now) having African, Asian, Hispanic, or American Indian ancestry."

Frequently, the question "How can a nation such as the United States embrace the diversity of so many cultures?" is asked. The answer is complex and best rests with education. As educators and parents, we must prepare our children to live and work harmoniously and productively in an increasingly multicultural society. As we approach the twenty-first century, American children need to develop a worldview that appreciates the richness of other cultures while at the same time preserving and celebrating their uniqueness. Children need to be provided with resources that allow for exploration and understanding of various people living within and outside our borders.

One of the key resources is literature that reflects cultural diversity, including books from and about other countries. It is important to expose children to the literary heritage of cultures around the world, including Native American, European, African, Asian, and Hispanic cultures (Norton, 1990). Children's books should include all kinds of people, in many different occupations, economic situations, lifestyles, and roles. Children who read a variety of traditional folklore develop an awareness of different languages and cultural backgrounds (Piper, 1986). The range of multicultural books can also help children better understand themselves and their relationship to others (Tway, 1989).

Creating a Multicultural Classroom

Teachers play an important role in creating a multicultural classroom where children can gain a sensitivity for the beliefs, values, and customs of others as well as take pride in their own heritage. Teachers set the tone for the acceptance of each student as an important member of the classroom community. The following guidelines may be helpful in establishing a community of learners where everyone feels as if they belong.

1. Use accepting language and be positive.
2. Build on students' strengths, not their weaknesses.
3. Provide encouragement and support.
4. Involve all students in classroom activities.
5. Demonstrate and communicate an appreciation for the culture and language of speakers of other languages.
6. Solicit help from parents to gain a better understanding of their children's culture.
7. Pair minority students with nonminority students. Both students will learn a great deal from the interaction.
8. Invite people from other cultures to be regular guests in your classroom.
9. Provide books, art, music, foods, and so on that represent a variety of cultures.
10. Celebrate holidays of other cultures, such as Kwanza, Chanukah, and Chinese New Year, in addition to the traditional holidays.
11. Be sensitive to and respect students' needs based on their traditions and customs.

Evaluating and Selecting Multicultural Literature

It is important that teachers, parents, and librarians select well-written books from a variety of genres that represent different cultures—Asian/Pacific (includes Japanese, Korean, Chinese, Vietnamese), African American, Hispanic (includes Mexican, Cuban, Puerto Rican), and Native American. This is not an easy task, because some cultural groups are underrepresented in children's books (Frederick, 1990). Recently, however, there has been a demand for publishers to produce more multicultural books and materials. The following sources can be helpful in locating good multicultural books: *Booklist* (American Library Association), *School Library Journal,* (R.R. Bowker), *Bulletin* (Council on Interracial Books for Children), *The Reading Teacher* (International Reading Association), *Language Arts* (National Council of Teachers of English), *The New Advocate* (Christopher Gordon Publishers), and *Horn Book Magazine* (Horn Book).

Teaching Multicultural Literature to Children in Grades K–8 (Harris, 1992) lists small and independent presses, large presses, organizations, journals, and a small group of bookstores that serve as good sources for multicultural children's literature. *Books Without Bias: Through Indian Eyes* (Slapin and Seale, 1988) is a good resource for books about Native Americans and has articles, essays, and poems written by Native Americans. *Books in Spanish for Children and Young Adults* (Schon, 1985) provides a guide for selecting Spanish-language books for Hispanic children. *Literature for Children about Asian and Asian Americans* (Austin and Jenkins, 1987) provides a guide for selecting literature about Asians and Asian Americans, arranged by nation and subdivided into genres.

Quality multicultural children's books can also be selected from lists of award-winning books (see Appendix A). The Coretta Scott King award, the best known of these, is awarded for outstanding African American literature. There are no other book awards specific to a culture.

Multicultural books for children should be selected using the same criteria as for any book: they should be of high literary and artistic quality, be age appropriate and reflect worthy themes. In addition, the books should:

1. Neither generalize nor present specific images, in text or illustrations, that establish or perpetuate stereotypes
2. Show respect for a variety of lifestyles
3. Reflect and validate the culture
4. Present positive images of minority characters
5. Provide accurate cultural details
6. Represent a variety of authors native and nonnative to the culture

Rudine Sims (1982) developed a classification system for books about African Americans that can also be applied to other multicultural books. The categories are as follows:

1. Socially conscious literature. Sims found that for socially conscious books, "the main goals of authors seemed to have been to create social conscience among white children—to encourage them to develop empathy, sympathy, and tolerance for black children" (p. 651). *Roll of Thunder, Hear My Cry,* by Mildred Taylor, is a good example of a socially conscious book.
2. Melting pot literature. These are usually picture books that present a homogeneous American culture and contain no racial conflict (p. 651). Ezra Jack Keats's *The Snowy Day* and *A Letter to Amy* are good examples of melting pot literature.
3. Culturally conscious books. These books are primarily (but not exclusively) written by authors native to the culture about which they are writing. They are usually more authentic and reveal the author's "insider" perspective. Patricia McKissock's *Flossie and the Fox*, Eloise Greenfield's *Me and Nessie,* and John Steptoe's *Mufaro's Beautiful Daughters* are good examples of culturally conscious books.

Providing a selection of books representing each of these types allows students to gain different perspectives about the cultures and experience the writings of both native and nonnative authors.

Using Multicultural Children's Books in the Classroom

There is growing interest in including multicultural education in classrooms throughout the United States, from preschool through high school. Researchers have found that children between the ages of 4 and 6 are the easiest to teach to be comfortable with and accepting of people of different races and cultures and that by age 9 children's attitudes become more difficult to change (Derman-Sparks, 1989). Many states and local school districts are responding to this need by developing and implementing literature-based curricula that include multicultural books, and publishers are including multicultural literature in basal readers. A plethora of teacher resource books that provide ideas for integrating multicultural children's books into the curriculum are available, and educators are publishing journal articles about teaching with multicultural literature (Norton, 1990). All of this effort is in the spirit of motivating teachers, parents, and librarians to share quality multicultural books with children.

There are many reasons to include quality multicultural children's literature in the curriculum (Rothlein and Wild, 1993).

1. Children can develop a sensitivity for others' beliefs, values, and customs. This is easily accomplished using books such as Lucille Clifton's *Three Wishes*, Elizabeth Fitzgerald Howard's *Aunt Flossie's Hats (and Crab Cakes Later)*, and Audrey Osofsky's *Dream Catcher*. These beautifully illustrated books give the reader an opportunity to share steadfast friendships and loving families as they experience their beliefs, values, and customs.

2. Children learn to understand and value the cultural and literary diversity that is part of our society. A good choice for this objective is *Children of the Great Muskeg*, a collection of writings and drawings of Native American children by Sean Ferris. Poetry also provides excellent insight into cultural and literary diversity. For example, Eloise Greenfield's *Night on Neighborhood Street* and *Honey, I Love and Other Love Poems* and Virginia Driving Hawk Sneve's *Dancing Teepees: Poems of American Indian Youth* contain powerful, sensitive, and diverse voices. *The Mouse Rap*, by Walter Dean Meyers, is a superb novel that reflects very clearly the importance of linguistic and cultural traditions in enriching society as a whole.

3. Children can recognize that there are similarities as well as differences among cultures: all children play games, celebrate holidays, and have basic needs. This is simply demonstrated in Mary Lankford's *Hopscotch Around the World*, which tells of 19 different versions of hopscotch, and Jan McPherson's *Chasing Games from Around the World*, which demonstrates simple games that children from other countries play. Books on friendship allow the reader to see that friends are basically the same, regardless of

their culture. Examples are Claire Murphy's *Friendship Across Artic Waters* and Patricia Polacco's *Mrs. Katz and Tush. Eskimo Boy: Life in an Inupiag Eskimo Villiage,* by Russ Kendall, demonstrates how 7-year-old Norman's life in a small Alaskan village is different from that of the readers and how it is the same. Tricia Brown's *Lee Ann: The True Story of a Vietnamese Girl* shares a Vietnamese tradition, the Tet celebration, giving the reader a sense of another culture and its celebrations.

4. Children can develop a sensitivity to the common needs and emotions of all people. Maxine Rosenberg's picture book, *Brothers and Sisters,* presents the needs and emotions shared by the siblings in three different families, one multicultural, one white, and one African American. It also portrays similarities and differences among people. Eleven-year-old Koya in Eloise Greenfield's *Koya DeLaney and the Good Girl Blues,* who thought she was afraid to show anger, finds herself in a situation where she gets angry in public. Gary Soto's *Baseball in April* is full of warmth, humor, and the experiences and emotions shared by all young people regardless of where they live.

5. Children can gain pride in their own culture. For example, in Susan Kuklin's *How My Family Lives in America,* children tell their own stories about the heritage that makes their families special. *Child of the Owl* and *Dragonwings,* by Laurence Yep, and *In the Year of the Boar and Jackie Robinson,* by Bette Bao Lord, help children learn to appreciate their own culture as they adjust to life in a new country.

6. Children can begin to understand the reason why people from other cultures immigrated to the United States. In Laurence Yep's *The Rainbow People,* immigrants tell about not being able to bring their families to America yet needing to be there themselves to work. *My Grandmother's Journey,* by John Cech, paints a vivid picture of a journey that begins in prerevolutionary Russia and ends in America. Jamie Gibson's *Hello, My Name Is Scrambled Eggs* and Barbara Cohen's *Molly's Pilgrim* serve as excellent catalysts for discussing the many reasons, including political repression, that people have left their countries and migrated to America.

7. Children can recognize and gain insights into the prejudices and difficulties people of various cultures often face. Mildred Taylor's books often include harsh but painfully accurate accounts of racial oppression. Her historical accounts of the close-knit Logan family in *The Song of the Trees, The Road to Memphis, Let the Circle Be Unbroken,* and *Roll of Thunder, Hear My Cry* speak of prejudice, injustice, and unfairness. In Nicholasa Mohr's *Felita,* a young Puerto Rican girl has no friends and even fears for her life because she lives in a neighborhood that would not accept a family from a different culture. *At the Crossroads,* by Rachel Isadora, portrays the injustice of apartheid as it keeps families separated for months at a time. Yoshiko Uchida's *A Jar of Dreams* and *The Best Bad Thing* tell of the Japanese American's experiences during the years of the Great Depression. Ossie Davis's *Just Like Martin,* set in Alabama during the early years of the

Civil Rights Movement, is told by a young African American boy who is caught up in the movement and struggles to practice nonviolence in a violent setting.

Books may not be a substitute for first-hand contact with other people, but they can help deepen and enrich our understanding of other cultures. This is particularly important for today's children, who live in such a pluralistic society. It is essential that they learn to respect and appreciate the diversity of all cultures.

Activities for Cultural Diversity

1. Obtain crayons that reflect the natural skin colors of people around the world. Have children use them to illustrate a character from a favorite book.
2. Obtain a copy of *The Whole Earth Holiday Book,* by Linda Polin and Aileen Cantwell, or *Small World Celebrations,* by Jean Warren. Tell students how various holidays are celebrated in different parts of the world. Select a holiday and have a celebration. Enter as many ethnic holidays as you and the class can name on a calendar. Throughout the year, recognize these holidays with an activity related to that culture.
3. Invite community members who have lived in other countries to tell the class about the customs and traditions there. Prior to their visits, ask the students to read books relating to the culture. Encourage the students to ask questions.
4. Similar themes are found in folk tales from different cultures. Read books such as *Yeh-Shen, A Cinderella Story from China,* retold by Ai-Ling Louie, *Lon Po Po: A Red Riding Hood Story from China,* by Ed Young, to the class and ask students to compare and contrast them with familiar Cinderella and Little Red Riding Hood stories. *The Story Teller's Sourcebook* (Read McDonald, 1992) is an annotated bibliography of folk tales from other countries.
5. Have children use multicultural learning aids, such as musical instruments and multicultural dolls, to dramatize their favorite stories (see Professional Resources).
6. Request from the Anti-Defamation League of B'nai B'rith (823 United Nations Plaza, New York, NY 10017) information on multicultural materials and issues. For example, *The Wonderful World of Difference* consists of 20 lessons (K–8) designed to help children explore the diversity and richness in the human family. Use these materials to reinforce what the students learn through readings of other cultures.
7. Show *The Rabbit Brothers,* by Robert Kraus (Anti-Defamation League: see 6, above), a cartoon filmstrip with an accompanying booklet about twin

rabbits—Joe, who dislikes all rabbits different from himself and is miserable, and George, who tries to find some good in all rabbits and is much happier. Allow time for discussion.

8. Using *Chasing Games from Around the World,* by Jan McPherson, teach the students simple games from other countries.

9. Using *Multicultural Cooking with Kids* (Lakeshore Learning Materials, (800) 421-5354), help the students prepare some of the 30 recipes. Discuss the cultures from which the recipes originate.

10. Show the students a passport and discuss its purpose. Let them see how the passport has been stamped to indicate the countries visited. Then help them make their own passports by stapling paper together to make a booklet. Take pictures of the students or ask them to bring in pictures of themselves. Glue the pictures in the passport and write in them the students' name, address, and place and date of birth. Every time they read a book about another culture, have them "log in" to that country by writing the country's name or drawing a picture that represents the country.

11. Organize an "International Day." Ask the children to bring in favorite foods of various cultures. Make dances, music traditions, clothing, and other customs part of the celebration. This is a good time to read Peter Spier's *People.*

12. Ask the students to compare themselves with a character from one of the multicultural books they have read. Use a Venn diagram (page 135) to illustrate this comparison. For example, have the students list adjectives that describe the book character in circle 1, adjectives that describe themselves in circle 2, list and adjectives that describe both in the area that overlaps.

13. Folk tales reflect the fundamental beliefs of the culture from which they originate. Ask the students to find a folk tale that represents their heritage and to present the tale to the class by reading it, acting it out, or making a television or puppet show.

14. Help the students create a trivia card game about characters, settings, and themes from the multicultural books they have read. For example, from the book, *Abuelo* by Arthur Dorros, the following trivia card could be made.

> Abuelo and Cassie flew over: (a) Mexico City, (b) Miami, Florida, (c) New York City

15. Ask students to read books from Ann Martin's Baby Sitters Club series published since 1986 (which include a Japanese American and an African American character), *Meet Addy,* the fifth book in the American Girl series (which features an African American character), and Jerry Spinelli's *Maniac Magee.* Discuss these books and evaluate how well the authors represent the cultures they present.

16. Remind the students that many of the stories they read were handed down from family to family. Ask them to think of and/or ask their parents about a story that has been passed down in their family. Allow time for them to share these stories. Books such as Julius Lester's *How Many Spots Does a Leopard Have* (African and Jewish folk tale for grades 4–6) or Sybil Hancock's *Esteban and the Ghost* (Spanish folk tale for grades K–3) may be helpful to promote this activity.

17. Encourage the students to read stories about families who have moved from one country to another, such as the characters in *In the Year of the Boar and Jackie Robinson,* by Bette Lord, or *Petanella,* by Betty Waterton. As a class project, write a short story about what it would be like to move from the United States to another country.

Children's Literature

*Cited in text.

Students with Special Learning Needs

General Disabilities

*Brown, Tricia. *Someone Special, Just Like You.* Photographs by Fran Oritz. Holt, Rinehart & Winston, 1984. (Grades K–2)

*Moss, Marissa. *But Not Kate.* Lothrop, Lee & Shepard, 1992. (Grades K–3)

Rosenberg, M. B. *My Friend Leslie: The Story of a Handicapped Child.* Lothrop, Lee & Shepard, 1983. (Grades K–3)

*Stein, Sara Bonnet. *About Handicaps: An Open Family Book for Parents and Children Together.* Walker, 1974. (Grades 1–4 with additional text for parents)

Thompson, M. *My Brother, Matthew.* Woodbine, 1992. (Grades 1–5)

Ward, B. R. *Overcoming Disability.* Franklin Watts, 1989. (Grades 1–5)

Wood, J. R. *The Man Who Loved Clowns.* G.P. Putnam. (Grades 3–6)

Mental Retardation

Amenta, C. A. III. *Russell Is Extra Special: A Book About Autism for Children.* Magination, 1992. (Grades K–3)

Anders, F. *A Look at Mental Retardation.* Lerner, 1976. (Grades 3–6)

Bergman, T. *We Love, We Laugh, We Cry.* Gareth Stevens, 1989. (Grades 1–6)

Berkus, C. W. *Charlsie's Chuckle.* Woodbine, 1992. (Grades K–6)

*Cairo, Shelley, Jasmine Cairo, and Tara Cairo. *Our Brother Has Down's Syndrome.* Photographs by Irene McNeil. Annick, 1991. (Grades 1–3)

Kroll, V. L. *My Sister, Then and Now.* Carolrhoda, 1992. (Grades 1–3)

Litchfield, A. B. *Making room for Uncle Joe.* Whitman, 1992. (Grades 2–5)

O'Shaughnessy, E. *Somebody Called Me a Retard Today . . . and My Heart Felt Sad.* Walker, 1992. (Grades 1–3)

Rabe, B. *Where's Chimpy?* Whitman, 1992. (Grades Pre-S–2)

*Wright, Betty Ren. *My Sister Is Different.* Illustrated by Helen Cogancherry. Raintree, 1981. (Grades 1–4)

Learning Disabilities

Aiello, B., and J. Shulman. *Secrets Aren't Aways for Keeps.* Illustrated by Loel Barr. Twenty-Five Century, 1988. (Grades 4–6)

Avi. *Man from the Sky.* Orchard/Jackson, 1992. (Grades 3–6)

Betancourt, J. *My Name Is Brin Brian.* Scholastic, 1993. (Grades 3–6)

Birdseye, Tom. *Just Call Me Stupid.* Holiday, 1993. (Grades 3–6)

Cassedy, S. *M.E. and Morton.* Thomas Y. Crowell, 1987. (Grades 4–6)

Dunn, K. B. and A. B. Dunn. *Trouble with School.* Woodbine, 1993. (Grades 1–5 and parents)

Dwyer, K. M. *What Do You Mean I Have a Learning Disability?* Walker, 1991. (Grades 5–9)

Fassler, J. *One Little Girl.* Human Sciences, 1969. (Grades Pre-S–3)

Gehret, J. *The Don't Give Up Kid.* Verbal Images, 1990. (Grades 1–3)

Janover, C. *Josh, A Boy with Dyslexia.* Illustrated by Edward Epstein. Waterfront, 1988. (Grades 3–6)

*Kraus, Robert. *Leo the Late Bloomer.* Photographs by Jose Aruego. Simon & Schuster, 1971. (Grades K–1)

*Lasker, Joe. *He's My Brother.* Albert Whitman, 1974. (Grades 1–3)

Rosenberg, M. B. *My Friend Leslie.* Lothrop, Lee & Shepard, 1983. (Grades 1–3)

Visual Impairments

Alexander, S. H. *Mom Can't See Me.* Photos by George Ancona. Macmillan, 1990. (Grades 3–6)

Bergman, T. *Seeing in Our Special Ways.* Gareth Stevens, 1989. (Grades 2–5)

*Chapman, Elizabeth. *Suzy.* Illustrated by Margery Gill. Bodley Head, 1982. (Grades K–2)

Davidson, M. *Helen Keller.* Hastings, 1989. (Grades 2–4)

Litchfield, A. B. *A Cane in Her Hand.* Whitman, 1992. (Grades 1–3)

MacLachan, P. *Through Grandpa's Eyes.* HarperCollins, 1980. (Grades 2–4)

*Raskin, Ellen. *Spectacles.* Atheneum, 1968. (Grades K–2)

Yolen, J. *The Seeing Stick.* HarperCollins, 1975. (Grades K+)

Hearing Impairments

Arthur, C. *My Sister's Silent World.* Children's Press, 1979. (Grades 2–4)

Aseltine, L., Mueller, et al. *I'm Deaf and It's Okay.* Whitman, 1992. (Grades 1–4)

*Booth, B. D. *Mandy.* Lothrop, Lee & Shepard, 1991. (Grades 1–3)

*Levine, E. S. *Lisa and Her Soundless World.* Human Sciences, 1974. (Grades 1–5)

Litchfield, A. B. *A Button in Her Ear.* Whitman, 1992. (Grades 1–3)

———. *Words in Our Hands.* Whitman, 1992. (Grades 2–4)

St. George, J. *Dear Dr. Bell . . . Your Friend Helen Keller.* Putnam, 1992. (Grades 1–4)

Sullivan, M. B., L. Bourke, and S. Regan. *A Show of Hands: Say It in Sign Language.* HarperCollins, 1992. (Grades 2–6)

Walker, Lou Ann. *Hand, Heart and Mind.* Dial, 1994. (Grades 5–9)

Physical and Health Impairments

Alexander, S. H. *Mom's Best Friend.* Macmillan, 1992. (Grades 1–3)

Bergman, T. *On Our Own Terms.* Gareth Stevens, 1989. (Grades 1–3)

Bernstein, J. E., and B. Fireside. *Special Parents, Special Children.* Whitman, 1992. (Grades 3–7)

*Carlson, Nancy. *Arnie and the New Kid.* Puffin, 1990. (Grades Pre-K–2)

Caseley, J. *Harry and Willy Carrothead.* Greenwillow, 1991. (Grades K–3)

Dugan, B. *Loop the Loop.* Greenwillow, 1992. (Grades 1–3)

Durant, P. R. *When Heroes Die.* Viking, 1992. (Grades 2–4)

Emmert, M. *I'm the Big Sister Now.* Whitman, 1992. (Grades 2–6)

Fassler, J. *Howie Helps Himself.* Whitman, 1975. (Grades 1–3)

Gallico, P. *The Snow Goose.* Knopf, 1992. (Grades 9+)

Gellman, E. *Jeremy's Dreidel.* Kar-Ben, 1992. (Grades 1–3)

Getz, D. *Almost Famous.* Holt, 1992. (Grades 2–4)

Girard, L. W. *Alex, the Kid with AIDS.* Whitman, 1992. (Grades 2–5)

*Green, C. J. *Emmy.* Lerner, 1992. (Grades 1–3)

Hamm, D. J. *Grandma Drives a Motor Bed.* Whitman, 1992. (Grades Pre-S–3)

Helfman, E. *On Being Sarah.* Whitman, 1992. (Grades 1–3)

Henriod, L. *Grandma's Wheelchair.* Whitman, 1992. (Grades 1–3)

Jordan, M. *Losing Uncle Tim.* Whitman, 1992. (Grades 2–6)

Kesey, K. *The Sea Lion.* Illustrated by Neil Waldman. Viking, 1991. (Grades 4–6)

Kiementz, J. *How It Feels to Live with a Physical Disability.* Simon & Schuster, 1992. (Grades 4–6)

Lasker, J. *Nick Joins In.* Whitman, 1980. (Grades 1–3)

*Merrifield, Margaret. *Come Sit by Me.* Illustrated by Heather Collins. Women's Press, 1990. (Grades K–3)

Muldoon, K. M. *Princess Pooh.* Whitman, 1992. (Grades 2–5)

Osofsky, A. *My Buddy.* Holt, 1992. (Grades 1–3)

Powers, M. E. *Our Teacher's in a Wheelchair.* Whitman, 1992. (Grades Pre-S–3)

Rabe, B. *The Balancing Girl.* Dutton, 1981. (Grades Pre-S–2)

Roy, R. *Move Over, Wheelchairs Coming Through!* Clarion, 1985. (Grades 4–6)

*Russo, Marisabina. *Alex Is My Friend.* Greenwillow, 1992. (Grades K–2)

Schwartz, C. *Lee, the Rabbit with Epilepsy.* Woodbine, 1989. (Grades Pre-S–2)

*Thompson, M. *My Brother Matthew.* Woodbine, 1992. (Grades 1–3)

Behavior Disorders

*Bradman, Tony. *Michael.* Macmillan, 1990. (Grades K–3)

Gehret, J. *Eagle Eye: A Child's View of Attention Deficit Disorders.* Illustrated by Susan Covert. Verbal Images, 1991. (Grades 4–6)

Moss, M. *But Not Kate.* Lothrop, Lee & Shepard, 1992. (Grades K–3)

*———. *Shelley the Hyperactive Turtle.* Illustrated by Carol Schwartz. Woodbine, 1989. (Grades K–3)

Bilingual

Avery, C. E. *Everybody Has Feelings: A Photographic Essay.* Open Hand, 1992.

Bailey, D. *Los Osos.* Steck-Vaughn, 1992.

Belpre, P. *Perez y Martina: Un Cuento Folklorico Puertorriqueño.* Viking, 1966.

Borlenghi, P. *From Albatross to Zoo: An Alphabet Book in Five Languages.* Scholastic, 1992.

Brown, R. *Alphabet Times Four: An International ABC.* Dutton, 1991.

Day, A. *Carlito en el Parque Una Tarde.* Farrar, Straus & Giroux, 1991.

Ehlert, L. *Moon Rope: A Peruvian Folktale.* Harcourt Brace Jovanovich, 1992.

Ets, M. H., and A. Labastida. *Nueve Dias Para Navidad.* Viking, 1987.

Freeman, D. *Un Bolsillo Para Corduroy.* Viking, 1978.

Heller, R. *Las Gallinas No Son Las Unicas.* Grosset & Dunlap, 1992.

Keats, E. J. *Silba por Willie.* Viking, 1964.

Levinson, R. *Mira Como Salen Las Estrellas.* Dutton, 1985.

Mayorga, D. *David Juega al Escondite en Celebraciones.* Lerner, 1989.

————. *David Juega al Escondite en Cuentos Folkloricos.* Lerner, 1989.

————. *David Juega al Escondite en Vacaciones.* Lerner, 1989.

Scieszka, J. *¡La Verdadera Historia de Los Tre Cerditos!* Viking, 1989.

Shulevitz, U. *El Tesoro.* Farrar, Straus & Giroux, 1978.

Singer, I. B. *Por Que Noe Eligio la Paloma.* Farrar, Straus & Giroux, 1973.

Va, L. *A Letter to the King.* HarperCollins, 1987.

Winter, J. *Diego.* Knopf, 1991.

Zemach, M. *Siempre Puede Ser Peor.* Farrar, Straus & Giroux, 1976.

English as a Second Language (ESL) Students

*Ada, Alma Flor. *The Gold Coin.* Atheneum, 1991. (Grades 1–3)

*Allyn, Carole L., and Lois Webb. *The Multicultural Cookbook for Students.* Oryx, 1992. (Grades 1–6)

*Baylor, Byrd. *Hawk, I'm Your Brother.* Scribner's, 1976. (Grades 3–5)

*Carle, Eric. *The Mixed-Up Chameleon.* Crowell, 1984. (Grades K–3)

*Coronado, Rosa. *Cooking the American Way.* Lerner, 1982. (Grades 1–5)

*Dooley, Norah. *Everybody Cooks Rice.* Carolrhoda, 1991. (Grades 1–5)

*Elhert, Lois. *Moon Rope.* Harcourt Brace Jovanovich, 1992. (Grades 1–3)

*Ets, Marie Fall, and Aurora Labastida. *Nine Days to Christmas.* Puffin, 1987. (Grades K–3)

*Feelings, Muriel. *Jambo Means Hello: Swahili Alphabet Book.* Dial, 1974. (Grades K–2)

*————. *Mojo Means One: Swahili Counting Book.* Dial, 1971. (Grades K–2)

*Garland, Sherry. *The Lotus Seed.* Harcourt Brace Jovanovich, 1993. (Grades 1–4)

*Garza, Carmen Lomas. *Family Pictures/Cuadros de Familia.* Children's Press, 1990. (Grades K–3)

*Greenfield, Eloise. *My Doll, Keisha.* Black Butterfly, 1991. (Grades K–3)

*Howard, Elizabeth. *Aunt Flossie's Hats.* Clarion, 1991. (Grades K–3)

*Johnson, Angela. *When I Am Old With You.* Orchard, 1990. (Grades 1–3)

*McKissack, Patricia. *Flossie and the Fox.* Dial, 1986. (Grades K–1)

*————. *A Million Fish . . . More or Less.* Knopf, 1991. (Grades 1–3)

*————. *Mirandy and Brother Wind.* Illustrated by Jerry Pinkney. Knopf, 1988. (Grades 2–4)

*Polin, Linda, and Aileen Cantwell. *The Whole Earth Holiday Book.* Scott, Foresman, 1983. (Grades 1–5)

*Ringgold, Faith. *Tar Beach.* Crown, 1991. (Grades K–3)

*Strete, Craig Kee. *Big Thunder Magic.* Greenwillow, 1990. (Grades K–3)

*Yellow Robe, Rosebud. *Tonweya and the Eagles and Other Lakota Indian Tales.* Dial, 1979. (Grades 3–6)

Cultural Diversity

Asia

Adams, E. B., ed. *Blindman's Daughter.* Seoul International, 1992. (Grades 1–3)

————,ed. *Korean Cinderella.* Seoul International, 1992. (Grades 1–3)

Baillie, A. *Little Brother.* Viking, 1992. (Grades 3–7)

Breckler, R. K. *Hoang Breaks the Lucky Teapot.* Houghton Mifflin, 1992. (Grades 2–4)

*Brown, T. *Lee Ann: The Story of a Vietnamese-American Girl.* Illustrated by Ted Thai. Putnam, 1991. (Grades 2–4)

*Cohen, B. *Molly's Pilgrim.* Illustrated by Michael J. Deraney. Lothrop, 1983. (Grades 1–3)

DeJong, M. *The House of Sixty Fathers*. HarperCollins, 1956. (Grades 5–8)

Garland, S. *The Lotus Seed*. Harcourt Brace Jovanovich, 1993. (Grades 2–4)

*Gilson, J. *Hello, My Name Is Scrambled Eggs*. Illustrated by John Wallner. Lothrop, 1985.
    (Grades 1–3)

Girard, L. *We Adopted You, Benjamin Koo*. Albert Whitman, 1989. (Grades 2–6)

Hamanaka, S. *The Journey: Japanese Americans, Racism, and Renewal*. Orchard, 1990.
    (Grades 5+)

Haskins, J. *Count Your Way Through Korea*. Carolrhoda, 1989. (Grades 1–4)

Havil, J. *Treasure Nap*. Houghton Mifflin, 1992. (Grades 2–4)

Ho, M. *The Clay Marble*. Farrar, Straus & Giroux, 1991. (Grades 4–6)

Hong, L.T., reteller. *How the Ox Star Fell from Heaven*. Albert Whitman, 1991. (Grades K–6)

Hoyt-Goldsmith, D. *Hoang Anh: A Vietnamese-American Boy*. Holiday, 1992. (Grades 3–7)

Laurin, A. *The Perfect Crane*. Harper & Row, 1981. (Grades 2–5)

Lee, J. M. *Silent Lotus*. Farrar, Straus & Giroux, 1991. (Grades 2–4)

*Lord, B. *In the Year of the Boar and Jackie Robinson*. Illustrated by Marc Simont. Harper-
    Collins, 1984. (Grades 4–6)

*Louie, A. *Yeh-Shen: A Cinderella Story from China*. Putnam, 1990. (Grades K–3)

MacMillan, D., and D. Freeman. *My Best Friend Duc Tran: Meeting a Vietnamese-American
    Family*. Simon & Schuster, 1987. (Grades 2–5)

Meltzer, M. *All Times, All Peoples: A World History of Slavery*. HarperCollins, 1980.
    (Grades 5+)

———. *The Chinese Americans*. HarperCollins, 1980. (Grades 5+)

Moffett, E. *Korean Ways*. Seoul International, 1986. (Grades K+)

*Namioka, L. *Yang the Youngest and His Terrible Ear*. Little, Brown, 1992. (Grades 3–7)

Pinkwater, M. *Wingman*. Bantam, 1992. (Grades 4–7)

Quayle, E., reteller. *The Shining Princess and Other Japanese Legends*. Arcade, 1989.
    (Grades K–5)

Say, A. *The Bicycle Man*. Houghton Mifflin, 1982. (Grades 3+)

———. *El Chino*. Houghton Mifflin, 1990. (Grades 2–8)

———. *Tree of Cranes*. Houghton Mifflin, 1991. (Grades 2–6)

Surat, M. M. *Angel Child, Dragon Child*. Raintree, 1983. (Grades 3–6)

Tan, A. *The Moon Lady*. Macmillan, 1992. (Grades 1–4)

Tran Khan Tuyet. *The Little Weaver of Thai-Yen Village*. Children's Press, 1987. (Grades
    2–9)

*Uchida, Y. *The Best Bad Thing*. Macmillan, 1983. (Grades 4–7)

———. *The Happiest Ending*. Macmillan, 1985. (Grades 3–7)

———. *The Invisible Thread*. Simon & Schuster, 1991. (Grades 3–6)

*———. *A Jar of Dreams*. Macmillan, 1981. (Grades 4–7)

Wallace, I. *Chin Chiang and the Dragon's Dance*. McElderry, 1984. (Grades K–4)

Wartski, M. C. *A Boat to Nowhere*. Westminster John Knox, 1980. (Grades 4–8)

Wolkstein, D. *White Wave: A Chinese Tale*. HarperCollins, 1979. (Grades K–6)

Yashima, T. *Umbrella*. Viking, 1955. (Grades K–3)

Yee, P. *Roses Sing on New Snow: A Delicious Tale*. Macmillan, 1991. (Grades 1–6)

———. *Tales from Gold Mountain: Stories of the Chinese in the New World*. Macmillan, 1990.
    (Grades Pre-S+)

*Yep, Laurence. *Dragonwings*. HarperCollins, 1975. (Grades 7+)

*———. *Child of the Owl*. HarperCollins, 1977. (Grades 7+)

———. *The Lost Garden: A Memoir*. HarperCollins, 1991. (Grades 3–7)

*———. *The Rainbow People*. HarperCollins, 1989. (Grades 3–7)

————. *The Star Fisher.* Morrow, 1991. (Grades 3+)

————. *Tongues of Jade.* HarperCollins, 1991. (Grades 3–7)

*Young, E., trans. *Lon Po Po: A Red Riding Hood Story from China.* Putnam, 1989. (Grades K–4)

Africa

Aardema, V. *Traveling to Tondo: A Tale of the Nkundo of Zaire.* Knop, 1991. (Grades K–4)

————. *Why Mosquitoes Buzz in People's Ears: A West African Tale.* Dial, 1975. (Grades Pre-S–3)

Adoff, A. *All Colors of the Race.* Lothrop, Lee & Shepard, 1990. (Grades 5+)

————. *Malcolm X.* HarperCollins, 1985. (Grades 3+)

————. *My Black Me: A Beginning Book of Black Poetry.* Dutton, 1974. (Grades 3+)

Archer, Jules. *They Had a Dream.* Viking, 1993. (Grades 5+)

*Armstrong, W. *Sounder.* HarperCollins, 1969. (Grades 4–6)

Belton, S. *From Miss Ida's Porch.* Four Winds, 1993. (Grades K–3)

Berger, T. *Black Fairy Tales.* Macmillan, 1974. (Grades K–4)

Blume, J. *Iggie's House.* Dell, 1986. (Grades 3–6)

Brenner, B. *Wagon Wheels.* Harper & Row, 1984. (Grades 2–5)

Bryan, A. *Beat the Story-Drum, Pum-Pum.* Macmillan, 1987. (Grades 3–6)

————. *Sing to the Sun.* HarperCollins, 1992. (Grades 2+)

Bunting, E. *How Many Days to America: A Thanksgiving Story.* Houghton Mifflin, 1988. (Grades 2–5)

Burgess, B. H. *Oren Bell.* Delacorte, 1991. (Grades 2–5)

Cameron, A. *Julian's Glorious Summer.* Random House, 1987. (Grades 2–4)

Campbell, B. *Taking Care of Yoki.* HarperCollins, 1986. (Grades 3–7)

*Clifton, L. *Three Wishes.* Illustrated by Michael Hays. Doubleday, 1992. (Grades 1–3)

Collier, J., and C. Collier. *Jump Ship to Freedom.* Delacorte, 1981. (Grades 4–6)

Courlander, H., and G. Herzog. *The Cow-Tail Switch and Other West African Stories.* Holt, 1988. (Grades 2–4)

Crews, D. *Bigmama's.* Greenwillow, 1991. (Grades K–3)

Davidson, M. *The Story of Jackie Robinson, Bravest Man in Baseball.* Parachute, 1988. (Grades 4–8)

*Davis, O. *Just Like Martin.* Simon & Schuster, 1992. (Grades 4–6)

Ellis, V. F. *Afro-Bets First Book About Africa.* Just Us, 1990. (Grades Pre-1–4)

Ferris, J. *Go Free or Die: A Story about Harriet Tubman.* Carolrhoda, 1988. (Grades 3–5)

*Fox, P. *Slave Dancer.* Macmillan, 1982. (Grades 5+)

Fritz, J. *Brady.* Puffin, 1987. (Grades 5–9)

Gerson, M. J. *Why the Sky Is Far Away: A Nigerian Folktale.* Little, Brown, 1992. (Grades K–4)

Golenbock, P. *Teammates.* Harcourt Brace Jovanovich, 1990. (Grades 2–5)

Greaves, N. *When Hippo Was Hairy and Other Tales from Africa.* Barron's, 1991. (Grades 3+)

Greenfield, E. *Grandpa's Face.* Philomel, 1988. (Grades Pre-S–3)

*————. *Honey, I Love: And Other Love Poems.* Dial, 1978. (Grades 1–3)

*————. *Koya De Laney & Good Girl Blues.* Scholastic, 1992. (Grades 1–3)

————. *Mary and McLeod Bethune.* HarperCollins, 1977. (Grades 2–5)

*————. *Me and Nessie.* HarperCollins, 1975. (Grades 1–4)

*————. *Night on Neighborhood Street.* Harper & Row, 1991. (Grades 1–4)

————. *Rosa Parks.* HarperCollins, 1973. (Grades 1–5)

————. *She Come Bringing Me That Little Baby Girl.* Lippincott, 1975. (Grades K–3)

————. *Sister.* HarperCollins, 1974. (Grades 5+)

———. *Talk about a Family.* HarperCollins, 1991 (reissued). (Grades 2–5)

Hamilton, V. *The All Jahdu Storybook.* Harcourt Brace Jovanovich, 1991. (Grades 3+)

———. *The Bells of Christmas.* Harcourt Brace Jovanovich, 1989. (Grades Pre-S+)

———. *Cousins.* Philomel, 1990. (Grades 5+)

———. *Drylongso.* Harcourt Brace Jovanovich, 1992. (Grades 1–3)

———. *The People Could Fly: American Black Folktales.* Knopf, 1985. (Grades K–12)

———. *Zeely.* Macmillan, 1967. (Grades 5–7)

*Hancock, S. *Esteban and the Ghost.* Dial, 1983. (Grades 1–3)

Hopkinson, D. *Sweet Clara and the Freedom Quilt.* Knopf, 1993. (Grades 1–3)

*Howard, E. F. *Aunt Flossie's Hats (and Crab Cakes Later).* Clarion, 1991. (Grades K–3)

Hudson, W., and V. W. Wesley. *Afro-Bets Book of Black Heroes from A–Z: An Introduction to Important Black Achievers.* Just Us, 1988. (Grades 3–6)

Isadora, R. *Ben's Trumpet.* Greenwillow, 1979. (Grades 1–4)

*———. *At the Crossroads.* Greenwillow, 1991. (Grades 1–4)

———. *Over the Green Hills.* Greenwillow, 1992. (Grades 2–4)

Johnson, A. *One of Three.* Orchard, 1991. (Grades K–3)

*Keats, J. *A Letter to Amy.* HarperCollins, 1968. (Grades K–3)

*———. *The Snowy Day.* Viking, 1962. (Grades K–3)

*Lester, J. *The Knee-High Man and Other Tales.* Dial, 1985. (Grades 2–5)

*———. *How Many Spots Does a Leopard Have? And Other Tales.* Scholastic, 1989. (Grades 2–6)

*McKissack, P. C. *Flossie and the Fox.* Dial, 1986. (Grades 1–3)

———. *Mary McLeod Bethune: A Great American Educator.* Children's Press, 1985. (Grades 4–7)

Meltzer, M. *All Times, All Peoples: A World History of Slavery.* HarperCollins, 1980. (Grades 5–9)

———. *The Black Americans: A History of Their Own Words.* HarperCollins, 1984. (Grades 7+)

Mennen, I., and N. Daily. *Somewhere in Africa.* Dutton, 1992. (Grades 1–4)

Mitchell, M. K. *Uncle Jed's Barbershop.* Simon, 1993. (Grades K–3)

Mollel, T. M. *A Promise to the Sun: An African Story.* Little, Brown, 1992. (Grades 1–3)

Musgrove, M. *Ashanti to Zulu: African Traditions.* Dial, 1976. (Grades K–4)

Myers, W. D. *Brown Angels.* HarperCollins, 1993. (Grades K–3)

*———. *The Mouse Rap.* Harper & Row, 1990. (Grades 3–5)

Patterson, L. *Martin Luther King, Jr. and the Freedom Movement.* Facts on File, 1989. (Grades 4–8)

Petry, A. *Harriet Tubman: Conductor on the Underground Railroad.* Marshall Cavendish, 1991. (Grades 5+)

Pickney, A. D. *Seven Candles for Kwanza.* Dial, 1993. (Grades K–3)

Rappaport, D. *Escape from Slavery: Five Journeys to Freedom.* HarperCollins, 1991. (Grades 4–7)

Rochelle, Belinda. *Witness to Freedom.* Lodestar, 1993. (Grades 3–7)

San Souci, R. D. *Sukey and the Mermaid.* Four Winds, 1992. (Grades 1–3)

Schermbrucker, R. *Charlie's House.* Viking, 1989. (Grades 1–3)

Scioscia, M. *Bicycle Rider.* HarperCollins, 1983. (Grades 2–6)

Slote, A. *Finding Buck McHenry.* HarperCollins, 1991. (Grades 3–7)

Smothers, E. F. *Down in the Piney Woods.* Knopf, 1992. (Grades 1–4)

Smucker, B. *Runaway to Freedom.* HarperCollins, 1979. (Grades 4–8)

*Spinelli, J. *Maniac Magee.* Little, Brown, 1990. (Grades 4–7)

Stanley, D. *Shaka King of the Zulus.* William Morrow, 1988. (Grades 4–6)

*Steptoe, J. *Mufaro's Beautiful Daughters: An African Tale*. Lothrop, 1987. (Grades K–4)

Stolz, M. *Go Fish*. HarperCollins, 1991. (Grades 2–6)

———. *Stealing Home*. HarperCollins, 1992. (Grades 3–6)

Taylor, C. J. *How Two-Feather Was Saved from Loneliness*. Tundra, 1990. (Grades 1–5)

*Taylor, M. *Let the Circle Be Unbroken*. Dial, 1981. (Grades 7+)

*———. *The Road to Memphis*. Dial, 1990. (Grades 2–5)

*———. *Roll of Thunder, Hear My Cry*. Dial, 1976. (Grades 5+)

*———. *Song of the Trees*. Dial, 1988. (Grades 2–5)

Thomas, J. C. *Brown Honey in Broomwheat Tea*. HarperCollins, 1993. (Grades K–3)

Walker, A. *Langston Hughes, American Poet*. HarperCollins, 1974. (Grades 2–5)

Wisniewski, D. *Sundiata: Lion King of Mali*. Clarion, 1992. (Grades K–3)

*Waterton, B. *Pettranella*. Camden House, 1991. (Grades 1–3)

Yarbrough, C. *Cornrows*. Putnam, 1981. (Grades 2–6)

Hispanic

Baden, R. *And Sunday Makes Seven*. Albert Whitman, 1990. (Grades 3–6)

Bardot, D. *A Bicycle for Rosaura*. Kane/Miller, 1991. (Grades 2–4)

*Blume, J. *Iggie's House*. Dell, 1986. (Grades 2–5)

Brusca, M. C. *On the Pampas*. Holt, 1991. (Grades 2–4)

Burchard, S. H. *Sports Star, Fernando Valenzuela*. Harcourt Brace Jovanovich, 1982. (Grades 2–5)

Buss, F. L. *Journey of the Sparrows*. Lodestar, 1991. (Grades 5–9)

Delacre, L. *Arroz con Leche: Popular Songs and Rhymes from Latin America*. Scholastic, 1989. (Grades Pre-S–3)

———. *Veligante Masquerader*. Scholastic, 1993. (Grades 1–3)

*Dorros, A. *Abuela*. Dutton, 1991. (Grades K–3)

Fern, E. *Pepito's Story*. Yarrow, 1991. (Grades Pre-S–3)

Fradin, D. B. *New Mexico in Words and Pictures*. Children's Press, 1981. (Grades 2–5)

Garza, C. L. *Family Pictures*. Children's Press, 1990. (Grades 1–7)

Haseley, D. *Ghost Catcher*. HarperCollins, 1991. (Grades 1–5)

Hayes, J. *The Day it Snowed Tortillas*. Mariposa, 1982. (Grades 4–8)

Hewett, J. *Hector Lives in the United States Now: The Story of a Mexican-American Child*. HarperCollins, 1990. (Grades 2–5)

Holman, F. *Secret City, U.S.A.* Scribner's, 1990. (Grades 3–5)

Krumgold, J. *And Now Miguel*. HarperCollins, 1987. (Grades 5+)

Macmillan, D., and D. Freeman. *My Best Friend Martha Rodriguez: Meeting a Mexican-American Family*. Julian Messner, 1986. (Grades 3–6)

Martel, C. *Yagua Days*. Dial, 1987. (Grades Pre-S–2)

Maury, I. *My Mother the Mail Carrier/Mi Mama, la Cartera*. Feminist Press, 1976. (Grades K–4)

Meltzer, M. *The Hispanic Americans*. HarperCollins, 1982. (Grades 5+)

*Mohr, N. *Felita*. Dial, 1979. (Grades 3–6)

O'Dell, S. *Carlota*. Dell, 1989. (Grades 5+)

Perl, L., and A. F. Ada. *Piñatas and Paper Flowers: Holidays of the Americas in English and Spanish*. Houghton Mifflin, 1985. (Grades 3–6)

Politi, L. *Song of the Swallows*. Scribner's, 1987. (Grades 1–4)

Shalant, P. *Look What We've Brought You from Mexico: Crafts, Games, Recipes, Stories, and Other Cultural Activities from Mexican-Americans*. Julian Messner/Simon & Schuster, 1992. (Grades 4–6)

*Soto, G. *Baseball in April and Other Stories.* Harcourt Brace Jovanovich, 1992. (Grades 5+)
———. *The Skirt.* Delacorte, 1992. (Grades 3–5)
Stanek, M. *I Speak English for My Mom.* Albert Whitman, 1989. (Grades 2–5)
Taylor, T. *Maria: A Christmas Story.* Harcourt Brace Jovanovich, 1992. (Grades 7+)
Walker, P. R. *The Pride of Puerto Rico, the Life of Roberto Clemente.* Harcourt Brace Jovanovich, 1988. (Grades 4–8)
Winter, J. *Diego.* Knopf, 1991. (Grades K–4)

Native Americans

Baylor, B. *Hawk, I'm Your Brother.* Scribner's, 1976. (Grades 1–5)
Bierhorst, J. *The Lightning Inside You: And Other Native American Riddles.* Morrow, 1992. (Grades 2–4)
Bruchac, J., and J. London. *Thirteen Moons on a Turtle's Back, a Native American Year of Moons.* Philomel, 1992. (Grades 2–5)
Clymer, E. *The Spider, the Cave and the Pottery Bowl.* Peter Smith, 1992. (Grades 1–6)
Cohen, C. L., adapt. *The Mud Pony: A Traditional Pawnee Tale.* Scholastic, 1988. (Grades K–4)
Crowder, J., and F. Hill. *Stephanie and the Coyote.* Upper Strata, 1969. (Grades 3+)
Curry, J. L. *Back in the Beforetime: Tales of the California Indians.* McElderry, 1987. (Grades 3–5)
Dial, A. *Lumbee.* Chelsea House, 1992. (Grades 5+)
Dixon, A. *How Raven Brought Light to People.* McElderry, 1992. (Grades 2–4)
Ekoomiak, N. *Artic Memories.* Holt, 1990. (Grades 3–6)
Feest, C. F. *The Powhatan Tribes.* Chelsea House, 1990. (Grades 5+)
*Ferris, S. *Children of the Great Muskeg.* Black Moss/Firefly, 1991. (Grades 3–5)
Fixico, D. L. *Urban Indians.* Chelsea House, 1991. (Grades 5+)
Freedman, R. *Buffalo Hunt.* Holiday, 1988. (Grades 3–6)
———. *Indian Chiefs.* Holiday, 1987. (Grades 3–5)
Fritz, J. *The Good Giants and the Bad Pukwudgies.* Putnam, 1982. (Grades 3–7)
Garbarino, M. S. *Seminole.* Chelsea House, 1989. (Grades 5+)
Goble, P. *Beyond the Ridge.* Chelsea House, 1989. (Grades 2–4)
———. *Dream Wolf.* Chelsea House, 1990. (Grades 1–4)
———. *The Gift of the Sacred Dog.* Bradbury, 1984. (Grades 2–5)
———. *The Girl Who Loved Wild Horses.* Macmillan, 1986. (Grades K–3)
———. *Star Boy.* Macmillan, 1983. (Grades 2–4)
Highwater, J. *Moonsong Lullaby.* Lothrop, Lee & Shepard, 1981. (Grades Pre-S–3)
Hirschfelder, A. B., and B. R. Singer. *Raising Voices: Writings of Young Native Americans.* Scribner's, 1992. (Grades 3–5)
Hobbs, W. *Bearstone.* Atheneum, 1989. (Grades 3–6)
Hoyt-Goldsmith, D. *Totem Pole.* Holiday, 1990. (Grades 3–7)
Keegan, M. *Pueblo Boy: Growing Up in Two Worlds.* Cobblehill, 1991. (Grades 2–6)
*Kendall, R. *Eskimo Boy: Life in an Inupiag Eskimo Village.* Scholastic, 1992. (Grades 2–6)
McDermott, G. *Arrow to the Sun: A Pueblo Indian Tale.* Viking, 1974. (Grades 1+)
———. *Flecha al Sol: Un Cuento de los Indios Pueblo.* Puffin, 1991. (Grades Pre-S–3)
Melody, M. E. *Apache.* Chelsea House, 1989. (Grades 5+)
Merrell, J. H. *Catawbas.* Chelsea House, 1989. (Grades 5+)
O'Dell, S. *Black Star, Bright Dawn.* Houghton Mifflin, 1988. (Grades 5–9)
O'Dell, S., and E. Hall. *Thunder Rolling in the Mountains.* Houghton Mifflin, 1992. (Grades 5–9)

*Osofsky, A. *Dreamcatcher.* Orchard, 1992. (Grades 3–5)

Oughton, J. *How the Stars Fell into the Sky.* Houghton Mifflin, 1992. (Grades 2–4)

Paulsen, G. *The Night the White Deer Died.* Delacorte, 1990. (Young adult)

Peters, R. M. *Clambake: A Wampanoag Tradition.* Lerner, 1992. (Grades 3–6)

Red Hawk, R. *A, B, C's: The American Indian Way.* Sierra Oaks, 1988. (Grades 3–6)

———. *Grandfather's Origin Story: The Navajo Indian Beginning.* Sierra Oaks, 1988. (Grades 3–6)

Regguinti, G. *The Sacred Harvest: Ojibway Wild Rice Gathering.* Lerner, 1992. (Grades 3–6)

Rodanas, K. *Dragonfly's Tale.* Clarion, 1991. (Grades 1–4)

Rollings, W. H. *Comanche.* Chelsea House, 1989. (Grades 5+)

Ruoff, A. L. *Literatures of the American Indian.* Chelsea House, 1991. (Grades 5+)

Schneider, M. J. *Hidatsa Indians.* Chelsea House, 1989. (Grades 5+)

Seattle, Chief. *Brother Eagle, Sister Sky.* Dial, 1991. (Grades 1–5)

Shemie, B. *Houses of Bark: Tipi, Wigwam and Longhouse.* Tundra, 1990. (Grades 3–7)

*Sneve, V. D. H., sel. *Dancing Teepees: Poems of American Indian Youth.* Holiday, 1989. (Grades 3–6)

Taylor, C. J. *How Two-Feather Was Saved from Loneliness: An Adenaki Legend.* Tundra, 1990. (Grades 1–5)

Tratzer, C. E. *Nez Perce.* Chelsea House, 1992. (Grades 5+)

Wunder, J. R. *Kiowa.* Chelsea House, 1989. (Grades 5+)

Yolen, J. *Sky Dogs.* Harcourt Brace Jovanovich, 1990. (Grades 2–4)

Young, E. *Moon Mother.* HarperCollins, 1993. (Grades K–3)

Other Cultural Diversity Books

*Cech, J. *My Grandmother's Journey.* Illustrated by Sharon McGinley-Nally. Bradbury, 1991. (Pre-S–4)

Hoffman, P. *Meatball.* HarperCollins, 1991. (Pre-S–2)

Isadora, R. *City Seen from A to Z.* Greenwillow, 1983. (Grades K–3)

Kelly, E. *Happy New Year.* Carolrhoda, 1984. (Grades K–4)

Knight, M. B. *Who Belongs Here? An American Story.* Illustrated by A. S. O'Brien. Tilbury, 1993.

*Murphy, C. R. *Friendship Across Arctic Waters: Alaskan Cub Scouts Visit Their Soviet Neighbors.* Lodestar, 1991. (Grades 3–5)

*Polacco, P. *Mrs. Katz and Tush.* Bantam, 1992.

*Polon, L., and A. Cantwell. *The Whole Earth Holiday Book.* GoodYear, 1983. (Grades 1–6)

*Rosenberg, M. B. *Brothers and Sisters.* Clarion, 1991. (Grades Pre-S–3)

*Spier, P. *People.* Doubleday, 1980. (Grades 1–3)

*Warren, J. and E. S. McKinnon. *Small World Celebrations: Multicultural Holidays to Celebrate with Young Children.* Warren, 1988. (Grades 1–6)

Professional Resources

*Cited in text

Students with Special Learning Needs
General Disabilities

Bos, C. S., and S. Vaughn. *Strategies for Teaching Students with Learning and Behavior Problems,* 2nd ed. Allyn & Bacon, 1991.

Bower, E. M., ed. *The Handicapped Child in Literature.* Love, 1980.

Gloeker, T., and C. Simpson. *Exceptional Students in Regular Classrooms.* Mayfield, 1988.

Hagner, D. *Working Together.* Brookline, 1993.

Itard, J. M. G. *The Wild Boy of Aveyron.* Translated by G. Humphrey and M. Humphrey. Prentice-Hall, 1962 [1806].

Kozol, J. *Rachel and Her Children: Homeless Families in America.* Fawcett, 1988.

Lerner, J. *Learning Disabilities: Theories, Diagnosis, and Teaching Strategies.* Houghton Mifflin, 1988.

Mercer, C., and M. Mercer. *Teaching Students with Learning Problems,* 3rd ed. Macmillan, 1989.

Smith, D. D. *Teaching Students with Learning and Behavior Problems,* 2nd ed. Prentice-Hall, 1988.

Smith, D. D., and R. Luckasson. *Introduction to Special Education: Teaching in an Age of Challenge.* Allyn & Bacon, 1992.

Stone, A., and S. Stone, *The Abnormal Personality Through Literature.* Prentice-Hall, 1965.

Turnbull, A. *Families, Professionals, and Exceptionality: A Special Partnership,* 2nd ed. Macmillan, 1990.

Communication Disorders

Caldwell, E. *Tobacco Road.* Dutton, 1947.

Melville, H. *Billy Budd.* Macmillan, 1975.

Emotional Disturbance/Behavior Disorders

Axline, V. M. *Dibs in Search of Self.* Ballantine, 1986.

Greenfield, J. *A Child Called Noah: A Family Journey.* Holt, 1972.

Kesey, K. *One Flew Over the Cuckoo's Nest.* Viking Penguin, 1977.

MacCracken, M. *A Circle of Children.* Dutton, 1975.

Plath, S. *The Bell Jar.* Bantam, 1975.

Sachs, O. *The Man Who Mistook His Wife for a Hat: And Other Clinical Tales.* HarperCollins, 1987.

Sheehan, S. *Is There No Place on Earth for Me?* Houghton Mifflin, 1982.

Stryon, W. *Darkness Visible: A Memoir of Madness.* Random House, 1990.

Hearing Impairments

Kisor, H. *What's That Pig Outdoors? A Memoir of Deafness.* Hill & Wang, 1990.

McCullers, C. *The Heart Is a Lonely Hunter.* Bantam, 1970.

Sachs, O. *Seeing Voices: A Journey into the World of the Deaf.* University of California Press, 1989.

Walker, L. A. *A Loss for Words: The Story of Deafness in a Family.* HarperCollins, 1987.

Learning Disabilities

Smith, S. *No Easy Answers: The Learning Disabled Child.* Bantam, 1981.

Stevens, S. H. *The Learning Disabled Child: Ways That Parents Can Help.* Blair, 1980.

Mental Retardation

Burke, C., and J. McDaniel. *A Special Kind of Hero: Chris Burke's Own Story.* Doubleday, 1991.

Kaufman, S. Z. *Retarded Isn't Stupid, Mom.* Brooks, 1988.
Keyes, D. *Flowers for Algernon.* Harcourt Brace Jovanovich, 1966.
Ling, M. H., S. McAnally, and C. Wieck, eds. *Case Management.* Brookline, 1992.
Mantle, M. *Some Just Clap Their Hands: Raising a Handicapped Child.* Adama, 1985.
Perske, R. *Don't Stop the Music.* Abingdon, 1986.

Physical and Health Impairments

Brown, C. *My Left Foot: The Story of Christy Brown.* Faber & Faber, 1990.
Callahan, J. *Don't Worry, He Won't Get Far on Foot.* Random, 1990.
De Ford, F. *Alex: The Life of a Child.* Dutton, 1986.

Visual Impairments

Bickel, L. *Triumph over Darkness: The Life of Louis Braille.* Ulverscroft, 1989.
Greenberg, J. *Of Such Small Differences.* Dutton, 1989.
Keller, H. *The Story of My Life.* Doubleday, 1951.
Kipling, R. *The Light That Failed.* Airmont, 1969.
*Litchfield, Ada B. *Words in Our Hands.* Albert Whitman, 1980.
*Sesame Street Staff. *Sesame Street Sign Language.* Random House, 1980.
Wagner, S. *How Do You Kiss a Blind Girl?* Charles C. Thomas, 1986.

English as a Second Language

Ambert, Alba, and Sara E. Melendez. *Bilingual Education: A Source Book.* Garland, 1985.
Anderson, Betty, and Rosie Webb Joels. *Teaching Reading to Students with Limited English Proficiencies.* Charles C. Thomas, 1985.
Appleberry, M. H., and E. A. Rodriguez. "Literary Books Make the Difference in Teaching the ESL Student." *Reading Horizons,* 28:112–116, 1988.
Appolt, J. E. "Not Just for Little Kids: The Picture Book in ESL Classes." *TESL Canada Journal,* 2: 87–88, 1985.
Bird, L. B., and L. P. Alvarez. "Beyond Comprehension: The Power of Literature Study for Language Minority Students." *Elementary ESOL Education News,* 10: 1–3, 1987.
Bowman, Barbara T. "Educating Language-Minority Children: Challenges and Opportunities." *Phi Delta Kappan,* 71: 118–120, 1989.
Boyle, Owen F., and Suzanne F. Peregoy. "Literacy Scaffolds: Strategies and First- and Second-Language Readers and Writers." *The Reading Teacher,* 44: 194–200, 1990.
Ching, Doris C. *Reading and the Bilingual Child.* International Reading Association, 1976.
*Collier, V. "How Long? A Synthesis of Research on Academic Achievement in a Second Language." *TESOL Quarterly,* 23: 509–532, 1989.
*Crawford, J. *Bilingual Education: History, Politics, Theory and Practice.* Crane, 1989.
*Crist, Barbara. "One Capsule a Week: A Painless Remedy for Vocabulary." *Journal of Reading,* 19: 147–149, 1975.
*Cummins, J. *Empowering Minority Students.* California Association of Bilingual Education, 1989.
*Delgado-Gaitan, C. *Literacy for Empowerment: The Role of Parents in Children's Education.* Falmer, 1990.
*Delgado-Gaitan, C., and H. T. Trueba. *Crossing Cultural Borders: Education for Immigrant Families in America.* Falmer, 1991.

Educational Research Service. *What We Know About Culturally Sensitive Instruction and Student Learning.* Arlington, VA, 1991.

Elley, W. B., and F. Mangubhai. "The Impact of Reading on Second Language Learning." *Reading Research Quarterly,* 19: 53–56, 1983.

Enright, D. S., and M. L. McCloskey. *Integrating English: Developing Classroom Language and Literacy Communities.* Addison-Wesley, 1988.

———. "Yes Talking! Organizing the Classroom to Promote Second Language Acquisition." *TESOL Quarterly,* 19: 431–453, 1985.

Feeley, Joan T. "Bilingual Instruction: Puerto Rico and the Mainland." *The Reading Teacher,* 30: 741–744, 1977.

*Freeman, D. E., and Y. S. Freeman. "Enriching Primary Language Print Resources." *CABE Newsletter,* 15: 8–9, 1992a.

*———. "Strategies for Promoting the Primary Languages of All Students." *The Reading Teacher,* 46: 552–558, 1993.

*Freeman, Y. S., and C. Cervantes. "Literature Books en Español for Whole Language." In K. S. Goodman Y. M. Goodman (eds.). *Occasional Papers: Program in Language and Literacy,* University of Arizona, 1991.

*Freeman, Y. S., and D. E. Freeman. *Whole Language for Second Language Learners.* Heinemann, 1992b.

*Forum. *George Washington University and the Center for Applied Linguistics: National Clearinghouse for Bilingual Education,* Forum, 1991.

Fritz, G. "What Works: Using Materials for Different Skill Levels." *WATESOL News,* 18: 9, 1987.

Genesee, Fred. *Learning Through Two Languages: Studies of Immersion and Bilingual Education.* Newbury, 1987.

*Goldenberg, C. "Low-Income Hispanic Parents' Contributions to Their First-Grade Children's Word-Recognition Skills." *Anthropology & Education Quarterly,* Vol. 18 No. 3: 149–179, 1987.

Hamayan, Else V., and Ron Perlman. *Helping Language Minority Students After They Exit from Bilingual/ESL Programs.* National Clearinghouse for Bilingual Education, 1990.

*Hough, Ruth A., Joanne R. Nurss, and D. Scott Enright. "Story Reading in the Regular Classroom." *The Reading Teacher,* 39: 510–514, 1986.

*Hudelson, S. "The Role of Native Language Literacy in the Education of Language Minority Children." *Language Arts,* 64: 827–840, 1987.

Johns, Kenneth M. *How Children Learn a Second Language.* Fastback 278. Phi Delta Kappa, 1989.

Johns, Kenneth M., and Connie Espinoza. *Mainstreaming Language Minority Children in Reading and Writing.* Fastback 340. Phi Delta Kappa, 1992.

Johnson, Donna M. "ESL Children as Teachers: A Social View of Language Use." *Language Arts,* 65: 154–163, 1988.

Kendall, F. *Diversity in the Classroom: A Multicultural Approach to the Education of Young Children.* Teachers College, 1983.

*Krashen, S. *Inquiries and Insights.* Alemany, 1985.

———. *Principles and Practices in Second Language Acquisition.* Pergamon, 1982.

*Krashen, S., and D. Biber. *On Course: Bilingual Education's Success in California Classrooms.* California Association of Bilingual Education, 1988.

Lindfors, J. *Children's Language and Learning,* 2nd ed. Prentice-Hall, 1987.

Lundsteen, S. W., and N. B. Tarrow. *Guiding Young Children's Learning*. McGraw-Hill, 1981.

McCauley, Joyce K., and Daniel S. McCauley. "Using Choral Reading to Promote Language Learning for ESL Students." *The Reading Teacher*, 45: 526–533, 1992.

Moustafa, Margaret. "Comprehensive Input PLUS the Language Experience Approach: A Longterm Perspective." *The Reading Teacher*, 41: 276–286, 1987.

————. "Picture Books for Oral Language Development for Non-English Speaking Children: A Bibliography." *The Reading Teacher*, 33: 914–919, 1980.

Moustafa, Margaret, and Joyce Penrose. "Comprehensible Input PLUS the Language Experience Approach: Reading Instruction for Limited English Speaking Students." *The Reading Teacher*, 38: 640–647, 1985.

National Council for Teachers of English Committee on Issues in ESL and Bilingual Education. *Position Statement*. National Council of Teachers of English, 1986.

Norton, D. "Language and Cognitive Development Through Multicultural Literature." *Childhood Education*, 62: 103–108, 1985.

*Olsen, L., and N. Mullen. *Embracing Diversity: Teachers' Voices from California Classrooms*. California Tomorrow, 1990.

Past, Kay Cude, Al Past, and Sheila Bernal Guzman. "A Bilingual Kindergarten Immersed in Print." *The Reading Teacher*, 33: 907–913, 1980.

Radencich, Marguerite C. "Books that Promote Positive Attitudes Toward Second Language Learning." *The Reading Teacher*, 38: 528–530, 1985.

*Ramirez, J. D. *Final Report: Longitudinal Study of Structured English Immersion Strategy, Early-Exit and Late-Exit Bilingual Education Programs (300-87-0156)*. U.S. Department of Education, 1991.

Saville-Troike, Muriel. *Foundations for Teaching English as a Second Language*. Prentice-Hall, 1976.

Sinatra, R. "Using Visuals to Help the Second Language Learner." *The Reading Teacher*, 34: 539–546, 1981.

Smallwood, B. A. "Children's Literature for Limited English Proficient Speakers, Ages 9–14." *WATESOL Working Papers*, 4: 67–87, 1988.

Stahl-Gemake, Josephine, and Francine Gustello. "Using Story Grammar with Students of English as a Foreign Language to Compose Original Fairy and Folktales." *The Reading Teacher*, 38: 213–216, 1984.

Strickland, D. S. *The Role of Literature in Reading Instruction: Cross-Cultural Views*. International Reading Association, 1981.

Sutton, Christine. "Helping the Nonnative English Speaker with Reading." *The Reading Teacher*, 42: 684–688, 1989.

Task Force on Racism and Bias in the Teaching of English. *Expanding Opportunities: Academic Success for Culturally and Linguistically Diverse Students*. National Council of Teachers of English, 1986.

Tompkins, E. G., and L. M. McGee. "Launching Nonstandard Speakers into Standard English." *Language Arts*, 60: 463–469, 1983.

*U.S. Department of Education. *The Condition of Bilingual Education in the Nation: A Report to the Congress and the President*. Washington, D.C., 1991.

Cultural Diversity

Ada, A. F., V. J. Harris, and L. B. Hopkins. *A Chorus of Cultures: Developing Literacy Through Multicultural Poetry*. Hampton-Brown, 1993.

Allen, J., E. McNeill, and V. Schmitt. *Cultural Awareness for Children.* Addison-Wesley, 1992.

*Austin, M. C., and E. C. Jenkins. *Literature for Children About Asians and Asian Americans.* Greenwood, 1987.

*Barringer, Felicity. "Census Shows Profound Changes in Racial Make-Up of the Nation." *New York Times.* March 11, 1991, pp. A1, B8.

Baker, G. C. *Planning and Organizing for Multicultural Instruction.* Addison-Wesley, 1983.

Banks, J. A. *Teaching Strategies for Ethnic Studies.* Allyn & Bacon, 1991.

Banks, J. A., and C. A. M. Banks. *Multicultural Education: Issues and Perspectives.* Allyn & Bacon, 1991.

Boyer, J. B. *Multicultural Education: Product or Process?* Kansas Urban Education Center, 1985.

Cech, M. *Globalchild: Multicultural Resources for Young Children.* Addison-Wesley, 1991.

Chu-Chanug, M., ed. *Asian and Pacific American Perspectives in Bilingual Education.* Teachers College, 1983.

Colangelo, N., D. Dustin and C. Foxley, eds. *Multicultural Nonsexist Education: A Human Relations Approach.* Kendall Hunt, 1985.

Crary, E., et al. *Historical Activity Guide.* Parenting Press, 1989.

Crawford, L. W. *Language and Literacy Learning in Multicultural Classrooms.* Allyn & Bacon, 1993.

Dames, S. "Massasoit, Moccasins, and Massacres: Teaching Anti-Biased Native American Curriculum." Unpublished, 1988.

*Derman-Sparks, L., and ABC Task Force. *Anti-Bias Curriculum: Tools for Empowering Young Children.* National Association for the Education of Young Children, 1989.

Fantini, M. D., and R. Cardenos, eds. *Parenting in a Multicultural Society.* Longman, 1980.

Frank, M., ed. *Newcomers to the United States: Children and Families.* Haworth, 1983.

*Frederick, H. V. "In Search of Multi-Ethnic Books." *Christian Science Monitor,* Feb. 21, 1990.

Glover, M. K. "A Bag of Hair: American First-Graders Experience Japan." *Childhood Education,* 66: 155–159, 1990.

Greenfield, F. *Games of the World.* UNICEF/Plenary, 1975.

*Harris, Violet, ed. *Teaching Multicultural Literature to Children in Grades K–8.* Christopher-Gordon, 1992.

Hirsch, E. D. Jr. *A First Dictionary of Cultural Literacy.* Houghton Mifflin, 1991.

Honey, E., et al. *Festivals: Ideas from Around the World.* Delmar, 1988.

Jenkins, E., and M. C. Austin. *Literature for Children about Asians and Asian Americans.* Greenwood, 1987.

Kendall, F. E. *Diversity in the Classroom: A Multicultural Approach to the Education of Young Children.* Teachers College, 1983.

Kitano, H. L. *Race Relations.* Prentice-Hall, 1980.

*Lankford, M. D. *Hopscotch Around the World.* Morrow, 1992.

Legg, P., and R. Harold. *Folk Costumes of the World.* Blandford, 1989.

Lewis, F. N., and J. Margold. *Children's World View: The Basis for Learning Activities.* Far West, 1981.

Lynch, E. W., and M. J. Hanson. *Developing Cross-Cultural Competence.* Brooks, 1992.

*Martin, D. "Wake Up: The American Dream Is Fading and Our Future Is at Risk." *Michigan School Board Journal,* 10, Oct. 1988.

*McPherson, Jan. *Chasing Games from Around the World.* Sleck-Vaughn, 1992.

Milford, S. *Hands Around the World: 365 Ways to Build Cultural Awareness and Global Respect.* Williamson, 1992.

Neugebauer, B., ed. *Alike and Different: Exploring Our Humanity with Young Children.* Exchange, 1987.

*Norton, D. E. "Teaching Multicultural Literature in the Reading Curriculum." *The Reading Teacher,* 44: 28–40, 1990.

*Piper, D. "Language Growth in the Multiethnic Classroom." *Language Arts,* 63: 23–36, 1986.

Ramsey, P. G., E. B. Vold, and L. R. Williams. *Multicultural Education: A Source Book.* Garland, 1989.

Ramsey, P. G. *Teaching and Learning in a Diverse World: Multicultural Education for Young Children.* Teachers College, 1987.

*Read McDonald, Margaret. *The Storyteller's Sourcebook: A Subject, Title and Motif Index to Folklore Collections for Children.* Gale Research Company, 1992.

*Rothlein, L., and T. Wild. *Read It Again! Multicultural Books for the Primary Grades.* Scott, Foresman, 1993.

Saracho, O. N., and B. Spodek, eds. *Understanding the Multicultural Experience in Early Childhood Education.* National Association for the Education of Young Children, 1992.

Schmidt, V. E., and E. McNeil. *Cultural Awareness: A Resource Bibliography.* National Association for the Education of Young Children, 1978.

*Schon, Isabel. *Books in Spanish for Children and Young Adults: An Annotated Guide.* Scarecrow, 1985.

Seelye, H. N. *Teaching Culture.* National Textbook, 1984.

*Sims, Rudine. *Shadow and Substance: Afro-American Experience in Contemporary Children's Ficton.* National Council for Teachers of English, 1982.

*Slapin, Beverly, and Doris Seale, eds. *Books Without Bias: Through Indian Eyes.* Oyate, 1988.

Tiedt, P., and I. Tiedt. *Multicultural Teaching: A Handbook of Activities, Information, and Resources.* Allyn & Bacon, 1986.

*Tway, E. "Dimensions of Multicultural Literature for Children." In M. K. Rudman, ed. *Children's Literature: Resource for the Classroom.* Christopher-Gordon, 1989, pp. 109–138.

Vold, E. B., ed. *Multicultural Education in Early Childhood Classrooms.* National Association for the Education of Young Children, 1992.

Williams, L. R., Y. DeGaetano, C. C. Harrington, and I. R. Sutherland. *Alerta.* Addison-Wesley, 1987.

Multicultural Learning Aids

Adoptive Families of America, 3333 Highway 100 North, Minneapolis, MN 55422, phone number: (612) 535-4829

Child Craft, P.O. Box 29149, Mission, KS 66201-9149, phone number: (800) 631-5657

Constructive Playthings, 1227 East 199 Street, Grandview, MS 64030, phone number: (800) 255-6124

First Step Ltd., Rt. 26 RR 1, Box 1425, Oxford, ME 04270, phone number: (800) 639-1150

Hammacher Schlemmer, 2515 East 43 Street, P.O. Box 182256, Chattanooga, TN 37422-7256, phone number: (800) 543-3366

Heritage Key, 6102 East Mescal, Scottsdale, AZ 85254, phone number (602) 483-3313
Nasco, Box 901, Ft. Atkinson, WI 53538-0901, phone number: (800) 558-9595
PlayFair Toys, P.O. Box 18210, Boulder, CO 80308, phone number: (800) 824-7255
Pleasant Co., P.O. Box 190, Middleton, WI 53562, phone number: (800) 845-0005
Teach-A-Bodies, 3509 Arcon Run, Ft. Worth, TX 76109, phone number: (817) 923-2380

PART III

Words and Worlds of Wonder: Interacting with Literature

CHAPTER 9 • **Responding to Literature Through the Language Arts**

CHAPTER 10 • **Responding to Literature Through the Arts**

CHAPTER 11 • **Celebrating Literature: Alternatives**

'Tis the good reader that makes the good book; in every book he finds passages which seem confidences or asides hidden from all else and unmistakably meant for his ear; the profit of books is according to the sensibility of the reader; the profoundest thought or passion sleeps as in a mine, until it is discovered by an equal mind.

Ralph Waldo Emerson
1803–1882

Whan children read, they do more than decode words. They bring their own set of needs, hopes, and dreams with them as they make their own special meaning from the printed text. Often, a work of literature will touch children in a special way. They will want to talk about a certain character or describe how they felt when reading a specific part. Children need an opportunity to pursue their feelings about what they have read. They need the chance to explore their ideas, interpretations, and opinions. They need the time to pose questions and speculate on alternatives. And they need time to retell the story as they mentally flip through the pages to relive the magic.

Several strategies for encouraging responses to literature have become increasingly popular. Louise Rosenblatt's (1978) theory of transaction between the reader and the text, for example, has become a major influence in teaching literature. According to Rosenblatt, children need an opportunity to respond aesthetically, to relate what they read to their own experiences, each interpreting the text based on their own background, each forging their own connections.

Other strategies have also been developed or adapted to involve students more actively in their responses to literature:

There has been a conceptual shift in the way many researchers and teachers think about reading, which gives students a much more active role in the learning and reading comprehension process. This shift is reflected in changes from packaged programs to experiences with books and from concentration on isolated skills to practical reading and writing activities.

Yet, improvements in higher-level reading skills cannot come about simply by an emphasis on reading instruction in isolation from the other work students do in school. To foster higher-level literacy skills is to place a new and special emphasis on thoughtful, critical elaboration of ideas and understandings drawn from the material students read and from what they already know.

(*Educational Testing Services*, 1985)

Many techniques and strategies have been developed to encourage children's responses to literature. Several of these are presented in this part of *Legacies*, with four main goals in mind: to surround children with a variety of literature, giving them the opportunity to read and share what they have read; to allow children to respond to literature through reading, writing, speaking, drama, and artistic endeavors; to encourage children to return to the literature they have read to make connections, create their own interpretations, and formulate their own conclusions; and to use literature as a springboard for discussion and problem solving.

These goals can be accomplished only in a classroom atmosphere that values reading and the exchange of ideas. Such a classroom will encourage reading and include many opportunities throughout the day for reading; provide a supportive, nonthreatening environment that encourages children to discuss ideas based on their readings, challenge their own interpretations, and explore alternatives; and involve students in activities that encourage responses to literature through all types of creative processes.

Years ago, while still in college, one of the authors visited an area in Central Florida called Cross Creek, the home of Marjorie Kinnan Rawlings. Moved by the beauty and stillness of the landscape, she tried to capture the scene in a drawing. Frustrated because she couldn't draw, she tried a different medium—poetry. While it was only a little better than the drawing, the poem was a catharsis—a way of internalizing a special moment, of making it her own for all time. Children need the same opportunity—a way to celebrate what they have read, to make it their own. Whether through a poem, a picture, or a dramatic interpretation, children need the chance to react and respond as they travel through the words and world of wonder that is literature.

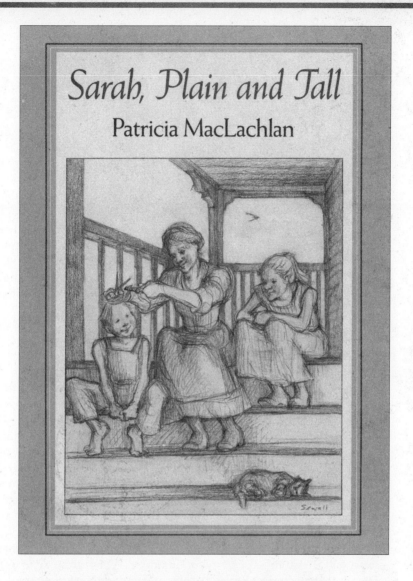

Sarah, Plain and Tall

Patricia MacLachlan

CHAPTER 9

Responding to Literature
Through the Language Arts

Good literature provides an excellent catalyst for thought, discussion, and writing, causing children to wonder, dream, and imagine. As children interact with the literature they read and hear, their reading, writing, thinking, and listening skills are developed. The strategies described in this chapter provide a framework that encourages students to approach literature from different perspectives, consider possibilities, and form their own conclusions.

Speaking and Listening

A discussion of literature can take many forms. Students may wish to tell others about a favorite book and/or author (book talks) or discuss one of a number of issues or ideas suggested by the literature with which they have been involved (literature circles). To facilitate the discussion of literature, in addition to describing book talks and literature circles, this section focuses on questioning techniques that encourage aesthetic responses (Rosenblatt), higher-level thinking responses (Bloom), interpretive responses (shared inquiry method), and divergent responses as well as two techniques that involve students in using literature as the catalyst for creative problem solving and as a basis for the discussion of moral dilemmas as suggested by the story.

Each of the strategies has a place in the curriculum, has its own benefits, and will enrich the discussion of literature. Which strategy to use and when to use it depends on the literary selection. Frequently, student questions and reactions will form the basis for discussion. Sometimes, the teacher's questions and responses will be the springboards for discussion. It is important to acknowledge that students need to be encouraged to respond in a variety of ways, to reflect on that which they read, and to be able to connect literature with their own lives.

To illustrate ways to implement these strategies, examples of questions reflecting the levels of Bloom's taxonomy and ways to use interpretive questioning strategies (shared inquiry) are included, based on Natalie Babbitt's *Tuck Everlasting*. *Tuck Everlasting* is the story of the Tuck family, who, through a strange trick of fate, discover that they are immortal. Most of the questions focus on the concept of immortality and were developed to help students gain insight into the importance of life and living each day to the fullest as they strive to make a difference in this world.

Book Talks

One of the most effective strategies for enhancing students' interest in literature is the book talk. In a sense, a book talk is an advertisement, a short vignette designed to arouse the students' interest in a specific book. In book talks, the teacher and/or students share some aspect of a book. A good time to use this technique is following independent reading, so students can share a book that has excited them in some ways.

A book talk can take many forms, including:

1. Reading several pages from the book. This can reflect an exciting part, a segment that involves foreshadowing of things to come, a part that excites the imagination, and so on.
2. Sharing an artifact box—a box containing several objects that relate to the book. Children begin to wonder what the objects mean and how they work together to weave a tale. For example, an artifact box about *Sadako and the Thousand Paper Cranes,* by Eleanor Coerr, the story of a young girl who contracts leukemia as a result of the radiation from atomic warfare, can include paper cranes and pictures of the bombing of Japan during World War II.
3. Sharing photographs that represent the time period in which the book is set. For example, pictures that reflect pioneer life can be used to introduce books such as *Prairie Songs,* by Pam Conrad, or *Sarah, Plain and Tall,* by Patricia MacLachlan. Pictures from books such as *Children of the Wild West* and *Cowboys of the Wild West,* by Russell Freeman, not only transport students to a fascinating time in history but allow them to see the West as it actually was.
4. Dressing as a character in the book and telling a little about yourself (as the character).
5. Delivering a one-minute radio or television commercial for the book.
6. Presenting a monologue from the book that introduces the character and/or other elements of the story.

Through book talks, teachers can introduce the students to genres, authors, and topics they may never seek on their own. One teacher reported that she had three copies of *Tuck Everlasting* in her classroom library, but her students never picked it up. After a book talk that focused on the subject of a magical spring and the promise of immortality, the book was never again on the shelf.

While book talks are fairly short, usually around five minutes, their effects are amazing. They are a wonderful way for students and teachers to share their love of favorite books/poems and introduce them to other students.

Literature Circles

Literature circles provide a forum for discussing selected literary works, themes, and/or topics in depth. The discussion can focus on a specific question the student wishes to pursue or on various elements of the book, such as how the author told the story or how the book dealt with the theme/topic.

It is important that the teacher uses questions and/or questioning techniques (described later in this chapter) that elicit interesting responses and help students formulate their own. Teachers should also guide students in holding discussions before they lead their own so they see ways to encourage ideas and explore them. Certain rules need to be established, such as the right of the individual to speak without fear of ridicule.

Introducing Literature Circles

Stimulating discussions don't just happen. Students need to learn how to respond to each other's ideas and be able to express their own attitudes, reflections, and reactions. The following steps can help teachers implement effective literature circles:

1. Involve students in a discussion of a book or portion of a book everyone has had the opportunity to read.
2. Ask a question that will stimulate discussion. For example, after reading portions of Jerry Spinelli's *Maniac Magee,* ask, "Do you consider Maniac a true hero? Support your answer."
3. As students respond to this question, model ways in which students can piggy-back on one another's answers as well as ways students can reflect on their classmates' responses and offer their own. Make sure students learn to agree or disagree with an *idea*—not with a person.
4. After the discussion is completed, involve students in an evaluation of the discussion process. Ask them questions such as: Did the classroom environment support the discussion? Were you encouraged to react to the questions? Did the discussion reflect your ability to listen and react to the remarks of others? Did the discussion reflect your ability to stick to the topic at hand?
5. Once students are familiar with discussion techniques, divide them into groups based on a specific book each has read and give them a prompt for their discussion.
6. As students take part in their literature circles, the teacher should observe the groups' progress and the dynamics of their interaction. Record individual strengths and weaknesses in terms of leadership, ability to express ideas, etc.
7. Reassemble the class and again involve students in an evaluation of the discussion process. (see step #4 above)
8. Steps #6 and #7 should be repeated several times until you know students' strengths and weaknesses. Create heterogeneous literature circle groups made up of approximately 6–8 students (smaller numbers in the earlier grades).

9. Once groups have been formed, assign each group a specific book or give book talks on specific books and allow each group to select the book they'd like to read. When selecting literature, select books by topic, author, etc., so that each group can ultimately bring a new perspective to a class discussion.

10. While it is suggested that you keep students in the same literature circle groups throughout the year, periodically you may wish to allow new groups to be formed based on individual book selections rather than group selections.

Prompts for Literature Circle Discussions

Listed below are just a few of the many ideas that can serve as springboards for literature circles:

1. Questions concerning the author's meaning
2. A comparison of plot, characters, mood, and so on with those in other books on the same topic or in other books by the same author or illustrator
3. Ideas concerning character motivation
4. A critique of the selection
5. The way the work changed ideas or views
6. Questions students would like to ask the author about his or her development of the story
7. Questions students wish to pursue concerning some aspect of the story

Literature circles can be part of the teacher's daily plans or the students or teacher can post an announcement to advertise the next literature circle and the books or topic that will be discussed. Often, a teacher can introduce students to a topic that will later be discussed in literature circles in whole class or small group lessons. For example, many of the activities developed in Chapter 3 can be used to introduce students to elements of literature. Another way to prepare for the literature circle is to have students make entries in their literary logs (page 294–296) or journal (page 292–294) that respond to the book they are reading and note favorite parts, questions, and comments. These entries will serve as excellent springboards for discussion. If a certain aspect of the story is to be discussed, students could prepare for the literature circle by creating a graphic organizer, such as a web or cluster of the topic/theme to help generate ideas and organize thoughts. The Literary Circle Discussion Web (page 280) works especially well with interpretive questions that require students to use the text to back up their responses. It helps them look at both sides of a situation to draw their own conclusion(s).

Discussing Literature: Questioning Strategies

Aesthetic Questioning

In recent years, any discussion of children's responses to literature has cited the work of Louise Rosenblatt's transactional theory (1976). She defines reading as a transaction between the reader and the text. Rosenblatt recognizes that each

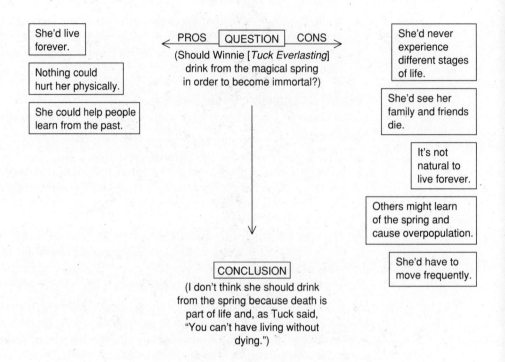

LITERARY CIRCLE
DISCUSSION WEB

PROS | QUESTION | CONS

(Should Winnie [*Tuck Everlasting*] drink from the magical spring in order to become immortal?)

She'd live forever.

Nothing could hurt her physically.

She could help people learn from the past.

She'd never experience different stages of life.

She'd see her family and friends die.

It's not natural to live forever.

Others might learn of the spring and cause overpopulation.

She'd have to move frequently.

CONCLUSION

(I don't think she should drink from the spring because death is part of life and, as Tuck said, "You can't have living without dying.")

Based on *Tuck Everlasting*, by Natalie Babbitt

person responds to literature based on his or her own background. She takes the position that readers can focus attention mainly on the information in the text (efferent) or on the reading experience itself as they feel the excitement, pathos, fear, joy, or any of the myriad of emotions that literature can tap (aesthetic). Rosenblatt (1982) believes that too often teachers ask questions that cause children to read and respond in a more efferent way. She advocates that children in the elementary schools be encouraged to read and respond more aesthetically. For this to happen, the teacher must introduce activities and questions that encourage children to respond to the literature in a very personal way.

Zarrillo (1991) developed an excellent tool to help teachers encourage children to transact with literature more aesthetically (p. 281). Questions and prompts, divided into three levels, can be used to stimulate both written and oral language. For example, children can use the questions as springboards for literature talks as well as for their personal writing journals. They can also be used during independent student–teacher conferences to give students an opportunity to talk about what they have been reading and how it affected them.

Higher-Level Thinking Questions

Many studies have been conducted about the types of questions teachers ask. A majority of questions often focus on the literal, lower levels of questioning, and students seldom engage in reasoning or formulating opinions (Goodlad, 1984). The report of the National Assessment of Educational Progress (1981) reported

AESTHETIC TEACHING: QUESTIONS AND PROMPTS

Level 1: Free response (most conducive to aesthetic reading)
   a. Write (or draw) whatever you want about what you just read.
   b. Does anybody have anything they want to say about what you just read?
Level 2: Reliving the reading experience
   2.1 Identifying vivid episodes
      a. Did anything seem especially interesting? Annoying? Puzzling? Frightening? Weird? Funny? Sad?
   2.2 Imaging and picturing
      a. Pretend you (were doing something a character did).
      b. Picture in your mind (an event or scene in the book).
      c. What would it feel like to (be a character in the book or participate in an event in the book)?
      d. What would (a scene in the book) have looked like (from the perspective of one of the characters)?
   2.3 Preference
      a. What was your favorite (or least favorite) part of the book?
Level 3: Interpreting the reading experience
   3.1 Personal associations
      a. Have you ever experienced what (a character in the book) experienced?
      b. Have you ever read a story (or seen a TV show or movie) where (event in the book) happened?
      c. Have you ever known anyone like (a character in the book)?
   3.2 Speculation
      a. What do you think will happen to (the characters in the book) in the future?
      b. What do you think would have happened if (an event in the book had been altered)?
      c. What do you think would happen to (the book's characters in a different setting)?
   3.3 Summative opinion
      a. Did you like the (name of the book)?
      b. What about the book led to your judgment?

Source: Zarrillo, James. "Theory Becomes Practice: Aesthetic Teaching with Literature." *New Advocate* 4, 1991.

that "students seem . . . genuinely puzzled at requests to explain or defend their points of view and that few students [show] evidence of well-developed problem-solving or critical thinking skills." Barell (1991) echoes this concern and describes the problems students have in thinking about concepts and issues in greater depth. As a result, the teacher must be willing to provide sufficient time for thinking about questions that ask students to think and perform higher-order mental functioning.

Bloom and colleagues (1956) developed the Taxonomy of Educational Objectives: Cognitive Domain to classify educational objectives according to the level of thinking required. These six levels—knowledge, comprehension, application, analysis, synthesis, and evaluation—are hierarchical, each depending on those below it.

Too often, students are involved in numerous questions and activities that require only cursory knowledge of the selected literature and little reflective thought. Since the taxonomy represents all levels of thinking, it enables the teacher to focus and plan questions and activities based on any literary work to stimulate all levels of thinking, especially those considered higher-level (analysis, synthesis, evaluation). This will increase the students' ability to think critically, understand human behavior and social issues, and reflect on their own values and beliefs.

This structure focuses on ways teachers and students can formulate questions that go beyond the simple "right" answers students generally are asked to find, although a certain level of knowledge and comprehension provides the background for more critical thinking. The questions cause readers to reflect on the literature, analyze, hypothesize, synthesize, and give evidence to support their evaluations.

The levels of questions, from least complex to most complex, are as follows:

1. Knowledge. Students recall facts and information. Activities and questions can be completed using only the information given. Knowledge questions or activities may include arranging the events of the story in sequence, recalling details about plot, characters, setting (Who said . . . ?), or identifying the main characters.
2. Comprehension. This is the lowest level of understanding, and it is made up of three skills: translation—stating an idea in one's own words; interpretation—summarizing; and extrapolation—extending ideas. Comprehension questions or activities may include explaining what happened, explaining the character's actions, describing a character's feelings or attitudes toward a situation, organizing and summarizing the story's events (What will happen next? How would you describe a favorite character or setting?), or illustrating a special event, character, or setting.
3. Application. Students apply information or knowledge in a new way. Application questions or activities may include giving examples of someone who has a problem similar to the one in the book (How could it be solved? How would the character's life be different if he or she lived 50 years

ago?), solving a problem presented in a different way, enacting a favorite scene from the story, or classifying the main characters (according to predetermined criteria).

4. Analysis. Students break down the whole into parts and examine the elements and their relationships. Questions encouraging analysis may include: Why is the story considered a good example of (name of genre)? How was the plot affected by the characters? How did the setting affect the plot? Activities may include analyzing the main character's motives or comparing the main characters from two related stories.

5. Synthesis. Students put parts together in a different way to produce something unique. Synthesis questions or activities may include developing a new ending, creating a diary as if you were the main character, writing a biopoem to describe a selected character, or creating a new character for the story and discussing how this character's presence will change the plot or affect other characters.

6. Evaluation. Students form judgments or opinions based on selected criteria. Evaluative activities may include judging the actions and behavior of a specific character, writing a review that discusses your evaluation of a story, defending the points of view of two different characters in the story. An example of an evaluative question is: Which character would you most like to know?

After students read *Tuck Everlasting* you could ask these example questions based on the strategy above.

1. Knowledge. Who said, "You can't have living without dying. So you can't call it living, what we got . . ."?

2. Comprehension. What does Tuck mean by that quote? Summarize Tuck's views about immortality. What would happen if Tuck couldn't convince Winnie to keep the spring a secret?

3. Application. What effect would immortality have on different aspects of society, such as technology, living conditions (housing, food, crime), and scientific research?

4. Analysis. Compare the attitudes concerning immortality of each of the following characters: Tuck, Mae, Miles, Jesse, the stranger, Winnie. What do these attitudes tell you about the kind of person each is?

5. Synthesis. Become immortality. What do you look like, taste like, smell like? How do you affect people? What do people think of you? Prepare a monologue to describe yourself as immortality.

6. Evaluation. If you were given the opportunity to become immortal, would you choose to do so? Explain.

Interpretive Questioning: Shared Inquiry

The Great Books Foundation established Junior Great Books to provide a liberal arts program through the reading and discussion of outstanding literary works. The foundation publishes paperback sets of literary works and offers training courses to prepare and certify teachers and discussion leaders to conduct great books groups.

The program is based on shared inquiry, a method through which groups discuss and explore ideas offered by the classics. In shared inquiry, participants discover for themselves certain meanings in the literature, and they must be able to support their views with facts and evidence from the writings. Shared inquiry helps develop critical thinking skills, encourages divergent answers, models an inquiry style of learning, provides a framework for classroom discussion, helps students interpret what they read, and promotes independent and reflective thought.

Shared inquiry can be based on any quality work of literature representing any genre. Interpretation can focus on words or passages or on the entire work. Before the discussion, students should read the selection a second time, or as an alternative, listen to it being read aloud (in pairs, small groups, or as a class) or listen to a taped version.

Shared inquiry is conducted as follows.

1. Before beginning the first shared inquiry discussion, students should be familiar with the rules: each participant must have read the selection; only the selections that everyone has read can be discussed; opinions must be backed with evidence from the selection; and the teacher or leader can only *ask* questions, not answer them.
2. Prior to the discussion, develop questions that make students think for themselves. The questions must pose a real problem about the meaning or idea of the story and reflect your doubts as well. The questions must be specific and clear. The initial question should be interpretive (explaining character motives, making connections between passages, giving opinions about meaning, etc.). Subsequent related questions can be factual (one correct answer), interpretive, or evaluative (based on individual values and choice of action).
3. Students must read a specific selection before the group discussion. Encourage them to read the selection a second time.
4. Seat students in a circle for the discussion. This organization has been found to stimulate discussion.
5. Have students write down the question you ask. Give a set time (approximately one to two minutes) for each student to formulate an interpretive answer.
6. As students respond, ask frequent follow-up questions to challenge them and encourage in-depth answers, as well as to give them the opportunity to explain their views more clearly.
7. Try to call on each participant at least three times during the discussion. A seating chart can help you keep track of respondents.
8. At the end of the discussion (usually about 20 minutes), attempt to bring the group to resolution. To do this, repeat the initial interpretive question and call on students to repeat their answers. Try to call on those students

who participated less during the discussion. At this point, all participants should have an answer and should be able to support it.

After students have read *Tuck Everlasting*, the following example questions based on shared inquiry might be asked.

1. Making connections between passages. Throughout the story, the author refers to a toad. What is the significance of the toad to the story?
2. Opinion as to meaning. What does Tuck mean when he says, "... we got to talk, and the pond's the best place. The pond's got answers."
3. Character motives. Is the stranger's motivation in solving the mystery of the Tuck family always based on greed?
4. Why something is put in an unusual way. Why doesn't the author give the stranger with the yellow suit a name?

For more information about Junior Great Books and Shared Inquiry, contact the Great Books Foundation (35 East Wacher Dr.; Suite 2300, Chicago, IL 60601-2298; (1-800-222-5870).

Divergent Questioning

Most questions students are asked to answer are convergent in nature—have one right answer. Divergent questions generate a variety of responses, based on students' backgrounds, perceptions, and creativity. Divergent questions can have a tremendous impact on the way children interact with literature. They can:

> Provide a risk-free environment, since there are no "right" answers
> Encourage the development of critical and creative skills
> Encourage students to manipulate the observations and ideas gained
> through reading
> Look at various literary genres in new, meaningful ways
> Arouse interest
> Encourage students to participate in discussions
> Give students insights as they approach information in innovative ways
> Give students new perspectives into reasoning and problem solving
> Encourage students to ponder their own questions and pursue incongruities, discrepancies, and meaning

The following questioning formats can be adapted to a variety of books; however, it is important that the questions selected are relevant to the literary work and cause children to interact with the text.

1. List all the words you can think of to describe _____.
2. What are all the possible solutions for _____?
3. List as many _____ as you can think of.
4. How many ways can you come up with to _____?
5. How would _____ view this?

6. What would _____ mean from the viewpoint of _____?
7. How would this look to _____?
8. How would _____ describe _____?
9. How would you feel if you were _____?
10. How would _____ feel it if were human?
11. What would _____ do?
12. You are a _____. Describe your feelings.
13. How is _____ like _____?
14. I only know about _____. Explain _____ to me.
15. What ideas from _____ are like _____?
16. What _____ is most like _____?
17. What would happen if there were more (or less) _____?
18. Suppose _____ happened. What would be the results?
19. What would happen if _____ were true?
20. Imagine if _____ and _____ were reversed. What would happen?

Another form of divergent questions is "What if" questions. They encourage students to look at literary works and imagine the implications if various elements of the work were changed in some way, giving them another way of seeing the importance of the author's choice and the way various elements interact. "What if" questions also give students ideas about transformations they could make in literature and offer ideas for their writings. After modeling "What if" questions, encourage students to create some of their own as a springboard for classroom and group discussion.

"What if" questions might include:

1. What if this story took place 50 years earlier (or later)?
2. What if the story were told from the viewpoint of (a different character)?
3. What if (one specific incident from the story) had had a different outcome?
4. What if (the main character) were a different gender?
5. What if you were the main character? What would you do?
6. What if (a character from a different story) visited (the characters in the story currently being read)? What advice would he or she give?
7. What if the events in this story could actually happen? What effects would it have on life as we know it?

Creative Problem Solving

Creative problem solving (CPS) is a technique that approaches problem solving through the use of imagination (Parnes, 1977). It provides a framework for problem solving that encourages generating as many solutions as possible. Creative problem solving results in innovative problem solving and helps promote more creative thinking in general. Many industries and businesses train their employees in CPS and its importance in education is now being recognized.

In almost every literary work, there is some problem that must be solved. Often, students are faced with similar problems in their lives. As the literary work brings the problem to the surface, students can work individually or as a group to generate alternatives to help solve the problem. Literature also reflects universal problems, such as crime, pollution, and aging. Students have an opportunity to apply CPS skills to real-word problems. The framework provided by CPS will encourage students to use their imagination in problem solving to formulate solutions that might not have been apparent from the beginning.

The steps in CPS are as follows.

1. Fact finding. Students are provided with the "mess" (problem). They collect as much information as possible about the mess and try to find out all the facts relating to it.
2. Problem finding. Students view the mess and the information gathered from different perspectives to focus on the main problem that needs to be solved. The problem is stated using the formula IWWMI (In What Ways Might I . . .).
3. Idea finding. Students brainstorm, listing as many ideas as they can to solve the problem. The rules for brainstorming include:
   a. Defer judgment
   b. Hitchhike on the ideas of others
   c. Quantity produces quantity
4. Solution finding. Students list the most appropriate criteria for evaluating the ideas that were generated. The following matrix can be used to help evaluate the possible solutions.

ALTERNATIVE SOLUTIONS	CRITERIA					TOTAL
	1	2	3	4	5	
1.						
2.						
3.						
4.						
5.						
6.						
7.						
8.						

They list the alternative solutions and evaluate each one according to the criteria selected. The solutions are ranked on a scale of 1 to N (N being the number of alternatives listed), with 1 being the best solution. The points are added for each alternative to find the solution that best meets the criteria.

5. Acceptance finding. Students create a plan of action to explain how they would carry out the chosen solution, keeping in mind the needs of those who will ultimately be evaluating the plan.

Many literary works, such as *The Hundred Dresses,* by Eleanor Estes, *The Great Gilly Hopkins,* by Katherine Paterson, *Dragonwings,* by Laurence Yep, *In the Year of the Boar and Jackie Robinson,* by Bette Bao Lord, and *The New Kid on the Block,* by Jack Prelutsky, deal with moving and starting over. The following example of creative problem solving deals with problems related to moving.

1. **Fact finding:** Based on the work of literature read and children's knowledge, brainstorm the problems caused by moving and list them on a chart or chalkboard. Have students create a list of questions dealing with the problem of moving so they can get as much information as possible. What problems are caused by moving? How did people feel when they have to move? How does moving affect the family?

2. **Problem finding:** Change the fact finding responses into problem statements. For example: In what ways might we find new friends? In what ways might we make a move from another country easier? In what ways might we learn to get around a new city? Have students select the "best" problem.

3. **Idea finding:** Generate as many ideas as possible to help solve the problem. For example, if the problem selected were "In what ways might we make new friends?" ideas might include join a club, join a sports group such as Little League, become involved in after-school activities, and invite classmates to your home after school to play.

4. **Solution finding:** Place the ideas on the matrix, select criteria on which to base them, and prioritize the solutions, rating them one through the number of solutions you have. The criteria might include the fastest way to make friends or the easiest solution to implement (see page 289).

5. **Acceptance finding:** Develop a plan of action for implementing the best solution.

Discussion of Moral Dilemmas

Laurence Kohlberg formulated his approach to moral education as a result of his belief that certain universal, ethical principles must be considered when making decisions involving moral questions. Kohlberg (1971) identified fixed stages of moral development through which all people pass, although not everyone stops at the same stages along the way. He also found that most people do not act solely on the basis of their own personal stage of reasoning; instead, most decisions are based on group identification. Therefore, in the high-

ALTERNATIVE SOLUTIONS	CRITERIA				TOTAL
	Fastest Way	Most comfortable	Most effective	Most interesting to me	
1. Join school clubs	3	2	3	4	12
2. Join band	5	4	4	5	18
3. Invite classmates home	1	5	2	3	11
4. Go to local park	4	3	5	2	14
5. Join baseball team	2	1	1	1	5 *

*The solution with the lowest total rates the best

est level of moral development, the individual makes decisions based on certain moral principles regardless of others' thoughts or decisions. Kohlberg found that teachers can help students reach higher levels of moral reasoning through the discussion of situations in which universal values come into conflict. The key word in Kohlberg's technique is *reasoning*: "Basic to the understanding of Kohlberg's theory is the realization that it is a cognitive approach . . . suggesting that educators attempt to develop moral *reasoning* rather than moral *behavior.* Sophisticated moral reasoning usually leads to ethical behavior, and educators should be concentrating on reasoning" (Maker, 1982, p. 140). The discussion of moral dilemmas stresses thought processes and patterns of thinking.

Many of the books students read include moral dilemmas that the characters face. These dilemmas can be discussed using the steps outlined below. Often students face similar dilemmas, and the discussion will help them in the reasoning of their own dilemma. Periodically, involve students in problem solving to encourage alternatives not considered in the original dilemma as it was presented. This will make them more aware of the choices open to all of us.

Moral dilemmas can be presented in numerous ways. When selecting dilemmas for classroom discussion, use the following criteria: a central character must decide between alternatives; there are only two or three alternatives from which to choose; society provides at least some support for any of the alternatives; and at least one moral issue is involved. Use the following steps to augment the discussion:

1. Present the dilemma. There are many ways to present a dilemma to students. For example, you may read the dilemma aloud, students may read it individually, or the dilemma can be role-played.
2. Clarify facts and issues. Encourage students to list the facts of the situation, summarizing events, characters involved, and possible alternatives.
3. Choose an alternative. Have students decide which alternative the main character should follow and give at least three reasons for their decision. They should do this individually and in written form.
4. Small group discussion. By a show of hands, find out which alternatives students selected. If the class is fairly split on the issues, divide them into groups depending on their position. If a majority of the class selected the same position, place some students in the group that took an alternative position or place them in groups depending on their reason for their position. (Those students who have a similar reason can be placed together.) Have groups discuss the position they took and focus on the most important reasons for taking the position.
5. Class discussion. Seat students in a circle to promote group interaction. Allow time for the students to discuss their positions and their reasons for them. Initiate discussion by having each group summarize their position and reasons for it or stimulate a general discussion with the questions: "What should the character do? Why?"

    During this discussion, it is important to be nonjudgmental and to encourage all students to participate and interact. Ask questions to help students clarify their own reasons and perceptions of the issue.
6. Reevaluate positions. Encourage students to think about the facts, issues, and reasons discussed and then individually record what they think the main character should do, and the most important reason for taking this position. If they changed their original position, encourage them to write about what caused them to look at the issue differently. Do not attempt to reach a class consensus.

    When students have completed their papers, compare responses to their earlier responses to see if any ideas changed. You may also record the stage of moral reasoning as reflected by students' responses.

Many books deal with prejudice and discrimination and the need to take a stand. Schultz's Dilemma (see page 291) ties in with a study of prejudice and persecution and especially with a study of the literature of the Holocaust. Books such as *Number the Stars,* by Lois Lowry, and *The Devil's Arithmetic,* by Jane Yolen, are excellent springboards for discussion of Schultz's dilemma. Begin the discussion by reading the dilemma aloud or have students role-play the situation. During class discussion, ask questions that encourage students to focus and clarify responses. For example, have them explain their statements, focus on a moral issue, determine universal consequences (e.g., What would happen if the same situation happened in this country?), give reasons behind a statement, or explain the responses of another student.

SCHULTZ'S DILEMMA

During the late 1930s and early 1940s, Germany invaded and conquered Austria, Poland, France, the Netherlands, Norway, and Denmark. Throughout these countries and in Germany, Jewish people were routinely forced into ghettos and later transported to concentration camps and killed. This was known as Hitler's "Final Solution." By the time the war had ended, more than 6 million Jewish men, women, and children had been killed.

Living in Germany at this time were two families who had been friends for six years, since their oldest children had been born. The Rosen family was Jewish; their friends, the Schultzes, were not. Both families knew what was being done to the Jewish people and the Rosens decided they had to escape from Germany if they were to survive.

The Rosens, along with other Jewish families, tried to develop a plan that would lead them to safety, but they soon realized that no matter what they did, they would be discovered. The trains and all other forms of transportation were guarded by Nazi soldiers. All routes out of their city were blocked. Time was running out. Already, many of their Jewish friends had been rounded up in the middle of the night, never to be heard from again.

Finally, the Rosens had an idea, the only one they felt had a chance of working. In the middle of the night, they dressed their young children—Stephen, age 6, Adam, age 4, and the baby, Rachael, age 2—and quietly left their home. In the shadows, they made their way to the Schultz home and knocked at the door. They begged the Schultzes to hide them in the basement of their home, knowing the Schultzes were the only ones they could trust.

Mr. Schultz and his wife knew they had to make a decision. If they allowed the Rosens to stay with them, they risked death for themselves and their own children. The Nazi soldiers were ordered to shoot on sight anyone found aiding a Jewish person. They had witnessed such an execution only a few weeks earlier. On the other hand, they knew that if they didn't help their friends, the Rosens would be transported to concentration camps and meet certain death. They looked at the faces of the Rosen children, so young and innocent. Then they thought of their own children tucked safely in bed.

Readers as Writers

For too long, reading and writing were taught as isolated subjects far removed from one another. Children were not expected to write until they could read. Recently, changes in the approach to teaching children writing have occurred. We now realize that just as children learn to read by reading, they learn to write by writing. Children are now encouraged to write daily, and each child is an author. Even if the "writing" is in the form of a picture they explain, a line of "scribble" they can decode, or a sentence using invented spelling, they have created meaning and, as such, are authors.

One of the most important aspects of writing instruction today is the use of literature. For students to become better writers, they must be immersed in good literature. Thus they begin to associate sounds and symbols and become aware of and appreciate what is meant by *story*. Literature serves as a model and a stimulus for writing (Calkins, 1986); in fact, the author actually becomes the teacher. By reading or listening to a story being read, children learn how to write. When they write, they use their knowledge of story structure and other literary techniques they have gathered through their involvement with good literature.

The strategies described here involve children in connecting their reading with their writing. These strategies include journal writing, literary logs, the writing process, and the language experience approach. These strategies encourage children to respond to what they read. Literature thus becomes a catalyst for writing and inspires readers to write their own literary interpretations and original pieces.

Journals

A variety of journals, developed for different purposes, can be kept to encourage students to respond to literature. Journal writing promotes understanding and insights as students react personally to literature. It fosters language skills and skills in critical and creative thinking. Students should have an opportunity to write daily and to share their responses in large or small group discussion.

Book Response Journals

After children read independently or hear a story or poem read aloud, they are encouraged to react to the literature in some way. Younger students may respond through illustrations or short sentences. Older students may describe how the work affected them, pursue a question, or speculate on a motive. They may wish to write about how the events parallel happenings in their own lives. Students are led to examine what makes the book or poem special. Book response journals are very personal and can serve as a catharsis. Often, journal entries lead to a piece that students take through the writing process to publication. Since it is impossible for teachers to read and react to each journal entry, they may wish to divide students into five groups and each day of the week collect the journals of one group. They can explain that while they will read all entries (unless students ask that certain ones not be read), they will respond to only one. Teacher responses should be encouraging and validate students' feelings. Journal entries should not be evaluated with a letter grade or marked for mechanical errors.

Students might have difficulty deciding what to write about, especially when they first begin. The suggestions in Aesthetic Questioning (pages

279–281) serve as an excellent springboard for journal responses, as do the following questions:

> How did the book/poem make you feel?
> What did it remind you of?
> How did the writer's choice of words affect you?
> What part did you like best?
> Which character would you select for a friend? Which character reminds you of yourself or a family member?
> What surprised you?
> What makes this unique?
> What was the book/poem's message to you?
> What would you like to find out more about?
> What part of the book/poem would you change?
> What does the book/poem make you wonder about?
> What in the book/poem do you feel strongly about?
> What do you think the author was trying to say or make you think about?
> What caused the characters to act as they did? What would you have done under similar circumstances?
> What other stories does this book/poem remind you of?

Dialogue Journals

A dialogue journal is a written conversation, allowing students to communicate with their teacher. It empowers students by providing them an opportunity to initiate the "conversation" based on what is important to them at the time and their need to express it. Dialogue journals can be written on a variety of topics; this section focuses on those related to literature.

In a dialogue journal, the students react to a specific event, character, or element based on the way it affected them. As with other types of journals, younger children may respond with a picture, brief phrase, or sentence to which the teacher can respond. The teacher then responds to the content of what the students communicate. The response should encourage students to continue to write about their ideas, interpretations, and insights; ask a few questions to encourage further exploration of the subject; and be brief—a sentence or two is sufficient.

The dialogue journal is not a forum for improving grammar or other mechanical writing skills, although the teacher's modeling of correct spelling and grammar in his or her response will not be lost on the students, who modify their spelling and writing. Dialogue journals are a way for students to discuss their feelings and ideas openly in a private, risk-free way. Dialogue journals can also be written between two students who share their ideas and opinions about specific topics related to what they have read.

Learning Logs

Learning logs are tied more closely to content areas; they work well when students are involved in an integrated thematic approach. Students may keep a separate learning log journal for each unit. In learning logs, students are encouraged to ask questions about the subject/topic being explored that might serve as the basis for future reading and research; form predictions and hypotheses about the topic and examine them based on future study, reading, and research; and organize information learned throughout the unit. Learning logs give students ownership over their own learning as they pursue information and understandings to answer questions that pique their curiosity. Furthermore, they encourage students to make connections as they gather, organize, analyze, synthesize, and evaluate the information they uncover.

Simulation Journals/Literary Letters

In simulation journals, students take on the persona of a character from literature and write journal entries or letters from the character's viewpoint. This type of writing gives students additional insights into characters, character motivation, and how events and setting shape character. Other students and/or the teacher should be encouraged to reply to the letters students write as the character. Often the ideas and conclusions expressed in the letters and simulation journal entries can focus for small group and whole class discussions.

Literary Logs

Students should be encouraged to keep a log of the books they read. The literary log can take many forms, based on the students' level. Students should be encouraged to react to what they have read, write any questions they have, and share their feelings and ideas about the literary work. Literary logs can be used as a springboard for class discussions of a specific book or poem and can be used during student–teacher conferences to help teachers assess how children are reading and reacting to literature.

Literary logs should be brief so they are not viewed as a chore. Pages 295 and 296 show examples of intermediate-level and primary-level literary logs. Younger children can respond to literature through pictures. You may wish to duplicate the log and keep copies easily assessible in a central area. Students can keep completed logs in a separate section of their notebook or in a special folder.

The Writing Process

As children react to literature in their journals and literary logs, they are often inspired to expand the ideas and/or create their own stories and poems. A knowledge of the writing process will not only help children revise and edit their writing, but also suggest ways of generating topics for their writing, help them recognize those elements and techniques that make writing effective, and help them explore a variety of avenues for sharing their work with others.

In recent years there has been a tremendous amount of research to determine the best way to teach writing. Donald Graves (1983), in his landmark *Writ-*

**INTERMEDIATE-LEVEL
LITERARY LOG**

Name: _____ Date: _____

Title: _____

Author: _____

Genre: _____

General impressions, comments, or questions:

1. _____

2. _____

3. _____

4. _____

5. _____

General recommendation: _____

_____

---

ing: Teachers and Children at Work, focused on classroom practices based on the implications of research concerning how children learn to write. From his work and the work of others emerges the realization that writing is a process. Previously, the product itself was emphasized, and writing was a cornucopia of isolated exercises and practice writings. The writing process, however, emphasizes the dynamic and interactive experiences that writers follow as they create their own meaning. In this holistic approach, children are given the opportunity to write meaningful texts.

The writing process includes five stages; it is important that children be familiar with each step: prewriting, drafting, revising, editing, and publishing (Graves, 1983). The process approach gives children an opportunity to select their own topics, thereby giving them ownership of their writing. It encourages students to write for real audiences and gives them an opportunity to write collaboratively and share what they have written. Each student writes daily, and the generation of ideas takes precedence over the mechanics of writing in the initial stages so they feel free to generate ideas with fluency without fear of breaking any rules.

**PRIMARY-LEVEL
LITERARY LOG**

Name: _____ Date: _____

Title of book: _____

Author: _____

I (liked) (did not like) the book because: _____

_____

_____

_____

One question I have is: _____

_____

_____

While students are involved in the writing process, the teacher should be a facilitator, modeling strategies, leading minilessons to help develop specific skills, and holding writing conferences (see Chap. 12) in which students discuss their writing, their progress, and any specific problems they have.

To help organize their writing, students should keep a writing folder (see page 297) that contains a personal dictionary and thesaurus; an editing checklist; a list of writing ideas, to which they continuously add (see page 299); a list of writings they took through the writing process that were ultimately "published" (see p. 300); a section to keep work in progress; and a list of skills they have mastered and those they need help with (see page 301).

According to Hansen (1987), the following elements are essential to the writing process.

1. Time. Students need to be given time, on a daily basis, to write. Ideally, they should write at a regularly scheduled time. Traditionally, writing programs include exercises in spelling, grammar, handwriting, and punctuation, in addition to writing papers on assigned topics that are graded. However, researchers (e.g., Atwell, 1987) have recently compiled more realistic information about what "real" writers actually do. The writing process allows students to follow a process that is similar to that followed by "real" writers.

(Back Cover)

My Stories

Title	Date
The True Story of the Three Bears	9/24
The Hungry Alligator	10/15
My Scariet Halloween	10/30
Taylor and Me	11/14

My Writing Folder

By Ken Adams

(Front Cover)

(Inside Folder)

Writing Skills

1. I begin each sentence with a capital letter.

2. I indent each paragraph.

3. I use a Thesaurus to find new words.

(Inside Folder, Front and Back)

EDITING CHECKLIST

Name: _____ Date: _____

Title of writing _____

Capitalization
- ☐ Does each sentence begin with capital letter?
- ☐ Are proper nouns (name of a person, place or thing) capitalized?
- ☐ Are the first word and all other important
- ☐ words in the title capitalized?

_____

Punctuation
- ☐ Does each sentence end with a period, question mark, or exclamation point?
- ☐ Do quotation marks indicate beginning and end of what someone says?
- ☐ Is an apostrophe used to show ownership or to make contractions?
- ☐ Are commas used to separate words in a list?
- ☐ _____
- ☐ _____

Ideas to Write About

My summer vacation
How my brother broke his arm
Grandpa's store
I learned to swim
School
My best friend, John

2. Choice. Students need the freedom to choose their topics and to feel in control of their writing. They soon learn that it is their responsibility to decide what to write about. As Donald Graves (1985) so poignantly stated, "The most important thing children can learn is what they know and how they know it."

3. Response. As part of the writing process, teachers and peers *respond* to the writers, not only on the finished product but also on their drafts. Also, teachers move among the students, responding and teaching as they write.

4. Structure. The writing process works best in classrooms with structures. According to Jane Hansen (1987), teachers who like order can often get a writing program organized more easily than those who are not organized. Once the writing process is organized, students know what to do—from choosing a topic, to editing a draft, to sharing with classmates.

5. Community. Developing a writing community in which students have an opportunity to share and listen to others share is very important to this whole process. Students value their own contributions as well as the contributions of others.

Perhaps one of the best ways to help students become comfortable with the stages of the writing process is to have the class work on a group composition. The teacher describes each stage and, based on a specific topic, has groups practice each step of the process. Students may dictate the story to the teacher, who writes it on a chalkboard or an overhead transparency. The teacher can then model ways to revise the draft—additions, deletions, organization, and so on. Students then proofread the composition for mechanical errors and spelling. The revised, edited story can then be rewritten and copies made for each child to keep.

Steps in the Writing Process

1. **Prewriting:** This is perhaps the most important stage and one that is too often neglected. During prewriting, children must choose a topic, consider the purpose for their writing and the audience, and generate ideas for writing. Teachers can encourage children to select topics from the list of ideas they have been collecting in their writing notebooks or react to literature they have read or listened to.

   To assist children in prewriting, the teacher can model his or her own way of selecting a topic about which to write. Many of the ideas can be associated with literature children have read or listened to. For example, after reading *Tuck Everlasting*, by Natalie Babbitt, with the students, one teacher decided to write a paper about the metaphor comparing life to a wheel. After reading *Alexander and the Terrible, Horrible, No Good, Very Bad Day*, by Judith Viorst, one class decided to write their own version of the flip side: *Alexander and the Terrific, Wonderful, Extremely Good, Very Excellent Day*.

   Students can be taught specific strategies to help them generate ideas for their writing. Younger students can be encouraged to draw pictures to help organize ideas; students can talk with other students about their ideas; they can read books on their selected topic; and they can conduct interviews with those who might have information on the topic. Graphic organizers, such as listing, clustering, cubing, and mapping (see pages 302–303), are important to the writing process. Each graphic organizer should be described and modeled by the teacher. Students should be guided and encouraged to use these organizers.

2. **Drafting:** In this stage, students write on their selected topic, trying to get down as many ideas as possible. All rules are suspended and the only goal is fluency. It is important that students mark their paper "draft" to help them realize this is part of the process of writing, not the finished product. It also shows that the writing is in progress and that it is not to be graded or marked for mechanical errors. Students should double-space their drafts to provide space for revisions.

IDEAS FOR TOPICS I CAN WRITE ABOUT

1. _____
2. _____
3. _____
4. _____
5. _____
6. _____
7. _____
8. _____
9. _____
10. _____
11. _____
12. _____
13. _____
14. _____
15. _____
16. _____
17. _____
18. _____
19. _____
20. _____

PIECES I HAVE WRITTEN

TITLE   DATE

1. _____

2. _____

3. _____

4. _____

5. _____

6. _____

7. _____

8. _____

9. _____

10. _____

11. _____

12. _____

13. _____

14. _____

15. _____

16. _____

17. _____

18. _____

19. _____

20. _____

WRITING SKILLS I HAVE LEARNED

1. _____
2. _____
3. _____
4. _____
5. _____
6. _____
7. _____
8. _____
9. _____
10. _____
11. _____
12. _____
13. _____
14. _____
15. _____
16. _____
17. _____
18. _____
19. _____
20. _____

Often, the most difficult part of writing is the first paragraph. Sharing a variety of types of writing from literature will help children recognize different leads. Graves (1983) suggests that children experiment with a variety of introductions to see which works best.

3. **Revision:** During this stage, children revisit what they have written and both individually and in groups try to improve their draft. Once students have made any changes, they form writing groups to share their writings with others. Writing groups are an excellent way to help children recognize what makes writing most effective. Writing groups should be composed of three or four students. Some teachers use the same writing groups all years while others allow groups to form spontaneously when

GRAPHIC ORGANIZERS

Listing. Ask students to select a topic and list all the ideas, words, and related phrases they can think of. They can then read through their list, cross out words that don't fit, and try to group related words. They can then summarize the ideas and use this summary as the topic sentence for their writing.

Clustering/Webbing. Have students write a topic in the center of a sheet of paper and circle it. Have them write as many ideas, words, and phrases as they can that relate to the circled word and circle each of these. (In webs, the words are not generally circled.) Have them connect the circles to the one in the middle. Have them rearrange their cluster/web by grouping like ideas, then select one of the ideas to use as the basis of their writing. For example, a cluster done of "curiosity," based on *Curious George*, by H. A. Rey, might look like this:

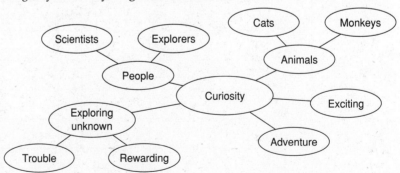

The 5 Ws and the H. Based on a selected topic, have students ask Who, What, Where, When, Why, and How. Have them list the questions and answers on a chart. Responses might come from their imaginations, from reading, or from interviews.

GRAPHIC ORGANIZERS (*continued*)

Topic: _____

Question: *Response*

Who

What

Where

When

Why

How

Cubing. Have students select a topic. Have them spend several minutes describing it, comparing it, associating it, analyzing it, applying it, and arguing for or against it. This will generate a tremendous bank of words, phrases, metaphors, and similes for their writing. To familiarize students with this technique, go through each perspective together on a selected subject. For example, after reading a book on the subject of survival, use the term *survival* or *courage* as the topic for cubing.

Story Mapping. A story map is "a unified representation of a story based on a logical organization of events and ideas of central importance to the story and the interrelationships of these events and ideas" (Beck and McKeown, 1981). A story map can be used to help students achieve a mindset for reading the story, as a framework for discussion following the story, or as a way to help plan their own writing. "In story maps, specific relationships of story elements are made clear. Main ideas and sequences, comparisons of characters, and cause–effect relationships are some of the features of stories that can be shown in maps" (Burns, Roe, & Ross, 1988).

To familiarize students with this technique, each student can create his or her own map, or a class map can be developed. For example, in *Curious George*, the story's events can be mapped using outlines of Africa and the United States. Or shapes representing balloons can be cut out and filled with events from the story, then organized into the correct chronological order.

To help students create a story map, ask them "What happened first in the story?" Write their responses on the board and continue until the entire story has unfolded and the main events have been identified. Students can then copy or rewrite the items listed onto their story maps.

students are ready to revise. It is important that groups be heterogeneous and represent different strengths and weaknesses.

To help students understand the role of the writing group, you may wish to share an example of a work on the chalkboard and go through different strategies for improving it. Each time you model the revision stage, select only a few skills on which to focus. For example, students can learn about sentence expansion, substitution of one word for a more descriptive one, deletions, or additions. Or you may wish to model the way sentences and/or paragraphs can be manipulated to make the writing more effective. Modeling can also focus on questions the writer may ask others of his or her writing: Which lead did you like best? Is there a better word I can use instead of _____? Does my piece make sense? Is there anything else you'd like to know? Did the content seem organized?

In the writing groups, the writer first reads his or her piece aloud to the group. The group then comments on the strengths of the piece, being as specific as possible. The group then asks the writer questions and can make suggestions for improvement. The writer asks specific questions of the group and then discusses what he or she plans to change.

The writer makes revisions and can then share the new draft with the writing group. The stages of drafting and revision are circular, rather than linear, and continue until the writer feels his or her piece is ready for the next stage.

To make students aware of the importance of word choice, teachers should encourage them to keep their own dictionary and thesaurus in their writing folder and continuously add to them. For overused words, such as *said* or *nice*, students can compile a list of more descriptive, dynamic words.

Minilessons (see Chap. 12) are an excellent strategy that allow the teacher to work with individuals or small groups of students who need help with specific skills, as evidenced by their writing. The significance of minilessons is that the skill being taught has meaning for the student because it is something he or she needs to learn to improve his or her current writing project. Previously, skills were taught because they were on the next page of the textbook; therefore, they had little or no meaning to the students, nor did the students have a chance to apply the skill in a meaningful context.

4. **Editing:** In this stage, students put their writing into final form. Whereas in earlier stages the attention was on content, in this stage the mechanics of writing and spelling are the main focus. The writer is the main editor, and it is his or her responsibility to locate and correct errors. The teachers may wish to provide students with an editing checklist to keep in their writing folders, such as the one on page 306. This checklist will remind students to focus on specific mechanics and to mark errors with standard proofreader's marks. Depending on the students' level, this checklist can be made more or less complex, and additions can be made as students learn new rules about the mechanics of writing. Once students have proofread their own piece they may ask others in their writing group to proofread it. Finally, the story can be rewritten in final form and made ready for the last stage.

   To help students better understand the process of proofreading, the teacher can model the practice using a piece on the chalkboard or overhead. He or she should model how the piece is read first for meaning and then word for word to find errors. Use of the various editing marks (see page 307) can be modeled. The use of minilessons in this stage is extremely important for students who need help with specific writing mechanics and spelling skills.

5. **Publishing:** This is the final stage of the writing process and the point at which the piece can be evaluated. Publishing refers to any way the writing may be shared. Students may read their finished piece sitting in a special "author's chair." Work may be posted on bulletin boards, read over the school's closed television network, or transcribed onto an audio tape. Encourage students and assist them in submitting final writing products to a magazine that publishes the work of young writers. What a thrill to see their work and name in print! Keep copies of these magazines in the school and classroom libraries so students can read the published work of their peers. Magazines that publish children's writing are listed on pages 308–310. Address can be found in Appendix D.

EDITING CHECKLIST

Name: _____ Date: _____

Title of writing _____

Capitalization

☐ Does each sentence begin with capital letter?

☐ Are proper nouns (name of a person, place, or thing) capitalized?

☐ Are the first word and all other important words in the title capitalized?

☐ _____

Punctuation

☐ Does each sentence end with a period, question mark, or exclamation point?

☐ Do quotation marks indicate the beginning and end of what someone says?

☐ Is an apostrophe used to show ownership or to make contractions?

☐ Are commas used to separate words in a list?

☐ _____

☐ _____

Additional Checks

☐ Did I read the writing word for word to check for all errors?

☐ Were the spellings of words checked?

☐ Did I avoid commonplace words that say nothing, like *nice, good,* and *said*?

☐ Are all sentences complete?

☐ Are all paragraphs indented?

☐ Is the writing well organized?

☐ _____

☐ _____

☐ _____

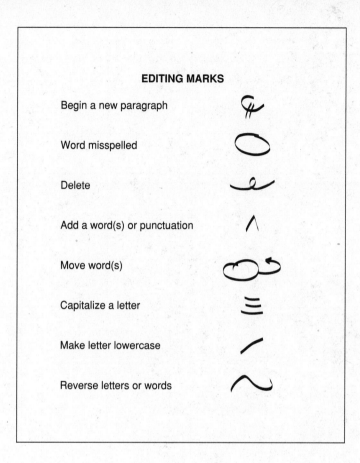

Writings can also be bound into book form. A student-made book should include a page entitled, "Something About the Author," with a brief blurb about the writer and a picture. If someone other than the author illustrated the text, a similar "Something About the Illustrator" page should be included. Directions for creating a variety of books are given in Appendix F. A special portion of the classroom library should be dedicated to books that were written by the students.

Each class should have a publishing center where children can type their stories or bind their books into various forms that have previously been made (pop-up books, little books, big books, etc.). Books can also be created by punching holes in the left corner and connecting the pages with a large circular ring. Each page should be covered with contact paper to ensure durability. If possible, recruit parent volunteers to help make hardbound books and help students with typing. You may establish certain times of the week when volunteers will help students bind final drafts.

(text continues, page 311)

Magazines that publish student work

Magazine	Grade level	Focus	Art	Book reviews	Contest responses	Essays	Creative fiction	Crafts & hobbies	Jokes & riddles	Letters	Poems	Questions	True stories
						Type of student work published							
Bear Essential News for Kids	Pre-K–7	Consumer issues									x		
Boy's Life	2–12	Boys' life	x					x	x	x			x
Chart Your Course!	4–6	Gifted students	x	x		x	x	x	x	x	x		
Chickadee	Pre-K–3	General	x										
Child Life	3–6	Health	x						x		x		
Children's Album	3–8	Student writing, arts & crafts	x			x	x	x	x	x	x	x	x
Children's Digest	3–5	Health	x			x			x		x	x	
Children's Playmate	1–3	Health	x						x		x	x	
Cobblestone	4–9	History	x					x		x			
Creative Kids	K–12	Student writing	x	x		x	x	x			x		x
Cricket	1–6	General	x		x	x	x			x			x
Daybreak Star	4–8	Native American life	x			x	x			x	x		x
Faces	4–9	Anthropology	x							x	x		

From: *The Reading Teacher,* 47:1, 1993.

(continued)

Magazines that publish student work (continued)

Magazine	Grade level	Focus	Art	Book reviews	Contest responses	Essays	Creative fiction	Crafts & hobbies	Jokes & riddles	Letters	Poems	Questions	True stories
						Type of student work published							
Free Spirit	5–12	Growing up & gifted				×	×					×	×
Highlight for Children	Pre-K–6	General	×				×		×	×	×		×
Hopscotch	3–6	Girl's life								×	×		
Humpty Dumpty's Magazine	Pre-K–1	Health	×									×	
Jack and Jill	1–4	Health	×						×		×	×	
Kid City	1–4	General			×				×				
Kidlife and Times	1–8	Imagination	×		×		×						
Merlyn's Pen	7–12	Student writing				×	×				×		×
National Geographic World	3–12	Children of the world	×							×			
Odyssey	3–8	Space & astronomy	×		×					×		×	
Owl	3–6	Environment	×		×	×			×	×			
P3	K–9	Ecology	×							×	×		
Prism	5–12	Student writing & gifted				×	×			×	×		×
Ranger Rick	1–6	Nature								×		×	

(continued)

Magazines that publish student work (continued)

Magazine	Grade level	Focus	Type of student work published										
			Art	Book reviews	Contest responses	Essays	Creative fiction	Crafts & hobbies	Jokes & riddles	Letters	Poems	Questions	True stories
Sesame Street Magazine	Pre-K–1	School preparation	x							x	x		
Shoe Tree	1–9	Student writing	x	x		x	x				x		x
Sports Illustrated for Kids	3–7	Sports	x						x	x	x		
Stone Soup	1–8	Student writing	x	x			x				x		x
Surprises	Pre-K–6	Home activities					x	x	x				
3-2-1 Contact	3–8	Science and technology			x							x	
Turtle Magazine	Pre-K–K	Health	x										
Wee Wisdom	K–6	Values	x			x	x	x			x		x
Zillions	3–7	Economics		x						x		x	

The following items should be available in your publishing center.

Writing paper
Computer/printer
Typewriter
Pens/pencils
Markers
Glue
Contact paper
Blank books (pop-up, little books, big books, etc.)
Construction paper
Rings
Staplers
Scissors
Dictionary
Thesaurus

Activities for the Writing Process

Literature is an excellent source for inspiring individual, group, and class stories. The following activities will help foster the reading–writing connection. In addition, the activities listed for each genre in Chapter 1 include many ideas for writing.

1. Students can learn a tremendous amount about the writing process by reading and discussing specific works of literature. Based on a favorite book, discuss how the author may have selected the topic for the story; how he or she developed it; why the author included or did not include certain information; how the author achieved the mood that was set; and the way specific word choices affected the story.
2. Share information about authors, where they get their ideas, and their process for writing. Many author biographies are available. Other references are *Something About the Author* and L. B. Hopkins's *Books Are by People* and *More Books by More People.* These include detailed information about many children's authors. In addition, many companies have audio-visual materials available on different authors (see Chap. 10).
3. Create a group book on a specific topic being studied. For example, a study of animals could involve groups researching and writing about a specific animal and illustrating their pages. The book pages and cover can be cut into the form of the animal subject. Or read *Anamalia,* by Graeme Base, and, using it as a model, have groups of students create their own alliteration page. Bind the pages to create "Anamalia II."

4. Have students write transformations of their favorite folk tales. For example, after reading a version of *The Three Little Pigs* and Jon Scieszka's *The True Story of the 3 Little Pigs!*, have students read another folk tale and write "The True Story of _____"

5. Have students use specific literary techniques as a model for their own writing. For example, in Natalie Babbitt's *Tuck Everlasting*, the prologue begins:

> The first week of August hangs at the very top of the summer, the top of the live-long year, like the highest seat of a Ferris wheel when it pauses in its turning. The weeks that come before are only a climb from balmy spring, and those that follow a drop to the chill of autumn, but the first week of August is motionless and hot. It is curiously silent, too, with blank white dawns and glaring noons, and sunsets smeared with too much color. Often at night there is lightning, but it quivers all alone. There is no thunder, no relieving rain. These are strange and breathless days, the dog days, when people are led to do things they are sure to be sorry for after.

Have students create their own picture of August or another month, "showing" what it is like using figurative language, rather than simply "telling."

6. Have students rewrite a favorite story by manipulating one of the elements. For example, they can create a new exploit for the title character of Jerry Spinelli's *Maniac Magee* or rewrite a scene from Katherine Paterson's *The Great Gilly Hopkins* from the viewpoint of another character.

7. Have students write their own ending to a story whose ending they didn't agree with.

8. Have students create a diary as if they were the main character in a book they have read.

9. Create a class anthology of favorite poems or works of favorite poets. Have students create a class anthology of their own poetry.

10. Have students create their own book or big book based on a predictable book they have read. For example, after reading Ezra Jack Keats's *Over in the Meadow*, an illustrated Appalachian counting rhyme book, have students create another version for the numbers 1–10 or continue the rhyme using 11–20.

11. Have students create the text for wordless picture books, such as *Tuesday*, by David Wiesner.

12. Have students select a scene from a book and create a dialogue between themselves and one of the characters.

13. Have students write a letter to the author/illustrator of a favorite literary work.

14. After being introduced to works in a specific genre, have students write a brief story or poem of that genre.

15. Have students discuss how the theme of a specific literary work impacted them. For example, after reading *The Bridge to Terabithia*, by Katherine Paterson, they might write about friendship, courage, or death.

16. After reading books of fantasy, have students create a strange new world and describe it such that it becomes real to the reader.

The Language Experience Approach

The language experience approach (LEA) is a method of teaching reading based on translating personal experiences into written text and then reading them. This approach involves stimulating oral expression, writing it down, reading it back, and then using the written material as the basis for developing reading and other language arts skills. It is simply teaching reading via compositions developed with a child or a group of children. Literature is the perfect stimulus for LEA.

The LEA has many advantages. One of the most significant is that it integrates all of the language arts skills—listening, speaking, reading, and writing. Second, although the LEA is often associated with beginning reading, it can be used successfully with upper-grade students in the beginning stages of reading, students whose backgrounds are not standard English, high school dropouts, adult basic literacy learners, and students who are learning English as a second language. The LEA actually begins wherever the child is in terms of language development. It bridges the gap between "home language" and "school language." Along the same track, the basal reader is often criticized because the language patterns used are not typical of the way children actually speak; this is because of the controlled vocabulary that is used. The LEA does not limit vocabulary to high-utility words and is therefore much more natural and typical of children's speech. Another advantage is that students are motivated to read the selections because the text is centered around them and something familiar to them. Finally, the LEA is very inexpensive. A pencil, marker, or chalk and paper or chalkboard are the necessary equipment.

The LEA is implemented as follows.

1. The students' thinking is stimulated, for example by reading a story; experiencing an event such as a field trip, a special holiday, a cooking activity, or a science experiment; or displaying an interesting picture or photograph.

2. The students discuss the event and listen as others express their ideas and thoughts. The ideas and thoughts are written on a large piece of chart paper or on the chalkboard. The final result is a story that interests the children *and* that they can read and understand, because the words, the information provided, and the text are all familiar. The children are the authors! This process enables children to understand better that the books and stories they read are someone else's ideas, experiences, or fantasies.

3. Once the story has been written, it can be used to teach a variety of reading skills. For example, to work on punctuation skills, decisions can be made about punctuation as the sentences are being written. You can demonstrate that if the sentence asks something a question mark is used,

if it tells something a period is needed, and if something is being said by someone quotation marks are used. Activities such as these make learning more meaningful than simply putting in punctuation marks on a skill sheet or workbook page. In addition, these skills can be transferred to other materials the students are reading.

Activities for the Language Experience Approach

The following activities can be initiated using LEA stories to encourage children to become actively involved in the reading process.

1. Have students use predictable books as a model for their own LEA stories/poems.
2. Have students make an individual book of each of their stories, or collect the stories over time and make them into one book. To make the books, have the children copy the stories from the wall chart or chalkboard onto smaller sheets of paper. Staple the pages together and make a construction paper cover. (Books can also be made following the directions in Appendix F.) Or punch holes in the chart paper and use large metal rings to hold the pages together. For more durability, the pages can be laminated. The books can be catalogued into the school library or classroom library, thus allowing each student to have his or her copy of the book to read at school or at home. Students enjoy lying or sitting on the floor reading the collection of stories or you can use this book in much the same way as a big book (see Chap. 5). Big books can also be made by neatly printing or typing the text of the stories onto separate sheets of paper and then having the children illustrate each page. These books can then be used during shared reading time.
3. Make a cassette tape to accompany each story. A student, group of students, a parent, or a volunteer can help. The tape, along with the book, can be put in the library or the listening center for other children to enjoy.
4. Encourage students to read their books to other students in class or in another class.
5. Develop a class newspaper using the LEA stories as well as other news items, advertisements, and so on. This could be done on a monthly basis to allow parents to enjoy the rich stories developed by the class.

Children's Literature

*Cited in text
*Babbitt, Natalie. *Tuck Everlasting*. Farrar, Straus & Giroux, 1975.
*Base, Graeme. *Animalia*. Harry Abrams, 1986.
*Coerr, Eleanor. *Sadako and the Thousand Paper Cranes*. Putnam, 1977.
*Conrad, Pam. *Prairie Songs*. Harper & Row, 1985.

*Estes, Eleanor. *The Hundred Dresses*. Illustrated by Louis Slobodkin. Harcourt Brace Jovanovich, 1944.

*Freeman, Russell. *Children of the Wild West*. Clarion, 1983.

*———. *Cowboys of the Wild West*. Clarion, 1985.

*Keats, Ezra Jack. *Over in the Meadow*. Scholastic, 1971.

*Lord, Bette Bao. *In the Year of the Boar and Jackie Robinson*. HarperCollins, 1984.

*Lowry, Lois. *Number the Stars*. Houghton Mifflin, 1989.

*MacLachlan, Patricia. *Sarah, Plain and Tall*. Harper & Row. 1987.

*Paterson, Katherine. *The Bridge to Terabithia*. Harper, 1977.

———. *The Great Gilly Hopkins*. Harper, 1978.

*Prelutsky, Jack. *The New Kid on the Block*. Greenwillow, 1984.

*Scieszka, Jon. *The True Story of the 3 Little Pigs* Viking, 1989.

*Spinelli, Jerry. *Maniac Magee*. Harper, 1990.

*Viorst, Judith. *Alexander and the Terrible, Horrible, No Good, Very Bad Day*. Macmillian, 1987.

*Wiesner, David. *Tuesday*. Clarion, 1991.

*Yep, Laurence. *Dragonwings*. HarperCollins, 1975.

*Yolen, Jane. *The Devil's Arithmetic*. Viking, 1988.

Professional Resources

*Cited in text

*Atwell, Nancy. *In the Middle*. Boynton, 1987.

*Barell, J. *Teaching for Thoughtfulness: Classroom Strategies to Enhance Intellectual Development*. Longman, 1991.

Baskwell, Jane, and Paulette Whitman. *A Guide to Classroom Publishing*. Scholastic, 1986.

*Beck, I. L., and M. G. McKeown. "Developing Questions that Promote Comprehension: The Story Map." *Language Arts*, 58: 913–918, 1981.

*Bloom, Benjamin S., ed. *Taxonomy of Educational Objectives: Handbook I: Cognitive Domain*. McKay, 1956.

*Burns, P., B. Roe, and E. Ross. *Teaching Reading in Today's Elementary Schools*. Houghton Mifflin, 1988.

*Calkins, Lucy. *The Art of Teaching Writing*. Heinemann, 1986.

Calkins, Lucy, and S. Harwayne. *Living Between the Lines*. Heinemann, 1991.

Chomsky, Carol. "Approaching Early Reading Through Invented Spelling." In L. B. Resnick and P. A. Weaver, eds. *Theory and Practice of Early Reading*, vol. 2. Earlbaum, 1979, pp. 43–65.

Cullinan, Bernice E., ed. *Children's Voices: Talk in the Classroom*. International Reading Association, 1993.

Educational Testing Services. *National Assessment of Educational Programs: Reading Report Card*. Report no. 15-R-01. 1985.

Ennis, R. H. "Goals for a Critical Thinking Curriculum." In A. Costa, ed. *Developing Minds: A Resource Book for Teaching Thinking*. Association for Supervision and Curriculum Development, 1985.

*Goodlad, J. *A Place Called School*. McGraw-Hill, 1984.

Graves, Donald H. "All Children Can Write." *Learning Disability Focus*, 1: 36–43, 1985.

*———. *Writing: Teachers and Children at Work*. Heinemann, 1983.

Graves, Donald H., and J. Hansen. "The Author's Chair." *Language Arts*, 60: 176–183, 1983.

Handbook on Interpretive Reading and Discussion. Great Books Foundation, 1984.

Hansen, Jane. *When Writers Read.* Heinemann, 1987.

*Hopkins, L. B. *Books Are by People: Interviews with 104 Authors and Illustrators of Books for Young Children.* Citation, 1969.

*———. *More Books by More People: Interviews with 65 Authors of Books for Children.* Citation, 1974.

*Kohlberg, Lawrence. "Stages of Moral Development as the Basis for Moral Education." In C. M. Beck, B. S. Crittenden, and E. V. Sullivan, eds. *Moral Education: Interdisciplinary Approaches.* Newman, 1971.

*Krathwohl, David R., Benjamin Bloom, and Bertram B. Masia. *Taxonomy of Educational Objectives. Handbook II: Affective Domain.* McKay, 1964.

Lloyd, Pamela. *How Writers Write.* Heinemann, 1989.

*Maker, June C. *Teaching Models in Education of the Gifted.* Aspen, 1982.

Marzano, Robert J., R. S. Brandt, C. S. Hughes, B. F. Jones, B. Z. Presseisen, S. C. Rankin, and S. Suhor. *Dimensions of Thinking.* Association for Supervision and Curriculum Development, 1988.

*National Assessment of Educational Progress. *Reading, Thinking & Writing.* Educational Testing Service, 1981.

*Parnes, Sidney J. "Guiding Creative Action." *Gifted Child Quarterly,* 21: 460–472, 1977.

Parry, Jo Ann, and David Hornsby. *Write On: A Conference Approach to Writing.* Heinemann, 1989.

Peterson, R., and M. Eeds. *Grand Conversations: Literature Groups in Action.* Scholastic, 1990.

Read, Carol. "Pre-School Children's Knowledge of English Phonology." *Harvard Educational Review,* 41: 1–34, 1971.

Smith, Frank. "Reading Like a Writer." *Language Arts,* 60: 558–567, 1983.

Something About the Author: Facts and Pictures About Authors and Illustrators of Books for Young Children. Gale Research (annual volumes).

Turbill, Jan. *No Better Way to Teach Writing.* Heinemann, 1982.

*Rosenblatt, Louise M. "The Literacy Transaction: Evocation and Response." *Theory into Practice,* 21: 268–277, 1982.

———. *Literature as Exploration.* Noble & Noble, 1976 [1938].

*———. *The Reader, the Text, the Poem: The Transactional Theory of the Literary Work.* Southern University Press, 1978.

Wasor-Ellam, Linda. *Start with a Story: Literature and Learning in Your Classroom.* Heinemann, 1991.

*Zarrillo, James. "Theory Becomes Practice: Aesthetic Teaching with Literature." *The New Advocate,* 4: 221–223, 1991.

FABLES

ARNOLD LOBEL

CHAPTER 10

Responding to Literature Through the Arts

Children are natural actors, and they love to pretend. Literature is the perfect vehicle for encouraging these special qualities. As children retell stories they step into the pages of books and step out into worlds of limitless possibilities. The first section of this chapter offers a variety of approaches and strategies for encouraging the dramatic as students become very special characters, take part in spectacular adventures, and visit incredible new worlds.

Often, we tend to focus on the words of literature. But there is another, very important element that works along with the words to convey mood and meaning—the illustrations. The second half of the chapter focuses on children's artistic responses to literature. Various activities encourage students to be visual learners as they take students back into books to explore the illustrations and how they affect the story and the reader. The activities also introduce students to many of the artists whose work have given us unforgettable images and encourage students to experiment with various types of artistic media.

Dramatic Responses

A well-planned, effective literature program provides opportunities for children to experience, interact with, and respond to literature. Many teaching strategies that provide these opportunities, such as reading aloud, independent reading, shared reading, and storytelling, are discussed in other chapters. This chapter focuses on teaching strategies that provide children with opportunities to interact and respond *orally* to literature through creative drama, story theater, reader's theater, choral reading, and puppetry.

Creative Drama

Creative drama is an enjoyable, rewarding oral language activity that can be done with a single scene or an entire book. The stories selected should have a great deal of action and movement. This strategy can be used with students of all ages. Drama allows the students to become a specific character in a specific setting. The students can express real feelings in a safe situation because they are pretending to be someone else. It allows them to use all of their senses. For example, they can almost hear, see, smell, feel, and taste what Donald Crews's and his family's summer trip to *Bigmama's* house was like as they act out riding on the train to Cottendale, getting water in a bucket from a well, or digging worms to go fishing. Students get a sense of what it was like to grow up in Harlem as they float over New York City with Cassie of Faith Ringgold's *Tar Beach* or imagine what it is like to join the crowd in Chris Van Allsburg's *The Polar Express*.

To prepare for creative drama, students must first have experience with mime. Warm-up activities should be developed to allow students to become comfortable with mime and to help them develop skill in the technique. The following activities can be used, with some adaptation, with students in the elementary grades. Encourage students to rehearse in front of a mirror and concentrate on every facial and body movement.

Activities for Drama

1. Pretend you are walking through snow, mud, or high grass.
2. Pretend you are eating something you detest.
3. Mime an activity that you do every day, such as brushing your teeth, making the bed, or fixing a sandwich. Include every move you make when you are actually involved in the activity.
4. Mime the action of a player in your favorite sport.
5. Mime an emotion, such as terror, surprise, worry, or impatience. See if the audience knows what you are feeling.
6. Become a wild animal. Move as that animal might move. See if the audience knows what type of animal you are.
7. Imagine you are looking in the mirror and become the mirror image of your partner, doing what he or she does.
8. Become a robot, moving as a robot might move.

In creative drama, the dialogue is created by the players regardless of the source—a simple story, folk tale, poem, short story, or chapter of a book. The player decides which character and scenes of the story are important, who will play the parts, and where it will take place. For example, in Ed Young's *Lon Po Po: A Red Riding Hood Story from China,* one corner of the room might be the scene of Shang, Tao, and Paotze's house where Po Po came and another corner may represent the scene where they went to the gingko tree.

Creative drama is informal and should be enjoyed. McCaslin (1990) recommends that teachers and librarians keep the following in mind as they implement drama:

- Drama should be based on a piece of literature the children enjoy.
- Lines are not written or memorized. Instead, the dialogue is created by the players.
- Improvisation and imagination are essential.
- Pantomime and movement by the players is important.

Reflections of. . .

Sam Leaton Sebesta

In regard to drama as a means to evoke literary awareness, these three things I know.

First, the imagination must be fed. If it is neglected in education in deference to rote memory and abstraction, it will be fed anyway, often by the sound and fury of a "zap" culture where violence and shouting supplant judgment. When we use an appropriate form of drama to extend response to literature, we feed the imagination as a force to help humanity solve problems and weigh consequences.

Second, drama develops empathy. When you have played at being Monobozoh, Anansi, Urashima Taro, Anne Frank, Harriet Tubman, or any character other than yourself, you have bonded with that character. Empathy, the bond across time and culture, proves possible.

The third thing I know is that drama is accessible. Never mind the product: the finished script, the memorized lines and blocked action, the frozen performance before an audience. That's fine if it's your intent. But drama as a process comes closer to feeding imagination and arousing empathy. Start small. Be the character and say what she or he might have said, as written or as made up by you as a result of what you are reading. Or mime the character's actions as described or implied in the literature. Add other characters and you begin to examine, as if under a microsocope, the complexity of relationships—contrast, conflict, or mutual purpose. Reflect on the process. Is it authentic? Re-enact: can you make it better? From these small beginnings, you can create scenes and, if you so choose, a whole drama.

Two things I have learned about drama as a process. The first is to trust that a shift will take place from self-consciousness or showing off toward wonderful concentration upon character and situation. One of my students described it thus: "I played Icarus and I didn't know what I was doing until I began falling out of the sky, and then suddenly I *was* Icarus. I *became* Icarus falling toward the sea!" The second is that the measurement people, who often dominate what is done in education, have a dickens of a time putting a meter on drama, but now they are starting to realize the effect of the drama process on reader response, comprehension skills, amount and quality of voluntary reading, and attitudes toward literacy.

- Props are not necessary but may be used to help create a particular scene or character. Scenery and costumes *are not* used.
- Drama is a process, not a product. The performances are for the benefit of the players, not the audience. In fact, different groups of children may dramatize the same piece of literature in different parts of the classroom simultaneously.

Books become more real to children as they identify with and act out characters through creative drama. Due to its spontaneous and improvisational nature, creative drama can be used frequently to respond to favorite stories, folk tales, poems, and so forth.

Story Theater

Closely related to creative dramatics is story theater. In this technique, stories or poems are read or told while they are being mimed. Materials that lend themselves best to story theater contain quite a bit of action. Folk tales, myths, fables, and legends are particularly suited to story theater.

For example, children enjoy miming *Mufaro's Beautiful Daughters,* the folk tale by John Steptoe. In this beautifully illustrated Caldecott Honor book there are two beautiful daughters—one kind and considerate, the other selfish and spoiled. When the king decides to select a wife, both sisters are considered. Only because of the king's cleverness is he able to sort out which sister is kind and someone he wants to marry.

It is important to select an appropriate text for story theater. In addition to folk tales, myths, legends, and fables, contemporary stories, such as *Hey, Al,* by Arthur Yorinks, or *If You Give a Mouse a Muffin,* by Laura Joffe Numeroff, provide good materials for story theater. Poems can also be used. Poems particularly well suited to story theater include narrative poems like "My Shadow," by Robert Louis Stevenson, and "Casey at the Bat," by Ernest L. Thayer.

Deciding how to divide the text is part of the creative process of story theater. It is possible to have a narrator; characters can do their own narration in addition to their dialogue; or some players can do the action as others read. There are many options.

Once the selection for the story is made it must be carefully analyzed. Students must be able to visualize the setting, characters, and action. Even if only part of the story is used, the students should be familiar with the entire work to understand better the characters, their motivation, and how they might think and move. Gestures, posture, and facial expressions must be well planned to recreate the mood of the story.

If the narration is told rather then read, follow the guidelines outlined for storytelling (Chap. 7). If the narration is read, follow the guidelines described for reading aloud (Chap. 4).

Readers Theater

Some stories contain a large amount of dialogue that determines the plot and action. Readers theater is an excellent technique to use with these stories. In readers theater, a narrator describes the action while other students read the dialogue. Props and other media are not important for this technique—the story is revealed through the characters' portrayal and the narration.

Since readers theater necessitates creation of a script based on the story, reading and writing skills are enhanced. The narrator's part must be developed to help introduce the characters, describe the plot, and simplify the narrative passages. The dialogue in the story should not be changed, although it may be shortened. When preparing the script, it is often helpful to script part of the story and have the students compare the original and the script. Then work with the class on scripting a portion of the text. Finally, allow pairs of students to write the script based on a certain part of the story. Allow time for students to help edit each portion of the script. As students write the script, you may need to question them to be sure they understand how their portion fits in with the entire story and to ensure that their piece keeps with the story line and tone.

When students participate in readers theater, they read from their scripts. However, they must have ample opportunity to rehearse before performing the story for others, so they feel comfortable with what they read. With younger children, it is often advisable for the teacher to play the narrator. Older students will easily assume this role.

Students must be familiar with the entire work, not just the portion used for readers theater. This will make them more sensitive to their character. Remind students that to become the character, they must assume his or her voice inflections and accent. Guide students in their understanding and interpretation of the characters and their movements, tone of voice, dialects, and so on.

Students can prepare for readers theater by first developing skill in speaking with different inflections or accents. Provide them with situations in which they can practice this skill. For example: "You are the owner of a plantation in the Deep South. Your crops will be destroyed unless the rains come;" "You are an elderly woman, praying for a visit from your son;" "You are a young child who has just learned that he or she must move to the other side of the country, far from friends and family;" "You are a salesperson, trying to persuade a reticent audience to buy a special chair you have developed;" "You are living in a large urban area. It is cold and dark outside. You are alone at home, when suddenly you hear noises."

You can create your own scripts or purchase them from Readers Theatre Script Service (see Professional Resources). Books that lend themselves well to readers theater include those in which the plot is developed and the characters are revealed through dialogue. Try to choose books that will not need a great deal of adaptation. The following stories (or portions) lend themselves well to readers theater: The Little House series, by Laura Ingalls Wilder, *Charlotte's Web,* by E. B. White, and *The Borrowers,* by Mary Norton. Most books suitable for storytelling are also adaptable, provided they meet the criteria listed earlier.

After a story has been prepared, arrange for an audience of other students, school staff, or parents to attend the production. Try to have the presentation videotaped. Children love to see themselves on television, and videotaping provides an excellent opportunity for self-appraisal.

Choral Reading

Choral reading is an effective and enjoyable way for children to participate in and share poetry as well as prose. A large or small group of children reads in unison, in parts, in solo, or in a combination of these. Choral reading helps strengthen student literacy in a nonthreatening way, because less able readers are carried along by better readers.

A common reading text is needed for choral reading. This can be provided with transparencies, handouts, text written on the chalkboard, or multiple copies of the same text. The text may be divided into different parts, with different groups reading different roles. It is advantageous to have a leader who can "conduct" the group, using hand or head signals to indicate a change in parts, volume, tempo, and so on.

Choral reading of poetry helps children learn to appreciate the sounds, feelings, and magic of poetry. The 1989 Newbery Award–winning *Joyful Noise: Poems for Two Voices*, by Paul Fleischman, is written for choral reading. The 14 poems in this collection use two voices, sometimes alternating, sometimes together. They offer listeners a look at what insects might think of themselves and their world. Shel Silverstein's "Boa Constrictor" and Eve Merriam's "Catch a Little Rhyme" are also appropriate for choral reading as are most poems.

To implement choral reading, the following steps are recommended:

1. Choose an appropriate selection.
2. Read the selection as a group until everyone is familiar with it.
3. Determine how the text will be divided.
4. Decide who will speak what lines.
5. Read the entire selection as arranged.
6. Have students practice reading with expression, thinking about parts that should be softer or louder, slower or faster, and so on.
7. Reread until the selection flows with the intended rhyme.
8. If possible, tape the reading, critique it, and refine it.

Puppetry

Puppets have long been a favorite prop for children to use when acting out their favorite stories. Puppets seem to give children the freedom to express themselves when they may otherwise be reluctant. Children learn to project their voices and take on the role of their character through puppetry. For example, a very quiet child may use a loud, booming voice when playing the wolf in *The Three Little Pigs*.

Some stories are more appropriate than others to interpret through puppetry. The setting that would be required and how the characters could be made into puppets should be considered. Cumulative, repetitive stories, such as *Henny Penny, The Three Bears,* and *The Three Billy Goats Gruff,* are easily adapted for puppetry. Picture books such as Leo Lionni's *Alexander and the Wind-Up Mouse* or William Steig's *The Amazing Bone* are also well suited, because they contain a lot of dialogue and action.

Puppets can be purchased or students can construct their own. When they create their own puppets, students develop not only their dramatic ability but also their creativity. Many different types of puppets can be made: paper bag puppets, stick puppets, sock puppets, finger puppets, paper plate puppets, cloth puppets, and so on (see pages 325–326). A variety of interesting materials should be provided for children to make puppets.

Puppet shows can be given anywhere—behind a blanket or sheet hung across a rope, behind a table or desk with a blanket thrown over it, behind a box, and so forth. A more elaborate puppet stage can be purchased or made, with a stage and a curtain to draw.

Ross (1980) suggested the following guidelines to make puppet productions successful:

- Keep the production short, because puppets have limited actions and voices may be hard to hear. This will help maintain the audience's interest.
- Use a narrator, when appropriate, to describe the setting and passage of time and to help move the action along.
- Have students improvise their parts, rather than memorize them. Do not write out the scripts.
- Provide music to help tie the performance together and to create effects.
- Observe the ceremonies appropriate to a real play. Introduce the play and players, have puppets take curtain calls at the end, darken and lighten the room, have different acts, and so on.

Music and Movement

Music is an integral part of children's lives; they sing and chant as they work and play. Therefore, it is important that connections be made between literature and songs, jingles, lyrics, and composers. It can be fun! It can be as simple as marching with Drummer Hoff in *Drummer Hoff*, by Ed Emberly, or learning a simple square dance after reading *Barn Dance*, by Bill Martin, Jr. and John Archambault. Musical literature and activities can be added as they fit with ongoing topics or themes. Books with musical themes are listed on pages 327–328.

Students can also develop lyrics and music to accompany a piece of literature. For example, they could develop an appropriate piece of music to be played at Sadako's monument in Japan's Hiroshima Peace Park as described in the epilogue in *Sadako and the Thousand Paper Cranes*, by Eleanor Coerr.

Books such as *Mary Wore Her Red Dress and Henry Wore His Green Sneakers*, by Merle Peek, and *Oh, A-Hunting We Will Go*, by John Langstaff, draw students into joining in with the chants.

Music teachers can be a valuable resource in connecting music and literature. Discuss your themes with the music teacher so he or she can provide appropriate music, dances, movement, or chants to complement the theme.

Simple musical instruments can be made from boxes, sticks, sandpaper, and pots and pans. Allow students to create instruments to accompany the reading of a specific book.

Combining good books and music can help enhance the enjoyment of reading and the arts. Classrooms that integrate music into the literature program provide a joyful feeling, making reading even more enjoyable.

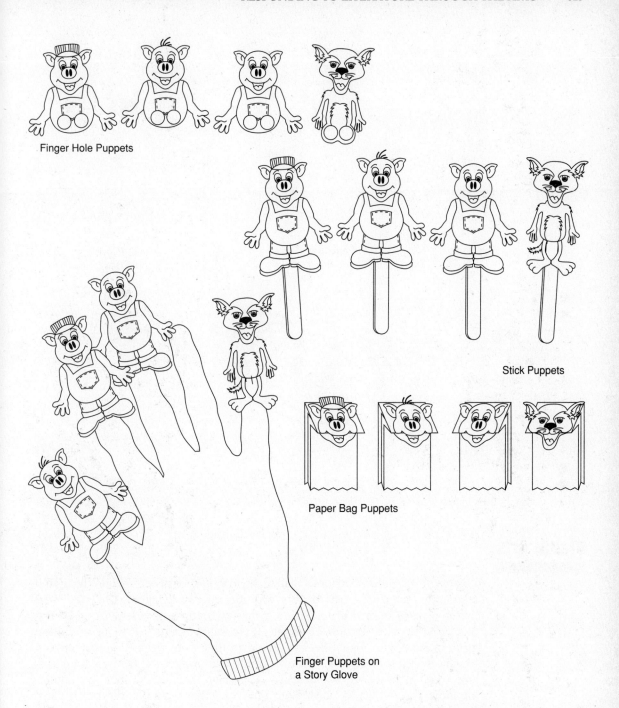

Finger Hole Puppets

Stick Puppets

Paper Bag Puppets

Finger Puppets on
a Story Glove

Stick Puppet   Paper Bag Puppet   Finger Puppet
                                                (with tabs)

Sock Puppet   Paper Plate Puppet   Cloth Puppet

Visual Arts

Illustrators of children's books realize the importance of conveying, through illustrations, the excitement, beauty, and meaning of the story. Children today live in a visual world of television, computers, movies, videotapes, and toys that provide visual stimuli. Therefore, it is a natural transition to make children more in tune with visual literacy to aid in their comprehension of the story. Much of what is done in school concerning comprehension focuses on reading and writing; however, we need to remember that illustrations are another medium from which to learn about the world. For example, through Tatsuro Kiuchi's illustrations in *The Lotus Seed,* by Sherry Garland, the reader senses the emotional strife of a Vietnamese family that was forced from their homeland to escape a devastating civil war. Lynne Cherry's *A River Ran Wild*, about the environment over different time periods, is another example of a book that con-

PICTURE BOOKS WITH MUSICAL THEMES

Books about musical performances	Author	Type of performance
Song and Dance Man	Ackerman	Vaudeville
The Paper Crane	Bang	Flute
The Traveling Men of Ballycoo	Bunting	Musicians
Sing, Pierrot, Sing	de Paola	Singing, mandolin
The Bremen Town Musicians	Grimm and Grimm	Singing
The Little Moon Theater	Haas	Singing, drum, horn, tambourine
Pages of Music	Johnston	Composer, orchestra
I Like Music	Komaiko	Concert hall
Looking for Daniela	Kroll	Singing, guitar
The Philharmonic Gets Dressed	Kuskin	Orchestra
The Bunny Play	Leedy	Band
Ty's One-Man Band	Walter	Washboard, tin pail
Elbert's Bad Word	Wood	Opera, oboe
Bravo, Minski	Yorinks	Singing

Books about musical enjoyment	Author	Type of music
Air Mail to the Moon	Birdseye	Singing and shaving
Hester in the Wild	Boynton	Humming
Jolly Mon	Buffett and Buffett	Singing
Granpa	Burningham	Singing
Busy Monday Morning	Domanska	Singing
Chester and Uncle Willoughby	Edwards	Singing
The Scarebird	Fleischman	Harmonica
Bearymore	Freeman	Old phonograph
The Maggie B	Haas	Singing, violin
Alfie Gives a Hand	Hughes	Singing
Apt. 3	Keats	Harmonica
By the Light of the Silvery Moon	Langner	Singing
Up and Down on the Merry-Go-Round	Martin & Archambault	Carousel
Lizard's Song	Shannon	Singing
The Piney Woods Peddler	Shannon	Singing
Follow the Drinking Gourd	Winter	Singing

Books about child musicians	Author	Instrument
Dear Daddy . . .	Dupasquier	Piano
Rondo in C	Fleischman	Piano
Ben's Trumpet	Isadora	Trumpet
A Piano for Julie	Schick	Piano
Music, Music for Everyone	Williams	Accordion
Something Special for Me	Williams	Accordion

PICTURE BOOKS WITH MUSICAL THEMES *(continued)*

Books About Music and Dance		*Accompaniment*
Oliver Button Is a Sissy	de Paola	None
Katie Morag and the Two Grandmothers	Hedderwick	Fiddle
Max	Isadora	Record
Barn Dance!	Martin & Archambault	Fiddle
Frog Goes to Dinner	Mayer	Dance band
The Relatives Came	Rylant	Dance band
Ragtime Tumpie	Schroeder	Ragtime
Books about music in nature		*Type of music*
Georgia Music	Griffith	Insects
17 Kings and 42 Elephants	Mahy	Animals
Listen to the Rain	Martin & Archambault	Rain
Nicholas Cricket	Maxner	Insects
Nightdances	Skofield	Nature
Sophie's Knapsack	Stock	Nature
The Song	Zolotow	Nature

veys a strong message through the illustrations as well as the text. Photographs have become a popular visual medium. Russell Freedman's, *Cowboys of the Wild West* for example, provides a history of the West through photographs that give a vivid and memorable portrayal of a time long gone. This section provides information about artists, artistic styles, and media as well as activities to aid children in becoming more visually literate.

About the Artist

Several series aimed at primary-grade students, such as Art for Children, by Ernest Raboff, and Getting to Know the World's Greatest Artists, by Mike Venezia, provide information about artists' life and work. More appropriate for intermediate grades are Florian Rodari's Weekend With series, in which the reader is invited to spend the weekend with an artist to learn about him or her, and First Impressions, by Ann Waldron.

Kimihito Okuyama's Art Play series, which introduces children to modern artists by focusing on one piece of art, appeals to all ages. The Portraits of Women Artists for Children series, by Robyn Montana Turner, is appropriate for primary and intermediate readers. It features the lives of female artists. Individual picture book biographies, such as Johnny Alcorn's *Rembrandt's Beret* and Robin Richmond's *Introducing Michelangelo,* will familiarize students with artists' works and accomplishments.

Reflections of. . .

Natalie Babbitt

Marcia Brown said once that illustrators don't often make good writers and writers even more rarely make good illustrators. And yet many of us try to do both. There are a number of reasons for this, the most obvious being the desire to control the whole thing. Collaboration can be harrowing, and feuds are commonplace. Lewis Carroll wasn't at all happy with John Tenniel's interpretations of his beloved Alice, and J. R. R. Tolkein refused to let illustrators anywhere near his Hobbits. But another reason for trying to be all things to a story is that in the beginning, when we are children, we experience a book as a unity. The illustrations are jelly to the text's peanut butter, the flavor of the one blending with the flavor of the other to make a new flavor neither can have all by itself. It's all very well to be peanut butter alone, or jelly alone, but much more satisfying to be both. I am always very cross when a favorite childhood book is reissued with different pictures from the ones I remember. This is not peanut butter and jelly; it's peanut butter and something incompatible, like cucumbers.

Then, too, writers see their characters in their heads as they write, and they see their settings as well. I've always thought that writing a story was like being the whole production crew of a play: casting director, set designer, lighting engineer, costume designer, and certainly director and producer. It's all very visual—inside one's head. So it's not surprising that there is frequently a desire to put all that on the paper along with the words. And by the same token, an illustrator might have a fondness for drawing lions, say, or pigs, and, not wishing to wait around for somebody to provide a story with lions or pigs as characters, will write his own.

People known primarily as illustrators often do their own writing. Maurice Sendak is the best, though by no means the only, example. People known primarily as writers somewhat less often make their own pictures. But what is this "primarily" business, after all? I, for instance, began in the field as an illustrator, and had no interest at all in writing. I only began to write because you can't make pictures for stories if you don't have stories to make pictures for. But I have long since been typecast as a writer. Well, Marcia Brown is probably right: nobody does the two things equally well. Writing, even if you do see pictures in your head, is mainly a left-brain exercise, while illustrating is a right-brain exercise. And we are told by those in the know that in each of us, one or the other half of the brain is dominant.

To me, the division in the field between writing and illustrating is finally less interesting than the division between realistic fiction and fantasy. Good fantasy and good realism are two separate roads towards the same truths and I for one would like to see more done to explain the difference. It is a philosophical difference at bottom, and merits looking into. In the meantime we all bumble along, trying hard to do what we do as well as we can, whatever the category, whichever half of the brain, whatever the philosophy. And once in a while something good is produced. Not often enough, by any means, but we do try.

Artistic Styles

Children learn to identify distinctive features of particular illustrators. For example, once they have experienced the illustrations of Faith Ringgold in *Tar Beach*, it is easy to recognize her work in *Aunt Harriet's Underground Railroad in the Sky*. In both books, they will recognize the flying people in their brightly colored clothing with distinctive features.

Illustrations can be realistic or representative, impressionistic, expressionistic, surrealistic, abstract, folk or naive, cartoon. Realistic or representative style accurately portrays the world as we see it. Jim Lamarche's luminescent paintings in *Mandy*, by Barbara Booth, give the reader a rare insight into the world of a very special deaf child and her grandmother. Readers feel the love and warmth of their relationship through the illustrations that show them baking chocolate chip cookies, dancing, reading books, and walking through the grass together.

Impressionistic style is exemplified by such artists as Monet and Pissarro, in which there is an emphasis on light. Maurice Sendak used this style in Charlotte Zolotow's *Mr. Rabbit and the Lovely Present*, in which the rabbit and the little girl wander through the countryside looking for presents of yellow, green, blue, and red for the little girl's mother. The illustrations in *Anno's Journey*, by Mitsumasa Anno, are another good example of impressionistic art.

Expressionistic style allows the illustrator to incorporate his or her own self-expression, rather than what he or she sees. Usually expressionistic art incorporates characters that are out of proportion, brightly colored, and childlike. Vera Williams's *A Chair for My Mother* provides a good example of expressionistic art, with its shockingly bright colors and distorted body positions of the grandmother and mother.

Surrealistic art generally presents fantasy images in unnatural juxtapositions. Anthony Brown's *Changes* provides an excellent example of surrealistic art. Joseph, the young boy in the story, begins to see changes in his world while his father is away picking up his mother and the new baby. The armchair becomes a gorilla, a shadow under the sofa looks like an alligator, and a tea kettle becomes a cat with ears and a tail. When the new baby and his parents arrive, Joseph's fantasy world disappears and only love remains.

Abstract art emphasizes qualities that have little or no direct representation of the objects. Instead, the emphasis is on the feeling or mood of the setting and/or characters. Leo and Diane Dillon illustrated the 1976 Caldecott Award–winning *Why Mosquitoes Buzz in People's Ears*, by Verna Aardema, with abstract art, conveying the feelings evoked by this African tale by distorting reality.

Naive, primitive, or folk art is used to represent the time during which a story took place and the culture represented. A good example is Barbara Cooney's illustration in the *Ox-Cart Man*, by Donald Hall, in which she uses

Early American art to express the culture of early nineteenth-century New England. Tony Johnston's *The Quilt Story*, illustrated by Tomie de Paola, is another good example of this style.

Children love cartoons, and some artists select this style of illustration. Dr. Seuss's *The Cat in the Hat* and *Horton Hatches the Egg* are good examples of this style of illustration, as is Ruth Kraus's *A Very Special House*, illustrated by Maurice Sendak.

Artistic Media

Today a wide variety of media is used to illustrate children's books. Illustrators are experimenting with new and interesting formats and media. Good examples are the books illustrated in black and white, such as Chris Van Allsburg's *Jumanji* and Robert McCloskey's *Blueberries for Sal*. David Macaulay's award-winning *Black and White* demonstrates the innovations in book illustrations. There are four stories in this book, each illustrated using different media and colors. Some of the media commonly used in children's books are collage, printing, painting, drawing, and photographs.

Collage

Collage is a popular medium for illustrating children's books. A variety of materials, such as patterned wallpaper, fabric, and newspaper clippings, are cut out, assembled into unified illustrations, and pasted down. Materials such as lace, buttons, bark, grass, leaves, feathers, and clay also work well for collage. Ezra Jack Keats is well-known for using collage to illustrate his books. The best example is the award-winning *The Snowy Day*, in which he used patterned and textured papers along with pen and ink to capture young Peter as he played in the snow. Other good examples of illustrations using collage include Mem Fox's *Hattie and the Fox*, Eric Carle's *The Very Hungry Caterpillar*, *The Very Busy Spider*, and *The Very Quiet Cricket*, and Leo Lionni's *Frederick, Inch by Inch, Little Blue and Little Yellow*, and *Matthew's Dream*.

Printing

Printing includes techniques such as woodcuts, block prints, linoleum prints, and lithography. Woodcuts were one of the first means of producing illustrations. In woodcutting, the nonprinting areas are cut away, leaving a raised surface. This is inked and pressed on paper to print the design. Marcia Brown's *Once a Mouse* and *All Butterflies* are excellent examples of books illustrated using woodcuts.

Painting

Painting may be done using acrylics, watercolors, tempera, oils, gouache, and so on. The vast majority of children's books are illustrated using this medium. In the 1993 Caldecott Award–winning *Tuesday*, by David Wiesner, blue and green watercolors are used effectively as the frogs take off on their lily pads to explore. Watercolors can be used to reflect moods, as demonstrated by Ronald Himler in *The Wall*, by Eve Bunting. The bluish grey watercolors set the somber tone when a little boy and his father visit the Vietnam War memorial to find the name of the boy's grandfather who was killed. In *Angelita's Magic Yarn*, Doris Lechner used watercolor illustrations to highlight the bright colors and wavy lines of the weavings of Angelita and the people of Oru.

Barbara Cooney's *Miss Rumphius* is an example of the use of acrylic paints to create clear, beautiful colors that capture the blue and purple blooming of the lupines throughout the Maine landscape. Max Velthuijs illustrated *Crocodile's Masterpiece* using a more opaque paint. His illustrations show the power of imagination through scenes on white canvas that change whenever Elephant closes his eyes and thinks of a new image.

Drawing

Drawings may be done using pen and ink, pastels (colored chalk), colored pencils, crayons, and charcoal pencils. Often artists use a combination of these media. A good example is Caryn Yacowitz's Chinese folk tale, *The Jade Stone* in which ink and watercolor painting are combined on handmade rice paper to elicit the look of ancient hand-colored Oriental woodblock prints.

Ann Grifalconi illustrated *Osa's Pride* using brilliant chalk. The reader can sense the beauty of the African world and the nurturing love of Osa's grandmother through her illustrations.

Photography

Photographs, whether black-and-white or color, can be beautiful, dramatic, and highly effective. Photography is an art of composition in which the photographer creates an arrangement of objects to create an appealing photograph. Photographs are often used in informational books to portray something realistically and accurately. Seymour Simon successfully uses photographs in *Galaxies* to provide accuracy as well as a sense of beauty. Tana Hoban uses bright, clear-colored photographs of common objects in *Is It Larger? Is It Smaller?* and *Of Colors and Things*. This is very effective because children can see what real colors and objects look like. Photographs such as those by Barbara Rogasky in *Light and Shadow*, Myra Cohn Livingston's book of poetry, can be used to demonstrate how light and shadow can change the everyday world into a world of mystery and beauty. *Lincoln: A Photobiography* and *Eleanor Roosevelt: A Life of Discovery* are two of the many outstanding books by Russell Freedman who uses photography to bring his subjects to life and help the reader reach a deeper level of understanding.

Children as Artists

Students should not only look at and interpret the work of other artists, they should also use art to make their own creations (Galda and Short, 1993). There are some excellent books available for primary and intermediate readers that provide students with information about techniques and materials. For example, Kim Solga has created the Art and Activities for Kids series. One of the books in this series, *Paint!*, provides easy-to-follow suggestions for painting, drawing, and making prints. Isidro Sanchez provides basic information about watercolor techniques and encouragement to try the techniques in *I Draw, I Paint: Watercolor*. *I Am an Artist*, by Pat Lowery Collins, reminds the reader that art is a way of looking at the world and that we are all artists when we take the time to look at the beauty around us. She encourages children to get involved with art.

Activities for Visual Literacy

Once the students have been introduced to the works and artistic styles of different artists and the media they use, encourage them to get involved in art by initiating some of the following activities.

1. Have students make a collage illustration to represent a favorite story.
2. Make a large class mural using a variety of media—watercolors, tempera paints, pen and ink, collage, and so forth.
3. Use *Tar Beach*, by Faith Ringgold, as an example of the use of a quilt border as a way of illustrating a book. Ask the students to write a short story and design a quilt border around it. Remind them that the illustrations in the quilt should relate to their story.
4. Provide students with pages of a simple story text without illustrations. Ask them to read the text and make an illustration to accompany the text. Allow time for students to share their illustrations.
5. Read a story aloud or have students read a book independently, then have them create a book jacket (different from the book cover) for it.
6. As a class project for National Book Week in November, decorate as many doors as possible with the theme from a selected book. Have students work in cooperative learning groups. For example, one group may decorate one door with five flying geese to represent the theme of *Kenji and the Magic Geese*, by Ryerson Johnson, while another decorates a door with frogs on lily pads to represent the theme of *Tuesday*, by David Wiesner. This project requires the cooperation of other teachers and the administration.
7. Make a class quilt by providing each student with a 6 × 6-inch square of white paper. Ask them to illustrate a favorite character or setting from a book they have read and to include the name of the book and author on

the square. When the squares are completed, fit them together on a bulletin board or large wall area.

8. Ask students to decide what media were used in their favorite illustrated book and then to share why they like the illustrations in that book.

9. Collect children's books about artists, such as *Claude Monet,* by Ann Waldron, *A Weekend with Picasso,* by Florian Rodari, *Introducing Michelangelo,* by Robin Richmond, *Rembrandt's Beret,* by Johnny Alcorn, *Rosa Bonheur,* by Robyn Montana Turner, and *Frida Kahlo,* by Malka Drucker. Assign books to groups of students and ask each group to present a visual report on the artist. Encourage creativity.

10. Robyn Montana Turner's Portraits of Women Artists for Children series for middle-grade readers features selected artists from different countries and those who have used different artistic styles and media, as follows.

Artist	Location	Style
Faith Ringgold	France, South America, New York	Folk art, acrylic, story quilts/sculpture
Georgia O'Keefe	New Mexico, Wisconsin, New York	Abstract art, watercolors
Frida Kahlo	Mexico, New York, San Francisco	Folk art, murals, oil painting
Rosa Bonheur	France, Western Europe	Oil painting
Mary Cassatt	France, Philadelphia, Italy	Impressionism, pastels

a. Obtain children's books illustrated by these authors and locate on a map where they lived or worked. Discuss how the locations may have influenced their illustrations.

b. Investigate the period of time when these artists live/lived. Make a time line.

c. Ask the students to choose one illustration by one artist and write a critique of it.

Children's Literature

*Cited in text

*Aardema, Verna. *Why Mosquitoes Buzz in People's Ears.* Illustrated by Leo and Diane Dillon. Dial, 1975.

*Ackerman, Karen. *Song and Dance Man.* Illustrated by Stephen Gammell. Knopf, 1988.

*Alcorn, Johnny. *Rembrandt's Beret.* Tambourine, 1991.

*Anno, Mitsumasa. *Anno's Journey.* Putnam, 1981.

*Bang, M. *The Paper Crane.* Greenwillow, 1985.

*Birdseye, T. *Air Mail to the Moon.* Illustrated by Stephen Gammell. Holiday House, 1988.

*Booth, Barbara. *Mandy.* Illustrated by Jim Larmarche. Lothrop, Lee & Shepard, 1991.

*Boynton, S. *Hester in the Wild.* Harper & Row, 1979.

*Brown, Anthony. *Changes.* Knopf, 1991.

*Brown, Marcia. *All Butterflies.* Scribner's, 1974.

*———. *Once a Mouse.* Scribner's, 1961.

*Buffet, J., & Buffett, S. J. *Jolly Mon.* Illustrated by Lambert Davis. Harcourt Brace Jovanovich, 1988.

*Bunting, Eve. *The Traveling Men of Ballycoo.* Illustrated by Kaeth Zemach. Harcourt Brace Jovanovich, 1983.

*———. *The Wall.* Illustrated by Ronald Himler. Clarion, 1990.

*Burningham, J. *Granpa.* Crown, 1984.

*Carle, Eric. *The Very Busy Spider.* Philomel, 1984.

*———. *The Very Hungry Caterpillar.* World, 1968.

*———. *The Very Quiet Cricket.* Philomel, 1990.

*Cherry, Lynne. *A River Ran Wild.* Harcourt Brace Jovanovich, 1992.

*Coerr, Eleanor. *Sadako and the Thousand Paper Cranes.* Paintings by Ronald Himler. Putnam, 1977.

*Collins, Pat Lowery. *I Am an Artist.* Millbrook, 1992.

*Cooney, Barbara. *Miss Rumphiu.* Viking, 1982.

*Crews, Donald. *Bigmama's.* Greenwillow, 1991.

*de Paola, T. *Oliver Button is a Sissy.* Harcourt Brace Jovanovich, 1979.

*———. *Sing, Pierrot, Sing.* Harcourt Brace Jovanovich, 1983.

*Drucker, Malka. *Frida Kahlo.* Bantam, 1991.

*Domanska, J. *Busy Monday Morning.* Greenwillow, 1985.

*Dupasquier, P. *Dear Daddy. . . .* Bradbury, 1985.

*Edwards, P. K. *Chester and Uncle Willoughby.* Illustrated by Diane Worfolk Allison. Little, Brown, 1987.

*Emberly, Ed. *Drummer Hoff.* Simon & Schuster, 1974.

*Fleischman, Paul. *Joyful Noise: Poems for Two Voices.* Illustrated by Eric Beddows. Harper & Row, 1988.

*———. *Rondo in C.* Illustrated by Janet Wentworth. Harper & Row, 1988.

*Fleischman, S. *The Scarebird.* Illustrated by Peter Sis. Greenwillow, 1987.

*Fox, Mem. *Hattie and the Fox.* Illustrated by Patricia Mullins. Bradbury, 1988.

*Freeman, R. *Cowboys of the Wild West.* Clarion, 1985.

*———. *Eleanor Roosevelt: A Life of Discovery.* Clarion, 1993.

*———. *Lincoln: A Photobiography.* Clarion, 1987.

*Freeman, D. *Bearymore.* Viking, 1976.

*Garland, Sherry. *The Lotus Seed.* Illustrated by Tatsuro Kiuchi. Harcourt Brace Jovanovich, 1993.

*Grifalconi, Ann. *Osa's Pride.* Little, Brown, 1990.

*Griffith, H. *Georgia Music.* Illustrated by James Stevenson. Greenwillow, 1986.

*Grimm, J., & Grimm, W. *The Bremen Town Musicians.* Illustrated by Janina Domanska. Greenwillow, 1980.

*Haas, I. *The Little Moon Theater.* Atheneum, 1981.

*———. *The Maggie B.* Macmillan, 1975.

*Hall, Donald. *Ox-Cart Man.* Illustrated by Barbara Cooney. Viking, 1979.

*Hedderwick, M. *Katie Morag and the Two Grandmothers.* The Bodley Head, 1985.

*Hoban, Tana. *Is It Larger? Is It Smaller?* Greenwillow, 1985.

*———. *Of Color and Things.* Greenwillow, 1989.

*Hughes, S. *Alfie Gives a Hand.* Mulberry, 1983.

*Isadora, R. *Ben's Trumpet.* Greenwillow, 1979.

*———. *Max.* Macmillan, 1976.

*Johnson, Ryerson. *Kenji and the Magic Geese*. Simon & Schuster, 1992.

*Johnston, Tony. *Pages of Music*. Illustrated by Tomie de Paola. Putnam, 1988.

*———. *The Quilt Story*. Illustrated by Tomie de Paola. Putnam, 1985.

*Keats, Ezra Jack. *Apt. 3*. Macmillan, 1971.

*———. *The Snowy Day*. Viking, 1962.

*Komaiko, L. *I Like Music*. Illustrated by Barbara Westman. Harper & Row, 1987.

*Kraus, Ruth. *A Very Special House*. Illustrated by Maurice Sendak. Harper, 1953.

*Kroll, S. *Looking for Daniela*. Illustrated by Anita Lobel. Holiday House, 1988.

*Kuskin, K. *The Philharmonic Gets Dressed*. Harper & Row, 1982.

*Langner, N. *By the Light of the Silvery Moon*. Lothrop, Lee & Shepard, 1983.

*Langstaff, John. *Oh, A-Hunting We Will Go*. Illustrated by Nancy Winslow Parker. Heath, 1986.

Larrick, Nancy. *Let's Do a Poem*. Delacorte, 1991.

———, ed. *Mice Are Nice*. Illustrated by Ed Young. Philomel, 1990.

*Lechner, Doris. *Angelita's Magic Yarn*. Farrar, Straus & Giroux, 1992.

*Leedy, L. *The Bunny Play*. Holiday House, 1988.

*Lionni, Leo. *Alexander and the Wind-Up Mouse*. Pantheon, 1969.

*———. *Frederick*. Pantheon, 1967.

———. *Inch by Inch*. Astor-Honor, 1962.

*———. *Little Blue and Little Yellow*. Astor-Honor, 1959.

*———. *Matthew's Dream*. Knopf, 1991.

*Livingston, Myra Cohn. *Light and Shadow*. Illustrated by Barbara Rogasky. Holiday, 1992.

*Macaulay, David. *Black and White*. Houghton Mifflin, 1990.

*Mahy, M. *17 Kings and 42 Elephants*. Illustrated by Patricia MacCarthy. Dial, 1987.

*Martin, Bill Jr., and John Archambault. *Barn Dance*. Illustrated by Ted Rand. Holt, 1986.

*———. *Listen to the Rain*. Illustrated by James Endicott. Henry Holt, 1988.

*———. *Up and Down on the Merry-Go-Round*. Illustrated by Ted Rand. Henry Holt, 1988.

*Maxner, J. *Nicholas Cricket*. Illustrated by William Joyce. Harper & Row, 1989.

*Mayer, M. *Frog Goes to Dinner*. Scholastic, 1974.

*McCloskey, Robert. *Blueberries for Sal*. Viking, 1963.

*Merriam, Eve. "Catch a Little Rhyme," in *It Doesn't Always Have to Rhyme*. Atheneum, 1964.

*Norton, Mary. *The Borrowers*. Illustrated by Beth and Joe Krush. Harcourt Brace Jovanovich, 1953.

*Numeroff, Laura Joffe. *If You Give a Mouse a Muffin*. Illustrated by Felicia Bond. Scholastic, 1991.

*Okuyama, Kimihito. Art Play series. Abrams.

*Peek, Merle. *Mary Wore Her Red Dress and Henry Wore His Green Sneakers*. Ticknor & Fields, 1985.

*Raboff, Ernest. Art for Children series. Harper & Row Junior Books.

*Richmond, Robin. *Introducing Michelangelo*. Little, Brown, 1991.

*Ringgold, Faith. *Aunt Harriet's Underground Railroad in the Sky*. Crown, 1993.

*———. *Tar Beach*. Crown, 1992.

*Rodari, Florian. *A Weekend with Picasso*. Rizzoli, 1991.

*———. Weekend With series. Rizzoli.

*Rylant, C. *The Relatives Came*. Illustrated by Stephen Gammell. Bradbury, 1985.

*Sanchez, Isidro. *I Draw, I Paint: Watercolor*. Barron's, 1991.

*Schick, E. *A Piano for Julie*. Greenwillow, 1954.

*Schroeder, A. *Ragtime Tumpie*. Illustrated by Bernice Fuchs. Little, Brown, 1989.

Sendak, Maurice. *Where the Wild Things Are*. Harper, 1963.

*Seuss, Dr. (Theodore S. Geisel). *The Cat in the Hat*. Random, 1957.

*———. *Horton Hatches the Egg*. Random, 1940.

*Shannon, G. *Lizard's Song*. Illustrated by Jose Aruego and Ariane Dewey. Greenwillow, 1981.

*Silverstein, Shel. "Boa Constrictors," in *A Light in the Attic*. Harper, 1981.

*Simon, Seymour. *Galaxies*. Morrow, 1988.

*Skofield, J. *Nightdances*. Illustrated by Karen Gundersheimer. Harper & Row, 1981.

*Solga, Kim. *Paint!* North Light, 1991.

*Steig, William. *The Amazing Bone*. Farrar, Straus & Giroux, 1976.

*Steptoe, John. *Mufaro's Beautiful Daughters*. Lothrop, 1987.

*Stevenson, Robert Louis. *My Shadow*. Illustrated by Red Rand. Putnam, 1990.

*Stock, C. *Sophie's Knapsack*. Lothrop, Lee & Shepard, 1988.

*Thayer, Ernest L. *Casey at Bat*. Illustrated by Wallace Tripp. Putnam, 1980.

*Turner, Robyn Montana. Portraits of Women Artists for Children series. Little, Brown.

*———. *Rosa Bonheur*. Little, Brown, 1991.

*Van Allsburg, Chris. *Jumanji*. Houghton Mifflin, 1981.

*———. *The Polar Express*. Houghton Mifflin, 1985.

*Velthuij, Max. *Crocodile's Masterpiece*. Farrar, Straus & Giroux, 1991.

*Venezia, Mike. Getting to Know the World's Greatest Artists series. Children's Press.

*Waldron, Ann. *Claude Monet*. Abrams, 1991.

*———. First Impressions series. Abrams.

*Walter, M. P. *Ty's One-Man Band*. Illustrated by Margot Tomes. Scholastic, 1980.

*White, E. B. *Charlotte's Web*. Illustrated by Garth Williams. Harper & Row, 1952.

*Wiesner, David. *Tuesday*. Clarion, 1991.

*Wilder, Laura Ingalls. Little House series. Illustrated by Garth Williams. Harper & Row.

*Williams, Vera. *A Chair for My Mother*. Greenwillow, 1982.

*———. *Something Special for Me*. Greenwillow, 1983.

*———. *Music, Music for Everyone*. Greenwillow, 1984.

*Wilner, Isabel, comp. *The Poetry Troupe: An Anthology of Poems to Read Aloud*. Scribner's, 1977.

*Winter, J. *Follow the Drinking Gourd*. Alfred Knopf, 1988.

*Wood, A. *Elbert's Bad Word*. Illustrated by Audrey Wood & Don Wood. Harcourt Brace Jovanovich, 1988.

*Yacowitz, Caryn. *The Jade Stone*. Holiday, 1992.

*Yorinks, Arthur. *Hey, Al*. Illustrated by Richard Egielski. Sunburst, 1986.

*———. *Bravo, Minski*. Illustrated by Richard Egielski. Michael di Capual Farrar/Straus/Giroux, 1988.

*Young, Ed. *Lon Po Po: A Red Riding Hood Story From China*. Philomel, 1989.

*Zolotow, Charlotte. *Mr. Rabbit and the Lovely Present*. Illustrated by Maurice Sendak. Harper, 1962.

*———. *The Song*. Illustrated by Nancy Tafuri. Greenwillow, 1982.

Professional Resources

*Cited in text

Champlin, C. *Storytelling with Puppets*. American Library Association, 1985.

Coger, L. I. and M. R. White. *Readers Theatre Handbook: A Dramatic Approach to Literature.* Scott, Foresman, 1982.

Flower, C. *Puppets, Methods, and Materials.* David, 1983.

*Galda, Lee, and Kathy Short. "Visual Literacy: Exploring Art and Illustration in Childrens Books." *The Reading Teacher*, 46: 506–516, 1993.

Marantz, Sylvia. *Picture Books for Looking and Learning.* Oryx, 1992.

*McCaslin, N. *Creative Drama in the Classroom*, 5th ed. Longman, 1990.

Moss, J. *Focus on Literature: A Context for Literacy Learning.* Owen, 1990.

Planter, W. *Musical Story Hours: Using Music with Storytelling.* Library Professional, 1989.

*Ross, R. R. *Storytellers*, 2nd ed. Merrill, 1980.

Stoyer, S. *Readers Theatre: Story Dramatization in the Classroom.* National Council of Teachers of English, 1982.

Swartz, L. *Dramathemes: A Practical Guide for Teaching Drama.* Heinemann, 1988.

Watson-Ellam, L. *Start with a Story: Literature and Learning in Your Classroom.* Heinemann, 1991.

Sources for Scripts for Readers Theater

Barchers, Suzanne. *Readers Theatre for Beginning Readers.* Teacher Ideas Press, 1993.

Fredericks, Anthony D. *Frantic Frogs and Other Frankly Fractured Folktales for Readers Theatre.* Teacher Ideas Press, 1993.

Institute for Readers Theatre, P.O. Box 17193, San Diego, CA 92117.

Laughlin, M. K., and K. H. Latrobe. *Readers Theatre for Children.* Teacher Ideas Press, 1990.

*Reader's Theatre Script Service, P.O. Box 178333, San Diego, CA 92177.

...and now
Miguel

By JOSEPH KRUMGOLD
ILLUSTRATED BY JEAN CHARLOT

CHAPTER 11

Celebrating Literature: Alternatives

Reading aloud, shared reading, individual reading, and storytelling are just a few techniques that bring children and the world of literature together by stimulating their imagination and creating a desire to read. As students enjoy and are touched by books, they should have an opportunity to share their treasures with classmates through peer sharing. Children delight in telling their friends about a wonderful book, just as adults love to turn their friends on to a book they just couldn't put down.

Traditionally, however, the desire to share books has been stifled, because students are asked write meaningless, often laborious reports. These reports take the excitement and creativity out of sharing by asking for a plot summary or a description of the main characters. Ironically, the very reports teachers have used to stimulate reading and sharing have caused a negative attitude toward books.

Book reports do have a place in the curriculum. They provide a vehicle through which the reader interacts with the characters and the plot. Students need a way to react to a particular story, whether their reaction is written, artistic, dramatic, or oral. Reports can be formal or informal, but they must give students an opportunity to talk about books rather than merely evaluate them.

The following ideas for extending and sharing literature provide alternatives to the traditional book report and are designed to motivate and inspire students and to make book sharing a natural outgrowth of reading.

Multimedia Alternatives

Video Broadcasts

Because television has such an impact on students, we can use the motivating qualities of this medium to bring literature to life. Many schools have a television studio set up to present opening exercises and announcements. Why not involve your students in creating short vignettes dealing with literature that can be videotaped and shown over closed circuit television? In this way, students can share their love of literature while satisfying their love for the dramatic. There are unlimited possibilities for videotaping, including:

- Readers theater, story theater, storytelling
- Dramatizations of special events, stories, and poems
- Advertisements for selected books
- Parade of characters (in which students dress as their favorite characters and introduce themselves)
- "Meeting of the Minds"—characters from various books on a similar subject discuss specific topics
- Book talks
- Monologues presented by a book character
- Interviews with literary characters
- Interviews with book authors (in which students research the author and take his or her persona)
- Sharing special projects students have created based on literature
- Sharing original stories and poems modeled from literature
- Rap and other musical renditions of favorite tales
- A miniseries to present a favorite story—each day a little more of the story is shared
- A theme program that shares books on a specific topic or theme
- A talk show format (literature circle) in which children discuss a special book

Radio Days

The golden days of radio can be relived as students create their own radio programs. Programs can be based on a specific book, author or illustrator, theme, or a combination of these. Students need to plan a format for their program and select roles. For example, several students can do a readers theater based on a specific event from a literary work. Others can be involved in an interview with the author, while others write and present commercials that are interspersed throughout the program. The commercials can be appropriate to the book. For example, if the radio program is based on Jerry Spinelli's *Maniac Magee,* students can write an advertisement for Maniac Sneakers. If the book is historical fiction, advertisements for products appropriate to the time can be created. Once the program has been taped, make several cassette copies to share with other classrooms.

Listening Library

Start a collection of stories and poems on cassette. As you introduce students to stories through read-aloud and shared reading, make tapes of the stories so students can listen as they follow along in the book. The listening library may also include tapes of stories students have written to accompany wordless picture books or various renditions of favorite tales that have been put to music. Label the tapes carefully and catalog them so students can select the ones they wish to hear. Be sure they know how to locate the accompanying literature as well.

Book Week

Celebrate National Book Week by organizing activities related to the books the children have read. Give them an opportunity to create a classroom in which they are enveloped in literature. The classroom may reflect a cornucopia of literature or a specific theme or author. For example, decorate the classroom door in the likeness of the class's favorite book character. Imagine walking up to the door to be greeted by the Cat in the Hat! Students can create puppets or dress dolls to represent characters. Grinches, Thing One and Thing Two, Bartholomew Cubbins, and other Seuss creations can fill the room and serve as props for student plays, mimes, and other dramatic activities. Students can create their own artistic model representations of green eggs and ham or the hats of Bartholomew Cubbins. Videos and filmstrips of Dr. Seuss stories can be shown. As a culminating activity, they can dress as their favorite character and parade through the school. Imagine children watching as their favorite characters stroll by and deliver invitations to a Dr. Seuss Fantasy Festival! At the festival, storytelling and student dramatic presentations can be the main events, and refreshments can reflect the theme.

Slide Show

Have students create their own slide show based on a specific book by taking photographs of book illustrations or photographic representations of the plot. For example, for E. B. White's *Charlotte's Web*, students can take pictures from the text or go to the zoo or a farm and photograph a pig, a sheep, or a goose. Characters such as Charlotte can be made from pipe cleaners or clay. Students can then make an audiocassette that tells the story and correlates with the pictures. Slide shows can be put into a literature corner to give students an opportunity to enjoy them time and time again.

Time Capsule

Discuss with students the purpose of a time capsule: to preserve information for the future. In this case, the time capsule would allow students in another era to become aware of the books enjoyed by children today. Brainstorm about the items they might put into a time capsule that would be representative of a favorite book. For example, for Don Freeman's *Corduroy*, they might include a small teddy bear with green overalls and a missing button. For Laura Ingalls Wilder's *Little House in the Big Woods*, they might include a letter that could have been written by Laura Ingalls telling a friend about her life or they could create an illustration representative of a selected scene. Each student should decide on a favorite book, select memorabilia, and provide the following information: title; author/illustrator; publisher/date of publication; summary of the story; and reason for selecting the book. This information can be captured on audiocassette.

Have students create their own time capsule that relates to the book in some way. For example, if they select *Corduroy*, they might make a time capsule in the shape of a bear, cutting out a pattern from a paper bag and stapling the sides together after inserting all the memorabilia. Get permission from the school principal to bury the time capsule(s) and be sure they are in waterproof containers to preserve their contents. Prepare a map that gives the location of the time capsule and the date it is to be opened. Present this map to the school's principal with the stipulation that it be turned over to each succeeding principal until the specified time.

Literary Newspaper

Students can create a classroom literary newspaper, each student developing a specific section relating to a book they have read. For example, assign students comic strips, editorials, classified ads, advice columns, headlines, sports, advertisements, and book reviews. The articles can be based on actual events as related in the story or an elaboration, as in the *Island News* (see page 344) based on *Island of the Blue Dolphins,* by Scott O'Dell. For *Corduroy*, students could write the headline, "Corduroy Loses Button in Department Store," and write a humorous column related to the book, or they could take the story a step further and develop other events that might have occurred but didn't.

Another type of newspaper is a monthly book review, in which students write reviews of books they have read. In preparation, have students read reviews from publications such as local newspapers and children's magazines. Reviews must include bibliographic information—title, author, illustrator, publisher, date of publication, number of pages, and age appropriateness. They should also include a summary of the plot and the students' reactions based on specific details. Have students, as a class, devise a rating scale and symbols to evaluate the books, such as:

$\ominus$ = Ho-hum—a real sleeper
$\bigcirc$ = OK, but could be replaced
$\oplus$ = Good book
$\bigstar$ = *Must read*

Computer Technology

Advances in computer technology provide students with a rich array of resources that improve reading and writing skills and allow them to read and respond to literature in a variety of ways. One popular use of the computer is word processing, which encourages free writing of ideas and greatly reduces the frustration often associated with revising and editing. In addition, word processing programs provide spell checks and grammar checks to help children

ISLAND NEWS

By Ken Meinbach

Vol 1   March 14, 1993

Tragedy on Island of the Blue Dolphins

Today on the island, an unfortunate event occurred. Chief Chowig, who rules the island, was killed in a battle. The Russian hunter who makes trades with us for the hides of animals, shot the chief when he refused to take just one chest of treasures for the skins. A battle was fought between us and the Russian with the help of the Aleuts. They emerged victorious. We hope no tragedy like this ever occurs again.

Karana and Ramo – Alone

After a storm, all people of the island prepared to leave. When everyone had boarded, Ramo realized he had forgotten his spear. He went back to the village to retrieve it. Karana went after him. While they were gone, the boat left, leaving them behind. They are now on the island alone.

Wild Dogs!

Karana and Ramo spotted a pack of wild dogs today. They built a house with a fence around it in order to protect themselves from the dogs. We hope it works out for them. Later Karana plans to build a device that will shoot an arrow into any dog that approaches the fort. Good luck to them both.

Dog Found

Today on the island Karana found a big gray dog. The dog has been shot with an arrow. Karana named him Rontu which means "Fox Eyes." Rontu was a little frightened at first, but is now getting used to Karana.

with the mechanics of writing so they can focus more on the content. As students read literature and use it as a model for their own writing, or as they create their own books and poetry, word processing programs allow them to create "professional" copy.

Programs such as *Children's Writing and Publishing Center* provide an opportunity for students to create stories and newsletters. A variety of software programs allow students to create their own newspapers, brochures, and even big books. *The New Print Shop,* for example, contains a vast selection of computer graphics with which students can make their own greeting cards, signs, posters, and stationery. *Superprint II: The Next Generation* provides a tremendous wealth of graphic designs and eight different size prints. Students can use this program to create their own minibooks as well as big books.

Another excellent use of computers to connect students and literature is *The Semantic Mapper,* which allows students to construct semantic maps based on stories they are reading, and *The Literary Mapper,* which provides semantic maps based on individual books. These maps can be used in the prereading stage to ascertain and stimulate background knowledge; during the reading stage as students, for example, compare and contrast ideas suggested; and during postreading as a graphic organizer to help students organize thoughts and generate ideas for writing based on their reactions and reflections.

The ability to network with other computers (interactive telecommunications) around the world is another benefit of using computers with a literature program. Through linkage with a modem and the telephone, students can have a dialogue with other students, sharing their ideas, reflections, book recommendations, stories and poems. Not only does this provide students with an unlimited audience, it also allows for cultural exchange and promotes understanding among students from diverse backgrounds.

Many software packages are available based on specific works of literature. They can be used with a variety of groupings, from individual to small group to the entire class. Many major publishers of supplementary literature and companies that specialize in computer software, such as Broderbund and Tom Snyder Productions, offer listings of literature-based software packages.

CD-ROM offers further opportunity for children to become actively involved with the literature they read. Recent literature programs using CD-ROM allow students to interact with stories, ask questions, learn the meaning of specific words, manipulate elements, and create their own endings.

With today's technology, the possibilities are endless!

Activities to Heighten Awareness and Interest

1. Compile a book of quotations by selecting and illustrating favorite quotations from a specific book

You shall not stir out of your house today!
(Calpurnia, Act II, Scene 2)

His life was gentle, and the elements so mixed in him that Nature might stand up and say to all the world, "This was a man!"
(Anthony, Act V, Scene 5)

2. Create caricatures of favorite characters
3. Write to an author. Authors' addresses can be found in books such as Anne Commire's *Something About the Author* and *Yesterday's Authors for Children.*
4. Design a bulletin board to depict a particular book or book theme
5. Create a book jacket with a clever cover and inside blurb to lure readers
6. Conduct a debate based on an issue related to the story
7. Create a peepbox. Inside a shoe box, design a scene from the story. Punch a hole in the lid so the scene can be viewed when the lid is put back on the box.

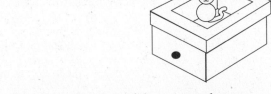

8. Develop a time line of the events of a story
9. Create a lost or found advertisement to recover a character or an item from a story

10. Make a collage to reflect a story theme or action
11. Indicate a book's setting on a world map posted in the classroom

12. Retell a story with musical accompaniment. Choose music that best reflects the story line and mood.
13. Become involved in a "Meeting of the Minds"—a discussion between the main characters of different books
14. Interview a book's main character

15. Research a book's author/illustrator, take on the persona, and let others interview them
16. Create a mural to retell a story
17. Create a book of interesting facts based on readings from informational books

18. Design a mosaic from pasta shapes, shells, fabrics, peas, or beans to symbolize a book in some way
19. Create a wanted poster for a character in a book; include a clever reward

20. Create a missing persons poster based on a character in a book

21. Participate in a panel discussion (literary circle) among several students who have read the same book

22. Compare a book with the movie or television version
23. Imagine they are creating a movie based on a favorite book. Have them cast the movie and give reasons for their selections.
24. Write a 25- or 10-word telegram that one character might send to another
25. Write a 25-, 15-, or 10-word telegram summarizing a favorite book/poem
26. Create flannel board characters and retell the story using them
27. Create a humorous skit between a person who is trying to sell a book and an uncooperative customer
28. After reading a nonfiction book about how to make something, create a chart showing the procedure and share it along with the finished product
29. Create a story map by sketching the main events of a story and then writing a brief phrase or sentence to describe each sketch
30. Create a comic book, cartoon, or comic strip based on a favorite character or story event
31. Prepare a mock trial in which a character is charged with a "crime" relating to the story. For example, try Jack (Lorinda Bryan Cauley's *Jack and the Beanstalk*) for trespassing or Wanda (Eleanor Estes's *The Hundred Dresses*) for exaggerating.

32. Create paper plate characters and retell a story or special event
33. Create an artifact book report by filling a paper bag with items related to a story; retell the story through these items
34. Create a "literary world bank" by illustrating words significant to a story in a way that their meaning becomes evident. For example:

35. Create Venn diagrams to compare characters, setting, authors, and illustrators
36. Create an illustrated folder for a specific book and use it to hold all papers related to that book
37. Create class awards to be given annually to a favorite book/character, author, and/or illustrator
37. Create a recipe for writing a fable, folk tale, or tall tale
39. Make a chapter of a favorite book into a play
40. Mime a favorite scene from a folk tale
41. Create a riddle based on a favorite book/poem
42. Retell a story in rebus fashion
43. Create a greeting card based on a book, with a short message to the class from one of the book's characters
44. Design a cereal box based on a specific story/poem. Send the designs to cereal companies.
45. Write a book review and send it to a children's magazine
46. Prepare a cliffhanger report—tell just enough to get others interested!
47. Write a horoscope for a book's character
48. Create a scrapbook about important people, places, and events in a story or poem
49. Create an original poem based on a story
50. Create a political cartoon based on a literary work
51. Create a pop-up book about an event from a book of historical fiction
52. Make a papier-maché head of a story character
53. Make masks for different characters and introduce each or use in a dramatic interpretation
54. Make a flip book based on an event in a story
55. Design a diorama of a significant scene
56. Give a chalk talk about a book
57. Take photographs of local scenes similar to scenes in a book and arrange them into an attractive display
58. Set up a museum display based on artifacts and objects related to a book
59. Design a transparency about an important story event and share it
60. Create a salt map of a setting in a story
61. Create a ballad and perform a literary character or event
62. Role-play selected scenes or problems from a book
63. Give a dramatic reading of a favorite scene
64. Rewrite the lyrics to a popular song using words/phrases from a story

65. Produce a puppet show based on a literary work
66. Prepare a "This Is Your Life" in which a book's character is introduced to the people who influenced his or her life
67. Create a piñata whose design is related to a specific story. Fill it with candies and objects related to the story. Blindfold students and allow them to try to break it and enjoy the spoils!

Children's Literature

*Cited in text

*Cauley, Lorinda Bryan. *Jack and the Beanstalk*. Putnam, 1983.

*Estes, Eleanor. *The Hundred Dresses*. Illustrated by Louis Slobodkin. Harcourt Brace Jovanovich, 1944.

*Freeman, Don. *Corduroy*. Viking, 1968.

*O'Dell, Scott. *Island of the Blue Dolphin*. Dell, 1960.

*Seuss, Dr. (Theodore Seuss Geisel). *The Cat in the Hat*. Random House, 1957.

*Spinelli, Jerry. *Maniac Magee*. Harper, 1990.

*White, E. B. *Charlotte's Web*. Illustrated by Garth Williams. Harper & Row, 1952.

Wilder, Laura Ingalls. Little House series. Illustrated by Garth Williams. Harper & Row.

*Wilder, Laura Ingalls. *Little House in the Big Woods*. Harper & Row, 1971.

Professional Resources

*Cited in text

*Commire, Anne, ed. *Something About the Author: Facts and Pictures About Authors and Illustrators of Books for Young Children*. Gale Research, 1971–1989.

*———, ed. *Yesterday's Authors for Children*. Gale Research, 1977–1978.

Kiefer, Barbara, sel. *Getting to Know You: Profiles of Children's Authors Featured in Language Arts, 1985–1990*. National Council of Teachers of English, 1991.

Moen, Christine. *Better than Book Reports*. Scholastic, 1992.

Audio-Visual Materials

Films for the Humanities and Sciences, P.O. Box 2053, Princeton, NJ 08543-2053, phone number: (800) 257-5126 (Video collections of outstanding literature and more)

Houghton Mifflin, Wayside Road, Burlington, MA 01803, phone number: (800) 225-3362 (Author videotapes)

Live Oak Media, P.O. Box AL, Pine Plains, NY 12567, phone number: (518) 398-1010 (Read-alongs, recorded books, videos, sound filmstrips)

Simon & Schuster, 15 Columbus Circle, New York, NY 10023, phone number: (800) 223-2348 (Book and cassette packages)

Society for Visual Education, Department BV, 1345 Diversey Parkway, Chicago, IL 60614-1299, phone number: (800) 829-1900 (Filmstrip and videocassette packages, software, and more)

Sundance, P.O. Box 1326, Newtown Road, Littleton, MA 01460, phone number: (800) 343-8204 (Book and cassette packages, filmstrips, video)

The Trumpet Club, 666 Fifth Avenue, New York, NY 10103, phone number: (800) 826-0110 (Author interview cassette tapes)

Weston Woods, Weston, CT 06883 (Films, filmstrips and more)

Software

Kuchinskas, G., and M. C. Radencich.
The Semantic Mapper.
Gainesville, FL,
Teacher Support Software, 1990.
Teacher Support Software, 1035 N.W. 57 Street,
Gainesville, FL 32605, phone number: (904) 332-6404

Kuchinskas, G., and M. C. Radencich.
The Literary Mapper.
Gainesville, FL,
Teacher Support Software, 1990.
Teacher Support Software, 1035 N.W. 57 Street,
Gainesville, FL 32605, phone number: (904) 332-6404

The Learning Company.
The Children's Writing and Publishing Center.
Freemont, CA,
The Learning Company, 1989.
The Learning Company,
6493 Kaiser Drive, Freemont, CA 94555,
phone number: (510) 792-2101

Lloyd, D. and B. Lee.
The New Print Shop.
Novato, CA,
Broderbund, 1990.
Broderbund, 17 Paul Drive, San Rafael, CA 94903-2101,
phone number: (415) 382-4600

Pelican Software.
Superprint II. The Next Generation.
Scholastic, 1989.
Scholastic, 555 Broadway, New York, NY 10012,
phone number: (212) 343-6100

Tom Snyder Productions,
80 Coolidge Hill Road,
Watertown, MA 02172,
phone number: (800) 342-0236

PART IV

Windows to the World: The Literature-Based Curriculum

CHAPTER 12 • **A Literature-Based Reading Program**

CHAPTER 13 • **Literature and the Curriculum: A Thematic Approach**

CHAPTER 14 • **Assessment and the Literature-Based Curriculum**

CHAPTER 15 • **Reaching Beyond the Classroom**

The world of books is the most remarkable creation of man. Nothing else that he builds ever lasts. Monuments fall; nations perish; civilizations grow old and die out; and, after an era of darkness, new races build others. But in the world of books are volumes that have seen this happen again and again, and yet live on, still young, still as fresh as the day they were written, still telling the hearts of men of the hearts of men centuries dead.

Clarence Day
Introduction to The Story of the Yale University Press

Becoming a Nation of Readers (Anderson et al., 1985), a national report on reading research and practices, confirmed that 70 percent of children's reading instruction time is spent on seat work, such as skill sheets and workbooks. Further, students were actively involved in actual reading for an average of only seven minutes of regular classroom reading time.

These findings and the results of similar research appear to have made an impression on the educational community. In reviewing the current educational trends in teaching reading and perusing new educational publications, we have noticed that conventional methods of reading instruction are being challenged. Today's reading curriculum puts real books by real writers into the students' hands. In many areas, reading trade books has become the core of the reading curriculum. In many other areas, trade books are used to supplement the more conventional reading program.

As literature becomes an integral part of classroom reading, the benefits to students are tremendous. Perhaps the greatest benefit is that it can foster a lifetime love of reading. Often, children who previously disliked reading become immersed in reading a good book and discover that reading can be pleasurable. Although children have no control over the subject matter when they read basal readers, they can make their own selections when trade books are adopted. Good literature has been written on almost every conceivable topic, and a child can usually find a book that matches his or her interests and needs.

Good literature also provides a model for oral and written language. Because of the constraints usually imposed on the basal reader, the beauty of language is often lost. As children read good literature, they can hear the poetry of the words and become aware of the magic that is created by the right word choice.

Too often, in teaching reading, we emphasize, and isolate, the skills needed for effective reading. While practice in reading is necessary, as is skill development, many skills can be learned as the book is read, rather than in a structured, isolated lesson. Learning this way is more meaningful, and students retain the skills more readily. Research has shown, for example, that using literature has a positive effect on vocabulary development and comprehension (Cohen, 1968).

Good literature allows the reader to experience the story vicariously and empathize with the characters. As they read, children learn about other people, about themselves, and about life. They discover that others have often experienced similar joys, sorrows, and fears, and they gain insight into solving their problems and dealing with their own world.

Finally, and perhaps the most viable reason for using literature in the classroom, is that it works! Children love it! Teachers love it! Bader et al. (1987) reported that "the use of children's literature to teach children had a strong effect upon student's achievement and interest in reading—much greater than the traditional methods used to teach children how to read."

Part IV of *Legacies* illustrates ways to incorporate literature throughout the curriculum as the heart of an integrated approach to learning. This approach directly coincides with whole language, a philosophy in which children become totally immersed in all aspects of language. "Whole language surrounds children with literature. . . . It enriches children's lives with a tremendous variety of experiences and enables children to enjoy those experiences as if they were participants. It uses excellent form and written expression and is relevant to children's interest and needs . . ." (Brountas, 1987). Through a whole language philosophy, all aspects of language are taught developmentally. Writing, reading, speaking, and listening are not taught as isolated contents, nor are their implicit skills taught in isolated lessons. Instead, these aspects of language are integrated through various approaches and strategies, described in earlier chapters, such as reading aloud, shared reading, sustained silent reading, storytelling, and activities for responding to and sharing literature. It is important to remember that a well-balanced curriculum includes using many such approaches.

Chapter 12 describes the components of a literature-based reading program and illustrates ways to combine the elements and approaches intrinsic to a literature-rich program to create a two-hour language arts block in which literature is the springboard for learning. Sample schedules and lesson plans are included, and the chapter details ways to weave skill development, based on student needs, into the program. Finally, the chapter describes the organization of the classroom and classroom library which together provide an environment that is stimulating, efficient, and brimming with literature.

Chapter 13 describes the development of thematic units to expose students to a variety of literature and genres, extend their interests, arouse their curiosity, provide opportunities to uncover discrepancies in information, and stimulate their desire to learn more. No matter what the concept or idea being explored, there are usually excellent examples of literature on the subject. An extensive annotated list of sources to help locate literature specific to a subject is included to facilitate creation of your own thematic units. Four sample thematic units are provided to illustrate the variety and scope of units.

In a literature-based program, process takes precedence over product, and student development and learning cannot simply be measured by traditional tests. Therefore, various types of alternative assessments need to be used to measure student growth in language. Chapter 14 describes many of the forms of authentic assessment that lend themselves to a literature-based program. These assessments, from informal to formal, from teacher observations to student self-evaluation, together give a multidimensional, indepth look at students' processes, growth, and attitudes toward learning.

Chapter 15 looks at the various community resources available to augment the literature-based curriculum. The chapter details the use of the school and public library and makes many suggestions for involving parents in their child's education. The main goal is to encourage parents to read with their children and make reading good literature an important part of home life.

From the time words were first printed, people realized that books had the ability to affect thoughts and feelings. Regardless of the label we assign to the use of literature in the classroom, the main ingredient for success is the use of real reading and real writing for real-life purposes. As a result, we bring the beauty of the written word to the forefront and empower students in the selection of words that will give meaning to their ideas and allow them to express new ideas and create new images.

References

Anderson, R. C., et al. *Becoming a Nation of Readers.* National Institute of Education, 1985.

Bader, L., J. Veatch, and J. L. Eldredge. "Trade Books or Basal Readers?" *Reading Improvement,* 24: 62–68, 1987.

Brountas, Marie. "Whole Language Really Works." *Teaching K–8,* November–December, pp. 57–60, 1987.

Cohen, D. "The Effect of Literature on Vocabulary and Reading Achievement." *Elementary English,* 45: 209–213, 217, 1968.

CHAPTER 12

A Literature-Based Reading Program

Through the literature-based reading program, various elements combine to provide children with a literature-rich, developmentally appropriate program that integrates all aspects of language arts. The literature-based reading program is based on a whole language philosophy, which is rooted in three main beliefs (Cullinan, 1992):

> that children learn to read by actually reading full texts, not worksheets; that reading is a part of language learning; and that learning in any one area of language helps learning in other areas. Children learn best when language is whole, meaningful, and functional. The language of literature becomes the heart of reading and writing programs; thus, whole language and literature are inseparable. (p. 426)

Teachers sometimes have difficulty coming to terms with whole language because they assume it is something you "do." Actually, whole language is a philosophy that suggests certain methodologies—approaches and techniques—that place meaning making at the center of learning. In the whole language philosophy, students work at their own developmental level, learn through modeling, and share responsibility for their own learning. Evaluation is ongoing, based on a variety of assessments that offer positive feedback and provide a multidimensional look at children's progress. Literature and the literature-based program are intrinsic to the whole language philosophy, helping children discover connections and motivate learning. The teacher who believes in the whole language philosophy has a most crucial role; namely, setting up a literature-rich, child-centered classroom environment filled with meaningful activities that provide for social interaction.

Literature-based programs seem to be spreading quickly as teachers and administrators recognize the tremendous advantages of using literature throughout the curriculum. This chapter focuses on the elements and components needed to create a literature-based reading program and helps organize a program that will promote effective instruction as students become immersed in reading and writing.

Components of a Literature-Based Reading Program

Most of the approaches and strategies discussed in previous chapters and others listed below, are vital to the literature-based reading program. They provide opportunities for students to become familiar and interact with quality literature and empower students with the responsibility for making their own meanings and connections. While certainly not the only elements of a literature-based reading program, the following elements enhance a love for literature and provide for active involvement and an integrated literature-based program:

1. Introducing students to a variety of genres and surrounding them with literature
2. Involving students in the elements of good literature
3. Reading aloud
4. Sharing reading experiences
5. Independent reading
6. Storytelling
7. Literature discussions and book talks
8. Critical and creative thinking experiences; problem solving
9. Interacting with and responding to literature
10. The writing process
11. Journal writing
12. Language experience approach
13. Dramatic interpretations
14. Artistic responses
15. Sharing literature
16. Social interaction/cooperative learning
17. Directed reading
18. Across the curriculum activities
19. Skill development
20. Authentic assessment

When creating a literature-based reading program, these elements can be used in conjunction with a variety of techniques, including the creation and use of interdisciplinary units (described later in this chapter and in Chap. 13)— novel units, genre units, author/illustrator units, and thematic units—to encourage students to become immersed in all aspects of the literature and to develop skills in language arts and skills associated with all areas of the curriculum. The elements can also enhance the other components of the literature-based reading program described below as well as augment a basal reading approach to reading instruction.

Teacher-Directed Activities (Strategy Lessons)

Teachers need time to teach specific skills, whether to the entire class or to groups of students. Skills should be introduced and taught only as they are appropriate to the literature being discussed: "In whole language programs, direct instruction is sometimes referred to as strategy lessons. Reading strategy instruction builds upon the prior knowledge and language strengths of the learner, and helps students integrate and become more flexible in their use of efficient and effective strategies" (Slaughter, 1988). Students should be actively involved in reading and writing during most of the time allotted for reading. A smaller percentage of class time should be set aside for teacher-directed activities (strategy lessons).

Strategy lessons can focus on specific skills, introduce a specific book or author, or teach a specific concept. They can also take the form of a directed reading activity or other techniques that involve students in reading, discussing, and interacting with what they have read. Whatever focus the strategy lesson takes, it is a time when the teacher can pull the class together to introduce or teach a skill or concept when it is meaningful and relevant to the reader/writer.

Directed Reading Activity

Directed reading is one strategy used to guide students through reading a specific selection. There are five stages.

1. Providing background information. Students are provided with vocabulary and concepts that facilitate their understanding of the text. Vocabulary and concept development, for example, can be enhanced as students create a web or cluster of a concept or issue related to the story. This stage also helps children connect their own background knowledge to that which the story is about.
2. Setting the purpose for reading. This stage is often referred to as prereading. Statements and questions are designed to motivate reading and provide a purpose for reading, thereby increasing comprehension. Students may be asked to make predictions that are later readdressed and discussed or may be asked to read to find out something in particular.
3. Reading the selection. The selection can be read aloud or silently, based on student abilities. If the selection is read aloud with young children, a big book can be used to encourage choral reading and word recognition.
4. Discussing the selection. Discussion can be oral or written in writing journals. If questions are asked they should generally be more interpretive and require higher-level thought processes. Often it is necessary to follow a discussion question with related questions to ensure student understanding and to give students an opportunity to express their thoughts and feelings.
5. Developing skills. Skill development should emphasize a balance among decoding skills, comprehension skills, and interest. Activities should be designed to integrate various content areas and stimulate creative and critical thinking. Further reading can be stimulated by suggesting books with a similar theme or topic or books by the same author/illustrator.

Individual and Group Activities

It is vital that students have an opportunity to initiate their own activities and take responsibility for completing them. Daily Record Sheets (pages 364–365) give students an opportunity to record their daily activities and free the teacher to facilitate learning. As a facilitator, the teacher guides students as they make decisions about their own learning. Allowing students to make decisions, solve problems, and take responsibility for their own learning better prepares them for the work demands of the real world (Schweinhart, 1987).

Activities developed by the teacher should take into account the importance of the connection between literature and all aspects of life. Concepts from other curriculum content areas, such as science, social studies, and math, can be integrated with the skills of language arts along with those concepts being stressed though the literature. Art, music, and drama can be enhanced through well-developed activities. Activities can take the form of literature circles, book talks, journal writing, or any number of the elements discussed earlier that are inherent to a literature-based reading program. Students may analyze illustrations, create their own stories and poems modeled after the literature, compose music to accompany text, dramatize events, and so on. Activities should encourage students to return to the book, think critically, solve problems, and respond aesthetically.

Activities should be designed to provide for independent reading and independent work as well as small group work. Children need to learn to work together cooperatively for a common goal, completing activities developed by students as well as by the teacher. Many excellent sources, such as *Structuring Cooperative Learning* (Johnson, Johnson, and Holubec, 1987), outline ways to establish cooperative learning groups. It is important that the teacher be aware of the structuring and implications of cooperative learning so students can reap the tremendous benefits of this type of grouping.

When developing activities, it is vital to remember that not all students will be reading the same book at any given time. There will be times when each student is reading a different selection based on a common theme or author and when students will be divided into groups, each group reading a different selection. Activities can be developed to allow students to share the information and insights gained from their readings. Students might form discussion groups, or a classroom discussion might ensue. This process allows students of different abilities and different interests to feel as if they are the experts on a specific book and their contributions to the discussion are extremely valuable.

Minilessons and Modeling

Throughout the day, there will be opportunities to work with individuals and small groups on a specific skill. These minilessons allow the teacher to work

DAILY RECORD SHEET: REQUIRED ACTIVITIES

Name: _____

Directions: Fill in the number of each required activity you

complete, the date, and any comments.

Activity number: _____ Date: _____

Student comments: _____

_____

_____

Teacher comments: _____

_____

_____

Activity number: _____ Date: _____

Student comments: _____

_____

_____

Teacher comments: _____

_____

_____

Activity number: _____ Date: _____

Student comments: _____

_____

_____

Teacher comments: _____

_____

_____

DAILY RECORD SHEET: OPTIONAL ACTIVITIES

Name: _____

Directions: Fill in the number of each optional activity you

complete, the date, and any comments.

Activity number: _____ Date: _____

Student comments: _____

_____

_____

Teacher comments: _____

_____

_____

Activity number: _____ Date: _____

Student comments: _____

_____

_____

Teacher comments: _____

_____

_____

Activity number: _____ Date: _____

Student comments: _____

_____

_____

Teacher comments: _____

_____

_____

with only those students who need a specific lesson at a specific time, based on their reading and writing. For example, several students may have used dialogue writing in their journal entries but do not understand how quotation marks establish the speaker. The teacher would meet with these students, using the teachable moment to explain the mechanics of quotation marks. A teacher may also recognize that certain students have completed their work and need additional stimulation. A minilesson may be set up to help these students develop an independent project based on a related interest or select related literature and create an informal literature circle when they have completed their readings.

Modeling

Modeling is a powerful tool. It can be used with the entire class, with small groups during minilessons, and with individuals. This technique allows the teacher to model any number of things, from formulating interpretive questions to responding to literature, to writing and revising a rough draft, to constructing meaning from a text, and so on. As students observe the process the teacher has modeled, they begin to experiment with the same process in their own work. One form of modeling encompasses and extends the benefits of reading aloud, while demonstrating to students the thinking processes essential to effective reading. These processes include guessing word meanings, using background information, making and changing predictions, becoming emotionally involved, summarizing, and making mental pictures.

In this modeling, often refered to as "think alouds," the teacher reads a selection and verbalizes the mental processes that usually are silent. As he or she models the thinking skills necessary for effective reading, students should begin to identify these skills to help them with their own reading and reading comprehension. A modeling lesson using H. A. Rey's *Curious George* might take the following form:

Teacher reads:	"This is George. He lived in Africa. He was very happy. But he had one fault. He was too curious."
Teacher says:	I wonder what *curious* means. Well, I see George eating a banana. Perhaps it means he eats too much. [guessing word meaning]
Teacher reads:	"The man put his hat on the ground, and of course George was curious. He came down from the tree to look at the large yellow hat."
Teacher says:	*Curious* must have nothing to do with eating too much. Maybe it means he likes to find out things. [guessing word meaning] I wonder what the man looks like. He must be quite large if he wears such a big hat. [making mental pictures]

Teacher reads: "The man picked him up quickly and popped him into a bag. George was caught."

Teacher says: Poor George is being kidnapped; he must be so frightened. I'd scream and kick a hole through the bag. [becoming emotionally involved]

George is clever. I bet he'll figure out a way to escape. [making predictions]

The teacher continues in this manner, reading and modeling the thinking skills that good readers use automatically. As students become more aware of the processes, they can write down the skills being modeled and then model these same skills as they read aloud with a partner.

The overhead projector is quite helpful for demonstrating/modeling certain skills and techniques. For example, the teacher may put a portion of his or her own writing or a student's writing (no names) on a transparency and model specific skills, such as ways to expand sentences or organize by moving sentences and paragraphs.

Teacher-Student Conferences

Throughout the day, as students work independently and in groups, the teacher has the opportunity to meet with students for individual conferences. These conferences allow the teacher to assess student progress and offer tremendous insights into students processes and skill development. A checklist of reading and writing skills that can be used as part of the conference are included in Chapter 14. Conferences should be perceived as a pleasurable experience in which the teacher and student establish a dialogue and openly express opinions and ideas. One-to-one conferences should be held at most weekly and at least once every two weeks. The teacher may ask students to sign up for a conference date or may schedule the conferences. The conference should last approximately 5–10 minutes. After each conference, a Conference Log (pages 368 and 371) should be completed as a reminder of what transpired.

The Reading Conference

A reading conference can provide important information concerning students' interests, attitudes toward reading, and growth in specific reading and thinking skills. The reading conference can include the following.

1. A discussion of a selection the student read. You should be an active part of the discussion; don't just ask questions. The discussion may focus on the author/illustrator, any elements of the selection, concepts or issues suggested by the selection or may be based on the student's feelings and attitudes toward the selection and why he/she chose the book (aesthetic responses).

CONFERENCE LOG: READING

Name of student: _____ Date: _____

Name of book selection: _____

Rating scale: Rating is on a scale of 1 (poor) to 5 (excellent)

1. Attitude toward reading	1	2	3	4	5

2. Comprehension skills

Overall understanding	1	2	3	4	5
Context clues	1	2	3	4	5
Main ideas	1	2	3	4	5
Analysis/interpretation	1	2	3	4	5
Inferences	1	2	3	4	5
Evaluation	1	2	3	4	5

3. Oral reading

Fluency	1	2	3	4	5
Word attack	1	2	3	4	5
Reading with emotion/expression	1	2	3	4	5

4. Strengths: _____

5. Weaknesses: _____

6. Student reading log

Student has read _____ books in _____ weeks.

Student has selected books from a variety of genres:

Yes _____ No _____

Types of books selected: _____

7. Student activities (comments): _____

8. Suggestions/recommendations to the student: _____

_____

2. Questions to assess the student's comprehension of the selection. Ask a few well-focused questions that involve the student in higher-level thinking. If he or she seems to have a problem, conduct an additional assessment to evaluate which comprehension skills need remediation.

3. Oral reading, in which the student selects a specific part of the selection to read aloud. The section may be a favorite part, a part that surprised him or her, a part that made him or her laugh, and so on.
4. A discussion of the activities the student has completed or is working on. The discussion can focus on the selection process for optional activities, the plan of attack for completing work, the student's interests, and so on.
5. A check of the student's Independent Reading Log (Chap. 6) to establish his or her choices in reading.
6. Recommendations and suggestions for additional reading. Suggestions may be based on student, author/illustrator preferences, a specific topic or theme, and so on. Recommendations may also be made for specific skill development.

The Writing Conference

Similar to the reading conference, the writing conference focuses on the student's progress in writing. Students should bring their writing folders to the conference. The writing conference can address the following.

1. Student's understanding of the stages of the writing process.
2. Student's ability to initiate and develop topics for writing.
3. Student's ability to revise and edit his or her writing. By perusing student folders it will be evident what skills of revision/editing students are comfortable with and which skills need further development.
4. Student's writing skills—whether content or mechanics. The conference may focus on how well the writing is organized, the effectiveness of the lead, the effectiveness of the concluding paragraphs, the student's ability to make the subject come alive, the student's ability to use the mechanics of writing, and so on.
5. Recommendations and suggestions for improving content and/or a specific skill in writing mechanics. Recommendations might include reading specific literature that may serve as a model for the student's writing, such as a selection that "shows" rather than "tells," a selection that includes excellent use of figurative language, a selection that includes an excellent lead.
6. With younger children, student's discussion of a pictorial response to a story or poem. The teacher can help the student write the text to accompany the picture.
7. Discussion of questions that help students reflect on the writing process and their progress, such as:
   a. Tell me about your piece.
   b. How did you determine what you would write about?
   c. What do you like best/least about your piece?
   d. What will you do to the piece next?
   e. Does the piece reflect the feelings you want it to reflect?

   f. How is this piece similar to/different from your other writings?

   g. What problems have you encountered in writing this piece?

   h. What is the easiest/most difficult thing for you in terms of writing?

   i. How have you revised the piece so far?

   j. How do you feel about your lead? What other leads have you tried?

   k. How do you feel about your ending? What other endings have you tried?

   l. What would you like me (or others in your writing group) to listen for?

   m. Do you have any questions about your writing?

Sample Literature-Based Reading Schedules

The literature-based reading schedule is a suggested framework for implementing a balanced, developmentally appropriate curriculum in the primary and intermediate grades. The two-hour time block integrates the language arts, reading, writing, speaking, and listening. It allows for direct teaching of skills and inclusion of the elements necessary to a literature-based reading program. Most important, it includes those approaches that motivate reading and promise to instill a lifelong love of reading.

The schedule must be flexible. Of paramount importance is a sensitivity to the students' needs and interests. The schedule should be adjusted based on what is done during the various components of the literature-based reading program. For example, while a specific time is set aside for reading aloud, it is possible that reading aloud might form part of a teacher-directed lesson one day. While there is time set aside for independent reading, this might be incorporated into independent and group activities.

The general schedule (page 372) can be adapted to almost any classroom. It details the two-hour language arts block while showing time allotments for other content areas. For primary grades, the amount of time for independent reading, writing process, and independent activities may be shortened because of the students' attention spans, and reading aloud may take place several times a day rather than in one longer period. Similarly, the intermediate schedule may dedicate more time to independent reading, writing, and independent activities. The sample plans and accompanying schedule for a primary literature-based program (pages 373–378) and for an intermediate literature-based program (pages 379–385) clarify the adaptations needed for the different levels.

Sample Literature-Based Reading Lessons

The following weekly plans illustrate how the components of a literature-based reading program work together to create a reading program in which literature is at the heart of the curriculum. The weekly primary plan is based on *Corduroy*, by Don Freeman, and the weekly intermediate plan is based on *Bridge to Terabithia*, by Katherine Paterson. Following each weekly plan is a daily schedule to suggest one way to provide for a two-hour language arts block and to integrate the language arts with the rest of the curriculum.

CONFERENCE LOG: WRITING

Name of student: _____ Date: _____

Title of story/poem: _____

Rating scale: Rating is on a scale of 1 (poor) to 5 (excellent)

1. Understanding of the writing process

Ability to initiate topics	1	2	3	4	5
Prewriting skills	1	2	3	4	5
Ability to write rough draft	1	2	3	4	5
Revision skills	1	2	3	4	5
Editing skills	1	2	3	4	5

2. Writing skills—content

Overall organization	1	2	3	4	5
Experiments with leads	1	2	3	4	5
Ability to elaborate ideas	1	2	3	4	5
Ability to use most effective words	1	2	3	4	5
Ability to delete	1	2	3	4	5
Effectiveness of ending	1	2	3	4	5
Other _____	1	2	3	4	5

3. Writing skills—mechanics

Capitalization	1	2	3	4	5
Punctuation skills	1	2	3	4	5
Dialogue writing	1	2	3	4	5
Other _____	1	2	3	4	5

4. Strengths: _____

5. Weaknesses: _____

6. Student writing journal (comments): _____

_____

7. Suggestions/recommendations to the student: _____

_____

GENERAL SCHEDULE

8:30–8:50   Opening
Students work alone or with partners to complete activities unfinished from the previous day. They may also begin new self-directed activities. Activities may include journal writing, book-related activities, newspaper or magazine research, choral reading, or silent reading time.

8:50–9:10   Language Arts: Teacher-Directed Activity (Strategy Lessons)
Whole class activity related to a skill in reading, writing, thinking, or listening or an activity that introduces children to a book or poem, its author/illustrator, or some element of it

9:10–9:50   Language Arts: Required/Optional Activities
Students work independently and in small groups on specific book-related projects; students participate in literature circles

Teacher is involved with minilessons and student–teacher conferences

9:50–10:05   Read-Aloud Time/Storytelling
Teacher reads or does a storytelling of a book or poem related to the book(s) the students are reading as part of their language arts program

10:05–10:25   Writing Process
Students write in journals, react to the literature they've been involved with, meet with writing groups, move through steps of the writing process

Teacher is involved with observing students and groups

Teacher is involved with student–teacher conferences

10:25–10:40   Sharing/Author's Chair
Students share their writing and projects
Students give book talks, creative dramatic book related presentations, and so on

10:40–11:00   Independent Reading/Paired Reading/Sustained Silent Reading

11:00–11:30   Recess/Physical Education

11:30–12:00   Lunch

12:00–1:00   Math

1:00–2:00   Social Studies/Science/Health (Theme Activities)

2:00–2:30   Special Classes—Music, Art, Computers, Library, Foreign Language, and so on

2:30–3:00   Closure
Students and teacher review the day's activities. The class generates a summary statement about the activities. Students transcribe the summary onto a personal calendar or a minibook which they take home to share with parents (see Appendix F).

SAMPLE PLAN FOR A PRIMARY READING SCHEDULE

This sample plan is based on *Corduroy,* by Don Freeman, the story of a department store bear who is finally adopted by a little girl.
Whole Group Teacher-Directed Activities (approximately 20 minutes per day): Time schedules may vary from class to class.

MONDAY

MATERIALS NEEDED
A copy of *Corduroy*
A piece of corduroy fabric (green, if possible)
A note to parents telling them you'd like their child to bring a stuffed bear to school and why

PROCEDURES

1. Prereading: Tell the students that you are going to read a story about a special bear named Corduroy. Tell them to listen as you read the story to see if they can decide how Corduroy got his name.
2. Read-aloud: Read the story aloud.
3. Critical thinking: Discuss how Corduroy got his name. Following this discussion, show the children a piece of corduroy. Allow time for them to feel it.
4. Questioning: Ask the following discussion questions:
   a. Where did Corduroy live?
   b. What reasons did Lisa's mother give for not buying the bear?
   c. Why do you think Corduroy waited until the store closed to go looking for his button?
   d. How do you think Corduroy felt when Lisa sewed his button on?
   e. Why was it important to Corduroy for Lisa to buy him?
   f. Do you think this story is true? Why or why not?
5. Parent involvement: Give students the note for their parents requesting them to bring their stuffed bears to class the next day. Explain to the students what the note says.

TUESDAY

MATERIALS NEEDED:
Bears brought from home
A copy of *Corduroy*
Large pieces of chart paper
A marker

PROCEDURES

1. Sharing: Allow time for the students to introduce and share their bears.

(continued)

WEDNESDAY

MATERIALS NEEDED:
Sentence strips (prepared from the sentences dictated on Tuesday) adhered to 12 × 18-inch sheets of paper. Adhere one sentence strip per sheet of paper. Tape sheets in correct order along the chalkboard.
Scotch or masking tape
Bears brought from home

PROCEDURES

1. Shared reading: Group the students and their bears together as they choral read the sentences on the large sheets of paper.
2. Skill development: Remove the sheets of paper from the chalkboard and assign one sheet to each student or small group. Tell them to draw an illustration that represents the text written on the sheet of paper.
3. Skill development: When everyone is finished with the illustrations, as a group, tape the story back on the chalkboard in the correct sequence.
4. Shared reading: Choral read the story.

THURSDAY

MATERIALS NEEDED:
A copy of a big book, which you have made using the large sheets from the chalkboard that contain the story of Corduroy (see Chap. 5)
Small plain pieces of paper taped over all the nouns on each page of the big book text
Scotch tape or masking tape
Bears brought from home

PROCEDURES

1. Skill development: Gather the students and their bears together. Explain that you have made a big book from the story they wrote and illustrated about Corduroy and that you have covered all the names that represent a person, place, or thing. These words are called nouns. Tell them that they should fill in the word that is covered as you read the story together.
2. Dramatization: Choral read the story, allowing the students to fill in the covered words as you read. Remove the paper covering the word after the students supply the word.
3. Dramatization: Ask the students to think about all the things Corduroy did in the story. Students take turns miming something from the story while others guess what is being mimed.

(continued)

FRIDAY

MATERIALS NEEDED:
The big book of *Corduroy*
A copy of *A Pocket for Corduroy*
Bears brought from home
Refrigerated roll of sugar cookies (available in the refrigerated sections of most grocery stores)
Small circle to cut parts of the cookies (e.g., the top from a bottle)
Cookie sheet
Oven or toaster oven
Pot holders
Spatula

PROCEDURES

1. Shared reading: Choral read the big book about Corduroy.
2. Read-aloud: Read *A Pocket for Corduroy* to the class and their guest bears.
3. Critical thinking: Discuss this book and then ask the students to compare and contrast it with *Corduroy.*
4. Have a party for the students and their bears by serving "bear paw cookies" and juice. To make the cookies, use already prepared sugar cookie dough. Make one large circle for the paw and five smaller circles for the claws. Place them on the cookie sheet. Attach the five smaller circles to the large circle as illustrated and bake in the oven or toaster oven. Remove the sheet from the oven with a pot holder. Allow cookies to cool. Remove them with a spatula. Each child will then have a giant bear paw cookie.

REQUIRED ACTIVITIES

1. Make a cassette tape of *Corduroy* (Don Freeman's version), the big book version, and *A Pocket for Corduroy.* Allow students to listen to these tapes and follow along in the appropriate book.
2. Cut pieces of paper in the shape of Corduroy. Allow students to use these bear-shaped pieces of paper to write their own story about Corduroy. Provide time for the students to share these stories.

(continued)

3. Tell the students to pretend they are Corduroy and that they are still in the department store wishing for someone to take them home. Ask them to create a poster to display beside Corduroy that would convince customers to take Corduroy home with them.

4. Provide students with instruction on how to do a webbing or clustering (see Chap. 9). Then discuss with them the concept of friendship and how Lisa and Corduroy became friends. Next, assign a webbing or semantic activity on the word *friendship,* to be prepared by each student. Provide a time for the students to share their webbings or mappings.

OPTIONAL ACTIVITIES

1. Provide construction paper, crayons, paints, sample party invitations, and so on. Tell the students to make an invitation for someone (parent, grandparent, neighbor, stuffed bear), inviting them to come to school for the party on Friday. (*Note:* The time, place, and date will need to be provided.)

2. Provide construction paper, pieces of fabric (especially corduroy), glue, buttons, and yarn and tell the students to create their own bear.

3. Collect newspaper advertisements from toy stores, catalogs, and magazines. Provide plain sheets of 8-1/2 × 11-inch white paper. Ask the students to make an alphabet book of their favorite toys. Tell them to put a large *A* and a small *a* on the top of the first page. Then have them find a toy they would like that begins with the letter *A,* cut it out, and paste it on the *A* page. Have them continue throughout the alphabet. Finally, staple the pages into a book. The students may paste more than one toy on each page. Provide a large envelope for each student working on this project to keep the pages and cutouts together.

4. Provide paper bags, tongue depressors, assortments of cloth or scraps, and glue. Tell students to work in small groups to make puppets representing the characters in *Corduroy* and then present a puppet show to the class.

5. Provide materials for the students to make a new cover for *Corduroy.* Hang these covers on the bulletin board so others can see them.

6. Tell the students to design a Corduroy bookmark to use as they read other bear books such as *Beady Bear* and *Bearymore,* by Don Freeman, or the following:

   A Bear Called Paddington, by Michael Bond
   Ask Mr. Bear, by Marjorie Flack
   Bear by Himself, by Geoffrey Hayes
   Bear Hunt, by Anthony Browne
   Bear Mouse, by Berniece Freschet

(continued)

> *Bear Party,* by William Pene DuBois
> *The Bears' Bazaar,* by Michele Cartlidge
> *The Bears' House,* by Marilyn Sachs
> *The Bear's Toothache,* by David McPhail
> *Brown Bear, Brown Bear, What Do You See?,* by Bill Martin
> *Ernest and Celestine,* by Gabrielle Vincent
> *Fix-It,* by David McPhail
> *The Three Bears,* by Paul Galdone
> *Winnie the Pooh,* by A. A. Milne

PRIMARY SCHEDULE

8:00–8:50   Opening
Students set up a display of their favorite stuffed animals.

8:50–9:10   Teacher-Directed Activities (Strategy Lessons)
Teacher rereads *Corduroy,* modeling emotions as he or she reads. Students are involved in a language experience activity in which they retell *Corduroy* in their own words. Once the story is written, the teacher cuts it apart and students put it in order again and then choral read it.

9:10–9:50   Required/Optional Activities
Learning stations may be set up to facilitate individual and group activities. These stations are based on the required and optional activities suggested in the sample plan. Students can be organized into groups and a schedule set as to which groups visit the required stations. Students should also have the option of choosing among optional stations and activities.

> Group 1—Students use construction paper, pieces of fabric (especially corduroy), glue, buttons, and yarn to create their own bears.
> Group 2—Students create a poster to display beside Corduroy to convince customers to take Corduroy home with them.
> Group 3—Students listen to a cassette tape of *Corduroy* at the listening center.
> Group 4—Students create paper bag puppets based on *Corduroy* and work on a puppet show that retells the story.
> Group 5—Students create invitations to a "Bear Jamboree" the following week. The party will feature foods related to bears (honey sandwiches, bear paw cookies), root "bear" floats, and so on. Students will share their favorite stuffed animals and read related books with their guests.

(continued)

9:50–10:05   Read-Aloud
Teacher reads *Ira Sleeps Over,* by Bernard Waber, and students discuss the friendship between the children in the story and their stuffed animals, as well as the students' own friendships with their stuffed animals.

10:05–10:25   Writing Process
Journals—Several students write in their journals as if they were Corduroy, explaining how they feel when they are left in the store and how they feel when they are taken home. Journal entries may be in the form of picture responses.

Big Book—A small group of students creates a big book modeled after the phrase in the book, "Could this be a _____, I've always wanted a _____."

Fact Book—Several students create a "Bear's Book of Facts," based on information they have discovered about bears.

10:25–10:40   Sharing/Author's Chair
Students who wish to read their journals, big books, fact books, and so on and share the projects they have completed.

10:40–11:00   Independent Reading
Students read books from the classroom library or books they have brought from home. Several copies of *Corduroy* and other related books are available.

11:00–11:30   Recess

11:30–12:00   Lunch

12:00–12:45   Math

12:45–1:00   Read-Aloud
The teacher reads *Frog and Toad Are Friends,* by Arnold Lobel.

1:00–2:00   Social Studies—Theme of "Friendship"
1:00–1:20   Teacher-Directed Activity
The teacher explains to the class how a cluster or web is created. Students create a cluster or web on the topic of friendship.

1:20–2:00   Independent/Group Activities
  Group 1—Students create a mural on the topic of friendship and what it means to them.
  Group 2—Students create a language experience story (with the teacher's help) on special friendships.
  Group 3—Students write a letter to a special friend.
  Group 4—Students discuss the importance of friendship and how to be a friend. They are encouraged to use information they have gained from the literature that deals with friendship.
2:00–2:30   Special Classes (Art, Music, Languages, and so on)

2:30–3:00   Closure

SAMPLE PLAN FOR AN INTERMEDIATE READING SCHEDULE

This sample plan is based on Katherine Paterson's *Bridge to Terabithia*, a moving tale of friendship and courage as a young boy comes to terms with tragedy.

Teacher-Directed Activities: Time schedules will vary from class to class. Besides involving students in the activities listed, give students an opportunity to read *Bridge to Terabithia* in class.

Materials Needed: Each student will need a copy of *Bridge to Terabithia*.

MONDAY

INTRODUCTION

1. Prereading: Ask students: "What do you think Terabithia might be?" "Where do you suppose *Terabithia* is located?"
2. Read-aloud: Read Chapter 1 of the book to students.
3. Skill development: Discuss the concept of foreshadowing.
   Reread the sentence: "He thought later how peculiar it was that here was probably the biggest thing in his life and he had shrugged it off as nothing."
4. Predicting: Ask students: "What do you think Jess might have meant by that statement?" "Why might this be the biggest thing in his life?"
5. Ask students to look for other examples of foreshadowing in Chapter 1. Discuss each and what events might be foreshadowed.

TUESDAY

Shared inquiry (see Chap. 9): (For this lesson to be successful, students should have completed Chapter 3 of *Bridge to Terabithia*.) Involve students in a shared inquiry strategy. As impetus for the discussion, ask them: "Did Jess ask Leslie to race because he didn't think she was a threat or because he felt it was only fair?"

WEDNESDAY

SETTING ANALYSIS

1. Webbing: Collectively, make a web of Terabithia.

(continued)

2. Ask students to skim the book, looking for words they believe best describe Terabithia. Ask them to add these words to the classroom web.
3. Ask: "Which words most effectively help you create a mental picture of Terabithia?" Discuss their selections.
4. As a class or in smaller groups, write a cinquain, haiku, or an acrostic to describe Terabithia.

THURSDAY

FIGURATIVE LANGUAGE

1. Read several examples of similes from *Bridge to Terabithia* and write them on the board.
2. Ask students what similarities they can find in these examples (i.e., use of the words *as* or *like,* a comparison of two unlike things).
3. Discuss the use of similes and how they affect the images we receive from the written word.
4. Allow time for students to locate similes in the book and write their favorite ones on the board.
5. Using a few of the similes as models, have students make up their own. For example, "He [Jess] didn't worry about a shirt because once he began running he would be hot as popping grease." What can students substitute for "popping grease"?

6. Discuss what makes a simile effective (i.e., the comparison fits the setting and mood). Make a list of the criteria for writing good similes and evaluate the ones the students created.
     A similar procedure can be used to enhance understanding of other types of figurative language, such as metaphor, personification, and hyperbole.

(continued)

FRIDAY

THEME

1. Explain to students that people deal with death and tragedy in different ways but that they all go through similar stages.
2. As a class, create a story map that illustrates the stages Jess went through from the time he learned Leslie had died (see Chap. 8).
3. Have students research the stages of dealing with death and compare these stages with the map they have developed. (Research can include talks with professionals, such as doctors and nurses, or with those who have had to deal with death.)

REQUIRED ACTIVITIES

1. After reading Chapters 1–6 of *Bridge to Terabitha,* discuss in literature circles the relationship Jess had with his family and specific friends. After reading Chapters 7–13, compare how Jess's relationships changed and give possible reasons for these changes.
2. Create your own Terabithia. Describe it using any form you prefer: poetry, drama, art, music.
3. After completing *Bridge to Terabithia,* respond to one or more of the following in your writing journal or in discussion groups:
   a. In what ways did Jess's life change after meeting Leslie?
   b. Agree or disagree with the following statement, "It's dangerous to have a best friend."
   c. What lessons did Jess learn from Leslie? Which lesson do you feel is the most valuable? Why do you believe this to be valuable?
   d. What did Terabithia represent to Jess? to Leslie? to you?
   e. Look at the illustrations. Choose your favorite. How does the illustration reflect the mood of the story? How does the illustration reflect details from the story? What information or feelings did you gain from the illustration that you didn't gain from the text?
4. You are Jess. Write and deliver a eulogy for Leslie.
5. How did the book's ending affect you?

OPTIONAL ACTIVITIES

Students may contract to complete a certain number of activities or you may decide how many must be completed.

1. Read another book by Katherine Paterson. Compare the two books, based on setting, characters, themes, and your reaction to each.
2. In a group, recreate *Terabithia* in mural form.
3. Retell one of the conflicts Jess and Leslie had with Janice. Explain the conflict first from Janice's viewpoint and then from Jess's or Leslie's.
4. Using a book of quotations, select one on the subject of friendship that best reflects the relationship between Leslie and Jess. Illustrate

(continued)

5. Listen to "Free to Be You and Me." This was the same song Jess and Leslie sang in music class. Rewrite a verse as if you were one of the book's characters.

INTERMEDIATE SCHEDULE

8:30–8:50   Opening
Students go to the library, work in journals, or work at computer stations on a newspaper based on *Bridge to Terabithia*.

8:50–9:10   Teacher-Directed Activity (Strategy Lesson)
Students are introduced to the concept of figurative language. The teacher reads several examples of similes from *Bridge to Terabithia* and writes them on the board. Students look for similarities in the examples (use of the words *as* or *like*, a comparison of two unlike things). Students discuss the use of similes and how they affect the images the reader receives from the written words. Students locate similes in the book and share a favorite one by writing it on the board or an overhead transparency. Students write a simile of their own to share and discuss.

9:10–9:50   Required/Optional Activities
Students may be given a list of required and optional activities, as listed in the sample unit. From this list, students become involved in the required activities and are encouraged to select a specific number from the optional activities. Students are encouraged to create their own optional activity related to the book, based on a specific interest.

In lieu of the optional activities based on *Bridge to Terabithia*, students may be involved in independent reading of other books dealing with the cycle of life, such as *Tuck Everlasting*, by Natalie Babbitt. In literature circles and book talks, they share insights gained from their additional reading.

9:50–10:05   Read-Aloud Time
The teacher reads aloud from *The Fall of Freddie the Leaf*, by Leo Buscaglia, which is allegory illustrating the delicate balance between life and death.

10:05–10:30   Writing Process
Students write journal entries based on their reactions to the book(s) they have been reading. Their entries can be based on their responses or can take the viewpoint of one of the characters and express his or her feelings.

(continued)

Several students may write a sequel to *Bridge to Terabithia*, while others continue their work on a "Bridge to Terabithia" newspaper.

10:30–10:40   Author's Chair
Students share their journal entries, sequels, and newspaper articles.

10:40–11:00   Independent Reading

11:00–11:30   Physical Education

11:30–12:30   Math

11:30–12:30   Math

12:30–1:00   Lunch

1:00–2:00   Social Studies/Science/Health—Thematic Connections
For several weeks, students have been working on a science/social studies unit focusing on the cycles of life of human and nonhuman organisms.

2:00–2:30   Special Classes—Music, Art, Languages, and so on.

2:30–3:00   Closure

Creating Literature-Based Lessons and Units

A variety of types of literature-based units can be developed to add continuity, make learning more meaningful, and aid students in making connections. Literature-based units can take the form of novel/book units, author/illustrator units, genre units (see Chap. 1), or thematic units (see Chap. 13). These units can contain many of the elements intrinsic to the literature-based reading program and can be used in conjunction with the many components of the reading program.

Novel/Book Unit

Each literary work has its own special elements that should guide the way it is developed. One of the best approaches to help provide ideas for activities and discussion topics is bookwebbing. Bookwebbing can involve student input, although with younger children it is more difficult at first. To begin the process, give a short book talk, or read a short portion of the work. Then help students brainstorm ideas that tie into the book. When you and students have shared all the ideas you can think of, list the various curricular areas and see if this sparks additional ideas. A bookwebbing for *The Jolly Postman and Other People's Letters*, by Janet and Allan Ahlberg, is shown below.

Once ideas for each curricular area have been recorded on the completed web, develop activities that correlate with the ideas. See pages 385–388 for a book unit on *The Jolly Postman*. The ideas developed can then be part of your daily schedule and will help you integrate all curricular areas. Thematic units can also be developed based on the book web. For example, *The Jolly Postman* can be part of a thematic unit on folk tales, communication, or letter writing.

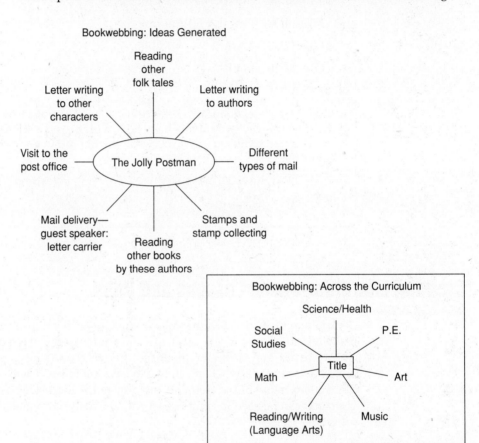

Bookwebbing: Ideas Generated

- Reading other folk tales
- Letter writing to other characters
- Letter writing to authors
- Visit to the post office
- The Jolly Postman
- Different types of mail
- Mail delivery— guest speaker: letter carrier
- Reading other books by these authors
- Stamps and stamp collecting

Bookwebbing: Across the Curriculum

- Science/Health
- Social Studies
- P.E.
- Math
- Title
- Art
- Reading/Writing (Language Arts)
- Music

Author/Illustrator Unit

To involve students in this type of unit, it is important that they be exposed to a rich variety of books written and/or illustrated by the person being honored. You may wish to introduce several books through book talks. In addition, selections for read-aloud, storytelling, literature circles, and so on should be based on one or several of the author's/illustrator's work.

BOOK UNIT FOR *THE JOLLY POSTMAN AND OTHER PEOPLE'S LETTERS*, BY JANET AND ALLEN AHLBERG

The Jolly Postman delivers all types of letters to characters of your favorite folk tales, including The Three Bears, the Giant from *Jack and the Beanstalk*, and the Big Bad Wolf!

READING/LANGUAGE ARTS

1. Read aloud the folk tales whose characters get mail from the Jolly Postman.
2. Read aloud additional folk tales and have students select a character with whom to correspond. Brainstorm different types of mail people receive: personal letters, invitations, bills, advertisements, requests for donations, and so on.
3. Have students write a letter to Janet and Allen Ahlberg, the authors of *The Jolly Postman* (via William Heinemann Ltd., 10 Upper Grosvenor Street, London WIX 9PA.)
4. Have students collect examples of the various types of mail they receive and classify them by their purposes. (Suggest they leave the bills at home!)
5. Have students *become* the letter they have written to a favorite friend or relative and tell about their life from the time they were created to the time they were delivered, opened, and read.
6. Have students create a book for the Piper Press that tells what happened next in one of their favorite folk tales.
7. Create a story from the villain's point of view. For example, Cinderella's step-sisters might explain that they were mean to Cinderella because of all the horrible tricks she played on them when they first lived together.

MATH

1. Have students graph the prices of first-class stamps since the early 1900s. Have them form some inferences about the future prices of stamps.
2. With students, create prices for each of the Hobgoblin supplies advertised in the letter to the witch in the gingerbread house. Have each student make a list of supplies for the witch to buy (with quantities indicated). Have them pass their list to other students so that each can compute the witch's bill.
3. Goldilocks received a £1 note. Have students bring in examples of money from other countries and compute their equivalent worth in dollars and cents.

(continued)

MUSIC

1. Teach students songs often associated with many of their favorite folk tales, such as "Who's Afraid of the Big Bad Wolf." Have students create instruments to accompany their songs. Books such as *Making Musical Things* (Wiseman, 1979) give directions for making all sorts of musical instruments.
2. Divide students into groups based on their favorite folk tale. Have them create a dance for a character in this tale. For example, they might create a wedding dance for Cinderella or a fireside dance for Rumpelstiltskin. Have them select a piece of classical music to accompany the dance. For example, the wedding dance might be used with Bach's "Concerto for Harpsichord and Strings."

SCIENCE/HEALTH

1. Mail delivery has certainly improved since the days of the Pony Express. Share information with students about the Pony Express and discuss the dangers the Pony Express riders were exposed to.
2. Take a field trip to the local post office. What methods and equipment are used to make mail delivery so much faster today? Have students discuss the improvements in the mail system over the years. Have them create a futuristic mail system.
3. Make a list of all the animals that are characters in folk tales on a large chart similar to the one below. Assign each group of students a different animal to research. Have them find out what qualities the animal exhibits in the folk tales and what qualities it actually has. When all groups have completed their portion of the chart, see what conclusions students can draw.

Animal	Qualities in Folktale	Actual Qualities

(continued)

SOCIAL STUDIES

1. Involve students in reading folk tales from different countries. Have them discuss the different customs and values they learned about the culture as a result of reading the folk tales.
2. Read several versions of the same folk tale. Have students compare them and decide which they prefer and why.
3. Encourage students to start a class stamp collection. Have them bring in used stamps from mail received at home. When you have a large amount of different types of stamps, have students categorize them. Each group of students can be responsible for mounting the stamps of a certain category and labeling the country of origin. Each group can share their most interesting stamp with the rest of the class and locate, on a map, the country of origin. Have them learn whatever they can about what is depicted on the stamp. Put all group pages together into an album.
4. Have students design a stamp to commemorate what each believes is the most important event of that year. Before students begin, brainstorm different events of the past year. Hold a contest and have the class vote on one stamp to send to the postmaster general. Compose a letter explaining why your class thinks the event is so important and why it should be remembered on a stamp.

ART

1. Have students create a big book of their favorite folk tale. They may wish to create their own illustrations or create collages using magazine pictures.
2. Have students design stamps that commemorate some of their favorite folk tale characters.
3. Have the school's art teacher teach students how to create their own stationery using sponge printing.
4. Have students design a picture postcard (similar to the one Jack sent to the Giant) that depicts something special about their city. Have them send it to a family member or friend who lives in a different state.
5. Have students create and deliver invitations asking their family to attend a folk tale fair. Have students dress as their favorite folk tale characters. Have them create puppets and dramatize various stories. Have them decide on the menu and make and serve food items appropriate to the different folk tales, such as *giant* sub sand*wiches*, *gingerbread* cookies, and Cracker *Jacks*.

(continued)

PHYSICAL EDUCATION

1. In groups, have students create a game in honor of a favorite folk tale. For example, they might make up a game called "Cast a Giant Shadow" to see who can make the biggest shadow figure appear on a wall. Ask each group to teach the game to the rest of the class and take time to play it.
2. Introduce a relay race in which students pass a letter instead of a baton.

Teacher-directed activities (strategy lessons) can be developed to involve students in comparing and analyzing the work of the author/illustrator, and independent and group activities can involve students in reading and discussing specific works. Students should be involved in research of the author/illustrator, which often helps them understand the author's/illustrator's work and motivation.

Students can create a bulletin board that include a picture of the author/illustrator surrounded by books jackets (originals and student-made). A book shelf next to the bulletin board should contain a variety of books by this author/illustrator so they can be read during independent reading. The classroom door can also be decorated to reflect the author's/illustrator's work.

Students should be encouraged to write to the author/illustrator if he or she is still alive and letters can be sent via the publisher. In their letters, students should ask questions they really want answered. These questions can be based on their research of the person and their reading of his or her work. Letters can also contain personal reactions to the literary works.

A day can be set aside for a party to honor the author/illustrator. A videotape, film, or filmstrip based on the work of a specific author/illustrator can be shown. Students can dress up as characters created by the author/illustrator and hold a parade through the school. A videotape can be made of students introducing themselves and telling about themselves as the character they've chosen. Foods can be served that are appropriate to the stories and characters. Students can create their own entertainment through creative dramatics, readers theater, or story theater, based on specific stories and events.

Additional activities to honor the author/illustrator include: the creation of buttons and bumper stickers; short readings over the school public address system or closed circuit television; a display set up in the school library; sharing specific books/poems with other classrooms; creating cassette tapes to accompany books; and creating big books with student illustrations to accompany original text.

Literature and the Basal Reading Program

The basal reading program approach to teaching reading is the most widely used approach in U.S. schools today. Most reading programs consist of a set of graded texts, with one or two readers for each succeeding grade level through sixth or eighth grade. In addition to the graded texts, the series includes the following:

1. Teacher's manuals with detailed lesson plans for directed reading activities
2. Skill sheets for practicing and reinforcing skills
3. Diagnostic and prescriptive materials and activities for assessing progress and meeting curriculum objectives
4. Record-keeping systems for systematically recording students' progress
5. Supplementary materials, such as puppets, big books, duplicating masters, parent suggestions, computer programs, and other selected materials

As with any reading program, the basal reading series has advantages and disadvantages. The first major advantage is that the series provides the scope and sequence of skills to be mastered and a systematic way to teach and review these skills. Second, the explicitly detailed teacher's manuals contain many valuable suggestions that save much planning time. Finally, the basal reader series covers all areas of reading, including word recognition, comprehension, and oral and silent reading. Thus, overemphasis or underemphasis of any one area can be avoided.

Although the series provides for many aspects of teaching reading, it does have some disadvantages that need to be considered. First, most series today, while providing quality literature, often offer only segments of the whole. As a result, the full impact of the work is lost and often, too, so is the magic. Older reading programs often include controlled vocabulary, which leaves stories dull and boring, offering little literary merit. Second, many teachers follow the teacher's manual word for word, without considering the special needs of particular students. Often, teachers believe they must do every activity, even though some may not be appropriate or necessary for their students; thus, they misuse time that could be spent on more interesting and appropriate activities. Finally, teachers often believe the basal series is a complete reading program. As a result, they may not offer the variety of experiences that are essential to a well-balanced reading program. In fact, Bernice Cullinan (1987) reports that even though 80–90 percent of classrooms across the United States use the basal reading series as the core instructional material, no basal was ever intended to be a completely self-contained program.

Reform Movement

Educators are recognizing the need to include more children's literature in the classroom reading program. This movement was reinforced by the following explicit recommendations about basal readers and their use reported in *The Report Card On Basal Readers* (1988) (based on a study by the Commission on Reading, 1985).

(text continues on page 391)

Reflections of . . .

Sam Leaton Sebesta

"If you really believe in children's books, you wouldn't be associated with basal readers," declared the garden party guest. I turned green and pretended to be part of the topiary. That gives time for reflection and it's pleasant except for the bees. Why *do* I work on basal readers, anyway?

First, to help with selection. I put in grabbers, instantly recognized by some and instantly enjoyed by as many as possible. Then I put in more challenging items, those that take more teaching and mulling over. At every grade level I try to include every genre—fanciful and realistic, fiction and nonfiction, classic and modern. I try to represent all ethnic groups and a full range of multiculturism. When I work on basal anthologies, I am trying to provide samplers to generate and broaden interests. To the child and teacher I indicate that the whole books from which the samples are taken stand there waiting.

Others at the garden party do not accept this purpose. Self-selection proponents maintain that children always must be free to make their own choices in reading. I argue that freedom of choice exists only where there is knowledge of options. There are still some skills-first proponents who want basal content rigged so that it can't distract from phonemic segmentation, structural analysis, and a whole poppy field of comprehension strategies. I tell them that we've been down that path before, many times.

Second, I work on basal teacher guides to promote transaction. Transaction means that author and reader work together to create meaning. So reading is not passive. In the words of the best transactional theorist, Louise M. Rosenblatt, "reading is a performing art."

I take that idea more literally than do many of my colleagues. I want to see more mime, direct point-of-view talk, role playing, creative drama, and readers theater in basals and in *all* literature teaching. I want to see more evocation/engagement/transaction through the humanities. There has been entirely too much sit-and-discuss and write-answers-to-comprehension-questions in reading, together with too much let's-find-the-literary-elements in literary study. So I am, I suppose, a revolutionary hiding here in a shrub, waiting to load basal readers with suggestions to promote transaction.

Finally, I work on basals to broaden assessment. In this psychometric age, the majority of educational leaders treasure only what they can measure. Reading programs live or die on the basis of a number: what reading achievement score do children get when they're taught with them? But that number is an illusion. It does not tell us whether the children want to read and are likely to continue reading, nor does it tell anything about the quality of their literary selection and transaction. It does not tell whether literature and the connected humanities function in their lives to make them more joyful and useful.

The basals are not alone in the fallacy of measurement. I think they are open to change. Wide use and constant revision make change feasible. I want to be part of that.

Those are my reasons for being involved in basals, and I'll continue to pursue them, or stay here peacefully in the topiary.

1. Teachers should not be required to use any program they find professionally objectionable.
2. No adoption of any basal should exclude the possibility of teachers' modifying its use or using alternate materials and methods.
3. Publishers should immediately discontinue the practice of revising and censoring selections from children's literature.
4. Publishers should change the way teachers are treated in teacher's manuals of basals. They should be addressed as professionals and supported in their exercise of professional judgment.
5. School authorities should establish criteria for reading instructional materials and should not adopt materials that do not meet their criteria.
6. In all aspects of development, selection, and use of basals and alternate methods and materials, the needs and welfare of the students must be placed above all other considerations.
7. School authorities, legislatures, foundations, professional organizations, and others should encourage innovation within and outside basals through funding research and experimental programs in schools.

Publishers are attempting to include more literature selections in basal reading programs and to make the language more like normal conversation. Recent editions reflect a trend of introducing characters and settings from various backgrounds and races that include a variety of roles. Although publishers are making progress in including children's literature in the reading program, what has been called the "basalization" of children's literature is often found. That is, the publisher has revised the literature selections to fit its own constraints; as a result, often the original author would not recognize his or her story if a different title were used. Since such reading programs form the backbone of most reading classes, it makes sense to extend the reading program to include real literature. In other words, the answer to developing and maintaining a well-balanced reading program for those using basal readers seems to be a marriage between the basal reading program and literature.

Extending the Basal Reading Program

If the basal reader is to be used as an integral part of the reading program, much can and should be done in the classroom to extend the basal and provide students with approaches and strategies that will foster a love of reading, bring good literature to the forefront, and involve students in actual reading a greater percentage of the time.

One of the most frequently expressed complaints is that there is little time during the reading program to do anything other than the activities included in the basal. This is easily resolved by using pretests and posttests. All students *do not* need to do all the activities suggested in the basal; in fact, the tremendous amount of skill sheets and questions is usually counterproductive in terms of encouraging students to read and fostering a love of reading. Pretests and posttests are excellent diagnostic tools that help provide a profile of student strengths and weaknesses. Rather than teaching the entire class a certain lesson or skill, small groups or individuals can be pulled out for minilessons and the other students can be allowed to read independently or work alone or in small groups. This approach also allows time to work on specific skills as they are needed and provides time to hold conferences with individuals, to teach minilessons, and to assess students' progress.

Many of the readers, especially those published recently, include a greater number of selections from classic and contemporary literature. These selections should be used to encourage students to read the entire work as well as other books based on a similar theme or by the same author. Many readers have incorporated strategies such as read-aloud and storytelling into their lessons; yet, reading is still taught and viewed as an isolated skill. Little is done to help students make the connections between reading and the other components of language—writing, listening, and speaking. Nor are connections being made between reading and other content areas. In addition, students are given little opportunity to take an active part in their own education, and few associations are encouraged between reading and real-life purposes, problems, and needs.

The use of thematic units can help alleviate many of these concerns. Many basal reading programs group their literary selections thematically. Depending on the year's objectives, appropriate literary selections from the reader can be chosen to augment units of study in content areas such as social studies and science. Even if the reader is not arranged thematically, it doesn't preclude the use of certain works with a thematic lesson.

The following section outlines possible ways of extending a selection (*Sarah, Plain and Tall* from *Sometimes I Wonder*, Book 4, Scott, Foresman, 1989) using many of the approaches, activities, and strategies mentioned throughout this book (see Chap. 13 for related information, books, and activities).

1. Introduction. Have students web a main theme or concept from Patricia MacLachlan's *Sarah, Plain and Tall* (the story of a young woman who journeys West to begin a new life in the frontier). Themes might include pioneer life, the westward movement, loneliness, or survival. Encourage students to generate questions and activities they would like to pursue based on the completed web.
2. Read-Aloud. Read other books or poems dealing with the theme or concept selected. For example, if "pioneer life" is selected, read *Little House on the Prairie*, by Laura Ingalls Wilder. If "survival" is selected, read *Julie of the Wolves*, by Jean George, or *Island of the Blue Dolphin*, by Scott O'Dell. When reading aloud, model comprehension and critical thinking strategies, such as predicting, evaluation, and context clues.
3. Dramatics. Students may want to recreate a favorite scene or chapter from a related book. Groups of students may want to prepare a readers theater or a story theater (see Chap. 10). Chapter scenes from any of the Little House series lend themselves especially well to readers theater, since the narrator describes the action while the students read the dialogue.

4. Independent Reading. Along with the students, bring in books and other written materials related to the theme or concept selected, materials of a similar genre, or materials written by the same author(s) being studied. Although students have the freedom to select their own reading materials, they might decide to read one of the related materials if the books are easily accessible.

5. Writing Process. Although students select their own topics for writing, many may react to something read or discussed in the literature. Students will also be involved in writing throughout the two-hour block. Writing activities are woven throughout the activities portion as well as in minilessons and teacher-directed activities.

6. Teacher-Directed Whole Class/Large Group Activities (Strategy Lessons). Use a shared reading approach or present a specific skill the entire class or large group needs. Either activity may be based on the basal selection and appropriate activities from the reader. However, choose only those that *best* meet objectives and student needs.

7. Activities. Have students work independently or in small groups on activities to extend the literature, whether from the basal reader or another literary source. Activities may be categorized as required and optional so students have choices. Include activities that cause students to think critically and creatively and to analyze literary elements or genres and that are based in large part on questions and interests generated by the students. Allow time for literature circles and discussions.

Allot time for independent reading of books related to the concept or theme being explored. Students may read to find answers to questions or to complete specific activities developed by both students and teachers, or just for the fun of it!

As students work and read independently or in groups, conferences may be held with individual students or minilessons may be taught to small groups, based on student needs. For example, students might have kept a diary of life on the prairie. Their writing might have indicated a need to know how to use quotation marks. The teacher might create a minilesson to teach this.

The main goal should be to involve students in reading and writing. The more they read and write and the more they enjoy both, the more fluent they will become. This is a circular pattern that can be directly affected by the way reading and writing are approached in the classroom. No matter what materials are used to help achieve the reading objectives, whether literature or basal, students can be involved with language and begin to make connections between reading and aspects of the world in which they live.

Organizing the Literature-Based Classroom and Materials

In the literature-based reading program, there is a tremendous amount of activity going on at one time. There are students working independently and in small groups, involved in minilessons and conferences, involved at various

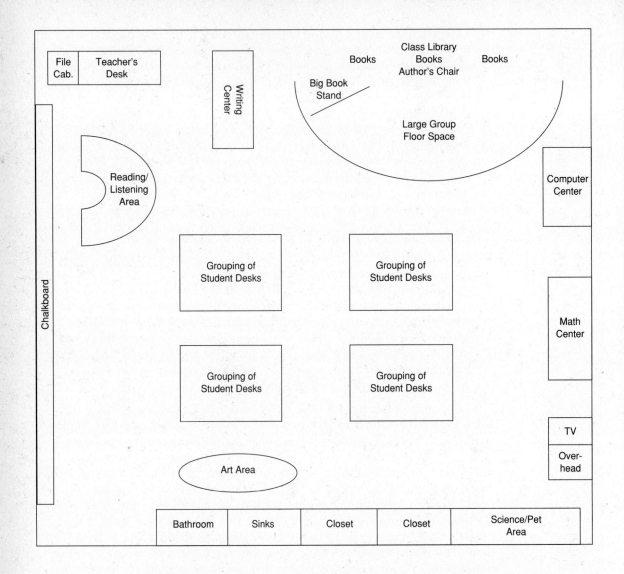

centers, visiting the classroom library and listening stations, reading independently and with peers. The students are constantly involved in activities that require movement and regrouping. Therefore, a well-organized learning environment is essential. Although the students are empowered with many choices, they must have a routine when it comes to moving about the classroom and using the various equipment and materials. Without this routine and structure, little can be achieved.

Many features enhance the literature-based reading program. The diagrams above (*left:* primary classroom; *right:* intermediate classroom) offer ways to organize a classroom to provide for these features and others basic to all

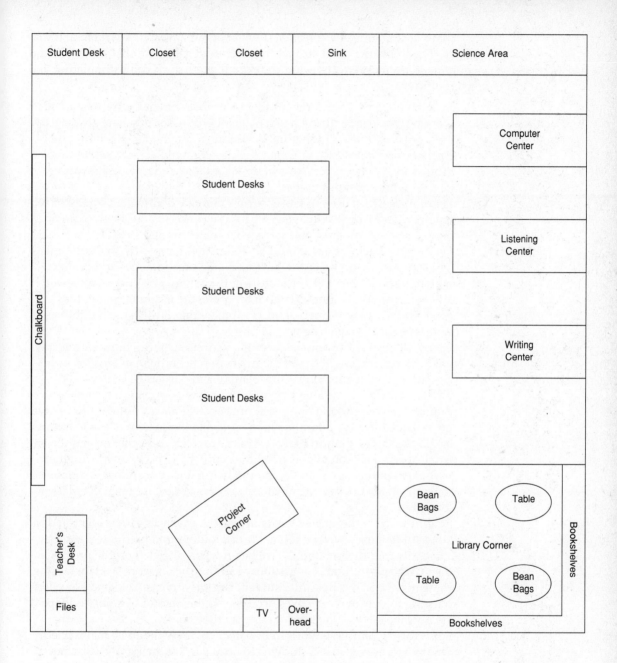

classrooms: learning centers, listening center, classroom library, independent reading area, conference area, student desks/tables, television/video, writing/publishing center, student files/folders, author's chair, large group area, chart and chart holder (primary), stand for big books (primary), overhead projector, bulletin boards, computer center, and art materials and supplies.

Many factors must be considered when organizing the classroom and materials. The following need special consideration to ensure that materials and equipment are most effective and the organization is visually stimulating and space-efficient.

1. *Student Groupings.* The room arrangement must be conducive to students working independently, in pairs, in small groups, or in whole group activities. Workstations or individual desks can accommodate the individual workers, but tables and/or clusters of desks should accommodate small groups and conferences. Areas of desks or tables or large circle areas are best for whole group activities.

2. *Furniture Selection.* Round tables permit more flexibility than square or rectangular tables, especially where space is a concern. Low shelves can often double as room dividers and storage for materials and supplies.

3. *Equipment.* Specific areas should be designated for audiovisual equipment and computers. Rules need to be established immediately for working with this equipment. Once established, they should be posted, reviewed, and enforced. For example, if students are in the listening center, they need to know how to operate the equipment and how to rewind the cassette tape for the next listener.

4. *Type of Activities.* The noise level of the various activities must be considered when arranging the classroom. There must be a quiet area for activities such as independent reading, conferencing, listening centers, and writing. However, the area where students are rehearsing storytelling or dramatizing or working on special projects will have a hum of productive noise. Because space allocation is so critical to the success of the literature-based classroom, platform areas or lofts are often created to extend the existing space. This solution also separates quiet and noisy areas. Another way of extending space and accommodating noisier activities is to move them to a patio or area outside the classroom, where others will not be interrupted.

5. *Student Work.* A designated easily accessible area needs to be identified to store student logs, writing folders, work folders, and journals so students can easily find their materials and begin where they left off the previous day. Large plastic crates or cardboard storage boxes work well for storing these materials. It is helpful if student work is alphabetized and placed in hanging folders in these boxes. Crates or boxes should be color-coded and clearly labeled with the type of material they hold.

   Some form of individual record of daily activities should be maintained. One simple way is to ask students to keep a log of their daily activities (see pages 364–365). In this log, both the teacher and the student react to the work being completed. This log can be kept in one of the folders, such as the work folder, for easy reference.

6. *Writing Materials.* Writing materials need to be stored near the writing/publishing center, perhaps on a low book shelf in plastic containers or brightly covered shoe boxes. Materials in this area should include dictionaries, thesauruses, lined paper, typing paper, construction paper,

glue, pens, pencils, scissors, markers, crayons, contact paper, rings for binding books, general hardbound covers, and hardbound books.

7. *Display Area.*

Students' Work. Bulletin boards and room dividers can be used to display students' work; it can be hung from the ceiling or displayed on doors and walls; or it can be pinned on a clothesline. Tables around the room and the tops of file cabinets can hold projects students are working on. Completed projects can be lent to the library for display or put on a traveling museum cart that is shared with other classrooms.

Books. Books that students are currently reading, related to topics under study, or by specific authors/illustrators can be shelved in plastic baskets. They can be arranged on low book shelves for easy access and labeled with the title and author. If possible, this shelf should be near a bulletin board that correlates to a featured theme, author/illustrator, or book (see page 398).

Big Books. It is suggested that you obtain a stand that holds the book and allows you to turn the pages easily. For storing big books, you may wish to use a storage ladder or clothes hanger and simply hang the books over the rungs.

Magazines/Newspapers. These materials lend themselves to being hung over the rungs of a clothes hanger. Skirt hangers can be used to hang the different sections of the newspaper. Keep sources current and have an area in the classroom library available for storing back issues (see page 399).

8. *Monitoring Students.* Not all activities can be completed at individual desks, therefore the overall organization of who will do what and when is important so that various centers and spaces do not become too crowded. For example, if one of the planned activities requires using the listening center and it can only accommodate six students, plan activities so that no more than six students will be at the center at one time yet all students will have the opportunity to go to the listening center at some time. One way to organize this is to color-code the areas of the room and provide colored wristbands (available in most sporting goods stores) to designate where students will go. If the listening center can accommodate six people, then only six wristbands would be the same color as that center. Usually in a literature-based classroom, students can choose among a variety of areas in which to work and among a variety of activities. Therefore, if the listening center is full, the student simply makes another selection and returns at a later time.

9. *Classroom Library.* In a literature-based classroom, perhaps the most important factor is the use of the library and the organization of the classroom library. For this reason, the next section is dedicated to organizing and using the classroom library.

In summary, in a literature-based classroom where students are continually reading, writing, thinking, collaborating, creating, and making choices, the overall success relies on identifying developmentally appropriate activities and then organizing the environment so it is conducive to learning.

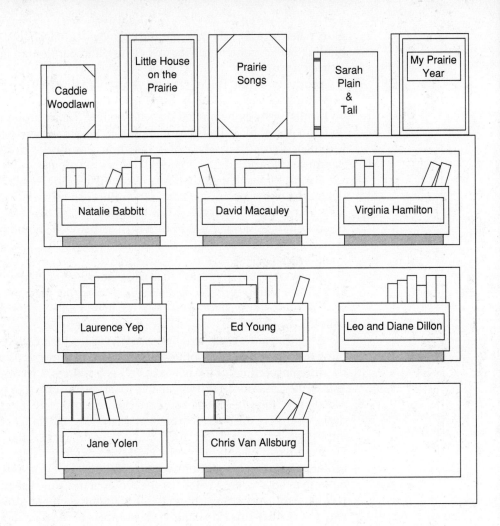

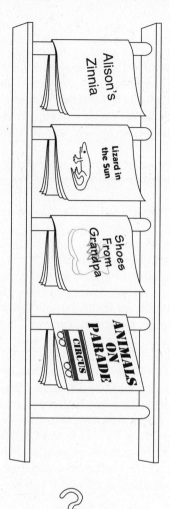

The Classroom Library

Children should be surrounded daily by good books. The classroom library is the perfect place to house all types of reading material, from classics to students' own published works, from national periodicals to local newspapers. A room filled with a variety of exciting books and an adult who encourages students to read is the perfect combination for creating an atmosphere that nurtures a love of reading.

The following activities will aid you and your students in organizing a classroom library:

1. Collecting reading materials. Materials can be gathered for the classroom library in many ways.
   a. Plan and hold a book fair. Many publishing companies, local children's bookstores, and local book companies will help set up and stock a book fair. Consult the yellow pages in the telephone directory for such companies. Often the companies will, based on the percentage of sales, give the school books or money to purchase books for the classroom library.

      Book fairs can be much more than simply a display of books. They can involve the entire school family: faculty, students, friends, and relatives. For example, invite storytellers (parents, grandparents, etc.), local authors and student authors to speak about books they've written, or "storybook characters" to greet students; display student-created book advertisements, book covers, and book reviews; provide donated food items that represent certain books or book characters, such as Curious George Frozen Bananas and Babar the Elephant Peanut Butter Cookies.
   b. Encourage parents and relatives to donate books and magazines. Place a sticker inside each book with the name of the person who donated the book and the person in whose name it was donated. In this way, the book will serve as a lasting tribute.

THIS BOOK IS DONATED IN HONOR OF

_____

By _____

Date _____

   c. Organize a traveling library so classrooms can share books. Each classroom can select a variety of books from their collection to be included in the traveling library. These books can be kept in a large plastic bin to allow for easy access and ease in transport. Label each book in the traveling library with a classroom identification mark and put a cardholder in the back of the book, so it can be checked out just as in the regular library. Members of the participating classrooms should establish rules for the traveling library.

   d. Most public libraries allow classroom teachers to check out a substantial number of books at one time. Take advantage of this, so you can add to the classroom library every few weeks.

   e. Collect a variety of reading materials from various sources. Brochures can be collected from travel and governmental agencies. Student volunteers can take turns bringing in the daily newspaper and weekly magazines.

   f. Provide the necessary information for students who would like to take part in book clubs. Several companies have book clubs through which students can purchase books at discounted prices. These include Arrow Scholastic Book Club, Scholastic Book Club, Inc., Jefferson City, MO 65102; Troll Book Clubs, #2 Lethbridge Plaza, Mahway, NJ 07430 (201-529-4000); and Trumpet Club, P.O. Box 604, Holmes, PA 19043 (1-800-826-0110). Bonus points are awarded for each book ordered; these points can be accumulated and used to select books for the classroom library.

   g. Include any books written by students. This reinforces the importance placed on their reading *and* writing.

2. Organizing the library. The classroom library must be organized so students can locate books easily and efficiently. As books are collected, fill out and file three cards—subject, title, and author—for each book. Older students can help, using the school library's card catalog for help in setting up the cards. Cards can be alphabetized in boxes (e.g., shoe boxes) or in a Rolodex.

    Give the books call numbers, just as in the regular library. Code fiction books with an *F* for fiction and the first letter of the author's last name. Code biographies with a *B* and the first letter of the subject's last name. Organize nonfiction books according to the Dewey Decimal Classification System. Place a sticker with the book's call number on the bottom of the book's spine. You can also put different-colored pieces of tape on the spine to indicate genres; this will make classifying and shelving the books easier.

3. Checking out books. Ask your school librarian to help you obtain cardholders. Have students decorate them, and then attach one to the end page of each book. Place a card that lists the author and the title in the cardholder. Remember to leave room on the card for the name of the student checking out the book, the date the book is checked out, and the date it is returned. The book card on page 402 provides a sample.

OWL MOON

F

Yol

Yolen, Jane

Name	Date Out	Date Due

When a book is checked out, stamp both the card and the cardholder with the date the book is due. Have the class establish rules for dealing with late, lost, and damaged books. Teach students the procedure for checking out books, and show them how the books are organized. Schedule specific times when students are permitted to check out books, and post these times to avoid confusion. Each month, select student librarians who are responsible for helping students locate and check out books as well as for shelving books that have been returned.

4. Setting up the classroom library. Place bookshelves in an easily accessible area of the classroom. Label shelves so there is a place for fiction, biogra-

phies, and nonfiction. Establish an area for materials such as newspapers, periodicals, and reference books.

5. Reading area. A special reading area can be decorated and furnished with large pillows and carpeting so students can get comfortable as they become engrossed in their reading. A reading room such as the "Green Dragon Castle" can be constructed using refrigerator cartons and lots of imagination. The reading room can be changed throughout the year to reflect the themes being studied or different genres.

Children's Literature

*Cited in text

*Ahlberg, Janet, and Allen Ahlberg. *The Jolly Postman and Other People's Letters.* Heinemann, 1986.

*Babbitt, Natalie. *Tuck Everlasting.* Farrar, Straus & Giroux, 1970.

*Bond, Michael. *A Bear Called Paddington.* Illustrated by Peggy Fortnum. Houghton Mifflin, 1960.

*Browne, Anthony. *Bear Hunt.* Atheneum, 1980.

*Buscaglia, Leo. *The Fall of Freddie the Leaf.* Slack, 1982.

*Cartlidge, Michele. *The Bears' Bazaar.* Lothrop, 1980.

*DuBois, William Pene. *Bear Party.* Viking, 1951, 1963.

*Flack, Marjorie. *Ask Mr. Bear.* Macmillan, 1968.

*Freeman, Don. *Beady Bear.* Viking, 1954.

*———. *Bearymore.* Viking, 1957.

*———. *Corduroy.* Viking, 1968.

*———. *A Pocket for Corduroy.* Viking, 1978.

*Freschet, Berniece. *Bear Mouse.* Illustrated by Donald Carrick. Scribner's, 1973.

*Galdone, Paul. *The Three Bears.* Scholastic, 1973.

*George, Jean. *Julie of the Wolves.* Harper & Row, 1976.

*Hayes, Geoffrey. *Bear by Himself.* Harper & Row, 1976.

*Lobel, Arnold. *Frog and Toad Are Friends.* Harper, 1970.

*MacLachlan, Patricia. *Sarah, Plain and Tall.* Harper & Row, 1985.

*Martin, Bill. *Brown Bear, Brown Bear, What Do You See?* Holt, Rinehart & Winston, 1983.

*McPhail, David. *The Bear's Toothache.* Little, Brown, 1972.

*———. *Fix-It.* Dutton, 1984.

*Milne, A. A. *Winnie-the-Pooh.* Illustrated by Ernest H. Shepard. Dutton, 1926.

*O'Dell, Scott. *Island of the Blue Dolphins.* Dell, 1960.

*Paterson, Katherine. *Bridge to Terabithia.* Illustrated by Donna Diamond. Thomas Y. Crowell, 1977.

*Rey, H. A. *Curious George.* Houghton Mifflin, 1973.

*Sachs, Marilyn. *The Bears' House.* Illustrated by Louis Glanzman, Doubleday, 1971.

*Vincent, Gabrielle. *Ernest and Celestine.* Greenwillow, 1982.

*Waber, Bernard. *Ira Sleeps Over.* Houghton Mifflin, 1972.

*Wilder, Laura Ingalls. *Little House on the Prairie.* Illustrated by Garth Williams. Harper & Row, 1935.

Professional Resources

*Cited in text

*Commission on Reading. *Becoming a Nation of Readers: The Report of the Commission on Reading.* National Institute of Education, 1985.

Coordinating Council of the National Reading Initiative. *Celebrating the National Reading Initiative.* California State Department of Education, 1988.

*Cullinan, Bernice, ed. *Children's Literature in the Reading Program.* International Reading Association, 1987.

*———. "Whole Language and Children's Literature." *Language Arts,* 69: 426, 1992.

Fredericks, Anthony D. *Involving Parents Through Children's Literature: Grades 1–2.* Libraries Unlimited, 1992.

Fredericks, Anthony D., and Elaine LeBlanc. *Letters to Parents.* Good Year Books, 1986.

Goodman, Kenneth. *What's Whole in Whole Language?* Heinemann, 1986.

*Goodman, Kenneth, Patrick Shannon, Yvonne Freeman, and Sharon Murphy. *Report Card on Basal Readers.* Richard C. Owen, 1988.

Goodman, Yetta, Wendy H. Hood, and Kenneth S. Goodman. *Organizing for Whole Language.* Heinemann, 1991.

Hart-Hewins, Linda, and Jan Wells. *Read It in the Classroom!* Heinemann, 1992.

Hancock, Hoelie, and Susan Hill. *Literature-Based Reading Programs at Work.* Heinemann, 1988.

Hansen, Jane. *When Writers Read.* Heinemann, 1987.

*Johnson, Roger, David Johnson, and Edythe Johnson Holubec, eds. *Structuring Cooperative Learning: Lesson Plans for Teachers.* Interaction, 1987.

Pappas, Christine, Barbara Kiefer, and Linda Levstik. *An Integrated Language Perspective in the Elementary School.* Longman, 1990.

Petty, Walter, Dorothy C. Petty, and Richard T. Salzar. *Experience in Language.* Allyn & Bacon, 1989.

Routman, Regie. *Invitations.* Heinemann, 1991.

*Schweinhart, Lawrence J. "When the Buck Stops Here." *High/Scope Resources,* Fall: 1, 9–13, 1987.

*Slaughter, Helen B. "Indirect and Direct Teaching in a Whole Language Program." *The Reading Teacher,* October: 30–34, 1988.

Slavin, R. E. *Cooperative Learning: Theory, Research, and Practice.* Prentice-Hall, 1990.

*Wiseman, Ann. *Making Musical Things.* Scribner's, 1979.

The Talking Earth

JEAN CRAIGHEAD GEORGE

CHAPTER 13

Literature and the Curriculum:
A Thematic Approach

Our literature incorporates all that we are and all that we hope to be. It includes the knowledge of ages past and present and dares us to imagine the future. Literature is the perfect vehicle for making connections as we strive to understand our world and our place in it. Literature can help bridge the gap between classroom lessons and reality, adding perspective to the curriculum and giving dimension to concepts and themes.

A thematic approach combines a variety of materials, activities, and content areas to teach a specific concept, idea, or theme, thus offering a multidisciplinary as well as interdisciplinary approach to learning. And literature, no matter what the genre, adapts easily to this process.

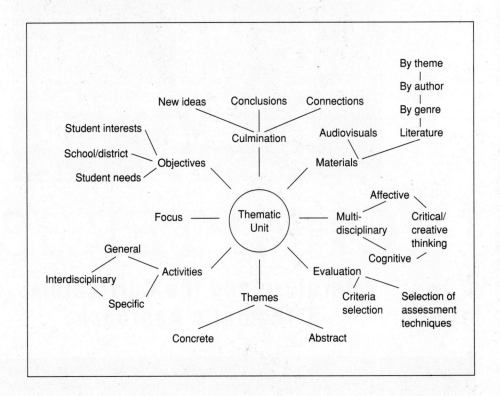

Toward a Thematic Approach

When using a thematic approach to learning, the following features should be considered and developed:

- Theme. Select an appropriate theme reflecting text topics, student interests, experiences, issues, or problems.
- Focus. Develop a one-sentence focus statement that summarizes the direction and intent of the unit.
- Objectives. Identify three or four specific objectives you wish students to master by the completion of the unit. These can be tied to state and county objectives and competencies.
- Materials and Resources. It is advantageous to determine all the necessary materials and resources after the unit has been written. This way, you avoid limiting yourself to a few familiar items.
- Initiating Activity. Introduce the unit with an activity that is highly motivational.
- General Activities. Develop activities you wish to use throughout the unit. For the most part, these activities will be broad-based, covering the range of curricular areas and reflecting elements of a literature-based program.
- Discussion Questions. Include a variety of open-ended questions that help students think about the topic in varied and divergent ways.
- Literature Selections. Select books related to the topic of each thematic unit. For literature selection you may wish to develop a prereading activity, a variety of cross-curricular learning activities, and open-ended discussion questions. Select books from a variety of genres.
- Culminating Activity. The culminating activity is a project or activity that engages students in meaningful summarization of their discoveries and leads to new ideas, understandings, and connections.
- Evaluation. Devise appropriate means of evaluating student progress throughout the unit. Avoid relying on formal pencil and paper tests; select criteria to measure growth. Use conferences, logs, and student journal writing as well.
- Related Works of Literature. Select books that relate to the theme and make these available for independent reading and reading aloud.

The following provides a more detailed description of several of these components.

Choosing a Theme

The theme can come from many sources. It's important to be open to the variety of themes that can be developed. Of course, one of the most important criteria is student interest, which is heightened when students are given an opportunity to suggest their own ideas for thematic units and activities.

A theme capable of generating a full, holistic thematic unit is usually a topic, an issue, or a problem.

Topics

Usually a thematic unit is based on a specific area of discovery in the science or social studies curriculum. Topics are often selected from the classroom textbook, but students' suggestions can also be used.

Listed below are topics that are universally taught at the designated grade levels and covered in major textbook series.

SCIENCE	SOCIAL STUDIES
Grades 1–3	*Grades 1–3*
Animals and how they grow	Neighborhoods and communities
The seasons	Transportation
Dinosaurs	Growing up
Weather	Family life
Plants and how they grow	Holidays and celebrations
Staying healthy	Sports and sportsmanship
The changing earth	Native Americans
Earth, sun, and moon	Communication
Magnetism, light, and heat	Urban and rural life
Simple machines	Citizenship
	Heroes and heroines
	Friendship
Grades 4–6	*Grades 4–6*
Systems of the body	Legacies of ancient worlds
Inventors and the inventive process	America's geography
Environment	Discovery and exploration
Oceanography	Becoming a nation
Life cycles (webs and chains)	Pioneer life
Work and energy	War and peace
Electricity, sound, and light	Multicultural understanding
The solar system	Career awareness
The changing earth	Economics
Exploring space	Leadership
	The State of . . . (individual state)

Issues

An issue is a condition or statement about which individuals take sides. Issues allow students to determine the different points of view, learn about them, and take a stand or make a point. Typically, issues come out of students' experiences or concerns, perhaps as precipitated by local or national current events. It is important that you be aware of local, statewide, national, and international issues. Listen to students talk in the halls, on the playground, and in the cafete-

Reflections of . . .

Jean Craighead George

Ever since my father asked me why the sky is blue and I found the answer after a long search, I have been a nature writer.

Nature writing is a poetic interpretation of nature with a scientific point of view. Seeing poetry in the blue sky, as does a poet, and asking questions of the sun and air, as does an empirical scientist, not only gave me the answer to Dad's question, but when I put it down on paper the effort became a piece of nature writing.

Nature writing is a new genre of literature which had its beginning in the eighteenth century, when Carlos Linneas devised his binomial system of nomenclature enabling laypeople to name plants and animals easily. Giving a name to a thing brings it to life. With names like *Vulpes fulva* (red fox) and *Quercus alba* (white oak), writers began to see a more depthful world and pursue it.

Although nature writing began in England, it flourished in wild America; John and William Bartram, Henry David Thoreau, John Burroughs, and John Muir are a few of the great innovators of nature writing. I read their books or they were read to me as a child. Then came the modern nature writers—Sally Carrighar, Rachael Carson, and Annie Dillard. I read, hiked, canoed, studied birds and animals, and wrote.

Having grown up in a scientific family, I knew well the empirical method of research and how it enhanced your point of view. I brought into my home red foxes, raccoons, crows, falcons, robins, turtles, frogs; raised them in freedom without cages; and gathered data about them. My stories and articles could be enchanting and poetic, but a fox had to walk like a fox, have young at the proper time, and eat what foxes eat. I was somewhat thrown off course when I discovered my red fox preferred ice cream to chicken, but concluded, who doesn't? I was also learning while I kept and observed my wild guests that there were "languages" among other animal species, intense emotions, and the power to reason. Some creatures were not all instinct.

When I asked primatologist C. R. Carpenter what this new knowledge meant, he said, "We are closer than we think." I agreed when my pet crow placed the lid of a coffee can on the top of the sliding board, stepped into it and did something he could do no other way—slide down the incline with my kids.

At the same time I had these pets, the field of animal behavior had come into its own. There were investigations into animal communications, cognitive activities, and senses. I lapped them up, contacted the researchers, and as I learned, my animal characters had more depth. *Julie of the Wolves, The Cry of the Crow,* and *The Talking Earth* reflected my new knowledge. The Thirteen Moons series infused animal behavior into the seasons of the moon.

Then the day came when a little girl appeared at my front door with a dead robin in her hand.

"Who murdered the robin?" she asked sadly. As I stood looking down on her bright young face, I thought back to the day my father asked me why the

(continued)

sky was blue. It was time to write an ecological mystery. Over the next seven months, *Who Really Killed Cock Robin?* clattered out of my old typewriter.

With that behind me I could see ecological mysteries everywhere—the strange disappearance of a huge alligator (*The Missing 'Gator of Gumbo Limbo*), the mystery of bugs that could not grow up, become mature, mate, and have young. What diabolical killer was that, I asked myself, tracked it down, and wrote *The Fire Bug Connection*. And so, I guess, another genre of literature was born when a little girl asked a question—the ecological mystery.

A few years ago I answered my granddaughter Rebecca's first question of nature, a real stumper from a 4-year-old: "What is winter, Grammy?" My answer—*Dear Rebecca, Winter Is Here*—is my first ecological mystery for the very young,—a picture book.

I have been to the Arctic again to write *Julie,* the sequel of *Julie of the Wolves*; I have hiked the awesome redwood forests of California to research a book about the spotted owl; and I have watched water life mysteriously appear in the manmade pond in my backyard. Nature writing is forever.

ria. What issues interest them and could be developed into a multifaceted thematic unit? That built-in interest can help ensure the success of any resultant unit, sustaining it over an extended period. Following is a list of issues that could serve as focal points for the development of thematic units.

GENERAL	SPECIFIC
Pollution	Cafeteria menus
Landfills	Shopping malls
Environment	Classroom behavior
Water quality	Homework
Chemical weapons	Allowance
Toxic wastes	Dealing with siblings
Care of the elderly	Curfews
Health care	Playground use
Air quality	Clothes made in America
Nuclear power	Shopping
Animal research	Testing and grading
Water use	Police brutality
Offshore drilling	
Waste disposal	
The economy	
Food prices	

Problems

Usually stated in the form of a question, problems typically involve matters of concern characterized by uncertainty or difficulty. The intent is for students to understand what the problem is and the various means by which it can be solved. Students should be provided with many opportunities for presenting and solving problems that have meaning for them. It is not important that students arrive at one, final answer. The goal is for them to engage in a variety of self-initiated options for investigating a problem. The processes of problem solving are infinitely more important than the products that result. Any of the following problems, posed by a class of fifth-grade students, could be developed into a thematic unit.

How can we save energy at our school?
How can we deal with the depletion of the ozone layer?
How can we feed the people of the world?
What can be done about overpopulation?
How can we prevent oil spills and other ecological disasters?
How can we save endangered wildlife?
How can we take advantage of solar power?
How can we improve the quality of the air we breathe?
How can we achieve racial harmony?
How can we take care of the homeless?
How can we ensure adequate health care for everybody?
How much aid should we give to other countries?
How can we improve our education system?

Materials and Resources

One of the distinct advantages of thematic units is that they can encompass a wide variety of materials and resources. Work to incorporate as many different kinds of learning tools as possible into your thematic units. We offer several suggestions for your consideration.

Printed Resources

What makes thematic units so dynamic is that they open up worlds of reading possibilities for students. Students can begin to understand the universality of reading through a variety of printed materials. Students can explore a topic through several media: newspapers, pamphlets, notices, travel guides, junk mail, journals, letters, maps, advertisements, brochures, flyers, encyclopedias, dictionaries, magazines, booklets, journals, and catalogs.

Audio/Visual Resources

It is important to consider including visual resources in a thematic unit. These can include videos, films, filmstrips, movies, slide programs, or overhead transparencies. Obviously, these resources can help students expand their appreciation for and understanding of a topic. (One of the best sources of videos and filmstrips in elementary science and social studies is the *Educational Services Catalog*, National Geographic Society.)

Literature Resources

Of course, the core of a thematic unit taught according to whole language philosophy consists of the books chosen for that unit. Following are some places, people, and publications that can help you select and obtain relevant children's literature.

I. Printed Resources. The following resources provide good leads for locating appropriate literature for your classroom.
    a. *Eyeopeners*, by Beverly Kobrin, is an annotated bibliography of more than 500 nonfiction books in a variety of areas. Included are activities and projects for each book as well as suggestions on how to incorporate nonfiction books effectively into any curriculum.
    b. "Outstanding Science Trade Books for Children" (National Science Teachers Association), is an annotated bibliography of the best science books of the past year. Included are write-ups on a variety of science-related books in several different areas.
    c. "Notable Children's Trade Books in the Field of Social Studies" (National Council for the Social Studies) is an annotated bibliography of the best social studies books published in the past year. Books included in this list emphasize human relations, present original themes or perspectives on traditional topics, have a pleasing format, and are highly readable.
    d. Publisher's catalogs list a panorama of children's books in science. Two of the most complete catalogs are *Literature-Based Classroom Catalog* (Scholastic) and *Master Catalog* (Perma-Bound).
    e. "Children's Choices" (International Reading Association), is a compendium of the most popular books of the past year as selected by students themselves. Each year more than 10,000 youngsters are surveyed on the fiction and nonfiction books they enjoyed most during the past year. An annotated bibliography is prepared, reprints of which can be obtained free of charge.
    f. *Science Through Children's Literature*, by Carol Butzow and John Butzow, offers several specific activities for each of 33 fiction books with science themes. Methods of extending science into other areas of the curriculum are also suggested.
    g. *Social Studies Through Children's Literature*, by Anthony D. Fredericks, provides 32 instructional units using an activity-centered approach to social studies. Both fiction and nonfiction books, along with a host of other resources, are used, and there is an extensive annotation of children's literature.

h. *Thematic Units: An Integrated Approach to Teaching Science and Social Studies,* by Anthony D. Fredericks, Anita Meinbach, and Liz Rothlein, presents designs, strategies, and implementation methods for the whole language classroom along with 28 exciting units in science and social studies that are based on use of literature.

i. *The Bookmaster,* by Donna Phillips, is a computer program that helps teachers identify children's trade books that can best supplement the science and social studies curriculum. The program is extremely user-friendly and can easily be used by students (for use on Macintosh computers).

j. *Focus Units in Literature,* by Joy F. Moss, offers 13 units, suggestions for read-aloud, sample questions for discussion, and additional activities.

k. Additional resources:
1. *A to Zoo—Subject Access to Children's Picture Books,* by Carolyn W. Lima
2. *Booklist Magazine*
3. *Children's Books in Print*
4. *Children's Literature in the Reading Program,* by Bernice Cullinan
5. *Fiction, Folklore, Fantasy, and Poetry for Children,* by S. S. Dreyer
6. *BookLinks*
7. *Best Books for Children: Preschool Through the Middle Grades,* by J. T. Gillespie and C. B. Gilbert
8. *A Critical Handbook of Children's Literature,* by Rebecca Lukens
9. *Adventuring with Books: A Booklist for pre-K to Grade 6,* by Diane Monson
10. *Through the Eyes of a Child: An Introduction to Children's Literature,* by Donna Norton
11. *Children's Literature from A to Z: A Guide for Parents and Teacher,* by J. C. Stott
12. *The Scott, Foresman Anthology of Children's Literature,* by Zena Sutherland and Myra Cohn Livingston
13. *The New Read-Aloud Handbook,* by Jim Trelease
14. *The WEB: Wonderfully Exciting Books*
15. *Children and Books,* by Zena Sutherland and May Hill Arbuthnot
16. *Literature for the Young Child,* by Eileen M. Burke
17. *The Bookfinder,* by Sharon S. Dreyer (American Guidance Services, 1990).

II. *Librarians.* School and public librarians can provide invaluable information on fiction and nonfiction books, keeping you up-to-date on some of the latest releases in children's literature.

III. *Book Clubs.* Several book clubs provide various kinds of books (often at very inexpensive prices) for students. Many of the clubs have incentive programs by which, after students have purchased a requisite number of books, the students or their teachers are entitled to a selection of free books for the classroom library. Four of the most popular book clubs are: Scholastic Book Clubs, Troll Book Club, The Trumpet Club, and Weekly Reader Paperback Clubs.

IV. *Neighborhood Sources.* One of the easiest ways to obtain books for the classroom is to shop at garage sales, yard sales, and neighborhood flea markets.

The sources for trade books are unlimited. Taking advantage of the variety of books available and the number of places they can be obtained is a significant factor in the creation of successful thematic units.

Community Resources

Students see thematic units as positive extensions of traditional learning that expand their learning arena far beyond the confines of the classroom. When teachers incorporate local community resources into thematic units, they give their students learning opportunities that far exceed what any textbook or curriculum guide can provide. Two types of community resources to consider in the development of thematic units are guest speakers and field trip sites.

Guest Speakers

People in the local community can add immeasurably to the effectiveness of a thematic unit. Besides sharing a wealth of experiences with students, community people can demonstrate to students that science and social studies are parts of their daily lives that can be shared and enjoyed by all. Inviting people from the local community to share their experiences with the class makes literature come alive for students by underscoring its practical applications.

The following are possible guest presenters to consider as resources for selected thematic units:

Doctors	4-H club leaders
Local authors	Early inhabitants of the community
Shop/store owners	Nurses
People with unusual hobbies	Travelers
College professors	Exchange students
Newspaper reporters	Roofers
County agents	Train conductors
Environmental group leaders	Engineers
Representatives of local industries	Community workers
Commercial pilots	Pharmacists
Sanitation workers	Electricians
High school science teachers	College students
Park rangers	Veterinarians
Plumbers	High school students
Astronomers	Musicians
Computer operators	Gardeners
Zoologists	Environmentalists

TV meteorologists
Ecologists
Farmers
Construction workers
Cooks
Bakers
Carpenters
Artists
Pet store owners
Masons
Restauranteurs

Factory workers
Medical laboratory workers
Biologists
Butchers
Auto mechanics
Dieticians
Landscapers
Architects
Weavers
Tree surgeons
Chefs

Field Trips

Field trips are marvelous opportunities for students to see how elements of a thematic unit apply to the real world. In addition, field trips can enhance specific aspects of certain literature selections, providing students with important extensions of concepts learned in the pages of a book.

Though the possibilities are innumerable, here are some sites to consider visiting:

Factories
Colleges
Recreational places
Airports
Museums
Theaters
Zoos
Planetariums
Graveyards
Libraries
Nature trails
Backyard of the school
Sports arenas
Beaches
Farms
Aquariums
Post offices
Nursing homes
Radio/TV stations
Fast-food restaurants
Amusement parks
Flea markets
Fire/police stations
Shipyards
Wildlife sanctuaries
Parks

Lakes
Churches/synagogues
Mortuaries
Historical sites
Airports
Natural history museums
Lumberyards
Retirement centers
Power stations
Music stores
Supermarkets
Hospitals
Power plants
Ethnic restaurants
Greenhouses
Hardware stores
Department stores
Banks
Sanitation areas
Caves
Orchestra halls
Fish hatcheries
SPCA offices
Train stations
Newspaper offices
Garden centers

Drug stores   Machine shops
Festivals   Quarries
Printers   Service stations
Recycling centers   Historical societies

Activites

The crux of any thematic unit is the selection of a wide variety of meaningful activities. The possibilities are innumerable. We believe the selection of activities should be dictated by three major criteria:

1. Activities should be holistic in nature. That is, they should incorporate the tenets of whole language, challenging students to use reading, writing, speaking, and listening skills. Filling in the blanks on a commercial worksheet is not an appropriate activity; designing a questionnaire, interviewing selected community workers, and tabulating the data is an appropriate activity.
2. Activities should be "hands-on—minds-on." Any activity in a thematic unit should allow students to manipulate data or information with their hands as well as their minds.
3. Above all, activities should be meaningful and reflect student needs and interests. Activities based on works of literature should take students back into the books, as they analyze, synthesize, evaluate, solve problems, and make connections.

The activities fall into one of the following categories:

1. Initiating Activity. This is usually a single activity designed to "kick off" the thematic unit. The activity should alert students to some of the components of the unit, tap into their background experiences, and motivate their participation in the unit.
2. General Activities. The variety of these activities should provide a broad-based experience with the theme and address its major topics. These activities should be cross-curricular, designed to last various periods of time. It is appropriate to offer a selection of short-term projects (lasting less than one day), mid-term projects (lasting two or three days), and long-term projects (lasting one week or longer).
3. Literature-Specific Activities. These are the activities designed specifically for identified books in the thematic unit. Included with each literature selection should be a prereading activity (designed to alert students to some of the elements of a book and tap into their prior knowledge), writing activities (in which students record ideas, thoughts, responses, or extensions of a book), a variety of learning activities that tie the book into various areas of the curriculum, and appropriate questions.
4. Culminating Activity. The culminating activity should be a project or series of activities that gives students a meaningful format in which to sum-

marize their discoveries. The intent is for students to design and develop a product synthesizing their experiences with the general topic.

Topics for activities can be generated as students create webs based on a selected idea, concept, or theme. Webbing creates a framework for the integration of content areas and encourages students to use their own creativity, imagination, and interests to shape the curriculum. The topics and subtopics generated from this exercise can serve as a springboard to readings in a variety of genres and can aid in the planning of activities and research (both teacher- and student-directed) that enhance growth in the cognitive and affective domains. The following steps will help you and your students create a web, such as the one on page 453

(text continues on page 421)

A Centennial Tribute to Lois Lenski

Sam Leaton Sebesta

In the mid-1950s I taught fourth grade in Salina, Kansas, in a school where many of the children were called deprived and later labeled underprivileged and even later disadvantaged and then at-risk. I'd say the same of our textbooks, especially of the social studies textbook. It had the title *Human Use Geography,* as I recall, but my students and I never found anything human in it. It divided the United States into regions. Then it named major crops and industries and gave a passing nod to rivers and cities. Years later, when I met one of my former students, who was now 40, I asked him if he remembered anything from *Human Use Geography* and he said, "Yes. I remember that Kansas was lavender. I wondered about that all year."

In about November of that first year of teaching fourth grade, I stumbled on the classroom library. It was on the floor of the supply closet under the shelf for putting overshoes. Among the classroom library books was *Strawberry Girl,* by Lois Lenski. The teacher next door told me that it had won a prize. So I took it out and discovered that it was about Florida, which was in one of the regions we were attempting to study in *Human Use Geography.*

The next afternoon we laid aside *Human Use Geography* and I began reading *Strawberry Girl* aloud to my fourth-graders. It started with the Slaters's cow damaging the orange trees that belonged to a new family called the Boyers. Right off, it was clear that the Boyers and the Slaters weren't going to get along. The Slaters didn't like fences or selling things. Mrs. Slater said, "Why, nothin' won't grow here in Floridy." We knew she was wrong. *Human Use Geography* had told us that lots of things were grown and sold in Florida. We spent most of the afternoon finding out what the Boyers were going to do about those Slaters, the Florida crackers who cut down fences and let their pigs destroy the Boyers's strawberries. At the end we were satisfied, sort of. The Slaters were going to sell out and work for the phosphate company. But we felt sorry for their son, Shoestring. He seemed to be coming around to the Boyers's way of thinking. We were sorry the book ended there where it did.

(continued)

I went to the city library and found other regional stories by Lois Lenski. We read *Boom Town Boy* and *Cotton in My Sack*. By the time we reached *Prairie School* we were very fond of Lois Lenski, but here she disappointed us. *Prairie School* has a tornado at the beginning and it doesn't do anything. Now, it so happened that this was the year when a tornado hit Salina, Kansas. We had all crouched in the school basement while it tore down a trailer park on the other side of town. We felt that Lois Lenski hadn't taken her tornado seriously enough. We had a notion to write to her to straighten her out. I wish we had, but today I remember the incident because it shows the personal involvement children may have with an author they have never met.

Lois Lenski recognized the value of children's interests. She was a teacher at heart and she wanted to impart information. But she knew what many education professors and textbook writers still do not know today: that young people will learn what interests them and pass unseeingly by whatever does not interest them. So Lenski, the clever teacher, found ways to make information interesting.

Consider her visual art. She began as an artist who illustrated other authors' books. When she came to illustrating her own, with *Skipping Village* in 1927, she had developed a firm drawing and drafting style that showed precisely the actions and settings described in her text. *Skipping Village* is nostalgic and idyllic. Its 17 chapters take us through a year in a small town called Greenhill when, at least in retrospect, life seemed stable and perfect. It is a long book filled with mild incidents, but we are made willing visitors by drawings that show every activity on Greenhill's nameless streets. Today the book might be called an ethnography for its vivid visual detail.

Lenski's visual art dominates the Mr. Small books. Compare them with some of today's nonfiction for young children. They are less elaborate. They have no color plates, no fold-outs, no pop-ups. But they are not simple. *The Little Train* is man-to-man (well, we now say person-to-person) about diagraming and naming the parts on a train engine and how to get coal from the coal hopper to the tender. *The Little Fire Engine* is no simplified toy but a real one right down to the pump controls and a nozzle with two handles. Lenski was not alone in this precision. There were other authors and illustrators who led the way out of the chug-chug putt-putt choo-choo school to a more realistic, complex literature for early childhood. But Lenski was one of the forerunners.

There is something about Lois Lenski that defies categorization. After all, she wrote and illustrated about 90 books. There are the Mr. Small books and the Davy books, which I would call nonfiction for early childhood, although the card catalog classifies them differently. There are seven historical novels for young people. I approached these with wonder. I'd never heard anyone refer to them, yet there they were, taking up a substantial part of the shelf. Some of them are between 300 and 400 pages long. There are the Regional America books—15 of them by my count—for which Lenski is probably best remembered. And there are the Roundabout America books, for which I have a special fondness because they are in simple language that almost all of my fourth-graders could read. There are poetry collections, a Bible story, an al-

(continued)

phabet book, and Christmas stories. Truly, Lois Lenski was the Balzac of children's literature. She wouldn't stop until she'd covered the whole gamut of childhood and her homeland.

In all these works, Lenski's drawings, large and small, give credibility: "See," they say, "this is how it looked." They give specificity. The specifics are most important in the historical and regional stories, because without them children would be at a loss. Lois Lenski knew this. Her full-page drawings and double-page spreads are packed with detail matched to text. But even more helpful are the small insets: for example, a miniature sketch of a New Hampshire commercial shop in 1732 in the first chapter of *Ocean-Born Mary* and a generous number of quarter-page sketches to anchor the action and setting in *Strawberry Girl. My fourth-graders culd not read the Regional America books by themselves, but they poured over the drawings, absorbing information.*

There is an amazing amount of research behind the Lenski books. That, in itself, does not ensure literary distinction. Each year brings books intended for young readers by authors who know their subject well but do not know how to make it interesting. They might take as their model Lois Lenski's Indian Captive: The Story of Mary Jemison, a book that would still fascinate upper-grade children lucky enough to run across it and that still is praised by anthropologists for its rich detail about eighteenth-century Senecan culture. It is based on a true account: two years in the life of a blond child of European descent who was kidnapped by the Senecas, never to return to her own people. How does Lenski manage this story without resorting to stereotypes, never savaging or sentimentalizing Native American life but showing the child's gradual assimilation? How does she provide all the necessary background, drawn from research that includes diverse customs and settings and even the Senecan language, without once failing to move the action forward? *Indian Captive* is a classic that needs to be rediscovered.

The Regional America books and the easier Roundabout America series are based on research too, this time on-site research of the kind highly valued by modern anthropologists and ethnographers. The accountsf of Lois Lenski's travels and how she became absorbed into the regional families she wrote about are numerous and inspiring. What other author has written 90 books, each oned based on a different sphere of documental or on-site research?

Pay tribute to Lenski's plotting. In the Lois Lenski collection at the University of North Carolina is a single handwritten page wherein Lenski outlined her first regional story, *Bayou Suzette.* It contains a main idea, the main scenes, and a surprise ending. The outline gives a clue to Lenski's unity, the drive shaft she used to kee the plot moving from first page to last: for example, the conflict between two families in *Strawberry Girl,* the isolation of *Indian Captive,* and the poverty and ill-treatment by bosses in *Cotton in My Sack.*

Lenski was also a master of subplots. She knew that children require briefer problems and solutions as they read. They won't postpone all their interest in outcome from page 1 to page 200. In *Blueberry Corners,* for example, the main plot is a struggle in mid-nineteenth-century Connecticut between Puritans and materialism. One subplot shows this struggle in microcosm:

(continued)

Becky, the daughter of a parson, wants a blue muslin delaine gown but she doesn't get one. Instead, she is given a plain, severe linsey woolen gown. What will happen? Will she learn that her wish is foolish or will her wish eventually be granted? Lenski lets her readers wonder as the major plot brings resolution. The same book, *Blueberry Corners,* demonstrates Lenski's gift for vignette. Brief incidents bring young readers satisfaction, a whole incident tucked into two or three pages. On page 20 a small sister disappears on a trip to town, to be found one page later in a pool of molasses—she'd been too curious about what the hogshead barrel contained. Sometimes these vignettes have the quality of folk tale. In *Blueberry Corners* a pet horse pretends to go lame when someone steals him so the thief will bring him back. But the horse does his own bit of thievery: he puts his head through the kitchen window and consumes a whole plate of sugared doughnuts. Lois Lenski's books are alive with these small incidents—subplots and vignettes. They came from her vast research, her planning, and her knowledge that children need constant payoff as they read. Her imagery is vivid. She can show you a Yorkshire hog in *Corn-Farm Boy* "so old she's got three wrinkles across her nose." The alligator blocking the corduroy road in *Strawberry Girl* "rose up on his feet, kept his head turned toward the intruders, and his mouth partly open. He lifted his tail to one-half his length, ready to flay an unwelcome visitor. . . ."

Now we come to a problem: Lenski's critics. In her own day some of them thought her books were "too grimly realistic." Ironically, some modern commentators think the opposite. They find her plots, subplots, and vignettes too genteel for her regional or historical topics. Apparently, you can't win.

There's a story about Lenski that sheds some light on the matter. In the 1950s Connecticut was flooded and Lenski wanted to write a book about children in the flood. But at first she backed off, saying that the topic was too tragic for a chiodren's book. Eventually she changed her mind and wrote *Flood Friday,* but her concern remained. From first to last, there is a struggle in tone in the Lenski books. We want them to be happy, to prove to children that life in any time and region can be a joyful experience. But we want them to be credible. We want them to be honest.

In her first notable book, *Skipping Village,* everyone is breezy and happy, give or take a couple of isolates. But wait! Midway through the book Polly James, the eight-year-old central character, catches pneumonia and almost dies. Her suffering is downplayed, to be sure, and it is only through the headshaking and handwringing of the adults that the seriousness is portrayed. But it's there.

In *Indian Captive* the tone is many shades darker throughout, and there is a scene (or perhaps a lack of one) that shows Lenski's struggle with grim realism. A young man is forced to run the gauntlet as Mary Jemison, the Indian captive, watches. Apparently, the gauntlet consists of two lines of Senecan warriors who lash out at the young man with their weapons. To prove his mettle, he must complete the run. Lenski skirts over the incident but shows its aftermath. The young man nearly bleeds to death and is saved only by the ministrations of the Indian women.

Poverty, illness, and physical abuse are all present in the regional stories

(continued)

but outcomes are usually hopeful. Lenski's tone usually says, "See? These are things you can overcome." Still, there are exceptions, particularly in the latter part of Lenski's career. In the accident near the conclusion of *Peanuts for Billy Ben*, published in 1952, the hero is crushed beneath several hundred-pound bags of peanuts. His father says, "That's all I've been thinking about—my good big crop! I forgot my little boy—my little boy." Billy's three months in the hospital cost the family all their profits, and there the book ends. At least two of the other regional stories of the 1950s, *We Live in the South* and *Corn-Fed Boy*, feature children with incurable physical conditions.

I mention this dilemma in Lenski's realism because of its relevance today. How many times I have heard a colleague or student say, "This book is not suitable for children!" Lois Lenski encountered but did not solve that issue.

In summary, Lois Lenski wrote a lifetime about rural, small-community America in its many times and places. She drew upon primary sources. She thus contributes to our sense of tradition, our Americana. Her central characters are all children, showing that children and childhood may play central roles in the drama of life. She exemplified ways to make local color literature interesting while informative. Many modern writers of children's realistic fiction and nonfiction owe their craft to Lois Lenski's model.

Will her work continue to be read? Will there be a Lenski Bicentennial in 2093 A.D. to celebrate her continuing readership? I checked to see if her works are listed in the current edition of *Children's Books in Print*. I found the Mr. Small books and picture book editions of two Lenski poems. The historical novels, the Roundabout America series, and the Regional America books are, with one exception, out of print. The one exception is *Strawberry Girl*, showing once again the staying power of the Newbery Award.

I checked libraries and grew more hopeful. In libraries many Lenski books still are available. Quite a few are checked out. Those found on the shelves look as though they've been busy. I know that more often than in the past, children rely on adults to guide them in choosing what to read. I know, too, that modern children have an increased need to share their literary experience with their peers and adults. So I hope that not too far away fourth-graders and their teachers are laying aside their *Human Use Geography* or its modern manifestation in order to spend a pleasant, informative afternoon with Lois Lenski.

1. Determine the idea, concept, or theme to be explored.
2. Display a variety of materials related to the idea, concept, or theme and allow time for students to peruse the materials.
3. Write the idea, concept, or theme in the middle of a large piece of chart paper or the chalkboard.
4. Involve students in a brainstorming session, as they call out words related to the central term.
5. Write down the words generated and connect them to the central term, attempting to arrange words (topics and subtopics) under appropriate head-

ings. Arrange and rearrange the words and continue brainstorming until the web reflects all possible ideas.

6. Copy the web onto a piece of butcher paper or chart paper and display it so students can refer to it from time to time.

Thematic Units

This section contains sample thematic units developed to illustrate how literature can be used to supplement and enhance units of study. Two primary themes and two intermediate themes are included. At each level, one theme generally classified as social studies and one theme generally classified as science are described; however, the units are multidisciplinary in nature. The activities section has two parts: the general activities can be completed without the use of any particular book, while the specific activities are designed to be used with designated books or books of a specific genre. The activities section helps develop the unit objectives and guides students as they explore the focus of the theme. When developing your own thematic units, remember to take into account your own students' needs, interests, and motivation in selecting literature and planning the unit. The following provide a format to help you design your own thematic units.

THEMATIC UNIT PLAN SHEET

Theme/Topic: _____

Focus: _____

Objectives: (select three to four significant objectives)
1. _____
2. _____
3. _____
4. _____

Materials and Resources:
1. _____
2. _____
3. _____
4. _____
5. _____

Initiating Activity:
_____
_____

General Activities:
1. _____
2. _____
3. _____
4. _____
5. _____
6. _____

Discussion Questions:
1. _____
2. _____
3. _____
4. _____
5. _____
6. _____

Culminating Activity:
_____
_____
_____

Evaluation Techniques:

1. _____
2. _____
3. _____
4. _____

Related Works of Literature
1. _____
2. _____
3. _____
4. _____
5. _____
6. _____

Literature Specific Activities
(complete for each book used)

Title: _____

Author: _____

Prereading Activity: _____
_____
_____

Activities Related to Book:
1. _____
2. _____
3. _____

Questions Related to Book:
1. _____
2. _____
3. _____
_____
_____

Primary Level (Social Studies)

Theme: China

Focus: Students will become familiar with Chinese culture by learning about the customs, foods, language, literature, art, and so forth.

Objectives: On completion of this thematic unit, students will:

1. Be familiar with a variety of Chinese foods
2. Create Chinese characters to represent words such as *one, two, three, up, down*
3. Locate China on a world map
4. Describe some similarities and differences between Chinese literature and American literature
5. Be familiar with many Chinese customs
6. Describe the differences and similarities between the architecture of Chinese homes and of American homes
7. Speak a few words in Chinese by being able to sing "Happy Birthday" in Chinese
8. Be familiar with Chinese cooking and eating utensils

Materials

1. Abacus
2. Collection of books relating to China (see Related Literature, (pages 431–432)
3. Cardboard and scissors for a tangram
4. Menu from a Chinese restaurant
5. Wok
6. Selection of vegetables
7. Student copies of the following: *Tikki Tikki Tembo,* by Arlene Mosel; The *Weaving of a Dream,* by Marilee Heyer; *Passport to China,* by Stephen Keeler
8. Variety of Chinese foods
9. Chopsticks
10. Art materials for a Chinese dragon: paper, tissue paper, glue, crayons, markers
11. Samples of rice foods
12. Pictures of brocades
13. Large map of the world

Initiating Activity

Write *China* on the chalkboard. Ask the students to illustrate or write sentences or phrases about what they know about China. Allow 15 minutes for this activity. Then organize the students into small groups and allow them to share their information.

General Activities

It is not necessary, nor is it suggested, to use all of these activities. They are intended as a guide to illustrate the scope of activities that can be developed. Selection should be based on student needs, interests, and objectives.

1. Although the Chinese language is written in the same way throughout China, it is spoken in many different ways. Recently, the People's Republic of China declared Mandarin Chinese the official language. Teach the students to sing "Happy Birthday" in Chinese to help them better understand what the Chinese language is like.

    Happy Birthday

    (Zuni Shenri)

    English words: Hap py birth day to you

    Pinyin (system for writing Chinese words in English):

       Zhu ni   Sheng ri   kuai le

    English sounds: joo nee shung rr kwai leh

2. Most classrooms have an abacus. Show the abacus to the students and point out that this tool was created by the ancient Chinese to add, subtract, multiply, divide, and calculate square and cube roots. If you haven't taught them how to use the abacus, demonstrate it. Provide time for students to experiment with the abacus.

3. The Chinese do not have a written alphabet to form words like the English alphabet. Instead, they use a character (called *zi* in Chinese) to represent a word or idea. For example, the characters in the box below represent the

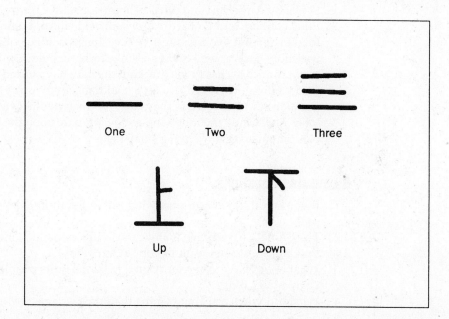

English words indicated. Obtain copies of *Chinese Writing: An Introduction*, by Diane Wolff, or *Chinese Calligraphy*, by Chiang Yee, to help students investigate the art of Chinese writing in greater depth.

4. Every country seems to have its own versions of popular folk tales and nursery rhymes. In China, for example, there is *Yeh-Shen, A Cinderella Story from China*, in which Yeh-Shen (Cinderella) wishes for pretty clothes to wear to a festival. Her stepmother has killed her magical fish, so Yeh-Shen wishes on the bones of the fish for pretty clothes. Suddenly, she is dressed in beautiful gold and feathers, and she goes to the festival. As she hurries from the festival, she leaves her golden slipper. A wealthy merchant finds the slipper and marries Yeh-Shen. Her wicked stepmother and stepsister are buried beneath an avalanche of heavy stones. Read other Chinese folk tales, such as *The Fox That Wanted Nine Golden Tales*, by Mary Knight, or Diane Wolkstein's *8,000 Stones: A Chinese Folktale* and *The Magic Wings*. Use books such as Robert Wyndham's beautifully illustrated *Chinese Mother Goose Rhymes*, which has Chinese calligraphy decorating the borders of the pages, and Ray Wood's *The American Mother Goose* to compare and contrast the Chinese and American versions of these rhymes.

5. The Chinese developed the tangram, a puzzle with only seven pieces that is used to make pictures of birds, fish, houses, and many other things. Provide pieces of cardboard and enlarged pieces of the puzzle (see the following tangram; tangrams are also available commercially). Allow time for each student to trace the puzzle's pattern pieces on the cardboard and cut them out. Then ask the students to create a design, using the tangram puzzle pieces. Share these designs.

6. Many people enjoy Chinese food. Using books such as *Chinese Food and Drink*, by Amy Shui and Stuart Thompson, and *Creative Wok Cooking*, by Ethel Graham and Richard Ahrens, provide information about Chinese food in general, food and festive occasions, cooking equipment, how to use chopsticks, and so on. If possible, bring in menus from Chinese restaurants. Discuss foods the students may have tasted that are considered Chinese. Then prepare for a cooking activity using a wok. Woks are popular in China because they cook food very quickly and do not use a lot of fuel. Using the following recipe, prepare enough stir-fried vegetables that everyone will get a small taste.

Discussion Questions

1. If you could travel to China, what is the first thing you would want to see?
2. The Chinese have made many contributions to the world. Which contribution is most important to you? Why?
3. What books have you read related to China or its people? Which did you enjoy most? Why?
4. What did you learn about China that most surprised you?

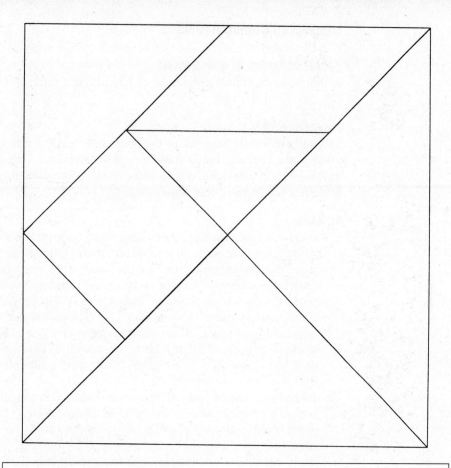

STIR-FRIED VEGETABLES

4 tablespoons vegetable oil
2 cloves garlic
6 cups vegetables (green beans, broccoli, mushrooms, pea pods, bean sprouts, Chinese celery, cabbage, etc.)
1 cup chicken broth
1 teaspoon salt
1 teaspoon sugar
2 teaspoons cornstarch in 2 tablespoons cold water

Heat oil in the wok. Brown and discard the garlic. Stir-fry the vegetables for three minutes. Add the chicken broth, salt, and sugar. Cover and steam over moderate heat for three minutes or until the vegetables are tender, but still bright and crisp. Stir the cornstarch mixture and add it to the wok. Cook, stirring, until the sauce thickens. Serve at once.

Literature-Specific Activities

Tikki Tikki Tembo, by Arlene Mosel

A charming folk tale that tells about Tikki Tikki Tembo and how his long name almost cost him his life.

Prereading Activity

Show the children the cover of the book and read the title to them. Then write Tikki Tikki Tembo's entire name on the chalkboard. Discuss why they think anyone would have such a long name. Ask them to share their full names and how they might have been shortened.

Activities

1. Tikki Tikki Tembo had a very long name because it was the custom in China many years ago to give the firstborn and honored sons long names. Have the students find out how the names they were given were decided. On a large piece of chart paper, write each student's name and a brief explanation of how he or she got this name. When complete, this could become a newspaper, "How We Got Our Names," which could be duplicated and sent home. As an addition to or variation of this activity, ask the students to find out what their name means. For example, *Tikki tikki tembo-no sa rembo-chari bari ruchi-pip peri pembo* means "the most wonderful thing in the whole wide world."

2. Tikki Tikki Tembo and Chang ate rice cakes. Discuss other foods that are typically Chinese. Make a list of these foods. Discuss who in the class has eaten these foods and who has not. Obtain a variety of foods from a Chinese restaurant and have a tasting party. Include egg rolls, wonton soup, chow mein, Chinese noodles, and fortune cookies. Have the children experiment with chopsticks.

3. One of the illustrations in *Tikki Tikki Tembo* is a picture of the Chinese Dragon, which symbolizes good fortune, strength, and wisdom and is present at most celebrations, especially at the New Year's parade. It is believed to keep the evil spirits away for the coming year. Provide students with a large sheet of paper, scraps of tissue paper, glue, crayons, markers, and so on. Ask them to create their own Chinese Dragon.

4. Show the students the illustrations depicting Tikki Tikki Tembo's house and other houses in his village. Discuss how these houses are similar to and different from the houses in which the students live.

5. Write *Tikki tikki tembo-no sa rembo-chari bari ruchi-pip peri pembo* on the chalkboard. Develop a pencil (or chopstick) tapping rhythm to accompany this name. As the story is read aloud, have the students tap out this rhythm each time you read his name.

6. Parts of the story about Tikki Tikki Tembo were real or could actually have happened, but some of what happened was make-believe. After you finish reading the story, discuss the concepts of real and make-believe. On

the chalkboard, make a list of those things the students believe could have happened and those that were make-believe.

7. Tikki Tikki Tembo and his brother Chang were eating rice cakes as they stood by the well. Rice is very popular in China. Make a list of all the different products or dishes the students have eaten that are made with or from rice (e.g., rice pudding, rice cereal). If possible, have students bring in samples of rice foods for a "rice day" tasting party.

Discussion Questions

1. Do you think Tikki Tikki Tembo's original name was a good one? Why or why not?
2. How do you think Tikki Tikki Tembo's brother, Chang, felt about having such a short name?
3. Tikki Tikki Tembo's name almost cost him his life. What other disadvantages are there to having such a long name?
4. At the end of the book it says, "And from that day to this the Chinese have always thought it wise to give all their children little, short names instead of great, long names." Do you believe this custom was inspired by Tikki Tikki Tembo? Explain.

The Weaving of a Dream, by Marilee Heyer

A classic tale of love, loyalty, greed, and envy. It is based on an ancient Chinese legend. Using this book, select appropriate activities for your students from the following.

Prereading Activity

Ask the students to discuss some of their dreams and illustrate one of them. On completion of the story, compare illustrations.

Activities

1. The widow thought the best life for her would be living in a beautiful palace like the one she saw in the painting. Using large sheets of paper, have the students create a picture of their dream place.
2. Display pictures of brocades or bring in a real one. Ask students to draw a pattern for a brocade they would like to have.
3. Discuss the students' feelings toward the two sons, Leme and Letuie, who took the box of gold and went to the big city instead of returning home. Make a list of adjectives on the chalkboard describing these two boys: greedy, selfish. Next, ask the students to describe their feelings about Leje, the son who returned the brocade to his mother. Make another list on the chalkboard of words describing Leje: caring, loyal. Finally, discuss these descriptive words and have the children prioritize the qualities based on which they feel are most important for a friend to possess. Have the students also determine which is the most undesirable trait for a friend to possess.

4. *The Weaving of a Dream* is a folk tale based on an ancient Chinese legend. Read other Chinese legends. For example, Jeanne Lee's *Legend of the Li River* explains the mysteries of nature, such as the magical hills that line the Li River. Her *Legend of the Milky Way* provides an ancient Chinese explanation for the phenomenon of the galaxy. Have the class write a folk tale based on one of the legends they like best.

Discussion Questions

1. Leje gave his mother the idea to do a weaving of the painting. Was this a good idea? Explain.
2. If you met the first two sons, what would you say to them about taking the gold from the fortuneteller instead of helping their mother?
3. Leme and Letuie, the first two brothers, return to their home to find a beautiful palace and garden instead of their hut. How did they react to this? Why didn't they talk to their mother and Leje who were sitting in the garden?

Passport to China, by Stephen Keeler

A nonfiction book that provides the reader with a complete, in-depth understanding of life in China and its role in today's world.

Prereading Activity

Locate China on a world map. Engage students in a discussion about China. What have they read in the paper about China? What customs, foods, and holidays are they familiar with?

Activities

1. Divide the topics presented in the table of contents—people, pastimes and sports, transportation—among the students. Ask them to research their assigned topic based on the community in which they live. Next, ask them to write the information in a brief, concise manner, illustrating or inserting photographs whenever possible. When all students have completed this assignment, develop a table of contents and put it together as a book, "A Passport to (the name of your community)."
2. After studying the information in *Passport to China,* ask students to identify one thing they like about China and one thing they do not like. Discuss reasons for their likes and dislikes.
3. China is the world's third largest country; as a result, there are big differences, depending on where you are, in weather, vegetation, population, and so on. After looking at the maps and pictures in this book, ask the students to select an area of China they would most like to visit and tell why they selected it.
4. The following Chinese traditions, customs, or rules are very different from those in the United States. Discuss each one to determine its advantages and disadvantages.

   a. People do not own their own homes.
   b. The government offers generous benefits to couples who have only one child and penalizes couples who have more than one.
   c. It is common for three generations of a family (grandparents, parents, and children) to live in the same house, which is usually very small.
   d. There are almost no privately owned cars. Until recently, owning a car was not allowed.

Discussion Questions
   1. Compare life in China with life in the United States.
   2. In which country would you prefer to live? Why?
   3. What is the most interesting fact you learned about China?
   4. If you could adopt one Chinese custom, which would you select?

Culminating Activity
Hold an "Images of China" day, on which students create skits, pantomimes, and demonstrations to describe their favorite Chinese customs or legends.

Evaluation
The final culminating product can be evaluated according to the following criteria:

   1. Does it reflect an understanding of China's culture and legends?
   2. Does it allow viewers to gain a better understanding of China's culture and legends?
   3. Does the content of the project illustrate the differences and similarities between Chinese and American cultures and legends?
   4. Does the project show creativity?

Related Literature

*Cited in text

Fiction

Birdeye, Tom. *A Song of Stars: An Asian Legend.* Illustrated by Ju-Hong Chen. Holiday, 1990.

Bishop, Claire Huchet. *The Five Chinese Brothers.* Illustrated by Kurt Weise. Scholastic, 1938.

Demi. *The Empty Pot.* Holt, 1990.

*Heyer, Marilee. *The Weaving of a Dream.* Viking Kestrel, 1986.

Jensen, Helen Zane. *When Panda Comes to Our House.* Dial, 1985.

Kendall, Carol. *The Wedding of the Rat Family.* Illustrated by James Watt. McElderry, 1988.

*Knight, Mary. *The Fox That Wanted Nine Tails.* Illustrated by Brigitte Bryan. Macmillan, 1969.

Leaf, Margaret. *Eyes of the Dragon.* Illustrated by Ed Young. Lothrop, 1987.

*Lee, Jeanne. *Legend of the Li River.* Holt, Rinehart & Winston, 1983.

*————. *Legend of the Milky Way*. Holt, Rinehart & Winston, 1982.
*Louie, Ai-Ling. *Yeh-Shen: A Cinderella Story from China*. Illustrated by Ed Young. Philomel, 1982.
Mahy, Margaret. *The Seven Chinese Brothers*. Illustrated by Jean and Mou-Sien Tseng. Scholastic, 1990.
*Mosel, Arlene. *Tikki Tikki Tembo*. Illustrated by Blair Lent. Holt, Rinehart & Winston, 1968.
Wang, Rosalind C. *The Fourth Question: A Chinese Tale*. Illustrated by Ju-Hong Chen. Holiday, 1991.
*Wolkstein, Diane. *The Magic Wings: A Tale from China*. Illustrated by Robert Andrew Parker. Dutton, 1983.
*————. *8,000 Stones: A Chinese Folktale*. Illustrated by Ed Young. Doubleday, 1972.
*Wood, Ray. *The American Mother Goose*. Illustrated by Ed Hargis. Lippincott, 1940.
*Wyndham, Robert, comp. *Chinese Mother Goose Rhymes*. Illustrated by Ed Young. World, 1968.
Young, Ed. *Lon Po Po: A Red Riding Hood Story from China*. Philomel, 1989.

Informational Books

*Graham, Ethel, and Richard Ahrens. *Creative Wok Cooking*. Ottenheimer, 1976.
*Keeler, Stephen. *Passport to China*. Watts, 1987.
Sadler, Catherine Edwards. *Two Chinese Families*. Photographs by Alan Sadler. Atheneum, 1981.
*Shui, Amy, and Stuart Thompson. *Chinese Food and Drink*. Bookwright, 1987.
*Wolff, Diane. *Chinese Writing: An Introduction*. Holt, Rinehart & Winston, 1975.
*Yee, Chiang. *Chinese Calligraphy*, rev. ed. Harvard University Press, 1973.

Primary Level (Science)

Theme: Dinosaurs

Focus: Students will explore prehistoric times to expand their knowledge of dinosaurs.

Objectives: On completion of this thematic unit, students will:

1. Know the names of at least ten dinosaurs
2. Distinguish between plant-eating dinosaurs and meat-eating dinosaurs
3. Understand how scientists know as much as they do about dinosaurs
4. Know when dinosaurs lived
5. Identify dinosaurs that lived on land versus prehistoric creatures that lived in the sea or flew in the air
6. Compare various sizes, weights, and body shapes of dinosaurs

Materials

1. *Science Adventures: Dinosaurs,* by Kayne Quinn and Jan Hutchings
2. Plastic dinosaur figures
3. Clay for making dinosaur models
4. Dinosaur model sets (available in most toy stores)
5. Chicken or turkey bones
6. Collection of books relating to dinosaurs (see Related Literature at the end of this section)
7. Student copies of the following: *If the Dinosaurs Came Back,* by Bernard Most, *Danny and the Dinosaur,* by Syd Hoff, *The Secret Dinosaur,* by Marilyn Hirsh, and *Dinosaurs,* by Kathleen Daly

Initiating Activity

Purchase three to four medium-sized watermelons and paint them white. Hide them in a "dinosaur nest" somewhere on the playground before the start of the lesson. Tell the students they must find the dinosaur's nest to begin the dinosaur unit. Once they find the "eggs," cut them open and share them with the group. After returning to the classroom have the students draw pictures of imaginary creatures that may have laid those "eggs."

General Activities

It is not necessary, nor is it suggested, to use all the activities included. They are intended as a guide to illustrate the scope of activities that can be developed. Selection should be based on student needs, interests, and objectives.

1. Provide students with large paper bags. Have them create a paper bag puppet to represent their favorite dinosaur. Next, have students create skits with the puppets (e.g., a fight between a meat eater and a plant eater).
2. Tell students to use the names of dinosaurs to create new names for foods (e.g., fabrosaurus french fries, megalosaurus milkshakes, stegosaurus spaghetti). Then have them write a menu for lunch using these "new foods." Allow time for students to share their menus.
3. Scientists have proposed several reasons for the dinosaurs' disappearance (the earth became too cold, there wasn't enough food, etc.). Have students research these reasons and then divide them into groups, each group supporting one of the reasons. Provide time for them to discuss and defend their positions.
4. Ask the students to pretend they want a dinosaur for a pet. Ask them to identify the dinosaur they would want and tell how they would capture and tame it.
5. Using a variety of sources, list some dinosaurs and their lengths on the chalkboard. To help students understand how long the different dinosaurs were, measure their exact lengths with a ball of yarn (in which you have previously tied knots every 5 feet). Count by fives as the yarn is unrolled. Use a meter stick to convert these lengths to meters.

6. Have students become paleontologists (a scientist who specializes in finding and studying ancient fossil remains) by bringing clean chicken or turkey bones to school. Place each bone in wet, packed sand to make an imprint. Remove the bone and pour plaster of paris into the imprint (or mold). Let it harden and then remove it from the sand. Have students label and display their fossils.

7. Have students pretend they want to move Tyrannosaurus Rex, the largest of the meat-eating dinosaurs, which weighed approximately eight tons and was over 20 feet high, from a zoo in New York City to a zoo in Paris, France. Provide time for a brainstorming session on how this could be done.

8. Give each student a large piece of butcher paper and have them draw their favorite dinosaur and color or paint it. Place a second sheet of paper under the first sheet and staple them together loosely, leaving a small opening for stuffing. Stuff the dinosaur with crumpled newspaper and add legs, horns, tails, and so on. Label and display these stuffed dinosaurs.

9. Ask students to create riddles about dinosaurs (e.g., What is the best way to get a piece of paper out from under a dinosaur? Wait until it moves.) Compile these riddles into a class booklet, "Dinosaur Riddles."

10. Have students take on the role of a particular dinosaur. If possible, mime the dinosaur, in addition to giving one clue at a time:

    I weigh _____.
    I am _____ tall.
    I eat _____.

    Allow four clues. If students haven't guessed the dinosaur after four guesses, have the dinosaur-student provide the answer.

11. Plan a field trip to a museum of natural history to see dinosaur skeletons.

12. Provide students with plastic dinosaur figures, clay, dinosaur model sets, and so on. As a class, create a display or diorama that depicts a prehistoric time when dinosaurs roamed the world.

Discussion Questions

1. Do you wish dinosaurs were still living today? Explain.
2. How do we know all that we know about dinosaurs today?
3. How are certain animals living today similar to the dinosaurs of the past?
4. Why do you think dinosaurs became extinct?

Literature-Specific Activities

If the Dinosaurs Came Back, by Bernard Most

An imaginative and charming fantasy about a boy who dreams about having a dinosaur of his own and all the things they will be able to do, from pushing rain clouds back, to getting kites from trees. Using this book, select appropriate activities for your students from the following.

Prereading Activity

Read the title and ask children to complete the phrase. "If the dinosaurs came back . . ."

Activities

1. Select one of the dinosaurs that are illustrated and named on the last page of the book and draw its shape on a sheet of construction paper. Cut out the dinosaur and, using it as a pattern, make pages and construction paper covers for student dinosaur books. Allow students to use these materials to write their own stories about "if dinosaurs came back." Provide time for the students to share their stories.
2. Tell students to use the last page of the book (where all the dinosaurs are pictured) as a guide and go back through the story to see how many dinosaurs they can recognize and name.
3. Ask students to select one of the dinosaurs in the story and write a letter to it saying why they would like it to come back or why they wouldn't.
4. Tell students to pretend it is possible to bring back the dinosaurs; first, however, they must convince their community that it is a good idea. Divide students into pairs and ask them to create a full-page newspaper advertisement that will convince the community. Display these advertisements.

Discussion Questions

1. If you had a dinosaur for a pet, what things would you like to do with it?
2. What was the most/least useful thing the dinosaur did with the boy?
3. What things in the story could really happen if the dinosaurs came back?

Danny and the Dinosaurs, by Syd Hoff

This fantasy book describes the joys of having a dinosaur as a pet.

Prereading Activity

After sharing the book's cover, ask students to predict what they think Danny and the dinosaurs will do in the story.

Activities

1. Ask students to pretend they have a dinosaur like Danny's and it gets lost. Have each student create a reward poster to get his or her dinosaur back.
2. Tell students to create their own list of activities for their pet dinosaur to do. Then ask them to illustrate their pet dinosaurs. Compile the illustrations and lists into a class booklet, "Our Dinosaur Pets."
3. Have students conduct a survey among their classmates and neighbors, asking: "If you had a dinosaur at home, what one job or task would you like it to do?" Have students compile the responses into a list by listing the person's name and what they'd like the dinosaur to do, it:

Name of Interviewee	*Job or Task*
Mother	Wash windows

Duplicate this list and give each participant a copy.

Discussion Questions
1. Would you like to have a dinosaur as a pet? Explain.
2. What would you need (food, shelter, etc.) for a pet dinosaur?
3. What would you name your pet dinosaur?
4. How do you think your neighbors would react to having a pet dinosaur in the neighborhood?

The Secret Dinosaur, by Marilyn Hirsh
This fantasy book explains the difficulty Bill and Jane have in trying to hide a hungry dinosaur.

Prereading Activity
Read the title and ask each student to create an imaginary dinosaur. Allow time for sharing. Put pictures together and create a flip book (see Appendix F).

Activities
1. Tell students to write a letter to their parents and neighbors convincing them it would be beneficial for the students if they could keep the dinosaur described in this book as a pet.
2. Ask students to make a list of the places in their neighborhood they might hide a dinosaur. Allow time for them to share and discuss their lists of hiding places.
3. Create a contest in which students illustrate a good hiding place for a dinosaur. Allow one week for them to submit their ideas. Then display all the ideas and have students vote on the best illustrations in different categories, such as most original, silliest, most unusual, most practical. Provide blue ribbons for the winners.

Discussion Questions
1. Why did Bill and Jane want to keep their dinosaur secret?
2. What pets would be easy/difficult to hide?
3. What would happen if you tried to hide a dinosaur in your neighborhood?

Dinosaurs, by Kathleen Daly
This informational book provides the names and kinds of dinosaurs, their habitats, size, weight, and so on.

Prereading Activity
Have students cluster/web the word *dinosaur*. They can add to this web on completion of this book.

Activities

1. Tell students to pretend they could add another page with another dinosaur to this book. Create an imaginary dinosaur by drawing a picture of it and then writing a paragraph describing it. In the description, include the name of the dinosaur, its length, weight, and height, what it eats, where it lives, who its enemies are, and so on. Compile all of these illustrations and descriptions into a book, "Our Imaginary Dinosaur Friends."
2. Tell students that after reading the book they should select one dinosaur and, using an encyclopedia, do additional research. Ask them to write a brief report of their findings and share it with their classmates.
3. Provide students with science books, encyclopedias, and other reference books and ask them to investigate reptiles living today that bear some resemblance to dinosaurs (i.e., crocodiles, turtles, lizards). Tell them to make a chart listing these reptiles and include the similarities and differences (i.e., what they look like, where they live, and what they eat).

Name of Reptile	Similarities	Differences
Turtle	Four legs	Pulls head under shell

Discussion Questions

1. Which dinosaur would you like to learn more about?
2. Which dinosaur would have the greatest chance of survival if it were alive today? Explain.
3. What dinosaur features are evident in some animals you see today?
4. What is the most interesting idea you learned about dinosaurs from this book?

Culminating Activity

There is at least one dinosaur name for each letter of the alphabet. Assign one letter to each student or group of students and tell them to find a dinosaur whose name begins with that letter. Have them draw the dinosaur and write a one-page summary describing it. The summary should include the pronunciation of the dinosaur's name, its size, where it lived, what it ate, and so on. Finally, compile these reports into an "ABC of Dinosaurs."

Evaluation

The culminating product can be evaluated using the following criteria:

1. Do the illustrations and text reflect an understanding of the main types of dinosaurs and their characteristics?
2. Does the student-made alphabet book allow the reader to gain a better understanding of the variety of dinosaurs and their characteristics?
3. Are the illustrations creative?

Related Literature

*Cited in text

Andrews, Roy Chapman. *All About Dinosaurs.* Illustrated by Thomas W. Voter. Random House, 1953.

Arnold, Caroline. *Dinosaurs Down Under: And Other Fossils from Australia.* Clarion, 1990.

———. *Dinosaur Mountain: Graveyard of the Past.* Photographs by Richard Hewett. Clarion, 1989.

Barton, Byron. *Bones, Bones, Dinosaur Bones.* HarperCollins, 1990.

———. *Dinosaurs, Dinosaurs.* Crowell, 1989.

Branley, Franklin M. *Dinosaurs, Asteroids, and Superstars: Why the Dinosaurs Disappeared.* Illustrated by Jean Zallinger. Thomas Y. Crowell, 1982.

Brown, Marc, and Stephen Krensky. *Dinosaurs Beware! A Safety Guide.* Atlantic Monthly, 1982.

Carrick, Carol. *What Happened to Patrick's Dinosaur.* Clarion, 1986.

Carroll, Susan. *How Big Is a Brachiosaurus?* Platt & Monk, 1986.

Cobb, Vickie. *The Monsters Who Died: A Mystery About Dinosaurs.* Illustrated by Greg Wenzel. Conrad-McCann, 1983.

Craig, Jean. *Discovering Prehistoric Animals.* Troll, 1989.

———. *Dinosaurs and More Dinosaurs.* Illustrated by George Solonevich. Four Winds, 1965.

*Daly, Kathleen. *Dinosaurs.* Illustrated by Greg and Tim Hildebrandt. Western, 1977.

Freedman, Russell. *Dinosaurs and Their Young.* Illustrated by Leslie Morrel. Holiday, 1983.

Gurney, James. *Dinotopia.* Turner, 1992.

*Hirsh, Marilyn. *The Secret Dinosaur.* Holiday, 1979.

*Hoff, Syd. *Danny and the Dinosaur.* Illustrated by Else Holmelund Minarik. Harper & Row, 1958.

Knight, David C. *"Dinosaurs" That Swam and Flew.* Illustrated by Lee J. Ames. Prentice-Hall, 1985.

Lasky, Kathryn. *Dinosaur Dig.* Morrow, 1990.

*Most, Bernard. *If the Dinosaurs Came Back.* Harcourt Brace Jovanovich, 1978.

Parish, Peggy. *Dinosaur Time.* Illustrated by Arnold Lobel. Harper & Row, 1974.

*Quinn, Kayne, and Jan Hutchings. *Science Adventures: Dinosaurs.* Price/Stern/Sloan, 1987.

Rowe, Erna. *Giant Dinosaurs.* Illustrated by Merle Smith. Scholastic, 1973.

Sattler, Helen Roney. *Dinosaurs of North America.* Illustrated by Anthony Rao. Lothrop, Lee & Shepard, 1981.

———. *The Illustrated Dinosaur Dictionary.* Illustrated by Pamela Carrol. Lothrop, Lee & Shepard, 1983.

———. *The New Illustrated Dinosaur Dictionary.* Lothrop, 1990.

Selsam, Millicent. *Tyrannosaurus Rex.* Harper & Row, 1978.

Shuttlesworth, Dorothy. *To Find a Dinosaur.* Doubleday, 1973.

Simon, Seymour. *New Questions & Answers About Dinosaurs.* Morrow, 1990.

———. *The Smallest Dinosaurs.* Crown, 1982.

Stanton, Harry. *Now You Can Read About Dinosaurs.* Illustrated by Bob Hersey. Brimax, 1984.

Zallinger, Peter. *Dinosaurs and Other Archosaurus.* Random House, 1986.

Zim, Herbert. *Dinosaurs.* Illustrated by James G. Irving. Morrow, 1954.

Intermediate Level (Geography)*

Theme: From Sea to Shining Sea: America's Geography

Focus: Students will become aware of various geographical features in the United States and the ways in which humans interact with their environment.

Objectives: On completion of this thematic unit, students will:

1. Describe the various geographical features in the United States
2. Explain the ways these geographical features were created
3. Make connections between geographical features and lifestyles
4. Recognize the role people play in protecting their physical environment

Note: The general activities in this unit encourage students to discover the geography of the United States through a study of the features and regions of the land. Most of the activities, however, can be adapted to the study of individual states.

Materials

1. Recording of "America the Beautiful"
2. Magazines, especially *National Geographic* and similar periodicals
3. *Where in the U.S.A. Is Carmen Sandiego?* (computer software)
4. Informational books concerning the geography of the United States
5. Class almanac and atlas
6. Books of poetry about the United States
7. Student copies of the following: *Julie of the Wolves,* by Jean Craighead George, *The Talking Earth,* by Jean Craighead George, . . . *and now Miguel,* by Joseph Krumgold
8. Class copy of a book concerning legends/tall tales of America, such as *Yankee Doodle's Cousins,* by Anne Malcolmson
9. Copies of regional paintings that depict life in America
10. Camera, slide film, and slide projector
11. Cassette tape and player
12. Video camera (optional)
13. Poster board, butcher paper
14. Large relief map of the United States

*The authors wish to acknowledge the contributions of Robert Gray and Terri Rowan to the creation of this unit.

Initiating Activity

Play "America the Beautiful" to the class. Give out a copy of the song (p. 441) and give students time to practice singing it. Discuss the lyrics, especially those referring to the geographical features of the United States.

Discuss with students what is meant by the term *geographical features* (mountains, rivers, forests, canyons, valleys, mesas, beaches, plains, marshes, deserts, etc.). Divide students into groups and have them cut out pictures from magazines that represent the vast variety of geographical features found in the United States. Once all pictures have been cut, have each group divide its pictures by type of feature and label each grouping. Create and post a class list of geographical features found in the United States.

Assign each group a different geographical feature and ask the group to go through the pictures to select one or two that best represent that feature. Make slides of these pictures, organize the slides, and create a slide show called "From Sea to Shining Sea." With the help of the school's music teacher, create a cassette tape of the class singing "America the Beautiful" to accompany the slides.

General Activities

1. Our land has been shaped by various natural phenomena. Group students by phenomenon (earthquakes, rivers and glaciers, erosion, wind, volcano eruption, etc.). Have each group research its phenomenon to create a demonstration that illustrates the ways this phenomenon has shaped the land. Books such as *Land Masses,* by Caroline Arnold, and *Volcanoes* and *Earthquakes,* by Seymour Simon, can help with this.

   You may wish to introduce this activity with the following demonstration to show what happens during an earthquake. Cut a shallow, rectangular box (bottom of a shirt box) in half. Put the box together by overlapping the two sides. Fill the box with sand and smooth the sand with your hand. Choose two students and have each take a side of the box and slowly pull the box apart. Then have them push it back together. Discuss the changes that occurred in the sand. (Did it form hills or valleys?) Explain that sometimes two parts of the earth's crust push against each other or pull apart. This causes an earthquake. On a relief map, point out areas in the United States that have frequent earthquakes. Discuss what changes in the land's geography are caused by these quakes.

2. Have the class create a large floor map of the United States. Group the students and assign each group a different physical feature of the United States. (Use the list of features generated in the initiating activity.) Have each group research its feature, select a specific example of this feature (the Painted Desert, the Sierra Nevada Mountains, Carlsbad Caverns, etc.), and learn its location in the United States and how it was created. Have each group create a symbol that represents the physical feature assigned. Encourage each group to present a skit that teaches the class about the feature, its location, and its effect on the land and people around it. Students

America, the Beautiful

Music by Samuel A. Ward   Words by Katherine Lee Bates

1. O beau - ti - ful for spa - cious skies. For am - ber waves of grain.
2. O beau - ti - ful for pil - grim feet. Whose stern im - pas - sioned stress.

For pur - ple moun-tains maj - es - ties A - bove the fruit - ed plain!
A thor - ough fare for free - dom beat A - cross the wil - der - ness!

A - mer - i - ca! A - mer - i - ca! God shed his grace on thee,
A - mer - i - ca! A - mer - i - ca! God mend thine ev - 'ry flaw,

And crown thy good woth broth - er - hood From sea to shin - ing sea!
Con - firm thy soul in self - con - trol, Thy li - ber - ty in law!

3.   O beautiful for heroes proved In liberating strife,
      Who more than self their country loved, And mercy more than life!
      America! America! May God thy gold refine,
      Till all success be nobleness, And ev'ry gain divine!

4.   O beautiful for patriot dream That sees, beyond the years,
      Thine alabaster cities gleam Undimmed by human tears!
      America! America! God shed His grace on thee.
      And crown thy good with brotherhood, From sea to shining sea!

should place the symbols they created in the correct locations on the large class map.

3. Have each student select one of the geographical features found in the United States and write a haiku (see page 63) about it. You may wish to read some haiku to the class to familiarize students with this poetic form. Have students illustrate their haiku with photographs.

4. Involve students in the computer program *Where in the U.S.A. Is Carmen Sandiego?*

5. Contact a local environmentalist and ask him or her to speak to the class on the subject of environmental protection. Have students prepare interview questions for the environmentalist to help them learn the dangers facing our environment and what each individual can do to prevent the destruction of our natural resources.

6. As a class, have students select and research one of the ways the geography of our land is being destroyed. Divide students into groups. Ask each group to focus on a central problem that needs to be solved and brainstorm ways to solve it. Have students in each group list the most appropriate criteria for evaluating the ideas and, based on these criteria, select the best solution to the problem. Ask each group to create a plan of action to explain how to carry out the solution chosen. Have the different groups share the problems they selected and their plans of action for solving them. Students may write to the following for information:

   The Natural Resources Defense Council
   40 West 20th Street
   New York, NY 10011

   The Environmental Defense Fund
   1616 P Street, N.W.
   Suite 150
   Washington, D.C. 20036

7. Have students create a graph to show what percentage of the United States is mountain, desert, rivers, and so on. They can also graph the population density of these geographical areas. What generalizations can be formed?

8. Divide students into groups. Assign each group a different national park. Have students write letters to the head of each park department to learn about the natural resources in the park, its physical features, and what is being done to protect the area. See pages 443–444 for a listing of parks.

9. The physical features of the United States support recreational activities such as skiing, hiking, and rafting. Have each student select a physical feature and list the activities associated with it. Have each make a chart describing and illustrating the health benefits and dangers associated with the activity. Allow time for students to share their charts.

10. Using a map of the United States, have students use yarn to divide the

AMERICA'S NATIONAL PARKS

The U.S. national park system consists of 49 national parks and more than 300 other preserves. Addresses of the national parks follow.

ALASKA

Denali National Park: P.O. Box 9, McKinley Park, AK 99755

Gates of the Arctic National Park: P.O. Box 74680, Fairbanks, AK 99707

Glacier Bay National Park: P.O. Box 140, Gustavus, AK 99826

Katmai National Park: P.O. Box 7, King Salmon, AK 99613

Kenai Fjords National Park: P.O. Box 1727, Seward, AK 99664

Kobuk Valley National Park: P.O. Box 287, Kotzebue, AK 99752

Lake Clark National Park: 222 West Seventh Avenue, No. 61, Anchorage, AK 99513-7539

Wrangell-St. Elias National Park: P.O. Box 29, Glennallen, AK 99588

ARIZONA

Grand Canyon National Park: P.O. Box 129, Grand Canyon National Park, AZ 86023

Petrified Forest National Park: Petrified Forest National Park, AZ 86028

ARKANSAS

Hot Springs National Park: P.O. Box 1860, Hot Springs, AR 71902

CALIFORNIA

Channel Islands National Park: 1901 Spinnaker Drive, Ventura, CA 93001

Lassen Volcanic National Park: P.O. Box 199, Mineral, CA 96063

Redwood National Park: Drawer N, 1111 Second Street, Crescent City, CA 95531

Sequoia and Kings Canyon National Parks: Three Rivers, CA 93271

Yosemite National Park: P.O. Box 577, Yosemite, CA 95389

COLORADO

Mesa Verde National Park: Mesa Verde National Park, CO 81330

Rocky Mountain National Park: Estes Park, CO 80517

FLORIDA

Biscayne National Park: P.O. Box 1369, Homestead, FL 33030

HAWAII

Haleakala National Park: P.O. Box 369, Makawao, Maui, HI 96768

Hawaii Volcanoes National Park: P.O. Box 52, HI 96718

KENTUCKY

Mammoth Cave National Park: Mammoth Cave, KY 42259

MAINE

Acadia National Park: 87 North Rioley Street, Houghton, ME 49931

MINNESOTA

Voyageurs National Park: U.S. 53 International Falls, MN 56649

MONTANA

Glacier National Park: West Glacier, MT 59936

NEVADA

Great Basin National Park: Baker, NV 89311

NEW MEXICO

Carlsbad Caverns National Park: 3225 National Parks Highway, Carlsbad, NM 88220

AMERICA'S NATIONAL PARKS (continued)

NORTH DAKOTA

Theodore Roosevelt National Park: P.O. Box 7, Medora, ND 58645

OREGON

Crater Lake National Park: P.O. Box 7, Crater Lake, OR 97604

SOUTH DAKOTA

Badlands National Park: P.O. Box 6, Interior, SD 57750

Wind Cave National Park: Hot Springs, SD 57747

TENNESSEE

Great Smoky Mountains National Park: Gatlinburg, TN 37738

TEXAS

Big Bend National Park: Big Bend National Park, TX 79834

Guadalupe Mountains National Parks: 3225 National Parks Highway, Carlsbad, NM 88220

UTAH

Arches National Park: 125 West 200 South Moab, UT 84532

Bryce Canyon National Park: Bryce Canyon, UT 84717

Canyonlands National Park: 446 South Main Street, Moab, UT 84532

Capitol Reef National Park: Torrey, UT 84775

Zion National Park: Springdale, UT 84767

VIRGIN ISLANDS

Virgin Islands National Park: P.O. Box 806, St. Thomas, U.S. Virgin Islands 00801

VIRGINIA

Shenandoah National Park: Route 4, P.O. Box 348, Luray, VA 22835

WASHINGTON

Mount Ranier National Park: Tahoma Woods, Star Route, Ashford, WA 98304

North Cascades National Park: 2105 Highway 20, Sedro-Woolley, WA 98284

Olympic National Park: 600 East Park Avenue, Port Angeles, WA 98362

WYOMING

Grand Teton National Park: Drawer 170, Moose, WY 83012

Yellowstone National Park: P.O. Box 168, Yellowstone National Park, WY 82190

United States into regions. (There are many ways the United States can be divided. Have students consult various books and reach a class concensus.) Discuss and list the states in each region.

Ask students to develop computation problems for others to solve based on the area of each region or the distances between cities, states, and geographic features.

11. Every state and region has its own poetry. Locate a book of poetry, such as *America Forever New*, compiled by Sara and John E. Brewton, that includes poems which capture the geography and spirit of the United States. Make class copies of each poem selected, read the verses aloud, discuss the meaning and mood of the poem, and involve students in a choral reading. Have students select a favorite poem to illustrate. Create a bulletin board called "From Sea to Shining Sea," highlighting the poems and illustrations.

12. Ask students to select a region of the United States and imagine what the area will be like in the year 2525 if pollution, environmental waste, and

other such problems that affect the geography of the land are allowed to go unchecked. Have students capture this in an editorial cartoon. Have them establish selection criteria and select two cartoons to send to a local newspaper. Bind all cartoons into a class book.

13. Read aloud portions of books about various geographical regions. For example, Jean Craighead George (HarperCollins) has written a series that includes *One Day in the Desert, One Day in the Alpine Tundra, One Day in the Prairie,* and *One Day in the Woods.* Assign groups of students their own regions and have them create their own "One Day in the _____" books.

14. Have each student select a different state and find the derivation of its name, its slogan (e.g., Florida is the "Sunshine State"), its state flower, and its state bird. Allow time for students to share their findings and discover how many of the state names and slogans were influenced by the state's geography.

    Have students design sandwich boards in the shape of their state. The front of each sandwich board should include the state's name and an original slogan that reflects the influence of one of the state's significant geographical features. Students can create borders using state flowers or birds.

    Have students create a living map by positioning themselves so that their sandwich boards take on the shape of the United States. Videotape the map as it is being formed.

15. Obtain copies of paintings depicting regions of the United States by American scene painters such as Andrew Wyeth, Thomas Benton, Grant Wood, Georgia O'Keeffe, and John Curry. Ask students to make inferences about the land and the lifestyles of the people based on these pictures. Discuss how the land and lifestyles have changed over the ages and the reasons for these changes.

16. Read several tall tales to students and discuss the characteristics of the genre: Do the stories reflect the regions of the United States? What factual information was included? What geographical features are explained? You might wish to read tall tales such as *Mike Fink,* by James Cloyd Bowman, or *Paul Bunyan* and *Pecos Bill,* by Steven Kellogg. Have each student create a tall tale to explain one geographical feature of the United States.

Discussion Questions

1. Which geographical feature in the United States do you find the most interesting? Why?
2. Which geographical features are most evident in your city or state?
3. How are our lives affected by the geography of the land?
4. What causes phenomena such as earthquakes, volcanoes, and glaciers?
5. How do phenomena such as earthquakes, volcanoes, erosion, and glaciers affect the geography of the land?
6. What inventions were created out of a need for people to live and interact with various geographical features in the United States?

7. What are the most significant problems affecting the geography of our land?
8. What impact does our lifestyle have on the environment? What can we do to help protect the physical features of our land?
9. What single sentence and/or word would best describe the geography of the United States?
10. How will the geography of the United States change over time? Explain.

Literature-Specific Activities

Julie of the Wolves, by Jean Craighead George

This is the story of Julie, alone and lost on the North Slope of Alaska. Juile is accepted by a pack of wolves and survives with their help.

Prereading Activity

Discuss with children whether they have ever been lost. If so, what did they do?

Activities

1. Have students create charts illustrating the signs in nature that act as a compass (e.g., the North Star, moss on trees).
2. Have students read informational books about Alaska. Discuss the accuracy of the details in *Julie of the Wolves*. Ask students to determine which geographical features in Alaska are the most difficult to contend with. Then have them create a humorous newspaper article called "10 Tips for Surviving America's 49th State."
3. Ask each student to write a dialogue between Julie and her father after she discovered he was responsible for killing the wolf.
4. Discuss the song Julie sang to the spirit of Amaroq at the end of the story. Have students debate whether Julie was right when she said "the hour of the wolf and the Eskimo is over."

Discussion Questions

1. If humans succeed in killing off the wolves of the Arctic, how will this affect the balance of nature?
2. What did Miyax take with her when she ran away? What purpose did each object have? Is there anything else she might have taken that would have helped her survive? Explain.
3. What do you think is the most important lesson Julie learned from the wolves? What did she learn about herself and about Eskimo customs?
4. What single word would you use to describe the geography of Alaska's Northern Slope?

The Talking Earth, by Jean Craighead George

Billie Wind journeys into the wilderness of the Everglades and discoverie she must listen to the land and its animals to survive.

Prereading Activity

Discuss what the students think the title of this book means. Can the earth really talk? How?

Activities

1. Group students and have each group read the legends of a different American Indian tribe. Have each group prepare a visual display that depicts one way the tribe learned to adapt to the land.
2. Ask each student to select five animals and present a humorous speech to describe what each animal could teach us to help us survive in our own world.
3. Have students debate this question: "Can a person believe in scientific explanations and still believe in the legends of his or her people?"
4. Ask students how the land "talked" to Billie. Select one of the ways and research it further.

Discussion Questions

1. What dangers did Billie Wind overcome during her journey?
2. What is meant by "the balance of nature"? What did Billie witness in the Everglades that illustrates the way humankind is upsetting this balance of nature?
3. What skills did Billie have that allowed her to survive in the Everglades alone?
4. What was the most important lesson Billie learned from the "mission" on which Charlie Wind sent her?

. . . and Now Miguel, by Joseph Krumgold

Miguel is finally allowed on the long, hard sheep drive to the Sangre de Cristo Mountains in New Mexico. The fulfillment of his wish brings disturbing results.

Prereading Activity

Ask students whether they have ever wished for something that came true in a way that surprised them. If so, have them tell what happened.

Activities

1. Ask students to research the customs of the Mexican Americans and illustrate a favorite custom in a style similar to that in this book.
2. Have students create free verse poems that describe the view from the mountains as Miguel began to climb them.
3. Have students locate the Sangre de Cristo Mountains on a map. Have each student research this area to find and share three facts that he or she finds the most interesting.
4. Miguel explained that his family had raised sheep in his area long before the founding of the United States. Discuss with students why the area was

so ideal for raising sheep. Divide students into groups and give each group a different region of the United States. Have each group create a map of its region that creatively indicates the animals and/or crops that grow best in the area.

5. Have students read about different mountain types (domes, faulted, etc.) to discover what type the Sangre de Cristo mountains are. Discuss with students the English translation of the Spanish name *Sangre de Cristo*, which is "Blood of Christ." Ask students why they think the mountains were given this name. Have them find out what natural elements or phenomena contributed to this choice of a name.

Discussion Questions

1. Why did Miguel accept the news about being allowed to go on the sheep drive with mixed emotions?
2. Why is it so important to Miguel that he be allowed to go on the sheep drive?
3. What are some of the hardships and responsibilities that go along with raising sheep?
4. Why have so many generations of Miguel's family continued to raise sheep? What are the advantages and disadvantages of their way of life?

Culminating Activities

"Showcase-Your-State Day." The following activities will help students discover the wonders in their own backyard! Celebrate your state with a special day in which the products of these activities are highlighted.

1. Have students imagine they are travel agents, planning a seven-day trip around their state for children their age. Group students and have each group:
   a. List the cities their "clients" should visit
   b. List the sites in each city (emphasizing any special geographical features) clients should visit
   c. Decide how clients will travel from place to place
   d. Plan a day-by-day itinerary
   e. Compute the expenses of the trip (travel, accommodations, food, entertainment, etc.)
2. Have each group prepare a travel brochure to advertise the trip planned in Activity 1. The brochure should include:
   a. An itinerary
   b. Pictures of the cities and places to be visited
   c. A map outlining the routes that will be taken, showing the forms of transportation to be used

    d. Suggested clothing and items needed for the trip

    e. Any especially interesting facts about the cities/state

    f. The trip's cost

3. Have students keep diaries of their imaginary seven-day trips around the state. Encourage them to include impressions and reactions, not just a listing of places visited.

4. Invite speakers who have lived in your city or state for many years. Have them discuss changes they have seen over the years (the land, the people, the industries, etc.). Videotape these "oral histories."

5. Have students write letters to their local chamber of commerce to learn about the businesses and industries of their city or state. Letters requesting information can also be sent to tourism bureaus in various cities.

6. Have students research and prepare recipes that highlight foods native to your state. Have them create their own state recipe books.

7. Encourage students to read biographies of famous sons and daughters of the state. Have them complile a "Who's Who of _____ (name of state)" book.

8. Have students design picture postcards to represent the state's geographical features. Have each student write a note to a friend on the back of his or her card, describing the feature pictured. Ask students to design and include stamps that symbolize the state.

9. Divide students into groups and have each group create a three-dimensional replica of one of the state's most interesting geographical features.

10. Have students (in groups) prepare and present 60-second commercials to persuade others to visit the state. Videotape commercials, if possible, and send them to your state's Department of Tourism.

Evaluation

A final evaluative project can involve students in an analysis and synthesis of the knowledge they have gained. You may wish to select one of the following projects to help assess student growth.

1. Have students add their own verses about America's geography to "America the Beautiful."

2. Ask students to create collages that reflect the variety of geographical features found in the United States and/or their state.

3. If each student could live anywhere in the United States, where would each go? Have students deliver persuasive speeches that would convince their parents to move.

4. Ask students to think of all the ways we are fighting environmental pollution and attempting to prevent the destruction of our country's landforms. Have each student select the method he or she feels is the most effective and write a "letter to the editor" to try to persuade others to support this effort.

Related Literature

*Cited in text

Realistic Fiction and Historical Fiction

Blos, J. W. *A Gathering of Days: A New England Girl's Journal, 1830–1832.* Scribner's, 1979. (New Hampshire)

Cleaver, V., and B. Cleaver. *Dust of the Earth.* Harper, 1975. (South Dakota)

———. *The Kissammee Kid.* Lothrop, Lee & Shepard, 1981. (Florida)

———. *Where the Lilies Bloom.* Harper & Row, 1969. (Appalachia)

Conrad, P. *Prairie Songs.* Harper & Row, 1985. (Nebraska)

Ellison, L. W. *The Tie that Binds.* Scribner's, 1981. (Alabama)

*George, Jean Craighead. *Julie of the Wolves.* Harper & Row, 1972. (Alaska)

*———. *The Talking Earth.* Harper & Row, 1983. (Everglades, Florida)

*Krumgold, Joseph. *. . . and now Miguel.* Harper & Row, 1953. (New Mexico)

O'Dell, S. *Zia.* Houghton Mifflin, 1976. (California)

Paulsen, G. *The Winter Room.* Orchard, 1989. (Minnesota)

Robertson, K. *In Search of a Sandhill Crane.* Viking, 1975. (Michigan)

Sargent, S. *Seeds of Change.* Bradberry, 1989. (Georgia)

Spear, E. G. *Sign of the Beaver.* Houghton Mifflin, 1983. (Maine)

Wilder, L. I. Little House series. Harper & Row. (Midwest–West)

Williams, V. B. *Stringbean's Trip to the Shining Sea.* Greenwillow, 1988. (Kansas, Pacific Ocean)

Nonfiction

*Arnold, C. *Land Masses.* Franklin Watts, 1985.

Arnold, P., and P. White. *How We Named Our States.* Criterion, 1965.

Coburn, D. *A Split Is a Piece of Land: Landforms in the U.S.A.* Messner, 1978.

*George, J. C. *One Day in the Alpine Tundra.* Harper & Row, 1984.

*———. *One Day in the Desert.* Harper & Row, 1983.

*———. *One Day in the Prairie.* Harper & Row, 1986.

*———. *One Day in the Woods.* Harper & Row, 1988.

Muller, J. *The Changing Countryside.* Macmillan, 1979.

Seddon, T., and J. Bailey. *The Physical World.* Doubleday, 1987.

*Simon, S. *Earthquakes.* Morrow, 1991.

*———. *Volcanoes.* Morrow, 1988.

Where in the U.S.A. Is Carmen Sandiego? (computer program). Broderbund, 17 Paul Drive, San Rafael, CA 94903-2101; 800-521-6263.

Poetry

*Brewton, Sara, and John E. Brewton. *America Forever New.* Thomas Y. Crowell, 1968.

Parker, E. *Here and There: 100 Poems About Places.* Thomas Y. Crowell, 1967.

Traditional Literature: Tall Tales

Blair, W. *Tall Tale America: A Legendary History of Our Humourous Heroes.* Coward, McCann and Geoghegan, 1944.

*Bowman, James Cloyd. *Mike Fink.* Little, Brown, 1957.

*Kellogg, Steven. *Paul Bunyan.* Morrow, 1984.

*———. *Pecos Bill.* Morrow, 1986.

Malcolmson, A. *Yankee Doodle's Cousins.* Houghton Mifflin, 1941.

Stoutenburg, A. *American Tall Tales.* Viking, 1966.

Intermediate Level (Social Studies)

Theme: Pioneer Life

Focus: Students will become aware of the changes and challenges facing the pioneers who settled the American West and will understand how the pioneer spirit affects their own lives.

Objectives: On completion of this thematic unit, students will:

1. Describe the "pioneer spirit" and relate how it affects their lives today
2. Relate the contributions of some of the great pioneer leaders
3. Express insights into pioneer life gained through their reading of historical fiction, nonfiction, and biographies
4. Create works of art, music, and drama to retell the story of America's pioneers

Materials

1. Slides of artwork depicting pioneers and pioneer life
2. Copies of songbooks or records that convey the spirit of the West
3. Small pieces of fabric for making a patchwork quilt
4. Large map of the United States
5. Photographs of pioneers and their journey west
6. Butcher paper
7. Student copies (or at least one teacher copy) of the following: *Sarah, Plain and Tall,* by Patricia MacLachlan, *Little House on the Prairie,* by Laura Ingalls Wilder, and *Prairie Songs,* by Pam Conrad
8. A collection of informational books on pioneer life (see Related Literature at the end of this unit)
9. A collection of biographies of famous pioneers of the past and present

Note: At the end of the unit, hold a "Pioneer Festival" in which participants are transported to the days of the pioneers' settlement of the American West. Recreate a scene from pioneer times and have students dress in pioneer garb. Many of the activities in this unit yield products that can be shared during the festival. For example, decorate the room with student crafts, artwork, and writings. Simulate a campfire and have students sit around the "fire," singing songs, retelling stories of pioneer days, and presenting original monologues, skits, stories, and poems. Serve the foods prepared in the cooking class. Invite parents, school administrators, and other classes.

Initiating Activity

Have students imagine they are living in the early 1800s and are embarking on a journey by covered wagon across the continent. Ask each student to choose ten personal items to take on this journey. Once students have listed their items, have them cut their lists to five items and defend their selections. This activity will help them prioritize values and become more aware of the problems facing the pioneers who settled the American West.

General Activities

1. With students, create a thematic web of pioneer life (page 453). Once the web is complete, ask students to each compose five questions they'd like to have answered concerning pioneer life. Many of these questions can form the basis for research, projects, and classroom discussion.

2. Hang butcher paper around the classroom. Throughout the unit, allow students to draw pictures and write words on it that reflect their perceptions of pioneer life.

3. Display artwork that depicts life in the Old West and the days of the pioneers. Take photographs of artwork in books, such as Russell Freeman's *Cowboys of the Wild West* and *Children of the Wild West*, and display them in the form of slides or pictures. Have students select favorite pictures and then try to recreate them; have them write brief biographies of the artists and share their feelings about the works of art and what they represent.

4. Have each student select and learn a favorite song about pioneer life. Then have the students teach their songs to small groups of students so they can sing it at the festival campfire. (Many pioneer songs can be found in *America Sings,* by Carl Carmer. Songs may include "Old Dan Tucker," "Davy Crockett," "Cumberland Gap," "Goodbye Old Paint," and "Home, Home on the Range."

5. Involve students in problem solving based on difficulties encountered during a wagon train trip. For example, students might wish to target the problem of leadership, and one of their ideas might center on the need for rules on a wagon train.

6. Provide each student with a 12 × 12-inch piece of fabric. On this piece of fabric, each student should illustrate a scene from pioneer life for a patchwork quilt of the Old West. Information on quilting can be obtained from books such as *The Quilt Story,* by Tony Johnson, or *The Quilt,* by Ann Jonas.

7. Hold a cooking class in which students make some of the foods discussed in the books about pioneer life. Students will have to research the foods to find recipes. A collection of these recipes can be combined to create a "Pioneer Cookbook."

8. Involve students in a simulation of decision making on a wagon train using *Pioneers* (Interact, P.O. Box 997-589, Lakeside, CA 92040).

9. With students, brainstorm a list of today's pioneers. Have each student select one pioneer, read a biography of his or her life, and create a chart to il-

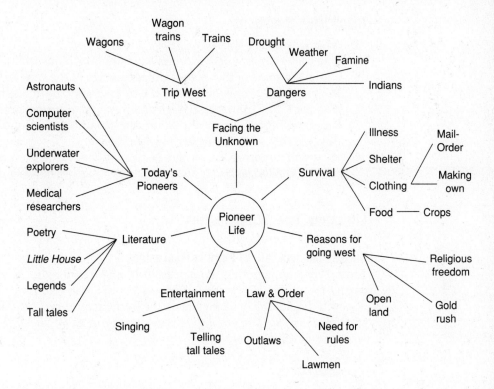

lustrate the dangers he or she faced. What connections can they make between the Old West's pioneers and today's pioneers?

10. Have students read about the hardships facing past or present pioneers and write papers to discuss "the best of times and the worst of times."

11. Have students research one of the famous trails that took settlers west in the 1800s (e.g., the Oregon Trail, the Santa Fe Trail, the Donner Pass). Trace the trail on the classroom map. In groups, students can summarize and/or dramatize any interesting stories connected with the trail and place the summaries in the appropriate locations on the map.

12. Have students read about one of today's pioneers, then become that person and role-play a highlight of his or her life.

13. Have students select one of the following topics: clothing, crops, food, encounters with native tribes, disease, or other factors affecting pioneer life. Have them locate information on the topic and share the information through poetry, art, music, or drama.

14. Create a time capsule that might have been left by the pioneers of the 1800s. It might contain pictures, letters, artwork, crafts, pieces of cloth, copies of songs, or poetry that reflect life at that time.

Discussion Questions

1. What is "pioneer spirit"?
2. What determines whether or not a person is a "pioneer"?
3. Who were some of the most famous pioneers of the American West? What are the greatest contributions of the pioneers of the American West?
4. Who are today's pioneers? What are their greatest contributions?
5. Compare the pioneers of the American West with the pioneers of today. How are they alike? How are they different?
6. What will tomorrow's pioneers be like? What do you think will be their greatest challenges?

Literature-Specific Activities

Sarah, Plain and Tall, by Patricia MacLachlan

Sarah Wheaton, a young woman from Maine responds to an ad in the paper asking for a wife. This is the touching story of Sarah's journey to the West and about the beginning of a new life on the frontier, one very different from the life she knew. *Sarah, Plain and Tall* was awarded the 1986 Newbery Medal for outstanding children's literature.

Prereading Activity

Ask students whether they have ever had to move from one part of the country to another or from one country to another. Discuss the pros and cons of moving and put students' responses on the board or on a chart. As students read *Sarah, Plain and Tall*, ask them to determine what Sarah felt were the pros and cons of her move.

Activities

1. Have students list details of frontier life as described in the book and then look through informational books to compare the details. Have them write brief papers to explain why *Sarah, Plain and Tall* is considered historical fiction.
2. Have students create charts comparing the differences between life in Maine and life on the frontier as discussed in the book. Items compared can include animals, plants and vegetation, transportation, dangers, and weather.
3. Have students list clues and formulate hypotheses as to the part of the American frontier in which Sarah settled. Each student should locate this area on a class map and then research it to see if the facts back up his or her hypothesis.
4. Create a class book of illustrations for *Sarah, Plain and Tall* that reflects students' perceptions of the prairie.

Discussion Questions
1. What would you enjoy most about life on the prairie?
2. What would you enjoy least about life on the prairie?
3. What caused Sarah to move to the prairie? What other reasons would cause people to move to the West?
4. Where could people go today if they wanted to move for the reasons you gave in the above question?

Little House on the Prairie, by Laura Ingalls Wilder

This is one book in the Little House series which relate the true story of Laura Ingalls and her family as they travel by covered wagon through the West. In *Little House on the Prairie*, Laura and her family work together to build a new life, only to be forced by the government to leave their land, which rightfully belonged to the Indians.

Prereading Activity

The illustrations in *Little House on the Prairie* are by Garth Williams, who followed the same route west as did Laura Ingalls and her family. Divide the class into groups and assign each group a different picture to analyze. Based on the picture, what predictions can each group make about life in the West? Allow groups to share their pictures and predictions. After the book has been read, see which predictions were most accurate.

Activities
1. After students have read *Little House on the Prairie,* have each decide which character best exemplifies the "pioneer spirit" and write a persuasive speech to convince others of the appropriateness of this choice.
2. On a class map of the United States, trace the route Laura and her family followed. Help students compute the time it would take to travel this route using different modes of transportation.
3. Read another of the Little House books. Compare daily life in each. For example, in which book did life appear to be easier? Why? In which was life more dangerous? Why?
4. The pioneers did not have the appliances and tools we have today, and they had to adapt available materials to accomplish a multitude of tasks. Have students imagine they are living in the 1800s and decide which modern-day appliances they would most like to have. Have students find pictures of the appliances and create advertisements to sell them to the pioneers of the 1800s.
5. Have each student invent a children's game that can be made with any material described in *Little House on the Prairie.* Have students make their games and teach others in the class to play with them.
6. Ask students to imagine what the Osage chief might have said to his tribe

and to the other tribes to persuade them to ride off in peace rather than make war. Simulate a debate, selecting pairs of students to take either the chief's side or that of one of Indians who believes war is the only answer.

Discussion Questions

1. In the book, Charles Ingalls says, "There's no great loss without some gain." Do you agree with this? Explain. Based on your knowledge of pioneers of the American West, do you think most of them would agree with this quote? Why or why not?
2. What were some of the greatest dangers faced by the pioneers who settled the West?
3. Are families better off today or during the time described in *Little House on the Prairie*? Defend your answer.
4. The Ingalls family began a new life only to be forced to leave their new home after a year. Did the government have the right to force them to leave? Explain your answer.

Prairie Songs, by Pam Conrad

This is the story of a family living on the Nebraska prairie. Louisa, the main character, provides insights into prairie life and its paradoxical qualities.

Prereading Activity

Have students analyze the illustration on the title page and describe the people, particularly their dress. Ask students to imagine and discuss the type of life these people must have led. Record these ideas and compare them to what students uncover from reading the book to see how accurate they were.

Activities

1. Louisa describes a soddy in great detail. Have students use sod to create a small soddy based on her description. Students should put the soddy outside and, for several weeks, record the daily temperature inside and outside the soddy. Ask the students what they discovered and why they think pioneers lived in this type of shelter.
2. Louisa speaks admiringly of Emmeline and often compares her mother to Emmeline. Have each student fold a piece of paper in half lengthwise and list Emmaline's qualities on one side and those of Louisa's mother on the other. Have students place asterisks next to the ten qualities they believe are most important for survival in pioneer days. Have students rank the importance of the qualities they chose. In large groups, discuss the rankings and try to reach a consensus. Ask students which qualities on the list are most admired today and what this tells them about our values.
3. Have students create and deliver monologues that one of the characters might have delivered to describe life on the prairie.
4. Have students consider the problems described in the book and create a "Survival Guide" for a person traveling to the West in the 1850s.

Discussion Questions

1. What was the main quality Emmeline lacked that would have better enabled her to survive in the pioneer West?
2. Which qualities did the pioneers of the American West possess that would be most important for today's pioneers?
3. Louisa described the prairie as "the comfort of a blank wall without too many things on it, or a stretch of clean, flawless sand down at the river." What does she mean by this? Have you ever seen a place that would fit this description? Where?
4. Could you survive in pioneer days? Why or why not?

Culminating Activity

Read "The Pioneer" with students and discuss its theme and the mood it evokes. Group students and let each group select one of today's pioneers. Ask each to create a poem from the pioneer's perspective to describe his or her feelings about the accomplishments and contributions made. The original poem may be used as a model.

The Pioneer

Long years ago I blazed a trail
Through lovely woods unknown till then
And marked with cairns of splintered shale
A mountain way for other men;
For other men who came and came;
They trod the path more plain to see,
They gave my trail another's name
And no one speaks or knows of me.
The trail runs high, the trail runs low
Where windflowers dance or columbine;
The scars are healed that long ago
My ax cut deep on birch and pine.
Another's name my trail may bear,
But still I keep, in waste and wood,
My joy because the trail is there,
My peace because the trail is good.

Arthur Guiterman, from *I Sing the Pioneer*

Evaluation

1. Did the student's original poem reflect an understanding of the accomplishments and contributions of today's pioneer?
2. Did the students understand the changes and challenges facing the pioneer?
3. Did the students capture the "pioneer spirit?"
4. Was the poem creative?

Related Literature

*Cited in text

Historical Fiction

Aldrich, R. *A Lantern in Her Hand.* New American Library, 1983.
Brink, C. *Caddie Woodlawn.* Macmillan, 1936.
*Conrad, Pam. *Prairie Songs.* Harper & Row, 1985.
Dalgliesh, A. *The Courage of Sarah Noble.* Scribner's, 1954.
Defelice, C. *Weasel.* Macmillan, 1990.
Harvey, B. *My Prairie Year.* Holiday, 1986.
*MacLachlan, Patricia. *Sarah, Plain and Tall.* Harper & Row, 1985.
Wilder, L. I. Little House series. Harper & Row.
*Wilder, Laura Ingalls. *Little House on the Prairie.* Illustrated by Garth Williams. Harper & Row, 1935.

Informational Books

*Carmer, Carl. *America Sings.* Knopf, 1942.
Felton, H. *Cowboy Jamboree—Western Songs and Lore.* Knopf, 1975.
Fisher, L. E. *The Oregon Trail.* Holiday, 1990.
*Freeman, R. *Children of the Wild West.* Clarion, 1983.
*———. *Cowboys of the Wild West.* Clarion, 1985.
Geis, Jacqueline. *Where the Buffalo Roam.* Ideals, 1992.
Grant, B. *Famous American Trails.* Rand McNally, 1971.
Hammer, T. *The Advancing Frontier.* Watts, 1986.
*Johnson, Tony. *The Quilt Story.* Illustrated by Tomie de Paola. Putnam, 1985.
*Jonas, Ann. *The Quilt.* Greenwillow, 1984.
Laycock, G., and E. Laycock. *How the Settlers Lived.* MacCay, 1980.
Levine, E. *If You Traveled West in a Covered Wagon.* Scholastic, 1986.
Place, M. *American Cattle Trails: East and West.* Holt, Rinehart & Winston, 1967.
Rounds, B. *The Treeless Plains.* Holiday, 1967.
Williams, D. *Grandma Essie's Covered Wagon.* Knopf, 1993.

Legends

Blair, Walter. *Tall Tale America: A Legendary History of Our Humourous Heroes.* Coward, McCann & Geoghegan, 1944.
Bowman, James C. *Pecos Bill.* Albert Whitman, 1964.
Shephard, Esther. *Paul Bunyan.* Harcourt Brace Jovanovich, 1952.
Stoutenburg, Adrien. *American Tall Tales.* Viking, 1966.

Poetry

Brewton, Sara, and John Brewton. *America Forever New: A Book of Poems.* Thomas Y. Crowell, 1968.
Guiterman, Arthur. *I Sing the Pioneer.* Dutton, 1926.
Lindsey, Vachel. *Johnny Appleseed and Other Poems.* Macmillan, 1928.
Sandburg, Carl. *Wind Song.* Harcourt Brace Jovanovich, 1960.
Wild, Peter, and Frank Graziano, eds. *New Poetry of the American West.* Logbridge Rhodes, 1982.

Lenski Books Cited
Bayou Suzette. Stokes, 1943.
Blueberry Corners Stokes, 1940.
Boom Town Boy Lippincott, 1948.
Corn-Farm Boy. Lippincott, 1954.
Cotton in My Sack. Lippincott, 1949.
Flood Friday. Lippincott, 1956.
Indian Captive: the Story of Mary Jemison. Stokes, 1941.
The Little Fire Engine. Oxford, 1946.
The Little Train. Oxford, 1940.
Ocean-Born Mary. Stokes, 1939.
Peanuts for Billy Ben. Lippincott, 1952.
Prairie School. Lippincott, 1951.
Skipping Village. Stokes, 1927.
Strawberry Girl. Lippincott, 1945.
We Live in the South. Lippincott, 1952.

Professional Resources

Audio/Visual Resources

National Geographic Society. *Educational Services Catalog.* 17th and M Streets NW, Washington, D.C. 20036; 800-368-2728.

Printed Resources

BookLinks. American Library Association.
Burke, Eileen M. *Literature for the Young Child.* Allyn & Bacon, 1990.
Butzow, Carol, and John Butzow. *Science Through Children's Literature.* Teacher Ideas Press, 1989.
Children's Books in Print. Bowker (annual).
Cullinan, Bernice. *Children's Literature in the Reading Program.* International Reading Association, 1987.
Dreyer, S. S. *Fiction, Folklore, Fantasy, and Poetry for Children.* Bowker, 1986.
Fredericks, Anthony D. *Social Studies Through Children's Literature.* Teacher Ideas Press, 1991.
Fredericks, Anthony D., Anita Meinbach, and Liz Rothlein. *Thematic Units: An Integrated Approach to Teaching Science and Social Studies.* HarperCollins, 1993.
Gillespie, J. T., and C. B. Gilbert. *Best Books for Children: Preschool Through the Middle Grades.* Bowker, 1985.
International Reading Association. "Children's Choices." *The Reading Teacher,* October (annual).
Kobrin, Beverly. *Eyeopeners.* Penguin, 1988.
Lima, Carolyn W. *A to Zoo: Subject Access to Children's Picture Books.* Bowker, 1985.
Lukens, Rebecca. *A Critical Handbook of Children's Literature.* Scott, Foresman, 1986.
Monson, Diane. *Adventuring with Books: A Booklist for Pre-K to Grade 6.* National Council of Teachers of English, 1985.
Moss, Joy F. *Focus Units in Literature.* National Council of Teachers of English, 1984.

National Council for the Social Studies. "Notable Children's Trade Books in the Field of Social Studies." *Social Education*, April/May (annual).

National Science Teachers Association. "Outstanding Science Trade Books for Children." *Science and Children*, March (annual).

Norton, Donna. *Through the Eyes of a Child: An Introduction to Children's Literature*. Merrill, 1983.

Phillips, Donna. *The Bookmaster*. Department of Education, Canisius College, 2001 Main Street, Buffalo, NY 14208-1098.

Stott, J. C. *Children's Literature from A to Z: A Guide for Parents and Teacher*. McGraw-Hill, 1984.

Sutherland, Zena, and May Hill Arbuthnot. *Children and Books*. HarperCollins, 1991.

Sutherland, Zena, and Myra Cohn Livingston. *The Scott, Foresman Anthology of Children's Literature*. Scott, Foresman, 1984.

Trelease, Jim. *The New Read-Aloud Handbook*. Penguin, 1989.

The WEB: Wonderfully Exciting Books. Ohio State University, 200 Ramseyer Hall, Columbus, OH 43210 (periodical).

Book Clubs

Scholastic Book Clubs, 2931 East McCarty Street, P.O. Box 7500, Jefferson City, MO 65102.

Troll Book Club, 2 Lethbridge Plaza, Mahwah, NJ 07498.

The Trumpet Club, P.O. Box 604, Holmes, PA 19092.

Weekly Reader Paperback Clubs, 4343 Equity Drive, P.O. Box 16628, Columbus, OH 43272.

THE MOON OF THE
GRAY
WOLVES

BY JEAN CRAIGHEAD GEORGE
ILLUSTRATED BY SAL CATALANO

CHAPTER 14

Assessment and the Literature-Based Curriculum

Assessment of student achievement has been an issue in educational circles for years. Most school districts and states use standardized tests as a systematic means for evaluating growth. Because of the importance and credibility given to test results, these standardized tests often determine the curriculum. Historically, in addition to standardized tests, teacher accountability and student progress have also been determined by teacher-made and basal-generated tests. Although they provide some insight into what facts students have internalized, unfortunately much of what is achieved in a literature-based program cannot be measured using such traditional methods. As a result, advocates of literature-based programs and the whole language philosophy are continually seeking and developing new assessment procedures to reflect student achievements in all areas of language: reading, writing, listening, and speaking.

Principles of Whole Language Evaluation

The following principles of whole language evaluation (Harp, 1993) guide the types of assessment strategies teachers can adopt to provide a more accurate picture of student progress, growth, and attitudes toward learning.

1. Assessment and evaluation strategies must honor the wholeness of language.
2. Reading and writing are viewed as processes.
3. Teacher intuition is a valuable assessment and evaluation tool.
4. Teacher observation is at the center of assessment and evaluation.
5. Assessment and evaluation in reading must reflect what we know about the reading process.
6. Assessment and evaluation in writing must reflect what we know about the writing process.
7. Norm-referenced achievement testing is of no help to the whole language teacher.
8. Assessment and evaluation instruments are varied and literacy is assessed in a variety of contexts.
9. Assessment and evaluation are integral parts of instruction.

10. Assessment and evaluation strategies are developmentally and culturally appropriate.
11. Assessment and evaluation occur continuously.
12. Assessment and evaluation must reveal children's strengths.

Forms of Authentic Assessment

Forms of assessment are needed that focus on process and not just product, although process cannot always be separated from product. For example, in writing, the focus must be on the writing process itself, how children select a topic, generate ideas for it, write and revise their rough drafts, edit, and publish. Yet, the finished piece is also important and is evaluated. Assessment must also focus on concepts rather than rote memorization. Information alone—having a bank of facts from which to draw—is not sufficient. Knowing what to do with information, how to apply it, how to manipulate it, how to make connections, and how to solve problems should be a major goal of education. Finally, evaluation and assessment needs to focus on growth in language and attitude. To be a valid measure of student achievement and change, evaluation cannot be consigned to a test or series of tests. Instead, evaluation should be ongoing as teachers observe, analyze, and interact with students (Marek and Howard, 1984). These activities can be categorized to provide a framework for evaluating whole language education. Students can be observed, analyzed, and interacted with using a combination of formal and informal procedures as illustrated in the chart on page 466. In formal procedures, some evaluation of an activity is recorded at regular intervals, while informal evaluation can occur any time you come into contact with your students. Informal evaluation is not planned or

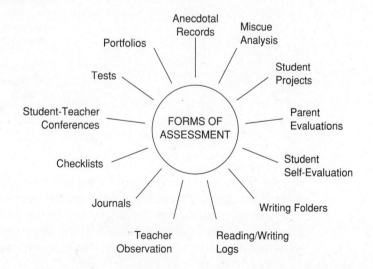

Anecdotal Records

Miscue Analysis

Portfolios

Student Projects

Tests

Student-Teacher Conferences

FORMS OF ASSESSMENT

Parent Evaluations

Checklists

Student Self-Evaluation

Journals

Writing Folders

Teacher Observation

Reading/Writing Logs

FORMAL AND INFORMAL ASSESSMENT

Activity	Informal	Formal
Observation	Watching and listening as student works alone, in groups, and in whole-class activities	Keeping anecdotal records
Interaction	Daily conversation with students	Asking planned questions to determine how students perceive concepts, internalize what has been discussed, read, written, and so on
		Conducting student-teacher conferences
Analysis	Listening to students and analyzing language skills and needs	Monitoring student compositions and written reactions
		Listening to student tapes of readings and conversations
		Monitoring student logs and checklists
		Evaluating student literature-based projects

recorded, although you may note what you learn informally, including dates, and use this information later to reinforce the formal evaluation.

Authentic assessment can take many forms, including anecdotal records, journals, writing folders, reading/writing logs, checklists, conferences, projects, miscue analysis, and evaluation by students and parents.

Anecdotal Records

Anecdotal records—brief descriptions of student behavior and performance—can be one of the most valuable evaluation tools. Anecdotal records can be a running list of each student's likes, dislikes, growth, and development. Yetta Goodman (1978) speaks of "kid watching" and the importance of watching children as they take part in various learning experiences and social interactions. Anecdotal records help teachers record these observations. Anecdotal records can be kept in a notebook or on index cards. Once reviewed for planning future instruction, they can be included in the students' folders or portfolios. Guidelines for keeping anecdotal records are as follows:

1. Don't try to write a description of each student's behavior and performance every day. Instead, focus on three to five students each day.
2. Be brief. Keep comments short and to the point.
3. Plan time at the end of the day to discuss your observations with students. This will make them more adept at self-evaluation.

Journals

Journal entries should reflect students' responses to literature, ability to express ideas, ability to react to specific works of literature, ability to organize thoughts and ideas, and growth in ability to make connections, form generalizations, and formulate new understandings and insights (see Chap. 9).

Writing Folders

Student writing samples, usually of work they have taken through the writing process, are an excellent gauge of student growth and development. Teachers can assess how well students are mastering the writing process as well as the mechanics of writing.

Reading/Writing Logs

Many of the logs and worksheets in this book are especially helpful in assessment. For example, the Independent Reading Log (Chap. 6) and Literary Logs (Chap. 9) work together to create a picture of student processes and development.

Checklists

Many of the skills and processes involved in reading, writing, thinking, and speaking can be placed on a checklist along with student names, as in the sample checklists on pages 469 and 470. Checklists will take different forms, depending on students' developmental levels, and can be used to indicate the introduction, reinforcement, and mastery of various skills and processes. Checklists are often extremely helpful in planning strategy lessons and minilessons. Students can also keep their own checklist, such as the one in Chapter 9 that lists the writing skills each has developed.

Student–Teacher Conferences

Teachers are encouraged to meet with students periodically to discuss their reading, writing, and growth in all areas of the curriculum. The conference logs teachers fill out (see Chap. 12) are excellent sources of information regarding student growth, skill development, attitudes, and motivation.

Student Projects/Literature-Based Activities

Throughout the literature-based reading program and the literature-based curriculum, students are involved in a variety of activities. Often they select activities from those offered and often they are encouraged to design their own activities. An assessment of the activities they select, the process they use to complete the activities, and the final products themselves are all part of the evaluation process. Forms such as Daily Record Sheets (Chap. 12) are excellent for recording student selections and work on these literature-related activities. Many projects result in audio and video tapes of student work; these, too, become assessment tools.

Miscue Analysis

Miscue analysis makes the teacher aware of the language cues and strategies children use when they read, giving them insight into each child's reading process. The strategy, originally proposed by Kenneth Goodman, was developed into the Reading Miscue Inventory (Y. Goodman and Burke, 1972) and later expanded *Reading Miscue Inventory: Alternative Procedures* (Y. Goodman, Watson, and Burke, 1988). Miscue analysis is based on listening to a student's oral reading and his or her retelling of the story. As the teacher records and analyzes the student's miscues he or she is provided with a detailed picture of the student's reading process. This information aids teachers in instructional planning and helps students understand their own reading processes.

Student Self-Evaluation

Self-evaluation is one of the most important evaluative measures, yet it is too often overlooked. Students need to examine their progress as they observe their own actions and processes, assess their interaction with the teacher and with other students, and analyze their work. When students participate in evaluating their own progress, they develop a sense of responsibility, which helps them assume some control over their own learning. Self-evaluation can take many forms. The simplest is the student–teacher discussion. For example, discussion

Grades 2–3 Writing Skills Checklist

Key	
I	Introduced
R	Reinforced
M	Mastered

Student	CAPITALIZATION:	Capitalize beginning of sentence	Capitalize proper nouns—names of people, places and things	Capitalize greeting and closing of a letter	Capitalize titles and initials	PUNCUATION:	Ends sentence with period, question mark, or exclamation point	Commas: between words in a series	Commas: between city and state	Commas: between day and year	Apostrophe: contractions	Apostrophe: possessives	WRITING PROCESS:	Uses prewriting techniques	Revising: reorganizes content	Revising: deletes information / adds information and details	Revising: experiments with leads and endings	Revising: uses conference techniques with self and peers	Editing: Edits for capitalization, punctuation, spelling and content	Publishing: publishes in different forms	Publishing: enjoys sharing

Grades K–1 Reading Skills Checklist

Key	
I	Introduced
R	Reinforced
M	Mastered

Student	**CONCEPTS OF PRINT:**	Recognizes print in environment	Holds book right side up	Turns pages from front to back	Tracts words in a sentence	Tracts sentences in a story	Makes letter/sound associations	Sight vocabulary	**EXPRESSION:**	Interprets story through drama/art	Reacts to story in journals	Reacts to story orally	**ATTITUDES:**	Aware of author/illustrator/has favorites	Enjoys reading and listening to literature	Chooses to read	Selects appropriate books	**FLUENCY:**	Participates in shared reading	Reads own page of big book	Recognizes words in predictable stories	Reads from LEA stories	**COMPREHENSION:**	Can retell story and details	Uses picture clues	Uses prior knowledge to predict	Predicts new endings	Recalls main idea

of a student's writing or literature-based activities might focus on the following:

1. Which of your pieces/activities do you think is your best work?
2. What makes this your best piece/project?
3. What problems did you encounter?
4. How did you solve them?
5. What goals did you set for yourself?
6. What are your goals for the next _____ week(s)?

Another type of student self-evaluation is the two-minute essay in which students are asked to react to "What I learned, what I still don't understand, questions I'd like to answer." This gives the teacher insight into the effectiveness of what the student has been doing and gives guidance for lessons and activities that students can pursue.

Finally, the student portfolio, discussed below, is an excellent strategy for encouraging students to assess their own work and make selections that represent their growth and learning.

Parent Evaluations

Often, we forget to include the parent's assessment of their child's growth. Parent input is extremely vital and should be sought. You may send home questionnaires that ask parents to react to questions whose responses will give a good indication of student interest and motivation. A sample questionnaire about students' reading attitudes is shown on page 472.

Portfolios

The portfolio is a powerful tool for documenting student development. A portfolio is a collection of various work samples and other informative materials that together give an in-depth look at a student's performance over the course of the year. A portfolio can include samples from all curricular areas. There are three basic types of portfolio designs.

1. Showcase. The significance of a showcase portfolio is the student's decisions as to what work samples go into it. For each work sample in the portfolio, the student should be encouraged to write a brief explanation about why it was included; this should go in the front of the portfolio. Teachers can establish certain criteria for selection. For example, at various intervals during the year, the teacher can ask students to select a writing piece that shows the most improvement; select two writing pieces that reflect different purposes (e.g., persuasive, narrative); select two writing pieces that reflect different genres; select the writing piece they learned the most from doing; select a piece that represents their best writing efforts.
2. Descriptive. A descriptive portfolio includes a majority of work chosen by the teacher and gives a good picture of the entire body of the student's work development.
3. Evaluative. All of the items in an evaluative portfolio are scored, rated, or evaluated.

PARENT QUESTIONNAIRE –READING ATTITUDES

Student _____

Date _____

Please respond to the following questions. Your answers will help me better help your son/daughter.

1. My child likes to be read to.   Yes   No

2. My child likes to read to me.   Yes   No

3. My child spends time daily   Yes   No
   reading independently.

4. My child likes to discuss what   Yes   No
   has been read.

5. My child likes to visit the library.   Yes   No

6. My child's favorite book is _____

7. My child's favorite author is _____.

8. My child likes to read about _____

_____

_____

_____

9. When it comes to reading, I have noticed that my child _____

_____

10. Additional Comments:

_____

_____

Parent Signature

Well-rounded portfolios include elements from each of the three types. A portfolio can be a single file folder or an accordion file, the latter providing room for a greater number of inclusions. Students and teachers add to their portfolios at various times throughout the year. Every item that goes into the portfolio should be labeled with the date it was completed. Whether the student will take the portfolio home at the end of the school year or whether it will remain on file until he or she leaves the school will influence what materials to include.

The portfolio can include a variety of materials, such as:

Skills checklists
Conference logs
Student self-evaluation essays
Student reading logs and response logs
Journal entries
Writing pieces (that have been through entire writing process)
Audio and video tapes of the student's reading and dramatic interpretations
Anecdotal records
Literature-based products or pictures of same
Work reports and samples (from other curricular areas)
Parent evaluations

To facilitate continued assessment and retrieval of needed information, all materials should be gathered in each student's individual journals, reading folders, tapes, and portfolios. The information provided through teacher and student observation, interaction, and analysis will be sure to move us away from the traditional testing procedures toward assessment procedures that provide an accurate, multidimensional assessment of student growth and needs. The possibilities for this type of assessment are limitless, the results gratifying.

Professional Resources

*Cited in text

Baskwill, J., and P. Whitman. *Evaluation: Whole Language, Whole Child.* Scholastic, 1988.

De Fina, Allan A. *Portfolio Assessment.* Scholastic, 1992.

Goodman, Kenneth S. *What's Whole in Whole Language?* Scholastic, 1985.

Goodman, Kenneth S., Yetta M. Goodman, and Wendy J. Hood, eds. *The Whole Language Evaluation Book.* Heinemann, 1989.

*Goodman, Yetta. "Kidwatching: An Alternative to Testing." *National Elementary School Principal,* 57: 41–45, 1978.

*Goodman, Yetta and Carolyn Burke. *Reading Miscue Inventory Manual: Procedures for Diagnosis and Evaluation.* Owen, 1972.

*Goodman, Yetta, Dorothy Watson, and Carolyn Burke. *Reading Miscue Inventory: Alternative Procedures.* Owen, 1987.

*Harp, Bill, ed. *Assessment and Evaluation in Whole Language Programs.* Christopher-Gordon, 1993.

Jagger, A. M., and M. T. Smith-Burkey, eds. *Observing the Language Learner.* International Reading Association, 1985.

Jasmine, J. *Portfolio Assessment for Your Whole Language Classroom.* Teacher Created Materials, 1992.

*Marek, A., and D. Howard. "A Kid-Watching Guide: Evaluation for Whole Language Classrooms." Occasional Paper No. 9, Tucson Program in Language and Literacy. University of Arizona, 1984.

Myers, Miles. *A Procedure for Writing Assessment and Holistic Scoring.* NCTE, 1980.

Valencia, Sheila-Heibert, Elfrieda Afflerbach, and Peter Afflerbach, eds. *Authentic Reading Assessement.* International Reading Association, 1993.

Yancey, Kathleen Blake, ed. *Portfolios in the Writing Classroom.* National Council of Teachers of English, 1992.

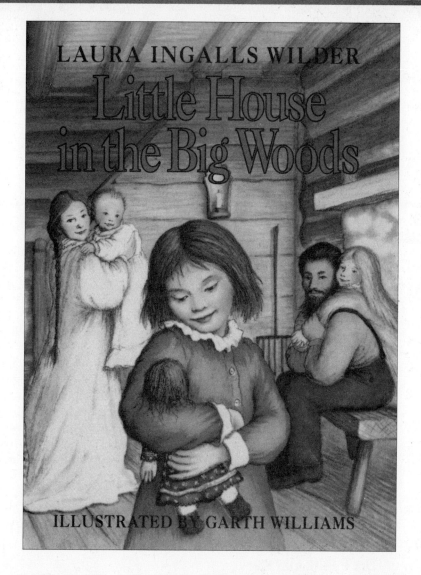

CHAPTER 15

Reaching Beyond the Classroom

Libraries

As children's love for literature and reading grows, they naturally want to read more. What better place to nourish this need than the library. Young children become familiar with the library by visiting it with their parents, finding special "treasures" to bring home and read, and listening during story hour, as librarians and storytellers bring books to life. Unfortunately, children do not all have the same advantages, and many come to school having had little or no contact with libraries.

It is important that students know how to find what they want and need in the library. In many libraries, computer technology is replacing card catalogs. Some systems are more sophisticated than others in the information provided; however, most systems are relatively simple to operate. Students should be given instruction in how to use the card catalog and/or computer.

Any book on literature for children would be incomplete without a discussion of the library and suggestions to encourage children, parents, and teachers to take advantage of the many quality books, materials, and activities available. The strategies described in this section will help you familiarize students with their local public library and the school library. Suggestions are also included to facilitate the planning and implementation of a classroom library.

The Public Library

The public library is a source of tremendous opportunities for children. In addition to making thousands of books available, public libraries host puppet shows, storytelling hours, author talks, travel documentaries, guest speakers, movies based on literature, and a vast variety of activities designed to educate, inform, and entertain—and all for free!

The following activities will help students and their parents become familiar with their local libraries:

1. It's all happening . . . at the library. What does your public library offer? Involve students in a "fact-finding mission" to learn what activities and events their local library hosts. Have students advertise monthly events through a school newsletter, parent bulletin boards, announcements, and "billboards."

2. Calendar of events. Select students each month to create a Calendar of Library Events bulletin board. Select a strategic location for the bulletin board, such as the cafeteria, so all students and parents will be sure to see it. Copies of the calendar can be sent home for parents as well. Encourage students to evaluate the activities and select the events they would like to attend.

3. Library field trip. Arrange a tour of the local public library. The tour should include an explanation of the organization of the library and procedures for checking out materials. Allow time for students to browse through the aisles of books, searching for those that capture their interest. If a student is having difficulty finding a book, have previously completed interest inventories handy (Chap. 2) so you can recommend appropriate materials.

   To check out books, students will need their own library card. Most libraries require that parents of minors complete and sign a form, since the parent is responsible for anything borrowed from the library. Before the field trip, determine the library's procedures and send parents appropriate forms to be completed if their child does not have a library card.

4. Scavenger hunt. Prepare a scavenger hunt appropriate to the students' abilities that asks students to locate certain materials in the library. Divide students into teams and award points for each item, with those items that are more difficult to find being worth more points. At the end of the time limit, determine which group has earned the most points. Allow groups to discuss what they found and how they went about finding each item. A sample scavenger hunt for grades 3–6 is shown on page 478.

5. Guest librarians. Invite local librarians to your classroom for a "story-sharing session" to introduce students to specific books on a selected theme or books that are new to the library.

The School Library

The school library is another excellent source of good literature. The library will seem more accessible to students as they become familiar with its organization and adept at locating specific works. As students become more comfortable with using the library, they will visit it more regularly, searching for both recreational reading materials and materials to help them fulfill assignments.

The following activities will aid students in using their school libraries:

1. Library play. After learning about the organization of the library and the Dewey Decimal Classification System, have students create a play that will introduce other students to the library and the variety of books found there. For example, they can design sandwich boards decorated with the number of a certain section of books and pictures representative of that section. Then, as that section, they can tell about themselves in prose or poem. The student introducing section 800–899 might say the following:

   For books that take you back in time,
   To ages long ago,

SCAVENGER HUNT

Directions: You and your team members have 30 minutes to locate the following items. Find as many of these items as you can.

A book for young children on colors	2 points
A nonfiction book on space	5 points
A mystery book for children your age	5 points
A book with maps of different countries	10 points
A magazine on the subject of science	5 points
A book that gives information about your state	5 points
A volume of a general encyclopedia	3 points
A biography of a famous artist	10 points
A volume of the *Readers' Guide to Periodical Literature*	10 points
A record, filmstrip, or cassette tape on any subject	5 points
A book that has won a Caldecott Award	3 points
A book illustrated using watercolors	3 points
Two books illustrated by the same illustrator	4 points

Total Possible Points: 70

The 800 section of the library
Is the place for you to go.
For books on travel to places
You've always wanted to see,
For books on history and geography,
The 800s is the place to be.

2. Library checklist. Distribute the checklist on page 480. Have students visit the library to discover which of these items are available. Students can then compare the school library to the local public library to determine which has more appropriate materials for them, which has a greater variety of materials, and which is easier to use and why.

3. Where in the library am I? Involve students in a library version of hide-and-seek. Hide several objects around the library and give students clues that will help them locate the objects and at the same time become more familiar with the materials in the library. For example:

    If you're searching for an outer-space book,
    This is the place that you should first look.
    (card catalog under "space")

Depending on their ability, students can create their own clues for classmates to solve.

4. Magical library tour. Have students develop maps of the school library and then lead a tour, pointing out the places and materials they've indicated on their maps. Copies of the maps can be distributed to students on the library tour. Special times can be set aside for the tour, and teachers can make tour reservations for their classes or for individual students.

5. Story hour. Establish a story hour, a read-aloud program in which you select students to read to younger students. Allow the reader to select the material for the story hour, making sure it is appropriate for those who will attend. A flier advertising the story hour and the book being read can be written and distributed weekly to teachers of the targeted age group. Encourage students to read their own published works as well as the works of well-known authors.

Parent Lending Library

Resource books for parents, teacher-made games, educational toys, videos, cassettes, and children's books are among the important components of a parent lending library. Ideally, this should be a place, perhaps within the confines of the school library, where parents can browse while they select appropriate materials. If it is part of the regular school library, the school librarian can monitor the process for checking out books. Parents can be encouraged to donate items to the resource library, such as toys and books, of which their children have grown tired. Families can enhance their parenting skills as well as helping their children develop important reading skills by reading some of the resource materials.

LIBRARY CHECKLIST

Directions: Using the list below, locate reference works that are available. As you find each of the materials, place a check in the box on the left, and indicate its location in the library.

☐ Card catalog _____

☐ Computer _____

☐ Dictionary _____

☐ Encyclopedia _____

☐ Familiar Quotations _____

☐ First Facts _____

☐ Thesaurus _____

☐ World Almanac _____

☐ *World Atlas* _____

☐ *Current Biography Yearbook* _____

☐ *Readers' Guide to Periodical Literature* _____

☐ *Twentieth Century Authors* _____

☐ *Webster's Biographical Dictionary* _____

☐ *Who's Who in America* _____

☐ Newspapers _____

☐ Magazines _____

☐ Microfilm _____

☐ Filmstrips _____

☐ Cassette tapes/records _____

☐ Photographic file _____

☐ *Something About the Author* _____

_____

☐ *Illustrators of Books for Young Children* _____

Parent Involvement

Importance of Parent Involvement

Most often, the parent is the first and most important teacher a child will ever have. The parents, not professional educators, teach many of the important basic skills. Imagine what life would be like today if you knew only what you had

been taught in school. Most likely, you learned many of the important lessons of life from a parent or caregiver, not from a teacher.

As the poem "Unity" so beautifully illustrates, success can be achieved when the teacher and parents work together.

Unity

I dreamed I stood in a studio
and watched two sculptors there.
The clay they used was a young child's mind,
And they fashioned it with care.
One was a teacher; the tools he used
Were books, and music, and art;
One, a parent with a guiding hand,
And a gentle, loving heart.
Day after day the teacher toiled,
With touch that was deft and sure
While the parents labored by his side
And polished and smoothed it o'er.

And when at last their task was done,

They were proud of what they had wrought.

For this thing they had molded in the child

Could neither be sold nor bought.

And each agreed he would have failed

If he had worked alone,

For behind the parent stood the school

And behind the teacher, the home.

Author Unknown

The significance of the teacher and parents sharing the responsibility of educating a child is recognized by many researchers. There is evidence, as measured by standardized tests, that parental involvement has strong effects on children's developing intelligence and achievement (Becher, 1982; Olmstead and Rubin, 1983). In addition, researchers have found that parent–teacher contact with the goal of providing at-home reading instruction resulted in gains on standardized tests (Garber, 1972; Iverson, Brownlee, and Walberg, 1981; Keele and Harrison, 1971; McKinney, 1977). Tizard, et al. (1982) found that children whose parents listened to them read at home had markedly higher reading attainment at ages 7 and 8 than children who did not receive such support.

Holdaway (1979) reports that children who are read to frequently begin to understand that stories have characters, settings, beginnings, middles, endings, and other important concepts needed for understanding what is read and heard. It is important for parents not only to read to their children but also to talk about the story and ask questions during the reading process (Becher, 1985; DeFord and Rasinski, 1986).

The Commission on Reading's report (Anderson et al., 1985), present, the following interpretations of current knowledge and research on parents and reading:

- "The single most important activity for building the knowledge required for eventual success in reading is reading aloud to children."
- "Research shows that parents of successful readers have a more accurate view of their children's performance."
- "Most children will learn how to read. Whether they will read depends in part upon encouragement from their parents. Several researchers recently studied the amount of reading that middle-grade students do at home. Those who read a lot show larger gains on reading achievement tests. They tend to come from homes in which there are plenty of books, or opportunities to visit the library, and in which parents and brothers and sisters also read."
- "The more knowledge children are able to acquire at home, the greater their chance for success in reading."
- "Wide experience alone is not enough, however. The way in which parents talk to their children about an experience influences what knowledge

the children will gain from the experience and their later ability to draw on the knowledge when reading."

- "A long-term study that followed children from age one to seven found that the content and style of the language parents used with their children predicted the children's school achievement in reading."

It is rare to find parents who are not interested in their children's education. Most parents, regardless of social class, want their children to be successful in school and in life (Brantlinger, 1985; Seginer, 1983). If this is true and if parent involvement is so important, why aren't more parents involved? Greenwood and Hickman (1991) have identified several barriers to parent involvement. First, many parents feel inadequate in their qualifications to help with academics. Second, more women than ever before are working outside the home, therefore they do not have time to become involved with their children's education. Third, some parents feel the school and the teacher are responsible for educating their child. Fourth, there are those few parents who do not want to be involved in the education of their child. Finally, some parents have negative feelings about the school life they experienced and are not particularly supportive if they believe their children are in a similar setting. If parents are reluctant to become involved in their children's education, teachers need to help them overcome this reluctance.

How to Achieve Successful Parent Involvement

There is much support for parental involvement in the literacy development of their children (Durkin, 1977; Goldfield and Snow, 1984; Greaney, 1980; Henderson, 1988; Topping, 1987). Educators have long realized that parents can be the most valuable resource available for better understanding the children with whom they work. It is therefore important that teachers and parents forge a strong link of communication. This communication needs to be honest, open, and frequent to build a bond of trust. Parents need to realize and believe the teacher has their child's best interest in mind when making decisions. It is important for teachers to remember that communication with parents may be just as important when students are in upper elementary grades as when they are in primary grades. Without frequent communication, it is virtually impossible to build and maintain good parental involvement (Goldenberg, 1989). Therefore, teachers need to develop strategies for communicating with parents, such as the following.

1. Strategically placed parent bulletin boards—at the door of the classroom or by the office, for example—can be effective. Weekly menus, upcoming meetings, events, and activities can be posted. For example, details of events such as a reading day at the mall or a puppet show at the local library can be posted. Parents soon look forward to checking the bulletin board to learn what is going on.

2. Parent newsletters (see p. 485) provide an excellent way to network with parents, especially those who are not able to stop by the school on a regular basis. The newsletters can provide information posted on the parent bulletin board, relate students' activities at school, and include ideas for at-home activities for parents and children to reinforce concepts being taught at school.

3. Telephoning parents on a regular basis to tell them something positive about their child can be a beneficial way to communicate with them. Be sure to call at a time that is convenient for the parents and to make the call short. If parents become accustomed to your calling and often hear a positive message, they will be much more receptive when you call to ask for their assistance or tell them of a problem with their child.

4. Meetings for groups of parents throughout the year can be helpful; however, they should be short and present useful information. A parent meeting is a good opportunity for the teacher to introduce himself or herself and to describe some of the activities and literacy events the children will be involved in throughout the year. Teachers may provide samples of children's work at these meetings and/or get the parents involved in some of the children's activities. One teacher read *Alexander and the Terrible, Horrible, No Good, Very Bad Day,* by Judith Viorst, to the parents at a parent open house and the parents commented on how much they enjoyed being read to. They said they had forgotten how enjoyable it was to be read to.

5. Parent–teacher conferences can provide an opportunity for parents and teachers to spend quality time together. Teachers can learn much about a child from the parents. It is important for the teacher, and perhaps even the parent, to share something positive about the child.

6. Various organizations have brochures and pamphlets designed for parents working with their children. Obtain samples and invite parents to borrow your copies or order their own. Most of these materials are free or inexpensive. Often schools buy these resources in bulk and distribute them to parents (see Appendix G). Some of these organizations also have video tapes that may be useful to show at parent meetings or to lend to parents.

7. Children can become involved in communication with parents by writing their own letters informing parents about what they are or will be doing at school. Teachers may devote part of a reading/writing period each week to this activity. Before writing, the class can brainstorm what they have done over the past week and list their accomplishments on the chalkboard. Children can then write the letters, share them with peers and/or teacher, ask for suggestions, make suggested revisions, and then present them to their parents. This also provides parents with an opportunity to see their children's work. It should be explained to the parents what the purpose of this activity is and that the letters may not be perfect.

8. Ongoing communication can be maintained by sending children's work home on a weekly basis. The teacher can attach a short note pointing out the child's stengths and weaknesses and how the parent might assist. Par-

**News Groups
First Grade
Mrs. C.**

Week of February 25, 1991

On Monday Chucky told us about his trip to Disney World. He went on the "Run Away Train" and in the submarine, Chucky told us that he said "Hell-o" to Mickey Mouse for Mrs. C. His Mom and Dad drove to Disney World and it took them two days. Richard showed us a clay bear he made. He put it in the oven so it would get hard. He made it at his baby sitter's house. Craig showed us a Canadian coin that his Mom got out of her bank. He had to trade a U.S. quarter for it. Amber told us that she got a new cat. The cat's claws had to be taken off. Now it can't go outside.

On Tuesday Brittany showed us a clown in a box that her Dad gave her. It is musical and can come out of the box. Chris F. showed us a Nintendo Power Magazine. He showed us how to get some clues. If you have a Nintendo you could use the magazine. Sarah brought in pictures of her dog. She brought in picture of Philip and herself when they were outside playing in the snow. Tamara showed us crystals she got from her friend's house. She found them in the woods. Mrs. C. told Tamara to always be sure she can see her house when she is in the woods because she could get lost.

On Wednesday Cherie showed us two dolls that came with a high chair and a stroller. It also came with food. The big doll could walk but the rechargeable battery was weak. Jacob told us he got a puppy. It is black and white. Craig thought it sounded like a border collie. Jacob's father named it Ottis. Lindsay showed us her Cabbage Patch Doll. Her grandma made a blanket for the doll. Lindsay said she has a bag of clothes for her doll.

Andrew told us his brother, Daniel, got a hair cut. Lauren brought in Snow White and the three Dwarfs. They move and they have little platforms that you can put them on. You can add on to this set. Her mother gave it to her on Valentine's Day.

On Thursday Alex showed beautiful rocks. She brought in a piece of special coal. Ten children examined them during the morning. Nichole showed us a newspaper article about her uncle's house that had a fire that started in the basement. Nichole read part of the article to us. Leif showed us another comic book his Uncle Ron wrote. Steven showed us a magic mirror book. It makes a reflection of pictures. We talked about things being symmetrical. Ken showed us a car. It was broken. It had a man inside. It was yellow, the number on it was one. There were stickers all over it. His Dad tried to fix it, it worked, and broke again. Dad will try again.

On Friday Elise showed us a colored pencil. You can take one color out and put in another color. It had about 9 or 10 colors. She got it from Renai Richardson's birthday. Robert told us he is in Level 5. He is a Gold Star. He likes reading *Together We Go*. Michael showed us twenty or thirty rocks, a horse and a parrot. It was called a rock garden. He showed us a rock necklace. Bree brought in little beads to make a necklace and a bracelet. You would need a lot to make a bracelet. Chris B. showed us 45 baseball cards. There were stickers with the baseball cads. He got them from his Grandma when she was visiting her two sisters in Florida.

ents can see their children's progress throughout the year, eliminating surprises at the end.

Parents need to feel successful in their endeavors with their children. To achieve this, provide specific tasks that all parents can accomplish. These tasks should be stated in a clear, concise manner and the parent should feel comfortable about doing them.

Giving feedback to the parent is essential. The parent needs to know if what he or she is doing is indeed beneficial. When possible, communicate with the parent about specific progress the child is making as a result of the parent's extra help or interest. Also, when a parent does something for the child or the class, express your appreciation by sending a thank you note or calling.

Parents also need to feel a sense of empowerment, to recognize they play a role in making decisions about their children's learning and instruction (Rasinski, 1989). Parents who feel empowered are much more likely to be actively involved and committed to the process of helping educate their child. Some schools have very active parent advisory groups that work closely with the teachers and administrators in making important decisions.

For any parent program to be successful, administrative support is imperative (Berninger and Rodriguez, 1989). If the administration does not show enthusiasm and support for parent involvement, then teachers and other staff may not see it as important.

Training programs that teach parents how to read aloud to their children, such as Parents as Partners in Reading, the Parent Readers Program, and the Intergenerational Reading Project (France, 1991; Jongsma, 1990; Somerfield, 1989) can be beneficial. Parents need and want to learn how to involve their children actively in story reading and how to use their voices and intonation to create different emotions appropriate to the plot of the story. Research strongly supports that with assistance from school, parents can learn to provide an environment that promotes and fosters literacy (France and Meeks, 1987; Walberg, 1984).

Parents may also be trained as individual tutors for children. Tutors can often help children expand their language and thinking in addition to teaching and practicing specific skills.

Most parents want to be treated as equals, not as clients or consumers (Lindle, 1989). Most beneficial for the child is for the parent and teacher to develop a true partnership in which they can sit down together and discuss what learning experiences would best benefit the child and how they can work cooperatively to accomplish these.

How Parents Can Help

Parents can serve as a wonderful source of information about their children. They can provide information about their children's out-of-school literacy development. Does the child like being read to? Does the child choose reading a book as an at-home activity? What does the child like to read about? Parents can also discuss the type of reading involvement they have with their child at home. The checklist on page 487 can help parents evaluate their reading involvement with their child and help them discover activities to do with their children.

Parents and other family members can be very effective classroom volunteers. It is important to involve not only parents but also grandparents, aunts, uncles, and other relatives.

Dear Parents,

The following checklist provides activities that encourage listening,

speaking, reading, and writing. Using the following scale, rate

yourself on each of the statements:

                                                          Sincerely,

1	2	3
Never	Sometimes	Frequently

_____   I listen to my child and answer his or her questions.

_____   I make time each day to talk with my child.

_____   My child and I go to the library and select books.

_____   I show my child that reading is important by reading
                books, magazines, newspapers, and so on.

_____   My child and I talk about books, magazines, or other
                things that we have read.

_____   I read aloud to my child.

_____   I limit TV viewing so that there is at least equal time
                for reading.

_____   I write messages to my child and encourage return
                messages in whatever form he or she chooses.

_____   I give and suggest reading and writing materials as
                gifts for my child.

In addition, you may wish to select a particular month as Visitor Reading Month. Send the letter on page 488 home inviting members of each family to be involved. Once the forms are returned, make a schedule of visitors and send it home with the students. It is good to follow up with a phone call at least two days before the visitor's presentation to confirm the time and date and to ask if any assistance is needed.

Traditional report cards and standardized tests are not used as widely today, with the whole language movement, as they once were to report students' progress. Today, educators are looking for assessment procedures that move beyond norm- or criterion-referenced tools and are focusing on evaluation that

Dear Parent,

This is "Visitor Reading Month" in our classroom, and we would like to invite someone from your family to participate. Mothers, fathers, grandparents, uncles, aunts, and cousins are invited. A checklist of activities you might like to do during your visit, along with a choice of days and times, is provided below. Please complete and return to me by _____ . We look forward to having a member of your family with us during "Visitor Reading Month."

                                 Sincerely,

— —

I _____ would like to participate in "Visitor Reading Month."
      name

I will be happy to:

_____ select a book and read it aloud to the class

_____ take a group of children to the school library

_____ monitor the classroom library and assist students as needed

_____ assist students with writing projects

_____ tell a favorite story

Other _____

Choice of day	Choice of time
_____	_____ 9:00 – 10:00 A.M.
_____	_____ 10:00 – 11:00 A.M.
_____	_____ 1:30 – 2:30 P.M.
	Other _____

It is not possible for me or members of my family to come to the classroom during "Visitor Reading Month." However, I would be happy to:

_____ donate a book for reading aloud

_____ share a game or activity my child enjoys

_____ send a snack for the children

Other _____

Signature: _____

Relationship: _____

involves more meaningful and functional reading. Fredericks and Rasinski (1990) believe parents should and can play a significant role in assessment. They provide the following six ideas for teachers who want parents to become partners in the assessment process.

1. At the beginning of the year, provide a way for the parents to state individual expectations of their child. Record the parents' expectations.
2. Solicit help from the parents in designing an assessment instrument that rates homework assignments. The assessment instrument can be attached to each homework assignment. Parents can respond to such factors as difficulty of the assignment, how well their child understood the assignment procedures, appropriateness of the assignment, and suggestions for improving the assignment.
3. Provide parents with a weekly or biweekly summary sheet on which they can record their own observations about their child's reading growth. You may want to prepare some questions ahead of time, such as: What were some positive things you noted in your child's reading this past week? What were some negative events? Keep a record of these sheets and refer to them regularly in home telephone calls or face-to-face conferences.
4. Develop a series of simple question sheets for parents to complete frequently. Each sheet should be designed to elicit parents' questions about their child's progress. Space should be included for your responses.
5. Ask parents frequently to compose lists of things their children have learned in reading. Direct parents to provide information on lessons or parts of lessons their children did not understand. Ask that these be submitted at intervals throughout the year and take time to discuss them with parents.
6. Provide opportunities for parents to visit the classroom and observe the reading program in action. Afterward, ask them to evaluate their child's performance in class and elicit their perceptions about their child's strengths or weaknesses. Record these parental observations and keep them in a portfolio for sharing later in the year.

Fredericks and Rasinski (1990) have designed two useful parental assessment tools—an Attitudinal Scale for Parents (p. 490) and an Observation Guide for Parents (p. 491). Send one or both periodically throughout the year.

Emphasize to parents the importance of reading aloud to their children and how this can help make them better readers at school. Vukelich (1984) reports that a 20-minute reading interaction time every day has helped children begin a lifelong reading habit. A study by Romotowski and Trepanier (1977) showed that children who are read to on a regular basis (at least four times a week for eight to ten minutes) exhibit a more positive attitude toward reading and show higher levels of achievement in reading than those not read to. For years, researchers have been documenting that children who have been read to or exposed to books learn to read earlier than those who have not had this experience (Doake, 1979; Durkin, 1966; Holdaway, 1979).

ATTITUDINAL SCALE FOR PARENTS

Child's name: _____ Date: _____

Please indicate your observation of your child's reading growth since the last report. Feel free to comment where appropriate.

A = Strongly agree
B = Agree
C = Disagree
D = Strongly disagree

My child: Comments

 1. Understands more of what he/she reads   A   B   C   D
 2. Enjoys being read to by family members   A   B   C   D
 3. Finds time for quiet reading at home   A   B   C   D
 4. Sometimes guesses at words, but they
    usually make sense   A   B   C   D
 5. Can provide a summary of stories read   A   B   C   D
 6. Has a good attitude about reading   A   B   C   D
 7. Enjoys reading to family members   A   B   C   D
 8. Would like to get more books   A   B   C   D
 9. Chooses to write about stories read   A   B   C   D
10. Is able to complete homework assignments   A   B   C   D

Strengths I see: _____

_____

_____

Areas that need improvement: _____

_____

_____

Concerns or questions I have: _____

_____

_____

To assist parents in getting involved with their children's literacy development, a letter such as the one on page 494 may be sent home to them. Remind parents to continue reading aloud even as their children grow older. Even adults love being read to. Teachers may want to select books from the suggested list of read-aloud books (Chap. 4) to send home with this letter.

In addition to reading aloud, there are other ways parents can help to promote literacy. The letter on page 493 provides some ideas to share with parents.

Parents can serve as resource people. It is important that teachers determine what expertise, knowledge, and experiences parents and/or other family members have that they may be willing to share with the class. For example, if the class is doing a thematic unit on Mexico, a parent or other family member

---

OBSERVATION GUIDE FOR PARENTS

_____

Child's name: _____

Date of last report: _____ Today's date: _____

The skills and attitudes you observed in your child on the last report have been recorded in the first column. Please place a check (√) next to those items in the second column that you have observed in your child since the last report.

My child:

_____	_____	1. Reads from a wide variety of materials, such as books, magazines, newspapers.
✓	_____	2. Takes time during each day to read in a quiet place
✓	_____	3. Talks with family members about the things he/she is reading
_____	_____	4. Finds reading to be an exciting way to learn about the world
✓	_____	5. Brings books and other reading materials from the school or public library
✓	_____	6. Seems to understand more of what he/she reads at home
_____	_____	7. Tries to discover new words and uses them in conversations
_____	_____	8. Seems to have developed higher-level thinking skills
_____	_____	9. Uses study skills (e.g., note taking, organizing time, etc.) regularly
_____	_____	10. Has shown improvement in his/her reading ability since the last report

My child would be a better reader if: _____

_____

_____

My child's greatest strength in reading is: _____

_____

_____

By the next report my child should learn: _____

_____

_____

_____
Signature

---

who has traveled to or lived in Mexico could enhance the study of Mexico. A simple survey in a newsletter can provide the teacher with a wealth of resources. The survey need only ask parents about their interests/expertise and whether or not they would be willing to share or demonstrate these. Teachers may want to include potential topics for the year on the survey and ask for other suggestions. This may trigger parents' ideas.

Parents who cannot participate in the classroom may be willing to help with other activities, such as:

- Collecting and developing materials for upcoming thematic units
- Collecting and organizing arts and crafts materials for an art project
- Preparing snacks for holidays and celebrations
- Calling and arranging for other parents to participate in field trips and other activities

Parent involvement opportunities that do not require the parent to be in the classroom are very important for the child as well as the parents and can prove to be invaluable to the teacher.

Parents can also become involved with their child's classroom by helping collect and/or donate materials. For example, they may purchase and donate paperback books, perhaps in honor of someone in the child's family or to celebrate a special occasion. Books as well as art and craft materials can often be found at garage sales. Parents can be informed in newsletters of items needed for the classroom and could become valuable collectors of these items.

Another after-school project that parents can plan and implement to benefit the school or classroom is a book fair in which books are sold and/or traded.

This book was donated by _____

in honor of _____

Additional Activities for Parents

The following activities that involve parents and the community can be initiated.

1. Have a "Picnic Reading Day." Invite family members to come on a particular day and time. Request that the children and family members pack a picnic lunch. In addition, ask each child to select several books that he or she would like to have read. The family members join the children for a picnic lunch as they read the book(s) together. If some children do not have a family member at the picnic, invite them to join other children and their family members.
2. Conduct a Read-a-Thon—a whole day to read! Have students bring pillows, blankets, and books from home. If weather permits, let them read outdoors. Ask parent volunteers to help supervise.
3. Invite parents and other interested people to "An Author's Night" to celebrate the young authors in the class. This could be combined with a potluck or dessert feast. Ask each child to read something he or she has written to the very appreciative audience.
4. Schools with lower-income families can participate in Reading Is Fundamental programs, in which each child is given a free book. For more infor-

Dear Parents,

As a parent, you are your child's first and most important teacher. There are many ways you can help your child to become a better reader. Following are some suggestions.

1. Be a reader yourself. If your child sees that you enjoy reading the newspaper or books on a regular basis, he or she will want to follow your example.
2. Involve your child in activities that involve looking at newspapers and magazines. For example, have a scavenger hunt in which you give your child a list of things to find in today's newspaper, such as:

   The temperature in Paris, France
   The temperature in a place where a relative lives
   Two words that begin with the first letter of your child's name
   A movie that is playing at a nearby theater
   A picture of someone your child can identify, such as the president of the United States

3. Help your child create his or her own home library.
4. Give your child books as gifts for birthdays and holidays.
5. Schedule regular library trips with your child.
6. Make sure your child reads every day. Encourage this by allowing him or her to stay up 15 minutes later at night if he or she is reading a book. Researchers have found that children who spend a least 30 minutes a day reading for enjoyment develop skills to be a better reader at school.
7. READ ALOUD TO YOUR CHILD. Studies have shown that 10–20 minutes of reading aloud each day can make your child a better reader. Jim Trelease has written an excellent handbook that provides information about reading aloud. It is entitled *The New Read Aloud Handbook* (Penguin, New York, 1989) and is available in most book stores.

Most of all, enjoy reading activities with your child. Reading aloud or independently provides a chance to do something together. HAVE FUN!

Sincerely,

---

mation, contact Reading Is Fundamental, 600 Maryland Avenue S.W. 1, Suite 600, Washington, D.C. 20560, (202) 287-3220.

5. Pizza Hut, Inc., sponsors an excellent reading incentive program called Book It! For more information, contact The Book It Program, c/o Pizza Hut, Inc., P.O. Box 2999, Wichita, Kansas 67201-0428, (800) 4-BOOK-IT.
6. At "Back to School Night," explain the reading and writing program to the parents. This can help alleviate problems and misunderstandings that

Dear Parents,

Reading to your child regularly is very important for developing his or her ability to read and fostering a love for reading. The following guidelines are important for making reading time profitable and enjoyable for both of you. So sit back, relax, and enjoy a good book with your child!

Sincerely,

1. Select from a variety of books that reflect your child's interests.
2. Try to set aside a special time each day for a story, perhaps at bed time, naptime, or after dinner.
3. Find a quiet, comfortable place to read.
4. Ask a few prereading discussion questions, such as: "Look at the cover. What do you think this book might be about?"
5. Be sure your child can see the illustrations as you read.
6. Read with expression. Gestures, sound effects, and voice inflections add interest to many books.
7. Encourage your child to participate in the reading when appropriate.
8. The main objective of reading to your child is to provide an opportunity to relax and enjoy the magic of good literature. However, a few appropriate questions can enhance your child's comprehension and interest. The following questions can serve as a guide.

   Which character would you most like to be friends with?
   How would you change the ending of the story?
   How would the story be different if it took place at a different time or place?
   Compare this story with other stories we have read on the same subject or other books written by the same author.

9. Stop at strategic points and discuss what your child thinks will happen next.
10. When the book is finished, allow your child to respond in some way, perhaps by making an illustration of a favorite character or part of the book or by making a puppet to role-play the story.

might occur later. Educate parents about research that supports the methods being used. Recruit parents who will volunteer, on a regular basis, to listen to the students read and read to them.

7. Create "Traveling Book Packs" for students to take home. Place a book, a related visual (e.g., puppet, toy), and suggested questions/activities in lunch boxes or backpacks. In lieu of questions, you may wish to include a journal in which students can respond in words or pictures to the book. Parents should also be encouraged to respond to the book by writing a journal entry. Parent volunteers may be willing to assist in making travel-

ing book packs. Every week have students take a different "Traveling Book Pack" home, where he or she can share it with the family. Allow time to share projects and information.

8. Invite parent volunteers to tape record a book or portion of a book so children can listen to it over and over again.

Professional Resources

*Cited in text

*Anderson, R. C., E. H. Hiebert, J. A. Scott, and I. Wilkinson. *Becoming a Nation of Readers: The Report of the Commission on Reading.* National Institute of Education, 1985.

*Becher, R. "Parent Education," in *Encyclopedia of Educational Research,* 5th ed. Macmillan/Free Press, 1982, pp. 1379–1382.

*———. "Parent Involvement and Reading Achievement: A Review of Research and Implications for Practice." *Childhood Education,* 62: 44–50, 1985.

*Berninger, J. M., and R. C. Rodriguez. "The Principal as Catalyst in Parent Involvement." *Momentum,* 20: 32–34, 1989.

*Brantlinger, E. A. "What Low-Income Parents Want from Schools: A Different View of Aspirations." *Interchange,* 16: 14–28, 1985.

*DeFord, D., and T. Rasinski. "A Question of Knowledge and Control in Teaching and Learning," in M. Sampson, ed. *The Pursuit of Literacy.* Kendall-Hunt, 1986.

*Doake, D. "Book Experience and Emergent Reading Behavior." Paper presented at Pre-convention Institute no. 24, Research on Written Language Development, International Reading Association Annual Convention, Atlanta, April 1979.

*Durkin, D. *Children Who Read Early.* Teachers' College Press, 1966.

*———. "Facts About Pre-First-Grade Reading," in L. O. Ollila, ed. *The Kindergarten Child and Reading.* International Reading Association, 1977.

*France, M. G. *An Examination of the Effects of an Intergenerational Reading Workshop on the Listening Comprehension of At-Risk Pre-Kindergarten Students.* Unpublished dissertation. Old Dominion University, Norfolk, 1991.

*France, M. G., and J. Meeks. "Parents Who Can't Read: What the Schools Can Do." *Journal of Reading,* 31: 222–227, 1987.

*Fredericks, A. D., and T. V. Rasinski. "Involving Parents in the Assessment Process." *Reading Teacher,* 44: 346–349, 1990.

*Garber, M. "The Florida Parent Education Program." ERIC Document Reproduction Service no. ED 058 953, 1972.

*Goldenberg, C. N. "Making Success a More Common Occurrence for Children at Risk for Failure: Lessons from Hispanic First Graders Learning to Read," in J. B. Allen and J. M. Mason, eds. *Risk Makers, Risk Takers, Risk Breakers.* Heinemann, 1989.

*Goldfield, B. A., and C. E. Snow. "Reading Books with Children: The Mechanics of Parental Influence on Children's Reading Achievement," in J. Flood, ed. *Promoting Reading Comprehension.* International Reading Association, 1984.

*Greaney, V. "Factors Related to the Amount and Type of Leisure Reading." *Reading Research Quarterly,* 15: 337–357, 1980.

*Greenwood, G. E., and C. W. Hickman. "Research and Practice in Parent Involvement: Implications for Teacher Education." *Elementary School Journal,* 91: 279–288, 1991.

*Henderson, A. T. "Parents Are a School's Best Friends." *Phi Delta Kappan,* 70: 148–153, 1988.

*Holdaway, D. *The Foundations of Literacy.* Ashton Scholastic, 1979.

*Iverson, B. K., G. D. Brownlee, and H. J. Walberg. "Parent–Teacher Contacts and Student Learning." *Journal of Educational Research,* 74: 394–396, 1981.

*Jongsma, K. "Intergenerational Literacy." *The Reading Teacher,* 39: 522–523, 1990.

*Keele, R., and G. Harrison. *The Effects of Parents Using Structural Tutoring Techniques in Teaching Their Children to Read.* Rand McNally, 1971.

*Lindle, J. C. "What Do Parents Want from Principals and Teachers?" *Educational Leadership,* 47: 12–14, 1989.

*McKinney, J. "The Development and Implementation of a Tutorial Program for Parents to Improve the Reading and Mathematics Achievement of Their Children." ERIC Document Reproduction Service no. ED 113 703, 1977.

*Olmstead, P. P., and R. I. Rubin. "Linking Parent Behaviors and Child Achievement: Four Evaluation Studies from the Parent Education Follow Through Program." *Studies in Educational Evaluation,* 8: 317–325, 1983.

*Rasinski, T. V. "Reading and the Empowerment of Parents." *The Reading Teacher,* 43: 226–231, 1989.

*Romotowski, J. A., and M. L. Trepanier. "Examining and Influencing the Home Reading Behaviors of Young Children." ERIC Document Reproduction Service no. ED 195 938, 1977.

*Seginer, R. "Parents' Educational Expectations and Children's Academic Achievement: A Literature Review." *Merrill-Palmer Quarterly,* 29: 1–23, 1983.

*Somerfield, B. *First Teachers: A Family Literacy Handbook for Parents, Policy-Makers, and Literacy Providers.* The Barbara Bush Foundation for Family Literacy, 1989.

*Tizard, J., W. N. Schofield, and J. Hewison. "Collaboration Between Teachers and Parents in Assisting Children's Reading." *British Journal of Educational Psychology,* 17: 509–514, 1982.

*Topping, K. "Paired Reading: A Powerful Technique for Parent Use." *The Reading Teacher,* 40: 608–614, 1987.

*Vukelich, C. "Parents' Role in the Reading Process: A Review of Practical Suggestions and Ways to Communicate with Parents." *The Reading Teacher,* 37: 472–477, 1984.

*Walberg, H. "Families as Partners in Educational Productivity." *Phi Delta Kappan,* 65: 397–400, 1984.

APPENDIX A

Children's Book Awards

Many awards, medals, and prizes are given each year for outstanding children's literature in the United States. The two best-known are the Newbery Medal and the Caldecott Medal. The Newbery Medal is awarded annually by the Children's Services Division of the American Library Association to honor the most distinguished contribution to literature for children published in the United States during the previous year. The Caldecott Medal is awarded annually to the illustrator of the most distinguished picture book published in the United States during the previous year. Other awards given to honor significant contributions in the field of children's literature are as follows:

1. The Laura Ingalls Wilder Award is given every three years to an author or illustrator whose books have made a substantial and lasting contribution to children's literature.
2. The International Reading Association Children's Book Award, started in 1975, is awarded annually to an author who shows universal promise in the field of children's literature.
3. The National Council of Teachers of English Award for Excellence in Poetry for Children is given every three years to a living American poet in recognition of his or her work of poetry.
4. The Coretta Scott King Award, founded to commemorate Dr. Martin Luther King, Jr., and his wife, Coretta Scott King, for their work in promoting peace and brotherly love, is given to an outstanding African American author and, since 1974, an African American illustrator of children's books. The awards are sponsored by the Social Responsibilities Round Table of the American Library Association.
5. The Hans Christian Andersen Award is given every two years to a living author who has made an important international contribution to children's literature. Since 1966 a medal has also been given to an outstanding illustrator.
6. The Children's Choice is a project of the International Reading Association and the Children's Book Council Joint Committee. The listing is a yearly selection by young readers of their favorite newly published books. The choices are published in the October issue of *The Reading Teacher*.

The Newbery Medal

1922 *The Story of Mankind,* by Hendrik Willem van Loon, Liveright
Honor Books: *The Great Quest,* by Charles Hawes, Little; *Cedric the Forester,* by Bernard Marshall, Appleton; *The Old Tobacco Shop,* by William Bowen, Macmillan; *The Golden Fleece and the Heroes Who Lived Before Achilles,* by Padraic Colum, Macmillan; *Windy Hill,* by Cornelia Meigs, Macmillan
1923 *The Voyages of Doctor Dolittle,* by Hugh Lofting, Lippincott
Honor Books: No record

1924   *The Dark Frigate,* by Charles Hawes, Atlantic/Little
Honor Books: No record

1925   *Tales from Silver Lands,* by Charles Finger, Doubleday
Honor Books: *Nicholas,* by Anne Carroll Moore, Putnam; *Dream Coach,* by Anne Parrish, Macmillan

1926   *Shen of the Sea,* by Arthur Bowie Chrisman, Dutton
Honor Book: *Voyagers,* by Padraic Colum, Macmillan

1927   *Smoky, the Cowhorse,* by Will James, Scribner's
Honor Books: No record

1928   *Gayneck, The Story of a Pigeon,* by Dhan Gopal Mukerji, Dutton
Honor Books: *The Wonder Smith and His Son,* by Ella Young, Longman; *Downright Dencey,* by Caroline Snedeker, Doubleday

1929   *The Trumpeter of Krakow,* by Eric P. Kelly, Macmillan
Honor Books: *Pigtail of Ah Lee Ben Loo,* by John Bennett, Longman; *Millions of Cats,* by Wanda Gág, Coward; *The Boy Who Was,* by Grace Hallock, Dutton; *Clearing Weather,* by Cornelia Meigs, Little; *Runaway Papoose,* by Grace Moon, Doubleday; *Tod of the Fens,* by Elinor Whitney, Macmillan

1930   *Hitty, Her First Hundred Years,* by Rachel Field, Macmillan
Honor Books: *Daughter of the Seine,* by Jeanette Eaton, Harper; *Pran of Albania,* by Elizabeth Miller, Doubleday; *Jumping-Off Place,* by Marian Hurd McNeely, Longman; *Tangle-Coated Horse and Other Tales,* by Ella Young, Longman; *Vaino,* by Julia Davis Adams, Dutton; *Little Blacknose,* by Hildegarde Swift, Harcourt

1931   *The Cat Who Went to Heaven,* by Elizabeth Coatsworth, Macmillan
Honor Books: *Floating Island,* by Anne Parrish, Harper; *The Dark Star of Itza,* by Alida Malkus, Harcourt; *Queer Person,* by Ralph Hubbard, Doubleday; *Mountains Are Free,* by Julia Davis Adams, Dutton; *Spice and the Devil's Cave,* by Agnes Hewes, Knopf; *Meggy Macintosh,* by Elizabeth Janet Gray, Doubleday; *Garram the Hunter,* by Herbert Best, Doubleday; *Ood-Le-Uk the Wanderer,* by Alice Lide and Margaret Johansen, Little

1932   *Waterless Mountain,* by Laura Adams Armer, Longman
Honor Books: *The Fairy Circus,* by Dorothy P. Lathrop, Macmillan; *Calico Bush,* by Rachel Field, Macmillan; *Boy of the South Seas,* by Eunice Tietjens, Coward; *Out of the Flame,* by Eloise Lownsbery, Longman; *Jane's Island,* by Marjorie Allee, Houghton; *Truce of the Wolf and Other Tales of Old Italy,* by Mary Gould Davis, Harcourt

1933   *Young Fu of the Upper Yangtze,* by Elizabeth Foreman Lewis, Winston
Honor Books: *Swift Rivers,* by Cornelia Meigs, Little; *The Railroad to Freedom,* by Hildegarde Swift, Harcourt; *Children of the Soil,* by Nora Burglon, Doubleday

1934   *Invincible Louisa,* by Cornelia Meigs, Little
Honor Books: *The Forgotten Daughter,* by Caroline Snedeker, Doubleday; *Swords of Steel,* by Elsie Singmaster, Houghton; *ABC Bunny,* by Wanda Gág, Coward; *Winged Girl of Knossos,* by Erik Berry, Appleton; *New Land,* by Sarah Schmidt, McBride; *Big Tree of Bunlahy,* by Padraic Colum, Macmillan; *Glory of the Seas,* by Agnes Hewes, Knopf; *Apprentice of Florence,* by Anne Kyle, Houghton

1935   *Dobry,* by Monica Shannon, Viking
Honor Books: *Pageant of Chinese History,* by Elizabeth Seeger, Longman; *Davy Crockett,* by Constance Rourke, Harcourt; *Day on Skates,* by Hilda Van Stockum, Harper

1936   *Caddie Woodlawn,* by Carol Brink, Macmillan
        Honor Books: *Honk, The Moose,* by Phil Stong, Dodd; *The Good Master,* by Kate
        Seredy, Viking; *Young Walter Scott,* by Elizabeth Janet Gray, Viking; *All Sail Set,*
        by Armstrong Sperry, Winston

1937   *Roller Skates,* by Ruth Sawyer, Viking
        Honor Books: *Phebe Fairchild: Her Book,* by Lois Lenski, Stokes; *Whistler's Van,*
        by Idwal Jones, Viking; *Golden Basket,* by Ludwig Bemelmans, Viking; *Winter-
        bound,* by Margery Bianco, Viking; *Audubon,* by Constance Rourke, Harcourt;
        The Codfish Musket, by Agnes Hewes, Doubleday

1938   *The White Stag,* by Kate Seredy, Viking
        Honor Books: *Pecos Bill,* by James Cloyd Bowman, Little; *Bright Island,* by Mabel
        Robinson, Random; *On the Banks of Plum Creek,* by Laura Ingalls Wilder, Harper

1939   *Thimble Summer,* by Elizabeth Enright, Rinehart
        Honor Books: *Nino,* by Valenti Angelo, Viking; *Mr. Popper's Penguins,* by
        Richard and Florence Atwater, Little; *"Hello the Boat!"* by Phyllis Crawford,
        Holt; *Leader by Destiny: George Washington, Man and Patriot,* by Jeanette Eaton,
        Harcourt; *Penn,* by Elizabeth Janet Gray, Viking

1940   *Daniel Boone,* by James Daugherty, Viking
        Honor Books: *The Singing Tree,* by Kate Seredy, Viking; *Runner of the Mountain
        Tops,* by Mabel Robinson, Random; *By the Shores of Silver Lake,* by Laura Ingalls
        Wilder, Harper; *Boy with a Pack,* by Stephen W. Meader, Harcourt

1941   *Call It Courage,* by Armstrong Sperry, Macmillan
        Honor Books: *Blue Willow,* by Doris Gates, Viking; *Young Mac of Fort Vancouver,*
        by Mary Jane Carr, T. Crowell; *The Long Winter,* by Laura Ingalls Wilder,
        Harper; *Nansen,* by Anna Gertrude Hall, Viking

1942   *The Matchlock Gun,* by Walter D. Edmonds, Dodd
        Honor Books: *Little Town on the Prairie,* by Laura Ingalls Wilder, Harper; *George
        Washington's World,* by Genevieve Foster, Scribner's; *Indian Captive: The Story of
        Mary Jemison,* by Lois Lenski, Lippincott; *Down Ryton Water,* by Eva Roe Gag-
        gin, Viking

1943   *Adam of the Road,* by Elizabeth Janet Gray, Viking
        Honor Books: *The Middle Moffat,* by Eleanor Estes, Harcourt; *Have You Seen Tom
        Thumb?,* by Mabel Leigh Hunt, Lippincott

1944   *Johnny Tremain,* by Esther Forbes, Houghton
        Honor Books: *These Happy Golden Years,* by Laura Ingalls Wilder, Harper; *Fog
        Magic,* by Julia Sauer, Viking; *Rufus M.,* by Eleanor Estes, Harcourt; *Mountain
        Born,* by Elizabeth Yates, Coward

1945   *Rabbit Hill,* by Robert Lawson, Viking
        Honor Books: *The Hundred Dresses,* by Eleanor Estes, Harcourt; *The Silver Pencil,*
        by Alice Dalgliesh, Scribner's; *Abraham Lincoln's World,* by Genevieve Foster,
        Scribner's; *Lone Journey: The Life of Roger Williams,* by Jeanette Eaton, Harcourt

1946   *Strawberry Girl,* by Lois Lenski, Lippincott
        Honor Books: *Justin Morgan Had a Horse,* by Marguerite Henry, Rand; *The
        Moved-Outers,* by Florence Crannell Means, Houghton; *Bhimsa, The Dancing
        Bear,* by Christine Weston, Scribner's; *New Found World,* by Katherine Shippen,
        Viking

1947   *Miss Hickory,* by Carolyn Sherwin Bailey, Viking
        Honor Books: *Wonderful Year,* by Nancy Barnes, Messner; *Big Tree,* by Mary and
        Conrad Buff, Viking; *The Heavenly Tenants,* by William Maxwell, Harper; *The*

Avion My Uncle Flew, by Cyrus Fisher, Appleton; *The Hidden Treasure of Glaston,* by Eleanore Jewett, Viking

1948   *The Twenty-One Balloons,* by William Pène du Bois, Viking
Honor Books: *Pancakes-Paris,* by Claire Huchet Bishop, Viking; *Li Lun, Lad of Courage,* by Carolyn Treffinger, Abingdon; *The Quaint and Curious Quest of Johnny Longfoot,* by Catherine Besterman, Bobbs; *The Cow-Tail Switch, and Other West African Stories,* by Harold Courlander, Holt; *Misty of Chincoteague,* by Marguerite Henry, Rand

1949   *King of the Wind,* by Marguerite Henry, Rand
Honor Books: *Seabird,* by Holling C. Holling, Houghton; *Daughter of the Mountains,* by Louise Rankin, Viking; *My Father's Dragon,* by Ruth S. Gannett, Random; *Story of the Negro,* by Arna Bontemps, Knopf

1950   *The Door in the Wall,* by Marguerite de Angeli, Doubleday
Honor Books: *Tree of Freedom,* by Rebecca Caudill, Viking; *The Blue Cat of Castle Town,* by Catherine Coblentz, Longmans; *Kildee House,* by Rutherford Montgomery, Doubleday; *George Washington,* by Genevieve Foster, Scribner's; *Song of the Pines,* by Walter and Marion Havighurst, Winston

1951   *Amos Fortune, Free Man,* by Elizabeth Yates, Aladdin
Honor Books: *Better Known as Johnny Appleseed,* by Mabel Leigh Hunt, Lippincott; *Gandhi, Fighter Without a Sword,* by Jeanette Eaton, Morrow; *Abraham Lincoln, Friend of the People,* by Clara Ingram Judson, Follett; *The Story of Appleby Capple,* by Anne Parrish, Harper

1952   *Ginger Pye,* by Eleanor Estes, Harcourt
Honor Books: *Americans Before Columbus,* by Elizabeth Baity, Viking; *Minn of the Mississippi,* by Holling C. Holling, Houghton; *The Defender,* by Nicholas Kalashnikoff, Scribner's; *The Light at Tern Rock,* by Julia Sauer, Viking; *The Apple and the Arrow,* by Mary and Conrad Buff, Houghton

1953   *Secret of the Andes,* by Ann Nolan Clark, Viking
Honor Books: *Charlotte's Web,* by E. B. White, Harper; *Moccasin Trail,* by Eloise McGraw, Coward; *Red Sails to Capri,* by Ann Weil, Viking; *The Bears on Hemlock Mountain,* by Alice Dalgliesh, Scribner's; *Birthdays of Freedom,* vol. 1, by Genevieve Foster, Scribner's

1954   *. . . and now Miguel,* by Joseph Krumgold, T. Crowell
Honor Books: *All Alone,* by Claire Huchet Bishop, Viking; *Shadrach,* by Meindert DeJong, Harper; *Hurry Home Candy,* by Meindert DeJong, Harper; *Theodore Roosevelt, Fighting Patriot,* by Clara Ingram Judson, Follett; *Magic Maze,* by Mary and Conrad Buff, Houghton

1955   *The Wheel on the School,* by Meindert DeJong, Harper
Honor Books: *The Courage of Sarah Noble,* by Alice Dalgliesh, Scribner's; *Banner in the Sky,* by James Ullman, Lippincott

1956   *Carry on, Mr. Dowditch,* by Jean Lee Latham, Houghton
Honor Books: *The Secret River,* by Marjorie Kinan Rawlings, Scribner's; *The Golden Name Day,* by Jennie Lindquist, Harper; *Men, Microscopes, and Living Things,* by Katherine Shippen, Viking

1957   *Miracles on Maple Hill,* by Virginia Sorensen, Harcourt
Honor Books: *Old Yeller,* by Fred Gipson, Harper; *The House of Sixty Fathers,* by Meindert DeJong, Harper; *Mr. Justice Holmes,* by Clara Ingram Judson, Follett; *The Corn Grows Ripe,* by Dorothy Rhoads, Viking; *Black Fox of Lorne,* by Marguerite de Angeli, Doubleday

1958   *Rifles for Watie,* by Harold Keith, T. Crowell
        Honor Books: *The Horsecatcher,* by Mari Sandoz, Westminster; *Gone-Away Lake,*
        by Elizabeth Enright, Harcourt; *The Great Wheel,* by Robert Lawson, Viking; *Tom
        Paine, Freedom's Apostle,* by Leo Gurko, T. Crowell

1959   *The Witch of Blackbird Pond,* by Elizabeth George Speare, Houghton
        Honor Books: *The Family Under the Bridge,* by Natalie S. Carlson, Harper; *Along
        Came a Dog,* by Meindert DeJong, Harper; *Chucaro: Wild Pony of the Pampa,* by
        Francis Kalnay, Harcourt; *The Perilous Road,* by William O. Steele, Harcourt

1960   *Onion John,* by Joseph Krumgold, T. Crowell
        Honor Books: *My Side of the Mountain,* by Jean George, Dutton; *America Is Born,*
        by Gerald W. Johnson, Morrow; *The Gammage Cup,* by Carol Kendall, Harcourt

1961   *Island of the Blue Dolphins,* by Scott O'Dell, Houghton
        Honor Books: *America Moves Forward,* by Gerald W. Johnson, Morrow; *Old Ra-
        mon,* by Jack Schaefer, Houghton; *The Cricket in Times Square,* by George Selden,
        Farrar

1962   *The Bronze Bow,* by Elizabeth George Speare, Houghton
        Honor Books: *Frontier Living,* by Edwin Tunis, World; *The Golden Goblet,* by
        Eloise McGraw, Coward; *Belling the Tiger,* by Mary Stolz, Harper

1963   *A Wrinkle in Time,* by Madeleine L'Engle, Farrar
        Honor Books: *Thistle and Thyme,* by Sorche Nic Leodhas, Holt; *Men of Athens,* by
        Olivia Coolidge, Houghton

1964   *It's Like This, Cat,* by Emily Cheney Neville, Harper
        Honor Books: *Rascal,* by Sterling North, Dutton; *The Loner,* by Esther Wier, McKay

1965   *Shadow of a Bull,* by Maia Wojciechowska, Atheneum
        Honor Book: *Across Five Aprils,* by Irene Hunt, Follett

1966   *I, Juan de Pareja,* by Elizabeth Borten de Trevino, Farrar
        Honor Books: *The Black Cauldron,* by Lloyd Alexander, Holt; *The Animal Family,*
        by Randall Jarrell, Pantheon; *The Noonday Friends,* by Mary Stolz, Harper

1967   *Up a Road Slowly,* by Irene Hunt, Follett
        Honor Books: *The King's Fifth,* by Scott O'Dell, Houghton; *Zlateh the Goat and
        Other Stories,* by Isaac Bashevis Singer, Harper; *The Jazz Man,* by Mary H. Weik,
        Atheneum

1968   *From the Mixed-Up Files of Mrs. Basil E. Frankweiler,* by E. L. Konigsburg,
        Atheneum
        Honor Books: *The Black Pearl,* by Scott O'Dell, Houghton Mifflin; *The Egypt
        Game,* by Zilpha Keatley Snyder, Atheneum; *The Fearsome Inn,* by Isaac Bashevis
        Singer, Scribner; *Jennifer, Hecate, Macbeth, William McKinley, and Me, Elizabeth,*
        by E. L. Konigsburg, Atheneum

1969   *The High King,* by Lloyd Alexander, Holt, Rinehart & Winston
        Honor Books: *To Be a Slave,* by Julius Lester, Dial; *When Shlemiel Went to Warsaw
        and Other Stories,* by Isaac Bashevis Singer, Farrar, Straus & Giroux

1970   *Sounder,* by William Armstrong, Harper & Row
        Honor Books: *Journey Outside,* by Mary Q. Steele, Viking; *Our Eddie,* by
        Sulamith Ish-Kishor, Pantheon; *The Many Ways of Seeing: An Introduction to the
        Pleasures of Art,* by Janet Gaylord Moore, Harcourt Brace Jovanovich

1971   *The Summer of the Swans,* by Betsy Byars, Viking
        Honor Books: *Enchantress from the Stars,* by Sylvia Louise Engdahl, Atheneum;
        Kneeknock Rose, by Natalie Babbitt, Farrar, Straus & Giroux; *Sing Down the Moon,*
        by Scott O'Dell, Houghton Mifflin

1972   *Mrs. Frisby and the Rats of Nimh,* by Robert C. O'Brien, Atheneum
        Honor Books: *Annie and the Old One,* by Miska Miles, Atlantic-Little; *The Headless Cupid,* by Zilpha Keatley Snyder, Atheneum; *Incident at Hawk's Hill,* by Allan W. Eckert, Little, Brown; *The Planet of Junior Brown,* by Virginia Hamilton, Macmillan; *The Tombs of Atuan,* by Ursula K. LeGuin, Atheneum

1973   *Julie of the Wolves,* by Jean C. George, Harper & Row
        Honor Books: *Frog and Toad Together,* by Arnold Lobel, Harper & Row; *The Upstairs Room,* by Johanna Reiss, Crowell; *The Witches of Worm,* by Zilpha Keatley Snyder, Atheneum

1974   *The Slave Dancer,* by Paula Fox, Bradbury
        Honor Book: *The Dark Is Rising,* by Susan Cooper, Atheneum

1975   *M. C. Higgins, the Great,* by Virginia Hamilton, Macmillan
        Honor Books: *Figgs and Phantoms,* by Ellen Raskin, E. P. Dutton; *My Brother Sam Is Dead,* by James Lincoln Collier and Christopher Collier, Four Winds; *The Perilous Gard,* by Elizabeth Marie Pope, Houghton Mifflin; *Philip Hall Likes Me, I Reckon Maybe,* by Bette Greene, Dial

1976   *The Grey King,* by Susan Cooper, Atheneum
        Honor Books: *Dragonwings,* by Laurence Yep, Harper & Row; *The Hundred Penny Box,* by Sharon Bell Mathis, Viking

1977   *Roll of Thunder, Hear My Cry,* by Mildred Taylor, Dial
        Honor Books: *Abel's Island,* by William Steig, Farrar, Straus & Giroux; *A String in the Harp,* by Nancy Bond, Atheneum

1978   *Bridge to Terabithia,* by Katherine Paterson, Crowell
        Honor Books: *Anpao: An American Indian Odyssey,* by Jamake Highwater, Lippincott; *Ramona and Her Father,* by Beverly Cleary, Morrow

1979   *The Westing Game,* by Ellen Raskin, Dutton
        Honor Book: *The Great Gilly Hopkins,* by Katherine Paterson, Crowell

1980   *A Gathering of Days: A New England Girl's Journal, 1830–32,* by Joan W. Blos, Scribner's.
        Honor Book: *The Road from Home: The Story of an Armenian Girl,* by David Kerdian, Greenwillow

1981   *Jacob Have I Loved,* by Katherine Paterson, Crowell
        Honor Books: *The Fledgling,* by Jane Langton, Harper & Row; *A Ring of Endless Light,* by Madeleine L'Engle, Farrar, Straus & Giroux

1982   *A Visit to William Blake's Inn: Poems for Innocent and Experienced Travelers,* by Nancy Willard, Harcourt Brace Jovanovich
        Honor Books: *Ramona Quimby, Age 8,* by Beverly Cleary, Morrow; *Upon the Head of the Goat: A Childhood in Hungary, 1939–1944,* by Aranka Siegal, Farrar, Straus & Giroux

1983   *Dicey's Song,* by Cynthia Voigt, Atheneum
        Honor Books: *The Blue Sword,* by Robin McKinley, Greenwillow; *Doctor DeSoto,* by William Steig, Farrar, Straus & Giroux; *Graven Images,* by Paul Fleischman, Harper & Row; *Homesick: My Own Story,* by Jean Fritz, Putnam; *Sweet Whispers, Brother Rush,* by Virginia Hamilton, Philomel

1984   *Dear Mr. Henshaw,* by Beverly Cleary, Morrow
        Honor Books: *The Sign of the Beaver,* by Elizabeth George Speare, Houghton Mifflin; *A Solitary Blue,* by Cynthia Voigt, Atheneum; *Sugaring Time,* by Kathryn Lasky, Macmillan; *The Wish Giver,* by Bill Brittain, Harper & Row

1985   *The Hero and the Crown,* by Robin McKinley, Greenwillow
Honor Books: *Like Jake and Me,* by Mavis Jukes, Knopf; *The Moves Make the Man,* by Bruce Brooks, Harper & Row; *One-Eyed Cat,* by Paula Fox, Bradbury

1986   *Sarah, Plain and Tall,* by Patricia MacLachlan, Harper & Row
Honor Books: *Commodore Perry in the Land of the Shogun,* by Rhoda Blumberg, Lothrop, Lee & Shepard; *Dogsong,* by Gary Paulsen, Bradbury

1987   *The Whipping Boy,* by Sid Fleischman, Greenwillow
Honor Books: *A Fine White Dust,* by Cynthia Rylant, Bradbury; *On My Honor,* by Marion Dane Bauer, Clarion; *Volcano: The Eruption and Healing of Mount St. Helens,* by Patricia Lauber, Bradbury

1988   *Lincoln: A Photobiography,* by Russell Freedman, Clarion
Honor Books: *After the Rain,* by Norma Fox Mazer, Morrow; *Hatchet,* by Gary Paulsen, Bradbury

1989   *Joyful Noise: Poems for Two Voices,* by Paul Fleischman, Harper & Row
Honor Books: *In the Beginning: Creation Stories from Around the World,* by Virginia Hamilton, Harcourt Brace Jovanovich; *Scorpions,* by Walter Dean Myers, Harper & Row

1990   *Number the Stars,* by Lois Lowry, Houghton Mifflin
Honor Books: *Afternoon of the Elves,* by Janet Taylor Lifle, Watts; *Shabanu: Daughter of the Wind,* by Suzanne Fisher Staples, Knopf; *The Winter Room,* by Gary Paulsen, Watts

1991   *Maniac Magee,* by Jerry Spinelli, Little, Brown
Honor Book: *The True Confession of Charlotte Doyle,* by Avi, Jackson/Orchard

1992   *Shiloh,* by Phyllis Reynolds Naylor, Atheneum
Honor Books: *Nothing But the Truth: A Documentation Novel,* by Avi, Jackson/Orchard; *The Wright Brothers: How They Invented the Airplane,* by Russell Freedman, Holiday

1993   *Missing May,* by Cynthia Rylant. Jackson/Orchard
Honor Books: *The Dark-Thirty,* by Patricia McKissack, Knopf; *Somewhere in the Darkness,* by Walter Dean Myers, Scholastic; *What Hearts?* by Bruce Brooks, HarperCollins

1994   *The Giver,* by Lois Lowry, Houghton Mifflien
Honor Books: *Crazy Lady!* by Jane Leslie, HarperCollins; *Eleanor Roosevelt: A Life of Discovery,* by Russell Freedman, Clarion; *Dragon's Gate,* by Laurence Yep, HarperCollins

1995   *Walk Two Moons,* by Sharon Creech, HarperCollins
Honor Books: *Catherine, Called Birdy,* by Karen Cushman, Clarion; *The Ear, the Eye and the Arm,* by Nancy Farmer, Jackson/Orchard

The Caldecott Medal

1938   *Animals of the Bible,* by Helen Dean Fish, illustrated by Dorothy P. Lathrop, Lippincott
Honor Books: *Seven Simeons,* by Boris Artzybasheff, Viking; *Four and Twenty Blackbirds,* by Helen Dean Fish, illustrated by Robert Lawson, Stokes

1939   *Mei Li,* by Thomas Handforth, Doubleday
Honor Books: *The Forest Pool,* by Laura Adams Armer, Longman; *Wee Gillis,* by

Munro Leaf, illustrated by Robert Lawson, Viking; *Snow White and the Seven Dwarfs,* by Wanda Gág, Coward; *Barkis,* by Clare Newberry, Harper; *Andy and the Lion,* by James Daugherty, Viking

1940 *Abraham Lincoln,* by Ingri and Edgar Parin D'Aulaire, Doubleday
Honor Books: *Cock-A-Doodle Doo . . . ,* by Berta and Elmer Hader, Macmillan; *Madeline,* by Ludwig Bemelmans, Viking; *The Ageless Story,* illustrated by Lauren Ford, Dodd

1941 *They Were Strong and Good,* by Robert Lawson, Viking
Honor Book: *April's Kittens,* by Clare Newberry, Harper

1942 *Make Way for Ducklings,* by Robert McCloskey, Viking
Honor Books: *An American ABC,* by Maud and Miska Petersham, Macmillan; *In My Mother's House,* by Ann Nolan Clark, illustrated by Velino Herrera, Viking; *Paddle-to-the-Sea,* by Holling C. Holling, Houghton; *Nothing at All,* by Wanda Gág, Coward

1943 *The Little House,* by Virginia Lee Burton, Houghton
Honor Books: *Dash and Dart,* by Mary and Conrad Buff, Viking; *Marshmallow,* by Clare Newberry, Harper

1944 *Many Moons,* by James Thurber, illustrated by Louis Slobodkin, Harcourt
Honor Books: *Small Rain: Verses from the Bible,* selected by Jessie Orton Jones, illustrated by Elizabeth Orton Jones, Viking; *Pierre Pigeon,* by Lee Kingman, illustrated by Arnold E. Bare, Houghton; *The Mighty Hunter,* by Berta and Elmer Hader, Macmillan; *A Child's Good Night Book,* by Margaret Wise Brown, illustrated by Jean Charlot, W. R. Scott; *Good Luck Horse,* by Chih-Yi Chan, illustrated by Plao Chan, Whittlesey

1945 *Prayer for a Child,* by Rachel Field, illustrated by Elizabeth Orton Jones, Macmillan
Honor Books: *Mother Goose,* illustrated by Tasha Tudor, Walck; *In the Forest,* by Maria Hall Ets, Viking; *Yonie Wondernose,* by Marguerite de Angeli, Doubleday; *The Christmas Anna Angel,* by Ruth Sawyer, illustrated by Kate Seredy, Viking

1946 *The Rooster Crows . . .* (traditional Mother Goose) illustrated by Maud and Miska Petersham, Macmillan
Honor Books: *Little Lost Lamb,* by Golden MacDonald, illustrated by Leonard Weisgard, Doubleday; *Sing Mother Goose,* by Opal Wheeler, illustrated by Marjorie Torrey, Dutton; *My Mother Is the Most Beautiful Woman in the World,* by Becky Reyher, illustrated by Ruth Gannett, Lothrop; *You Can Write Chinese,* by Kurt Wiese, Viking

1947 *The Little Island,* by Golden MacDonald, illustrated by Leonard Weisgard, Doubleday
Honor Books: *Rain Drop Splash,* by Alvin Tresselt, illustrated by Leonard Weisgard, Lothrop; *Boats on the River,* by Marjorie Flack, illustrated by Jay Hyde Barnum, Viking; *Timothy Turtle,* by Al Graham, illustrated by Tony Palazzo, Viking; *Pedro, The Angel of Olvera Street,* by Leo Politi, Scribner's; *Sing in Praise: A Collection of the Best Loved Hymns,* by Opal Wheeler, illustrated by Marjorie Torrey, Dutton

1948 *White Snow, Bright Snow,* by Alvin Tresselt, illustrated by Roger Duvoisin, Lothrop
Honor Books: *Stone Soup,* by Marcia Brown, Scribner's; *McElligot's Pool,* by Dr. Seuss, Random; *Bambino the Clown,* by George Schreiber, Viking; *Roger and the Fox,* by Lavinia Davis, illustrated by Hildegard Woodward, Doubleday; *Song of*

Robin Hood, edited by Anne Malcolmson, illustrated by Virginia Lee Burton, Houghton

1949   *The Big Snow*, by Berta and Elmer Hader, Macmillan
Honor Books: *Blueberries for Sal*, by Robert McCloskey, Viking; *All Around the Town*, by Phyllis McGinley, illustrated by Helen Stone, Lippincott, *Juanita*, by Leo Politi, Scribner's; *Fish in the Air*, by Kurt Wiese, Viking

1950   *Song of the Swallows*, by Leo Politi, Scribner's
Honor Books: *America's Ethan Allen*, by Stewart Holbrook, illustrated by Lynd Ward, Houghton; *The Wild Birthday Cake*, by Lavinia Davis, Illustrated by Hildegard Woodward, Doubleday; *The Happy Day*, by Ruth Krauss, illustrated by Marc Simont, Harper; *Bartholomew and the Oobleck*, by Dr. Seuss, Random; *Henry Fisherman*, by Marcia Brown, Scribner's

1951   *The Egg Tree*, by Katherine Milhous, Scribner's
Honor Books: *Dick Whittington and His Cat*, by Marcia Brown, Scribner's; *The Two Reds*, by William Lipkind, illustrated by Nicholas Mordvinoff, Harcourt; *If I Ran the Zoo*, by Dr. Suess, Random; *The Most Wonderful Doll in the World*, by Phyllis McGinley, illustrated by Helen Stone, Lippincott; *T-Bone, the Baby Sitter*, by Clare Newberry, Harper

1952   *Finders Keepers*, by William Lipkind, illustrated by Nicholas Mordvinoff, Harcourt
Honor Books: *Mr. T. W. Anthony Woo*, by Maria Hall Ets, Viking; *Skipper John's Cook*, by Marcia Brown, Scribner's; *All Falling Down*, by Gene Zion, illustrated by Margaret Bloy Graham, Harper; *Bear Party*, by William Pène du Bois, Viking; *Feather Mountain*, by Elizabeth Olds, Houghton

1953   *The Biggest Bear*, by Lynd Ward, Houghton
Honor Books: *Puss in Boots*, by Charles Perrault, illustrated and translated by Marcia Brown, Scribner's; *One Morning in Maine*, by Robert McCloskey, Viking; *Ape in a Cape*, by Fritz Eichenberg, Harcourt; *The Storm Book*, by Charlotte Zolotow, illustrated by Margaret Bloy Graham, Harper; *Five Little Monkeys*, by Juliet Kepes, Houghton

1954   *Madeline's Rescue*, by Ludwig Bemelmans, Viking
Honor Books: *Journey Cake, Ho!*, by Ruth Sawyer, illustrated by Robert McCloskey, Viking; *When Will the World Be Mine?* by Miriam Schlein, illustrated by Jean Charlot, W. R. Scott; *The Steadfast Tin Soldier*, by Hans Christian Andersen, illustrated by Marcia Brown, Scribner's, *A Very Special House*, by Ruth Krauss, illustrated by Maurice Sendak, Harper; *Green Eyes*, by A. Birnbaum, Capitol

1955   *Cinderella, or the Little Glass Slipper*, by Charles Perrault, translated and illustrated by Marcia Brown, Scribner's
Honor Books: *Books of Nursery and Mother Goose Rhymes*, illustrated by Marguerite de Angeli, Doubleday; *Wheel on the Chimney*, by Margaret Wise Brown, illustrated by Tibor Gergely, Lippincott; *The Thanksgiving Story*, by Alice Dalgliesh, illustrated by Helen Sewell, Scribner's

1956   *Frog Went A-Courtin'*, edited by John Langstaff, illustrated by Feodor Rojankovsky, Harcourt
Honor Books: *Play with Me*, by Marie Hall Ets, Viking; *Crow Boy*, by Taro Yashima, Viking

1957   *A Tree Is Nice*, by Janice May Udry, illustrated by Marc Simont, Harper
Honor Books: *Mr. Penny's Race Horse*, by Marie Hall Ets, Viking; *1 Is One*, by Tasha Tudor, Walck; *Anatole*, by Eve Titus, illustrated by Paul Galdone,

McGraw; *Gillespie and the Guards,* by Benjamin Elkin, illustrated by James Daugherty, Viking; *Lion,* by William Pène du Bois, Viking

1958 *Time of Wonder,* by Robert McCloskey, Viking
Honor Books: *Fly High, Fly Low,* by Don Freeman, Viking; *Anatole and the Cat,* by Eve Titus, illustrated by Paul Galdone, McGraw

1959 *Chanticleer and the Fox,* adapted from Chaucer and illustrated by Barbara Cooney, T. Crowell
Honor Books: *The House That Jack Built,* by Antonio Frasconi, Harcourt; *What Do You Say, Dear?* by Sesyle Joslin, illustrated by Maurice Sendak, W. R. Scott; *Umbrella,* by Taro Yashima, Viking

1960 *Nine Days to Christmas,* by Marie Hall Ets and Aurora Labastida, illustrated by Marie Hall Ets, Viking
Honor Books: *Houses from the Sea,* by Alice E. Goudey, illustrated by Adrienne Adams, Scribner's; *The Moon Jumpers,* by Janice May Udry, illustrated by Maurice Sendak, Harper

1961 *Baboushka and the Three Kings,* by Ruth Robbins, illustrated by Nicholas Sidjakov, Parnassus
Honor Book: *Inch by Inch,* by Leo Lionni, Obolensky

1962 *Once a Mouse . . . ,* by Marcia Brown, Scribner's
Honor Books: *The Fox Went Out on a Chilly Night,* by Peter Spier, Doubleday; *Little Bear's Visit,* by Else Holmelund Minarik, illustrated by Maurice Sendak, Harper; *The Day We Saw the Sun Come Up,* by Alice E. Goudey, illustrated by Adrienne Adams, Scribner's

1963 *The Snowy Day,* by Ezra Jack Keats, Viking
Honor Books: *The Sun is a Golden Earring,* by Natalia M. Belting, illustrated by Bernarda Bryson, Holt; *Mr. Rabbit and the Lovely Present,* by Charlotte Zolotow, ilustrated by Maurice Sendak, Harper

1964 *Where the Wild Things Are,* by Maurice Sendak, Harper & Row
Honor Books: *All in the Morning Early,* by Sorche Nic Leodhas, illustrated by Evaline Ness, Holt, Rinehart & Winston; *Mother Goose and Nursery Rhymes,* by Philip Reed, Atheneum; *Swimmy,* by Leo Lionni, Pantheon

1965 *May I Bring a Friend?* by Beatrice Schenk de Regniers, Atheneum
Honor Books: *A Pocketful of Cricket,* by Rebecca Caudill, illustrated by Evaline Ness, Holt, Rinehart & Winston; *Rain Makes Applesauce,* by Julian Scheer, illustrated by Marvin Bileck, Holiday; *The Wave,* by Margaret Hodges, illustrated by Blair Lent, Houghton Mifflin

1966 *Always Room for One More,* by Sorche Nic Leodhas, illustrated by Nonny Hogrogian, Holt, Rinehart & Winston
Honor Books: *Hide and Seek Fog,* by Alvin Tresselt, illustrated by Roger Duvoisin, Lothrop, Lee & Shepard; *Just Me,* by Marie Hall Ets, Viking; *Tom Tit Tot,* edited by Joseph Jacobs, illustrated by Evaline Ness, Scribner's

1967 *Sam, Bangs & Moonshine,* by Evaline Ness, Holt, Rinehart & Winston
Honor Books: *One Wide River to Cross,* by Barbara Emberley, illustrated by Ed Emberley, Prentice-Hall

1968 *Drummer Hoff,* by Barbara Emberley, illustrated by Ed Emberley, Prentice-Hall
Honor Books: *Frederick,* by Leo Lionni, Pantheon; *Seashore Story,* by Taro Yashima, Viking; *The Emperor and the Kite,* by Jane Yolen, illustrated by Ed Young, Harcourt Brace Jovanovich

1969   *The Fool of the World and the Flying Ship*, by Arthur Ransome, illustrated by Uri Shulevitz, Farrar, Straus & Giroux
Honor Book: *Why the Sun and the Moon Live in the Sky: An African Folktale*, by Elphinstone Dayrell, illustrated by Blair Lent, Houghton Mifflin

1970   *Sylvester and the Magic Pebble*, by William Steig, Windmill/Simon & Schuster
Honor Books: *Alexander and the Wind-Up Mouse*, by Leo Lionni, Pantheon; *Goggles!* by Ezra Jack Keats, Macmillan; *The Judge: An Untrue Tale*, by Harve Zemach, illustrated by Margot Zemach, Farrar, Straus & Giroux; *Pop Corn & Ma Goodness*, by Edna Mitchell Preston, illustrated by Robert Andrew Parker, Viking; *Thy Friend, Obadiah*, by Brinton Turkle, Viking

1971   *A Story, A Story*, by Gail E. Haley, Atheneum
Honor Books: *The Angry Moon*, by William Sleaton, illustrated by Blair Lent, Atlantic-Little; *Frog and Toad Are Friends*, by Arnold Lobel, Harper & Row; *In the Night Kitchen*, by Maurice Sendak, Harper & Row

1972   *One Fine Day*, by Nonny A. Hogrogian, Macmillan
Honor Books: *Hildilid's Night*, by Cheli Duran Ryan, illustrated by Arnold Lobel, Macmillan; *If All the Seas Were One Sea*, by Janina Domanska, Macmillan; *Moja Means One: Swahili Counting Book*, by Muriel Feelings, illustrated by Tom Feelings, Dial

1973   *The Funny Little Woman*, by Arlen Mosel, illustrated by Blair Lent, Dutton
Honor Books: *Hosie's Alphabet*, by Hosea, Tobias, and Lisa Baskin, illustrated by Leonard Baskin, Viking; *Snow-White and the Seven Dwarfs*, translated by Randall Jarrell from The Brothers Grimm, illustrated by Nancy Ekholm Burkert, Farrar, Straus & Giroux; *When Clay Sings*, by Byrd Baylor, illustrated by Tom Bahti, Scribner's

1974   *Duffy and the Devil*, by Harve and Margot Zemach, Farrar, Straus & Giroux
Honor Books: *Cathedral: The Story of Its Construction*, by David Macaulay, Houghton; *The Three Jovial Huntsmen*, by Susan Jeffers, Bradbury

1975   *Arrow to the Sun*, by Gerald McDermott, Viking
Honor Book: *Jambo Means Hello: A Swahili Alphabet Book*, by Muriel Feeings, illustrated by Tom Feelings, Dial

1976   *Why Mosquitoes Buzz in People's Ears*, by Verna Aardema, illustrated by Leo and Diane Dillon, Dial
Honor Books: *The Desert Is Theirs*, by Byrd Baylor, illustrated by Peter Parnall, Scribner's; *Strega Nona*, by Tomie de Paola, Prentice-Hall

1977   *Ashanti to Zulu*, by Margaret Musgrove, illustrated by Leo and Diane Dillon, Dial
Honor Books: *The Amazng Bone*, by William Steig, Farrar, Straus & Giroux; *The Contest*, by Nonny Hogrogian, Greenwillow; *Fish for Supper*, by M. B. Goffstein, Dial; *The Golem: A Jewish Legend*, by Beverly Brodsky McDermott, Lippincott; *Hawk, I'm Your Brother*, by Byrd Baylor, illustrated by Peter Parnall, Scribner's

1978   *Noah's Ark: The Story of the Flood*, by Peter Spier, Doubleday
Honor Books: *Castle*, by David Macaulay, Houghton; *It Could Always Be Worse*, by Margot Zemach, Farrar, Straus & Giroux

1979   *The Girl Who Loved Wild Horses*, by Paul Goble, Bradbury
Honor Books: *Freight Train*, by Donald Crews, Greenwillow; *The Way to Start a Day*, by Bryd Baylor, illustrated by Peter Parnall, Scribner's

1980   *Ox-Cart Man*, by Donald Hall, illustrated by Barbara Cooney, Viking

Honor Books: *Ben's Trumpet,* by Rachel Isadora, Greenwillow; *The Garden of Abdul Gasazi,* by Chris Van Allsburg, Houghton; *The Treasure,* by Uri Shulevitz, Farrar, Straus & Giroux

1981   *Fables,* by Arnold Lobel, Harper & Row
Honor Books: *The Bremen-Town Musicians,* by Ilse Plume, Doubleday; *The Grey Lady and the Strawberry Snatcher,* by Molly Bang, Four Winds; *Mice Twice,* by Joseph Low, Atheneum; *Truck,* by Donald Crews, Greenwillow

1982   *Jumanji,* by Chris Van Allsburg, Houghton Mifflin
Honor Books: *On Market Street,* by Arnold Lobel, illustrated by Anita Lobel, Greenwillow; *Outside over There,* by Maurice Sendak, Harper & Row; *A Visit to William Blake's Inn: Poems for Innocent and Experienced Travelers,* by Nancy Willard, illustrated by Alice and Martin Provensen, Harcourt; *Where the Buffaloes Begin,* by Olaf Baker, illustrated by Stephen Gammell, Warne

1983   *Shadow,* by Blaise Cendrars, translated and illustrated by Marcia Brown, Scribner's
Honor Books: *A Chair for My Mother,* by Vera B. Williams, Greenwillow; *When I Was Young in the Mountains,* by Cynthia Rylant, illustrated by Diane Goode, Dutton

1984   *The Glorious Flight Across the Channel with Louis Bleriot,* by Alice and Martin Provensen, Viking
Honor Books: *Little Red Riding Hood,* by Trina Schart Hyman, Holiday; *Ten, Nine, Eight,* by Molly Bang, Greenwillow

1985   *Saint George and the Dragon,* by Margaret Hodges, illustrated by Trina Schart Hyman, Little, Brown
Honor Books: *Hansel and Gretel,* by Rika Lesser, illustrated by Paul O. Zelinsky, Dodd, Mead; *Have You Seen My Duckling?,* by Nancy Tafuri, Greenwillow; *The Story of Jumping Mouse,* by John Steptoe, Lothrop, Lee & Shepard

1986   *The Polar Express,* by Chris Van Allsburg, Houghton Mifflin
Honor Books: *King Bidgood's in the Bathtub,* by Andrew Wood, Harcourt Brace Jovanovich; *The Relatives Came,* by Cynthia Rylant, Bradbury

1987   *Hey, Al,* by Arthur Yorinks, illustrated by Richard Egielski, Farrar, Straus & Giroux
Honor Books: *Alphabatics,* by Suse MacDonald, Bradbury; *Rumplestiltskin,* by Paul O. Zelinsky, Dutton; *The Village of Round and Square Houses,* by Anne Grifalconi, Little, Brown

1988   *Owl Moon,* by Jane Yolen, illustrated by John Schoenherr, Philomel
Honor Book: *Mufaro's Beautiful Daughters: An African Tale,* by John Steptoe, Morrow

1989   *Song and Dance Man,* by Karen Ackerman, illustrated by Stephen Gammell, Knopf
Honor Books: *The Boy of the Three Year Nap,* by Dianne Snyder, illustrated by Allen Say, Houghton Mifflin; *Free Fall,* by David Wiesner, Lothrop, Lee, & Shepard; *Goldilocks and the Three Bears,* by James Marshall, Dial; *Mirandy and Brother Wind,* by Patricia C. McKissack, illustrated by Jerry Pinkney, Knopf

1990   *Lon Po Po: A Red Riding Hood Story from China,* by Ed Young, Putnam
Honor Books: *Bill Peet: An Autobiography,* by Bill Peet, Houghton Mifflin; *Color Zoo,* by Lois Ehlert, Harper & Row; *Hershel and the Hanukkah Goblins,* by Eric A. Kimmel, illustrated by Trina Schart Hyman, Holiday; *The Talking Eggs,* by

Robert San Souci, illustrated by Jerry Pinkney, Doubleday
1991   *Black & White,* by David Macaulay, Houghton.
Honor Books: *Puss in Boots,* by Fred Marcellino, de Capua/Farrar; *"More, More, More" Said the Baby: 3 Love Stories,* by Vera B. Williams, Greenwillow
1992   *Tuesday,* by David Wiesner, Clarion
Honor Book: *Tar Beach,* by Faith Ringgold, Crown
1993   *Seven Blind Mice,* by Ed Young, Philomel
Honor Books: *The Stinky Cheese Man and Other Fairly Stupid Tales,* by Jon Scieszka, illustrated by Lane Smith, Viking; *Working Cotton,* by Sherley Anne Williams, illustrated by Carole Byard, Harcourt Brace Jovanovich
1994   *Grandfather's Journey,* by Allen Say, Houghton
Honor Books: *Peppe the Lamplighter,* by Elisa Bartone, illustrated by Ted Lewin, Lothrop; *In the Small Pond,* by Denise Fleming, Holt; *Owen,* by Kevin Henkes, Greenwillow; *Raven,* by Gerald McDermott, Harcourt; *Yo! Yes?* by Chris Raschka, Orchard/Richard Jackson
1995   *Smoky Night,* by Eve Bunting, illustrated by David Diaz, Harcourt
Honor Books: *Swamp Angel,* by Anne Isaacs, illustrated by Jerry Pinkney, Dial; *Time Flies,* by Eric Rohmann, Crown

The Laura Ingalls Wilder Award

1954   Laura Ingalls Wilder
1960   Clara Ingram Judson
1965   Ruth Sawyer
1970   E. B. White
1975   Beverly Cleary
1980   Theodor Geisel (Dr. Seuss)
1983   Maurice Sendak
1986   Jean Fritz
1989   Elizabeth George Speare
1992   Marcia Brown
1995   Virginia Hamilton

International Reading Association Children's Book Award

1975   *Transport 7-41-R,* by T. Degens, Viking
1976   *Dragonwings,* by Laurence Yep, Harper
1977   *A String in the Harp,* by Nancy Bond, McElderry/Atheneum
1978   *A Summer to Die,* by Lois Lowry, Houghton
1979   *Reserved for Mark Anthony Crowder,* by Alison Smith, Dutton
1980   *Words by Heart,* by Ouida Sebestyen, Atlantic/Little
1981   *My Own Private Sky,* by Delores Beckman, Dutton
1982   *Good Night, Mr. Tom,* by Michelle Magorian, Kestrel/Penguin (Great Britain); Harper (U.S.A.)
1983   *The Darkangel,* by Meredith Ann Pierce, Atlantic/Little
1984   *Ratha's Creature,* by Clare Bell, Atheneum

1985   *Badger on the Barger,* by Janni Howker, McCray
1986   *Second Novel Prairie Songs,* by Pam Conrad, Harper & Row
1987   Children's Book: *The Line Up Book,* by Marisabini Russo, Greenwillow
        Young Adult: *After the Dancing Days,* by Margaret I. Rostkowski, Harper & Row
1988   Children's Book: *The Third-Story Cat,* by Leslie Baker, Little, Brown
        Young Adult: *The Ruby and the Smoke,* by Philip Pullman, Random House
1989   Children's Book: *Rechenka's Eggs,* by Patricia Polaccko, Putnam
        Young Adult: *Probably Still Nick,* by Virginia Euwer Wolff, Holt
1990   Children's Book: *No Star Nights,* by Anna Egan Smith and Steven Johnson, Random House
        Young Adult: *Children of the River,* by Linda Crew, Delacorte
1991   Children's Book: *Is This a House for Hermit Crab?,* by Megan McDonald, illustrated by S. D. Schindler, Orchard
        Young Adult: *Under the Hawthorn Tree,* by Marita Conlon-McKenna, O'Brien Press (Ireland), Holiday (U.S.A.)
1992   Children's Book: *Ten Little Rabbits,* by Virginia Grossman, illustrated by Sylvia Long, Chronicle
        Young Adult: *Rescue Josh McGuire,* by Ben Mikaelsen, Hyperion
1993   Children's Book: *Old Turtle,* by Douglas Wood, illustrated by Cheng-Khee Chee, Pfeiffer-Hamilton
        Young Adult: *Letters from Rifka,* by Karen Hesse, Holt
1994   Younger Children: *Sweet Clara and the Freedom Quilt,* by Deborah H. Hopkinson
        Older Children: *Behind the Secret Window,* by Nellie Toll

National Council of Teachers of English Award for Excellence in Poetry for Children

1977   David McCord
1978   Aileen Fisher
1979   Karla Kuskin
1980   Myra Cohn Livingston
1981   Eve Merriam
1982   John Ciardi
1985   Lilian Moore
1988   Arnold Adoff
1991   Valerie Worth
1994   Barbara Ebsensen

The Hans Christian Andersen Award

1956   Eleanor Farjeon (Great Britain)
1958   Astrid Lindgren (Sweden)
1960   Erich Kästner (Germany)
1962   Meindert DeJong (U.S.A.)
1964   René Guillot (France)
1966   Author: Tove Jansson (Finland)

Illustrator: Alois Carigiet (Switzerland)
1968   Authors: James Krüss (Germany), Jose Maria Sanchez-Silva (Spain)
Illustrator: Jiri Trnka (Czechoslovakia)
1970   Author: Gianni Rodari (Italy)
Illustrator: Maurice Sendak (U.S.A.)
1972   Author: Scott O'Dell (U.S.A.)
Illustrator: Ib Spang Olsen (Denmark)
1974   Author: Maria Gripe (Sweden)
Illustrator: Farshid Mesghali (Iran)
1976   Author: Cecil Bødker (Denmark)
Illustrator: Tatjana Mawrina (U.S.S.R.)
1978   Author: Paula Fox (U.S.A.)
Illustrator: Otto S. Svend (Denmark)
1980   Author: Bohumil Riha (Czechoslovakia)
Illustrator: Suekichi Akaba (Japan)
1982   Author: Lygia Bojunga Nunes (Brazil)
Illustrator: Zbigniew Rychlicki (Poland)
1984   Author: Christine Nostlinger (Austria)
Illustrator: Mitsumasa Anno (Japan)
1986   Author: Patricia Wrightson (Australia)
Illustrator: Robert Ingpen (Australia)
1988   Author: Annie M. G. Schmidt (Netherlands)
Illustrator: Dusan Kallay (Yugoslavia)
1990   Author: Tornod Haugen (Norway)
Illustrator: Lisbeth Zwerger (Austria)
1992   Author: Virginia Hamilton (United States)
Illustrator: Kveta Pacovská (Czechoslovakia)
1994   Author: Michio Mado (Japan)
Illustrator: Jorg Muller (Switzerland)

Coretta Scott King Award

1970   *Martin Luther King, Jr.: Man of Peace,* by Lillie Patterson, Garrard
1971   *Black Troubador: Langston Hughes,* by Charlemae Rollins, Rand
1972   *17 Black Artists,* by Elton C. Fax, Dodd
1973   *I Never Had It Made,* by Jackie Robinson as told to Alfred Duckett, Putnam.
1974   Author: *Ray Charles,* by Sharon Bell Mathis, Crowell
Illustrator: The same title, illustrated by George Ford
1975   Author: *The Legend of Africana,* by Dorothy Robinson, Johnson
Illustrator: The same title, illustrated by Herbert Temple
1976   Author: *Duey's Tale,* by Pearl Bailey, Harcourt
Illustrator: No award
1977   Author: *The Story of Stevie Wonder,* by James Haskins, Lothrop
Illustrator: No award
1978   Author: *Africa Dream,* by Eloise Greenfield, Day/Crowell
Illustrator: The same title, illustrated by Carole Bayard
1979   Author: *Escape to Freedom,* by Ossie Davis, Viking
Illustrator: *Something on My Mind,* by Nikki Grimes, illustrated by Tom

Feelings, Dial

1980   Author: *The Young Landlords,* by Walter Dean Myers, Viking
Illustrator: *Cornrows,* by Camille Yarbrough, illustrated by Carole Bayard,
Coward

1981   Author: *This Life,* by Sidney Poitier, Knopf
Illustrator: *Beat the Story-Drum, Pum-Pum,* by Ashley Bryan, Atheneum

1982   Author: *Let the Circle Be Unbroken,* by Mildred Taylor, Dial
Illustrator: *Mother Crocodile: An Uncle Amadou Tale from Senegal,* adapted by
Rosa Guy, illustrated by John Steptoe, Delacorte

1983   Author: *Sweet Whispers, Brother Rush,* by Virginia Hamilton, Philomel
Illustrator: *Black Child,* by Peter Mugabane, Knopf

1984   Author: *Everett Anderson's Good-Bye,* by Lucille Clifton, Holt
Illustrator: *My Mama Needs Me,* by Mildred Pitts Walter, illustrated by Pat
Cummings, Lothrop

1985   Author: *Motown and Didi,* by Walter Dean Myers, Viking
Illustrator: No award

1986   Author: *The People Could Fly: American Black Folktales,* by Virginia Hamilton,
Knopf
Illustrator: *Patchwork Quilt,* by Valerie Flournoy, illustrated by Jerry Pinkney,
Dial

1987   Author: *Justin and the Best Biscuits in the World,* by Mildred Pitts Walter, Lothrop
Illustrator: *Half Moon and One Whole Star,* by Crescent Dragonwagon, illustrated
by Jerry Pinkney, Macmillan

1988   Author: *The Friendship,* by Mildred D. Taylor, illustrated by Max Ginsburg, Dial
Illustrator: *Mufaro's Beautiful Daughters: An African Tale,* retold and illustrated
by John Steptoe, Lothrop

1989   Author: *Fallen Angels,* by Walter Dean Myers, Scholastic
Illustrator: *Mirandy and Brother Wind,* by Patricia McKissack, illustrated by Jerry
Pinkney, Knopf

1990   Author: *A Long Hard Journey,* by Patricia and Frederick McKissack, Walker
Illustrator: *Nathaniel Talking,* by Eloise Greenfield, illustrated by Jan Spivey
Gilchrist, Black Butterfly

1991   Author: *Road to Memphis,* by Mildred D. Taylor, Dial
Illustrator: *Aida,* retold by Leontyne Price, illustrated by Leo and Diane Dillon,
Harcourt

1992   Author: *Now Is Your Time! The African-American Struggle for Freedom,* by Walter
Dean Myers, HarperCollins
Illustrator: *Tar Beach,* by Faith Ringgold, Crown

1993   Author: *The Dark Thirty: Southern Tales of the Supernatural,* by Patricia McKissack, Knopf
Illustrator: *The Origin of Life on Earth: An African Creation Myth,* by David A. Anderson, illustrated by Kathleen Atkins Wilson, Sights

1994   Author: *Toning the Sweep,* by Angela Johnson, Orchard
Illustrator: "Soul Looks Back in Wonder," by Tom Feeling, *A Collection of
African American Poets,* Editor: Phyllis Fogelman, Dial

1995   Author: *Christmas in the Big House, Christmas in the Quarters,* by Patricia and
Frederick McKissack, Scholastic
Illustrator: *The Creation,* by James E. Ransome, poem by James Weldon Johnson,
Holiday House

APPENDIX B
Resources for Teaching Literature

American Library Association. "The USA Through Children's Books." *Booklist* (May 1, 1986 and May 1, 1988).

Barton, B., and D. Booth. *Stories in the Classroom: Storytelling, Reading Aloud, and Roleplaying with Children.* Heinemann, 1990.

Bauer, C. *Handbook for Storytellers.* American Library Association, 1977.

Bowker, R. R. *Children's Books in Print.* Bowker (annual).

Bromley, K. D. *Webbing with Literature: Creating Story Maps with Children's Books.* Allyn & Bacon, 1991.

Brozo, William, and Carl Tomlinson. "Literature: The Key to Lively Content Courses." *The Reading Teacher* (September 1985), pp. 493–497.

Burke, E. M. *Literature for the Young Child,* 2nd ed. Allyn & Bacon, 1986.

Butler, Andrea, and Jan Turnbill. *Towards a Reading-Writing Classroom.* Heinemann, 1987.

Butzow, C. M., and J. W. Butzow. *Science Through Children's Literature: An Integrated Approach.* Teachers Ideas Press/Libraries Unlimited, 1989.

Calkins, Lucy. *The Art of Teaching Writing.* Heinemann, 1987.

Children's Book Council. *Children's Books: Awards and Prizes.* Children's Book Council, 1986.

Cott, J., ed. *Masterworks of Children's Literature.* New York: Stonehill, 1986.

Cullinan, Bernice E., ed. *Children's Literature in the Reading Program.* International Reading Association, 1987.

———. *Literature and the Child,* 2nd ed. Harcourt Brace Jovanovich, 1989.

Dreyer, S. S. *The Bookfinder: A Guide to Children's Literature About the Needs and Problems of Youth Aged 2 and Up.* American Guidance, 1984.

———. *Fiction, Folklore, Fantasy, and Poetry for Children.* Bowker, 1986.

Fox, C., and M. Sauer. *Celebrate Literature: A Literature Curriculum for Grades K–6.* Perfection Form, 1989–1990.

Fredericks, T., A. Meinbach, and L. Rothlein. *Thematic Units: An Integrated Approach to Teaching Science and Social Studies.* HarperCollins, 1993.

Gillespie, J. T., and C. B. Gilbert. *Best Books for Children: Preschool Through the Middle Grades.* Bowker, 1985.

Glazer, J. I. *Literature for Young Children,* 3rd ed. Merrill/Macmillan, 1991.

Goodman, Kenneth, Yetta M. Goodman, and Wendy Hood, eds. *The Whole Language Evaluation Book.* Heinemann, 1989.

Graves, Donald H. *Writing: Teachers and Children at Work.* Heinemann, 1983.

Hains, Maryellen, ed. *A Two-Way Street: Reading to Write/Writing to Read.* National Council of Teachers of English, 1982.

Hancock, Joelie, and Susan Hill. *Literature and Basal Reading Programs at Work.* Heinemann, 1987.

Hansen, J. *When Writers Read.* Heinemann, 1987.

Heard, G. *For the Good of the Earth and Sun: Teaching Poetry.* Heinemann, 1989.

Hearne, B. *Choosing Books for Children: A Commonsense Guide,* rev. ed. Delacorte, 1990.

Hickman, J., and B. E. Cullinan, eds. *Children's Literature in the Classroom: Weaving Charlotte's Web.* Christopher-Gordon, 1989.

Hopkins, L. B. *Pass the Poetry, Please!* rev. ed. Harper & Row, 1987.

Huck, Charlotte S., Susan Hepler, and Janet Hickman. *Children's Literature in the Elementary School,* 4th ed. Holt, Rinehart & Winston, 1987.

Hunt, Mary Alice, ed. *A Multimedia Approach to Children's Literature,* 3rd ed. American Language Association, 1983.

International Reading Association. "Children's Choices." *The Reading Teacher* (annually in October issue).

Jalongo, Mary Renck. *Young Children and Picture Books: Literature from Infancy to Six.* National Association for the Education of Young Children, 1988.

Johnson, Terry D., and Daphne R. Louis. *Bringing It All Together: A Program for Literacy.* Heinemann, 1990.

———. *Literacy Through Literature.* Methuen, 1985.

Kimmel, M. M., and E. Segal. *For Reading Out Loud! A Guide to Sharing Books with Children,* rev. ed. Delacorte, 1988.

Kulleseid, E. R. and D. S. Strickland. *Literature, Literacy, and Learning: Classroom Teachers, Library Media Specialists, and the Literature-Based Curriculum.* American Library Association, 1989.

Lindgren, M. V., ed. *The Multicolored Mirror: Cultural Substance in Literature for Children and Young Adults.* Cooperative Children's Book Center, 1991.

Lukens, Rebecca. *A Critical Handbook of Children's Literature,* 4th ed. Scott, Foresman, 1990.

Maker, C. June. *Teaching Models in Education.* Aspen, 1982.

Martin, D. *The Telling Line: Essays on Fifteen Contemporary Book Illustrators.* Delacorte, 1990.

McClure, A. A. *Sunrises and Songs: Reading and Writing Poetry in an Elementary Classroom.* Heinemann, 1990.

McGowan, Tom, and Meredith McGowan. *Children, Literature and Social Studies: Activities for the Intermediate Grades.* Special Literature Press, 1986.

———. *Integrating the Primary Curriculum: Social Studies and Children's Literature.* Special Literature Press, 1988.

Meinbach, Anita M., and Liz Rothlein. *Circles and Square Pegs.* Educational Impressions, 1989.

Meinbach, Anita M., Liz Rothlein, and Anthony D. Fredericks, *The Complete Guide to Thematic Units: Creating the Integrated Curriculum.* Christopher-Gordon, 1995.

Monson, Diane, ed. *Adventuring with Books: A Booklist for Pre-K to Grade 6.* National Council of Teachers of English, 1985.

Moss, J. F. *Focus on Literature: A Context for Literacy Learning.* Owen, 1990.

Norton, Donna E. *Through the Eyes of a Child: An Introduction to Children's Literature,* 3rd ed. Charles E. Merrill, 1991.

Noyce, Ruth M., and James Christie. *Integrating Reading and Writing Instruction in Grades K–8.* Allyn & Bacon, 1989.

Paulin, M. A. *Creative Uses of Children's Literature.* Shoestring, 1982.

Pellowski, A. *The World of Storytelling: A Guide to the Origins, Development, and Applications of Storytelling,* rev. ed. Wilson, 1990.

Peterson, L. K., and M. L. Solt. *Newbery and Caldecott Medal and Honor Books: An Annotated Bibliography.* G. K. Hall, 1982.

Rothlein, Liz, and Terri Christman. *Read It Again!* Scott, Foresman, 1989.

Routman, R. *Invitations: Changing as Teachers and Learners K–12.* Heinemann, 1991.

———. *Transitions: From Literature to Literacy.* Heinemann, 1988.

Rudman, M. K., ed. *Children's Literature: Resource for the Classroom.* Christopher-Gordon, 1989.

Rudman, M. K., and A. M. Pearce. *For Love of Reading: A Parent's Guide to Encouraging Young Readers from Infancy Through Age 5.* Consumers Union, 1988.

Russell, W. F. *Classics to Read Aloud to Your Children.* Crown, 1984.

Senick, G. J., ed. *Children's Literature Review,* vols. 1–7. Gale Research, 1984.

Somersand, Albert, and Janet Evans Worthington. *Response Guides for Teaching Children's Books.* National Council of Teachers of English, 1979.

Stott, J. C. *Children's Literature From A to Z: A Guide for Parents and Teachers.* McGraw-Hill, 1984.

Strickland, D. S., and L. M. Morrow, eds. *Emerging Literacy: Young Children Learn to Read and Write.* International Reading Association, 1989.

Sutherland, Zena, and May Hill Arbuthnot. *Children and Books,* 8th ed. Scott, Foresman, 1991.

Sutherland, Zena, and Myra Cohn Livingston. *The Scott, Foresman Anthology of Children's Literature.* Scott, Foresman, 1984.

Trelease, Jim. *The New Read-Aloud Handbook,* 2nd rev. ed. Penguin, 1989.

Tway, Eileen, ed. *Reading Ladders for Human Relations,* 6th ed. National Council of Teachers of English, 1981.

Winkle, L., ed. *The Elementary School Library Collection: A Guide to Books and Other Media,* 14th ed. Brodart, 1984.

Wood, K. D., with A. Moss, eds. *Exploring Literature in the Classroom: Contents and Methods.* Christopher-Gordon, 1992.

APPENDIX C
Publishers and Addresses

Abingdon Press, 201 Eighth Ave. S., Nashville, TN 37202

Addison-Wesley Pub. Co., Inc., Reading, MA 01867

Allyn & Bacon, Inc., 160 Gould St., Needham Heights, MA 02194-2310

American Guidance Service, Inc., 4201 Woodland Rd., Circle Pines, MN 55014-1796

Association for Childhood Education International (ACEI), 11501 Georgia Ave., Wheaton, MD 20902-1924

Atheneum Publishers, 115 Fifth Ave., New York, NY 10003

Atlantic Monthly Press, 19 Union Square West, New York, NY 10013

Avon Books, 105 Madison Ave., New York, NY 10016

Ballantine Books, Inc., 201 E. 50th St., New York, NY 10022

Bantam Books, 666 Fifth Ave., New York, NY 10103

R. R. Bowker Co., 121 Chanlon Rd., New Providence, NJ 07974

Bradbury Press, Inc. See Macmillan.

William C. Brown Group, 2460 Kerper Blvd., Dubuque, IA 52001

Cambridge University Press, 40 W. 20th St. New York, NY 10011

Carolrhoda Books, Inc., 241 First Ave. N., Minneapolis, MN 55401

CBS Educational Publishing, 383 Madison Ave., New York, NY 10007

Chelsea House Pub. Co., 95 Madison Ave., New York, NY 10016

Child's World, Inc., 1235 S. Broad St., Mankato, MN 56001

Children's Book Council, Inc., 568 Broadway Suite 404, New York, NY 10012

Children's Press, Inc., 5440 North Cumberland Ave., Chicago, IL 60656

Clarion. See Houghton Mifflin

Collier-Macmillan, Inc., 866 Third Ave., New York, NY 10022

Coward, McCann & Geoghegan. See Putnam.

Creative Education, Inc., 123 S. Broad St., Mankato, MN 56001

Thomas Y. Crowell Co. See HarperCollins.

Crown Publishers, Inc., P.O. Box 4397. Glendale, CA 91222-0397

Delacorte Press, 666 Fifth Ave., New York, NY 10103

Dell Publishing Co., 666 Fifth Ave., New York, NY 10103

Dial Books. See Penguin USA.

Dillon Press, Inc. See Macmillan.

Dodd, Mead & Co., 79 Madison Ave., New York, NY 10016

Doubleday & Co., Inc., 666 Fifth Ave., New York, NY 10107

Dutton Children's Books. See Penguin USA.

Faber & Faber. See HarperCollins. 50 Cross St., Winchester, MA 01890

Farrar, Straus & Giroux, Inc., 19 Union Square West, New York, NY 10003

The Feminist Press, 311 E. 94th St. New York, NY 10128

Follett Pub. Co., 1010 W. Washington Blvd., Chicago, IL 60607

Four Winds Press. See Macmillan.

Franklin, (Chas.) Press, 1575 Sodon Lake Dr., Bloomfield Hills, MI 48302

Garrard Pub. Co., 1607 N. Market St., Champaign, IL 61820

Golden Press, 8550 Third Ave., New York, NY 10022

Greenwillow Books, 1350 Ave of the Americas, New York, NY 10019

Grosset & Dunlap, Inc., 200 Madison Ave., New York, NY 10016

Harcourt Brace Jovanovich, Inc., 1250 Sixth Ave., San Diego, CA 92101

HarperCollins Children's Books, 10 E. 53rd St., New York, NY 10022

Harvard University Press, 79 Garden St., Cambridge, MA 02138

Harvey House, Pub., Inc., 1075 Arrowsmith, Eugene, OR 97402

Hastings House Pub., Inc., 141 Halstead Ave, Mamaroneck, NY 10543

Heinemann Educational Books, 361 Hanover St., Portsmouth, NH 03801-3959

Herald Press, 616 Walnut Ave., Scottdale, PA 15683

Holt, Rinehart & Winston, Inc., 521 Fifth Ave., New York, NY 10175; 1627 Woodland Ave, Austin, TX 78741

Houghton Mifflin Co., 1 Beacon St., Boston, MA 02108

Human Sciences Press, 233 Spring St., New York, NY, 10013-1578

Kestrel Books. See Viking Penguin.

Alfred A. Knopf, Inc., 201 E. 50th St., New York, NY 10022

Learning Corp. of America, 1350 Ave. of the Americas, New York, NY 10019

Library of Congress, Supt. of Documents, U.S. Government Printing Office, Washington, DC 20402; Div. of U.S. Government, Washington, DC 20540

J. B. Lippincott Co., East Washington Sq., Philadelphia, PA 19105

Lippincott Junior Books. See HarperCollins.

Little, Brown & Co., 34 Beacon St., Boston, MA 02106

Live Oaks Media, Box 34, Angramdale, NY 12503

Lodestar. See Dutton Children's Books.

Longman, Publishing Group, The Longman Bldg. 10 Bank St., White Plains, NY 10606-1951

Lothrop, Lee & Shepard Co. 1350 Ave. of the Americas, New York, NY, 10019

Macmillan Pub. Co., Inc., 866 Third Ave., New York, NY 10022

McDougal, Littell & Co., P.O. Box 1667, Evanston, IL 60204

McFarland & Co., Inc., Box 611, Jefferson, NC 28640

McGraw-Hill, Inc. See Universal Book Co.

David McKay Co., Inc., 2 Park Ave., New York, NY 10016

Charles E. Merrill Pub. Co., 936 Eastwind Dr., Westerville, OH 43081

Merrimack Publishers Circle, 47 Pelham Road, Salem, NH 03079

Julian Messner. See Simon & Schuster.

Methuen, Inc., 29 W. 35 St. New York, NY 10001-2291.

Morning Glory Press, 6595 San Haroldo Way, Buena Park, CA 90620

Morrow Junior Books, 1350 Avenue of the Americas, New York, NY 10019

New American Library, Inc. (NAL), 1633 Broadway, New York, NY 10019

W. W. Norton & Co., Inc., 500 Fifth Ave., New York, NY 10010

Pantheon Books, 201 E. 50 St., New York, NY, 10022

Parents Magazine Press, 685 Third Ave., New York, NY 10017

Parnassus Press. See Houghton Mifflin.

Penguin USA, 375 Hudson St., New York, NY, 10014

S. G. Phillips, Inc., P.O. Box 83, Chatham, NY 12037

Philomel Books, 200 Madison Ave., New York, NY 10016. See Putnam.

Pied Piper Productions, P.O. Box 320, Verdugo City, CA 91046

Pocket Books, Inc., 1230 Avenue of the Americas, New York, NY 10020

Prentice-Hall, Inc., 115 Columbus Circle, New York, NY 10023

Prometheus Books, 700 E. Amherst St., Buffalo, NY 14215

G. P. Putnam's Sons, 200 Madison Ave., New York, NY 10016

Raintree Publishers, Inc., 14018 Ashwood Rd., Shaker Heights, OH 44120

Rand, McNally & Co., P.O. Box 7600, Chicago, IL 60680

Random House, Inc., 225 Park Ave. South, New York, NY 10003

St. Martin's Press, Inc., 175 Fifth Ave., New York, NY 10010

Schocken Books, Inc., 201 E. 50th St., New York, NY 10022

Scholastic, Inc., 730 Broadway, New York, NY 10003

Scott, Foresman & Co., 1900 East Lake Ave., Glenview, IL 60025

Charles Scribner's Sons. See Macmillan.

Sierra Club. See Little, Brown.

Simon & Schuster Books for Young Children, 1230 Avenue of the Americas, New York, NY 10020

Stuart (Lyle), Inc., 120 Enterprise Ave., Secaucus, NJ 07094; see Carol Pub. Group.

Teachers College Press, Columbia University, 1234 Amsterdam Ave., New York, NY 10027

Time-Life Books, Inc., 777 Duke St., Alexandria, VA 22314

Triad Publishing Co., Inc., P.O. Box 13096, Gainesville, FL 32604

Troll Assoc., 100 Corporate Drive, Mahwah, NJ 07430

Tundra Books of Northern New York, P.O. Box 1030, 51 Clinton St., Plattsburgh, NY 12901

University of Chicago Press, 5801 S. Ellis Ave., 4th Flr., Chicago, IL 60637

Van Nostrand Reinhold Co., 115 Fifth Ave., New York, NY 10003

Viking. See Penguin USA.

Walker & Co., 720 Fifth Ave., New York, NY 10019

Frederick Warne & Co., Inc. See Penguin USA.

Warwick/Watts. See Franklin Watts, Inc.

Franklin Watts, Inc., 387 Park Ave. S., New York, NY 10016

Western Pub. Co., Inc., 8550 Third Ave., New York, NY 10022

The Westminster Press, 100 Witherspoon St., Louisville, KY 40202-1396

Weston Wood Studios, Inc., 389 New Town Tpke., Weston, CT 06880

Albert Whitman & Co., 6340 Oakton St., Morton Grove, IL 60053

Windmill Books, Inc. See Simon & Schuster.

APPENDIX D
Children's Periodicals

Bear Essential News for Kids. 2406 S. 24 St., Phoenix, AZ 85034
  Distributed without charge to children in Arizona, California, and Georgia. Advertises products and services of interest to families.

Boys' Life. 1325 Walnut Hill Lane, PO Box 152079, Irving, TX, 75015-2079; Braille ed.: Volunteer Services for the Blind, 919 Walnut St., Philadelphia, PA 19107
  Published by the Boy Scouts of America. Features articles about hobbies, sports, scouting, the dangers of drugs, science, careers, and adventure, as well as fiction and comics.

Chart Your Course! PO Box 6448, Mobile, AL 36660
  Magazine published by and for gifted, creative, and talented children. Includes prose, poetry, reviews, essays, puzzles, games, art, photos, comics, and letters.

Chickadee. 255 Great Arrow Ave., Buffalo, NY 14207
  A "see and do" magazine with animal stories, crafts, photographs, games, posters, and experiments.

Child Life. Children's Better Health Institute, 1100 Waterway Blvd., PO Box 567, Indianapolis, IN 46206
  Health tips, recipes, doctor's column, stories, and informative articles are the core of this magazine. Also included are puzzles and games.

Children's Album. 1320 Galaxy Way, Concord, CA 94520
  Features creative writing, arts, and crafts.

Children's Digest. Children's Better Health Institute, 1100 Waterway Blvd., PO Box 567, Indianapolis, IN 46206
  Presents articles on health, fiction, nonfiction, poems, cartoons, puzzles, recipes, and games for preteens.

Children's Playmate. Children's Better Health Institute, 1100 Waterway Blvd., PO Box 567, Indianapolis, IN 46206
  Teaches children about health and the value of good nutrition and exercise. Each issue includes recipes, articles, puzzles, stories, poetry, games, riddles, and jokes.

Cobblestone: The History Magazine for Young People. 30 Grove St., Peterborough, NH 03458
  A theme-related magazine containing stories, games, songs, articles, contests, maps, cartoons, poems, and recipes to encourage interest in and involvement with American history.

Creative Kids. PO Box 637, 100 Pine Ave., Holmes, PA 19043; PO Box 6448, 350 Weinacker Ave., Mobile, AL 36660-0448

> This award-winning magazine presents stories, poetry, limericks, activities, reviews, crafts, artwork, music, cartoons, puzzles, and photography by kids for kids.

Cricket: The Magazine for Children. Box 51145, Boulder, CO 80323-1145; PO Box 300, Peru, IL 61354

> Offers stories and pictures from all over the world to stimulate children's imaginations. Presents fantasy, history, science, adventure, and humor in articles, stories, poems, and puzzles.

Daybreak Star: The Herb of Understanding. United Indians of All Tribes Foundation, PO Box 99100, Seattle, WA 98199

> Written and edited by Native American students and adults. Each issue includes legends, drawings, and articles on housing, food, and clothing from a different geographical area.

Faces: The Magazine about People. 30 Grove St., Peterborough, NJ 03458

> A theme-related anthropology magazine including articles, photographs, folk tales, activities, and book and movie recommendations.

Free Spirit: News and Views on Growing Up. 123 N. Third St., Minneapolis, MN 55401

> A bimonthly magazine geared to bright and talented young people. Features topics such as friendship, goals, relationships with teachers and parents, and dealing with pressure.

Highlights for Children. PO Box 269, Columbus, OH 43272-0002; 910 Church St., Honesdale, PA 18431

> Includes factual articles, short stories, crafts, cartoons, riddles, puzzles, and word games.

Hopscotch. Box 164, Bluffton, OH 45817-0164

> Subtitled "The Magazine for Young Girls," it includes feature stories, biographical sketches, games, poems, and puzzles.

Humpty Dumpty's Magazine. Children's Better Health Institute, 1100 Waterway Blvd., PO Box 567, Indianapolis, IN 46206

> Contains health articles, stories, poems, recipes, and activity pages.

Jack and Jill. Children's Better Health Institute, 1100 Waterway Blvd., PO 567, Indianapolis, IN 46206

> Focus is good health. Includes stories, recipes, games, and puzzles.

Kid City. PO Box 51277, Boulder, CO 80322-1277; One Lincoln Plaza, New York, NY 10023

> Each issue follows a theme, such as school, pets, or movies, and includes games, contests, puzzles, and cartoons.

Kidlife and Times. PO Box D, Bellport, NY 11713

> Features stories and articles that encourage the reader to use imagination and reading skills.

Merlyn's Pen, The National Magazine of Student Writing. 98 Main St., East Greenwich, RI 02818

> Consists of stories, essays, poems, and plays submitted by young authors. Authors receive a personal response from the magazine within three weeks.

National Geographic World. 17th and M Sts N.W., Washington, DC 20036

Features color photographs, illustrations, and science articles about children around the world. Includes posters, games, puzzles, contests, and crafts.

Odyssey. 7 School St., Peterborough, NJ 03458

Focuses on space exploration and astronomy and includes articles, letters, drawings, questions, answers, and contest responses.

Owl: The Discovery Magazine for Children. 255 Great Arrow Ave., Buffalo, NY 14207; 56 The Esplanade, Suite 306, Toronto, ON, Canada M5E 1A7

Published by the Young Naturalist Foundation. A participation magazine about the environment that includes articles, photographs, puzzles, recipes, and experiments to encourage children to explore their world.

P3, The Earth-Based Magazine for Kids. PO Box 52, Montgomery, VT 05470

An ecology magazine designed to educate children about protecting and saving the natural world.

Prism. Box 030464, Ft. Lauderdale, FL 33303

Geared for gifted and talented youth who seek penpals or a place to publish.

Ranger Rick. 8925 Leesburg Pike, Vienna, VA 22184-0001

Published by the National Wildlife Federation, this magazine contains color photographs, articles on nature and people helping nature, and poetry. Includes crafts, riddles, and puzzles.

Sesame Street Magazine. PO Box 55518, Boulder, CO 80322-5518; One Lincoln Plaza, New York, NY 10023

Designed for preschool children, each themed issue contains activities dealing with the alphabet, counting, and prereading. Includes games, stories, and color drawings.

Shoe Tree. National Association for Young Writers, PO Box 452, Belvidere, NJ 07823

A literary magazine devoted to the encouragement of young authors. Features stories, poems, artwork, personal narratives, and book reviews.

Sports Illustrated for Kids. Time and Life Bldg., Rockefeller Center, New York, NY 10020

Features professional and amateur athletes, fiction, sports tips, puzzles, posters, and activities.

Stone Soup. PO Box 83, Santa Cruz, CA 95063

A literary magazine of students' stories, poems, artwork, and book reviews. Contains information for contributors in each issue.

Surprises. PO Box 236, Chanhassen, MN 55317

Created by two teachers to provide activities for children and parents to share at home. Includes puzzles, games, math problems, and listening exercises.

3-2-1 Contact. PO Box 53051, Boulder, CO 80322-3051; One Lincoln Plaza, New York, NY 10023

Includes articles, photographs, and illustrations on science and technology topics and contains crafts, games, activities, and contests.

Turtle Magazine for Preschool Kids. Children's Better Health Institute, 1100 Waterway Blvd., PO Box 567, Indianapolis, IN 46206

Combines fun and learning with an emphasis on health. Includes stories, poems, songs, games, and puzzles.

Wee Wisdom. Unity School of Christianity, Unity Village, MO 64065

A nondenominational magazine, also available in Braille, geared toward helping children develop values. Contains puzzles, crafts, stories, and poetry.

Zillions. PO Box 51777, Boulder, CO 80321-1777; 256 Washington St., Mt. Vernon, NY 10553

A *Consumer Reports* for children that teaches about economics and finance and helps children make moneywise decisions. Contains articles on items children buy, tests on toys, clothing and fashion ideas, movies, and good foods.

APPENDIX E
Teacher Periodicals

BookLinks. American Library Association, 50 E. Huron St., Chicago, IL 60611

Booklist. American Library Association, 50 E. Huron St., Chicago, IL 60611

The Bulletin of the Center for Children's Books. University of Illinois Press, 54 E. Gregory Drive, Champaign, IL 61820.

The Horn Book Guide to Children's and Young Adult Books. 14 Beacon St., Boston, MA 02180

The Horn Book Magazine. 14 Beacon St., Boston, MA 02180

Instructor. Scholastic Inc., P.O. Box 2039, Mahopac, NJ 10541

Language Arts. National Council for Teachers of English, 1111 W. Kenyon Rd., Urbana, IL 61801

The New Advocate. Christopher-Gordon Publishers, 480 Washington St., Norwod, MA 02062

The Reading Teacher. International Reading Association, 800 Barksdale Rd., P.O. Box 8139, Newark, DE 19714

Teacher. P.O. Box 2091, Marion, OH 43305

Teacher K–8. 40 Richards Ave., Norwalk, CT 06845

Writing Teacher. ECS Learning Systems, Inc., P.O. Box 791437, San Antonio, TX 78279

APPENDIX F

Binding Books

Dry-Mount Tissue Book

Materials:

Lightweight cotton fabric
Dry-mount tissue (available in photography shops)
Cardboard (medium-weight; needs to be heavier for larger books)
Scissors
Iron
Construction paper (one piece for the endpaper)
Lightweight white paper (for the pages of the book)
Needle and thread or long-arm stapler
Glue or paste

Directions:

1. Cut cloth to desired size of book.
2. Cut dry-mount tissue the same size as the cloth.
3. Cut cardboard about 1 inch smaller all the way around than the dry-mount tissue and cloth.
4. Cut the piece of cardboard in half.
5. Place the dry-mount tissue evenly on top of the cloth.
6. Place the two pieces of cardboard on top of the dry-mount tissue. Leave about 1/2 inch between the pieces of cardboard, placing them so there is an equal amount of dry-mount tissue and cloth on all sides.
7. Fold the cloth and dry mount at the corners and, with a hot iron, press them down to the cardboard. The heat of the iron allows the dry-mount to adhere the cloth to the cardboard.
8. After all four corners are folded and ironed down, do the same to the remaining sides.
9. Fold the book cover together, and iron the front and back to adhere the cloth to the cardboard more securely.
10. Using construction paper, cut one piece that is 1/2 inch smaller than the book cover.
11. Using the lightweight paper, make pages for the book. To do this, cut a pattern for the pages that is 1/4 inch smaller than the construction paper previously cut. Using this as a pattern, cut the number of sheets needed for pages.
12. Place the pages on top of the construction paper page and fold in the center. Staple or sew these pages together.

13. Rub glue or paste over the construction paper sheet and carefully adhere it to the inside of the book cover. Hold the book open for several minutes to dry.

Pop-Up Book*

Directions:

1. Cut a large sheet of construction paper in half.
2. Fold one of the halves in half.
3. Cut tabs about 2-1/4–2-1/2 inches deep along the fold.

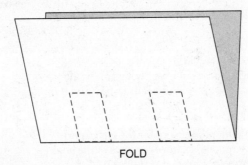

FOLD

4. Open the paper and push out these tabs to form the armature for the pop-up illustrations.
5. Measure illustrations so they do not overextend the book when the page is closed.
6. When the student has completed all pages, including all written work, and pop-ups are glued and dry, glue the book together.
7. After pages are glued, put pressure (with a heavy book) on the end where the tabs have been cut out, so the glue adheres well (about 15 minutes).
8. Stand the book on end with the pages separated and dry overnight.
9. Glue the cover and back to the book and attach the binding.
10. Apply all 3-D decorations after the cover and back are completely dry.

*With permission from Maddy Savin, Teacher of the Gifted, Pinecrest Elementary School, Dade County, Florida.

An Accordian Book

Directions:

Make a folding book by folding a roll of shelf paper accordion-style to make pages. To make a cover, paste or staple cardboard to the first and last pages. Punch holes in the sides of the covers and fasten with ribbon to close the book.

Triarama Book

Directions:

1. Use an 8 1/2 x 11 inch sheet of paper. Fold the right corner down to the lower left corner to form a triangle. Cut off excess paper.

2. Open and fold the left corner down, forming a triangle. Open.

3. Cut one of the folded lines to the center of the square.

4. Overlap the two triangles separated by the cut and glue to form a triarama.

Minibook (Little Book)

Directions

1. Begin with one 8 1/2 x 11 inch sheet of
   unlined paper or construction paper.

2. Fold in half, making folded creases tight. 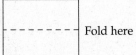 Fold here

3. Fold again.

4. Fold in half sideways.

5. Open to half a sheet (position 3).
   Hold with fold at the top and cut in
   the middle from fold to center.

6. Open the sheet completely.
   There should be 8 folded boxes.

7. Fold lengthwise.

8. Bring outer edges together.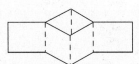

9. Form book. The book contains 4 pages,
   front and back for a total of 8 pages.

Flip Book

Directions

1. Use 8 1/2 x 11 inch paper or construction paper.

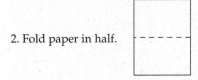

2. Fold paper in half.

3. Fold paper in half again.

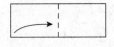

4. Fold in half sideways.

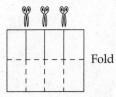

5. Open and cut to the center fold.

Fold

6. Fold cut pieces to center fold and make a crease.

7. You may wish to combine several pages, binding them together at the fold with binding tape or staples.

APPENDIX G

Resources for Parent Lending Library

Books

Cullinan, Bernice E. *Read to Me: Raising Kids Who Love to Read.* Scholastic, 1992.

Fredericks, Anthony D. *Involving Parents Through Children's Literature.* Grades 1–2. Libraries Unlimited, 1992.

———. *Involving Parents Through Children's Literature.* Grades 3–4. Libraries Unlimited, 1993.

———. *Involving Parents Through Children's Literature.* Grades 5–6. Libraries Unlimited, 1993.

———. *Involving Parents Through Children's Literature.* Preschool–K. Libraries Unlimited, 1993.

Hearne, Betsy. *Choosing Books for Children.* Delacorte, 1981.

Kummel, Margaret, and Elizabeth Segel. *For Reading Out Loud.* Dell/Delacorte, 1983.

Larrick, Nancy. *A Parent's Guide to Children's Reading,* 4th ed. Bantam, 1975.

Trelease, Jim. *The New Read-Aloud Handbook, 2nd ed.* Penguin, 1989.

Organizations

American Library Association, 50 East Huron Street, Chicago, IL 60611.

The Children's Book Council, P.O. Box 706, New York, NY 19276.

International Reading Association, 800 Barksdale Road, P.O. Box 8130, Newark, DE 19714-8139.

National Council of Teachers of English, 1111 Kenyon Road, Urbana, IL 61801.

Resources

Becoming a Nation of Readers: What Parents Can Do. Consumer Information Center, Department 459V, Pueblo, CO 81009.

Helping Your Child Use the Library. Consumer Information Center, Department 415Y, Pueblo, CO 81009.

The National Library Services for the Blind and Physically Handicapped, Library of Congress, Washington, DC 20542.

Reading Is Fundamental, Inc., Publication Department, Smithsonian Institution, 600 Maryland Avenue, SW, Suite 500, Washington, DC 20024.

CREDITS

Page 7   Paul Fleischman, *Joyful Noise,* HarperCollins Children's Books. Used with permission.

Pages 12-13 Christianna Cannon, *The Ally Alligator Alphabet Book,* Bright Elementary, Dade County Schools, Miami, Florida.

Page 36 Bronwyn Steinberg, Age 11, "What Is Prejudice," North Dade Center for Modern Languages, Teacher: Mrs. Marliese Hogan.

Page 37 Lauren Robinson, Age 12, "Acceptance," North Dade Center for Modern Languages, Teacher: Mrs. Marcus.

Page 38 Jennifer Herrera, Age 11, "I Am Prejudice," North Dade Center for Modern Languages.

Page 39 Jillian Robinson, Age 11, "What Is Prejudice," North Dade Center for Modern Languages.

Page 62 Greenfield, Eloise, "By Myself," from *Honey, I Love, and Other Love Poems,* HarperCollins Children's Books. Reprinted with permission.

Page 73 Donna Ogle, "K-W-L: A Teaching Model That Develops Active Reading of Expository Text," *Reading Teacher,* 2/86, pp. 564-570.

Page 109 Illustration by Ernest Crichlow from the cover of *Harriet Tubman: Conductor of the Underground Railroad* by Ann Petry. Every attempt was made to contact the illustrator without success.

Page 127 Mollie Hunter, *The Mermaid Summer,* HarperCollins Children's Books. Reprinted with permission.

Page 163 E. B. White, *Charlotte's Web,* Illustration copyright © 1980 by Garth Williams. Reprinted by permission.

Page 185 Eric Carle, *Do You Want to Be My Friend?,* HarperCollins Children's Books. Reprinted with permission.

Page 203 Ezra Jack Keats, *Peter's Chair,* HarperCollins Children's Books. Reprinted with permission.

INDEX

About Dying (Stein), 69
About Handicaps: An Open Family Book for Parents and Children Together (Stein), 236, 238
Abstract art, 330
Abstract thinking skills, 194
Abuela (Dorros), 23
Acceptance/belonging, 32–33, 233
Activities
    alphabet books, 14
    alternative methods for sharing literature, 346–350
    biographies, 78–79
    calender of genres, 113
    censorship, 154–157
    characterization element, 129–135
    concept books, 18
    counting books, 15
    cultural diversity, 251–253
    disabilities, children with, 237–238
    drama, 319
    easy-to-read books, 21–22
    ESL students, 244–246
    fables/folk tales, 54–55, 57
    historical fiction, 43–44
    independent reading, 209–210
    informational books, 71–72
    language experience approach, 314
    Mother Goose rhymes, 16
    myths/legends, 59
    picture storybooks, 23–24
    plot element, 136–139
    poetry, 67–68
    point of view element, 147–148
    predictable books, 20
    read-aloud program, 173
    realistic fiction, 30–37
    setting element, 140–143
    shared reading, 191–194
    student projects/literature-based, 468
    style and tone element, 150
    synthesis, 151–152
    teacher-directed, 361–363
    thematic units, 416–423
    theme element, 145–146
    toy books, 17
    unit plans, 113–124
    visual literacy, 333–334
    wordless picture books, 19
    writing, 311–313
Adventures of Tom Sawyer (Twain), 128
Aesop's Fables, 145
Aesthetic questioning, 279–281
Africa, 258–260
African Americans, 246
Aging, 27
AIDS (acquired immune deficiency syndrome), 237
Alexander and the Terrible, Horrible, No Good, Very Bad Day (Viorst), 22, 129, 147–148
Alex is My Friend (Russo), 236
All Butterflies (Brown), 331
All Shapes and Sizes (Hughes), 17
Alphabet books, 11–14, 80–81
Alternative methods for sharing/extending literature, 340–350
America Forever New (Brewton & Brewton), 63
Analysis and higher-level thinking questions, 283
And Then What Happened Paul Revere? (Fritz), 167
Anecdotal records, 467
Animalia (Base), 10, 12

Anne Frank: Beyond the Diary (van der Rol & Verhoeven), 167
Ann Martin's Baby Sitters Club series, 252
Anno's Alphabet (Anno), 12
Anno's Counting Book (Anno), 14
Anthropomorphic connections, 145–146
Appearance and realistic fiction books, 31
Application questions, 282–283
Arnie and the New Kid (Carlson), 236, 238
Art for Children (Raboff), 328
Artists, books about, 328
Art Play series (Okuyama), 328
Arts and literature
    dramatic responses, 318–326
    literature listings, 334–337
    professional resources, 327–328
    visual arts, 326–334
Ashanti to Zulu (Musgrove), 12
Asia, 239, 246, 256–258
Ask Mr. Bear (Flack), 224
Assessment
    authentic, 465–473
    biographies, 77–78
    fables, 56
    fantasy/science fiction, 48–50
    folk tales, 54
    genres and their elements, 151–152
    higher-level thinking questions, 283
    historical fiction, 43
    informational books, 70–71
    multicultural literature, 247–249
    myths/legends, 58–59
    picture storybooks, 23–24
    poetry, 64–65
    professional resources, 473–474
    read-aloud program, 173, 174
    realistic fiction, 30
    storytelling, 222–223
    whole language evaluation, 464–465
Ass in the Lion's Skin, The, (Aesop), 56
Attention span, 167
At the Crossroads (Isadora), 250
Audience reaction and storytelling, 221, 223
Audio/visual resources, 228–229, 340–341, 411–412
Aunt Flossie's Hats (Howard), 240, 249
Aunt Harriet's Underground Railroad in the Sky (Ringgold), 41
Authentic assessment, 465–473

Author/illustrator unit, 384, 388
Authors visiting classrooms, 207
Authors writing across genres, 111, 169
Awards, children's book, 497–512

Barn Dance (Martin, Jr.), 324
Basal reading program, 389–393
Baucis and Philemon, 57
Becoming a Nation of Readers, 355
Bedtime for Frances (Hoban), 128–129, 194
Behavior disorders, 255, 263
Best Bad Thing, The (Uchida), 250
Big books, 189–191, 195–201
Big Thunder Magic (Strete), 241
Bill Cosby; Making America Laugh and Learn (Woods), 75
Binding books, 525–529
Biographies, 74–80, 104–105, 182–183, 218, 238
Biopoem, 64
Birth of the United States, The (Asimov), 69
Blow, Bugle, Blow (Tennyson), 168–169
Blubber (Blume), 31
Book clubs, 413–414
Booklist (American Library Association), 247
Book/novel units, 383–388
Book response journals, 292–293
Books, selecting
    genres, exploring, 110–124
    independent reading, 205–207
    multicultural literature, 247–249
    read-aloud books, 167–170
    shared reading, 187–189
    storytelling, 217–218
Books in Spanish for Children and Young Adults (Schon), 248
Bookstore in the classroom, 207
Books Without Bias: Through Indian Eyes (Slapin & Seale), 248
Book talks, 277
Book Vine (publisher), 200
Bookwebbing, 383–384
Book week, 342
Borrowers, The (Norton), 46, 322
Bridge to Terabithia (Paterson), 27
Brothers and Sisters (Rosenberg), 250
Brown Bear, Brown Bear (Martin), 20
Budulinek, 51
Bulletin (Council on Interracial Books), 247

But Not Kate (Moss), 237, 238
By Myself (Greenfield), 62

Caddie Woodlawn (Brink), 40, 141–142
Caldecott medal, 503–509
Calender of genres, 113
Call It Courage (Sperry), 32, 34, 143
Cane in Her Hand, A (Litchfield), 238
Can You Imagine (Gardner), 15
Cartoons, 331
Cathedral (Macaulay), 70
Censorship, 152–157
Chair for My Mother, A (Williams), 330
Changes (Brown), 330
Characterization element, 128–135
Charlotte's Web (White), 46, 128, 143, 144, 322
Chasing Games from Around the World (McPherson), 249, 252
Checklists for reading skills, 467–470
Child of the Owl (Yep), 27, 250
Children of the Great Muskeg (Ferris), 249
Children of the Wild West (Freeman), 277
Children's Books in Print, 236
Children's Literature in the Elementary School (Huck, Hepler & Hickman), 63
Children's Press (publisher), 200, 226
Children's Writing and Publishing Center, 344
Child's Treasury of Animal/Seaside Verses (Daniel), 62
Choral reading, 322–323
Cinderella, 51, 147
Cinquain (poem), 63–64
Class President (Hurwitz), 172
Classroom climate, 165–167
Clerihew poetry, 64
Cloze technique, 191, 193
Clustering/webbing and graphic organizers, 302
Cock and the Jewel, The, (Aesop), 56
Collage, 331
Columbus, Christopher, 42
Come Sit by Me (Merrifield), 237
Commercial big books, 196–201
Communication skills, 217, 263
Community resources, 414–416
Comprehension, 282
Computers, 343, 345
Concept books, 17–18, 82–83

Conferences, teacher-student, 367–370, 371, 468
Conflicts and plot element, 136–137
Constance: A Story of Early Plymouth (Clapp), 41
Cookbooks, 241, 245
Cooking the Mexican Way (Coronado), 245
Coretta Scott King award, 511–512
Counting books, 14–15, 81
Cowboys of the Wild West (Freeman), 277
Creation myths, 57
Creative drama, 318–321
Creative problem solving (CPS), 286–288
Cricket, 206
Crocodile's Masterpiece (Velthuijs), 332
Crow and the Pitcher, The, (Aesop), 56
Cubing and graphic organizers, 303
Cultural diversity, 246–253
    activities, 251–253
    creating a multicultural classroom, 247
    literature listings, 256–262
    multicultural literature, 240–241
    professional resources, 266–268
    selecting multicultural literature, 247–249
    using multicultural books in the classroom, 249–251
Curious George (Rey), 366
Current events, 111

Daily record sheets, 363, 364–365
Dancing Teepees: Poems of American Indian Youth (Sneve), 249
Dear Mr. Henshaw (Cleary), 25, 27, 28
Death/dying, 27, 34, 69
Desdemona-Twelve Going on Desperate (Keller), 32
Devil's Arithmetic, The (Yolen), 36, 290
Dialogue journals, 293
Dicey's Songs (Voight), 33
Directed reading, 362
Disabilities, children with, 232
    activities, 237–238
    exploring genres, 36–37
    inclusion guidelines, 233–234
    literature for the inclusive environment, 234–237
    literature listings, 253–255
    professional resources, 262–264
Discrimination/prejudice, 36

Divergent questioning, 285–286
Doorbell Rang, The (Hutchins), 14
Drafting, 298, 302
Dragonwings (Yep), 41, 146, 250, 288
Dramatic responses to literature, 194,
    318–326
Drawings, 332
Dream Catcher (Osofsky), 249
Drummer Hoff (Emberly), 20, 324

Easy-to-read books, 20–22, 85–86
Eating the Alphabet (Ehlert), 12
Editing, 305, 306–307
Eleanor Roosevelt: A Life of Discovery (Freed-
    man), 75, 332
Elements of good literature
    characterization, 128–135
    literature listings, 157–158
    plot element, 135–139
    professional resources, 158
    setting, 140–143
    style and tone element, 149–150
    synthesis activities, 151–152
    theme, 143–146
Emmy (Green), 237
Emperor's New Clothes (Andersen), 145
Encounter (Yolen), 23, 42
Encyclopedias, 206
English as a Second Language (ESL), 239–240
    activities, 244–246
    inclusion in general education classroom,
        240–242
    literature listings, 242–244, 255–256
    professional resources, 264–266
Enormous Watermelon, The, 189
Eskimo Boy: Life in an Inupiag Eskimo Village
    (Kendall), 250
ESL. *See* English as a Second Language
Esteban and the Ghost (Hancock), 253
Everybody Cooks Rice (Dooley), 241, 245
Exactly the Opposite (Hoban), 17
Expressionistic style, 330

Fables, 56–57, 98
Fallen Spaceman, The (Harding), 47
Fall of Freddie the Leaf (Buscaglia), 22
Family Pictures/Cuadros de familia (Garza),
    240, 241
Family relationships, books on, 33–34

Fantasy/science fiction, 45–50, 93–96,
    179–180
Farm Concert, 194
Fast-Slow High-Low: A Book of Opposites
    (Spier), 17
Festival at school, storytelling, 224–227
Fiction. *See* Historical fiction; Realistic fiction
Field trips, 415–416
Figurative language, 61, 149
Fireflies! (Brinckloe), 22
First-hand experiences, 165
Fir Tree, The (Andersen), 145
Fisherman and his Wife, The, 51
Flannelboard Stories for the Primary Grades
    (Anderson), 224
Flannel characters, 224
Flight; Fliers and Flying Machines (Jefferies),
    70
Flossie and the Fox (McKissock), 248
Fly the Hot Ones (Lindblom), 70
Folk art, 330–331
Folklore, 180–182, 217–218
Folktales, 51–55, 96–98, 113–115
Foreshadowing, 138
Fox and the Grapes, The, (Aesop), 56
Franklin Delano Roosevelt (Freedman), 169
Freckle Juice (Blume), 31
Friendship, 34
Friendship, The (Taylor), 168
Friendship Across Arctic Waters (Murphy),
    249
Frog and Toad Are Friends (Lobel), 21
Fun of Cooking, The (Krementz), 69

Galaxies (Simon), 332
Gathering of Days, A (Blos), 140
Generations and realistic fiction books, 35
Genres
    biographies, 74–80, 104–105
    fantasy/science fiction books, 45–50,
        93–96
    historical fiction, 39–45, 91–93
    informational books, 68–74, 101–104
    picture books, 8–25, 80–88
    poetry, 60–68, 99–101
    professional resources, 106
    realistic fiction, 25–39, 88–91
    selecting a variety of genres, 110–124
    traditional literature, 50–60, 96–99

Geography in thematic approach to learning, 439–451

Getting to Know the World's Greatest Artists (Venezia), 328

Giver, The (Lowry), 47

Going to School in 1876 (Loeper), 69

Gold Coin, The (Ada), 242–244

Goodnight Moon (Brown), 17, 19

Graphic organizers, 298, 302–303

Great Books Foundation, 283

Great Gilly Hopkins, The (Paterson), 33, 129, 135, 149, 288

Great Kapok Tree: A Tale of the Amazon Rain Forest (Cherry), 168

Great Painters (Ventura), 70

Green Book, The (Walsh), 47

Growing up, 32

Gryphon House (publisher), 198

Guest speakers, 414–415

Guiness Book of World Records, 206

Haiku (poem), 63

Hamsters: All About Them (Silverstein), 69

Hans Christian Andersen award, 510–511

Harcourt Brace Javanovich (publisher), 198–199

HarperCollins (publisher), 201

Harriet Tubman: Conductor on the Underground Railroad (Petry), 169

Hatchet (Paulsen), 27

Have You Seen My Cat? (Carle), 169

Hawk, I'm Your Brother (Baylor), 241

Hearing impairments, 254, 263

Helen Keller Story, The (Peare), 75

Hello, My Name Is Scrambled Eggs (Gibson), 250

Henny Penny (Galdone), 51

Henry Wore His Green Sneakers (Peek), 324

He's My Brother (Lasker), 236

Hey, Al (Yorinks), 321

Hey Diddle Diddle (Paola), 16

Hi Cat! (Keats), 169

Higher-order thinking skills, 69, 281–283

Highlights, 206

Hippopotamusn't (Lewis), 173

Hispanic population, 239, 246, 260–261

Historical fiction, 39–45, 91–93, 179

Holdaway, Don, 186

Holidays of other cultures, 241

Honey, I Love and Other Love Poems (Greenfield), 62, 249

Hopscotch Around the World (Lankford), 249

Horn Hook Magazine (Horn Book), 247

House of Dies Drear (Hamilton), 41

How a Book Is Made (Aliki), 70

How Many Spots Does a Leopard Have (Lester), 253

How My Family Lives in America (Kuklin), 250

Hundred Dresses, The (Estes), 31, 168, 288

Hundred Penny Box, The (Mathis), 35

Husband Who Was to Mind the House, The, (Kipling), 51

I Draw, I Paint: Watercolor, I Am an Artist (Collins), 333

If I Were in Charge of the World and Other Worries (Viorst), 62

If You Give a Mouse a Muffin (Numeroff), 321

I'll See You in My Dreams (Jukes), 22, 27

Illustrations, 141, 189, 326–334, 384, 388

Impressionistic style, 330

In a Dark, Dark Woods, 189

Inclusion guidelines, 233–238, 240–242

Independent reading
    activities, 209–210
    establishing a period for, 208–209
    importance of, 204–205
    paired reading, 210–213
    professional resources, 213
    selecting reading materials, 205–207

Indian fables, 56

Informational books, 68–74, 101–104, 182

Intellectual freedom, 153

Interest inventories, 110–111, 112

International reading association children's book award, 509–510

Interpretive questioning, 276, 283–285

Interviewing techniques for exploring characters, 133

In the Dark, a Beginners's Guide to Developing and Printing Black and White Negatives (Davis), 70

In the Year of the Boar (Lord), 27, 253, 288

Introducing Michelangelo (Richmond), 328

Isis and Osiris, 58

Is It Larger? Is It Smaller? (Hoban), 17, 332

Island of the Blue Dolphins (O'Dell), 3

Jack and the Beanstalk, (Cauley), 51
Jackie Robinson (Lord), 27, 253, 288
Jade Stone, The (Yacowitz), 332
Jambo Means Hello: Swahili Alphabet Book
    (Feeling), 241
Jar of Dreams, A (Uchida), 250
Johnny Tremain (Forbes), 41
Jolly Postman and Other People's Letters, The
    (Ahlberg), 384
Jose Canesco: Baseball's 40–40 Man (Aaseng),
    75
Journals, 210, 292–294, 467
Joyful Noise: Poems for Two Voices (Fleis-
    chman), 63, 323
Julie of the Wolves (George), 3, 27
Jungle Book, The (Kipling), 173
Junior Great Books, 283
Just a Dream (Allsburg), 22
Just Like Martin (Davis), 250
Just So Stories, 173

Knights of the Kitchen Table (Scieszka), 46
Knowledge and higher-level thinking ques-
    tions, 282
Kohlberg's moral development approach,
    288–289
Koya DeLaney and the Good Girl Blues (Green-
    field), 250

Language arts and literature
    language experience approach, 313–314
    literature listings, 314–315
    professional resources, 315–316
    readers as writers, 291–294
    speaking and listening, 276–291
    writing process, 294–313
Language Arts (National Council of Teachers
    of English), 247
Language experience approach (LEA),
    313–314
Laura Ingalls Wilder award, 509
Learning aids, multicultural, 268
Learning disabilities, 254, 263
Learning logs, 293–294
Lee Ann: The True Story of a Vietnamese Girl
    (Brown), 250
Legends/myths, 57–59, 98–99, 115–119
Leo the Late Bloomer (Kraus), 22, 238
Let the Circle Be Unbroken (Taylor), 250

Librarians, 413
Libraries, 205–206, 397, 400–403, 476–480, 530
Life and Death (Zim & Bleeker), 69
Life and Words of John F. Kennedy, The (Wood),
    75
Light and Shadow (Livingston), 332
Limericks, 64
Limited English Proficiency (LEP) students,
    239
Lincoln: A Photobiography (Freedman), 75, 332
Lisa and Her Soundless World (Levine), 236,
    238
Listening library, 341
Literary logs, 294–296
Literary Mapper (software), 345
Literature-based reading programs, 187,
    273–274, 355–357, 360. *See also* Ele-
    ments of good literature; Language
    arts and literature; Literature listings;
    Thematic approach to learning
    alternative methods, 340–350
    arts and literature, 318–337
    basal reading program, 389–393
    conferences, teacher-student, 367–370, 371
    daily record sheets, 364–365
    disabilities, children with, 234–237
    library, classroom, 400–403
    literature listings, 403–404
    minilessons, 363, 366
    modeling, 366–367
    multicultural literature, 240–241, 246–251
    organizing, 393–399
    planning/scheduling, 370, 372–383
    professional resources, 404
    teacher-directed activities, 361–363
    units, 383–388
Literature circles, 278–279
*Literature for Children about Asian and Asian
    Americans* (Austin & Jenkins), 248
Literature listings, 124, 403–404
    alphabet books, 80–81
    alternative methods for sharing literature,
        350
    arts and literature, 334–337
    biographies, 104–105
    concept books, 82–83
    counting books, 81
    cultural diversity, 256–262
    disabilities, children with, 253–255

easy-to-read books, 85–86
elements of good literature, 157–158
ESL students, 242–244, 255–256
fantasy/science fiction, 93–96
historical fiction, 91–93
informational books, 101–104
language arts and literature, 314–315
Mother Goose rhymes, 81–82
picture storybooks, 86–88
poetry, 99–101
predictable books, 84–85
read-aloud program, 174–184
realistic fiction, 88–91
storytelling, 227–228
toy books, 82
traditional literature, 96–99
wordless picture books, 83–84
Little House series (Wilder), 133, 134, 322
Little Match Girl, The (Andersen), 145
Little Red Hen (Galdone), 19
Lives at Stake: The Science and Politics of Environmental Health (Pringle), 69
Log of books read, 210, 211, 467
London Bridge Is Falling Down (Spier), 16
Lon Po Po: A Red Riding Hood Story from China (Young), 251
Lotus Seed, The (Garland), 241, 326

Magic School Bus at the Waterworks (Cole), 10
Make Way for Ducklings (McCloskey), 171
Making and Using Big Books (Herald-Taylor), 195
Man Called Washington, A (Norman), 75
Mandy (Booth), 236, 238, 330
Maniac Magee (Spinelli), 27, 32, 129, 146, 252
Martian Chronicle, The (Bradbury), 48
Martin Luther King: The Peaceful Warrior (Clayton), 75
Mary Wore Her Red Dress (Peek), 324
M.C. Higgins the Great (Hamilton), 149
Me and Nessie (Greenfield), 248
Media, artistic, 331–332
Mental retardation, 253, 263–264
Midnight Ride of Paul Revere, The (Longfellow), 63, 167
Millions of Cats (Gag), 19
Minilessons, 363, 366
Miscue analysis, 468
Miss Nelson Is Missing, (Allard), 132

Miss Rumphius (Cooney), 332
Mitten, The (Brett), 173
Mixed-Up Chameleon, The (Carle), 245
Modeling, 366–367
Mojo Means One: Swahili Counting Book (Feeling), 241
Molly's Pilgrim (Cohen), 250
Monitoring students, 397
Monster Sandwich, A, 189
Monthly topics, 111
Moral dilemmas, 288–291
Mother Goose rhymes, 15–16, 81–82
Motivating students for independent reading, 206
Mouse Rap, The (Dean), 249
Mr. Rabbit and the Lovely Present (Zolotow), 330
Mrs. Katz and Tush (Polacco), 249
Mrs. Wishy-Washy, 189
Mufaro's Beautiful Daughters (Steptoe), 248
Multicultural Cookbook for Students, The (Allyn & Webb), 241, 245
Multicultural Cooking with Kids (Lakeshore Learning Materials), 252
Multicultural literature, 165, 240–241, 246–251. *See also* Cultural diversity
Multimedia alternatives for sharing literature, 340–345
Music and storytelling, 224, 324, 327–328
Musicians of the Sun (McDermott), 57
My Brother, Matthew (Thompson), 237
My Doll Keisha (Greenfield), 241–242
My Feet (Aliki), 17
My Grandmother's Journey (Cech), 250
My Hands (Aliki), 17
My Sister Is Different (Wright), 237
Mythology (Hamilton), 57
Myths/legends, 57–59, 98–99, 115–119

Nana Upstairs, Nana Downstairs (Paola), 27
National Assessment of Educational Progress, 281–282
National Association for the Preservation and Perpetuation of Storytelling (NAPPS), 220–221, 229
National Council of Teachers award for excellence in poetry for children, 510
National Story League (NSL), 229
National Storytelling Festival, 224

Native Americans, 42, 246, 248, 261–262

Nature myths, 57

New Advocate, The (Christopher Gordon Publishers), 170, 247

Newbery medal, 497–503

New Kid on the Block, The (Prelutsky), 288

New Print Shop, The (software), 345

Newspapers, 206, 343, 344

Night on Neighborhood Street (Greenfield), 249

Night Train, 189

Nine Days to Christmas (Ets & Aurora), 241

Nonfiction books, 169

Novel/book units, 383–388

Now One Foot, Now the Other (Paola), 27

Number the Stars (Lowry), 41, 290

Nursery rhymes, 15–16, 60–64, 81–82

Observation sheet for shared reading, 173, 192

Of Colors and Things (Hoban), 17

Oh, A-Hunting We Will Go (Langstaff), 324

Old Traveler, The, 51

Once a Mouse (Brown), 331

1, 2, 3 (Hoban), 14

On Market Street (Lobel), 12

Oral language development and storytelling, 217

Orchard Book of Nursery Rhymes, The (Sutherland), 16

Organizing literature-based classrooms, 393–399

Our Brother Has Down's Syndrome (Jasmine), 237

Over in the Meadow (Keats), 15

Owl Moon (Yolen), 22, 149

Ox-Cart Man (Hall), 330–331

Oxford Book of Nursery Rhymes (Opie), 16

Pablo Picasso (Raboff), 75

Painting, 332

Paired reading, 210–213

Pancake, The (Galdone), 51

Paper cutouts, 224

Parents
  assessing their child's growth, 471, 472
  ESL programs, 239–240
  involving, 480–495
  lending library for, 479, 530
  professional resources, 495–496

Participation in read-aloud program, 171–172

Pat the Bunny (Kunhardt), 16

Penguin USA (publisher), 199

People Could Fly, The (Hamilton), 52

Perfection Learning Corporation (publisher), 199–200

Perfect Person in Just Three Days (Manes), 32

Periodicals, children/teacher, 520–524

Petanella (Waterton), 253

Peter's Chair (Keats), 169

Phobe and the General (Griffin), 41

Photography, 332

Physical characteristics of characters, 129

Physical/health impairments, 254–255, 264

Picture Book of Eleanor Roosevelt (Adler), 169

Picture books, 8–11
  alphabet books, 11–14
  concept books, 17–18, 82–83
  counting books, 14–15, 81
  easy-to-read books, 20–22, 85–86
  literature listings, 80–88
  Mother Goose rhymes, 15–16, 81–82
  musical themes, 327–328
  predictable books, 19–20, 84–85
  professional resources, 106, 184, 460
  storybooks, 22–25, 86–88, 174–178
  toy books, 16–17, 82
  wordless, 18–19, 83–84, 205

Pinballs (Byars), 33

Planning/scheduling literature-based reading programs, 370, 372–383

Play Ball, Amelia Bedelia (Parish), 27

Plot element, 135–139

Poetry
  cultural diversity, 249
  exploring genres, 60–68
  literature listings, 99–101
  professional resources, 106, 388
  shared reading, 195
  storytelling, 218
  unit plans, 119–124

Point of view element, 146–148

Polar Bear, What Do You Hear? (Martin), 20

Polar Express (Van Allsburg), 319

Portfolios, 471, 473

Practicing reading, 204–205. *See also* Independent reading

Prairie Songs (Conrad), 41, 145, 277
Predictable books, 19–20, 84–85
Prejudice/discrimination, 36
Prereading discussions, 171
Prewriting, 298
Prince and the Golden Ax, The (Lattimore), 58
Printed resources, 411, 412–413
Printing techniques, 331
Problem solving, creative, 286–288
Professional resources, 106–107, 125, 404
  alternative methods for sharing literature,
      350
  arts and literature, 327–328
  assessment, 473–474
  cultural diversity, 266–268
  disabilities, children with, 262–264
  elements of good literature, 158
  ESL students, 264–266
  independent reading, 213
  language arts and literature, 315–316
  parents, 495–496
  read-aloud program, 183–184
  shared reading, 201
  storytelling, 228
Props in storytelling, 223–224
Publishing, 305, 307–311, 391, 515–519
Pull-out ESL programs, 239
Punctuation marks, 194
Puppets, 224, 324–326

Questioning strategies, 276–277, 279–286

Rabbit Brothers (Kraus), 251
Radio programs, 341
Rainbow People, The (Yep), 52
Ranger Rick, 206
Read-aloud program
  activities for, 173
  assessment, 174
  guidelines for, 170–173
  importance of, 164–165
  literature listings, 174–184
  preparing a, 165–170
  professional resources, 106, 183–184, 213,
      228, 496
Reading. *See also* Literature-based reading
    programs; Shared reading checklists,
    467–470

  choral, 322–323
  conferences, 367–369
  directed, 362
  independent, 204–213
  readers' theater, 321–322
  writing connected with, 291–294
Reading Teacher, The, 170, 174
Realistic fiction
  activities to use with, 30–37
  extending your knowledge of, 37–39
  literature listings, 88–91
  read-aloud program, 178–179
  self-understanding through, 25–30
Realistic stories, 218
Really Rosie, (Sendak), 9
Red Shoes, The (Andersen), 145
Reference books, 206
Reflections of . . .
  Babbitt, Natalie, 329
  Freedman, Russell, 4
  George, Jean C., 409–410
  Hopkins, Lee, 65
  Livingston, Myra, 66
  Lukens, Rebecca, 144
  Metzler, Milton, 76
  Myers, Dean, 26
  Sebesta, Sam L., 320, 390, 417–421
  Sendak, Maurice, 8–9
Reform movement for basal readers, 389,
    391–393
Rembrandt's Beret (Alcorn), 328
Repeated readings, 194, 204
Report Card on Basal Readers (Commission on
    Reading), 389
Revisions, 302, 304–305
Rhyming, 15–16, 60–64, 81–82
Rigby Education (publisher), 196–197
River Ran Wild, A (Cherry), 210, 326
Road to Memphis, The (Taylor), 250
Roll of Thunder, Hear My Cry (Taylor), 42, 248,
    250
Rose Blanche (Innocenti), 22, 41–42
Rosenblatt's transaction theory, 273, 279–
    280
Rosie's Walk (Hutchens), 196

Sadako and the Thousand Paper Cranes (Coerr),
    42, 277, 324

Sadat: The Man Who Changed Mid-East History (Sullivan), 75
Sally Ride, Astronaut: An American First (Behren), 75
Sam, Bangs and Moonshine (Ness), 136
Sarah, Plain and Tall (MacLachlan), 41, 277
Sarah Bishop (O'Dell), 41, 42
Save Queen of Sheba (Moeri), 42
Say Woof! The Day of a Country Veterinarian (Gibbons), 70
Scheduling/planning literature-based reading programs, 370, 372–383
Scholastic News Ranger, 206
Scholastic (publisher), 197
School Library Journal (R.R. Bowker), 247
Science fiction/fantasy, 45–50, 93–96, 179–180
Science in thematic approach to learning, 433–439
Scorpions, The (Myers), 32
Secret Garden (Burnett), 132–133
Self-evaluation, 222, 468, 471
Semantic Mapper (software), 345
Sesame Street Sign Language Fun, 238
Setting element, 140–143
Shapes and Things (Hoban), 17
Shared inquiry, 283–285
Shared reading
　activities, 191–194
　commercial big books, 196–201
　creating big books, 195–196
　guidelines for using big books, 189–191
　importance of, 186–187
　observation sheet, 173, 192
　poetry, 195
　professional resources, 201
　selecting books for, 187–189
Shelley the Hyperactive Turtle (Moss), 236
Shh! We're Writing the Constitution (Fritz), 41, 43
Simulation journals/literary letters, 294
Skills, teaching, 361–363
Slide shows, 342
Small World Celebrations (Warren), 251
Snap! Photography (Cooper), 70
Snowy Day, The (Keats), 10, 169, 190, 248, 331
Socially conscious literature, 248
Social studies in thematic approach to learning, 424–432, 452–461

Sociograms, 132–133
Someone Special, Just Like You (Brown), 236, 238
Song and Dance Man (Akerman), 167
Song of the Trees (Taylor), 250
Sound effects and storytelling, 221
Sounder (Armstrong), 36
Speaking and listening, 276
　book talks, 277
　dramatic responses to literature, 318–326
　literature circles, 278–279
　moral dilemmas, 288–291
　problem solving, 286–288
　professional resources, 106, 213, 263, 315–316
　questioning strategies, 279–286
Special learning needs. *See* Disabilities, children with
Spectacles (Raskin), 237, 238
Spontaneous reading, 167
Stat Ka'at (Madlee), 47
Stepsisters, 52
Stopping by Woods on a Snowy Evening (Frost), 10, 61
Story maps, 138–139, 303
Storyteller's Sourcebook (McDonald), 52, 251
Storytelling
　festival at school, 224–227
　guidelines for good, 221–223
　importance of, 216–217
　literature listings, 227–228
　preparing the story, 219–221
　professional resources, 228
　props, 223–224
　selecting the story, 217–218
Story theater, 321
Strategy lessons, 361–363
Structuring Cooperative Learning (Johnson, Johnson & Holubec), 363
Style and tone element, 149–150
Summer of the Swans, The (Byars), 36–37
Sundance (publisher), 197–198
Superprint II: The Next Generation (software), 345
Surrealistic art, 330
Survival and realistic fiction books, 34–35
Suzy (Chapman), 237
Sylvester and the Magic Pebble (Steig), 148
Synthesis activities/questions, 151–152, 283

Talking Earth, The (George), 27, 149

Tall tales, 52

Tar Beach (Ringgold), 319

Taxonomy of Educational Objectives: Cognitive Domain, 282

Teacher-directed activities, 361–363

Teaching Multicultural literature to Children in Grades K-8 (Harris), 248

Teammates (Golenbock), 23

Tenth Good Thing About Barney, The (Viorst), 27

Thematic approach to learning, 406
  activities, 416–423
  geography, 439–451
  materials/resources, 411–416
  professional resources, 106
  science, 433–439
  social studies, 424–432, 452–461
  theme, choosing a, 407–411

Theme element in stories, 143–146

Theme in thematic approach to learning, 407–411

Theseus and the Minotaur (Fisher), 57

Thinking, levels of, 282–283

This Time of Darkness (Hoover), 47

Three Little Ducks, 189

Three Wishes (Clifton), 249

Time capsules, 342

Time lines for exploring plot element, 136

Tinder Box, The (Andersen), 145

Tonweya and the Eagles and Other Lakota Indian Tales (Yellow Robe), 241

Topics in thematic approach to learning, 408

Tortoise and the Hare, The, (Aesop), 56

Toy books, 16–17, 82

Traditional literature, 50
  fables, 56–57
  folk tales, 51–55
  literature listings, 96–99
  myths/legends, 57–59
  professional resources, 106, 183–184, 228, 460
  read-aloud program, 180–182
  unit plans, 113–119

Transaction between reader and the text, 273, 279–280

Transitional bilingual programs, 239

Treasure Island (Stevenson), 171

Trouble with Elephants, The (Riddell), 241

True Story of the Three Little Pigs, The (Scieszka), 52

Trumpet Club (publisher), 198

Trumpet of the Swan, The (White), 37

Tuck Everlasting (Babbitt), 46, 129, 138, 149, 167, 276

Tuesday (Wiesner), 19, 138, 332

Twelve Dancing Princesses, The (Grimm Brothers), 51

Two Bags, The, 56

Two-way bilingual programs, 239

Ugh (Yorkins), 53

Ugly Duckling, The (Andersen), 145, 168, 221

Units, literature-based, 113–124, 383–388

Velveteen Rabbit, The (Williams), 46

Venn diagram, 135

Very Best Friends, The (Wild), 168

Very Busy Spider, The (Carle), 16, 19, 169, 189

Very Hungry Caterpillar, The (Carle), 16

Very Quiet Cricket (Carle), 169

Video and cassette tapes, 228–229, 340–341

Visit to William Blake's Inn (Willard), 62

Visual arts, 326–334

Visual discrimination skills, 193

Visual impairments, 254, 264

Vocabulary words, 193

Volcano: The Eruption and Healing of Mt. St. Helens (Lauber), 69

Wall, The (Bunting), 22, 332

War with Grandpa, The (Smith), 35

Water Sky (George), 27, 34

Weekend With series (Waldron), 328

Weekly Reader, 206

What Can She Be? A Newscaster (Goldreich & Goldreich), 70

What Do You See? (Martin), 20

When I Am Old With You (Johnson), 240

Where the Lilies Bloom (Cleaver), 33

Where the Wild Things Are (Sendak), 10, 22

Whole Earth Holiday Book, The (Polin & Cantwell), 241, 251

Whole language evaluation, 464–465

Why Mosquitoes Buzz in People's Ears (Aardema), 52, 330

Why There Is No Arguing in Heaven (Lattimore), 57

Wind in the Willows, The (Grahame), 140
Wind Song (Sandburg), 60, 121
Windy Nights (Stevenson), 60–61
Witch of Blackbird Pond, The (Speare), 42, 143
Women Artists for Children series (Turner), 328
Wonderful Flight to the Mushroom Planet (Cameron), 46
Word attack skills, 194
Wordless picture books, 18–19, 83–84, 205
Words in Our Hands (Litchfield), 238
Wright Brothers: How They Invented the Airplane (Freedman), 75
Wright Group (publisher), 197
Writing, 294–295
    activities, 311–313
    choice/response/structure, 297
    conferences, 369–370

drafting, 298, 302
editing, 305, 306–307
folder, 296, 299–301, 467
prewriting, 298
publishing, 305, 307–311
reading connected with, 291–294
revisions, 302, 304–305
time for, 296
Writing: Teachers and Children at Work (Graves), 294–295

Year in a River Valley/Nature Poems (Frank), 62
Yeh-Shen, A Cinderella Story from China (Louie), 251

Zlatch and the Goat and Other Stories (Singer), 51– 52